Vorwort

Crossover 2 – 6th edition, Ausgabe Baden-Württemberg ist konzipiert für Englischlernende an beruflichen Schulen, insbesondere an beruflichen Gymnasien. Band 2 bietet Stoff für die Jahrgangsstufen 1/2 und bereitet gezielt auf die Abiturprüfung vor.

Die sechs auf die Themen des Bildungsplans abgestimmten **Topics** sind wie folgt aufgebaut:

- **Overview** – Hinführung zum Thema und erste Themenwortschatzarbeit
- **Sections** – Texte und audiovisuelle Materialien mit vielfältigen kompetenzorientierten Aufgaben:
  - **Warm-up** – Anregung zum Sprechen
  - **Working with the text** – Leseverstehen und erweiterte Textarbeit
  - **Working with words** – Wortschatzerarbeitung
  - **Looking at language** – Grammatikthemen mit funktionalem oder formalem Ansatz
  - **Writing / Speaking / Listening** – gezieltes Training abiturrelevanter Aufgabenformate
  - **Crossover TV** – Hör-/Sehverständnistraining
- **Project** – schrittweise Anleitung zu selbstständiger Projektarbeit
- **Words in context** – der Themenwortschatz des jeweiligen *Topics* auf einen Blick, mit Übungsaufgaben zum Festigen
- **Skills** – intensives Methodentraining zu Lernstrategien und Prüfungsaufgaben
- **Consolidation & evaluation** – Rückschau auf das *Topic*, Bewertung des eigenen Lernstands und (in der PagePlayer-App) Aufgaben zur Vertiefung
- **Mock exam** – eine vollständige schriftliche und mündliche Musterprüfung pro *Topic*

In der Randspalte befinden sich Übersetzungen anspruchsvoller **Vokabeln**, die mit Zeilennummerierungen versehen sind.

8 **rise** *Aufstieg*	Fett gedruckte Wörter sind Lernwortschatz.
17 quirky *eigenwillig, unangepasst*	Nicht fett gedruckte Wörter dienen lediglich zum Verständnis des jeweiligen Textes.

Weitere Symbole und Verweise

🔊	Hörverstehen/Tracknummer
▶	Hör-/Sehverstehen / Nummer des Films
📱	Zusätzliches Material in der PagePlayer-App
S ▸	Verweis auf *Skills*-Inhalte
G ▸	Verweis auf die *Grammar summary*
Exam preparation	Aufgaben, die auf die Anforderungen der Prüfung ab 2024 vorbereiten

Topic 1 – The environment

Topic 2 – Technology

Topic 3 – Work and consumers

Topic 4 – The USA – a divided nation?

Topic 5 – The United Kingdom

Topic 6 – Equality

Zusatzmaterialien in der PagePlayer-App

Crossover 2 – 6th edition bietet eine neue Dimension des individuellen Lernens. Die zusätzlichen Materialien können zu Hause, unterwegs oder auch im Kurs mit dem Smartphone oder dem Tablet direkt aus dem Buch heraus angesehen und -gehört werden.

Und so können Sie die Materialien abspielen:

1 Laden Sie die kostenlose PagePlayer-App herunter. Sie können die Inhalte zu **Crossover 2 – 6th edition** kapitelweise auf Ihrem Smartphone oder Tablet speichern und jederzeit aufrufen.

2 Scannen Sie mit Ihrem Smartphone oder Tablet die ausgewählte Buchseite, die Verweise auf Audio- und/oder Videomaterialien enthält, sowie Seiten mit diesem Icon: . Das Material wird angezeigt und Sie können es direkt starten. Alternativ können Sie auf die Inhalte der App über das Medienmenü zugreifen.

Auf der PagePlayer-App finden Sie die folgenden Materialien:

- alle Audios und Videos zum Schülerbuch
- auf den *Overview*-Seiten (Auftaktseiten der *Topics*): Audiodateien mit *Background information* zu den einzelnen Sections, auch als Lesetexte verfügbar
- Checklisten zu *Writing*-Aufgaben (*argumentative texts* und *creative writing*)
- *Phrases* zu *Speaking*-Aufgaben zur Vorbereitung auf die Kommunikationsprüfung
- *Language for speaking*
- *Language for writing*
- auf den *Consolidation & Evaluation*-Seiten: Vertiefungsaufgaben zu jedem *Topic*

Topic 1 The environment

Section A
The human impact

Fact: Energy causes around 60% of total global greenhouse gas emissions. (Source: Sustainability Management School)

Section B
The need for energy

generating energy

climate crisis

Fact: Some scientists consider that we have entered a new geological epoch, the Anthropocene, which is characterized by the negative effects of human activity.

Planet Earth

renewables

Section F
Climate activism

school strikes

upcycling

"The greatest threat to our planet is the belief that someone else will save it."
– Robert Swan, environmental leader and public speaker

1 Read the facts and quotations about the environment above.

- **a** Which of them are totally new to you?
- **b** Which of them do you find surprising?

2 Rank Sections A–F on how interested you are in them.

3 The mind map shows you a preview of Topic 1. Copy it onto a piece of paper and add words and phrases from …

- **a** the facts and quotations above.
- **b** the Word bank opposite.
- **c** your own ideas.
- **d** Sections A–F you think are important.

Find information on each Section in the PagePlayer app!

emissions

advertising

biodiversity

fast fashion

Section C
Greenwashing

"Sustainability is now a big baggy sack in which people throw all kinds of old ideas, hot air and dodgy activities in order to be able to greenwash their products and feel good."
– Kevin McCloud, TV host and designer

Section D
The importance of forests

"Imagine a man without lungs. Imagine earth without the Amazon rainforest."
– Vinita Kinram artist and activist

Fact: Tropical rainforests cover less than 7% of Earth's landmass but are home to about 50% of all living things on the planet. (Source: Georgetown University)

Section E
The fashion industry

"Buy less. Choose well. Make it last."
– Vivienne Westwood, fashion designer

Fact: On average, an item of clothing is worn only 7 times before being thrown away (Source: www.sustainyourstyle.org)

4 Note a few key words to say what you expect to learn in each Section.

5 Make a "KWL" (Know, Want to know, Learned) list for the Topic.

6 With a partner, compare …

a your mind maps and say why you added words where you did.
b your rankings from exercise 2.
c what you expect to learn in Sections A–F.

Then compare with another pair.

7 Save your work for reviewing when you've finished the Topic.

Word bank

campaign *Kampagne, Aktion*
deforestation *Waldzerstörung*
extinction *Ausrottung, Aussterben*
fossil fuel *fossiler Brennstoff*
greenhouse gas *Treibhausgas*
overconsumption *Überkonsum*
pollution *(Umwelt-) Verschmutzung*
resource *Ressource, Rohstoff*
responsibility *Verantwortung*
waste *Abfall*

Section A The human impact

Warm-up

1 Work in groups of three or four. Estimate the position of the events in the list on the 24-hour model of the Earth's history.

collision of planets Earth and Theia forms our moon | Earth is formed | first bacteria appear | first fish appear | first humans appear | first land plants appear | first mammals appear | formation of the oceans | glaciers start to melt | significant increase in oxygen in the atmosphere

mammal *Säugetier*
glacier *Gletscher*

The history of the Earth*

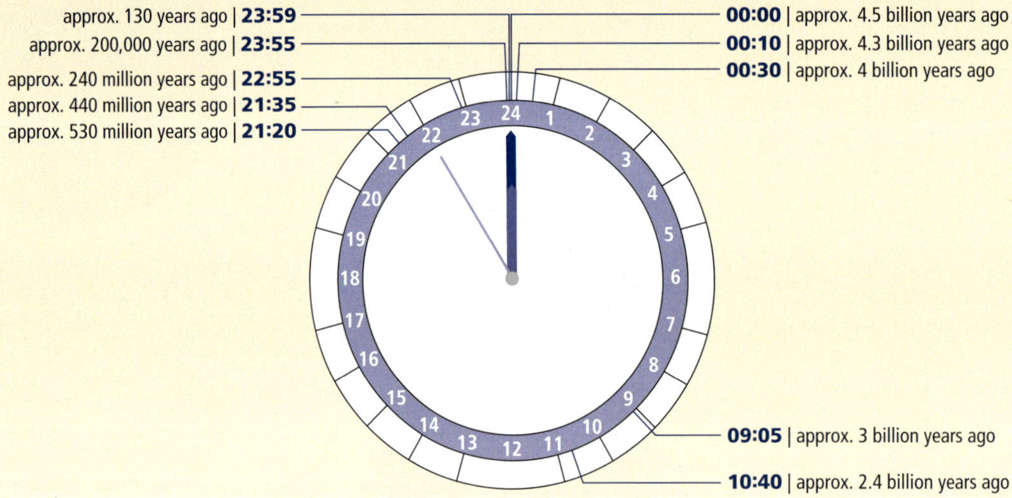

* not to scale

2 Check your answers on page 14. How accurate were your guesses? Which group had the closest estimates?

3 Did anything about the results surprise you? Explain why (not). What do you think the model tells us about the role of human beings in the Earth's history?

Before you read

4 Match the terms (1–7) from the text to the correct definitions (a–g).

1 deforestation
2 drought
3 extinct
4 force
5 fossil fuel
6 layer
7 species

a when a species no longer exists
b something which exercises power
c source of non-renewable energy such as coal, oil and natural gas
d the process of cutting down large numbers of trees
e a group of animals which have similar characteristics
f a long period of dry weather
g a level of material which has a different material above and/or below it

Conversation corner

Every month we ask an expert to break down for our readers an important topic affecting the world we live in. Today, our Young Globe reporter Kathy Chan is chatting to the environmentalist Ben O'Leary about the 'Anthropocene'.

02

Kathy An expert group of geologists claims that humanity's impact on planet Earth's climate and ecosystems has been so significant that it is necessary to declare that we have brought about a new geological epoch called the Anthropocene. Let's start at the beginning. So, Ben: what exactly *is* a geological epoch?

Ben Well, basically, it's a specific time in the Earth's history defined by an event which causes changes to rock sediment. So, for example, the end of the Cretaceous epoch, when dinosaurs were around, was caused by a meteorite crashing into Earth. The meteorite contained the metal iridium, which could subsequently be found in rock sediment. Scientists call these changes 'signals'. By the way, our current epoch is known as the Holocene.

Kathy OK. So why are geologists now talking about this new epoch, the Anthropocene?

Ben Because there have been a number of 'signals' to indicate that we are now in a new geological epoch, one that has been almost entirely brought about by humans. The term Anthropocene was coined in the year 2000 by the Nobel Prize winning scientist Paul Crutzen, who believes that it is important to change the name of the epoch to acknowledge the changes to the environment that humans have caused and, at the same time, to emphasize our great responsibility to look after the planet we live on.

Kathy I see! Would you say that officially declaring the start of the Anthropocene is also an attempt at a wake-up call to all of us to look after the environment?

Ben Yes, for sure. The scientists hope that if the Anthropocene is declared an official epoch, humans will appreciate the scale of what they are doing to the environment.

Kathy And is there a lot of evidence to back up their claim?

Ben Yes, a fair amount! They estimate that the new epoch began around 1950. At that time, there were a number of nuclear bomb tests dispersing radioactive elements around the world, which can be found in rock sediment. Furthermore, factors such as the advance of technology since the Second World War and a sharp rise in population numbers and consumption have made humanity a significant geological force.

Kathy Right. Is the burning of fossil fuels, like coal and natural gas, also a major contributing factor?

Ben Yes, definitely. The burning of fossil fuels has left a permanent layer of black carbon in sediment and glacial ice. It has also increased levels of climate-warming CO_2 in the atmosphere, which have led to extreme weather events, such as storms, drought and heatwaves, rising sea levels and bush fires. Plastic is another element that is likely to leave identifiable fossil records because we have put so much of it into the oceans that microplastic particles will most likely remain for many generations.

Good to know

Holocene
holo- = entire, whole
+ -cene = new or recent
= an entirely new geological epoch (or age)

Officially this is the current geological epoch of planet Earth, which has existed for around 12,000 years and has seen the beginning of human civilization.

Anthropocene
anthropo- = related to humans
+ -cene = new or recent
= a new geological epoch dominated by humans

7 to **claim** *behaupten*
9 to **declare** *verkünden*
9 to bring sth about *etw herbeiführen, etw verursachen*
16 subsequently *in der Folge*
17 **current** *aktuell, derzeitig*
22 **entirely** *völlig, ganz*
23 to coin sth *etw prägen*
25 to acknowledge sth *etw anerkennen, etw zugeben*
27 to **emphasize sth** *etw betonen, etw hervorheben*
32 to **appreciate** *anerkennen*
32 **scale** *Ausmaß, Umfang*
36 to disperse *(zer)streuen, verteilen*
38 **advance** *Fortschritt*
39 sharp *stark*
39 **consumption** *Verbrauch, Konsum*
44 **carbon** *Kohle(nstoff)*
44 glacial ice *Gletschereis*
46 **sea level** *Meeresspiegel*
47 identifiable *erkennbar, identifizierbar*
48 record *Aufzeichnung*

[51] to state a case *einen Fall darlegen*
[55] for the purpose of *zwecks*

Kathy Humans have clearly impacted the environment in a number of different ways. What other evidence are the scientists using to state their case?

Ben Another major factor is the rapid extinction of animals and plants. If this continues at the current rate, we could lose 75% of species over the next few centuries. There have also been drastic changes to land through deforestation and development for the purpose of feeding, housing and producing certain products for human consumption.

Kathy We humans have certainly done a lot of damage to our planet. Let's hope we can turn the Anthropocene into a positive new age both for humanity and the environment!

(615 words)

Working with the text

5 Work with a partner. Read the text and complete the following sentences.

1 Some geologists claim that human activity ...
2 ... signal the beginning or end of a geological epoch.
3 Paul Crutzen announced the start of the Anthropocene because ...
4 The Anthropocene was thought to have started when ...
5 Extreme weather events have been caused by ...
6 The planet will be left with only about a quarter of the current variety of species if ...
7 Humans have caused major changes to land through ...

Exam preparation

S ▸ Writing a summary, p. 81
S ▸ Words for tasks, pp. 79–80

6 Outline the evidence given in the text for the start of the Anthropocene.

Working with words

7 Complete the sentences with the correct prepositions from the list. There are more prepositions than you need.

about | as | by | down | for | in | of | on | to | up

marine *Meeres-*

1 The researchers backed ... their claims with scientific evidence.
2 An individual's carbon footprint is partly defined ... the different methods of transport they use, for example long-distance flights or trains.
3 Plastic waste on beaches has done a lot of damage ... marine wildlife.
4 The school clean-up initiative has had a positive impact ... both students and teachers.
5 The gases which cause global warming are known ... greenhouse gases.
6 Many recent climatic changes have been brought ... by human activity.
7 There has been a slight fall ... the amount of plastic waste produced each year.
8 The burning of fossil fuels has created high levels ... CO_2 in the atmosphere.

Speaking

8 Work in groups. Discuss whether declaring the start of the Anthropocene is an effective way to get people to start living more environmentally-friendly lives. Present your conclusions to the class.

Presentation

9 Work in groups. Each group chooses a different environmental topic for a short presentation to the class.

For **Air** and **Oceans** look at this page.
For **Forests** and **Population growth** look at File 1 on page 267.

Group A: Air

You are going give a group presentation about the air and how humanity is affecting the atmosphere.

Start by using the words in the list to help you create a mindmap or list of ideas. Then add your own ideas and do some research online.

air quality | atmosphere | to breathe in sth | carbon footprint | carbon monoxide | emissions | exposure to | exhaust fumes | factories | industrialization | ozone | particles | pollutant | pollution | radiation | respiratory problems

Questions

- Where can you find the best/worst air quality? Why is that?
- What factors affect the quality of the air?
- What effects does air pollution have on the environment and health?

respiratory *Atemwegs-*

Prepare and structure your presentation. If possible, find an image or images to illustrate it. Then give your presentation to the class.

Group B: Oceans

You are going to give a group presentation about the importance of the oceans and the dangers they face due to human impact.

Start by using the words in the list to help you create a mindmap or list of ideas. Then add your own ideas and do some research online.

to absorb | acidification | biodiversity | carbon dioxide | climate regulation | commercial whaling | coral reef | cruise ship | ecosystem | global warming | habitat | ice caps | marine wildlife | to melt | oil drilling/pipelines | overfishing | oxygen | plastic pollution | to regulate sth

Questions

- In what ways are the oceans important for human survival?
- What impact has climate change had on the oceans and what might this mean for humans in the future?
- In what ways are humans impacting the oceans?

acidification *Versäuerung*
whaling *Walfang*
habitat *natürlicher Lebensraum*

Prepare and structure your presentation. If possible, find an image or images to illustrate it. Then give your presentation to the class.

Writing

10 Assess which of the environmental problems facing humanity you think should be solved most urgently and give reasons for your answer.

Exam preparation

S ▸ Writing an argumentative text, pp. 167–172
Writing checklist

Section B The need for energy

Warm-up

1 Work in pairs. Look at the words in the word cloud and match the kinds of energy, e.g. biogas, to the correct source.

living organisms – movement – pre-historic plant or animal material – the sun – uranium – waste – water – waves – wind

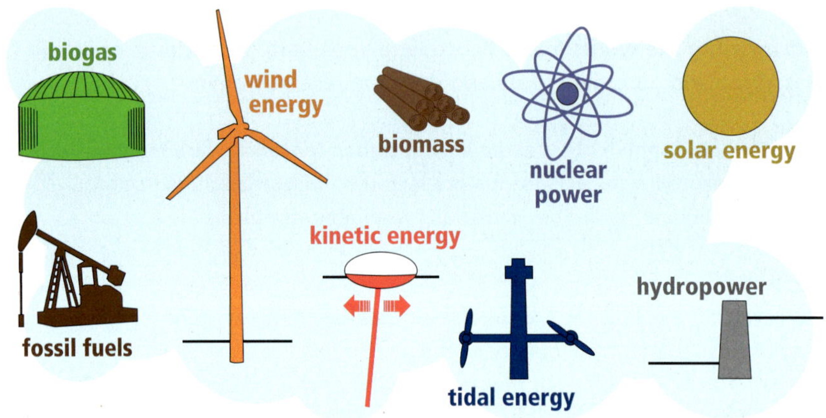

Working with the text

2 Read the information in the table on page 15 and complete the gaps using words from exercise 1. There are more items than you need.

Working with words

3 Match the highlighted words in the table on page 15 to the following definitions.

to **obtain sth** *etw erhalten, an etw gelangen*
to **remove sth** *etw entfernen, etw beseitigen*

1 can be trusted, not likely to stop working
2 to come from or be obtained from
3 to come to an end when there is none left
4 sb who actively promotes an idea or a cause
5 to get rid of sth, throw sth away
6 to remove or take sth out
7 extremely dangerous
8 substances that make air, water, soil, etc. dirty
9 to produce energy
10 enough, the necessary amount of something

Section A, exercise 1: answers

00:00: Earth is formed
00:10: collision of planets Earth and Theia forms our moon
00:30: formation of the oceans
09:05: first bacteria appear
10:40: significant increase in oxygen in the atmosphere
21:20: first fish appear
21:35: first land plants appear
22:55: first mammals appear
23:55: first humans appear
23:59: glaciers start to melt

Non-renewable energy sources	Renewable energy sources
Basic facts	
Energy sources derived from …[1] such as oil, coal and natural gas. Formed by ancient animals or plants which died and were buried in layers of rock that gradually (over millions of years) formed different kinds of fuels.	Derived from natural elements which won't run out, such as …[2] and sun.
Example(s)	
• …[3] is produced by splitting …[4] atoms. It is generated at power stations. Proponents claim that it is reliable and low-cost; power stations generally have a long lifespan. It does not create polluting gases or contribute to global warming. Furthermore, a small amount of fuel generates a large amount of energy and there is no need for mining or other environmentally-damaging methods of extracting energy. Waste is radioactive and it is difficult and expensive to dispose of safely; thermal pollution of wastewater can have damaging effects on local marine life. Moreover, accidents can be catastrophic and have wide-reaching effects (for example the Fukushima disaster).	• Wind energy: produced by turbines on land or in the sea. • …[5] : harvested through special panels, for example on rooftops or in fields. • …[6] : most commonly produced through hydroelectric dams in which water stored in a reservoir flows downwards and turns a turbine, which in turn generates power. • …[7] : an energy source which can be combusted to create heat or converted into biofuels. It is derived from living (or recently living) organisms, for example ethanol (made from materials such as corn or sugar cane). • …[8] : methane from animal manure or other organic material which has been digested.
Advantages	
• Cheap to find and produce energy. • Reliable: there are still plenty of sources around (for now). • Useful: used to produce plastic, which has multiple uses.	• Most sources are clean and inexpensive to run. • They will not run out.
Disadvantages	
• Non-renewable, meaning that at some point they *will* run out. • Environmental damage: pollution created by their production and use, for example by petrol for vehicles and smoke from factories. • Obtaining these resources can be dangerous for workers (for example mine workers). • Extracting oil though fracking can potentially poison drinking water supplies. • Drilling for oil on land or under the sea may disturb ecosystems and harm wildlife.	• Many ways of obtaining renewable energy are costly to set up and may be hazardous to wildlife. • They are also dependent on natural elements that cannot be controlled, such as sufficient wind or …[9]. • The use of crop plants to generate energy has been criticized on the grounds that the crops and land needed to produce them could otherwise be used to grow food.

to bury sth *etw vergraben, etw begraben*
gradual *schrittweise, allmählich*
to split *teilen, spalten*
power station *Kraftwerk*
lifespan *Lebensdauer*
thermal *thermisch, Wärme-*
wastewater *Abwasser*
moreover *überdies, zudem*

Good to know

In 2011, an earthquake and tsunami caused a major accident at the **Fukushima** nuclear power plant in Japan in which around 47,000 residents were evacuated.

to **harvest** *ernten*
in turn *wiederum, seiner-/ihrerseits*
to combust *brennen, verbrennen*
sugar cane *Zuckerrohr*
manure *Dung, Mist*
to digest *verdauen*
plenty (of) *reichlich, viel*
to **poison** *vergiften*
to drill *bohren*
crop *Nutzpflanze, Feldfrucht*
otherwise *ansonsten, andernfalls*

Good to know

Fracking (hydraulic fracturing) is a way of accessing oil and gas from underground rock by making cracks in it.

Crossover TV

The energy revolution at the end of the world

01

Good to know

The **Northern Isles** are two groups of islands – the Orkney Islands and the Shetland Islands – which belong to Scotland.

The **North Sea oil boom** occurred in the 1970s and '80s when oil and gas fields were discovered in the North Sea. However, over half of the North Sea oil reserves have now been extracted.

The COP 26 UN climate change conference took place in Glasgow, Scotland in 2021.

To reach **net zero** is to achieve the goal of being climate-neutral with zero greenhouse emissions.

Watching

4 You are going to watch a documentary about current and future energy sources on Scotland's Northern Isles.

Read the sentences below. Then watch the video and complete the sentences.

1 Fossil fuels have been important to the Northern Isles for many years because …
2 The Orbital 02 has the capacity to …
3 The power from Nova Innovation's sea floor turbines …
4 The advantage of tidal energy is that it is predictable because the amount of tidal power produced does not …
5 At the European Marine Energy Centre, tidal energy is converted into hydrogen, which is stored and …
6 The oil and gas terminal has provided the Shetland Islands with useful facilities and …
7 Excess electricity from the Viking Wind Project will be …
8 Many islanders are opposed to the Viking Wind Project because they say it's …
9 Greenpeace is campaigning against …
10 Some people think that if renewables aren't developed, the Islands will have to …

Speaking

5 **Partner A:** Look here. **Partner B:** Look at File 2 on page 268.

Study the graph and then do the tasks below.

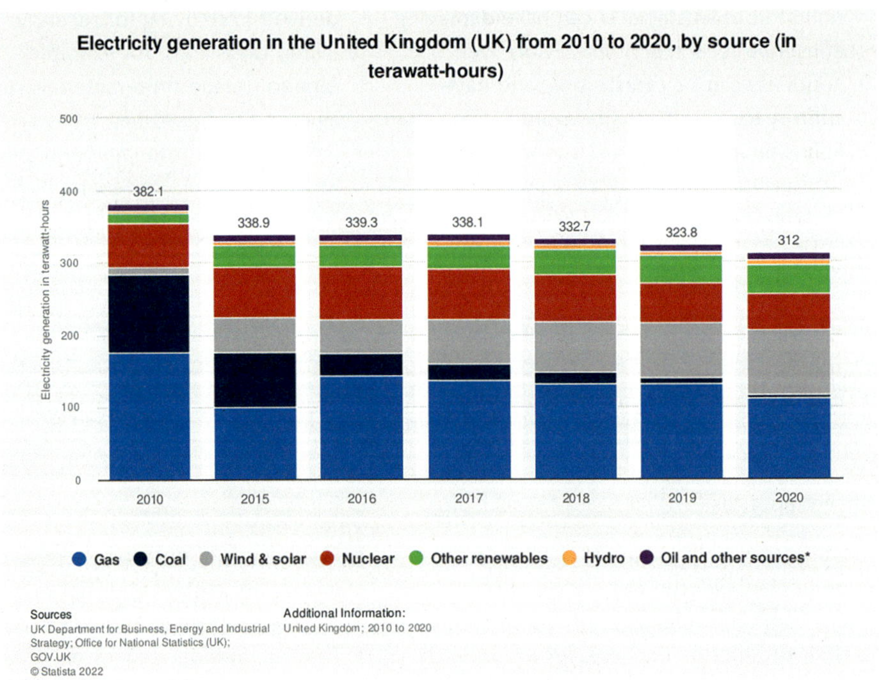

S ▸ Describing and analysing diagrams, pp. 43–44

1 Describe the graph to your partner. Explain the conclusions that can be drawn from the statistics.

2 Listen to your partner's description of their graph. Ask relevant questions about the statistics and your partner's conclusions about them.

6 Read the information about fracking and make a list of the pros and cons.

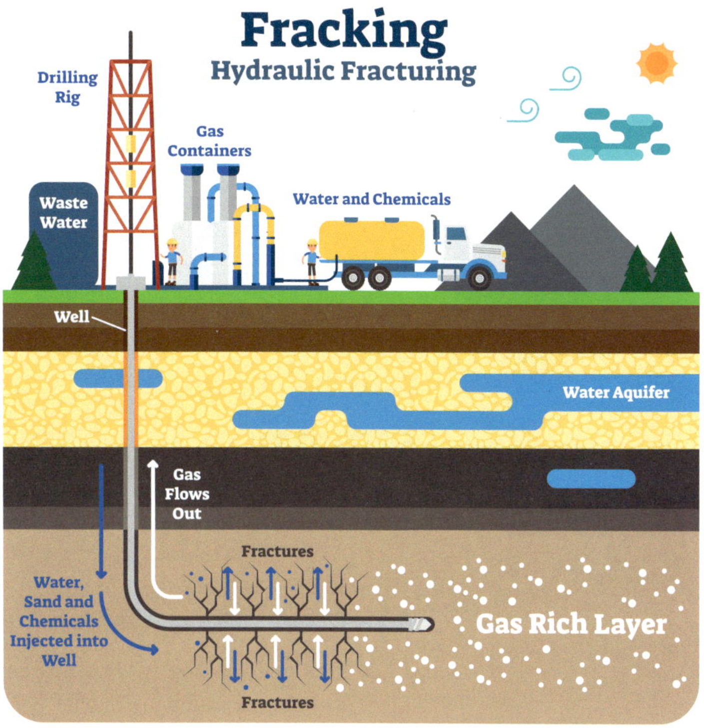

Fracking is used to extract oil or gas trapped inside layers of soft rock called shale rock. An alternative term for it is hydraulic (= using the pressure of water or any other liquid) fracturing (= breaking or cracking). During the fracking process, a high-pressure mixture of water, sand and chemicals is injected into the rock in order to release the gas. It is effective in accessing gas resources which are hard to reach through 'conventional' methods, and can be used to generate electricity with 50% fewer emissions than coal.

Fracking also has economic benefits: in the USA, for example, fracking has greatly increased domestic oil production and has brought down gas prices. At the same time, it has created thousands of jobs. Proponents of fracking claim that it is a way of providing energy security, as creating the infrastructure needed to obtain and store renewable energy is often still too expensive.

However, fracking is controversial and there are a number of environmental and safety concerns. Firstly, oil and gas are fossil fuels, and environmentalists worry that the economic benefits of fracking may stop governments and companies investing in renewable energy sources. Studies have also shown that there has been an increase in methane in the earth's atmosphere, which points to its release through drilling of shale gas. Fracking also requires large amounts of water at a huge environmental cost.

The drilling is thought by environmentalists to have caused ground tremors or even minor earthquakes in areas around fracking sites. It is also thought that the chemicals used may contaminate the groundwater – and drinking water.

Those responsible insist that they are monitoring safety and that tremors and contamination incidents are just the result of poor safety measures at certain sites.

well *Bohrloch*
aquifer *wasserführende Schicht*
shale *Schiefer*
to inject sth *etw einpressen*
tremor *Erschütterung, Beben*

7 An energy company is planning to start fracking in your area to meet increased energy needs. However, not everybody is happy about the idea. There will be a meeting in the town hall to discuss the proposal.

Hold the meeting in class with the following participants:

- the mayor of the town, who will host the debate and make sure all voices and audience questions are heard
- local politicians from two different parties: the party which has approved the fracking; and the opposition party which is against the idea
- owner/s of the land on which the fracking would happen
- representatives of the energy company
- residents of the area who want to voice their concerns about the fracking
- members of the audience who can ask questions

TIP

Make notes on the point of view and arguments of your role before you begin. Audience members should draft a few questions before and during the discussion.

Writing

8 Write a letter to the local newspaper giving your opinion on the debate and whether or not you think fracking in your area is a good idea.

Exam preparation

S ▸ Dealing with a creative writing task, pp. 126–128

Writing checklist

Section C Greenwashing

Warm-up

1 **Work in groups. Discuss the following questions. Share your results in class.**

1 Which everyday brands or products do you think are environmentally friendly? Why do you think that?
2 What examples of companies acting ecologically do you know? Do you think they are successful?
3 What do you think motivates companies to adopt a greener company policy?

Listening

03

Exam preparation

S ▸ Dealing with listening tasks, pp. 123–125

2 **You are going to listen to a radio show about how green everyday products really are. While listening, choose the correct answers (a, b or c).**

1 If a company has been involved in 'greenwashing', it has …
a contributed to a scheme to clean up the environment.
b used marketing to exaggerate how its products benefit the environment.
c taken steps to make its products or services more environmentally-friendly.

2 One main reason why companies greenwash their products or services is to …
a increase company profits.
b avoid fines for causing environmental damage.
c make a positive contribution to saving the environment.

3 A 'hidden trade off' is when a company …
a hires another company to deal with their environmental damage.
b pays the government of another country to dispose of their harmful waste.
c promotes one green aspect of their product to avoid mentioning the harm it is causing in another area.

4 If a company makes an irrelevant claim about the greenness of their product, it means that …
a the claim is false.
b the product doesn't make a significant contribution to global warming.
c the claim is probably true, but the company hasn't actually contributed to making the product green.

5 Claiming that a product is made of completely natural ingredients is …
a untrue, because no product is 100% natural.
b misleading, because natural products can also be harmful.
c dangerous, because some people may still have an allergic reaction to them.

6 The logo of an environmental organization on a product means that …
a it's a genuinely green product.
b the organization was involved in the invention of the product.
c you should be able to prove that the organization really has certified the product as environmentally-friendly.

7 According to Anthony, the fact that 'greenwashing' exists means that …
a society is increasingly interested in environmental issues.
b the majority of companies still don't care about the climate crisis.
c government pressure on companies to care for the environment is working.

Working with the text

3 Skim the text and answer the following questions in your own words.

S ▸ Reading difficult texts, pp. 39–40

1 What has ClientEarth found out?
2 What does it want policymakers to do?

'A great deception': oil giants taken to task over 'greenwash' ads

ClientEarth calls for tobacco-like health warnings on advertisements from fossil fuel firms

Some of the world's biggest fossil fuel companies have used advertising to "greenwash" their ongoing contribution to the climate crisis, according to files published by the environmental lawyers ClientEarth. They describe the practice as "a great deception".

The files compare the adverts produced by ExxonMobil, Aramco, Chevron, Shell, Equinor and others with the companies' operations and products, overall climate impact and progress toward climate-safe business models.

ClientEarth is calling on policymakers to ban all fossil fuel company ads unless they come with tobacco-style health warnings about the risks of global heating to people and the planet. Its lawyers lodged a complaint in 2019 alleging that BP's advertising campaigns had misled the public by focusing on the company's low carbon energy products, when more than 96% of its annual spend was on oil and gas. BP withdrew the ads before the complaint was assessed. ClientEarth said it was now putting other fossil fuel companies on notice over greenwashing adverts.

"We're currently witnessing a great deception, where the companies most responsible for catastrophically heating the planet are spending millions on advertising campaigns about how their business plans are focused on sustainability," said Johnny White, one of ClientEarth's lawyers.

"We need to reduce reliance on fossil fuels, but instead of leading a low-carbon transition these companies are putting out advertising which distracts the public and launders their image. Our research shows these adverts are misrepresenting the true nature of companies' businesses, of their contribution to climate change, and of their transition plans."

ClientEarth's analysis includes claims that:

ExxonMobil advertising suggested its experimental algae biofuels could one day reduce transport emissions, while it has no company-wide net zero target and its 2025 emission reduction targets do not include the vast majority of emissions resulting from its products.

Saudi Arabia's Aramco said it conducted business "in a way that addresses the climate challenge" yet it is the world's largest corporate greenhouse gas emitter and plans to continue exploring for more oil and gas, despite having reserves greater than those of Exxon, Chevron, Shell, BP and Total combined.

deception *Täuschung*
10 **operation** *Arbeitsablauf, Arbeitsgang, Betrieb, Geschäft*
12 policymaker *(politischer)* Entscheidungsträger/in
14 to lodge (a complaint) *(Beschwerde) einlegen*
14 to allege sth *jdm etw vorwerfen, jdm etw unterstellen*
15 to **mislead** *täuschen*
16 **annual** *jährlich*
16 spend *(sg) Ausgaben*
17 to **withdraw** *zurückziehen*
25 to **distract sb** *jdn ablenken*
26 to launder sth *(rein-) waschen*
32 **vast** *riesig, sehr groß*
34 to **conduct sth** *etw (durch) führen, etw leiten*
35 **emitter** *Emissionsquelle, Emittent*

Good to know

The **Paris Agreement** is an international treaty on climate change involving 196 countries. It was signed at the UN Climate Change Conference in Paris in 2015. One of its primary goals is to limit the global temperature increase to 1.5° C.

Chevron said it was "part of the solution" to climate change but does not have a net zero commitment or a strategy aligned with the Paris climate agreement. Its plans for carbon capture and storage cover less than 1% of its 2019 carbon emissions.

Shell said it was investing in "lower-carbon biofuels and hydrogen, electric vehicle charging, solar and wind power", but in 2020 it earmarked between $2bn and $3bn a year for low-carbon businesses, compared to $17bn on fossil fuels operations.

Norway's Equinor has talked of growing renewable capacity tenfold by 2026, but renewables are only planned to be 4% of its energy by that date.

ClientEarth said warnings on oil company adverts should state that fossil fuel products are the main cause of global heating and that companies must divulge how much they are spending on fossil fuels compared with their low-carbon businesses.

There are numerous campaigns in Europe and North America to ban fossil fuel advertising. The French parliament proposed a law in February to ban ads for fossil fuel products, and a Dutch law professor published a paper arguing that fossil fuel advertising is inherently harmful and misleading and should be banned.

A Shell spokesperson said: "Our target is to become a net-zero emissions energy business by 2050, in step with society's progress towards the goal of the Paris Agreement on climate change. Our short, medium and long-term intensity and absolute targets are fully consistent with the more ambitious 1.5C goal of the Paris Agreement. And our targets cover the full range of our own emissions and our customers' emissions."

A Chevron spokesman rejected ClientEarth's analysis. He said: "We engage in honest conversations about the energy transition. We believe the future of energy is lower carbon and are working to help the world achieve that goal. We are taking action to reduce the carbon intensity of our operations and assets, increase the use of renewables and offsets and invest in low-carbon technologies."

ExxonMobil, Aramco and Equinor did not respond to a request for comment.

The Guardian announced in January 2020 that it would no longer accept advertising from oil and gas companies.

(699 words) From: *The Guardian*, 19 April 2021

[40] **carbon capture and storage** *CO_2-Abscheidung und -Speicherung*

[43] to earmark sth for sth *etw für etw vorsehen*

[46] **capacity** *Kapazität, Leistung*

[46] tenfold *verzehnfacht*

[49] to divulge sth *etw offenlegen*

[53] to **propose sth** *etw vorschlagen, etw unterbreiten, etw darlegen*

[55] inherently *grundsätzlich, von Natur aus*

[59] **intensity** *Intensität*

[60] **consistent** *konsistent, widerspruchsfrei*

[63] to **reject** *ablehnen, zurückweisen*

[66] asset *Vermögen, Vermögenswert*

[67] **(carbon) offset** *Klimakompensation*

4 Read the text and do the following tasks.

S ▸ Writing a summary, p. 81

1 Outline BP's response to ClientEarth's accusation.
2 Point out the differences between the companies' advertising claims and reality (give 2 examples).
3 Describe the action taken regarding fossil fuel advertising in different regions and countries.
4 Examine the messages behind the statements given by fossil fuel companies.

5 Write an email to ClientEarth in which you comment on the examples of greenwashing advertising mentioned in the text.

Exam preparation

S ▸ Dealing with a creative writing task, pp. 126–128

Writing checklist

Working with words

6 Complete the sentences with the correct forms of the verbs in the box. The expressions are all from the article.

address | divulge | earmark | engage | launder | lodge | put | take

1 Local residents have … a complaint with the local council about the company's continued pollution of the river.
2 The government has … the company on notice over the emissions coming from their factories.
3 I think he wants to become a senior politician, so he'd better try and start … his image!
4 The new mayor said he wanted to … the issue of traffic and pollution in the city.
5 The funds have already been … for future green energy projects.
6 The authorities are insisting that the clothing brand … the level of emissions produced by their factories.
7 We are currently … in discussions with local government about improving access to public transport in the area.
8 Our manufacturers are … action to increase the amount of recyclable components in their products.

Speaking

7 Work in groups. Each group chooses to research either a greenwashing scandal or a company which is working hard to make a positive contribution to the environment. Present your research to the class.

Include information on …

Greenwashing scandals	Positive contributions to the environment
• the company • product/s and/or service/s involved	• the company • product/s and/or service/s involved
• how the scandal was uncovered (press, public, etc.) • the effect of the greenwashing scandal on the environment • response to the scandal and outcome	• what the company is doing/trying/ planning to do • the potential benefits • what the response has been so far

to uncover sth *etw aufdecken*

Writing

8 Comment on the following quote in relation to greenwashing, using examples from your research in exercise **7** to back up your arguments.

"Sustainability is now a big baggy sack in which people throw all kinds of old ideas, hot air and dodgy activities in order to be able to greenwash their products and feel good."

– Kevin McCloud, TV host and designer

Exam preparation

S ▸ Writing an argumentative text, pp. 167–172

dodgy *zwielichtig, verdächtig*

Writing checklist

Section D The importance of forests

Warm-up

1 Do the quiz in groups. If you don't know an answer, guess!

1 The Amazon rainforest contains … of the world's remaining rainforest.
   a 30% **b** 50% **c** 90%
2 Which country contains the largest area of the Amazon rainforest?
3 Name four other countries which contain parts of the Amazon rainforest.
4 Approximately how big is the area covered by the Amazon rainforest?
   a 1000 km^2 **b** 2,500,000 km^2 **c** 5,500,000 km^2
5 Approximately how many people live in the Amazon?
   a 50,000 **b** 300,000 **c** 30,000,000
6 The Amazon rainforest is sometimes referred to as the … of the Earth.
   a lungs **b** heart **c** brain
7 Name two major causes of deforestation in the Amazon.
8 Approximately how much of the Amazon rainforest has been destroyed over the past 50 years?
   a 3% **b** 17% **c** 50%
9 Roughly what percentage of the world's species can be found in the Amazon?
   a 10% **b** 30% **c** 50%
10 The Amazon creates up to 50% of its own … .
   a precipitation **b** wind **c** heat

precipitation *no pl* *Niederschlag/Niederschläge*

Working with the text

S ▸ Reading difficult texts, pp. 39–40

2 Skim the text and choose the correct answer (a, b or c).

One of the main causes of the transmission of animal viruses to humans is …
a a rise in extreme weather events.
b human development of natural areas.
c an increase in the amount of wildlife coming closer to human populations looking for food.

Rampant destruction of forests 'will unleash more pandemics'

Researchers to tell UN that loss of biodiversity enables rapid spread of new diseases from animals to humans

Rampant deforestation, uncontrolled expansion of farming and the building of mines in remote regions – as well as the exploitation of wild animals as sources of food, traditional medicines and exotic pets – are creating a "perfect storm" for the spillover of diseases from wildlife to people.

Almost a third of all emerging diseases have originated through the process of land use change, it is claimed. As a result, five or six new epidemics a year could soon affect Earth's population.

rampant *ungezügelt, grassierend*
to unleash sth *etw auslösen, etw entfesseln*
pandemic *Pandemie*
4 **mine** *Bergwerk, Mine*
4 exploitation *Ausbeutung, Abbau* (von Rohstoffen)
6 spillover *Übertragung*
7 to emerge *entstehen*
7 to originate *entstehen, seinen Ursprung haben*
8 epidemic *Epidemie, Seuche*

"There are now a whole raft of activities – illegal logging, clearing and mining – with associated international trades in bushmeat and exotic pets that have created this crisis," said Stuart Pimm, professor of conservation at Duke University. "In the case of Covid-19, it has cost the world trillions of dollars and already killed almost a million people, so clearly urgent action is needed."

It is estimated that tens of millions of hectares of rainforest and other wild environments are being bulldozed every year to cultivate palm trees, farm cattle, extract oil and provide access to mines and mineral deposits. This leads to the widespread destruction of vegetation and wildlife that are hosts to countless species of viruses and bacteria, most unknown to science. Those microbes can then accidentally infect new hosts, such as humans and domestic livestock.

Such events are known as spillovers. Crucially, if viruses thrive in their new human hosts they can infect other individuals. This is known as transmission and the result can be a new, emerging disease.

An example of such events is provided by the HIV virus, which in the early 20th century spread from chimpanzees and gorillas – which were being slaughtered for bushmeat in West Africa – to men and women and which has since caused the death of more than 10 million people. Other examples include Ebola fever, which is passed on by bats to primates and humans; the swine flu epidemic of 2009. [...]

"When workers come into rainforests to chop down trees, they don't take food with them," said Andy Dobson, professor of ecology and evolutionary biology at Princeton University. "They just eat what they can kill. So that exposes them to infection all the time."

However, not every emerging disease is caused by a single, major spillover event, stressed zoologist David Redding, of University College London. "In places where trees are being cleared, mosaics of fields, created around farms, appear in the landscape interspersed with parcels of old forest.

"This increases the interface between the wild and the cultivated. Bats, rodents and other pests carrying strange new viruses come from surviving clumps of forests and infect farm animals – who then pass on these infections to humans."

An example of this form of transmission is provided by Lassa fever, which was first discovered in Nigeria in 1969 and now causes several thousand deaths a year. The virus is spread by the rodent *mastomys natalensis*, which was widespread in Africa's savannahs and forests but now colonises homes and farms, passing on the disease to humans.

"The crucial point is that there are probably 10 times more different species of viruses than there are of mammals," added Dobson. "The numbers are against us and the emergence of new pathogens inevitable."

In the past many outbreaks of new diseases remained in contained areas. However, the development of cheap air travel has changed that picture and diseases can appear across the globe before scientists have fully realised what is happening.

"The onward transmission of a new disease is also another really important element in the pandemic story," said Professor James Wood, head of veterinary medicine at Cambridge University. "Consider the swine flu pandemic. We flew that around the world several times before we realised what was going on." [...]

10 a raft of sth *eine Fülle von etw*
10 to log *fällen*
10 to clear *räumen, roden*
11 bushmeat *Buschfleisch* (das Fleisch wildlebender Tiere)
16 to **cultivate sth** *etw anbauen; etw züchten*
17 **deposit** *Vorkommen*
18 countless *zahllose, unzählige*
20 livestock *Vieh*
21 to thrive *gedeihen, florieren*
25 to **slaughter** *schlachten*

Good to know

The **swine flu epidemic** was an influenza pandemic caused by a virus which spilt over from pigs to humans. It was thought to have originated from pigs in central Mexico. The pandemic lasted from January 2009 to August 2010.

29 to **chop down** *fällen*
31 to **expose** *aussetzen (einer Sache)*
36 to intersperse *durchsetzen*
36 **parcel** *Paket; Parzelle*
37 **interface** *Schnittstelle*
37 rodent *Nagetier*
38 pest *Schädling*
38 clump *Gruppe (Häuser, Bäume)*
47 **inevitable** *unausweichlich, unvermeidbar*
48 contained area *abgeschlossenes Gebiet*
51 onward *weiter, voran*
52 **veterinary (medicine)** *Tiermedizin*

58 **price tag** *Preisschild*
58 to dwarf *klein erscheinen lassen, in den Schatten stellen*
59 to **wipe** *wischen, wegwischen*
65 emergence *Auftreten, Entstehung*
66 to postpone sth *etw vertagen, etw verschieben*
67 to soar *steigen*
67 to strive *sich anstrengen*

In a paper published in *Science*, Pimm, Dobson and other scientists and economists propose setting up a programme to monitor wildlife, reduce spillovers, end the wildlife meat trade and reduce deforestation. Such a scheme could cost more than $20bn a year, a price tag that is dwarfed by the cost of the Covid-19 pandemic, which has wiped trillions of dollars from national economies round the world.

"We estimate that the value of prevention costs for 10 years to be only about 2% of the costs of the Covid-19 pandemic," they state. In addition, reducing deforestation – which is a major source of carbon emissions – would also have the benefit of helping the battle against climate change, add the researchers.

"The rate of emergence of novel diseases is increasing and their economic impacts are also increasing," states the group. "Postponing a global strategy to reduce pandemic risk would lead to continued soaring costs. Society must strive to avoid the impacts of future pandemics."

(790 words) From: *The Guardian*, 30 August 2020

3 Work in pairs. Create a flow diagram showing the chain of events which can lead to a new pandemic. Include the following information:

- factors which can facilitate a 'spillover' of disease
- chain of events which can lead to a pandemic
- example(s) of how previous pandemics might have spread
- why pandemics are becoming increasingly global
- solutions proposed by scientists

Use this example to help you.

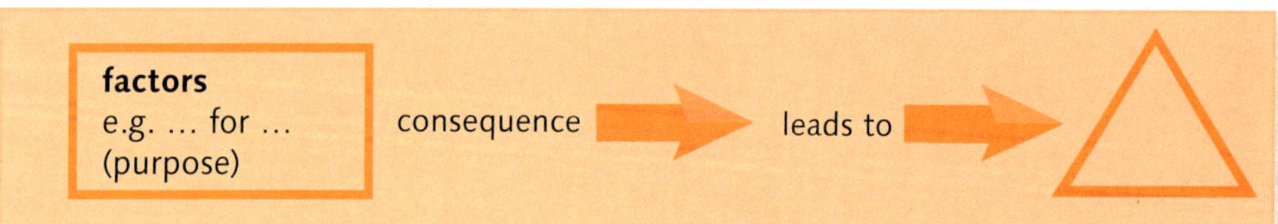

Compare your results with another pair and make any necessary additions or changes to your diagram.

Exam preparation
S ▸ Writing a summary, p. 81

4 Summarize the information given in the article. Use your flow diagram to help you.

Working with language

Remember

The passive is formed with ***to be*** (in the correct tense) + **past participle** (3rd form of the verb).

G ▸ The passive, p. 290

5 Work with a partner. Find examples of the passive in the text. When is the passive used?

6 Rewrite the following sentences using the passive. Decide whether or not you need to use *by*.

1. Participants at the climate conference discuss the issue of deforestation every year.
2. People have eaten bushmeat for hundreds of years.
3. The WHO will investigate the origin of the new virus.
4. Protesters blocked roads to the proposed new mine.
5. Virologists haven't seen this kind of virus before.

Research

7 Work in groups. Research products which are harmful to the rainforest. Find out why they are harmful. Present your results to the class.

S ▸ Describing and analysing diagrams, pp. 43–44

Writing

8 You are a member of a local environmental campaign group and your group is organizing a street protest about a local supermarket selling products which come from the Amazon rainforest and therefore contribute to deforestation. The organizers would like you to give a speech at the protest.

Write a speech using information from this Section. Include the following points.

- what the supermarket is selling and why the products are harmful to the environment
- how this may affect the planet and people's lives
- what your organization is trying to do and how people at the protest can help

Exam preparation

S ▸ Dealing with a creative writing task, pp. 126–128

Writing checklist

Skills training: Writing a speech

Before you start writing your speech, read and follow these tips.

1 Make notes on the following points:
- **Who** will your audience be? (adults / young people / kids? What do they know about the topic of your speech?)
- **What** will your speech be about? What points do you want to make?
- **Why** are you giving the speech? What do you want your audience to learn? What do you want them to feel/understand/do?
- **Where** will you give your speech? Will there be anything that you can use to illustrate your speech?
- **How long** should it last? How long can your audience concentrate for?

2 Brainstorm points you would like to make and information you would like to give in your speech. You may cut some of these later. It may be helpful to organize your thoughts in a list or mind map.

3 Divide your speech into three main parts: introduction, main body, conclusion.
- **Introduction:** How will you get your audience's attention (e.g. with a personal anecdote, a rhetorical question [= a question you don't expect an answer to, used for dramatic effect, e.g. *Do you want to buy products that destroy our planet?*], a short, funny story?). How will you lead your audience into the main part of the speech?
- **Main body:** Think about the main points you wish to make and how you can make them clear to an audience who might not know much about your topic. Avoid using long sentences or spending too long on one point.
- **Conclusion:** Sum up the points you made in the main body of your speech, but don't repeat them word for word. Try to use shorter, simpler sentences that the audience will remember when your speech is over.

How to say or write it

Introducing yourself
Hello everybody and welcome …
I'm … / My name's … from … (organization).
It's nice to see so many people here today.

Introducing the topic
I'm here to talk to you about … / I'd like to talk to you about …
The reason I'm here today is to … / I'm here today to tell you about …

Stating your aims
First, I'd like to tell you about … Then …
I'd like to start by explaining/introducing/outlining …
I'd like to take this opportunity to tell you / say a few words about …

Linking ideas
Let's move on to … / Let me turn to …
Another important aspect is …

Ending the speech
To sum up, …
Thank you all for listening / for your time.
Does anyone have a question? / Any questions?

Speaking

9 Deliver your speech to the class and give feedback on your classmates' speeches.

Section E The fashion industry

Warm-up

1 Look at the labels on your clothes and find out where they were made. Share the information with the class. Which countries were the most common?

2 Discuss the following questions in groups.

1. Where do you buy your clothes? Do you try to buy organic/ethical fashion or second-hand items? Why (not)?
2. Do you ever donate clothing to a charity or pass on clothes to friends or family members?
3. What environmental issues can you think of which are associated with the fashion industry?

toxic *giftig, Gift-*
arsenic *Arsen*
lead *Blei*
metric ton *Tonne (1000 kg)*
summit *Gipfel(treffen)*

Fast fashion fact sheet

Water consumption: ...[1]
The slightly better news: Attitudes seem to be changing: a recent survey in the UK found that 18 % of respondents decided against buying certain clothing items due to concerns about the environment.

Water pollution: ...[2]. It often contains toxic substances such as arsenic, mercury and lead and can harm both wildlife and the health of people living next to rivers. The contaminated water eventually reaches the sea and thus spreads around the globe.
The slightly better news: Campaigns such as Greenpeace's Detox My Fashion have led to fashion companies committing to banning toxic chemicals from their production lines within the next few years.

Textile waste: ...[3]
The slightly better news: Innovative new apps, clothes swapping and other community fashion projects are becoming more popular.

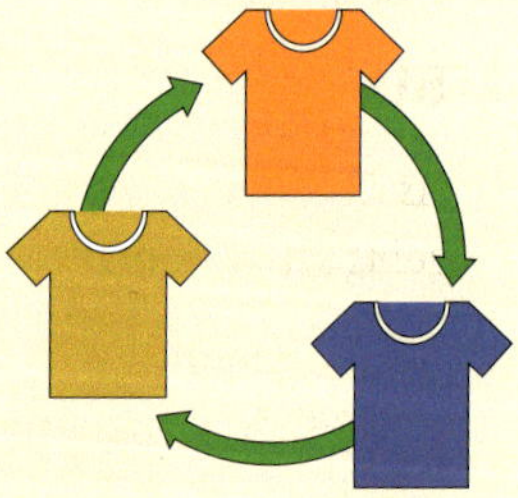

Air pollution: ...[4]
The slightly better news: Although clothing manufacturing in the UK produced approx. 306,000 metric tons of carbon dioxide emissions in 2019, this is almost 58 % less than in 1990 and 3.6 % less than in 2018.

Energy consumption: ...[5]
The slightly better news: At the G7 summit in 2019, 32 fashion companies including Chanel, Prada, H&M and Zara signed a pact to place more emphasis on sustainability in the industry.

Working with the fact sheet

3 Match the missing sentences (a–e) to the gaps (1–5) in the fact sheet on page 26.

a Fashion is responsible for 10% of greenhouse gas emissions.
b The fashion industry is one of the "thirstiest" industries: growing enough cotton to produce just one T-shirt requires about 2,700 litres of water!
c The fashion industry consumes more energy than both air travel and shipping.
d In the UK, about 13 million items of clothing end up in landfill annually.
e Around 90% of textiles factories in developing countries dump untreated wastewater from clothing dyes directly into rivers.

shipping *Schifffahrt*
landfill site *Mülldeponie*
dye *Farbe, Färbemittel*

Working with words

4 Match these definitions to words from the fact sheet.

1 a substance grown as a crop in countries such as India or Egypt in order to produce a clothing textile
2 a system of burying waste in between layers of earth
3 to get rid of waste in a careless way
4 the set of actions carried out to create a product, for example in a factory
5 to exchange an item or items with another
6 way of thinking or feeling towards something
7 a substance used to produce colour in fabrics

fabric *Gewebe, Stoff, Tuch*

Working with the text

5 Read the article and make notes on the following points.

- the different approaches to slow fashion mentioned in the article
- the issues they are trying to address
- issues not addressed by the start-ups

S ▸ Reading difficult texts, pp. 39–40

Resselling, repairing and 'swishing': the rise of sustainable fashion apps

04

As technology makes secondhand clothes more accessible, more shoppers in the UK are going green

A new generation of "slow fashion" apps is allowing people to experiment with clothes swapping and shopping secondhand.

Lauren Bravo, the author of How to Break Up with Fast Fashion, says: "Where a few years ago, buying secondhand could mean hours of trawling, tech is making the whole experience so much more efficient and more accessible." While charity shops have suffered sales declines of as much as a third, resale sites such as Loopster, Depop and Vinted have boomed in recent months.

Loopster, a website where people trade good-quality used children's and women's clothes, has recorded a meteoric 700% rise in sales from the beginning of 2020. Vestiaire Collective, an 11-year-old luxury hub where people sell pre-loved designer clothes and handbags, has reported a 101% increase, year on year, in the number of items posted for sale through its marketplace.

6 to trawl sth *etw durchkämmen, durchforsten*
8 to decline *zurückgehen, fallen, sinken*
8 **resale** *Weiterverkauf, Wiederverkauf*
12 **hub** *Knotenpunkt, Hauptumschlagplatz*
12 pre-loved *gebraucht*

15 alteration *Änderung*
16 to **launch** *(Produkt) auf den Markt bringen, einführen*
16 seamster/seamstress *Näher/in*
18 high-street *Durchschnitts-*
20 **token** *Gutschein*
22 gem *Juwel, Prachtstück*
23 to offload *abladen, abstoßen*
26 retailer *Einzelhändler/in*
26 goods *pl* *Waren, Güter*
29 conscience *Gewissen*
30 glorified *bessere/r/s*
33 **devastating** *verheerend*
33 **garment** *Bekleidung*
37 like-minded *gleichgesinnt*
38 to outgrow sth *aus etw herauswachsen*
42 to **loan** *ausleihen*
43 **fee** *Gebühr*
43 to **fund sth** *etw finanzieren*
51 to **treasure** *schätzen, pflegen*
52 intimacy *Vertrautheit*
55 proceeds *pl* *Einnahmen*
57 **circular** *kreisförmig, rund*

Sojo – a Deliveroo-like service for clothes repairs and alterations – has just launched a pilot in London. It connects customers to local seamster businesses through its app and bicycle delivery service.

And apps such as Nuw and Swopped now allow people to swap items, from high-street to designer, via their mobile phones. These platforms operate under a system of "swishing", which means you earn an equal value token for each item you swap and so there is no need to exchange directly with another user.

These platforms not only simulate the thrill of finding "new" gems but also offer alternatives to sending unwanted items to landfill or offloading donations at charity shops when they are closed. According to Wrap, an estimated 336,000 tonnes of used clothing gets thrown in the bin in the UK every year. Meanwhile, the charity retailer Barnardo's reported that goods left outside shops were costing the charity to clear.

"Charity shops need to be a two-way street," says Bravo. "It's not enough to use them to clear our wardrobes and our consciences; if we're going to use them as glorified recycling bins, we have to shop from them, too."

Nuw, which Aisling Byrne and friend Alison Kelly co-founded in 2015, was born in response to their guilt about the social and environmental costs of their favourite hobby: shopping. After seeing the devastating effects on garment workers while they were volunteering in India, the pair began lobbying for change.

"At university, avoiding fast fashion was really important to us, but we couldn't really afford any of the alternatives," Byrne says. So they started hosting clothes swapping events with like-minded people, using empty Dublin nightclubs. Nuw's community quickly outgrew its initial WhatsApp group. The social network now has nearly 8,000 members, with 2,500 monthly app users across the UK and Ireland.

Unlike most rental sites, where users profit – in some cases, greatly – from loaning their luxury items, Nuw members only pay the delivery cost of sending items; there's no rental fee. The Irish startup, which is funded by "tech for good" investors, focuses less on the commercial value of clothes than on the emotional significance each garment gathers as it is passed on, and the app includes an impact calculator that lets users track the carbon, waste and water offset created every time they swap.

"Our customers get the feeling like they're going into their friend's wardrobes, and just picking out things that they like," says Byrne. For Nuw members, seeing their treasured pieces reappear on social media with a new owner creates a sense of intimacy with someone they will never meet.

This is the idea behind the app Thrift+, which lets people send high-quality donations by post to be resold directly to other fashion lovers, with proceeds from each sale going to charity. The initiative, which launched this week, is designed to "power the circular fashion economy" says Joe Metcalfe, Thrift+'s co-founder and chief executive.

But the burden of going green shouldn't lie only on the consumer, says Emily Macintosh, the policy officer for textiles at the European Environmental Bureau and coordinator of the EEB's Wardrobe Change campaign, which urges the EC to actively reduce the footprint of textiles sold on the EU market. "We also need to put the responsibility on producers who are making massive amounts of money from this polluting, exploitative wasteful system."

While rental apps may present a welcome disruption to retail's ownership model, she adds, "it's not necessarily sustainable if the clothes that are being rented were produced using hazardous chemicals and they're all made from polyester".

"People are increasingly concerned about the environmental cost of fashion," says Jane Fellner, who runs Loopster. "And this has coupled with the financial impact of the pandemic – people are counting every penny they spend. Secondhand fashion is great for people's pockets and the planet."

(779 words) From: *The Guardian*, 29 January 2021

[59] burden *Last, Belastung, Bürde*
[61] to **urge sb** *jdn drängen*
[61] **EC (European Commission)** *Europäische Kommission*
[64] exploitative *ausbeuterisch*
[65] disruption *Störung, Behinderung, Unterbrechung*
[67] hazardous *gefährlich, Gefahr-*
[69] coupled with sth *mit etw verbunden*

6 State ways in which apps are attempting to solve environmental issues created by the fashion industry. Point out the shortcomings of the apps mentioned in the article.

Exam preparation
S ▸ Writing a summary, p. 81

Mediation

7 You work for a charity in your town/city which has its own second-hand clothes store. The charity is interested in developing new and practical ways to stop clothes being thrown away.

You read the article and decide to send an email to your boss summarizing the most important points in German.

S ▸ Mediation, pp. 257–259

Speaking

8 Work with a partner and talk about the following questions.

1 Which of the ideas from the article do you find the most interesting? Explain why.
2 What other slow fashion solutions have you heard of? Would you consider trying them out? Why (not)?

9 Work in groups. Do some research on the community environmental groups or projects that exist in your area. (e.g. clothes swapping or rental, carpooling, tool sharing, upcycling, etc.). Present the ones you like best to the class.

Writing

10 You have joined one of the community groups or projects from exercise 9. Write an article for your school magazine about what the project does and why you decided to join in. Inform other students about what you did and encourage them to do the same.

Exam preparation
S ▸ Dealing with a creative writing task, pp. 126–128

Writing checklist

Section F Climate activism

Warm-up

1 Have you or has anyone you know ever participated in climate activism? What did you/they do?

2 Work in groups. Look at the photos and logos of the climate activists and organizations below. Discuss which of them you know and what you know about them.

Luisa Neubauer

Xiuhtezcatl Martinez

Sea Shepherd

Extinction Rebellion

3 Now choose a person or organization you don't know or would like to know more about and do some research online. Share what you have found out with the class.

Working with words

4 Work with a partner. You have five minutes to make as many collocations about climate activism as you can using verbs from the list and phrases from the word cloud. If necessary, use your dictionary to help you.

to block | to break | to confront | to donate | to engage in | to file | to get | to glue | to go | to join | to make | to organize | to put | to spread

a lawsuit
involved with an organization on strike
money to environmental charities roads civil disobedience
the law a pledge to live a greener life politicians
pressure on the government the message on social media
a demonstration yourself to a public building
a beach clean-up

disobedience *Ungehorsam*
pledge *Zusage, Schwur Versprechen,*

Share your list with the class. Which pair found the most collocations?

Good to know

Climate justice is a term used to acknowledge the fact that, in general, disadvantaged communities (e.g. people of colour, indigenous people, people with low incomes, etc.) are far more vulnerable to climate change than wealthier, mainly white communities.

Speaking

5 Discuss the questions in a group, then share with the class.

1 Which form/s of activism, organizations or individual activists from exercises 1–4 do you find the most interesting and/or effective? Why do you think that?
2 What can individuals do to help the environment?
3 What do *you* do to help the environment?

6 Read and evaluate yourself according to the "Tree metaphor" below, then compare your answers with your group.

Tree metaphor

The **leaves:** Leaves may well know the latest trends in green fashion or diet, but they actually care more about their image than the environment. Disposable T-shirts sold in ridiculous amounts of plastic wrapping? If they're "in", you'll be completely blown away and order a whole box full online!

The **branches**: Branches are active in environmental activism and generally part of a network of people who really care about the environment. They follow several activists online and take part in as many campaigns as possible – from beach or park clean-ups to joining street protests with their lovingly-made banners. Branches are often very enthusiastic and might even encourage smaller twigs to grow and live a greener life. put pressure on companies to clean up their act and become more environmentally-friendly. Young trunks may look for careers in fields like conservation or environmental science.

The **twigs**: Twigs generally try to be environmentally-friendly – if it's not too much work! They might buy recycled paper and take their own bag to the supermarket, but if being green becomes too much effort; they'll probably just snap and do whatever is easiest – however environmentally-unfriendly it might be.

The **roots**: Roots might hide their commitment to living an environmentally-friendly life under the ground, but they have their principles and do whatever they can. They won't buy products which are known to be harmful to the environment or unethical and they get their clothes from second-hand shops wherever possible. Younger roots are often vegan and may sometimes experience conflict with older, meat-eating family members at mealtimes.

7 Now discuss the following questions:

1 How did your evaluation compare to your answers to exercise 5?
2 In what ways do/don't you act in an environmentally-friendly way?
3 Why do you honestly think this is, e.g. convenience, you don't really believe it helps, too expensive, …?
4 Do you feel you should change your behaviour? Why (not)?

Share your results with the class.

convenience *Bequemlichkeit*

Listening

05

8 You will hear a radio report about an unusual environmental activist in New York.

Exam preparation

S ▸ Dealing with listening tasks, pp. 123–125

While listening, take notes on the following points. You need not write complete sentences.

Topic

1 Jim O'Brien's message: …

Reactions on subway

2 reaction O'Brien wants from his listeners (2 aspects): …
examples: talk to family, friends, other passengers
3 how listeners usually react (2 aspects): …
4 positive reaction: …
5 Kent Bleeker's message's (2 aspects): …
example: it's too late

Teaching other activists

6 group O'Brien belongs to: …
7 O'Brien's speaking technique: …
8 reaction new speakers expect: …
9 issues for new speakers to mention (2 aspects): …
examples: worldwide crop failure, climate migrants
10 getting people to listen: …

Working with words

9 What do the underlined words and phrases mean? With a partner, take turns to explain them in your own words.

1 Jim O'Brien is a man with a mission.
2 He spends his time hollering at strangers on the subway.
3 What inspired him to pursue this unusual hobby?
4 Why don't I just sit down and mind my own business?
5 Have you ever had anyone heckle you?
6 This one guy … he's always badmouthing what I do.
7 … an old man who spends his time preaching the apocalypse.
8 … I would have appreciated a mentor guiding me.

Speaking

10 Work in groups. Discuss the following questions.

1 How would you react if someone started shouting about the climate emergency on a bus or train? Explain why.
2 Do you think Jim O'Brien's method of communicating his message to other people is effective? Why (not)?
3 Brainstorm ways to encourage people to act in more environmentally-friendly ways. Which do you think would be the most effective?

Research and presentation

11 Research an unusual climate solution and present it to the class. Choose one of the ideas below or your own idea. Include the following information.

- the aspect of the climate crisis the solution is aimed at
- the inventor(s) and how they came up with the idea (if possible)
- how the solution works
- the impact the idea could have / has already had
- your reasons for presenting this particular solution

Vermicomposting

This is a great way to turn your waste food into compost you can use to grow your own food (or houseplants!). Worms eat the leftover food, which turns into compost as it passes through and exits their body. This system can be used almost anywhere: Los Angeles city employees keep a plastic bin of live worms in their office to recycle their leftovers from lunch.

vermicomposting *Wurmkompostierung*
leftovers *Speisereste*

Carbon sequestration

Scientists are looking into ways to bury excess carbon dioxide and store it underground in places like depleted oil or gas fields. In order for this to work, it would be necessary to separate carbon dioxide from emissions, compress it and put it into an underground chamber for thousands of years. Sceptics point out the potential environmental effect if the gas leaked out of the ground.

carbon sequestration *CO_2-Abscheidung und -Speicherung*
depleted *erschöpft*
to **separate** *trennen, abspalten*
to compress *komprimieren*
chamber *Kammer*
to **leak** *auslaufen, lecken*

Turning plastic bottles into food flavouring

Researchers have managed to break down the materials used in plastic bottles using enzymes to convert them into vanilla flavouring (vanillin) to make the first valuable chemical brewed from waste plastic. Vanillin is used in food and cosmetics, but also in pharmaceuticals and cleaning products. Demand for vanilla exceeds supply, and vanillin is usually produced using chemicals derived from fossil fuels.

flavouring *Aroma(stoff)*
enzyme *Enzym*
to brew sth *etw brauen*
to **exceed** *überschreiten*
to derive *gewinnen, beziehen*

12 Discuss in class: If you could only implement one of these climate solutions on a wider scale, which would you choose and why?

Writing

13 Give your opinion on the statement below.

"It's far too late to save the environment now. There's nothing we can do. The planet is too far gone."

Exam preparation

S ▸ Writing an argumentative text, pp. 167–172

Writing checklist

Project Holding a climate conference

You are going to take part in a climate conference about the problem of plastic on the Galápagos Islands.

The Galápagos Islands
These are a group of islands in the Pacific Ocean, around 1,000km from the coast of Ecuador. The islands are famous for the many varieties of wildlife and marine species which inhabit them.

The problem of plastic
The Galápagos Islands are facing a number of environmental issues, and pollution from plastic waste is one of the most serious. Plastic can be found on the islands' beaches, in the seawater – even inside marine animals, which may swallow it or become tangled in the waste. Plastic waste includes everyday objects such as plastic bags, packaging, water bottles, toothbrushes and even clothing, arriving in the Galápagos from waste thrown into the ocean from all around the world. Even plastic which has been degraded by the sun or water can break down into tiny microparticles which can be easily absorbed by marine wildlife.

Aim of the conference

Environmentalists and scientists, political decision-makers and those with different commercial interests (Galápagos tourism, the plastics industry) should work together to reach a viable solution to the problem of plastic on the Galápagos Islands. The solution should be acceptable to all parties involved. A mediator will run the conference and ensure that all parties are given equal opportunities to state their case.

Before the conference

Step 1
Decide on the title and headline of the conference. This should reflect the conclusion you aim to reach.

Step 2
Divide the class into groups according to their roles. The conference participants are as follows:

The mediator: Look at File 3 on page 268.

Government representative(s): Look at File 22 on page 280.

Representative(s) of a packaging manufacturer: Look at File 12 on page 273.

Representative(s) of the tourist industry: Look at File 15 on page 275.

Local scientific researcher(s): Look at File 5 on page 269.

Representative(s) of a local environment group: Look at File 9 on page 271.

Member(s) of the press: Look at File 7 on page 270.

Preparing your role

Step 3

Read your role card and prepare yourself (= your character) for the conference:

- Brainstorm what you want to achieve and the points you wish to make.
- Make a list of questions that members of the press may ask and any points which other participants may use against you. Think about ways to respond to these.
- Write a short opening statement, introducing yourself and your organization.

Tip

Structure your notes in such a way that you will be able to find the relevant points quickly!

During the conference

Step 4

When the conference begins, the mediator briefly summarizes what will be discussed at the conference and each participant makes their opening statement.

Step 5

The discussion begins. Each speaker presents arguments and counterarguments.

Step 6

Once the mediator has ended the discussion phase, each speaker has the opportunity to make a closing statement.

After the conference

Step 7

The mediator sums up the main points and the conclusions reached.

Evaluating the conference

As a class, evaluate the conference by thinking about the following questions.

- Did the conference run smoothly?
- Were all sides of the issue evenly represented?
- Was the conclusion fair to everybody?
- Which arguments did you find most convincing?
- What went well and what could have been done better?

Tip

Don't forget that body language, gestures and the use of language can all contribute to making an argument convincing.

Reporting on the conference

Write a newspaper article about the conference including the following aspects.

- the setting and atmosphere in the conference room
- facts about the participants and topics discussed
- the main arguments presented
- at least one quotation and highlight from the conference
- the outcome(s) of the conference

S ▸ Dealing with a creative writing task, pp. 126–128

Climate conference checklist

✓ Have you clearly defined the aim of the conference?
✓ Have you prepared your roles carefully, noting down what you want to say?
✓ Has everyone had a chance to present their arguments?
✓ Have the members of the press had enough time to ask questions?
✓ Has the mediator summed up the main points and the conclusions?

06

Words in context

The climate emergency

to **declare a climate emergency** *den Klimanotstand ausrufen*
irreversible *unumkehrbar*
to **raise awareness (about sth)** *auf etw aufmerksam machen*
climate change *Klimawandel*
net zero *Netto-Null-*
carbon neutrality *Klimaneutralität*
carbon dioxide (CO_2) emissions *pl Kohlendioxidausstoße*
global warming *Erderwärmung*
agreement *Vereinbarung*

The UK, all the EU member states and a number of other nations have declared a climate emergency, stating that urgent action is needed to prevent potentially irreversible damage to the environment.

The aim of the declaration was to raise awareness about the issue of climate change and put pressure on global leaders and companies to stick to the climate goal of becoming net zero or achieving carbon neutrality. This means that they should eventually eliminate all carbon dioxide emissions. By doing this, global warming should be kept to the maximum of 1.5°C agreed on in the Paris Agreement in 2015. The agreement was renewed at the United Nations Climate Change Conference (COP 26) held in Glasgow in 2021.

The consequences of global warming

extinct *ausgestorben*
to **trap sth** *etw einfangen*
solar radiation *Sonneneinstrahlung*
to **thrive** *gedeihen*
atmosphere *Atmosphäre*
to overheat *(sich) überhitzen*
catastrophic *katastrophal*
extreme weather event *extremes Wetterereignis*
flooding *Hochwasser*
drought *Dürre*
heatwave *Hitzewelle*
hurricane *Wirbelsturm*
survival *Überleben*
endangered *bedroht*
pollination *Bestäubung*
crops *pl Anbaupflanzen*
deforestation *Entwaldung*
biodiversity *Artenvielfalt*
to **store sth** *etw speichern*
ecosystem *Ökosystem*
habitat *Lebensraum*

Of course, most life on Earth would be extinct without the greenhouse effect, because it traps the necessary amount of solar radiation to warm the atmosphere sufficiently, allowing life to thrive on the planet. However, an increase in greenhouse gases in the atmosphere leads to the overheating of the planet.

In fact, even a slight rise in global temperatures can have catastrophic effects on human lives, for example in the form of extreme weather events such as flooding, drought, heatwaves and hurricanes. It can also lead to the extinction of species vital to our survival. Perhaps the most well-known example are bees, of which a number of species are now endangered and which are essential for the pollination of crops and other plants. Their extinction would directly threaten our food supplies.

Deforestation contributes to both global warming and the loss of biodiversity. Trees store carbon, preventing greenhouse gases from being released into the atmosphere, and form part of essential ecosystems and habitats for species which provide us with nutrition and medicines.

The ever-increasing need for energy

overpopulated *überbevölkert*
energy *Energie*
fossil fuel *fossiler Brennstoff*
to **generate sth** *etw erzeugen*
to **extract sth** *etw gewinnen*
fracking *Fracking*
drilling *Bohren*
harmful *schädlich*
to **pollute sth** *etw verschmutzen*
non-renewable *nicht erneuerbar*
energy source *Energiequelle*
to **run out** *ausgehen*
carbon footprint *CO_2-Bilanz*
renewable *erneuerbar*
tidal energy *Gezeitenenergie*
biofuel *Biokraftstoff*

Planet Earth is overpopulated and the human population is continuing to grow: meaning that we have an ever-increasing need for energy. For decades, burning fossil fuels has been the primary method of generating energy. However, not only are many methods of extracting fossil fuels such as fracking or drilling harmful to the environment, burning them also pollutes the atmosphere and contributes to global warming. Fossil fuels are also a non-renewable energy source, meaning that at some point they will run out. In order to reduce our global carbon footprint, we need to generate energy through renewable sources like solar, wind, geothermal, tidal energy and biofuels.

Nuclear power: a double-edged sword

One alternative method of energy generation is nuclear energy, created by splitting uranium atoms. The advantage is that nuclear power stations don't produce any carbon dioxide. However, the waste they create is radioactive and extremely difficult to dispose of safely.

Furthermore, accidents such as the one at the Fukushima Nuclear Power Plant in Japan cause widespread damage. In 2011, an earthquake and tsunami caused reactor shutdowns, flooding and explosions, releasing radiation into the atmosphere and contaminated water into the Pacific Ocean. As a result of this, the German government decided to immediately close down eight of its nuclear plants and begin phasing out the operation of the remaining nine.

nuclear power *Atomkraft, -energie*
double-edged sword *zweischneidiges Schwert*
to **split sth** *etw spalten*
uranium atom *Uranatom*
nuclear power station *Kernkraftwerk*
waste *Abfall*
to **dispose of sth** *etw entsorgen*
to **cause damage** *Schaden verursachen*
earthquake *Erdbeben*
shutdown *Herunterfahren, Abschaltung*
radiation *Strahlung*
contaminated *(strahlen)verseucht*
to **phase out** *auslaufen lassen*

Overconsumption and plastic waste

Humans are consuming so many natural resources, that nature cannot regenerate sufficiently: it's essential that we start to live more sustainable lives. One way for ordinary consumers to do this is to use less packaging and more biodegradable products – and much less plastic. Most plastic can't be broken down – it doesn't rot like food or paper – so it stays in the environment for hundreds of years. Furthermore, single-use plastic products are thrown away after they have been used, often ending up in the oceans; in fact, the 'Great Pacific garbage patch' in the Pacific Ocean is thought to measure up to 15,000,000 km². Marine wildlife can get trapped or injured by the plastic, or mistake smaller pieces for food and eat them. Another issue is microbeads, which are found in personal hygiene products such as soap or toothpaste and are washed down household drains. These can end up in rivers and other water systems and cause plastic particle pollution.

overconsumption *Überkonsum*
plastic waste *Kunststoffmüll*
to consume *verbrauchen, konsumieren*
natural resource *Naturressource*
to **regenerate** *sich regenerieren*
sustainable *nachhaltig*
packaging *Verpackung(-smaterial)*
biodegradable *biologisch abbaubar*
to **break sth down** *etw abbauen*
to **rot** *verrotten*
single use *Einmalgebrauch*
garbage patch *Müllstrudel*
marine wildlife *Meerestierwelt*
to **injure sb** *jdn verletzen*
microbead *Mikrokügelchen*
particle *Teilchen*
drain *Abfluss*
plastic particle *Kunststoffpartikel*

Tackling climate change begins at home

Of course, much of the blame and responsibility for the climate emergency lies with multinational companies, whose factories pollute the atmosphere and whose advertising encourages us to consume much more than we actually need. However, we can put pressure on companies by simply not buying their products, or actively lobbying politicians and other leaders to ban the sale of substances which harm our planet. For example, increasing numbers of people are switching to plant-based diets to reduce the problems caused by factory farming and the meat industry which uses a large amount of resources, such as water, medicines and food. Large areas of land are being cleared in order to grow food for the animals, which is particularly worrying in areas which are vital for the survival of the planet such as the Amazon rainforest.

Although changing our diets to eat less meat, buying less single-use products and supporting climate activists won't solve the climate crisis, things are slowly changing and it's important not to give up!

to **tackle sth** *etw (z.B. ein Problem) angehen, etw bewältigen*
responsibility *Verantwortung*
factory *Fabrik*
to **lobby sb** *jdn (mit Lobbyarbeit) beeinflussen*
to **ban sth** *etw verbieten*
to **switch to sth** *zu etw wechseln*
plant-based diet *Pflanzenkost*
factory farming *Massentierhaltung*
meat industry *Fleischindustrie*
to **clear sth** *hier: abholzen*
Amazon rainforest *Amazonas-Regenwald*
to **change ones's diet** *seine Ernährung umstellen*
climate activist *Klimaschützer/in*
to **solve the climate crisis** *die Klimakrise lösen*

1 **Copy and complete the table with the missing words. Use your dictionary if necessary.**

Verb	Noun	Adjective
…	…	declared
…	… / emitter	
to be extinct	…	…
…	generation / …	
…	… / …	… / polluting
to radiate	…	
…	…	sustained / …

2 **Match prefixes from box A to box B to make words. Then complete the sentences with the correct words.**

A	B
de- | eco- | en- | ir- | over- (2x) | re- | un-	dangered | forestation | generate | heating | population | reversible | sustainable | system

1 The landscape in our region has changed a lot due to … to create fields for planting soya crops.
2 We need to look at providing easier access to birth control as a way of controlling … .
3 Environmental scientists are studying the complex … in nearby rivers and lakes.
4 If we continue taking too many natural resources from the planet, nature won't be able to … .
5 The conservation programme is trying to protect … species from going extinct.
6 We need to change our lifestyles so that we don't do … damage to the environment.
7 Endless economic growth is … because we will eventually run out of resources.
8 An increase in greenhouse gases in the atmosphere leads to the danger of the planet … .

3 **Find highlighted words and phrases in the text to match the definitions.**

1 a state in which carbon dioxide is no longer emitted
2 to keep something in a way that it cannot escape
3 a severe shortage of water
4 to remove or take out from something
5 the amount of greenhouse gases that are emitted through a person's daily life or by a company
6 to break into two or more parts
7 to decompose or break down, for example fruit that has been left out for too long
8 tiny pieces of plastic often found in cosmetic products
9 to try to deal with a problem or bad situation
10 keeping large numbers of animals in a small area in order to produce large amounts of animal products, such as meat or milk

Reading difficult texts

First things first: don't give up if you don't understand everything the first time you read through a text. We often concentrate too much on what we don't know or don't understand, which means that we can sometimes miss the meaning or content of the text. But you have only just begun dealing with the unknown text! Be patient and take things one step at a time – it is well worth it.

Use the following **reading strategies** to improve your reading skills. They will also help you to improve your **decoding skills** – working out on your own what new words and difficult text passages mean.

> **Good to know**
> **Reading strategies** help you to understand difficult texts.

At content level

Strategy 1: Using a variety of reading techniques

Depending on what your reading task is, there are two useful techniques you can apply in addition to detailed, intensive reading.

> **Good to know**
> **Skimming and scanning** techniques often overlap in the classroom.

Skimming
Aim: reading quickly to identify the general content of a text

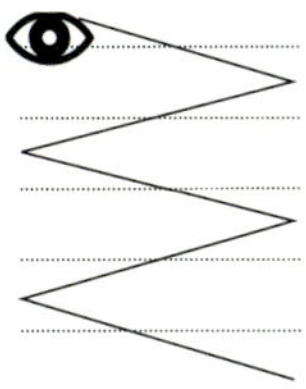

Scanning
Aim: looking for specific information

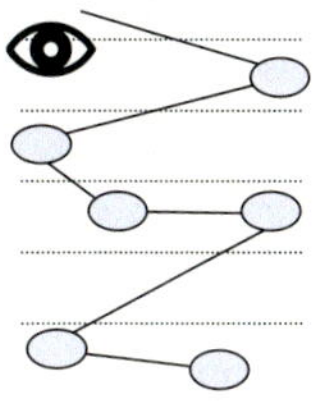

Exercise 1

Apply the correct reading technique for the following task on the text *'A great deception': oil giants taken to task over 'greenwash' ads* (pp. 19–20).

Look at the complete headline and state in a single sentence what you think the article is about. Then read the article and check whether your guess was correct.

Strategy 2: Using the context

Exercise 2

1 **Copy the following words and phrases in your exercise book. Write down (as far as possible) what they mean without using a dictionary to help you.**

deception · to take sb to task over sth · to allege · to withdraw · to witness · reliance · transition · to launder · capture · to divulge · inherently · offset

2 **Work out the rest of the meanings by looking at them in context.**

Read the text *'A great deception': oil giants taken to task over 'greenwash' ads* (pp. 19–20) and add any meanings that you can work out from the context.

You'll notice that when you are faced with new words in a text (and not just a list of words), you can often work out what they mean from the context. Texts that contain a number of unknown words are common in the upper years of secondary school. However, you don't need to understand every word to understand a text.

> **Good to know**
> If you understand the main ideas of the text, you don't need to spend time looking up every unknown word.

Strategy 3: 'Traffic light reading' (positive reading)

One technique recommended for understanding a text is known as 'traffic light reading': highlight in green the sections that you understand; highlight in yellow the words, groups of words or text passages that you are not completely sure about, but which you *think* you have understood from the context; and only highlight in red those things that you do not understand at all.

Exercise 3

Copy the text *'A great deception': oil giants taken to task over 'greenwash' ads* (pp. 19–20) and highlight it using the 'traffic light reading' technique.

The aim of positive reading is to show that you have a certain level of understanding of any text even when you don't know all the words. It also helps to give you an idea of your vocabulary skills – you shouldn't have too much red highlighting at all.

Strategy 4: Reading closely with a highlighter pen

Good to know

In your **written *Abitur*** exam, you will need to use **detailed reading** to help with **summary writing** tasks and especially **text analysis** tasks.

S ▸ Writing a summary, p. 81
S ▸ Dealing with a text analysis task, pp. 213–218

Read the reading comprehension tasks carefully and identify the important sections of photocopied texts using **highlighting** with a range of **colours** for the different tasks. Only mark key words to prevent the highlighting becoming confusing. You can also write **notes in the margin** (to summarize different sections).

Tip: If your book is school property, you can place a sheet of plastic film (overhead transparency) over the page and write on it with water-soluble ink. You can then clean the sheet after you have finished and re-use it again and again.

Exercise 4

Apply the close reading technique to the text *'A great deception': ...* (pp. 19–20).

At word level

Strategy 5: Using word formation patterns

Different prefixes and suffixes can help you to decode unknown words.
Example: *misrepresenting* → prefix *mis-* (= wrong or bad)

Strategy 6: Recognizing similarities to your mother tongue

Example: *algae* (l. 30) – Algen

Strategy 7: Using monolingual dictionaries

S ▸ Using a dictionary, pp. 41–42

This is especially helpful to check phrases such as *to lodge a complaint*.

Exercise 5

Apply the correct decoding strategy at word level on the following words from *'A great deception': ...* (pp. 19–20).

to lodge a complaint (l. 14) • to misrepresent (l. 26) • to invest (l. 42) • harmful (l. 55) • misleading (l. 55) • ambitious (l. 60)

Using a dictionary

Dictionaries are extremely important tools, but you need to learn how to use them – printed or online versions – correctly.

It doesn't matter whether you use a bilingual or a monolingual dictionary, you should *never* automatically choose the first translation or definition – you need to look carefully through the different options to find the right one for your context.

Good to know

For your **written *Abitur*** examination and when preparing for your **oral exam**, you will have access to a **bilingual** and a **monolingual dictionary** – and both of them are important!

Getting acquainted with a dictionary

First of all, you should get a general overview of the bilingual and monolingual dictionaries used in your school.

Exercise 1

Answer the following questions for both the bilingual and monolingual dictionaries.

1 Is there a section on how to use the dictionary? How is it structured?
2 Which abbreviations and symbols are used, and where can you find an explanation of what they mean?
3 Where can you find a list of irregular verbs?
4 Does the dictionary have any other lists?
5 Which topics have illustrations or diagrams?
6 Is there a section on grammar?
7 Does the dictionary provide any help with pronunciation?

Working with a dictionary

- **Working with texts:** Look up words if necessary.
- **Improve your vocabulary:** Create lists of word families.
- **Learn new phrases (idioms):** Monolingual dictionaries are particularly useful for doing this.

S ▸ Reading difficult texts, pp. 39–40

Bilingual dictionaries

Bilingual dictionaries will generally help you find the correct meaning quickly, but you must be careful to use them properly. Therefore, always ask yourself the following questions:

1 Am I looking for the right part of speech (noun, verb, adjective, adverb, etc.)?
2 Have I chosen the correct translation after reading through the whole dictionary entry carefully?

Exercise 2

Look up the English for the word *bemerken* and translate the following sentences.

1 *Er bemerkte zu spät, dass sie ihn bemerkt hatte.*
2 *„Das hätte ich wissen müssen", bemerkte er.*

Monolingual dictionaries

Good to know

Monolingual dictionaries contain more information than bilingual dictionaries. They present it in easy-to-understand language using vocabulary you've learned in earlier grades.

A good monolingual dictionary will show the following information for each entry:

- part of speech (e.g. noun, verb, adjective, adverb, etc.)
- irregular verb forms (e.g. *rise*, *rose*, *risen*)
- pronunciation and language variants (*BrE*, *AmE*, *AusE*, etc.)
- the different meanings of the word
- grammatical notes
- examples of use in context
- prepositions (e.g. on the internet)
- idioms that include the word
- synonyms
- how often the word is used in the language

pen·cil[1] /ˈpensəl/ *n* [C,U] an instrument that you use for writing or drawing, consisting of a wooden stick with a thin piece of black or coloured substance in the middle | *a sharp pencil* | *a blue pencil* | **in pencil** *a note written in pencil* | *a pencil sketch* → EYEBROW PENCIL; → see picture at OFFICE; → see picture at STATIONERY
pencil[2] *v* **pencilled, pencilling** *BrE*, **penciled, penciling** *AmE* [T] to write something or make a mark with a pencil: *a name pencilled on the envelope*
pencil sb/sth ↔ **in** *phr v* to make an arrangement for a meeting or other event, knowing that it might have to be changed later: *Pickford has been pencilled in as Robson's replacement.*
pencil case, pencil box *n* [C] a bag or box to carry pens and pencils in → see picture at CASE[1]
pencil pusher *n* [C] *AmE* someone who has a boring, unimportant job in an office
pencil sharpener *n* [C] a small instrument with a blade inside, used to make pencils sharp → see picture at STATIONERY
pencil skirt *n* [C] a long narrow straight skirt

From: *Longman Dictionary of Contemporary English*

Exercise 3

Look at the dictionary entry for the word *pencil* and identify the following information/elements:

a collocations (words that appear together frequently)
b definitions
c parts of speech
d example phrases
e pronunciation and frequency
f grammatical notes
g idioms
h reference to visual materials
i differences *BrE/AmE*
j prepositions

Exercise 4

Answer the following questions:

1 What part of speech is *pencil*?
2 Is *pencil* a countable or an uncountable noun?
3 What is the meaning of the word *pencil* in the following example? *"All right, let's pencil in 9 a.m. for our meeting in New York!"*
4 How frequently is the word used in spoken and written language?
5 Which term describing a person only exists in *AmE*?
6 What is the colour of the pencil case in your dictionary?

Decoding phonetic spelling

Good to know

You will have access to a monolingual and bilingual dictionary when preparing for the **spoken part** of your ***Abitur*** exam – the **oral exam**. Use the IPA to find out how to pronounce words you don't know.

Your dictionaries will also have a list showing the symbols used in the **International Phonetic Alphabet** (IPA) which are used to show exactly how a language sounds. The symbols used for the different sounds are based on the Latin writing system and the Greek alphabet. The pronunciation of each one is illustrated using an example. It is worth knowing where you can find the list of these symbols in your dictionary!

Exercise 5

Try and decipher this phrase written in the phonetic alphabet:

ðeə wəʊnt biː 'ɛni 'həʊm, wɜːk tə'deɪ ɪf juː kæn riːd ðɪs tɛkst!

Describing and analysing diagrams

Information that is based on figures can be visualized effectively in different ways. This makes it easier to take in and absorb the factual content.

The type of diagram used depends on the information that needs to be presented in a visual format. The words and phrases used to describe and interpret the information depend on what type of diagram is being discussed.

Good to know

Describing and analysing diagrams are a core element in the spoken part – the **oral exam** – of your ***Abitur*** examination.

Step 1: Deciding what type of diagram to use

Bar chart

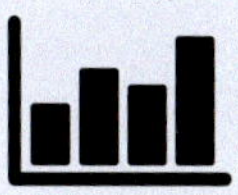

compares different values directly

Pie chart **Ring chart**

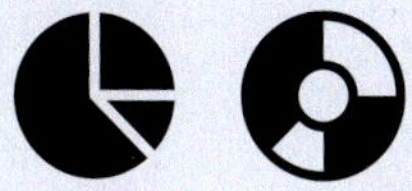

shows percentages adding up to 100%

Line graph

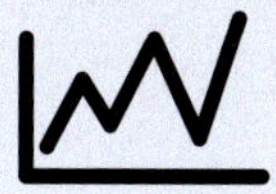

shows developments over a particular period of time

Exercise 1

Select the type of diagram that would be most suitable to show the following information.

1 level of deforestation over the past 12 months
2 Amazon rainforest tree cover by country in 2020
3 contribution of products which come from the Amazon rainforest to a supermarket's annual turnover
4 Amazon rainforest tree cover in hectares in Bolivia, Brazil and Colombia in 2020

Step 2: Describing diagrams

Start by summarizing the aim and content of the diagram. Specify what type of diagram you are dealing with and mention the source, the author and when it was published, if necessary. Give a short explanation of what the diagram shows.

The graph/chart is taken from … by …
It was published on … in …
The graph/chart is about … / deals with … / provides information about … / compares …
The graph/chart gives an overview of …
The graph/chart indicates/shows the development of …

to **publish sth** *etw veröffentlichen*
to **deal with sth** *sich mit etw befassen*
to **provide sth** *etw bieten*
to **indicate sth** *etw anzeigen, etw darstellen*

Exercise 2

While doing research for your speech on the threat to the Amazon rainforest (p. 25), you come across some diagrams on the internet which provide interesting general information on the issue.

Describe the three diagrams using the given phrases, and …
- give a short introduction to each diagram,
- explain briefly what it shows and
- prepare a detailed explanation of what information is shown in the diagrams.

▸ Research, p. 25

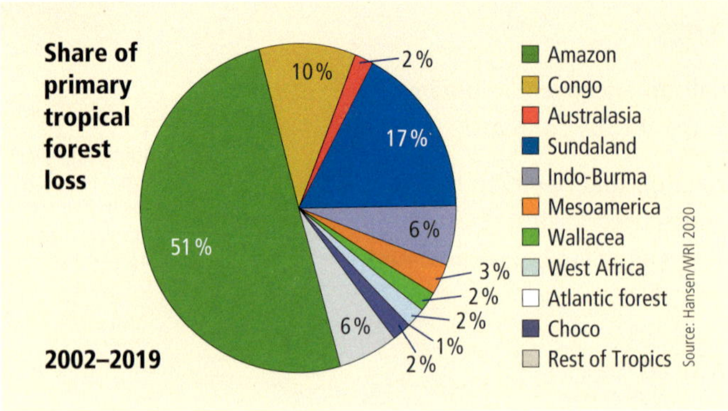

The pie chart is divided into … segments/sections …
Each segment represents …
The sections representing … and … constitute the majority …
… makes up the biggest/smallest segment.
more than / roughly / about twice as much as …
far less than …

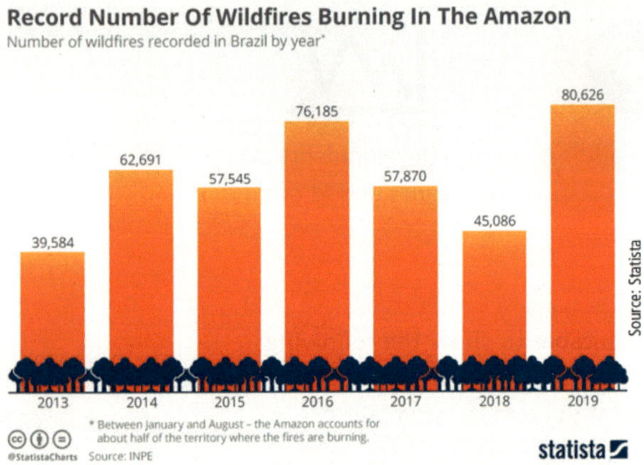

in comparison with / compared to …
in contrast to …
to rank first/second/…/last
the highest/lowest figure/score
no/little / a big difference between … and …
the vast majority / only a minority of …

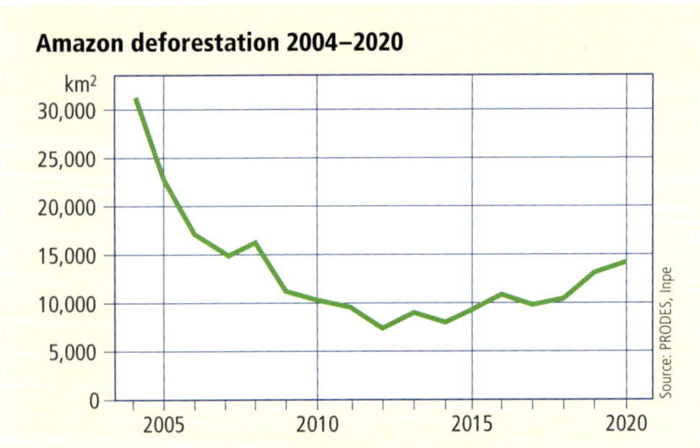

to reach a peak / a low point of …
to remain constant/stable
to increase/rise/grow / go up by … to …
to decrease/fall/drop / go down by … to …
an increase / a rise/growth …
sharp(ly)/steep(ly)/sudden(ly)/ constant(ly)/gradual(ly)/slight(ly)/ slow(ly)

Step 3: Analysing diagrams

by and large *im Großen und Ganzen*
to serve as sth *als etw dienen*
wake-up call *Weckruf, Alarmsignal*

Explain what conclusions can be drawn from the diagrams and specify how they fit into the overall context. Where possible, give some potential outcomes for the future.

By and large, it can be concluded that …
What surprises me most / does not surprise me is that …
The graph could serve as a wake-up call …

Exercise 3

1 Analyse the diagrams.
2 Use appropriate, meaningful information from the diagrams to provide supporting arguments for your presentation.

Review

1 Rank the Sections A–F in this Topic based on how interesting they were to you. Then, look back at your work on the overview of this Topic (pages 8–9) and how you ranked them there (page 8, exercise 2). Have your rankings changed? Share your results with a group and tell them what you found most interesting.

2 Look at your KWL list (page 9, exercise 5). Complete the "Learned" part of the list. Next, look at your "Want to know" list. What do you still want to know?

3 Make a list of ten words in the Topic that were new to you and you consider important to know. Then collect everyone's words and cluster them into groups. Finally, pick a word group and write a paragraph using all the words.

Evaluate

Do this task on your own. How much do you agree or disagree with the statements below? Rate each one on a scale of one to four. The references on the right show you which exercises you can review.

1 = totally disagree **2** = disagree **3** = agree **4** = totally agree

Section	Statement	
A	**1** I am able to summarize the impact of humanity on the environment.	▸ pp. 12–13, exercises 5–9
	2 I can discuss the effectiveness of declaring a new geological epoch.	▸ p. 12, exercise 8
	3 I can write an argumentative text about environmental problems.	▸ p. 13, exercise 10
B	**4** I can talk about renewable and non-renewable sources of energy.	▸ pp. 14–16, exercises 1–5
	5 I can participate in a debate on the pros and cons of fracking.	▸ p. 17, exercises 6–7
	6 I can write a letter to a newspaper expressing my opinion on fracking.	▸ p. 17, exercise 8
C	**7** I understand how 'greenwashing' works and can give examples.	▸ pp. 18–21, exercises 2–7
	8 I can write a comment on the practice of 'greenwashing'	▸ p. 21, exercise 8
D	**9** I can summarize the importance of forests for the planet.	▸ pp. 22–24, exercises 2–4
	10 I know how to use the passive.	▸ p. 24, exercises 5–6
	11 I can give a speech on products that contribute to deforestation.	▸ p. 25, exercises 7–9
E	**12** I can talk about how fast fashion contributes to the climate crisis.	▸ pp. 26–27, exercises 3–4
	13 I can explain the principles of slow fashion in German.	▸ p. 29, exercise 7
	14 I can write a magazine article about a slow fashion project.	▸ p. 29, exercise 10
F	**15** I can reflect on the ways in which my lifestyle affects the environment.	▸ p. 31, exercises 5–7
	16 I can understand a radio report about climate activism.	▸ p. 32, exercises 8–10
	17 I can give a presentation on unusual climate solutions.	▸ p. 33, exercises 11–12
	18 I can comment on whether it is too late to save the environment.	▸ p. 33, exercise 13
Skills	**19** I can read difficult texts.	S ▸ pp. 39–40
	20 I can use a dictionary.	S ▸ pp. 41–42
	21 I can describe and analyse diagrams.	S ▸ pp. 43–44

Consolidate

You want to go deeper into the topic of the environment and the climate crisis? Or you want to speed up your learning process? Scan this page with the PagePlayer app. There you'll find some suggestions for additional tasks.

Aufgabenteil I Hören

07

1 **You will hear an interview about plastic waste and recycling.**

While listening, choose the correct answers (a, b or c). There is only one correct answer.

1 Executives in the oil and plastic industry …
a have spent millions over the last decades on new recycling methods.
b have been aware for many years that most plastic isn't being recycled.
c have recently found out that the vast majority of plastic waste isn't being recycled.

2 Many plastic items aren't recycled because …
a the process is too complex.
b it's more expensive than manufacturing new plastic products.
c there aren't enough resources to collect, sort and melt them down.

3 Most plastic waste in recycling bins is usually …
a broken down and re-converted into oil or gas.
b melted down and made into new plastic objects.
c disposed of in non-environmentally-friendly ways.

4 The promotion of plastic recycling has been funded by …
a consumer groups.
b national governments.
c the oil and gas and plastics industries.

5 The researchers found …
a government documents showing that recycling isn't economically viable.
b research by activists showing that companies weren't actually recycling plastic waste.
c communications within the plastics industry stating that recycling isn't economically viable.

6 The real purpose of the ads is to …
a increase sales of plastic products.
b motivate the public to separate their rubbish more carefully.
c put pressure on the oil and gas and plastics industry to do more to protect the environment.

7 The recycling ads …
a increased public interest in recycling.
b caused a decline in the sales of plastic products.
c resulted in less consumer negativity towards plastic products.

8 Oil and gas and plastic companies have recently stated that they …
a will stop producing plastic straws and bags.
b are now serious about recycling their products.
c are going to spend billions of dollars on new recycling ad campaigns.

2 You will hear a radio interview with Yuki Yakomura, a scientist and writer on nutritional matters. 08

While listening, take notes on the following points. You need not write complete sentences.

1 What do studies about the reduction of emissions show (2 aspects)?: …
2 What kind of damage does intensive farming cause (2 aspects)?: …
example: *carbon sequestration*
3 What would happen if the meat industry was given up completely?: …
4 What problems related to cows can't be solved (2 aspects)?: …
5 What measures need to be taken to reduce meat consumption (2 aspects)?: …

3 You will hear five young people talking about their attitude towards taking action to prevent climate change. 09

While listening, match the headings A to G with the speakers 1 to 5. There are two more headings than you need.

Headings	
A	necessity: working together
B	criticism: other people's lifestyles
C	belief: getting involved
D	suggestion: integration not exclusivity
E	influence: large numbers of activists
F	solution: drastic measures
G	conflict: young versus old

Speaker	Heading

Aufgabenteil II Lesen und Schreiben

Aufgabenstellung

1 Outline why, according to the author, it is not enough for individuals to change their lifestyles in order to save the planet. (Material 1, pp. 48–49)

2 Analyse the means the author uses to convince the reader of her opinion. (Material 1, pp. 48–49)

3 Choose one of the following:

A "The revolution won't happen by people staying home and being good."

Discuss the author's statement and give your personal opinion on what is needed to combat climate change.

B You and some friends have founded a climate action group at your school. Write a speech to give in front of the school defining the group's goals and what you hope to achieve. Include arguments which support or disagree with the author's arguments in your speech.

Material 1

Big oil coined 'carbon footprints' to blame us for their greed. Keep them on the hook

Climate-conscious individual choices are good – but not nearly enough to save the planet. More than personal virtue, we need collective action.

Personal virtue is an eternally seductive goal in progressive movements, and the climate movement is no exception. People pop up all the time to boast of their domestic arrangements or chastise others for what they eat or how they get around. The very short counterargument is that individual acts of thrift and abstinence won't get us the huge distance we need to go in this decade. We need to exit the age of fossil fuels, reinvent our energy landscape, rethink how we do almost everything. We need collective action at every scale from local to global – and the good people already at work on all those levels need help in getting a city to commit to clean power or a state to stop fracking or a nation to end fossil fuel subsidies. The revolution won't happen by people staying home and being good.

But the oil companies would like you to think that's how it works. It turns out that the concept of the "carbon footprint", that popular measure of personal impact, was the brainchild of an advertising firm working for BP. As Mark Kaufman wrote this summer:

British Petroleum, the second largest non-state owned oil company in the world, with 18,700 gas and service stations worldwide, hired the public relations professionals Ogilvy & Mather to promote the slant that climate change is not the fault of an oil giant, but that of individuals. It's here that British Petroleum, or BP, first promoted and soon successfully popularized the term "carbon footprint" in the early aughts. The company unveiled its "carbon footprint calculator" in 2004 so one could assess how their normal daily life – going to work, buying food, and (gasp) traveling – is largely responsible for heating the globe.

The main reason to defeat the fossil fuel corporations is that their product is destroying the planet, but their insidious propaganda, from spreading climate-change denial to pushing this climate footprint business, makes this goal even more worthwhile.

Carbon footprints caught on, and I routinely see people on social media zooming in on individual consumption habits when climate chaos is under discussion. The goal of personal virtue is merely not to be part of the problem. It's not good enough for a bystander to say "I personally am not murdering this person" when someone is being stabbed to death before them (and those of us in the global north have countless ties to systems that are murdering the climate, so we are not exactly bystanders). The goal for those of us with any kind of resources of time, rights and a voice, must be being part of the solution, pushing for system change. To stop the murder.

Underlying this is a conflict in how we imagine ourselves, as consumers or as citizens. Consumers define themselves by what they buy, own, watch – or don't. Citizens see themselves as part of civil society, as actors in the political system. Too, even personal virtue is made more or less possible by the systems that surround us. If you have solar panels on your roof, it's because there's a market and manufacturers for solar and installers and maybe an arrangement with your power company to compensate you for energy you're putting into the grid.

In my own case, some of what I could tout as personal virtue is only possible because of collective action. I have 100% clean electricity at home because people organized to make that option and the solar and wind power behind it available. I do some of my errands by bicycle because the San Francisco Bicycle Coalition worked for decades to put bicycle paths across the city and otherwise make it safer to get about on two wheels. I can take public transit because there is public transit.

But individual and collective action don't have to be pitted against each other. Individual choices do add up (they just don't, in McKibben's terms, multiply). That vegan options are available at a lot of fast-food chains is because enough consumers have created a profitable market for them. We do influence others through our visible choices.

Vegetarian and vegan diets (and low-meat or no-red-meat diets) have become far more common, creating markets for new products and different menus. But they have not made the beef industry go away or reformed its devastating climate impact. Climate chaos demands we recognize how everything is connected. Seeing yourself as a citizen means seeing yourself as connected to social and political systems. As citizens we must go after the climate footprint of the fossil fuel corporations, the beef industry, the power companies, the transportation system, plastics, and so much more.

(789 words) Source: *The Guardian*, 23 August 2021

Mündlicher Teil Kommunikationsprüfung

Partner A: look here. **Partner B:** look at File 4 on page 269.

Partner A: Sequence 1 (your five-minute talk)

1 Describe the picture and the cartoon and interpret their messages.

2 Use the photo and cartoon as a starting point for an uninterrupted five-minute talk on climate change and the destruction of our planet.

CartoonStock.com

Partner A: Sequence 2 (you and the teacher / another student)

Discuss the following questions with your partner:

1 What changes – political and individual – need to be made to slow down global warming?

2 *"We have enslaved the rest of the animal creation, and have treated our distant cousins in fur and feathers so badly that beyond doubt, if they were able to formulate a religion, they would depict the Devil in human form."*
– William Inge, American playwright

What other "crimes" have we committed and how can we undo the harm that we have caused?

Topic 2 Technology

Section A
Genetically modified food

plant-based meat

Section B
Food production

"I want to put the animal agriculture industry out of business […] because it is the most destructive industry on Earth."
– Patrick Brown, CEO of Impossible Foods

Fact: Humans have been altering the genetic make-up of plants for millennia, keeping seeds from the best crops and planting them in following years.

feeding the world

Innovation

Section F
Artificial humans in literature and film

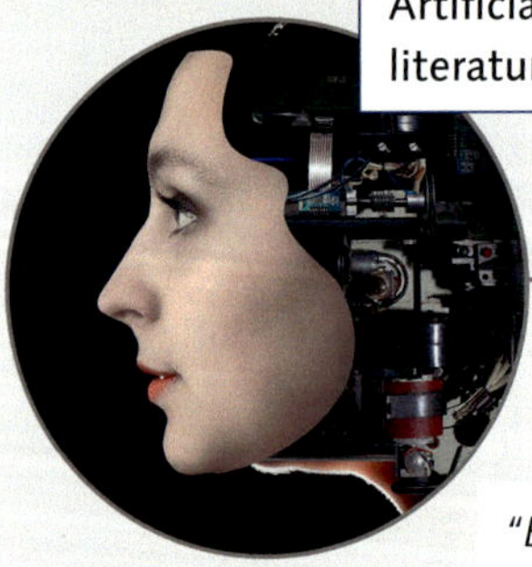

androids

"Before us sat the ultimate plaything, the dream of ages, the triumph of humanism – or its angel of death."
– *Machines Like Me* by Ian McEwan

1 Read the facts and quotations about technology above.

a Which of them are totally new to you?
b Which of them do you find surprising?

2 Rank Sections A–F on how interested you are in them.

3 The mind map shows you a preview of Topic 2. Copy it onto a piece of paper and add words and phrases from …

a the facts and quotations above.
b the Word bank opposite.
c your own ideas.
d Sections A–F you think are important.

Section C
Robots and artificial intelligence

Find information on each Section in the PagePlayer app!

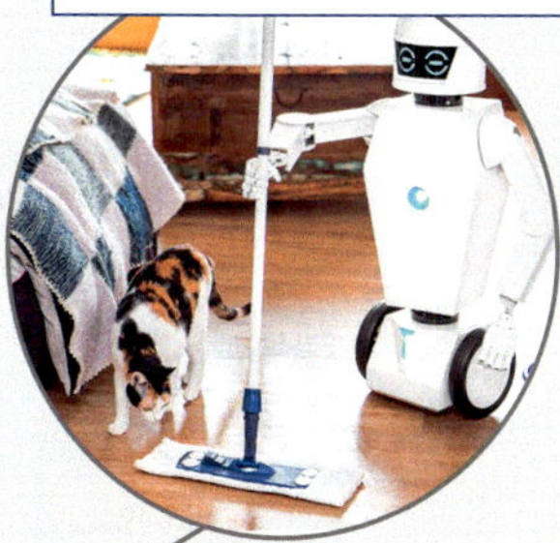

"There is a threat to people's jobs. But that threat is not the robots – it is the company decisions that are driven by a broader economic and political system of corporate capitalism."
– Dr Kate Darling, research specialist at MIT

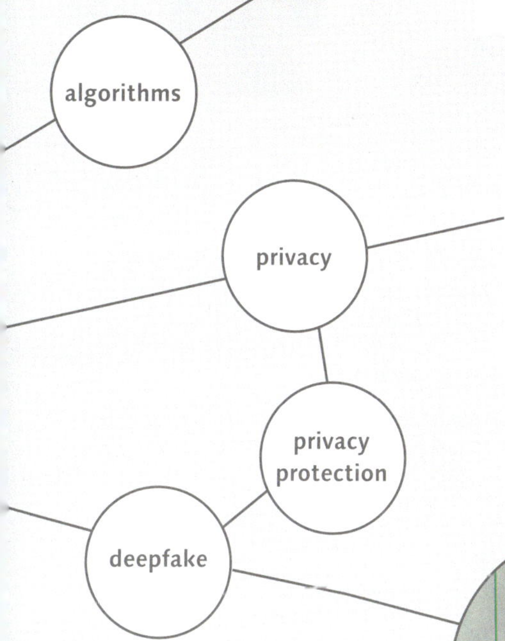

"Privacy protections in the United States are generally quite weak; when it comes to police purchases of private data, they are completely absent."
– *The Guardian*, 5 April 2021

Section D
The internet of things

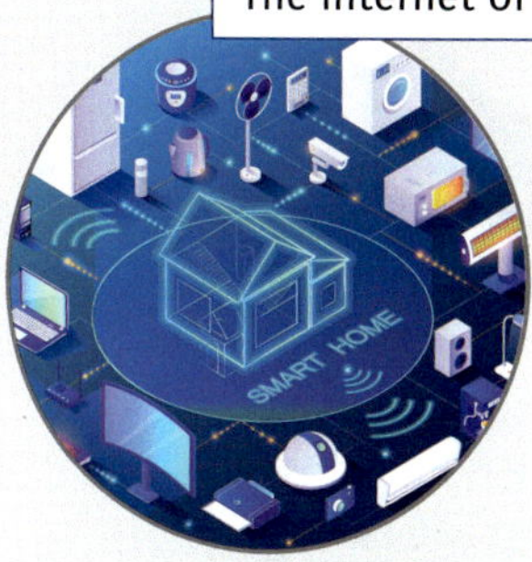

Fact: The first ever connected device was the ATM (Automatic Teller Machine or cash machine).

Section E
Digital manipulation

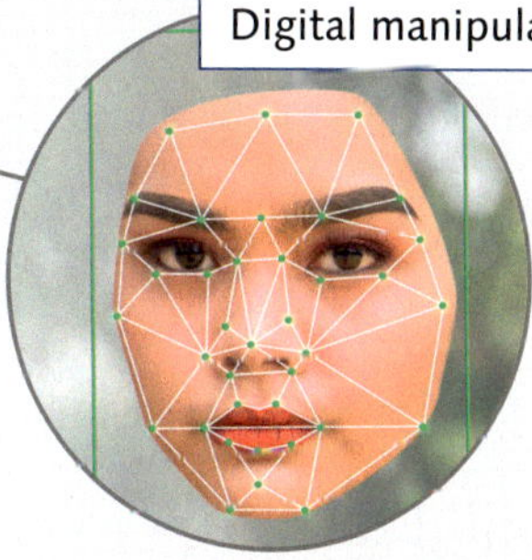

Fact: Deepfaking started in the dark corner of the internet in 2012.

"The more insidious impact of deepfakes, along with other synthetic media and fake news, is to create a zero-trust society, where people cannot, or no longer bother to, distinguish truth from falsehood."
– *The Guardian*, 13 January 2020

4 Note a few key words to say what you expect to learn in each Section.

5 Make a "KWL" (Know, Want to know, Learned) list for the Topic.

6 With a partner, compare …

- **a** your mind maps and say why you added words where you did.
- **b** your rankings from exercise 2.
- **c** what you expect to learn in Sections A–F.

Then compare with another pair.

7 Save your work for reviewing when you've finished the Topic.

Word bank

agriculture *Land, Agrarwirtschaft*
conscious *bewusst*
to **crossbreed** *kreuzen, durch Kreuzung züchten*
to **discredit sb/sth** *jdn/etw in Verruf bringen*
to **eradicate** *etw ausrotten*
to **expose sb/sth** *jdn/etw bloßstellen*
to **mimic sb** *jdn imitieren*
plausible *nachvollziehbar*
processed food *verarbeitete Lebensmittel*
threat *Drohung*
viable *lebensfähig*

Section A Genetically modified food

Warm-up

1 Decide on a scale of 1 to 10 how much you agree with the following statements (1 = totally disagree, 10 = totally agree).

I'm not worried at all. GM foods are harmless for animals and humans to eat.

Genetically modified foods are a serious risk to the environment.

The world's population is growing and GMOs are the only way to feed it in the future.

Hey, if it tastes better and isn't bad for me, I don't care what's in it.

Good to know

Genetically modified organisms (GMOs) are plants that have had their genetic structure changed artificially.

2 Compare your ideas about the statements with a partner.

3 Discuss the statements with another pair. Are there any statements that you all agree or disagree with?

Working with the text

S ▸ Reading difficult texts, pp. 39–40

genetic engineering *Gentechnik, Gentechnologie*

4 Read the text below and take notes on the following aspects:

Genetic engineering

- traditional methods
- modern methods
- dangers
- benefits

10

What's the deal with GM food?

Since humans began farming thousands of years ago, we have been altering the genetic make-up of plants continually. Seeds from the best crops were kept and planted the following year. We began crossbreeding varieties to make them stronger, better tasting and more resilient. Over time, we developed methods to produce the best food products to support the health and well-being of the population.

Some decades ago, scientists developed techniques to significantly speed up this process. Genes with specific traits could be transplanted into plant and animal DNA. Instead of the traditional methods, which transferred tens of thousands of genes each time, just a select few could be chosen. This process endeavoured to produce crops that were resilient to problems such as weeds, insects and disease.

[2] to **alter sth** *etw (ver)ändern*
[4] **variety** *Sorte, Art, Variante*
[5] **resilient** *widerstandsfähig*
[10] trait Eigenschaft
[12] to endeavour *anstreben, sich bemühen*

Farmers no longer had to spray their plants with herbicides to kill weeds: biotech crops can withstand being sprayed with chemicals that kill nearly every type of plant thanks to the special "tolerance" genes they carry.

The theoretical benefits of GM foods are obvious. When crops are stronger and more resilient, they produce more. This could end problems such as food shortages and malnutrition as sufficient food production could be ensured to feed everyone the world over. As well as this, the plants offer an environmentally friendly alternative to pesticides, causing less harm to surface and groundwater as well as wildlife. An end to world hunger and less pollution are good things, right? So, why the resistance to GM foods?

To begin with, some environmental scientists worry that genetically engineered crops are being developed too quickly, without adequate testing for long-term ecological impact. The seeds are released on millions of acres of farmland, making it impossible to reverse the process if serious problems are found later. A bigger issue is the evolution of insects which are impervious to pesticides. The genetically modified plants would be resistant to pests that no longer exist and would have to fight for survival against newly evolved super bugs. As a result, they may end up developing new toxins that cause more harm than good.

Nevertheless, increased yields of crops which are, at least in the short-term, resistant to pests and disease, could help solve the urgent problem of world hunger. Genetic engineering could offer plant varieties which grow on land that would otherwise not support farming. This might be because of drought conditions, polluted soils, or soils depleted of nutrients. Increased food production would naturally lead to decreased malnutrition and hunger. There are no difficulties in learning new techniques or understanding the new technology. Farmers would simply plant the seeds and witness the new features in the plants.

Although the solution seems obvious, and this technology has been around for some time, there is not likely to be an immediate end to world hunger. One problem is the large companies which currently dominate the GM industry. These multinationals are unwilling to devote resources to developing seed technology for subsistence farmers because the investment offers minimal return. These companies also own the patents for the key methods and materials, which stifles the free exchange of seeds and techniques which are vital to public agricultural research programmes.

A question posed by many critics is whether biotechnology is really the answer to ending world hunger, or whether it could be better dealt with by redistributing existing food supplies. Even advocates of genetic modification agree that biotech food production would be ineffective on its own. It would have to go hand in hand with soil and water conservation, pest management and other technologies that have yet to see the light of day.

It is possible that biotech foods will eliminate world hunger, and better the lives of all. Humans in the near future might dine on highly nutritious food that was produced without the use of herbicides or pesticides, using minimal water and causing little environmental damage. It is also possible that future generations will pay for accidents and errors in judgement in ways that we cannot possibly imagine. If we take a careful look at how, where and why we introduce genetically altered products, and if they are tested thoroughly, we will be able to judge their risks and benefits properly.

14 **herbicide** *Unkrautvernichtungsmittel*
15 to withstand *überstehen, widerstehen*
17 **obvious** *offensichtlich, klar*
19 to **ensure** *sicherstellen*
23 **resistance (to)** *Widerstand (gegen)*
25 adequate *ausreichend, angemessen*
25 **long-term** *langfristig, Langzeit-*
26 acre *Morgen* (ca. 4047m²)
27 to reverse sth *etw umkehren*
28 impervious *unempfindlich*
30 bug *(schädliches) Insekt*
31 **toxin** *Gift*
32 yield *Ertrag*
36 **nutrient** *Nährstoff*
39 to **witness** *(mit)erleben*
42 to **dominate sth** *etw beherrschen, etw dominieren*
43 to devote sth to sb/sth *etw für jdn/etw verwenden, jdm/etw etw widmen*
44 **investment** *Investition*
44 **return** *Ertrag, Rendite*
45 to stifle *unterdrücken*
49 to redistribute *umverteilen*
50 **advocate** *Befürworter/in*
55 to dine on sth *sich von etwas ernähren*
55 **nutritious** *nahrhaft*
58 **error in judgement** *Fehleinschätzung*
60 **thoroughly** *grundlich, aufmerksam*
61 **properly** *richtig, ordentlich, korrekt*

[67] **fortunate** *glücklich*
[69] to endorse sth *etw befürworten*

This is a field of promise and a topic for controversial debate. GM food is changing the food we eat and the world we live in. What effect is this technology already having on the environment and agriculture, and what effects can we expect to see in the future? Can farmers really use this technology to produce enough food for the Earth's ever increasing population without causing massive environmental damage? Will less fortunate nations ever benefit from this technology? We need to talk through this topic. The biggest mistake we could make would be to totally reject or endorse this new technology.

(802 words)

Writing

Exam preparation

S ▸ Writing a summary, p. 81

5 Summarize the pros and cons of genetic engineering related to modern methods of food production.

Working with words

6 Match the words (1–8) with the correct definitions (a–h).

1 herbicide
2 cross-breeding
3 weed
4 toxin
5 pollution
6 pest
7 malnutrition
8 drought

a a harmful insect or animal that attacks crops, etc.
b a long period of little to no rainfall which causes a shortage of water
c a substance that is used to destroy unwanted plants
d the condition that develops when a person does not get enough nutrients to stay healthy
e a wild plant that grows where it is not wanted
f to produce a plant or an animal by bringing two different species or varieties together
g a poison that originates in a plant or an animal
h something in the environment which is harmful to it

Looking at language

G ▸ Participle constructions, p. 296

7 Rewrite the following sentences, using the underlined words in participle constructions.

1 The engineered organisms that scientists produce by transferring genes are called transgenic.
The engineered organisms produced by transferring genes are called transgenic.
2 Biotech crops carry special genes that allow them to withstand the spraying of chemicals.
3 Some scientists are concerned about genetically engineered crops and claim that they are being released without adequate testing.
4 Breeders cross related organisms. In so doing, they transfer thousands of genes.
5 Biotech plants can increase crop yields and offer varieties that resist pests and disease.
6 Big companies are patenting key methods and materials and as a result they are stopping the free exchange of seeds and techniques.

Speaking

8 **Partner A:** Look here. **Partner B:** Look at File 6 on page 270.

Partner A: Sequence 1 (your five-minute talk)

1 Describe the photo and the cartoon and interpret their message.

2 Use the given material as a starting point for an uninterrupted five-minute talk on people's concerns about genetically modified food.

Exam preparation

Kommunikationsprüfung

S ▸ Describing and analysing cartoons, pp. 43–44

Phrases for speaking

Partner A: Sequence 2: (you and the teacher / another student)

Discuss the following questions with Partner B:

1 *"Practically every food you buy in a store for consumption by humans is genetically modified food. There are no wild, seedless watermelons. There's no wild cows."*
– Neil deGrasse Tyson, US astrophysicist, author and broadcaster

Why is genetically modifying food different to cross-breeding?

2 Will it be possible in the future to feed the Earth's population without genetically modified food products?

Writing

9 Write a blog post directed at a local supermarket chain convincing them of the advantages or disadvantages of genetically altered products, depending on your

Exam preparation

S ▸ Dealing with a creative writing task, pp. 126–128

Writing checklist

Section B Food production

1

2

3

4

5

6

Warm-up

1 In small groups, discuss the following questions.

- Which of these meals would you like, or not like, to eat? Explain why.
- What makes a meal appealing? What puts you off a certain kind of food? Collect ideas in your group.
- Does the environmental impact of the production of food play a role in your decisions? Why (not)?

Working with the text

S ▸ Reading difficult texts, pp. 39–40

2 Read the text below and on the following pages and take short notes on the following aspects:

Impossible Foods
- goals and how the company will reach them
- founding, investments, products, sales
- challenges and controversies

friggin' *infml verdammt*
creator *Schöpfer/in*
01 to **eradicate** *ausrotten*
06 deadly serious *todernst*
08 **roast** *gebraten*

"Let's get rid of friggin' cows" says creator of plant based 'bleeding burger'

Patrick Brown is on a mission: to eradicate the meat and fish industries by 2035. The CEO of Impossible Foods, a California-based company that makes genetically engineered plant-based meat, is deadly serious. No more commercial livestock farming or fishing. No more steak, fish and chips or roast dinners, at least not as you know them.

In their place, his company's scientists and food technicians will create plant-based substitutes for every animal product used today in every region of the world, he promises.

"I want to put the animal agriculture industry out of business. It's that simple. The goal is not because I have any ill will toward the people who work in that industry, but because it is the most destructive industry on Earth," Brown says.

The former Stanford University biochemistry professor started Impossible Foods in 2011 after a sabbatical researching intensive farming. The company has since attracted nearly $1.3bn (£960m) in investment. Jay Z, Katy Perry, Serena Williams and Trevor Noah all took part in the most recent $500m fundraising round in March last year, alongside leading financial institutions. The Silicon Valley firm's flagship Impossible Burger is on sale at thousands of restaurants in the US, Hong Kong and Singapore, including around 7,000Burger King chains, and the company has branched out into supermarkets during the pandemic.

The products are not cheap – a 5lb (2.25kg) family pack of Impossible Burger ground beef in the US costs about $65 (£48) – but the company aims to lower cost as it grows [...]. Impossible Pork and Impossible Sausage were added to its portfolio of GMO plant-based meat substitutes in 2020, part of the company's "worst first" approach that targets the most environmentally damaging livestock consumed by humans. Milk and fish equivalents are in development in its laboratories.

"To the outside world, Impossible Foods is a food company – but at its heart [it] is an audacious yet realistic strategy to turn back the clock on climate change and stop the global collapse of biodiversity," Brown wrote in the company's 2020 impact report. As part of his vision of the future, the 45% of the land surface of the Earth reserved for animal agriculture would be returned to nature. Deforestation, antibiotic resistance and overfishing could be overcome and reversed in some cases, Brown insists.

Although attitudes are changing to plant-based diets and growing numbers of Americans are eating less meat, Brown still has a mountain to climb to make his vision a reality. A January 2020 YouGov survey found more than two-thirds of US adults identify as meat eaters, while beef burgers were rated more highly than plant-based equivalents for taste.

But there's good reason to see the need for change. Millions of hectares of ecosystems are projected to disappear by the middle of the century to meet future demand for agriculture, animal feed and bioenergy. A 2018 study of life on Earth found that farmed poultry makes up around 70% of the birds on the planet. More than half of mammals are livestock, mainly cattle and pigs, and just 4% are wild animals.

"The entire cause of the catastrophic collapse of wildlife populations, which are less than a third of what they were 50 years ago, globally, is the use of animals as a food technology," Brown claims [...]. "Cows outweigh every remaining wild vertebrate on land by more than a factor of 10. Just the cows. We've literally totally replaced biodiversity with cows. Let's get rid of friggin' cows and let nature recover," he says.

Did Brown ever eat meat? Yes, until his early 20s, but he stopped when he realised he was only doing it for pleasure. Does he really mean all meat and fish could be substituted? What about chorizo? "No problemo." And what happens to livestock farmers? "They're not going to be in that business any more. But there's a lot of very reasonable solutions."

11 **substitute** *Ersatz*
14 ill will *böses Blut*
17 sabbatical *Studienurlaub*
19 **fundraising** *Spendensammeln, Geldbeschaffung*
20 alongside *neben*
23 to **branch out** *sich verzweigen*
31 audacious *kühn, verwegen*
35 to overcome *überwinden*
40 to **rate sth** *etw einstufen, etw bewerten*
43 to **project sth** *etw prognostizieren, vorhersagen*
45 **poultry** *Geflügel*
49 to **outweigh sth** *etw übertreffen*
49 vertebrate *Wirbeltier*
51 to **recover** *sich erholen*
54 to **substitute** *jdn/etw ersetzen*

57 **to crack a code** *einen Code knacken*
58 to decouple *abkoppeln, entkoppeln*
59 to **replicate** *nachbilden*
60 **texture** *Konsistenz, Beschaffenheit*
60 **sensation** *Gefühl, Empfinden*
60 **soy** *Soja*
60 heme *Häm*
61 yeast *Hefe*
66 **processed** *verarbeitet*
68 **loaf**, *pl* **loaves** *Laib*
69 **oven** *Backofen*
69 pretty much *(so) ziemlich, fast*
70 pejorative *abwertend*

But the rise of Impossible Foods, which claims to have "cracked meat's molecular code" and aims to decouple "meat" from animals, has not been without controversy. [...] Impossible Foods uses genetically modified ingredients to replicate the texture, taste and sensations of eating meat. Soy leghemoglobin – known as heme – produced by genetically modified yeast, is the key to replicating the "meaty" taste. The Impossible Burger even "bleeds" as it is cooked.

[...] In the US, the company has faced criticism from a number of organisations, including Friends of the Earth and the US Center for Food Safety, over concerns that the process to produce heme has not been properly tested and that the products are "overprocessed".

"It's ridiculous," says Brown. "Our foods are no more processed than the foods that people eat every day. Everything you eat, the little loaf of bread that maybe you baked in your own oven is processed in pretty much the exact same way as our food.

"Processed food is a pejorative term because people are used to applying it to foods that are basically sugar and salt and garbage. OK. But that image does not apply to our project progress with our food, which is very, very thoughtfully put together from healthy ingredients."

(855 words) From: *The Guardian*, 8 January 2021

Writing

Exam preparation

S ▸ Writing a summary, p. 81

3 Summarize how and why Patrick Brown wants to "eradicate the meat and fish industries by 2035".

Remember

When writing a summary based on one or more specific aspects of the text, be sure to only include information that is relevant to the task.

Working with words

4 Combine words from box A and box B to create collocations from the text.

A	B
animal | antibiotic | food | food safety | genetically modified | livestock | meat | milk | plant-based | processed | wildlife	eater | equivalent | farming | food | ingredients | meat | population | product | regulations | resistance | technician

5 Use collocations from exercise 4 to complete the gaps. Two items are not used.

More than 65% of American call themselves …[1] but this does not mean that these people would not be interested in substituting at least some of their beef burgers with …[2]. More and more people are starting to view their consumption of …[3] as a strain on the environment and are making different choices about what foods they eat. For many, the choice of a …[4] at the coffee shop is no big deal, in fact many now prefer oat or soy milk to cow milk. But the move away from actual meat is harder for some, especially when …[5] are used to create a more "meaty" feel. These people often fear that a lack of …[6] is causing them to put chemicals into their bodies that could potentially be harmful. The companies which produce these meatless products claim that their products are safe and no different than other …[7] that we consume every day. In the end, the decision has to be up to the consumer as to whether they trust traditional …[8], which sometimes causes detrimental …[9] in animal populations, over the relatively new world of plant-based equivalents.

oat milk *Hafermilch*

Listening

6 You will hear a podcast about marketing plant-based foods. While listening, mark the correct answer (a, b or c). There is only one correct answer.

11

Exam preparation

S ▸ Dealing with listening tasks, pp. 123–125

1 Plant-based meat is today much different to what it used to be because it …
- **a** feels and tastes more like real meat.
- **b** is no longer genetically engineered.
- **c** contains much fewer chemicals.

2 One main problem in attracting people to plant-based meat products is …
- **a** poor advertising.
- **b** the high cost.
- **c** the way it looks.

3 "Meat-free" is one of the least effective terms because it …
- **a** makes people suspicious of what the product contains.
- **b** puts the focus on what customers are not getting.
- **c** doesn't sound very appetizing to customers.

4 The restaurant chain's vegetarian chili was originally labelled …
- **a** "meat-free".
- **b** "spicy".
- **c** "low-fat".

5 Associating the vegetarian chili with Mexico was important because it …
- **a** conjured up ideas of flavour.
- **b** was foreign and exotic.
- **c** made people think of meat.

to **conjure sth up**
etw herbeizaubern

6 The name "Cumberland spiced sausage and mash" increased sales because …
- **a** "Cumberland" is a typical British name.
- **b** it suggested there was meat in the product.
- **c** it sounded like a traditional British meal.

7 In order to help the environment by selling more plant-based meats, marketing people are trying to attract …
- **a** more vegetarian and vegan consumers.
- **b** people who are trying to eat less meat.
- **c** meat eaters who are sceptical about these products.

Speaking

7 Discuss the questions with a partner.

- Patrick Brown says that the meat industry is "the most destructive industry on Earth". Do you agree with him? Explain your answers.
- Will plant-based meat products help to save the environment? Why (not)?
- Would you be prepared to swap real meat for plant-based meat? Give reasons.

Writing

Exam preparation

S ▸ Writing an argumentative text, pp. 167–172

Writing checklist

8 Taking the company Impossible Foods as a starting point, comment on the following quote.

> *"By eating meat we share the responsibility of climate change, the destruction of our forests, and the poisoning of our air and water. The simple act of becoming a vegetarian will make a difference in the health of our planet."*
>
> – Thich Nhat Hanh, Vietnamese Buddhist monk and peace activist

Section C Robots and artificial intelligence

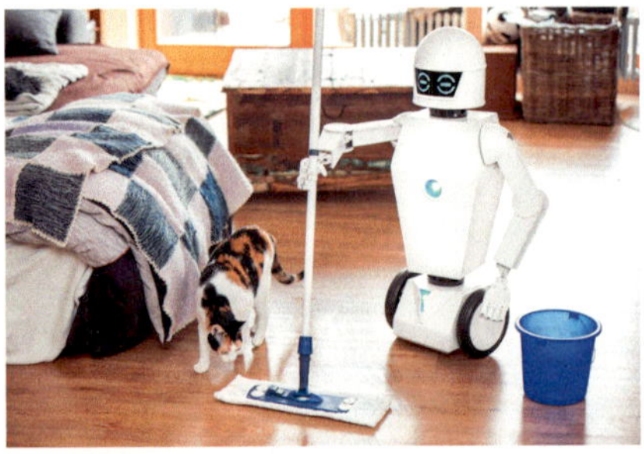

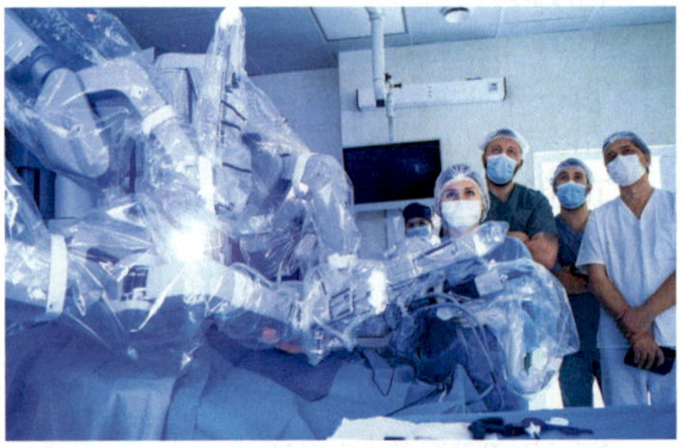

Good to know

Artificial intelligence (AI) is the science of programming machines or computers to reproduce human processes like learning or decision-making.

Warm-up

1 What areas are robots and artificial intelligence (AI) already being used in? Collect ideas in class.

2 Discuss in class: How do you feel about this development?

Crossover TV

Artificial Intelligence

02

Watching

3 You are going to watch a video about the development and future uses of artificial intelligence.
While watching, take notes on the following points. You need not write complete sentences.

1 intelligent algorithms: …
2 AI in our daily lives (2 aspects): …
Example: *cyber assistance to find information*
3 AI's promise of an efficient world (3 aspects): …
Example: *plan holidays*
4 significance of gaming (2 aspects): …
5 software in medicine: …
6 danger of fourth Industrial Revolution: …
7 threat of "super intelligence": …
8 definition of "super intelligence": …
9 definition of "social intelligence": …

4 Discuss these questions in class.

- What new aspects of AI have you learnt from the video?
- Has your opinion of AI changed after watching the video?

Working with the text

S ▸ Reading difficult texts, pp. 39–40

5 Read the text on the following pages and decide on the best summary of what Dr Darling says.

a We need to introduce much stricter regulations on how robots can be used in the future.
b Humans will be able to control robots in the same way as they control animals.
c Robots are not the problem because humans can choose how to use them.

AI ethicist Kate Darling: 'Robots can be our partners'

Dr Kate Darling is a research specialist in human-robot interaction, robot ethics and intellectual property theory and policy at the Massachusetts Institute of Technology (MIT) Media Lab. In her new book, *The New Breed*, she argues that we would be better prepared for the future if we started thinking about robots and artificial intelligence (AI) like animals.

What is wrong with the way we think about robots?

So often we subconsciously compare robots to humans and AI to human intelligence. The comparison limits our imagination. Focused on trying to recreate ourselves, we're not thinking creatively about how to use robots to help humans flourish.

Why is an animal analogy better?

We have domesticated animals because they are useful to us – oxen to plough our fields, pigeon delivery systems. Animals and robots aren't the same, but the analogy moves us away from the persistent robot-human one. It opens our mind to other possibilities – that robots can be our partners – and lets us see some of the choices we have in shaping how we use the technology.

But companies *are* trying to develop robots to take humans out of the equation – driverless robot cars, package delivery by drone. Doesn't an animal analogy conceal what, in fact, is a significant threat?

There is a threat to people's jobs. But that threat is not the robots – it is company decisions that are driven by a broader economic and political system of corporate capitalism. The animal analogy helps illustrate that we have some options. The different ways that we've harnessed animals' skills in the past shows we could choose to design and use this technology as a supplement to human labour, instead of just trying to automate people away.

Who should be responsible when a robot causes harm? In the Middle Ages, animals were put on trial and punished ...

We did it for hundreds of years of western history: pigs, horses, dogs and plagues of locusts – and rats too. And bizarrely the trials followed the same rules as human trials. It seems so strange today because we don't hold animals morally accountable for their actions. But my worry when it comes to robots is, because of the robot-human comparison, we're going to fall into this same type of Middle Ages animal trial fallacy, where we try to hold them accountable to human standards. And we are starting to see glimmers of that, where companies and governments say: "Oh, it wasn't our fault, it was this algorithm".

Shouldn't we hold robot manufacturers responsible for any harm?

My concern is that companies are being let off the hook. In the case of the cyclist killed by a self-driving Uber car in 2018, the back-up driver was held responsible instead of the manufacturer. The argument from the companies is that they shouldn't be responsible for learning technology, because they aren't able to foresee or plan for every possibility. I take inspiration from historical models of how we have assigned legal responsibility when animals cause unanticipated harm:

03 **breed** *Züchtung, Rasse*
07 subconscious *unterbewusst*
10 to **flourish** *florieren, blühen, gedeihen*
12 to domesticate sth *etw zähmen, etw domestizieren*
12 to plough *pflügen*
13 pigeon *Taube*
17 **equation** *Gleichung*
19 to conceal *verheimlichen, verstecken*
24 **supplement** *Ergänzung*
24 labour *Arbeit*
27 to **put sb on trial** *jdn vor Gericht stellen*
27 to **punish sb** *jdn bestrafen*
28 plague of locusts *Heuschreckenplage*
30 to **hold sb accountable (for sth)** *jdn (für etw) zur Rechenschaft ziehen*
33 fallacy *Irrtum, Täuschung*
34 glimmer *Schimmer, Schein*
37 to let sb off the hook *jdn aus der Verantwortung nehmen*
40 to **foresee sth** *etw voraussehen, etw vorhersehen*
42 to **assign sb sth** *jdm etw zuweisen*
42 **unanticipated** *unerwartet*

47 **cheetah** *Gepard*
50 **intimate** *intim, eng, persönlich*
51 **functionality** *Funktionalität*
52 **data set** *Datensatz*
52 to amass *anhäufen, ansammeln*
54 **racial bias** *rassistische Voreingenommenheit*
55 to reinforce *(ver)stärken, verfestigen*
55 to embed sth *etw integrieren, etw einbetten, etw einbauen*
56 companion *Begleiter/in*
57 societal *gesellschaftlich, sozial*
57 **loneliness** *Einsamkeit*
57 **care worker** *Pfleger/in*
59 supplemental *zusätzlich, ergänzend*
63 **conscious** *bewusst*
63 sentient *empfindungsfähig*
64 **predictor** *Indikator*
66 hypocrite *Heuchler/in*
67 to gravitate to sth *von etw angezogen werden*

for example, in some cases, we distinguish between dangerous and safer animals and solutions range from holding owners strictly responsible to allowing some flexibility, depending on the context. If your tiny poodle bites someone on the street, totally unexpectedly for the first time, you're not going to be punished like you would if it were a cheetah. But the main point is that unforeseeable behaviour isn't a new problem and we shouldn't let companies argue that it is.

What about privacy? Animals can keep your secrets, but a robot may not ...

These devices are moving into intimate spaces of our lives and much of their functionality comes from their ability to collect and store data to learn. There's not enough protection for these giant data sets these companies are amassing. I also worry that because a lot of social robotics deals with characters modelled on humans, it raises issues around gender and racial biases that we put into the design. Harmful stereotypes get reinforced and embedded into the technology. And I worry that we are looking to these robot companions as a solution to our societal problems such as loneliness or lack of care workers. Just as robots haven't caused these problems, they also can't fix them. They should be treated as supplemental tools to human care that provide something new.

Should we give rights to robots?

This often comes up in science fiction, revolving around the question of whether robots are sufficiently like us. I don't disagree that robots, theoretically, would deserve rights if they were to become conscious or sentient. But that is a far-future scenario. Animal rights are a much better predictor for how this conversation around robot rights is going to play out in practice, at least in western society. And on animal rights we are hypocrites. We like to believe that we care about animal suffering but if you look at our actual behaviour, we gravitate towards protecting the animals that we relate to emotionally or culturally. In the US you can get a burger at the drive-through, but we don't eat dog meat. I think it's likely we will do the same with robots: giving rights to some and not others.

(866 words) From: *The Guardian*, 17 April 2021

6 Explain the meaning of these quotes from the text within the context of the article.

1 "There is a threat to people's jobs. But that threat is not the robots – it is company decisions that are driven by a broader economic and political system of corporate capitalism." (ll. 20–22)
2 "Oh, it wasn't our fault. It was the algorithm". (ll. 34–35)
3 "My concern is that companies are being let off the hook." (l. 37)
4 "There's not enough protection for these giant data sets these companies are amassing." (ll. 51–52)
5 "Animal rights are a much better predictor for how this conversation around robot rights is going to play out in practice, at least in western society. And on animal rights we are hypocrites." (ll. 64–66)

7 Examine how Dr Darling presents her opinion and analyse how she tries to convince the reader of her point of view.

Exam preparation

S ▸ Dealing with a text analysis task, pp. 215–220

Working with words

8 Find the seven verb phrases and explain their meaning in the text.

1 to limit our imagination (l. 8)
2 to take … out of the equation (l. 17)
3 to hold sb/sth accountable ll. 30–31)
4 to cause sb harm (l. 42)
5 to hold sb responsible (l. 44)
6 to play out in practice (l. 65)
7 to gravitate towards sth (l. 67)

Speaking

9 **Partner A:** Look here. **Partner B:** Look at File 8 on page 271.

Partner A: Sequence 1 (your five-minute talk)

Situation: You are taking part in a youth forum on new developments in the field of artificial intelligence.

Use the given material as a starting point for an uninterrupted five-minute talk on our use of robots and artificial intelligence.

1 Describe and analyse the cartoon.

2 Comment on the quote and explain how it relates to the cartoon.

"Who do you want to replace when you grow up?"

"We are approaching a time when machines will be able to outperform humans at almost any task. I believe that society needs to confront this question before it is upon us: if machines are capable of doing almost any work humans can do, what will humans do?"
– Moshe Vardi, mathematician and computer scientist

Partner A: Sequence 2 (you and the teacher / another student)

Discuss the following questions with Partner B.

1 Why do some people see robots as a threat to humanity?

2 What do you imagine the future of robots to be? Compare the ideas from the video with the discussion of AI ethics in the article.

Exam preparation
Kommunikationsprüfung

S ▸ Describing and analysing cartoons, pp. 82–83
Phrases for speaking

Section D The internet of things

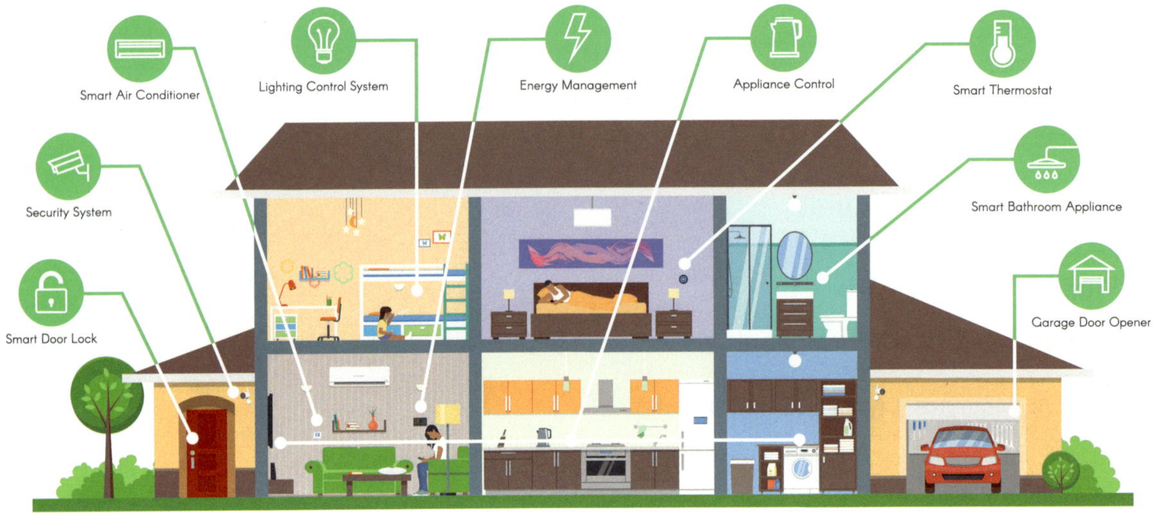

Warm-up

1 Look at the diagram and discuss these questions in small groups.

- What makes a home a "smart home"?
- Which of the applications do you know, have, or have you seen somewhere? How do they help?
- Which devices would you (not) like to have in your home? Why (not)?

Working with the text

S ▸ Reading difficult texts, pp. 39–40

2 Scan the text below and on the following pages and take notes on these aspects:

- tracking of people in their smart homes
- use of utility records
- privacy protection in the USA
- third-party data collection

utility records *pl* *Versorgungsdaten*

12

Your 'smart home' is watching – and possibly sharing your data with the police

06 key fob *Schlüsselanhänger*
10 bidder *Bieter/in*

You may have a roommate you have never met. And even worse, they are nosy. They track what you watch on TV, they track when you leave the lights on in the living room, and they even track whenever you use a key fob to enter the house. This is the reality of living in a "smart home": the house is always watching, always tracking, and sometimes it offers that data up to the highest bidder – or even to police.

This problem stems from the US government buying data from private companies, a practice increasingly unearthed in media investigations though still quite shrouded in secrecy. It's relatively simple in a country like the United States without strong privacy laws: approach a third-party firm that sells databases of information on citizens, pay them for it and then use the data however deemed fit. The Washington Post recently reported – citing documents uncovered by researchers at the Georgetown school of law – that US Immigration and Customs Enforcement has been using this very playbook to buy up "hundreds of millions of phone, water, electricity and other utility records while pursuing immigration violations".

"Modern surveillance" might evoke images of drones overhead, smartphones constantly pinging cell towers, and facial recognition deployed at political protests. All of these are indeed unchecked forms of 21st-century monitoring, often in uniquely concerning ways. Facial recognition, for instance, can be run continuously, from a distance, with minimal human involvement in the search and surveillance process. But the reporting on ICE's use of utility records is a powerful reminder that it's not just flashy gadgets that increasingly watch our every move; there's also a large and ever-growing economy of data brokerage, in which companies and government agencies, law enforcement included, can buy up data on millions of Americans that we might not even think of as sensitive.

Privacy protections in the United States are generally quite weak; when it comes to police purchases of private data, they are completely absent. This is one of the oddities of trying to update 18th-century rights to address 21st-century threats. At the time of the country's founding, the framers wrote about protecting things like our homes, our papers and other physical objects. Flash forward to today, and these categories fail to capture most of our intimate data, including the ins and outs of your daily routine captured by a nosy electronic roommate – or a data broker.

Courts have been slow to update these legal categories to include computers and other electronic records. But while we now have the same protections for our laptops as our paper records, the matter gets much less clear in the cloud. The documents and data we access remotely every day can end up in a gray zone outside the clear protections afforded in our homes and offices.

Whether it's our financial records, our phone records or the countless other records held about us by third parties, this data is generally open to police even without a warrant. This so-called "third-party doctrine" has come under more scrutiny in recent years, and there is some hope the courts will catch up with the changes in technology. Until they do, however, nearly all the data held about us by private companies remains completely exposed. Hence why utility records might end up in the hands of law enforcement via a private company, or how smart-home devices like thermostats and fridges could very well be sending off your data to be sold away.

While the recent Washington Post story focused on data brokerage and utility records, the smart-home phenomenon makes this problem of data sale and unchecked surveillance even worse. These gadgets are sold as flashy, affordable and convenient. But despite all that has been written about the speculative benefits of the so-called Internet of Things, these technologies are often terribly insecure

Good to know

Immigration and Customs Enforcement (ICE) is part of the Department of Homeland Security in the USA. Its role is to enforce the laws in the USA in connection with borders, immigration, customs and trade.

11 to **stem from** *herrühren von*
12 to **unearth sth** *etw ausgraben, etw aufstöbern*
13 shrouded in secrecy *geheimnisumwoben*
15 to deem *erachten, halten (für)*
16 to **cite sth** *etw zitieren, etw angeben*
18 using this very playbook *nach genau diesem Muster*
19 **violation** *Verstoß, Verletzung* (von Gesetzen, Rechten)
20 **surveillance** *Überwachung*
20 to evoke *auslösen, hervorrufen*
21 to deploy *einsetzen*
23 **concerning** *besorgniserregend*
26 flashy *auffällig, protzig*
26 gadget *Gerät, technischer Krimskrams*
27 **brokerage** *Börsenhandel*
28 **law enforcement** *Gesetzesvollzug, Polizeigewalt*
29 **sensitive** *sensibel, (Daten:) vertraulich*
33 framer *Verfasser/in*
34 flash forward *Vorausblende*
35 to **capture** *einfangen, erfassen*
36 **nosy** *neugierig*
37 **court** *Gericht(shof)*
47 **warrant** *richterliche Anordnung*
47 under scrutiny *auf dem/den Prüfstand*
50 hence *daher, folglich*
58 **insecure** *unsicher*

61 but *bloß, nur*
62 **absence** *Abwesenheit*
64 **deportation** *Abschiebung*
67 **restriction** *Beschränkung, Einschränkung*

and may provide few to no details to consumers on how they're protecting our data. Ring, Amazon's home security system, has documented surveillance ties with law enforcement; that is but one example. The more that smart devices are marketed in the absence of strong federal privacy protections, the more likely it's not just about hackers half a world away controlling your home's temperature – it'll also be about arrests and deportations with the help of smart-home data.

All of which means American citizens and lawmakers must remember that protecting modern privacy is not just a question of facial recognition bans and legal restrictions on smartphone data collection, for example. It's also a matter of regulating the appliances and smart devices that watch people in their homes – and reforming the giant industry that profits off buying and selling those systems' data.

(775 words) From: *The Guardian*, 5 April 2021

Exam preparation

S ▸ Writing a summary, p. 81

3 Point out how smart homes can be used in ways that violate privacy in the United States.

Working with words

4 Match the words (1–8) to the correct synonyms (a–h).

1 surveillance	**a** to chase
2 gadget	**b** device
3 to ban	**c** easy
4 utility	**d** to follow
5 to pursue	**e** to forbid
6 threat	**f** service
7 convenient	**g** danger
8 to track	**h** watching

5 Match the verbs with prepositions to complete the gaps in the advertisement. Make sure to use the correct form of the verb.

Verbs	Prepositions
to get | to turn	into | off | on | out | out of | to | up

When you leave your house in the morning, do you worry that you forgot to …[1] the coffee maker? When you …[2] bed last night, did you …[3] again to check that you had …[4] your alarm? If you're relaxing in your living room and start to feel cold, wouldn't it be nice if you didn't have to …[5] the couch to …[6] the thermostat?

Lots of people are now …[7] *SmartHomes* to help them …[8] their home …[8] a real smart home. Isn't it time for you to …[9] the most …[9] your home too?

Call now! It might …[10] to be the best decision you have ever made!

6 You have just moved into a smart home. Write a letter to a friend describing the things you (dis)like about living there using verbs and prepositions from exercise 5.

Listening

7 You will hear a radio report about smart homes in the USA. While listening, complete the following sentences.

13

Exam preparation

S ▸ Dealing with listening tasks, pp. 123–125

1 The smart homes of the future provide …
2 Janice Long doesn't think it is difficult to …
3 Smart home owners can control a large number of appliances easily by …
4 The apps help parents of teenagers to check …
5 Some people don't want to live in a smart home because …
6 The experience of real estate agents is …
7 Liz feels like she has a butler …
8 Liz's mother tries to avoid …

Presentation

8 Do some research on how digitalization and the Internet of Things are applied in one of the fields in the list. (Choose another area that you are interested in if you wish.) Prepare a five-minute presentation for the class.

- **consumer applications:** smart homes, care for the elderly, …
- **organizational applications:** medical and health care, transportation, …
- **industrial applications:** manufacturing, agriculture, …
- **infrastructure applications:** city management, energy management, …
- **military applications:** cyberwarfare, battlefield technology, …

Speaking

9 Discuss the pros and cons of the Internet of Things in class.

- Do we rely too heavily on technology? What happens when the systems fail?
- Does the Internet of Things mean that we no longer have any privacy?
- Is technology the answer to solving problems such as climate change and worldwide hunger?
- Is is possible to live without being connected in some way?

Writing

10 Choose <u>one</u> of the following options.

Exam preparation

S ▸ Writing an argumentative text, pp. 167–172

Writing checklist

A Comment on the following quote and how it relates to the text.

> *"A child born today will grow up with no conception of privacy at all. They'll never know what it means to have a private moment to themselves, an unrecorded, unanalysed thought. And that's a problem because privacy matters."*
> – Edward Snowden, Whistleblower

B You are doing a school exchange in California in the USA. There is a controversial discussion there about the regulation of information collected from smart homes and whether stronger privacy laws need to be introduced.

Write a letter to your local newspaper giving your opinion about smart homes and privacy.

S ▸ Dealing with a creative writing task, pp. 126–128

Writing checklist

Section E Digital manipulation

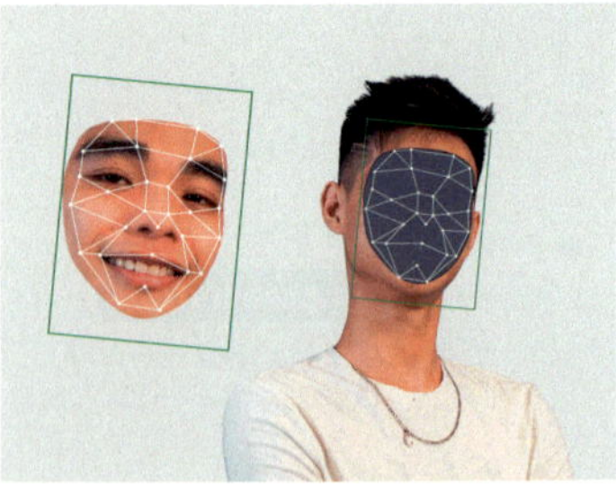

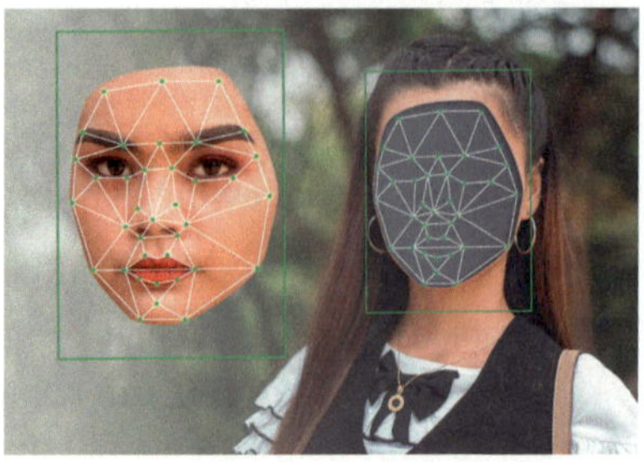

Good to know

Deepfake is a technique used to make a photo, video or an audio recording in which the face, voice and/or body of the person or thing is digitally altered to look like someone or something else.

Warm-up

1 Discuss these questions in small groups.

- Have you ever seen a deepfake photo, audio or video? What was it?
- How did you know it was a deepfake? Give reasons.
- What did you think of it? (funny, spooky, disturbing, ...)

Working with the text

2 Read the text and match the headings (A–F) to the correct sections (1–6).

to **undermine** *untergraben*
to wreak havoc *verheerende Schäden anrichten*

A	Will they undermine trust?
B	Will deepfakes wreak havoc?
C	What is a deepfake?
D	How do you spot a deepfake?
E	What's the solution?
F	Is it just about videos?

What are deepfakes – and how can you spot them?

AI-generated fake videos are becoming more common (and convincing). Here's why we should be worried.

1 ...

Have you seen Barack Obama call Donald Trump a "complete dipshit", or Mark Zuckerberg brag about having "total control of billions of people's stolen data", or witnessed Jon Snow's moving apology for the dismal ending to Game of Thrones? Answer yes and you've seen a deepfake. The 21st century's answer to Photoshopping, deepfakes use a form of artificial intelligence called deep learning to make images of fake events, hence the name deepfake. Want to put new words in a politician's mouth, star in your favourite movie, or dance like a pro? Then it's time to make a deepfake.

01 **artificial intelligence (AI)** *künstliche Intelligenz*
04 dipshit *infml Volldepp*
05 to brag about sth *mit etw angeben*
06 **apology** *Entschuldigung*
06 dismal *düster*

2 …

No. Deepfake technology can create convincing but entirely fictional photos from scratch. A non-existent Bloomberg journalist, "Maisy Kinsley", who had a profile on LinkedIn and Twitter, was probably a deepfake. Another LinkedIn fake, "Katie Jones", claimed to work at the Center for Strategic and International Studies, but is thought to be a deepfake created for a foreign spying operation.

Audio can be deepfaked too to create "voice skins" or "voice clones" of public figures. Last March, the chief of a UK subsidiary of a German energy firm paid nearly £200,000 into a Hungarian bank account after being phoned by a fraudster who mimicked the German CEO's voice. The company's insurers believe the voice was a deepfake, but the evidence is unclear. Similar scams have reportedly used recorded WhatsApp voice messages.

3 …

It gets harder as the technology improves. In 2018, US researchers discovered that deepfake faces don't blink normally. No surprise there: the majority of images show people with their eyes open, so the algorithms never really learn about blinking. At first, it seemed like a silver bullet for the detection problem. But no sooner had the research been published, than deepfakes appeared with blinking. Such is the nature of the game: as soon as a weakness is revealed, it is fixed.

Poor-quality deepfakes are easier to spot. The lip-synching might be bad, or the skin tone patchy. There can be flickering around the edges of transposed faces. And fine details, such as hair, are particularly hard for deepfakes to render well, especially where strands are visible on the fringe. Badly rendered jewelry and teeth can also be a giveaway, as can strange lighting effects, such as inconsistent illumination and reflections on the iris.

4 …

We can expect more deepfakes that harass, intimidate, demean, undermine and destabilise. But will deepfakes spark major international incidents? Here the situation is less clear. A deepfake of a world leader pressing the big red button should not cause armageddon. Nor will deepfake satellite images of troops massing on a border cause much trouble: most nations have their own reliable security imaging systems.

There is still room for mischief-making, though. Last year, Tesla stock crashed when Elon Musk smoked a joint on a live web show. In December, Donald Trump flew home early from a Nato meeting when genuine footage emerged of other world leaders apparently mocking him. Will plausible deepfakes shift stock prices, influence voters and provoke religious tension? It seems a safe bet.

5 …

The more insidious impact of deepfakes, along with other synthetic media and fake news, is to create a zero-trust society, where people cannot, or no longer bother to, distinguish truth from falsehood. And when trust is eroded, it is easier to raise doubts about specific events.

Last year, Cameroon's minister of communication dismissed as fake news a video that Amnesty International believes shows the country's soldiers executing civilians.

13 **from scratch** *ganz von vorne, von Grund auf*
20 **fraudster** *Betrüger/in*
21 to **mimic sb** *jdn nachahmen*
21 **insurer** *Versicherer*
22 **scam** *Schwindel, Betrug*
28 silver bullet *Königsweg*
28 **detection** *Entdeckung, Aufdeckung*
31 to lip-synch *synchronisieren*
32 patchy *fleckig, durchwachsen*
32 to **transpose** *austauschen*
33 to **render** *rendern (berechnen und ausgeben)*
34 **strand** *Strähne*
34 **fringe** *Rand*
35 giveaway *(verräterischer) Hinweis*
35 **inconsistent** *uneinheitlich, unstimmig*
36 **illumination** *Beleuchtung*
36 **reflection** *Reflexion, Spiegelbild*
36 iris *Iris, Regenbogenhaut*
38 to **intimidate** *einschüchtern, bedrohen*
38 to demean sb *jdn herabsetzen*
39 to spark *entfachen, entzünden*
43 **imaging** *Bildverarbeitung*
44 mischief *Unfug*
44 **stock** *Aktie, Anleihe*
46 **footage** *Film-/Bildmaterial*
47 to **mock sb** *sich über jdn lustig machen*
52 to **erode** *zerfressen, beschädigen*
53 **doubt** *Zweifel*
54 to dismiss sth as sth *etw als etw abtun*
55 to execute sb *jdn hinrichten*
56 civilian *Zivilist/in*

57 to **admit to sth** *etw zugeben, (ein)gestehen*
57 to boast *sich rühmen*
59 to cast doubt on sth *etw in Frage stellen*
60 **attorney** *(Rechts-)Anwalt/ Anwältin*
62 deniable *widerlegbar*
65 custody *Sorgerecht*
65 tribunal *Gericht(shof)*
68 vein *Vene, Ader*
68 gait *Gangbild*
77 provenance *Herkunft, Ursprung*
78 watermark *Wasserzeichen*
78 foolproof *idiotensicher*
79 tamper-proof *manipulationssicher*

Donald Trump, who admitted to boasting about grabbing women's genitals in a recorded conversation, later suggested the tape was not real. In Prince Andrew's BBC interview [...], the prince cast doubt on the authenticity of a photo taken with Virginia Giuffre, a shot her attorney insists is genuine and unaltered.

"The problem may not be so much the faked reality as the fact that real reality becomes plausibly deniable," says Prof Lilian Edwards, a leading expert in internet law at Newcastle University.

As the technology becomes more accessible, deepfakes could mean trouble for the courts, particularly in child custody battles and employment tribunals, where faked events could be entered as evidence. But they also pose a personal security risk: deepfakes can mimic biometric data, and can potentially trick systems that rely on face, voice, vein or gait recognition. The potential for scams is clear. Phone someone out of the blue and they are unlikely to transfer money to an unknown bank account. But what if your "mother" or "sister" sets up a video call on WhatsApp and makes the same request?

6 ...

Ironically, AI may be the answer. Artificial intelligence already helps to spot fake videos, but many existing detection systems have a serious weakness: they work best for celebrities, because they can train on hours of freely available footage. Tech firms are now working on detection systems that aim to flag up fakes whenever they appear. Another strategy focuses on the provenance of the media. Digital watermarks are not foolproof, but a blockchain online ledger system could hold a tamper-proof record of videos, pictures and audio so their origins and any manipulations can always be checked.

(892 words) From: *The Guardian*, 13 January 2020

Good to know

A **blockchain ledger system** is a data system which ensures that information is only accepted from and released to trusted parties.

S ▸ Writing a summary, p. 81

3 Use information from the text to complete this summary of *What are deepfakes – and how can you spot them?*

Deepfakes are made by ...[1] and are used to create fake events, like ...[2] or ...[3]. Deepfakes are not only videos. They can also be ...[4] or ...[5].

As the technology gets better, it gets harder and harder to ...[6]. In 2018 researchers noticed that the faces on deepfake videos ...[7], which made it possible recognize the videos as fake. As soon as the research was published, however, ...[8]. A bad deepfake is still pretty obvious, though. One can notice it because ...[9] or ...[10].

As deepfakes continue to improve in quality, we can expect that the harm that they can do will increase. Could a deepfake cause an international incident? Hopefully not, but there are plenty of problems that a deepfake video can cause. The bigger problem with deepfakes is that they create a society ...[11]. When this trust erodes, it can cause major problems. If a public figure gets caught on video doing something they should not be doing, they can simply ...[12]. In addition, as our society moves farther into the world of ...[13], deepfake could also cause problems by imitating biometric data, and the potential for scams grows.

In the end, the best answer may actually be AI. Artificial intelligence has already been used to ...[14] but new strategies are being worked on, including using blockchain to create ...[15], which can check original videos to ...[16].

Working with words

4 Find synonyms in the text for the words below.

fake (x3) | genuine (x2) | boast | fraud

Listening

5 You will hear a radio interview about deepfakes. While listening, take notes on the following points. You need not write complete sentences.

14

1 the reporter's definition of deepfake: …
2 evolution of deepfake since 2017: …
3 steps in process to manipulate a video (3 aspects): …
Example: *post-production clean-up*
4 examples of harmful and not harmful deepfakes (2 aspects): …
5 ethics of identity (2 aspects): …
6 deepfake videos potentially causing national security risks (2 aspects): …
7 misinformation apocalypse: …

Exam preparation

S ▸ Dealing with listening tasks, pp. 123–125

Mediation

6 Some friends have sent you links to deepfakes on the internet. They think they are funny and harmless. As you have just read the article *What are deepfakes – and how can you spot them?*, you don't agree with them.

Write a German blog entry summarizing the dangers that deepfakes present to our modern society.

S ▸ Mediation, pp. 259–261

Speaking

7 Read the quote from the radio interview and discuss the question below.

"And that's the danger here … it's not just the content, but it's that we can deliver it online, en masse to millions of people around the world, have it go viral, and before anybody gets around to figuring out that it's fake, we have a global nuclear meltdown."

- Who should be held responsible for regulating deepfake?
  - big tech companies that provide cloud computing and tools which make it possible to create deepfakes
  - social media platforms that make it possible to distribute deepfakes quickly
  - the people who create deepfakes
  - politicians and legislators
- How and why should deepfakes be regulated?

Writing

8 "'Seeing is believing' is a thing of the past."

Discuss this quotation taking into consideration the information about deepfakes in the article and the interview in this Section.

Exam preparation

S ▸ Writing an argumentative text, pp. 167–172

Writing checklist

Section F Artificial humans

Warm-up

1 In groups, discuss the following questions.

- What is the difference between a robot and an android?
- Have you ever come across a robot or an artificial human? Where? What was it like?
- Could you imagine living with an artificial human? Why (not)?

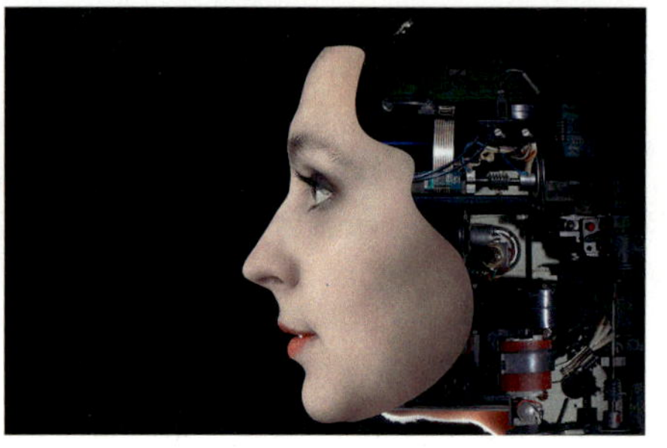

Working with the text

The 2019 novel *Machines Like Me*, written by the English author Ian McEwan, is set in the UK of the early 1980s. The historical reality in the novel, however, is different to the real world. The internet, social media and self-driving cars already exist. In this extract, the narrator, Charlie, has just bought an android called Adam.

2 Skim the extract and make short notes on the following.

- Adam's appearance
- what he is supposed to be able to do
- what he can't do

Machines Like Me

ONE

[...] I was among the optimists, blessed by unexpected funds following my mother's death and the sale of the family home, which turned out to be on a valuable development site. The first truly viable manufactured human with plausible intelligence and looks, believable motion and shifts of expression went on sale the week before the Falklands Task Force set off on its hopeless mission. Adam cost £86,000. I brought him home in a hired van to my unpleasant flat in north Clapham. I'd made a reckless decision, but I was encouraged by reports that Sir Alan Turing, war hero and presiding genius of the digital age, had taken delivery of the same model. He probably wanted to have his lab take it apart to examine its workings fully.

Twelve of this first edition were called Adam, thirteen were called Eve. Corny, everyone agreed, but commercial. Notions of biological race being scientifically discredited, the twenty-five were designed to cover a range of ethnicities. There were rumours, then complaints, that the Arab could not be told apart from the Jew. Random programming as well as life experience would grant to all complete latitude

01 blessed *gesegnet*
03 **viable** *realisierbar, durchführbar*
04 **motion** *Bewegung*
04 **shift of expression** *Ausdrucksänderung*
07 reckless *rücksichtslos, leichtsinnig*
08 presiding *führend*
10 corny *abgedroschen*
11 **notion** *Vorstellung, Auffassung*
13 **rumour** *Gerücht*
13 to **tell apart** *auseinander halten*
14 **random** *zufällig, beliebig*
14 to **grant** *gewähren, einräumen*
14 latitude *Spielraum, Freiheit*

in sexual preference. By the end of the first week, all the Eves sold out. At a careless glance, I might have taken my Adam for a Turk or a Greek. He weighed 170 pounds, so I had to ask my upstairs neighbour, Miranda, to help me carry him in from the street on the disposable stretcher that came with the purchase.

While his batteries began to charge, I made us coffee then scrolled through the 470-page online handbook. Its language was mostly clear and precise. But Adam was created across different agencies and in places the instructions had the charm of a nonsense poem. 'Unreveal upside of B347k vest to gain carefree emoticon with motherboard output to attenuate mood-swing penumbra.'

At last, with cardboard and polystyrene wrapping strewn around his ankles, he sat naked at my tiny dining table, eyes closed, a black power line trailing from the entry point in his umbilicus to a thirteen-amp socket in the wall. It would take sixteen hours to fire him up. Then sessions of download updates and personal preferences. I wanted him now, and so did Miranda. Like eager young parents, we were avid for his first words. There was no loudspeaker cheaply buried in his chest. We knew from the excited publicity that he formed sounds with breath, tongue, teeth and palate. Already, his lifelike skin was warm to the touch and as smooth as a child's. Miranda claimed to see his eyelashes flicker. I was certain she was seeing vibrations from the Tube trains rolling a hundred feet below us, but I said nothing.

Adam was not a sex toy. [...] He was advertised as a companion, an intellectual sparring partner, friend and factotum who could wash dishes, make beds and 'think'. Every moment of his existence, everything he heard and saw, he recorded and could retrieve. He couldn't drive as yet and was not allowed to swim or shower or go out in the rain without an umbrella, or operate a chainsaw unsupervised. As for range, thanks to breakthroughs in electrical storage, he could run seventeen kilometres in two hours without a charge or, its energy equivalent, converse non-stop for twelve days. He had a working life of twenty years. He was compactly built, square-shouldered, dark-skinned, with thick black hair swept back; narrow in the face, with a hint of hooked nose suggestive of fierce intelligence, pensively hooded eyes, tight lips that, even as we watched, were draining of their deathly yellowish-white tint and acquiring rich human colour, perhaps even relaxing a little at the corners. Miranda said he resembled 'a docker from the Bosphorus'.

Before us sat the ultimate plaything, the dream of ages, the triumph of humanism – or its angel of death. Exciting beyond measure, but frustrating too. Sixteen hours was a long time to be waiting and watching. I thought that for the sum I'd handed over after lunch, Adam should have been charged up and ready to go. It was a wintry late afternoon. I made toast and we drank more coffee. Miranda, a doctoral scholar of social history, said she wished the teenage Mary Shelley was here beside us, observing closely, not a monster like Frankenstein's, but this handsome dark-skinned young man coming to life. I said that what both creatures shared was a hunger for the animating force of electricity.

(741 words) Source: *Machines Like Me*, Ian McEwan

Good to know

The **Falklands Task Force** was a military group which successfully recaptured the Falkland Islands from the Argentine Army during the Falklands War (April–June 1982).

Alan Turing (1912–1954) was a British mathematician who worked on cracking secret German codes during World War II. He is considered by many to be the father of the modern computer, and the Turing Test is a way of measuring whether a machine shows intelligent behaviour. He never actually became "Sir Alan Turing".

24 to strew *streuen*
25 to trail *hier: schlängeln*
26 umbilicus *Nabel*
27 to fire sth up *etw anschmeißen (in Gang bringen)*
29 avid for *gierig nach*
31 palate *Gaumen*
36 factotum *Faktotum (Mädchen für alles)*
39 chainsaw *Kettensäge*
42 to **converse** *sich unterhalten*
44 fierce *bedrohlich*
45 pensive *nachdenklich*
45 hooded *halbgeschlossen*
46 to **drain of sth** *etw verlieren*
46 tint *Farbton*
47 to **resemble sb** *jdm ähneln*
47 docker *Hafenarbeiter/in*
54 doctoral scholar *Doktorand/in*
57 **animating** *belebend, beseelend*

Good to know

Mary Shelley was the author of the novel *Frankenstein*, published in 1818, which is considered one of the earliest examples of science fiction.

3 **Rewrite the following sentences from the text in your own words.**

1. The first truly viable manufactured human with plausible intelligence and looks … (ll. 3–4)
2. Twelve of this first edition were called Adam, thirteen were called Eve. Corny, everyone agreed, but commercial. (ll. 10–11)
3. Notions of biological race being scientifically discredited, the twenty-five were designed to cover a range of ethnicities. (ll. 11–12)
4. It would take sixteen hours to fire him up. (ll. 26–27)
5. We knew from the excited publicity that he formed sounds with breath, tongue, teeth and palate. (ll. 30–31)
6. I thought that for the sum I'd handed over after lunch, Adam should have been charged up and ready to go. (ll. 51–52)

Working with words

4 **Rewrite the sentences replacing the underlined words and phrases with synonyms from the text.**

1. Due to some unexpected money that came into my hands, I was able to afford to buy the robot that had just come on the market.
2. The first workable robot was developed in 1954 by George Devol.
3. When I decided to invest all my money in the newest technology, my friends thought it was a careless decision.
4. The idea that robots will someday be able to function in the same way as humans is absurd.
5. She went to the IT conference in order to have the chance to talk to some of the leading researchers in the field of Artificial Intelligence.
6. When the computer crashed, he didn't have a backup so he wasn't able to get back the information that was lost.
7. When the researcher came up with a way to program robots, her competitors tried to disgrace her so that no one would believe the work she had done.
8. Although the robot was able to change the way her face looked, she still did not have the capability to mimic human appearance.

Speaking

5 **With a partner, discuss your thoughts about Adam. Describe what you imagine the world would be like in this alternate reality with robot companions.**

Presentation

S ▸ Presentation, pp. 260–261

6 **Work in small groups. Choose a robot or humanoid from literature or films to research. Use the following questions as a guide and include any other information you find interesting. Present your findings to the class.**

1. What book or movie is the character from?
2. When was the book or movie written and when does it take place?
3. What is the story of the book or movie?
4. What is the character of the robot and how does it fit into the story?
5. Why and how was the robot created?

Project Creating a podcast

You are going to create a podcast about one specific aspect of technology that you have looked at in this Topic.

Step 1

Decide on your theme. Divide the class into groups, so that each of the following topics is covered by at least one group.

genetically modified foods | food production | digitalization | the internet of things | robots and artificial intelligence

Tip

Make sure that you choose a topic that you are interested in. If you are excited about your topic, your listeners will be too! If you're bored, they'll also be bored.

Step 2

Once your group has a topic, do some internet research and decide which specific theme within this heading you would like to present in your podcast.

Step 3

Choose what form of podcast you would like to create. Some possibilities are:

- educational podcast – focusing on teaching the audience
- interview podcast – featuring a host who interviews one or more people
- news summary podcast – summarizing the current news regarding your topic
- scripted non-fiction podcast – telling a true story about your topic
- scripted fiction podcast – telling a made-up story about your topic

Step 4

Write an outline describing what ideas you would like to include in your podcast.

Good to know

Make sure that you stay on topic. Think about this when creating your outline and make sure you stick to your outline when writing your script. You should also keep this in mind when editing.

Step 5

Use your outline to write a script. Create a storyline by starting with a set-up or introduction, leading to a confrontation, and finally ending with a solution. Try to answer these questions:

- What were the struggles and challenges?
- What lessons were learned?

Step 6

Record and edit your podcast. There are several free programs that you can download to edit your podcast once you've recorded it, and they are easy to use.

Step 7

Present your podcast to the class!

Podcast checklist

✓ Have you discussed your topic with your group, done your research and come up with an intriguing point of view?
✓ Have you made an outline of the structure of your podcast?
✓ Have you written and edited your script?
✓ Have you practised reading your text and prepared everything that you would like to record?
✓ Have you recorded the podcast?
✓ Have you edited the podcast together?

15

Words in context

genetically modified *genetisch verändert*
organism *Organismus*
gene *Gen*
crop *Getreide*
efficiency *Produktivität*
to **cross sth** *etw kreuzen*
resistance *Resistenz, Abwehr*
disease *Krankheit*
tolerance *Verträglichkeit*
herbicide *Unkrautvernichtungsmittel*
corn *Mais*
cotton *Baumwolle*
fertilizer *Dünger, Düngemittel*
nutritional value *Nährwert*
allergy trigger *Allergieauslöser*
human consumption *menschlicher Verzehr*

Genetically modified foods

Genetically modified (GM) foods are developed from organisms whose DNA or genetic material has been changed in a way that would not occur naturally, for example by introducing a gene from another organism. The majority of GM plants are crops that have been modified to improve their efficiency during growth, for example by crossing them with the genes of plants that have more resistance to disease or tolerance of herbicides and pesticides. GM corn, soybeans and cotton are common in the USA. Genetically modified plants can also reduce the production costs of foods because they are easier to grow and require fewer fertilizers. It is possible that in the future plants will be modified to increase their nutritional value or to reduce allergy triggers. GM foods are tested on a case by case basis to make sure they are safe, but they are highly controversial as many people do not trust that they are safe for human consumption or harmless for the environment.

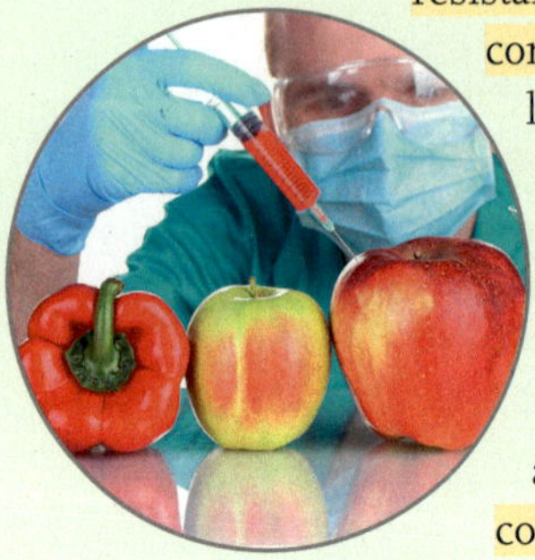

to comprise sth *etw umfassen, aus etw bestehen*
processing *Verarbeitung*
preservation *Konservierung*
preparation *Zubereitung*
packaging *Verpackung*
unsustainable *nicht nachhaltig, unhaltbar*
hunger *Hunger*
malnutrition *Mangel-, Unterernährung*
biofuel *Biokraftstoff*
agricultural *landwirtschaftlich*
food waste *Lebensmittelverschwendung*
plant-based meat *Fleisch, das aus pflanzlichen Zutaten hergestellt wird*

Industrial food production

The food industry itself is a complex supply chain that brings food to consumers around the world. It is comprised of a wide range of services including production, distribution, processing, preservation, preparation, packaging, and transport. It can range from small, family-run farms to large, industrial agricultural complexes and factories. Critics of modern food production claim that "Big Food", a term used for industrial farming and food production, is unsustainable and that changes must be made to solve problems such as hunger, malnutrition and long-term environmental damage. Among the most urgent problems caused by modern food production methods are damage to ecosystems by the increased production of biofuels; unsustainable agricultural practices such as industrial-scale meat production; lack of rights for small farmers and workers; and food waste, not only during production, but also at retailers and by consumers. Plant-based meat, using GM ingredients, may be one solution to the damage caused by breeding livestock on a large scale.

digitalization *Digitalisierung*
digital communication *digitale Kommunikation*
to **influence sb/sth** *jdn/etw beeinflussen*
to **appreciate sb/sth** *jdn/etw schätzen*
advance *Fortschritt*
to **disconnect** *abtrennen, die Verbindung unterbrechen*
superficial *oberflächlich*
to **interact** *interagieren, aufeinander eingehen*
face to face *persönlich*

Digitalization

Digitalization refers to the change in many aspects of human social life, which are now organized around forms of digital communication such as email, messaging and social media. There are many ways digitalization has influenced our modern world and the rate at which change is taking place is becoming faster and faster. While many people appreciate the advances which have made communication worldwide easier and faster, some believe that our world is too fast-moving and that it is increasingly difficult to disconnect from technology. In addition, some people claim that digitalization is creating a more superficial society in which people only know how to communicate via quick text messages and no longer know how to interact face to face.

The internet of things

The internet of things (IoT) refers to appliances and devices that have sensors, software and other technology that enable them to connect with other devices with the same technology. These networks can be used in order to make daily life more comfortable and convenient. So-called "smart homes" create a living space in which the devices and appliances within the home, including lights, thermostats, security systems, locks, cameras, etc., support each other and can be controlled remotely, usually by a smartphone app. There are many concerns about this new form of technology, not least of which is the unregulated collection, sale and distribution of personal data.

internet of things *Internet der Dinge*
appliance *(Haushalts-)Gerät*
device *Gerät, Apparat*
network *Netzwerk*
comfortable *bequem*
convenient *bequem, zweckdienlich*
thermostat *Temperaturregler*
security system *Sicherheitssystem*
remotely *aus der Ferne*
concern *Bedenken, Sorge*
personal data *persönliche Daten*

Artificial Intelligence

Artificial Intelligence (AI) is the science of programming machines or computers to reproduce human processes such as learning and decision-making. These "smart" computers are supposed to "think" like humans, mimicking their cognition. Many things that humans do, for example problem-solving, can also be done by computers although in a different way to humans. An ideal or, in other words, perfect machine would be flexible and able to take in the environment around itself and learn and react accordingly. The current state of AI includes machines that can successfully understand human speech and play strategic games such as chess, self-driving cars and computers that can process and analyse complicated data. While many find this development extremely exciting, there are others who find it dangerous and worry that computers, machines and robots will at the very least take over human jobs and at the worst, destroy humanity.

While AI has developed significantly over the years, there are still many problems associated with this technology, for example that computers are not able to perceive their environment with the same nuance as humans.

artificial intelligence *Künstliche Intelligence*
to **reproduce sth** *etw nachbilden*
decision-making *Entscheidungsfindung*
to **mimic sb** *jdn nachahmen*
cognition *Wahrnehmung, Erkenntnis*
problem-solving *Problemlösung*
accordingly *(dem)entsprechend*
to **process sth** *etw verarbeiten*
to **analyse sth** *etw analysieren*
to **destroy sth** *etw zerstören*
to **perceive sth** *etw wahrnehmen, etw erkennen*

Human robots

Although many companies and university researchers are working towards creating robots that are more and more human, and, in other words, more perceptive and mentally flexible, the science-fiction scenario that robots will replace humans is a long way off and is perhaps even impossible. According to some scientists, our modern film culture has ruined most people's idea of what robots are capable of. In many sci-fi movies, robots interact with humans (or aliens) in the same way that humans interact with each other. Through the development of AI and other technologies such as deepfake, robots and computers may give the impression of becoming more and more "human", but the technology is considered rudimentary by many researchers when compared with the actual abilities of human brains. This fact, however, does not stop humans from imagining a future, or alternate reality, where robots live among humans, as human companions. Is this our future? Only time will tell.

perceptive *scharfsinnig; einfühlsam*
science fiction *Science-Fiction*
scenario *Szenario, Drehbuch*
to **interact with sb/sth** *mit jdm/etw interagieren*
rudimentary *primitiv, unvollständig*
ability *Fähigkeit, Können*
brain *Gehirn*
to **imagine sth** *sich etw vorstellen*

1 Copy and complete the table with the missing words. The given words are all in the text. Use your dictionary if necessary.

Verb	Noun	Adjective
…	advancement	…
to appreciate	…	…
to compare	…	…
to destroy	…	…
to disconnect	…	…
to imagine	…	…
to influence	…	…
to interact	…	…
to perceive	…	…
…	preservation	…
…	processing / …	…
…	resistance	…

2 Fill in the gaps using highlighted words from the text.

1. Scientists who want to improve the characteristics of a specific plant often look for other … which have qualities that would benefit the plant.
2. One argument against GM foods is that by creating plants that would not naturally … , scientists are harming the environment.
3. Supporters of GM food believe that by creating disease-resistant plants, we can feed more people and eliminate the problem of … in our world.
4. Artificial Intelligence … human thought but it is not yet able to replicate human cognition.
5. Smart homes comprise a network of … that are able to connect to each other and understand the commands presented by humans.
6. Because the door locks on his house were linked to his smart home, he was able to unlock the doors … using an app on his smartphone.
7. While it is now quite common to have virtual meetings, many still prefer the more personal quality of … conversations.
8. Robot technology is still considered to be at a … level because robots are not able to … with humans on an equal cognitive level.

3 Match highlighted words from the text with the following definitions.

1. a chemical that is used to kill weeds
2. a device in a home that controls the heating and temperature
3. a plant that is grown on a large scale to provide food
4. only relating to the surface of sth, not having a deeper meaning
5. sth that causes sb to worry
6. the process by which knowledge and understanding is developed in the mind
7. the process of choosing which course of action to take
8. the quality of not being affected by sth
9. the science or practice of farming

Words for tasks

The verb used in the instructions to the task will help you understand exactly what you're expected to do to complete the task. For this reason, it's essential that you know what each of the verbs that occur in exam questions means.

The typical "question words" in the tables below cover three *Anforderungsbereiche*. The examples in **bold** refer to the reading texts in the book.

Good to know

The amount of personal input you are expected to provide increases according to the requirement sets.

Anforderungsbereich I: SUMMARY	*Reproduction* (reproduction of the materials provided)
Anforderungsbereich II: TEXT ANALYSIS	*Reorganization and transfer* (explanation, exploration and illustration of known topics using new questions)
Anforderungsbereich III: ARGUMENTATIVE/CREATIVE WRITING	*Reflection and problem-solving* (independent working out of solutions, interpretations and explanations)

Anforderungsbereich I + II

S ▸ Writing a summary, p. 81

Instruction	Examples	What's expected from you
General summary		
summarize	• *Summarize the (main points of the) article.* • *Sum up the text.* *Summarize the pros and cons of genetic engineering relating to modern methods of food production. (p. 54)* *Summarize why the switch to home working after Covid "will make gender equality worse". (p. 109)*	provide a condensed form of the most important points
Guided summary		
outline	• *Outline the information given by the author on …* • *Outline the arguments for and against …* *Outline the evidence given in the text for the start of the Anthropocene. (p. 12)*	present only the main points relevant to the task
describe	• *Describe … as depicted in …* *Describe the action taken regarding fossil fuel advertising in different regions and countries. (p. 20)*	describe the aspects precisely and in a structured manner
point out	• *Point out the author's ideas/opinion on …* *Point out the differences between the companies' advertising claims and reality. (p. 20)* *Point out the regulations that affect people who sell firearms in the USA. (p. 143)*	filter out the main aspects

state	• *State the reasons/information the author gives for/on ...* *State ways in which apps are attempting to solve environmental issues created by the fashion industry. (p. 29)*	clearly define certain aspects
illustrate	• *Illustrate the way in which ... differs from ...* *Illustrate things everyday consumers can do to become conscious consumers. (p. 101)*	use examples to demonstrate certain aspects

S ▸ Dealing with a text analysis task, pp. 213–218

Anforderungsbereich II

Instruction	Examples	What's expected from you
analyse **examine**	• *Analyse/Examine how the reader's interest in the text is aroused by its content and structure.* • *Analyse/Examine how the author tries to convince the reader of his/her point of view on the issue.* • *Analyse/Examine to what extent the picture/cartoon/graph relates to the text.* *Examine the messages behind the statements given by fossil fuel companies. (p. 20)* *Examine how Dr Darling presents her opinion and analyse how she tries to convince the reader of her point of view. (p. 62)*	describe aspects in detail using technical terms and explain their function with reference to the intended meaning of the text

S ▸ Writing an argumentative text, pp. 167–172

Anforderungsbereich III

Instruction	Examples	What's expected from you
comment on **give your opinion**	• *Comment on/Give your opinion of the writer's view on ...* • *Comment on the following quote in relation to greenwashing, ... (p. 21)* *Comment on the following quote and how it relates to the text. (p. 59)* *Write a letter to the editor in which you ... . Give your opinion on how the issue should be handled. (p. 243)*	present your own opinion in a structured way using arguments and examples
assess **evaluate**	• *Assess/Evaluate the impact/development/success of ...* *Assess which of the environmental problems facing humanity you think should be solved most urgently ... (p. 13)*	reach a carefully considered conclusion after weighing up all the advantages and disadvantages
discuss	• *Discuss the advantages/chances and disadvantages/risks of ...* • *Discuss whether ... is a blessing or a curse.* *Taking the text as a starting point, discuss this quotation. (p. 191)*	examine a complex topic from different viewpoints, considering the advantages and disadvantages
weigh up the pros and cons	• *Weigh up the pros and cons of ...* *Taking the text as a starting point, weigh up the pros and cons of using the name Aotearoa for New Zealand. (p. 188)*	

Writing a summary

You'll need to show you've correctly understood the content of a text to answer this type of question. What is the text about? What does it say about a certain topic? Depending on the focus of the question, you'll be asked either to write a **general summary** of the whole text or to summarize certain parts of it in a **guided summary**.

Good to know

In the ***Abitur*** exam, this type of task is designed to test your **understanding of a text** in the form of a **general** or **guided summary**.

Checklist for summaries

- You need to write a cohesive and structured text in the ***simple present*** tense.
- Structure your text according to the arguments presented in the original text.
- Leave out any examples or details.
- Do not include any quotes: either paraphrase them or use indirect speech.
- Stay objective: avoid giving your opinion on any points and just stick to what the text says.
- Your text should be around a quarter to a third of the length of the original.

G ▸ Reported speech, p. 288

General summary

1 Read the question through carefully.
Typical **instructions** for summaries might ask you to **summarize** or **outline** the main topic of a text.

2 Read the text through carefully and highlight the following:
a) the main point(s);
b) supporting arguments/facts.

Only highlight the most important concepts or phrases.

Exercise 1

Summarize the information given in the article about smart homes (pp. 64–66).

Introduction

The [text type + "title"] written by [author] in [year] informs the reader about / deals with [main topic].

Main body

The author …
… says/states/points out/claims/ believes/thinks/describes/ explains/argues/suggests that …
… doubts/asks whether …
… criticizes/analyses/tries to express …
… contrasts X with Y/compares X to Y …

Conclusion

In his/her concluding paragraph/sentence …
The author closes his/her [text type] stating …

S ▸ Words for tasks, pp. 79–80

Guided summary

The question might ask you to **restrict** your answer to certain aspects. Pay close attention to **how the task is worded** and **which verbs** are used.

Exercise 2

State the information the article gives on tracking and describe the role of utility records in the context of smart homes (pp. 64–66).

possible instructions

point out: filter information to a specific aspect

describe: describe one aspect precisely

state: clearly define one aspect (*summarize/outline*)

illustrate: use examples to demonstrate one aspect

S ▸ Words for tasks, pp. 79–80

Tip

You might have a task with one of the verbs *summarize* or *outline*, but asking you to concentrate on just one section of the text.

Describing and analysing cartoons

If you are asked to describe an image or a cartoon, concentrate on the main message, making sure you don't get lost in the details.

Example assignment

Describe and analyse the cartoon.
Compare it with the text.

"If I had to guess at what our biggest existential threat is, it's probably that."
– Elon Musk on Artificial Intelligence

THE TECHNOLOGY REVOLUTION

Step 1: Description

Describe what you can see in the image: look at all the aspects of the picture, but only include the elements which are important to understand the point it's trying to make.

the moon
three astronauts
a spaceship
~~*The moon is grey.*~~

Specify which object you're describing by stating clearly where it can be found in the image.

In the background*, there's a spaceship in the sky.*

G ▸ Present progressive, p. 283

Use the **present progressive** tense to describe what's happening in the image.
Be careful, though: the verbs ***be, seem, look*** and ***describe*** aren't generally used in the progressive tense.

The spaceship ***is disappearing****.*
~~*The spaceship disappears.*~~
The astronauts ***seem*** *surprised.*
~~*The astronauts are seeming surprised.*~~

Step 2: Interpretation

Interpret the image. If you think the image doesn't say very much, then mention this in your interpretation. You might also want to say if you think the image can be understood in different ways, or if it's unclear what it is trying to say.

The ***message*** *of the cartoon is* ***clearly*** *that society is too dependent on technology and the fact that it is playing a more and more dominant role in many people's lives leads to various risks.*

Step 3: Effect on you, and what you have to say about it

Make it clear what impact the image has on you: summarize its main point and give your own opinion on it.

I (don't) agree *with the message that society depends on AI too much.*

I (don't) find *the cartoon very funny/clever.*

Step 4: Relation to other source

If you are asked to, refer to the text you've been given (see above) and compare the image with the content of that text. State whether the text is supported by the image, or if it contradicts it.

The cartoon supports the quote, *with Elon Musk stating that humankind's existence could be at stake due to the potential of AI.*

Describing the picture
- The cartoon shows …
- The comic/cartoon consists of four frames/parts.
- The picture seems to show …
- The scene depicts …
- The caption / speech bubble says …
- In the foreground/background/centre, there is …
- On the left/right, there is …
- The person is (holding something / writing / walking away).
- It seems as if the person is (holding something / writing / walking away).

to **consist of** *bestehen aus*

to **depict** *darstellen*

Interpreting the picture
- The picture/cartoon deals with …
- The cartoon is intended to create …
- The (person in the centre) represents/shows/symbolizes …
- This shows/reveals/indicates …
- The impression of … is created.
- The point of the cartoon is / seems to be …
- The humour lies in the difference/misunderstanding/discrepancy/contrast/ parallels between ... and ...

point *Zweck*

Commenting on the picture
- I think … / In my opinion …
- The cartoon makes a fair point.
- The cartoon convinces / doesn't convince me, because …
- I agree with the cartoonist, but …
- The cartoonist is partly right.
- The cartoonist exaggerates a little / a lot.
- It forces you to think about …
- It has the effect of …

to **exaggerate** *übertreiben*
to **force sb** *jdn zwingen*

Comparing the picture with the text
- Although the cartoon/picture shows …, the text says …
- In the text we found out that …
- The picture supports the information in the text in the following way.
- The cartoon offers a completely different opinion to the text.

to **support** *unterstützen*

Exercise

Describe and analyse the cartoon. Compare it with the information given in the article "Your 'smart home' is watching – and possibly sharing data with the police" (pp. 64–66).

"Watch what you say. The appliances have ears."

Review

1 Rank the Sections A–F in this Topic based on how interesting they were to you. Then, look back at your work on the overview of this Topic (pages 50–51) and how you ranked them there (page 50, exercise 2). Have your rankings changed? Share your results with a group and tell them what you found most interesting.

2 Look at your KWL list (page 51, exercise 5). Complete the "Learned" part of the list. Next, look at your "Want to know" list. What do you still want to know?

3 Make a list of ten words in the Topic that were new to you and you consider important to know. Then collect everyone's words and cluster them into groups. Finally, pick a word group and write a paragraph using all the words.

Evaluate

Do this task on your own. How much do you agree or disagree with the statements below? Rate each one on a scale of one to four. The references on the left show you which exercises you can review.

1 = totally disagree **2** = disagree **3** = agree **4** = totally agree

	Section	**Statement**
▸ pp.52–54, exercises 1–4	**A**	**1** I understand genetic engineering related to crops and food.
▸ p.54, exercise 5		**2** I can summarize the pros and cons of genetic engineering related to food production.
▸ p.55, exercise 8		**3** I am able to describe photos and interpret cartoons.
▸ pp.56–58, exercise 1–3	**B**	**4** I understand how plant-based meats can revolutionize food production.
▸ p.59, exercises 7–8		**5** I can give my opinion on the use of plant-based meats.
▸ pp.60–62, exercise 1–2, 5–6	**C**	**6** I can talk about robots and how they can help us in our world.
▸ p.60, exercises 1–4		**7** I am able to talk about artificial intelligence, its development and influence on our daily lives.
▸ p.62, exercise 7		**8** I know how to analyse a text.
▸ p.63, exercise 9		**9** I can describe and analyse cartoons.
▸ pp.64–67, exercises 1–3, 7–8	**D**	**10** I am able to talk about smart homes and the internet of things.
▸ p.67, exercises 7–9		**11** I can talk about the privacy risks related to smart homes.
▸ pp.68–70, exercises 1–3	**E**	**12** I know how to discuss digital manipulation, especially related to deep fake.
▸ p.71, exercises 5–7		**13** I can talk about the dangers of deep fake and how it could or should be regulated.
▸ pp.72–74, exercises 1–2, 5–6	**F**	**14** I am able to discuss artificial humans in literature and film.
S ▸ pp.79–80	**Skills**	**15** I understand words for tasks and what is required of me.
S ▸ p.81		**16** I can write a summary.
S ▸ pp.82–83		**17** I describe and analyse cartoons.

Consolidate

You want to go deeper into the the topic of technology, and speed up your learning process? Scan this page with the PagePlayer app. There you'll find some suggestions for additional tasks.

Aufgabenteil I Hören

1 You will hear a radio interview with Eva Galperin, director of cybersecurity at the Electronic Frontier Foundation, about recent controversies surrounding Apple AirTags.

16

While listening, choose the correct answers (a, b or c). There is only one correct answer.

1 Apple AirTag tracking devices ...
- a are the size of a coin.
- b look like a normal key ring.
- c are designed to help parents track their kids.

2 The controversial discussions about Apple AirTags led to ...
- a a court banning them.
- b Apple warning their customers.
- c a minister publishing a warning to consumers.

3 Eva Galperin ...
- a works freelance for a NY court.
- b is an advocate for freedom rights.
- c works for an electronics company.

4 Apple AirTags are different to other trackers because they work using ...
- a Bluetooth.
- b the Find My app.
- c almost all Apple smartphones.

5 The concern about those devices is they can be used to ...
- a stalk other people.
- b reveal your identity.
- c track things you don't want to track.

6 Apple's promise to make improvements ...
- a was never turned into action.
- b was stopped by law-enforcement.
- c was insufficient in the eyes of Eva Galperin.

7 The "tracking-tracker" app that Apple released ...
- a required too much effort from the user.
- b is a good tool that can be used to identify tracking.
- c runs automatically in the background of an Android phone.

8 The interviewer wonders whether ...
- a all new technology is a danger to privacy.
- b legislators are a long way behind in regulating new technologies.
- c tech companies should be more aware of privacy issues related to new products.

17 **2** You will hear a radio interview with Sandy Wilson, an expert on Artificial Intelligence (AI).

While listening, take notes on the following points. You need not write complete sentences.

1 areas to consider when talking about AI (2 aspects): ...
Example: classificatory logistics
2 effects of AI on the labour market (2 aspects): ...
Example: crowd work
3 example of AI technology errors: ...
4 problems with training data sets (3 aspects): ...
5 Sandy's question: ...
6 Sandy's recommendation: ...

18 **3** You will hear an interview about possible downsides of alternative meat.

While listening, complete the following sentences.

1 Consumers should be careful with vegan alternatives because ...
2 When comparing fake meat with real meat ...
3 When Robert ate a vegan burger recently, ...
4 A vegan diet can be healthier if people ...
5 More important than a vegan diet is ...
6 The term "real" fish is controversial because ...

Aufgabenteil II Lesen und Schreiben

Aufgabenstellung

1 Summarize what the text says about using robots in care homes. (Material 1, pp. 87–88)

2 Analyse how the author tries to convince the reader of her attitude towards robots in care homes, referring to structure and language. (Material 1, pp. 87–88)

3 Choose one of the following:

A *"... it is more generally believed by people working in the field that programming even the basic skills required to build a beneficial human relationship – empathy and attachment – are nigh on impossible ... to reproduce in a robot."* (ll. 20–23).

Discuss the quote from the text.

B You are taking part in a youth conference on Artificial Intelligence. The question of using robots as carers for elderly people is a very controversial topic of discussion at the conference.

Write a blog entry for the conference website in which you comment on the recent trend of using robots in care homes.

Material 1

Would you want a robot to be your relative's carer?

As an evolutionary anthropologist I have spent more than a decade researching human interaction, and it is not an overstatement to say that the nature of our relationships with each other is one of the most critical factors in our health, happiness and life satisfaction. People who have strong, healthy relationships show a reduction in rates of mortality from chronic illness of 50% [...]. Having supportive friends reduces the risk of poor mental health but also contributes to recovery and a reduction in relapse among those who suffer from addiction.

Our need for each other is so critical to our survival that mechanisms in our body have been recruited to ensure we seek out relationships and strive to maintain them. This is most clearly represented by the phenomenon of bio-behavioral synchrony where, as two people interact in person, their behaviour, physiology and neurology synchronise. We all probably recognise the synchrony in behaviour that we see in the parent/child and romantic couples we know – the matching of gesture, voice tone and vocabulary – but this extends to their heart rate, blood pressure, body temperature, levels of circulating neurochemistry and brain activation patterns. As yet we do not fully understand what triggers this phenomenon but the fact that we see it in healthy interactions, and particularly where a close bond is present, suggests that it is fundamental to the ties that bind us and in all probability is key to the health benefits of social interaction.

Companion robots have been trialled in care homes in the UK and Japan, but it is more generally believed by people working in the field that programming even the basic skills required to build a human relationship – empathy and attachment – are nigh on impossible and prohibitively expensive to reproduce in a robot. [...]

Beyond this is the problem of our inbuilt ability to spot an imposter. Participants in a study led by the neuroscientist Thierry Chaminade were asked to interpret a range of emotions when displayed by a human face and a robot face. Functional MRI results comparing brain activity during the robot- and human-focused tasks showed increased neural processing during the robot task, required to interpret its expression. Another crucial area of the brain showed no activity at all when robots were the focus – the mirror neurones that fire when we perceive actions undertaken by a fellow human. The brain clearly identified it as alien.

Why does this matter? Surely even if we do not build a relationship with these robots they can feed us our pills, play us some music and even teach us a language, as the trialled robots can. But caring, even in this limited context, is rarely purely carrying out practical tasks. Caring is grounded in empathy. It is about reading someone's expression as we hand them their pills and knowing that they are having a hard day, or chatting about their birthday plans with family. It is about using our own life experience to offer them support and understanding. It is about that bio-behavioural synchrony. That meeting of human minds. The wonderful flood of neurochemicals that brighten our day and shore up our immune system.

In a way, this would not matter if we could be sure that, should robots be introduced into care homes, they would be used simply to supplement human care, not to replace it. Indeed, we may dream that as the robot completes practical tasks, humans are freed to spend time talking to their clients. But when adult social care is faced with a funding crisis, it is easy to see how care work could be automated rather than supplemented. After all, robots don't get ill, they don't take holidays, they don't leave for a new job and they can work 24/7.

If we allow robots into our care homes, we risk sleepwalking into an even larger social care crisis than we are now in. We are already beset by an epidemic of loneliness among older people, and we risk significantly worsening this, and their associated mental and physical health, if we withdraw the powerful medicine that is human contact. Replacing carers with robots yet again devalues what is valuable and skilled work, and abdicates the personal and social responsibility we owe to the most vulnerable in our society.

Now is the time to ask ourselves: would we be happy for our grandparents, our parents, even our children to be cared for by robots? Should you hesitate to answer yes to this question, then perhaps now is the time for us to pause and decide whether to continue down this path.

(774 words) Source: *The Guardian*, 10 September 2020

Mündlicher Teil Kommunikationsprüfung

Partner A: look here. **Partner B:** look at File 10 on page 272.

Partner A: Sequence 1 (your five-minute talk)

Situation: You are taking part in an international conference on modern technology and nutrition. Each participant is expected to give a five-minute opening statement.

Use the statistics below and cartoon opposite as a starting point to outline to your audience the controversy surrounding genetically modified food.

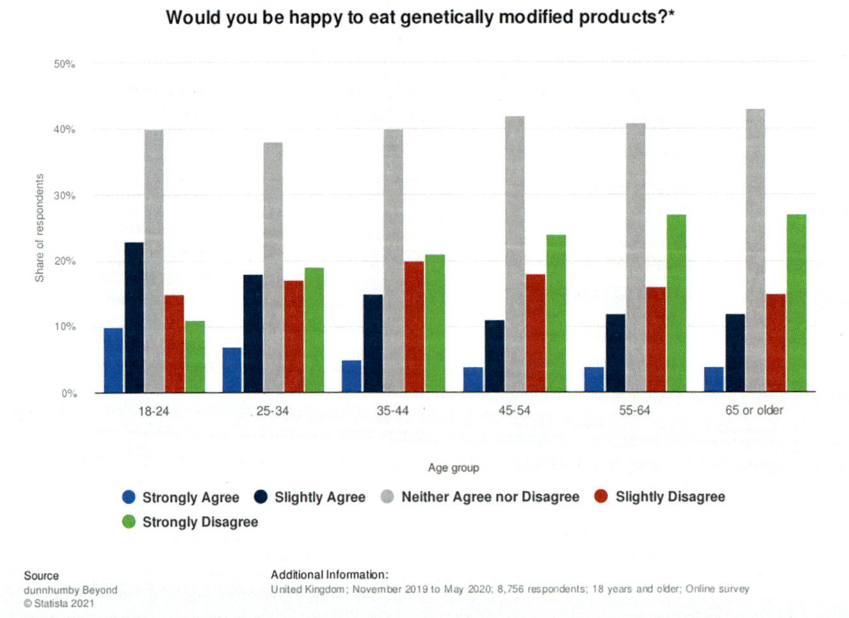

Describe and analyse the graph.

Describe and analyse the cartoon and say how it refers to the statistics.

Partner A: Sequence 2 (you and the teacher / another student)

Discuss the future of genetically modified food with your teacher / your partner.

1 Under what circumstances can you imagine a meaningful use of genetically modified foods?

2 How can the fight against hunger be won? Comment on the following quote.

> *"I'm against the theory of the multinational corporations who say if you are against hunger, you must be for GMO. That's wrong, there is plenty of natural, normal good food in the world to nourish the double of humanity. There is absolutely no justification to produce genetically modified food except the profit motive and the domination of the multinational corporations."*
>
> – Jean Ziegler, Swiss sociologist

Topic 3 Work and consumers

Section A
Advertising

consumers

influencers

Section B
Ethical consumption

Fact: Most consumers say they would pay more for meat and milk but in the end, a majority usually buys the cheapest product.

environmental impact

"People do not buy goods and services. They buy relations, stories, and magic."
– Seth Godin, US entrepreneur and author

cultural differences

Global economy

Section G
Intercultural competence in the workplace

respect

"Company cultures are like country cultures. Never try to change one. Try instead to work with what you've got."
– Peter Drucker, management consultant

1 Read the facts and quotations about work and consumers above.

- **a** Which of them are totally new to you?
- **b** Which of them do you find surprising?

2 Rank Sections A–G on how interested you are in them.

3 The mind map shows you a preview of Topic 3. Copy it onto a piece of paper and add words and phrases from …

- **a** the facts and quotations above.
- **b** the Word bank opposite.
- **c** your own ideas.
- **d** Sections A–G you think are important.

Find information on each Section in the PagePlayer app!

industry

connectedness

working from home

independent

life changes

Section C
Globalization

"Globalization is not a monolithic force but an evolving set of consequences – some good, some bad and some unintended. It is the new reality."
– John B Larson, US politician

Section D
Gender inequality

Fact: In most countries, women earn between 60 and 75% of men's wages – for the same work. (source: globalcitizen.org)

Section E
Generation Z

Fact: In 2019, Generation Z became the largest generation in the world, making up 32% of the global population. (source: New York Post)

"When well-being is on a better level, people have better chances to get a job. Employers see them as more capable of work."
– Minne Ylikanno, senior researcher at Finland's Social Insurance Institution

Section F
Unemployment and universal basic income

4 Note a few key words to say what you expect to learn in each Section.

5 Make a "KWL" (Know, Want to know, Learned) list for the Topic.

6 With a partner, compare …

a your mind maps and say why you added words where you did.
b your rankings from exercise 2.
c what you expect to learn in Sections A–G.

Then compare with another pair.

7 Save your work for reviewing when you've finished the Topic.

Word bank

compassionate *mitfühlend, barmherzig*
conscience *Gewissen*
convenient *bequem, praktisch*
crucial *wesentlich*
disruption *Störung, Unterbrechung*
to **emphasize sth** *etw hervorheben*
exhausted *erschöpft*
to **exploit sth** *etw ausbeuten*
freelance *selbstständig*
genuine *echt*
ignorance *Unwissenheit*
to **legislate** *Gesetze erlassen*

Section A Advertising

Warm-up

1 Work in groups of three or four and discuss the following questions.

- Where do you experience advertising in your everyday life?
- What do you like about advertising? Explain why.
- What do you dislike about advertising? Give examples.

Working with the text

S ▸ Reading difficult texts, pp. 39–40

2 Skim the text and then discuss with a partner: Who or what are the "beasts" (l. 20)?

It's genuine, you know?

In a central London hair salon last December, the fashion influencer Victoria Magrath [...] mingled among a few of her 849,000 [...] followers. Magrath – tall, with signature silver hair – was celebrating the launch of her book, *The New Fashion Rules*, at an event organized by her talent agency, Gleam Futures. She chatted easily, her high, delighted voice ringing out over the roar of the hairdryers and her manner so convincingly intimate that it was possible to think she knew her followers as well as they knew her. In a group discussion, a fan asked how her wedding plans were going, another if it was too late to start being a blogger. Magrath was encouraging: "Anyone can do it if they've got the right formula."

After nearly seven years in the game, Magrath is now part of the digital establishment – [...] high-end and dependable. Her content, spread across [a number of social media platforms] and her blog, is an old-school, manicured mix of fashion hauls, luxurious travel and commercial partnerships with brands from Armani to Reiss. Last year, she went on 36 trips, often gifted by PRs, on which her photographer boyfriend Alex [...] took pictures of her in Venetian gondolas and St Lucian waterfalls. "It's nice to keep the content flowing, that's the main reason we do it," she told her followers in the salon. "I love London, but there's only so many times I can keep taking pictures in Notting Hill."

Such is the life of a top-of-the-range influencer [...], who has to sustain an insatiable audience and satisfy platforms that reward constant posting. The beasts must be fed. But Magrath senses that change is afoot. The sheer volume of digital content has reached a point where everyone is becoming desensitized. "There's been a million makeup tutorials and a million fashion hauls," she told me. "People are a bit done with it."

[2] to mingle (among people) *sich (unter Leute) mischen*
[3] **signature** *charakteristisch, unverkennbar*
[5] **delighted** *froh, erfreut*
[5] roar *Gebrüll, Getöse*
[6] **manner** *Art, Wesen*
[9] to **encourage** *ermuntern, ermutigen*
[11] **dependable** *zuverlässig, verlässlich*
[12] manicured *gepflegt*
[13] haul *hier: Einkaufstour*
[19] to **sustain sth** *etw (aufrecht) erhalten*
[20] **insatiable** *unersättlich*
[21] to be afoot *im Gange sein*
[22] desensitized *abgestumpft*

Over the last decade, influencer marketing – the business of brands paying social media celebrities to advertise their wares – has become a well-established tactic. Influencers now have their own line on a brand's marketing-spend spreadsheet alongside TV, radio and so on. But as Magrath suggested, the industry is now entering a new phase. If phase one was hyperactive expansion – bump the follower count, boss the [...] algorithm, rack up the brand deals – then insiders say that phase two is about authenticity, about "coming back to quality again", as Dominic Smales, CEO of Magrath's agency Gleam Futures, told me.

In this new era of authenticity, influencers must display passion, a word that fills the air at Gleam. (It is the kind of office where instead of replying "yes" to a question, everyone says "100%!".) Magrath is like Gleam's head girl, a role model for others: "Victoria is really passionate about Dior, for example," said Smales. "She'll hang out with the people at Dior because she loves that brand, she loves what they do, for no payment or anything like that. Not everything is transactional, it's genuine, you know?"

Like many in the industry, Gleam have come to dislike the term "influencer", finding it both misrepresentative and degrading. They describe themselves instead as a "digital-first talent agency": if their talent have influence, that is simply a blessed by-product of their creative abilities. Gleam pride themselves on being able to distinguish between the hollow Instagrammers in it for fame and cash, and the genuine talent who have the potential to broaden and prolong their career beyond the transient limits of a social media platform (hence digital-*first*: their talent might start online, but they could go anywhere, do anything). "We want to represent the absolute crème de la crème," Lucy Loveridge, Gleam's head of global talent, told me. "In the UK, there's a lot of what I would call 'influencers'. There's less *talent*."

Back at the salon, after hugging the last of her followers goodbye, Magrath sat down to relax. She was still buzzing from the event: "I just feel like I have a massive family, to be honest." Her usually buoyant tone only slipped once, when talking about her audience's relentless expectations. Last Christmas, Magrath had decided not to do Vlogmas – a [...] tradition where vloggers post a video every day in December. Some of her followers expressed their displeasure. "I'm like, 'Well you got three blogposts, seven images, two videos and a multitude of tweets this week, so what more could I do, you know?'"

At Gleam, they often emphasize how hard their talent works: content-production is a grind, and a talent essentially does six jobs in one – producer, presenter, cameraman, editor, marketeer, PR. It looks easy, influencing – one long holiday with free clothes and a paycheck at the end – but as with many aspects of the industry, the image deceives. This year, said Magrath, was going to be all about stripping back the artifice. Honesty was in. "More honest portrayals of people's lives," she explained. "I kind of want to move that way as well."

(826 words) From: *The Guardian*, 5 April 2019

29 to bump sth *etw hochtreiben*
30 to boss sth *etw manipulieren*
30 to rack up sth *etw hereinholen, etw einbringen*
41 to **degrade sb** *jdn erniedrigen*
44 hollow *hohl, oberflächlich*
45 to **broaden sth** *etw erweitern*
45 to **prolong sth** *etw verlängern, etw herauszögern*
46 **transient** *vorübergehend*
52 buoyant *heiter, lebhaft*
53 **relentless** *unerbittlich, unbarmherzig*
59 grind *Schinderei, Plage*
59 **essentially** *im Wesentlichen*
62 to **deceive** *täuschen, (be)trügen*
63 to strip back sth *etw zurückdrängen*
63 artifice *Kunstgriff; Trick*

3 Read the text closely and then do the following tasks.

1 Describe Victoria Magrath's relationship with her fans.
2 Explain the nature of her relationship with the brands she promotes.
3 Point out the changes that are taking place in the world of influencers.

S ▸ Writing a summary, p. 81

S ▸ Words for tasks, pp. 79–80

4 Outline the differences between Victoria Magrath and traditional influencers.

Exam preparation

Working with words

5 Match the verbs (1–8) to the corrrect definitions (a–h).

1 to launch	**a** to found
2 to encourage	**b** to expand
3 to establish	**c** to lead someone to believe something that isn't true
4 to display	**d** to start an activity, especially for the first time
5 to distinguish	**e** to recognize or show the difference between things
6 to broaden	**f** to show
7 to emphasize	**g** to give special importance to something
8 to deceive	**h** to positively push someone to do something

6 Copy and complete the table.

Verb	Noun	Adjective
to launch	...	
to encourage	...	...
to establish	...	...
to display	...	
to distinguish	...	...
to broaden		...
to emphasize	...	...
to deceive	...	...

Looking at language

G ▸ Defining and non-defining relative clauses, p. 295

Remember

Do not use *that* in non-defining relative clauses!

7 Complete the sentences using suitable relative pronouns. Say whether each sentence is a defining or non-defining relative clause.

1. Ella Tidoff is a person ... followers consider her to be their friend.
2. People ... are interested in becoming bloggers should read her new book.
3. The party, ... was held at the TalentUnit agency, celebrated the launch of her new book.
4. Top influencers ... want to keep their followers have to stay ahead of the trends.
5. The marketing agency ... supports Ella uses the term 'talent' instead of 'influencer'.
6. Their employees, most of ... are under 30, use various social media platforms.
7. The people ... follow Ella regularly can sometimes expect too much of her.
8. Ella's boyfriend, ... is also her photographer, always accompanies her on her trips.

G ▸ Relative clauses and contact clauses, p. 295

Remember

When the relative pronoun is the **object** of a defining relative clause, you can leave it out.

8 Complete the sentences with a suitable relative pronoun where necessary.

1. Ella Tidoff is one of the influencers ... the TalentUnit agency manages.
2. Influencers ... work for TalentUnit prefer to be called 'talents'.
3. Ella is working on a travel blog ... she is going to post for her followers.
4. Influencers can become very rich when the companies ... sell the products are happy to pay them.
5. The book ... Ella has just published has lots of tips for new influencers.
6. People ... work in the influencing industry often have to do six different jobs.

Listening

Skills training: Dealing with multiple choice questions

- Always read through the questions carefully during the preparation time.
- If possible, cross out any answers on your answer sheet you are sure are wrong.
- Mark key words so you know what to listen for to find the correct answer.

9 You will hear an interview with a social media influencer. While listening, choose the correct answer (a, b or c). There is only one correct answer.

19

1 To advertise themselves on social media, companies are now hiring …
a ordinary people. b the Kardashians. c specialist ad agencies.

2 Leonie Hiller posts photos of coffee on her social media because …
a she loves the company's coffee.
b her friends persuaded her to do it.
c the company got in touch with her.

3 A microinfluencer is someone who …
a lives a normal, everyday life.
b only advertises products they like.
c only has a few thousand followers.

4 Consumer rights groups worry about influencers on social media because …
a they have so many young followers.
b there is far too much advertising on the internet.
c it is not always clear when they are promoting a product.

5 The Federal Trade Commission …
a doesn't have any guidelines about social media advertisings.
b checks social media platforms regularly to enforce its guidelines.
c says that influencers are responsible for marking advertising posts.

6 Leonie Hiller loves what she does but she …
a isn't interested in owning her own brand.
b doesn't consider herself a businesswoman.
c doesn't want to become a famous influencer.

7 Jessica Hayden says social media is changing people's behaviour because …
a capitalism has become a nightmare.
b real life and marketing are mixed up.
c people think their own lives are boring.

Exam preparation
S ▸ Dealing with listening tasks, pp. 123–125

blend *Mischung*
brew *Gebräu*
invoice *Rechnung*
the buck stops with sb *die Verantwortung liegt bei jdm*
extent *Umfang, Ausmaß*
guideline *Richtlinie*
disclosure *Offenlegung*
nightmare *Albtraum*
to get blurred *verschwimmen*

Speaking

10 Discuss the following questions with a partner:
- Would you buy a product because an influencer recommends it? Why (not)?
- Are influencers' vlogs different to other forms of advertising? Why (not)?

How to say or write it

Do you think that's true? I do/don't because …
How do you see it?
I don't think you can really say (that) …
I think … is probably true, but I don't agree with … (at all).

Writing

11 Comment on the following quote.

> *"People do not buy goods and services. They buy relations, stories, and magic."*
> – Seth Godin, US entrepreneur and author

Exam practice
S ▸ Writing an argumentative text, pp. 167–172
Writing checklist

Section B Ethical consumption

I'm happy to pay more for a product that has been produced sustainably.

When I go shopping, the most important thing is the price.

I sometimes think about how a product I want to buy has been produced.

Warm-up

1 With a partner, put the statements above in order from least to most environmentally friendly.

2 Discuss which statement most reflects the way you shop. Explain why.

Working with the text

S ▸ Reading difficult texts, pp. 39–40

3 Skim the text to find the difference between "conscious consumption" and "ethical consumption".

20

Good to know

Consumption is the act of buying and using products and services.

Consumerism is the belief that it is good for society and individuals to buy and consume large amounts of goods and services.

Is there such a thing as ethical consumption?

If you know that workers who make items of clothing for fast fashion companies are often treated and paid badly, and if you know that fast fashion is environmentally unsustainable, do you still buy that cool T-shirt? It is a real moral dilemma: fast fashion – using cheap materials and cheap labour to mass-produce the latest fashions – is just one of consumerism's numerous problems.

Acting as a conscious consumer, you would be aware of the negative impact of buying that T-shirt, and you would probably not buy it from one of the fast fashion companies, but rather try to find a more sustainable option. Maybe you would even choose to boycott the well-known fast fashion companies altogether.

"Conscious consumption" is a movement that encourages people to be aware of what they buy and to use their money to support brands that have the same values whenever possible. More and more people are jumping on this bandwagon, especially young people. It is also sometimes thought to be ethical consumption because it also encourages people to avoid unethical companies and to search for sustainable alternatives.

But "ethical consumption" is a contradictory term. Conscious consumption does not make a consumer an ethical consumer. Make no mistake: there is no such thing as ethical consumption under capitalism.

Because of this, just as zero-waste is impossible, being completely consequence-free in your purchases is also impossible. But you needn't have a guilty conscience about it.

[2] to **treat sb** *jdn behandeln*
[5] consumerism *Materialismus, Konsumverhalten*
[12] to jump on the bandwagon *auf den fahrenden Zug aufspringen*
[16] **contradictory** *widersprüchlich*
[20] **guilty** *schuldig*

As hard as you try, it is almost impossible to align this kind of morality with everyday reality. Although it is appropriate to do your best to support small businesses and to live as sustainably as possible, most of us still financially support giant corporations that we don't ethically agree with.

In our modern, globalized society, everything we do has negative consequences, whether intentional or unintentional. We all contribute to unethical consumption whether we want to or not: for example when we use a mobile phone which was made in a sweatshop to buy online some flowers that were grown with toxic pesticides and were picked by exploited migrant workers, and which were then delivered from thousands of miles away creating a massive carbon footprint as a result.

How unbelievably overwhelming it all is! Being environmentally aware and making informed purchases in every aspect of our lives, from groceries to takeouts, to necessities like soap and toothpaste, to clothing and medication: it is enough to stop you from even trying to be an ethical consumer. It feels completely futile. And it is sobering to realize that being able to make a choice between less and more sustainable products is often a question of price, which many people cannot afford to make.

If we separate conscious consumption and ethical consumption, however, we can make better choices because we don't have to see things as black or white, good or bad. This also gets rid of the idea that average individuals are responsible for the effects of capitalism. Rather, that responsibility rests fully with the mega-corporations and billionaires.

The fact is, we can make conscious consumption more inclusive. You don't have to reach a specific level of sacrifice to be considered a conscious consumer. No matter your socio-economic status, or the availability of sustainable brands, we can all contribute by doing the best we can with the knowledge we have, and by spreading that information to our peers, without judgement.

We can find information and vote with our wallet whenever possible but we can also be compassionate with ourselves. We shouldn't blame ourselves if we aren't able to change everything about our lifestyle overnight or if we can't afford to buy sustainable clothing or ethical products because of the price.

In conclusion, although our independent choices do make a difference, we should not forget to put pressure on large corporations who earn money by exploiting workers and the environment, and on the officials and politicians who have the power to change the rules. So, write emails, send letters, show up at meetings, get involved with legislation and protests: it all makes a difference.

(678 words)

22 **morality** *Moral (Wertesystem)*
25 **corporation** *Konzern*
29 sweatshop *Ausbeutungsbetrieb*
30 to **exploit sb** *jdn ausnutzen, jdn ausbeuten*
33 **overwhelming** *überwältigend*
34 takeout *AE* *Essen zum Mitnehmen*
35 **necessity** *Notwendigkeit*
36 futile *vergeblich*
37 sobering *ernüchternd*
46 **sacrifice** *Opfer*
49 **judgement** *Wertung*
50 **wallet** *Geldbeutel, Brieftasche*
51 **compassionate** *mitfühlend, barmherzig*

4 Read the text again and do the following tasks.

1 Explain the difference between conscious consumption and ethical consumption in your own words.
2 Point out why ethical consumption is not possible.
3 Illustrate things everyday consumers can do to become conscious consumers.

S ▸ Writing a summary, p. 81
S ▸ Words for tasks, pp. 79–80

5 **Examine how the author presents her opinion and analyse the means she uses to convince the reader of her position.**

Exam preparation

S ▸ Dealing with a text analysis task, pp. 215–220

Working with words

6 Match the words in box A to words in box B to create collocations.

A	B
carbon | conscious | ethical | fast | moral | negative | small | sustainable | zero	business | consumer | consumption | dilemma | fashion | footprint | impact | product | waste

7 Use the collocations from exercise 6 to complete the advertisement. One collocation is not used.

The best way to reduce your …[1] and turn your …[2] into a more positive one is to support …[3] like Clothes for the World! We are NOT …[4]: We don't use sweatshops, we pay our employees fairly, and we use recycled products to produce our wares, maintaining as much …[5] as possible. We create …[6] for the …[7], so that you don't have to struggle with the …[8] between fashion or saving the planet.

Watching

Crossover TV

Too cheap? The food price wars

03

upmarket *der gehobenen Kategorie*

8 You are going to watch a video about discount supermarket chains which offer food items at rock-bottom prices.
While watching the video, complete the sentences.

1 The world's biggest retailer is …
2 The German Schwarz Group owns … and …
3 Retailers put farmers under pressure by …
4 Two upmarket chains that push down prices are … and …
5 When farmers' deliveries have been turned down and agreed prices reduced, the farmers have …
6 Even though consumers say they're willing to pay a bit more for meat and milk, the majority of people …
7 Some call breaking up big retail chains or allowing governments to dictate prices …
8 Creating stricter laws to protect workers, animals, and the environment could …

Speaking

How to say or write it

The most important thing for me personally is …

It would be possible to …, but I don't think it would make sense to …

If I were a politician, I would make sure that …

9 In groups of three or four discuss the following questions from the video related to food pricing and sustainability.

1 How important is price versus sustainability to you, both personally and from an environmental standpoint?
2 Would it make sense to break up the big retail chain supermarkets? Why (not)?
3 How could governments dictate food prices? Is this a good idea? Why (not)?
4 What laws could or should be passed to protect workers, animals and the environment?

Writing

Exam preparation

S ▸ Dealing with a creative writing task, pp. 126–128

Writing checklist

10 As an exchange student at an English school, you are taking part in a project on ethical consumerism. Write an article for the school newspaper, assessing ideas on how to increase ethical consumption.

Section C Globalization

Warm-up

1 With a partner discuss whether you agree or disagree with the benefits and challenges of globalization listed below. What other benefits and challenges can you think of?

Benefits	Challenges
Access to new cultures	Loss of cultural identity
Spread of technology, innovation and products	Tariffs, taxes and export-import fees
Lower production costs	Exploitation of workers

Working with the text

2 Skim the text below and choose the most suitable summary.

a Covid-19 has killed off globalization completely.
b Covid-19 has forced companies to rethink where they source their materials.
c Covid-19 has helped to speed up globalization.

What bikes tell us about a changing global economy

The executives at Trek Bicycle can pinpoint the day they realized the bike market was going berserk. "April 12," says Eric Bjorling, the director of brand marketing for the company. "That's when we knew we had something on our hands."

Trek had originally believed this recession would be typical — and that demand for bikes would crash. But on April 12, the people at Trek noticed a record number of visitors to their website and an enormous volume of orders from retailers. They knew then that this recession was going to be different. The virus [had] made public transportation radioactive, so city dwellers [...] wanted alternative modes of transport. Gyms [were] closed, so fitness freaks [...] wanted to exercise outdoors. Young professionals with jobs [were] saving money by not going out, and they [had] extra cash to burn on durable goods. And everyone [was] mostly at home, bored as hell, looking for something to do.

"And the bicycle was sort of perfectly positioned to fit all those needs," Bjorling says.

Trek, like other bike manufacturers, has seen a surge in global demand. But [...] as Covid-19 spread through Asia, lockdowns derailed their supply chain. Bikes, like a lot of other products, stopped getting made. It has been the latest in a series of disruptions to global supply chains that has pushed companies like Trek to reevaluate how and where their products are getting made.

1 **executive** *Führungskraft*
1 to pinpoint sth *etw (genau) lokalisieren*
3 to go berserk *durchdrehen, ausrasten*
11 dweller *Bewohner/in*
14 **durable** *haltbar, langlebig*
18 to **derail** *entgleisen (lassen)*
18 **supply chain** *Lieferkette*

26 to **shift** *(sich) verlagern*
27 amalgamation *Zusammenschluss, Vereinigung*
27 spoke *Speiche*
27 derailleur *Umwerfer* (Kettenschaltung)
28 brake *Bremse*

In 1976, Dick Burke and Bevil Hogg founded Trek by making bikes in a small red barn in Waterloo, Wisconsin. I actually own an old Trek mountain bike that's red, white and blue and has two stickers that proudly declare "Handbuilt In The USA."

But in the late 1980s and early '90s, Bjorling says, Trek followed other bike manufacturers in shifting most of their production to China and Taiwan. Every bike is now an amalgamation of parts — wheels, spokes, seats, derailleurs, chains, brakes and so on — that are sourced from suppliers around the world. "The cycling industry is very supply chain dependent," Bjorling says. "You might have as many as 50 suppliers to make one bike."

Even if something is "manufactured" in the United States these days, it's often using parts made overseas. (Even my bike, which was made in the '90s, says "Bicycle Handbuilt In The U.S.A. Of Domestic And Foreign Parts" on one of the stickers.) These global supply chains, or "global value chains," have become the cardiovascular system of the world economy. According to the World Bank, over two-thirds of all global trade occurs through them.

39 cardiovascular system *Herz-Kreislauf-System*
46 **trillion** *Billion*
47 to revert *zurückkehren*
47 **nearshoring** *Produktions(zurück)verlagerung in die Nähe*
48 **offshoring** *Produktionsverlagerung ins Ausland*
51 **coffin** *Sarg*

Recently, however, it seems like everyone is reevaluating how and where supply chains function in the face of rising threats. A recent report from McKinsey Global Institute estimates that, over the next five years, companies will change their supply chains in a huge way. It estimates that "16 to 26 percent of exports, worth $2.9 trillion to $4.6 trillion in 2018, could be in play — whether that involves reverting to domestic production, nearshoring, or new rounds of offshoring to new locations."

In response to the recent disruptions to global supply chains, Carmen Reinhart, the chief economist of the World Bank, recently said, "Covid-19 is like the last nail in the coffin of globalization."

(535 words) From: *National Public Radio*, 25 August 2020

Working with the text

3 Read the text, then use the following sentence beginnings to complete a summary of the first six paragraphs.

- On April 12th, the people working at Trek realized that …
- At the beginning of the recession caused by the pandemic, they thought things would …
- But suddenly they … .
- Early on in the pandemic, however, lockdowns created … , which made it very difficult for Trek to …
- Over 40 years ago, the founders of Trek …
- But now Trek's bicycles, and actually most bicycles, are …

S ▸ Writing a summary, p. 81

4 Write three to five sentences summarizing the last three paragraphs of the article.

Working with words

5 Match the words in box A to words in box B to create collocations from the text.

A	B
city | global (x2) | perfectly | public | record | supply | world | young	chain | demand | dweller | economy | number | positioned | professional | trade | transportation

6 Use suitable collocations from exercise 5 to complete the paragraph below. Use the plural wherever necessary.

Because of the spread of Covid-19, many …[1] no longer wanted to use …[2] to get from their homes to their place of work. Additionally sport studios were closed and people had extra time on their hands and wanted to be outside. Many …[3] who had extra money to spend decided that buying a bike was a good solution. The bike industry seemed …[4] to accept this challenge, but because …[5] skyrocketed all at once, and bike manufacturers were dealing with a …[6] of orders, they suddenly had a problem. Lockdowns in countries around the world disrupted the …[7] and while the …[8] once seemed like an advantage for companies around the globe, it suddenly became a disadvantage because …[9] was nearly impossible.

Listening

7 You are going to listen to a podcast about globalization.

While listening, take notes on the following points. You need not write complete sentences.

1 reasons for debate about globalization (2 aspects): …
example: American movies and music
2 factors holding developing countries back (2 aspects): …
example: some African nations
3 advantages for companies in developed countries (2 aspects): …
examples: US automobile industry, call centres in India
4 benefits for developing countries (2 aspects): …
5 consequences in developed countries (2 aspects): …
example: US automobile factories in Mexico
6 negative effects in developing countries (2 aspects): …
example: clothing industry in Bangladesh
7 possible solutions (2 aspects): …

21

Exam preparation

S ▸ Dealing with listening tasks, pp. 123–125

silk *Seide*
detrimental (to) *schädlich (für)*
raw material *Rohstoff*
to take advantage of sth *sich etw zunutze machen, etw ausnutzen*
cost of living *Lebenshaltungskosten*
union *Gewerkschaft*
unskilled *ungelernt*

Research

8 Work with a partner: one partner researches the effects of globalization on workers in developing nations; the other partner focuses on developed nations. Make notes about the positive and negative effects of globalization and how unions and/or other organizations are involved.

9 Share your notes with your partner. Compare the positive and negative effects of globalization in both developing and developed nations.

Speaking

Exam preparation

Kommunikationsprüfung

S ▸ Describing and analysing cartoons, pp. 82–83

Phrases for speaking

10 **Partner A:** Look here. **Partner B:** Look at File 11 on page 273.

Partner A: Sequence 1 (your five-minute talk)

1 Describe the cartoon and explain how it relates to the quote.

2 Use the given material as a starting point for an uninterrupted five-minute talk on how globalization affects our everyday lives.

"AMERICAN PLASTIC WASTE ON A EUROPEAN BEACH... WOW! GLOBALIZATION WORKS!"

"Globalization is not a monolithic force but an evolving set of consequences – some good, some bad and some unintended. It is the new reality."
– John B Larson, US politician

Partner B: Sequence 2 (you and the teacher / another student)

Discuss the following questions with Partner A:

1 Is globalization going to get rid of cultural differences and make everybody the same?

2 What can be done to keep the negative effects of globalization to a minimum?

Writing

Exam preparation

S ▸ Writing an argumentative text, pp. 167–172

Writing checklist

Exam preparation

S ▸ Dealing with a creative writing task, 126–128

Writing checklist

11 Choose one of the following writing tasks.

A Comment on the following statement.

"Globalization benefits the big transnational corporations, but not the people who work for them."

B A British friend is planning to start a company selling electric cargo bikes made in the UK with 100% local components. He/She has sent you an email outlining the plan and asking what you think of his/her idea.

Reply to your friend by email stating your opinion.

Section D Gender inequality

*"Remember, you can do **anything**...
but for only 80 cents to every dollar earned by a man."*

Warm-up

1 Discuss the following questions with a partner.

- What is the gender gap?
- Have you experienced gender inequality in your life?
- What aspects of the gender gap are the photo and cartoon referring to?

Working with the text

2 Read the text and take notes on the following points.

1 the consequences of the pandemic for office workers
2 concerns about the change for gender equality
3 choices facing workers with caring responsibilities or disabilities
4 the responsibilities of employers towards their staff

Switch to more home working after Covid 'will make gender inequality worse'

22

The permanent switch to more home working following the pandemic will cause rising gender inequality in the workplace, according to experts, unless employers monitor their new working policies to make sure women aren't disadvantaged.

Traditionally, more women than men – particularly those with children or caring responsibilities – have requested flexible working. The switch to working from home necessitated by coronavirus lockdowns has [...] resulted in a permanent change in corporate culture, to the extent that the government is considering legislating to make home working the "default" option.

During Covid, millions of previously office-based employees enjoyed more family time and tasted life without the commute. Earlier in the pandemic, there were hopes that the wider adoption of remote working might remove the gender divide, while also reducing the so-called "maternity penalty" and getting rid of a culture of presenteeism.

Yet employment experts are warning that the hybrid working model favoured by most large businesses and organizations, allowing staff to split their time between home and their desks, could have unintended consequences for gender equality.

5 to **request sth** *etw (an)fordern, etw erbitten, um etw bitten*
6 to necessitate *erfordern, erforderlich machen*
8 to **legislate** *Gesetze erlassen*
8 **default** *Standard*
11 **adoption** *Übernahme, Aneignung*
12 **maternity** *Mutterschaft*
13 presenteeism *Präsentismus (Anwesenheitspflicht)*

Tip

Do not say "home office" in English; the correct phrase is **home working**.

23 to alleviate *lindern, abschwächen*
25 **substantially** *erheblich, im Wesentlichen*
26 **adverse** *nachteilig, ungünstig*
27 **accountancy** *Buchhaltung, Rechnungswesen*
27 occupier *Nutzer (von Räumlichkeiten)*
32 **pregnant** *schwanger*
32 screwed *gelinkt, reingelegt*
33 **pregnancy** *Schwangerschaft*
41 **hospitality** *Hotel- und Gaststättengewerbe*
44 to scupper *zunichte machen, scheitern lassen*
44 **promotion** *Beförderung*
52 to demote *degradieren*
58 onus *Verantwortung*
60 **seniority** *Führungsebene*
60 disparity *Ungleichheit, Missverhältnis*

"Employers now see that employees don't have to show face time," said Professor Cary Cooper, a psychologist from Alliance Manchester Business School. "The big question we don't have the answer to is, during this 15-month period, have enough men said to themselves life isn't just about work. Did they begin to reprioritize and understand how important the family is?"

Cooper, who is also president of the Chartered Institute of Personnel and Development, believes wider take-up of flexible working by men would alleviate gender inequality in the post-Covid workplace. "If they don't, then we have a problem, as women will be working substantially from home and the men will go in more days a week than the women, and that will adversely affect their career."

[The] accountancy firm Deloitte [has become] the latest large office-occupier to embrace an ultra-flexible future, telling its 20,000 UK employees they can decide when to visit the office.

Leaving the choice of workplace entirely in the hands of staff is a worry for Joeli Brearley, founder of the charity Pregnant Then Screwed, which supports women facing maternity or pregnancy discrimination. "Those with caring responsibilities or with disabilities will tend to stay at home and other employees will likely go into the office," she said.

"Those at home will look like they're less committed to their job, they won't have as good a relationship with their manager, the person that can promote them and give them a pay rise," Brearley said.

Jane* works in a managerial role in the hospitality sector in London, and requested a permanent move to remote working for part of the week, after successfully working from home during lockdown. However, the mother-of-one believes her flexible working arrangement has already scuppered a promotion. "I can show the results of my work, but it seems to be forgotten because I'm not there five days a week," Jane said. "It's that old-school mentality, that it doesn't matter what you do as long as you're in the office."

Since returning from maternity leave last summer, Siobhan*, who works in operations for a small company in the East Midlands, has occasionally worked from home because of a lack of childcare during the pandemic. Without any discussion, some of her responsibilities have been removed. "I feel like I've been demoted," Siobhan said. "It's not a reflection on the quality of my work. There hasn't been much support."

Most employment experts agree that organisations will have to monitor closely how new working policies are adopted by staff once coronavirus restrictions are lifted. "Companies have to take this seriously and build a cultural model in their organisation," said Katy Fridman, founder of talent platform Flexible Working People. "The onus is on the employer."

"There has to be encouragement across the board [for flexible working] from seniority to entry-level staff and whatever gender, so there isn't a disparity, or this could very well set women back."

---

* Not her real name

Women were more likely than men to reduce their flexible working demands to align with the perceived expectations of their manager or employer, according to a recent study by psychologists at the Behavioural Insights Team [...] which works with government.

“If we really care about diversity and inclusion, the study shows there is a difference, regardless of the reason behind it,” said Hannah Burd, principal adviser at the team. “We really encourage employers, whatever policy decision they make, to monitor the impact, and see if they do need to adjust it, to ensure women, or junior people, are getting more access to opportunities.”

(770 words) From: *The Guardian*, 19 June 2021

[63] **expectation** *Erwartung*

3 Summarize why the switch to home working after Covid "will make gender equality worse".

Exam preparation

S ▸ Writing a summary, p. 81

Working with words

4 Replace the underlined words with a suitable synonym from the list. You may have to change the form of some words.

ask for | change | experience | increase | introduce | keep an eye on | negative | plan | work environment

1. Lorrie has requested a move to remote working for three days a week.
2. Coronavirus lockdowns have caused a permanent change in the corporate culture in many companies.
3. If women work from home regularly and men go to the office more days a week, that will adversely affect women's careers.
4. According to experts, the permanent switch to more home working will cause rising gender inequality in the workplace.
5. Employers need to monitor their new working policies carefully to make sure women aren't disadvantaged.
6. During the pandemic, millions of office workers enjoyed more family time and tasted life without the daily commute.
7. Several companies have now adopted flexible working models for office staff.
8. My flexible working arrangement has already lost me an important promotion.

Looking at language

5 Rewrite the following quotes from the article using reported speech.

G ▸ Reported speech, p. 288

1. "Employers now see that employees don't have to show face time," said Professor Cary Cooper.
2. "If they don't, then we have a problem, as women will be working substantially from home and the men will go in more days a week than the women, and that will adversely affect their careers," Cooper continued.
3. "I feel like I've been demoted," Siobhan said. "It's not a reflection on the quality of my work. There hasn't been much support," she added.
4. "There has to be encouragement ... for flexible working ... so there isn't a disparity, or this could very well set women back," said Katy Fridman.
5. "We really encourage employers, whatever policy decision they make, to ... ensure women ... are getting more access to opportunities," said Hannah Burd.

Role-play

6 Work with a partner. You both work at a company which offers its employees the option to work from home. Partner A is the boss, Partner B is an employee. Role-play a meeting to discuss the best way to organize the employee's full- or part-time work from home.

Before doing the role-play, both partners should think about the following points and bring them up in the meeting.

- Why does Partner B want to work from home?
- How often does the employee want to work from home?
- What does working from home mean for Partner B's future in the company?
- How can the employee participate in in-office activities?

At the end of the discussion, Partner A should decide if Partner B's request is possible.

How to say or write it

A Hello, (name). Thank you for coming.

B Thank you for your time.

A I understand that you want to … . Maybe you could first explain why …

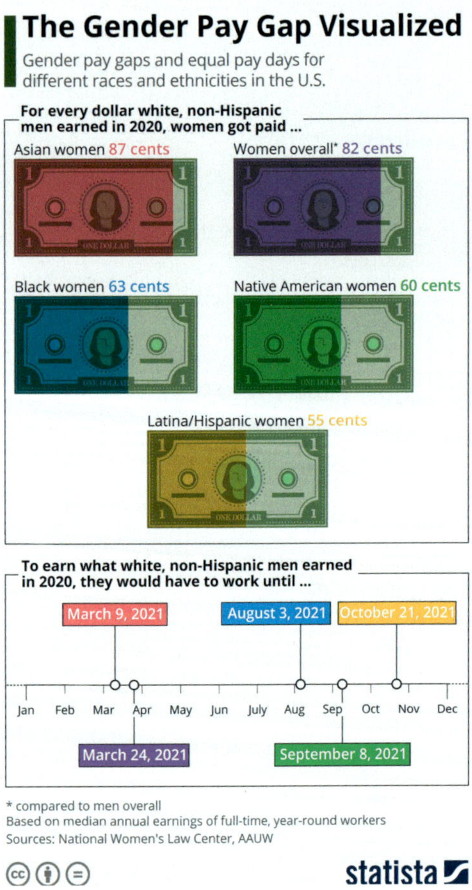

Research

7 First, use information from the infographic to complete the gaps in the following paragraph.

The …[1] gap shows the difference between what the average man and the average woman earn in one year. For example, in the USA, women overall earn …[2] for every dollar that a man earns. However, depending on what race or …[3] a woman is, the gap may be greater or smaller. …[4] women earn the least when compared to white men, earning only …[5] to every dollar earned by white men. Black women, who earn …[6] to every dollar earned by a man, are in the middle when comparing different ethnicities. …[7] women earn on average 60 cents to every dollar a man earns. Only Asian women generally earn …[8] than women overall. The …[9] day demonstrates exactly how much longer than a man a woman has to work in order to earn the same amount of money. For example, to earn what a …[10] man earned in 2020, the average woman had to work until …[11]. A Latina/Hispanic woman even had to work until …[12], which means that they have to work almost twice as long as a man to earn the same money for the same job.

8 Work in small groups. Choose a country within the EU and find out what the current gender pay gap is there. Present your findings to the class. Which country has the smallest gender pay gap? Which country has the largest?

Speaking

9 Discuss the following questions in your group, then share your ideas in class.

- What are the main drivers of the gender pay gap?
- What could be done to narrow the gender pay gap?
- Are political action and social change equally needed to breach the gap? Justify your opinion.

Section E Generation Z

Good to know

Generation Z is made up of people born between 1995 and 2012. **Millennials**, the generation before Gen Z, were born between 1980 and 1995.

Warm-up

1 Look at the word cloud and discuss the following questions with a partner.

- Which words describe you well and which words do not describe you at all?
- Which words are good words to describe Generation Z? Why?
- Which words don't describe your generation at all? Why?

If there are any words that you don't know, use a dictionary to look them up.

How to say or write it

I think … is a good/bad/ reasonable/perfect description of …

I don't think … applies to me/us at all. I'm / We're …

Working with the text

2 Rank the statements below according to how they relate to your ideas for your future. Use the emojis to help you.

a It is important to me to be successful in my job and to be the best among my colleagues.
b I would like to have a job that gives me financial stability.
c I would like a workplace that offers me lots of different opportunities.
d I am interested in working in some part of the digital world.
e How the company I work for impacts the world and society is very important to me.
f I have to be realistic about what the world is like and plan and prepare for the future.
g The cost of my education will influence my choices about my future.
h I would be happiest in a job where I have control over the kind of work I do and can create my own tasks.
i My parents have a big influence on the choices I make for my future.
j I would like a job where I can be independent and do things the way that I like.

3 Read the text on pages 108–109 and find the paragraphs (1–7) that best match the statements above. There are three more statements than you need. Compare your answers with a partner.

Gen Z @ Work

[1] leading edge *hier: die ältesten (dieser Generation)*
[9] to **adapt** *(sich) anpassen*
[9] to **challenge sb/sth** *jdn/etw herausfordern*
[11] **sophistication** *Ausgereiftheit, Erfahrung*
[13] to **customize sth** *etw anpassen, etw individuell gestalten*
[15] **tough** *hart, schwer*
[18] **generic** *generisch, allgemein, typisch*
[19] **in the aftermath of sth** *in der Folge von etw*
[21] **mindset** *Mentalität, Denkweise*
[26] to **miss out on sth** *etw verpassen*
[26] to **suffer from sth** *unter etw leiden*
[26] **intense** *intensiv*
[30] to have a lot in the hopper *eine Menge auf Lager haben*
[35] to leverage sth *etw wirksam einsetzen*
[40] **DIY (do-it-yourself)** *Heimwerker-, Heimwerken*
[44] **collaborative** *gemeinschaftlich, partnerschaftlich*

Good to know

FOMO = **f**ear **o**f **m**issing **o**ut

Introducing Gen Z [born 1995–2012]. The leading edge is already in their twenties. At 72.8 million strong [in the USA], Gen Z are making their presence known in the workplace, and organizations and leaders cannot afford to ignore them. [...] The time to get to know Gen Z is today. [...] We want to introduce you to their seven key traits:

1. **Phigital:** Gen Z is the first generation born into a world where every physical aspect (people and places) has a digital equivalent. For Gen Z, the real world and the virtual world naturally overlap. Virtual is simply part of their reality. The world of work has typically been slow to adapt to digital solutions and will be challenged like never before when it comes to finding its place in the phigital world. Ninety-one percent of Gen Z say that a company's technological sophistication would impact their decision to work there.

2. **Hyper-Custom:** Gen Z has always worked hard at identifying and customizing their own brand for the world to know. [...] From job titles to career paths, the pressure to customize has been turned up. This is going to be tough for the world of work, which has historically focused on trying to be fair and treating everyone the same. Fifty-six percent of Gen Z would rather write their own job description than be given a generic one.

3. **Realistic:** Growing up during the aftermath of 9/11, with terrorism part of everyday life, as well as living through a severe recession early on, has created a very pragmatic mindset when it comes to planning and preparing for the future. Colleges and universities were the first to struggle with this realistic attitude and the workplace is next. With idealistic Millennials as their frontline managers, the potential for gaps with Gen Z is huge. As Gen Z sees it, if you're going to survive or even thrive, you'd better get real about what it's going to take.

4. **FOMO:** Gen Z suffers from an intense fear of missing out on anything. The good news is that they will stay on top of all trends and competition. The bad news is that Gen Z will always worry that they aren't moving ahead fast enough and in the right direction. The workplace will be challenged by Gen Z, who will want to have a lot in the hopper at all times to be sure they aren't missing out. Seventy-five percent of Gen Z would be interested in a situation in which they could have multiple roles within one place of employment.

5. **Weconomists:** From Uber to Airbnb, Gen Z has only known a world with a shared economy. Gen Z will push the workplace to break down internal and external silos to leverage the collective in new convenient and cost-effective ways. More than just as employees, Gen Z will leverage the power of "we" in their role as philanthropists. Gen Z will expect to partner with their employers to fix the wrongs they are seeing in the world. Ninety-three percent of Gen Z says that a company's impact on society affects their decision to work there.

6. **DIY:** Gen Z is the do-it-yourself generation. Having grown up with YouTube, which can teach them how to do just about anything, Gen Z believes that they can do just about anything themselves. On top of that, they have been encouraged by their independent Gen X parents not to follow traditional paths. Gen Z is fiercely independent and will collide head-on with so many of the collaborative cultures that Millennials have fought for. Seventy-one percent of Gen Z said they believe the phrase "if you want it done right, then do it yourself!"

7. **Driven:** With parents who drilled into them that participation is not a real award and that there are winners and losers, a recession that pulled the rug out from their predecessors, and a rate of change that is hard to keep up with, it is no wonder that Gen Z is one driven generation. Gen Z is ready and hungry to roll up their sleeves. They will be more competitive as well as private than previous generations. Pressure will be on for companies to convince Gen Z that they are the winning team. Seventy-two percent of Gen Z said they are competitive with people doing the same job.

(855 words) From: *Gen Z @ Work*, by David Stillman and Jonah Stillman

48 **award** *Auszeichnung, Preis*
48 to pull the rug out from sb *jdm den Boden unter den Füßen wegziehen*
49 **predecessor** *Vorgänger/in, Vorläufer/in*
50 **driven** *besessen, ehrgeizig*
51 to roll up one's sleeves *die Ärmel hochkrempeln*

Mediation

4 You work in the Human Resources department of a German company. In order to help with recruiting young people, your boss has given you this book excerpt and has asked you to present the characteristics of Generation Z at your next department meeting. Summarize the most important points in German.

S ▸ Mediation, pp. 259–261

Working with words

5 Use the adjectives from the list to rewrite the sentences below. Make any other changes that are necessary

G ▸ Adjectives and adverbs, p. 293

collaborative | competitive | educated | idealistic | independent | innovative | pragmatic | sophisticated | traditional

1 Millennials are known for being good at working together, whereas members of Generation Z tend to work against their colleagues to get ahead.
2 Gen Z is considered more old-fashioned than Millennials because they prefer to work face-to-face, even though they are absolute digital natives.
3 People often think that the members of Generation Z want to work alone.
4 Many members of Generation Z have new ideas about how to conduct business and because of this are often entrepreneurial.
5 Generation Z is not a generation of dreamers, whereas, in contrast, Millennials are considered not to have a very realistic view of the future.
6 Marketers consider Generation Z to be one of the most knowledgable, experienced and mature generations in history.

Speaking

6 In a group, share and compare your ideas about yourself as compared to what the authors wrote about Generation Z. Then discuss as a class if you believe that the authors have correctly identified the traits of your generation.

Writing

7 Write an article for your school magazine in which you try to prepare your fellow students for the world of work and the challenges your generation faces when entering a career path while being surrounded by Gen X and Gen Y. Refer to the text *Gen Z @ Work* on pp. 108–109.

Exam preparation

S ▸ Dealing with a creative writing task, pp. 126–128

Writing checklist

Section F Unemployment and universal basic income

"IF EVERYONE IS GONNA GET A UNIVERSAL BASIC INCOME, WHAT'S THE POINT OF GETTING GOOD GRADES?"

Good to know

Universal basic income (UBI) is a scheme whereby a government provides its adult citizens with a regular payment of a fixed amount of money, regardless of their income or social status. The aim is to reduce poverty and replace other social benefit payments.

Warm-up

1 In groups, look at the cartoon and discuss the following questions.

1 What does this cartoon say about the concept of universal basic income?
2 Do you agree with the cartoon? Why or why not.

Listening

Skills training: Dealing with multiple matching tasks

Always read through the possible answers before you listen. The speakers will be in the order presented, but you will have to choose the correct answer.

1 The first time you listen, quickly take notes on key words. If the answer is clear, mark it the first time.
2 Double-check your answers the second time you listen.

23

Exam preparation

S ▸ Dealing with listening tasks, pp. 123–125

2 You will hear five speakers talking about their experience of being unemployed. While listening, match the headings (A–G) to the speakers (1–5). There are two more headings than you need.

A	problem: finding a new job because of age
B	consequence: self-worth has decreased
C	misconception: unemployed people are lazy
D	concern: added financial difficulties
E	solution: several part-time jobs
F	necessity: given up all extra activities
G	setback: nowhere to live

frugal *genügsam, bescheiden*

Working with the text

S ▸ Reading difficult texts, pp. 39–40

3 Scan the article on pp. 111–112 and decide if it is in support of or against universal basic income. Note down phrases that support your point of view. Find a partner and compare your conclusions about the tone of the article.

Does Finland show the way to universal basic income?

For two years Finland's government gave 2,000 unemployed citizens €560 a month with no strings attached. It was the first nationwide basic income experiment. The concept is slowly becoming difficult for people to ignore.

A "basic income guinea pig" — that's how Tuomas Muraja describes himself in the title of his book about the two years he received €560 a month from Finland's government. For four years the journalist had been looking for permanent work, attending job center classes and receiving state benefits alongside the odd freelance job, before he found out he had been selected for the country's universal basic income experiment, which began in 2017.

Muraja fondly remembers being a guinea pig. "It was a great relief because I got rid of all the bureaucracy," he recalls. "I didn't need to fill in any forms or attend any classes where they teach you how to make a CV and these kinds of things. I could concentrate [...] on my work, which is writing books and stories."

He certainly did. In those two years he published two books, wrote numerous articles and applied for 80 positions. Others he spoke to for *Basic Income Guinea Pig* had positive experiences too. One lady set up her own café, knowing she had guaranteed income. A university graduate could take low-paid internships to gain experience without having to worry.

A 'failed' experiment?

Yet Finland's basic income experiment has not caused a huge surge in support for the idea, either in Finland or abroad. Initial reports branded the scheme a "flop." While recent coverage of the long-term study, released earlier this month, has been more nuanced, much has focused on the minimal effect on employment prospects.

The "flop" tag is something Minne Ylikanno, senior researcher at Finland's Social Insurance Institution (Kela), which carried out the study, rejects. "I would say the experiment was a success," she says. "No other country in any part of the world has implemented a national basic income based on a law."

"It's fair to say that the result is that we can't see a very big employment effect, that's true. But the comment that it's a failure, I would say that's not fair."

The findings were based on comparing the 2,000 unemployed participants who had received the €560 a month from January 2017 to December 2018 with a control group of 173,000 who did not. There was only a small statistical difference between the study group and the control group in the number of people who found work after two years.

Economic benefits could come from well-being

Where there was a significant statistical difference, however, was in how happy each of the two groups felt. The people who received €560 a month reported much lower levels of insecurity and stress.

"The well-being was at a higher level than in the control group, and it really was a significant increase in most dimensions of well-being," reports Ylikanno.

[2] **with no strings attached** *ohne Auflagen*
[4] **guinea pig** *Meerschweinchen; Versuchsperson*
[7] **odd** *gelegentlich*
[10] **relief** *Erleichterung, Entlastung*
[11] to **recall** *sich erinnern*
[21] to **brand sth** *etw kennzeichnen, mit seinem Zeichen versehen*
[23] nuanced *differenziert*
[27] to **implement sth** *etw einführen, etw umsetzen, etw einsetzen*
[38] **insecurity** *Unsicherheit*

[43] **secure** *sicher*
[71] **trial** *Versuch, Studie*
[79] momentum *Schwung, Fahrt*

For Tuomas, this should be the point people concentrate on most when examining the study. "The main important thing is that those who received the basic income felt better, mentally. When you are secure and free, you feel better."

The idea of a guaranteed basic income has gained attention around the world in recent years.

Even if people are looking for economic gains, argues Ylikanno, increasing people's well-being is a good place to help long-term unemployed people to find work.

"When well-being is on a better level, people have better chances to get a job. Employers see them as more capable of work," she says.

Moving beyond the headline cost

But for governments and politicians examining whether a basic income is worth it, how much the scheme might cost is still the factor they overwhelmingly focus on.

That's a point made by Professor Bernhard Neumärker, director of the Department for Economic Policy at the University of Freiburg and a supporter of universal basic income.

"When it comes to basic income, the science is a long way behind society," he says. "Politicians feel uncertain about it, so find easy arguments, such as saying everyone will become lazy or that there is no way to finance it. Then it's case closed, next topic."

But he argues increasing public pressure could force politicians to begin to think differently about the problem, particularly in the wake of the coronavirus crisis.

"Germany and other EU countries were of the opinion everything was going well without basic income," states Professor Neumärker, "so why have it?"

"Now the crisis has shown things are becoming serious for the traditional and, in my view, outdated social welfare state. I would argue that if we properly organized basic income, then in the face of digitalization, new developments and crises, it is one of the few promising and sustainable models for a modern market economy."

Number of basic income tests increasing

There is still a long way to go from Finland's experiment. New trials will also need to look at larger groups, people already in employment, and take place over a longer period.

But other countries will be able to provide more data. Spain is offering a form of basic income to poorer people who lost work because of coronavirus. Kenya is conducting a 12-year study.

"Finland will go on with experiments in social policy," predicts Muraja, "which is a good thing."

The number of guinea pigs is growing, and so too might be momentum for basic income.

(904 words) From: *Deutsche Welle*, 30 May 2020

Writing

4 Read the text again and do the following tasks.

1. Describe the specific universal basic income experiment in Finland.
2. Explain why many reports about this experiment were negative.
3. Describe the emotional effect UBI had on the participants.
4. Compare and contrast the views of politicians on UBI and what might have changed their opinions.
5. Describe what the next steps are for UBI.

5 Outline the criticism towards the UBI-experiment in Finland and its emotional effect on the participants.

6 Analyse how the cartoon on page 110 corresponds to the article.

Exam preparation

S ▸ Writing a summary, p. 81

Exam preparation

S ▸ Dealing with a text analysis task, pp. 213–218

Looking at language

7 Complete the paragraph using the correct adjective or adverb form of the words in the list.

clean | drastic | easy | entire | extreme | high | inevitable | profound | quick | regular | unnecessary | wide

Some people believe that a universal basic income set at $1000 per adult per month and $300 per child per month would almost …[1] eliminate poverty in the USA. The high poverty level in Brazil decreased to the lowest level in almost 50 years after $100 a month had been duly given to about a quarter of the population starting in March 2020. Namibia's UBI programme …[2] reduced household poverty rates from 76% of residents before the trial started to 37% after one year. Child malnutrition rates experienced a …[3] drop, from 42% to 17% in six months. Participants in India's UBI trial said that UBI payments helped to …[4] improve their health by making medicine more …[5] affordable, improving sanitation, gaining access to …[6] water, eating more …[7] and reducing their anxiety levels.

However, one study estimated that $1000 per month for every adult in the United States would …[8] cost just over $3.8 trillion per year, which was almost 80% of the tax revenue from the exact year that the study was held. Some of the …[9] costs would be efficiently mitigated by getting rid of other …[10] assistant programmes but the …[11] held belief is that the …[12] costs would not be offset enough.

Remember

Adjectives are used to describe a noun (person or thing).

Adverbs are used to describe a verb, an adjective or complete sentences.

G ▸ Adjectives and adverbs, p. 293

Speaking

8 Divide the class into six groups, with each group researching one of the countries below. Find out how that country has implemented universal basic income and if it has been successful. Present your findings to the class.

India | Iran | Japan | Kenya | Namibia | United States (Alaska)

S ▸ Presentation, pp. 260–261

9 Work with a partner. One of you is in favour of UBI and the other is against it. Debate the issue of Universal Basic Income with your partner using arguments found in the article, your research and your classmates' presentations.

Section G Intercultural competence in the workplace

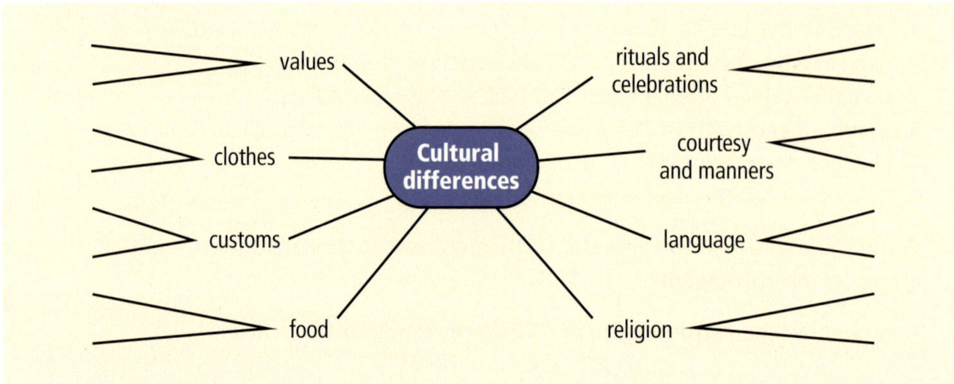

Warm-up

1 Work in groups of four and create a mind map using the template above. What kind of cultural differences, regardless of culture, can you think of in these categories? Add them to the mind map

2 Compare your results with another group.

Working with the text

3 Divide up the countries below in your group of four. Each member of the group reads the text and makes notes on the cultural differences that the business person mentioned experienced in his/her country.

Mongolia

Japan

Mexico

South Korea

Cultural complexity: the etiquette of doing business abroad

It's mid-afternoon in downtown Ulaanbaatar, Mongolia. Five or six guests are sat around a restaurant table waiting to share fermented mare's milk with you to celebrate the closing of an important business deal. It's a scenario ripe with possibilities for cultural cock-ups and etiquette faux pas, which entrepreneur Will Tindall recalls only too well.

Refusing to down your fair share of the toe-curling concoction, famed for being the tipple of choice of Genghis Khan and his troops, will not only be socially embarrassing, it could cost you the deal you've been working for months to broker.

"If you were to not drink it or have any sort of reaction to that initial taste, it would definitely lower your standing within a meeting," says Tindall, co-founder of Emerging Crowd. "And you're very much expected to have a shot each time someone has spoken."

[2] mare *Stute*
[3] **ripe** *reif*
[4] cock-up *infml (folgenschwerer) Fehler, Fehltritt*
[6] to down sth *etw herunterschütten* (trinken)
[6] toe-curling *hier: extrem peinlich*
[6] concoction *Gebräu, Machwerk*
[7] tipple of choice *Lieblingsgetränk*
[8] to **broker** *makeln, vermitteln*
[11] to have a shot *ein Gläschen trinken*

Of course, it's very hard to keep your head after 15 shots of fiery alcohol, and Tindall says even after living and doing business in the country for more than a year he left the meeting without a clue what had been said or what had actually happened. Any SME owner serious about exporting overseas, however, should be prepared for a culture clash or two, particularly in emerging markets unfamiliar with western customs.

Tindall says he has a weighty portfolio of embarrassing blunders made during his last six years living and working in Asia. But despite becoming fairly accustomed to the rituals of business meetings in Hong Kong and Singapore, he says nothing could prepare him for Tokyo.

Tindall remembers his first meeting in the Japanese capital 10 years ago, with a very senior and well known individual in an international bank. He was told to give a little bow upon taking the man's business card and it seemed all was going well. That was until he began to make notes about who the person was on the card.

"At that point I saw this guy's face change to a very strange shade of red. My actions went down incredibly badly. Although I was giving this business card lots of respect, the idea of writing on it was definitely frowned upon. When I went to leave and try to shake his hand, he turned his back on me. It was embarrassing but then I quickly realised that was also because they don't really shake hands."

It may have been awkward, but it taught him a valuable lesson about Japan's reverence for the mighty business card. They are incredibly important in Japan, Tindall says. If you are doing business there and have a card which is also translated on the other side, you will receive immediate kudos from the recipient. They love the extra effort that you go to, he adds, but warns to make sure you know which way up the Japanese language side is facing. Handing someone an upside down card is also considered rude.

Thankfully, most hosts will be sympathetic to your cultural ignorance, providing you make the effort. Having the ability to laugh at yourself if you make a mistake and apologising is key to recovering from a particularly awkward blunder, he says.

For Louis Barnett, the founder of Louis Barnett Chocolates, the biggest hurdle was understanding that in some countries doing business is as much a personal event as it is professional.

The 22-year-old entrepreneur, who started his British chocolate company at the tender age of 12, was initially flummoxed by the reaction to his typically hard-nosed business talk. After expressing his professional concern about a matter and sticking to the cold hard facts in a meeting with his partners in Mexico, he was surprised that the reaction was one of offence. By neglecting to ask the client about his personal life – his wife and kids – he had inadvertently antagonised his hosts.

Because overseas clients will be as unprepared for your way of doing business as you are for theirs, it is crucial you do your homework first and get one step ahead before meeting in person. Barnett found help and support from the British Chambers of Commerce, who have experts on the ground with an understanding of the culture of that nation and the ways UK exporters may have to adapt to doing business there. The chambers, he explains, has a wide reaching spider web of networks and contacts, from buyers and distributors to lawyers, who will help you understand the country's market.

13 fiery *feurig, scharf*
15 **not a clue** *keine Ahnung*
17 **clash** *Konflikt, Zusammenstoß*
19 weighty *gewichtig*
19 blunder *(blöder) Fehler*
21 **accustomed** *gewöhnt, gewohnt*
25 **bow** *Verbeugung*
27 **shade** *Schattierung, (Farb-)Ton*
29 to **frown upon sth** *etw missbilligen*
32 **awkward** *unangenehm, peinlich*
33 reverence *Verehrung*
33 mighty *mächtig*
35 kudos *Ansehen*
35 **recipient** *Empfänger/in*
40 to **make the effort** *sich die Mühe geben*
42 **hurdle** *Hürde, Hindernis*
46 **tender** *zart*
46 **initially** *anfangs, anfänglich*
46 flummoxed *perplex*
48 to **stick to sth** *bei etw bleiben, sich an etw halten*
49 **offence** *Beleidigung*
49 to **neglect sb/sth** *jdn/etw vernachlässigen*
50 inadvertent *unbeabsichtigt, versehentlich*
50 to antagonise sb *jdn verärgern*

[59] reputable *angesehen*
[59] grooming *Körperpflege*
[61] to **stock** *einlagern, vorrätig halten, am/auf Lager haben*
[62] to **dip** *(ein)tauchen*
[68] **venture** *Vorhaben, Unternehmen, Wagnis*
[72] sole (of your foot) *(Fuß-) Sohle*
[76] **latter** *letztere/r/s*
[76] **negotiation** *Verhandlung, Vermittlung*
[77] to **resolve sth** *etw (auf) lösen*
[79] rapport *gutes Verhältnis*
[79] **collaboration** *Zusammenarbeit, Gemeinschaftsprodukt(ion)*
[81] slack *Leerlauf*
[83] to **offend sb/sth** *jdn/etw verletzen, kränken*
[83] **sensibility** *Befindlichkeit, Feinfühligkeit*

Bulldog Skincare is already a reputable brand of male grooming products in the UK, but it is fast becoming equally well known abroad, with around 14,000 retailers stocking the product range across 13 countries. Its founder, Simon Duffy, first dipped his toe in the overseas market in 2010 with a lucrative deal in Sweden. After the company's success in Scandinavia, Bulldog had the confidence to throw its net wider, branching out to as far as the US and Australia.

One of their most interesting exporting experiences was breaking into the South Korean market. He hesitates to call it a challenge though, despite the vast cultural differences. He claims with thorough research and preparation, any exporting venture is totally manageable – you just have to be sensitive to the differences.

Duffy recommends ediplomat.com, which features a helpful section about cultural conventions, such as how to meet and greet people, as well as information about names, titles, and even acceptable body language such crossing your legs, eye contact and showing the soles of your feet.

"Certain conventions which are encouraged in the west can come across as confrontational in Korea," Duffy explains. "One of the things we tried to avoid was phrasing questions that required a yes or no answer, as Koreans try to avoid the latter. The negotiation process has a completely different rhythm. Things take longer to be resolved but that isn't a sign of a lack of momentum – you have to be prepared for several visits to build trust."

Once that rapport is built, however, then collaboration will become easier. Duffy adds that because they are making the best efforts to do the right thing, their partners are also cutting them a lot of slack.

"They are meeting us in the middle now which is important and we value that," he says. "We are very conscious that we don't want to offend the local sensibilities but we are aware that they are reaching out to us and finding common ground."

(1070 words) From: *The Guardian*, 27 October 2014

S ▸ Writing a summary, p. 81

4 Using your notes from exercise 3, write a two to three-sentence summary of each experience.

Working with words

Remember

Idioms are phrases or expressions that have a meaning that is different to the individual words. The meaning is often figurative.

5 Match the idiomatic phrases (1–10) to the correct definitions (a–j).

1 to cost you sth
2 to keep your head
3 to frown upon sb/sth
4 to dip your toe in sth
5 to throw your net wider
6 to break into a market
7 to cut sb a lot of slack
8 to meet sb in the middle
9 to reach out to sb
10 to find common ground

a to begin working in a new business area
b to compromise on sth
c to contact sb
d to dislike sb/sth
e to find sth people agree on
f to involve a larger number of people in what you are doing
g to lose sth due to a certain situation or action
h to make sth easier for sb because of a special situation
i to stay calm
j to try sth new to see if it works

6 Use the phrases in exercise 5 to complete the sentences below. Write your own sentences for the two phrases that you don't need to use.

1 Because dressing inappropriately at the office is ..., the bank decided to create a dress code.
2 I know he hasn't been very friendly today but he has had a really hard week – maybe you should ...
3 She should take a few courses in her new line of study so she can ... before completely changing her major.
4 If you're looking for a new job, you should ... to Martin – his company is looking for new employees.
5 The negotiations took a very long time but eventually they were able ... and come to an agreement.
6 Lily needs ... and start looking for jobs in other cities.
7 Her boss was very impressed that she ... throughout the meeting, even when the client started shouting at her.
8 If you don't learn to control your temper in meetings, it could ... your job!

Research

7 Divide the class into groups, with each group looking into one of the countries from the list.

Croatia | Egypt | India | Nigeria | Poland | Romania | Russia | Serbia | Syria | Turkey

Research what cultural differences exist between Germany and the country your group has chosen.

Writing

8 Choose <u>one</u> of the following tasks.

Exam preparation

S ► Dealing with a creative writing task, pp. 126–128

Writing checklist

A A friend of yours, who has lived in Germany his/her whole life, is interested in working in another country. He/She has just been offered a job in one of the countries from the list (see exercise 7). He/She is not sure about how he/she will cope with the cultural differences and asks you for your help.

Write an email to your friend, weighing up the pros and cons of accepting the job in the country you have chosen from the list. Use the information about cultural differences you have learned in this Section to help you.

B During a *Cultural Awareness Week* at your school, you are asked to write an English article for your online school magazine about the topic.

Write an article commenting on the importance of intercultural competence at the workplace. Use what you have learned in this Section, including the message of the cartoon.

"I think he wants you to pull his finger Mr President"

Project Creating an advertisement

You are going to create your own advertisement for a product. In doing so, your group will be competing against other advertising agencies to get the contract for the advertising campaign.

But first of all, you are going to study adverts to analyse the techniques they use.

Step 1

With a partner, choose three print advertisements from magazines and/or newspapers and analyse them. Look at the information in the infographic below and answer the following questions about the ads.

- What is being advertised?
- Who is the target group for the ad? Why do you think that?
- Which advertising techniques are being used?
- What feelings and/or associations does the ad cause?
- What does the ad say about people who buy this product?

Advertising techniques

Association: Using images (like a cartoon character or a famous person) so that the consumer associates the good feelings from the image with the product.

Call to action: Telling the consumer what to do. "Buy this!"

Claim: Telling the consumer about how the product can help him or her.

Humour: Ads that make the consumer laugh, catch their attention and are memorable.

Hype: Using words like "fantastic" or "amazing" to make the product seem more interesting.

Prizes: Giving the consumer the chance to win a prize.

Must-have: Giving the impression that the consumer "must-have" the product to be interesting/successful/popular.

Fear: Giving the impression that without this product, the consumer might have a big problem – for example bad skin.

Sales and discounts: Making it look like the consumer is getting a special deal on the price.

Repetition: Repeating a message so that the consumer remembers it.

Special ingredients: Pointing out what is special and different about a product to make it more appealing to consumers.

Testimonials/Endorsements: Featuring someone, especially a famous person, to say how good the product is.

Step 2

Present the ads that you chose to the class and explain the conclusions you came to when answering the questions. Compare the different advertisements. What are the similarities between them? What are the differences?

Step 3

Now you are going to create your own advertisement and compete with other agencies (groups) to get the advertising campaign for the product. So, first of all, you need to decide as a class on one product you all want to advertise.

car

chewing gum

fashion brand

fast food restaurant

perfume

toothpaste

Step 4

Divide the class into five advertising agencies. Each agency will create its own print ad for the product and compete against the others for the contract.

Tip

Keep the advertising techniques from the previous page in mind. Also use the information that you gained from the ads that you analysed to guide you.

Step 5

In your group, describe the product and make sure you know exactly what you are selling. What qualities make this product special? Why should the customer buy this product? Make sure you identify your target group. Age? Gender? Lifestyle?

Step 6

Think of a catchy slogan to sell your product. Do you want it to be serious, humorous, stylish, … ?

Step 7

Design and produce your ad using suitable techniques from the previous page.

Tip

Don't try to use all the techniques, but if you don't use any of them, your ad will be missing something.

Step 8

Present your ad to the company (the rest of the class) to compete for the contract.

Step 9

Decide in class which ad is the best and should win the contract.

Advertisement checklist

- ✓ Have you described the product thoroughly and agreed on the qualities that make it special?
- ✓ Have you identified your target group?
- ✓ Have you thought of a catchy slogan for your product?
- ✓ Have you designed your ad, using a number of different advertising techniques?

24

Words in context

Advertising and marketing

advertising *Werbung*
commercial break *Werbeblock, (TV-/Radio-) Werbung*
internet ad *Online-Werbung*
billboard *Plakatwand, Werbetafel*
leaflet *Prospekt, Werbezettel*
to **persuade sb to do sth** *jdn dazu bringen, etw zu tun*
advert *Anzeige, Werbespot*
to **influence sb** *jdn beeinflussen*
target audience *Zielgruppe*
brand *Marke*
to **broadcast sth** *senden (im Rundfunk)*

Advertising is all around us, almost all the time, but it's something that most people take for granted as a part of life. At home, we watch television adverts during commercial breaks, we see print advertising in the newspaper or in magazines, and internet ads even reach us while we're scrolling on social media or following influencers. Outside, billboards, shop windows and leaflets persuade us to buy products or services. Although some adverts do have entertainment value, the main aim of marketing companies is to influence their target audience. Using subtle techniques, ads tell us: 'your life will be better if you purchase this product'. Smiling faces, picture-perfect models, bright colours and engaging music make us believe that we too can only be satisfied if we try a new brand of yoghurt or book a package holiday to the Maldives. Advertisements broadcast to children are particularly powerful, as they can be more easily persuaded that a new toy or game will change their lives.

Ethical consumption

consumer *Verbraucher/in*
material comfort *materieller Wohlstand*
debt *Schulden*
to **purchase sth** *etw kaufen, erwerben*
economic model *Wirtschaftsmodell, ökonomisches Modell*
delivery *Lieferung, Zustellung*
sustainability *Nachhaltigkeit*
energy intensive *energieintensiv*
waste *Abfall, Müll*
to **go out of fashion** *aus der Mode gehen, altmodisch werden*
ethical consumption *ethischer Konsum*
environmental impact *Umweltbelastung*

We live in a consumer society where a high standard of living is commonly measured by our ability to afford luxury goods. Shopping has become a recreational activity, and material comfort is a higher priority for society than ever before. These factors play a big role in the increasing debt among young people who cannot afford the lifestyle they pursue. And purchasing goods isn't enough anymore: our economic model relies on quick delivery of a vast variety of goods. But this huge economic activity has negative consequences in terms of sustainability. Production and delivery are highly energy intensive. Fast fashion, especially, encourages waste as every season clothes go out of fashion and are discarded. Ethical consumption is a movement that urges consumers to think about the human and environmental impact of their purchases.

Pros and cons of globalization

globalization *Globalisierung*
interaction *Zusammenwirken, Beeinflussung*
growth *Zunahme, Wachstum*
free trade agreement *Freihandelsabkommen*
goods *pl Ware(n)*
service *Dienstleistung*
to **facilitate sth** *etw ermöglichen, erleichtern*
communications technology *Kommunikationstechnik*
transportation *Transport*
job loss *Arbeitsplatzverlust, Stellenabbau*
unemployment *Arbeitslosigkeit*
uncontrolled competition *ungeregelter Wettbewerb*
trade barrier *Handelsschranke, Handelshemmnis*
border control *Grenzkontrolle*

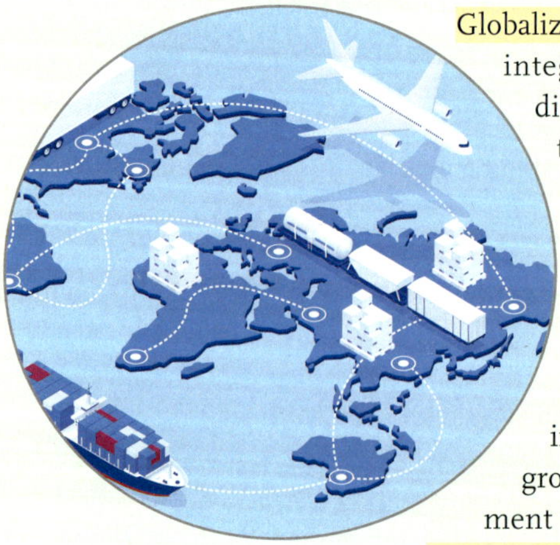

Globalization is the worldwide phenomenon of integration and interaction between different countries, primarily through trade. The Industrial Revolution in the 18th century advanced this growth in integration hugely, and since the end of World War II, free trade agreements have allowed goods and services to be sold all around the world. On the one hand, sharing information worldwide has facilitated groundbreaking progress in the development of communications technology and transportation, and has allowed poorer countries to benefit from world-class products and ideas. On the other hand, globalization has contributed to job losses and widespread unemployment, as uncontrolled competition has meant that small businesses struggle to survive. The responsibility is on politicians to implement laws to protect the most vulnerable workers, even if that means putting up trade barriers or strict border controls.

Gender inequality at work

Despite the granting of women's suffrage in most EU countries last century, women still do not have as equal an experience as men in the workplace. Traditional gender roles generally dictate that women must choose between having a family and a career, as they generally tend to do more than their fair share of household chores and have more caring responsibilities. Even when women are given adequate maternity leave and affordable childcare, they are often discouraged from following the same career paths as men. The glass ceiling means that women occupy a tiny proportion of leading positions in the world's top companies. Most women report instances of being taken less seriously than men at work, and in the worst cases, women are even harassed or bullied in the workplace because of their gender. Although politicians are working to fix instances of discrimination and injustice like the gender pay gap, substantial work is yet to be done to correct the root causes of the gender imbalance so that women are seen as equal at work.

suffrage *Wahlrecht*
gender role *Geschlechterrolle*
fair share *gerechter Anteil*
household chores *Hausarbeiten*
maternity leave *Mutterschutz*
to **follow a career path** *eine berufliche Laufbahn einschlagen*
glass ceiling *gläserne Decke (unsichtbare Barriere, die Frauen am beruflichen Aufstieg hindert)*
to **harrass sb** *jdn belästigen*
to **bully sb** *jdn mobben*
discrimination *Diskriminierung*
gender pay gap *geschlechtsspezifische Lohngefälle*
root cause *Grundursache*
gender imbalance *Ungleichgewicht zwischen den Geschlechtern*

New trends in the workplace

As technology develops and globalization continues, trends in the workplace are constantly changing. In the past, a worker might have one job for life, but this concept has all but disappeared, as casual staff in retail and hospitality make up a huge proportion of the working population. Generation Z is a generation of workers known for their adaptability, but widespread job insecurity caused by recessions and the coronavirus pandemic has pushed new workers to take on flexible working like never before. The gig economy allows freelance workers to work when it suits them, but the lack of permanent contracts means that exploitation is more difficult to police, and workers suffer from a lack of benefits such as holiday pay, health insurance and social security contributions. Self-employment can offer a better work-life balance than traditional employment, but this often means working longer hours for less pay. Trade unions are now much less common than in the past, as individual workers are less inclined to take industrial action over short-term contracts.

job for life *Lebensstellung*
casual staff *Aushilfskräfte*
retail *Einzelhandel*
job insecurity *Arbeitsplatzunsicherheit*
gig economy *Gig Economy (auf Freiberuflern basierendes Wirtschafts-modell)*
freelance worker *Selbstständige/r*
permanent contract *unbefristeter Vertrag*
health insurance *Krankenversicherung*
social security contribution *Sozialversicherungsbeitrag*
self-employment *Selbstständigkeit*
work-life balance *ausgewogenes Verhältnis zwischen Berufs- und Privatleben*
trade union *Gewerkschaft*
industrial action *Arbeitskampfmaß-nahmen*
short-term contract *kurzfristiger Vertrag*

Unemployment

Unemployment is often a sign of an economy which is struggling or which is unable to deal with current trends in customer demands or labour supply. If a person is of working age and is qualified to work, but cannot find paid work, they are considered unemployed. The psychological effects of long-term unemployment can be very damaging apart from the financial difficulties that being made redundant can cause. There are several social and economic reasons for unemployment: demand for goods and services might be decreasing, or labour supply might be increasing. Current trends towards automation mean that it is likely that unemployment figures will rise in the near future, especially in the manufacturing and service industries, as robots will be able to do much of the work that employees currently do.

unemployment *Arbeitslosigkeit*
supply *Angebot*
working age *erwerbsfähiges Alter*
long-term unemployment *Langzeitar-beitslosigkeit*
to **be made redundant** *entlassen werden*
demand *Nachfrage*
automation *Automatisierung*
manufacturing industry *Fertigungsin-dustrie, produzierendes Gewerbe*
service industry *Dienstleistungs-gewerbe*

1 **Complete the sentences with a word from the same word family as the word in brackets.**

1 … success is often measured by the ability to afford luxury items. (economy)
2 … at work gives everyone the same opportunities to succeed. (equal)
3 Fast fashion has a hugely damaging … impact. (environment)
4 Many people value experiences over … goods. (material)
5 Parents and carers, especially, need … in terms of their working hours. (flexible)
6 Self-employment allows people to choose their own working hours, but has higher job … than traditional employment. (insecure)
7 The city centre is now full of … buildings as locals have chosen to move to the suburbs. (commerce)
8 The most important quality for a successful career in IT is … , as systems are always changing. (adaptable)
9 There are many … factors which make it difficult to escape the cycle of poverty. (society)
10 Working in the entertainment … looks very glamorous, but only the very best singers and actors are successful. (industrial)

2 **Match words from box A to box B to make collocations. Then match them to the headings below.**

A	B
career | gender (x2) | gig | glass | health | household | holiday | industrial | job | maternity | short-term | social security | trade | work-life	action | balance | ceiling | chores | contract | contributions | economy | imbalance | insurance | leave | path | pay | pay gap | role | security | union

Gender inequality	Trends in the workplace
career path, …	…

3 **Complete the sentences with suitable verbs from the list. The phrases are all in the text.**

afford | contribute | follow | go | implement | influence | offer | persuade | put up | urge

1 It is easier to … children to buy a product than it is to convince adults.
2 Marketing companies try to … a target audience to follow a particular brand.
3 If people spend money on a lifestyle they cannot … , they will end up in debt.
4 Fast fashion is unsustainable because things … out of fashion so quickly and they have to be replaced.
5 Environmental activists … consumers to think about the impact of their purchases.
6 Globalization has … to a redistribution of work around the world.
7 If the government … a new law, the police must enforce it.
8 The protesters want the government to … trade barriers to protect local farmers.
9 Many young people feel pressure to … the same career path as their parents.
10 Generation Z often look for employers that … a good work-life balance.

Dealing with listening tasks

Apart from English lessons, there is one important thing you can do to improve your listening skills, and that is to listen to spoken English outside the classroom. English-language **music, films** and **TV series** are freely available, and **podcasts** are also very useful.
However, don't listen passively to something playing in the background while you're doing something else – it's much better to set yourself shorter listening times and to concentrate actively on what is being said.

Good to know

The written ***Abitur*** exam contains a listening exercise (duration: **30 minutes**).

Text types

You might be asked to listen to one of the following types of text in your listening exam: **radio, television and internet recordings of news programmes, interviews, speeches, conversations, discussions** and **background reports**.

Procedure

The listening section of your *Abitur* examination contains either three or a maximum of four listening texts with different task formats. You'll be given a short reading time before the listening task and some time for writing your answers after it. You'll hear each listening text twice.

Good to know

In your ***Abitur*** exam, you will have access to a **monolingual** and a **bilingual dictionary**.

Strategies

Before the listening

First things first: to make sure that nothing stops you doing your best in the listening test, it's important that you are ready to listen in a relaxed but, at the same time, concentrated and active way. Get any distracting thoughts out of your head!

- Read the task carefully.
- Activate any previous knowledge you have on the subject matter: it'll be useful.
- Highlight important key words.
- Even if there are some words you don't recognize, only look up key vocabulary – preparation time is extremely valuable!

During the listening

Don't panic if you don't understand everything during the first (or even second!) listening – at this stage of your school career, you shouldn't be too worried if there are a few words you don't understand. You'll miss the conclusion if you stop listening half-way through. Your understanding of the general meaning of longer passages of text will help you deal with any minor issues with individual words.

- Write down some short key points in English during the first listening.
- Complete these notes as you listen to the text for the second time.
- To save time, use symbols, abbreviations and shortened forms of the words.

After the listening task

- Quickly write out in full any points that are heavily abbreviated so that you understand the important content later.
- Don't ever leave any sections of closed tasks unanswered. If you don't know the answer, make a sensible guess – it might be right.

How to say or write it

Symbols

= ≠	(not) the same as
→	and so / therefore
+	and

Abbreviations

e.g.	for example
km	kilometres
w, w/o	with, without

Shortened word forms

govt	government
imp!	important
GB	Great Britain

Task formats

Exercise

Use the listening strategies to do the following listening tasks. They follow the format of the ***Abitur*** exam as a single audio file including all the instructions and time for preparation and your answers.

25

Task 1: "OK, boomer" (*multiple matching*)

You will hear five speakers talking about "OK, boomer", a phrase used by teenagers and young adults to show older people, especially the baby boomer generation, that they don't understand Millennials and Generation Z.

Exam preparation

While listening, match the aspects A to G with the speakers 1 to 5. There are two more aspects than you need.

You now have time to read the assignment.

A	generational harmony
B	embarrassing comments
C	insulting reply to "OK, boomer"
D	challenges facing the older generation
E	prejudice against young adults
F	prejudice against baby boomers
G	underlying feelings of the phrase

Speaker	**1**	**2**	**3**	**4**	**5**
Aspect					

Now listen to the recording again.

25

Task 2: The resale sneaker industry (*multiple choice*)

You will hear an interview dealing with the question of how much money is too much money to spend on a pair of sneakers.

Exam preparation

While listening, choose the correct answers (a, b or c). There is only one correct answer.

You now have time to read the assignment.

1 A sneakerhead is a person who …
- **a** owns a resale shoe company.
- **b** aims for the lowest price for a pair of sneakers.
- **c** may pay a huge amount of money for a pair of sneakers.

2 Bloomberg BusinessWeek has announced that the value of sneakers …
- **a** will rise.
- **b** is now first class.
- **c** has led to more careful examination.

3 Ann Hebert …
  a handed in her notice to Nike.
  b tried to prevent her son's purchase from becoming public.
  c was president and general manager of Nike North America.

4 During the global pandemic, …
  a people wore more sneakers.
  b people bought more sneakers.
  c the resale sneaker industry grew.

5 COVID-19 has led to …
  a redundancies.
  b an increase in sneaker apps.
  c the opening of the platform StockX.

6 Sneaker companies …
  a sell their sneakers to StockX.
  b sometimes limit the production of certain sneakers.
  c push the demand for certain sneakers by driving prices.

7 Michael Sykes believes that …
  a donations should be considered.
  b StockX halted the raffle for the Doernbecher Jordan 1.
  c the Doernbecher Jordan 1 was sold at a price of $2 million.

Now listen to the recording again.

Task 3: The gender pay gap (*sentence completion / short answers*)

25

Exam preparation

You will hear an interview about the gender pay gap.

While listening, add the correct information.

You now have time to read the assignment.

1 The gender pay gap is the difference between the average … of working men and working women.
2 Fact about educational level of women in the EU compared to men: …
3 Working … hours a week means you should take home less pay per month, not … pay per hour.
4 Examples of traditional fields concerning gender-specific responsibilities (name three): …
5 Definition of the term 'glass ceiling' according to the expert: …
6 Long-term impact of the gender pay gap on women (name two aspects): …
7 Measures taken by the European Union to close the gender pay gap (name two): …

Now listen to the recording again.

Good to know

A change in the format, as in task 3, only occurs in the ***Abitur*** in exceptional cases for functional reasons. For practice purposes, however, all four possible task formats are presented here even though the ***Abitur*** examination generally only consists of three listening texts.

Dealing with a creative writing task

Good to know

As part of your ***Abitur*** exam, you have the choice of whether to write a **written discussion** or **comment**, or to do a **creative writing task.**

This task involves something known as text-based writing, i.e. you are expected to produce a written response to a given text. You will be told clearly what sort of text (**text type**) you should write, as well as from which **perspective** it should be written, who it is aimed at (**audience**) and for which **purpose**. The given text may also contain diagrams, images or cartoons.

In the exam you might be asked to write a **speech**, an **article**, a **letter** or an **email**. Pay attention to the instructions given, as you will be expected to stick to the formal criteria for the given text type.

Step 1: Planning

Careful planning is just as important as actually writing the text itself. The following tips will help you with your planning:

- **Brainstorming:** Collect all your ideas and write them down as keywords.
- **Selection:** Limit the scope if necessary by removing any unimportant or inappropriate aspects.
- **Structure:** Sort your ideas/arguments into a clear, logical order.
- **Visualization aids:** Use these to help you prepare. You'll find a selection on the following pages.

Exercise 1

1 Read the text *Gen Z @ Work* on pp. 108–109.

2 Collect and structure ideas and arguments for the following creative writing task by making use of and expanding the Venn diagram on p. 128.

Write an article for your school magazine in which you try to prepare your fellow students for the world of work and the challenges your generation faces when entering a career path while being surrounded by Gen X and Gen Y. Refer to the text *Gen Z @ Work* on pp. 108–109.

In the PagePlayer app, you'll find the specific criteria, tips and *language help* for the different **text types**.

S ▸ Writing an argumentative text (Steps 3–6), pp. 168–171

Step 2: Writing

Make sure that you always keep at the back of your mind the **perspective**, **purpose** and **audience** you're writing for. You need to stay creative but within this framework!

Regardless of the type of text, you should always stick to the tried and tested structure of factual writing: introduction – body – conclusion. Included in this is organizing the text using paragraphs, starting each paragraph with a topic sentence and using appropriate linking words.

Exercise 2

1 Identify the text type, perspective, purpose and target audience for the writing task in exercise 1 above.
2 Write a text according to the instructions given.

Step 3: Checking

Check your draft version for content and language accuracy.

S ▸ Step 7, p. 172

Graphic organizers

Visualization aids can help you to organize information and to point out the connections between the different aspects of a topic or issue.

Mind map

Aim: brainstorming, creating a clear overview

A mind map will help structure your initial thoughts and will show connections between ideas, particularly in terms of hierarchies.

Define the central concept, then add branches reaching out in a circle to the most important ideas and then add further ideas, depending on their importance, as sub-branches coming off from those.

Tip

Use **colours** to mark the content and add different **symbols** – there are all kinds of possibilities to structure your mind map as your want.

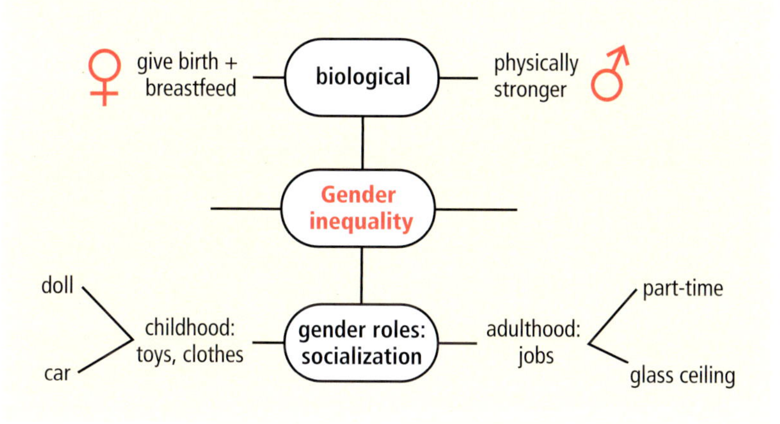

Fishbone diagram

Aim: describing cause and effect

On the right-hand side (head), enter the issue and then the main factors as bones coming out diagonally. Then collect ideas as to what the possible causes of each factor could be (further branching). After assigning a weighting to each 'bone', the main cause should become clear.

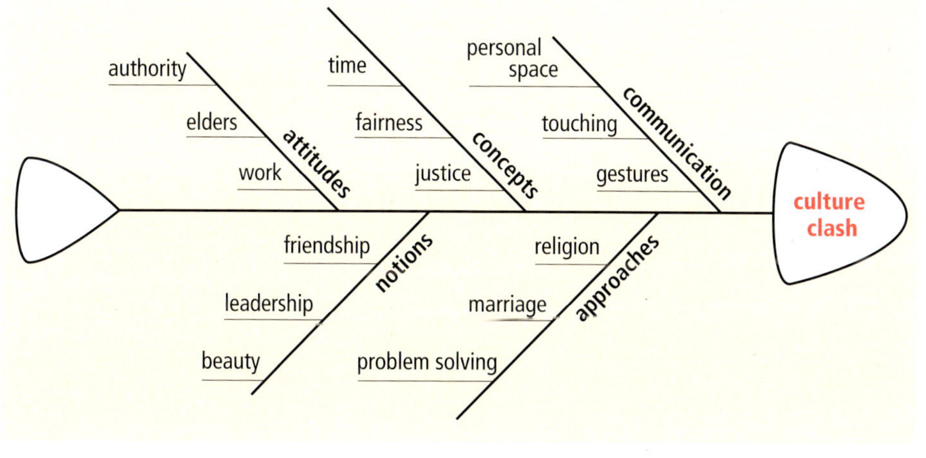

Venn diagram

Aim: showing relationships

A Venn diagram is a simple and clear way of showing common features and differences, e.g. your own experiences in comparison with the aspects of a text. Venn diagrams can also be expanded using further circles (e.g. in this case *Gen X*, *baby boomers*).

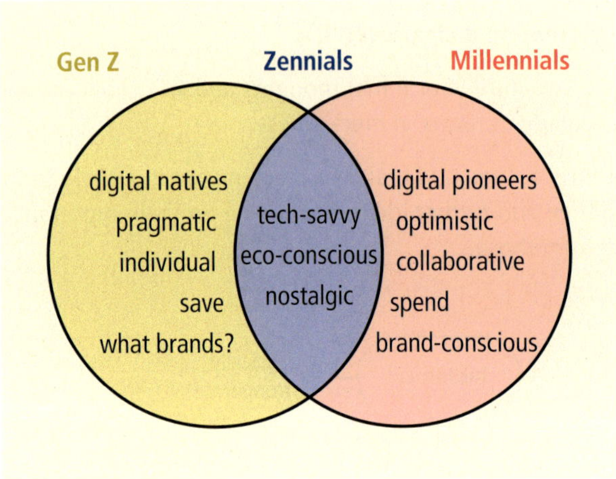

Flow chart

Aim: visualizing processes

Linking arrows show the process in action or define the path. Flow charts can be used in decision-making processes which explore alternative options and define outcomes. Each shape has a specific function (see below).

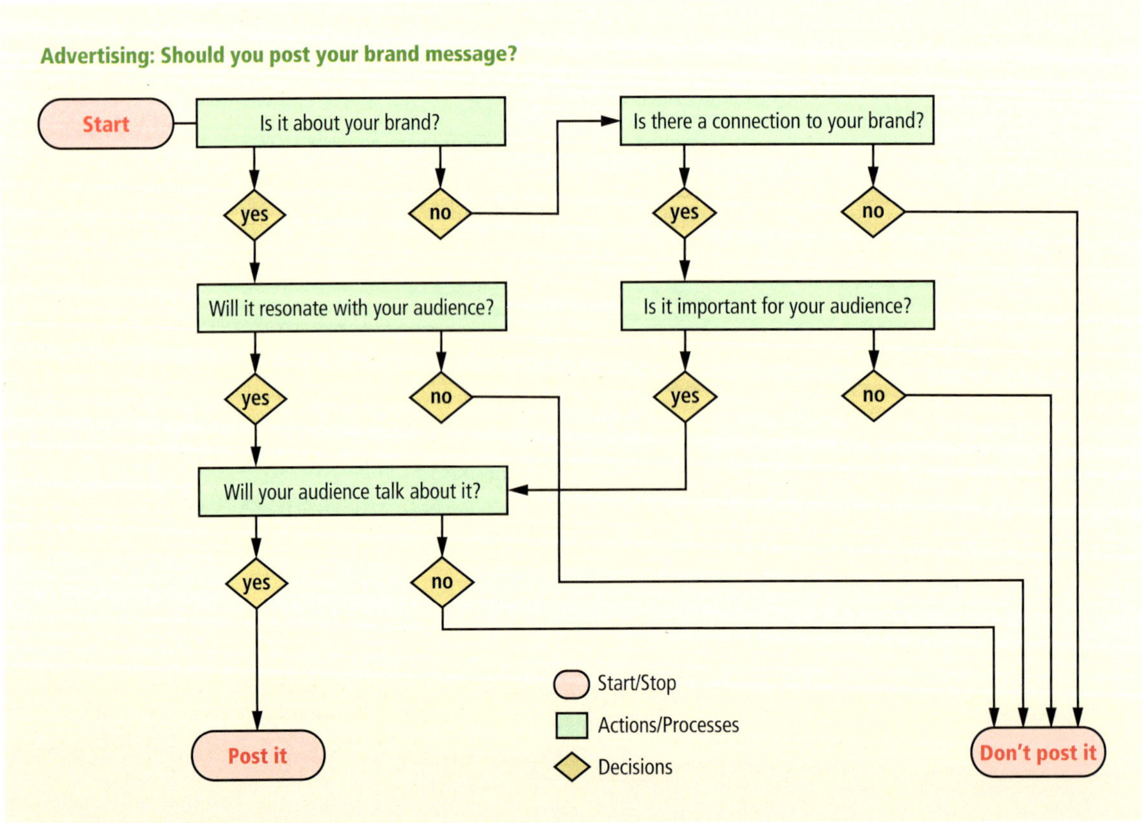

Review

1 Rank the Sections A–G in this Topic based on how interesting they were to you. Then, look back at your work on the overview of this Topic (pages 90–91) and how you ranked them there (page 90, exercise 2). Have your rankings changed? Share your results with a group and tell them what you found most interesting.

2 Look at your KWL list (page 91, exercise 5). Fill out the "Learned" part of the list. Next, look at your "Want to know" list. What do you still want to know?

3 Make a list of ten words in the Topic that were new to you and you consider important to know. Then collect everyone's words and cluster them into groups. Finally, pick a word group and write a paragraph using all the words.

Evaluate

Do this task on your own. How much do you agree or disagree with the statements below? Rate each one on a scale of one to four. The references on the right show you which exercises you can review.

1 = totally disagree **2** = disagree **3** = agree **4** = totally agree

Section	Statement	
A	**1** I can talk about advertising and social media influencers.	▸ p. 93, exercise 4
	2 I know how to write a summary.	▸ pp. 92–93, exercises 1–3
B	**3** I can define conscious and ethical consumption.	▸ pp. 96–97, exercises 1–4
	4 I know how to analyse a text.	▸ p. 97, exercise 5
	5 I know how to deal with creative writing tasks.	▸ p. 98, exercise 10
C	**6** I can summarize the main points of a text about globalization.	▸ pp. 99–100, exercises 2–4
	7 I can talk about the advantages and disadvantages of globalization.	▸ p. 101, exercises 7–9
	8 I know how to describe and analyse cartoons.	▸ p. 102, exercise 10
D	**9** I understand and can talk about the gender gap.	▸ pp. 103–105, exercises 1–3
	10 I can rewrite sentences in reported speech.	▸ p. 105, exercise 5
	11 I can talk about working from home and the gender pay gap.	▸ p. 106, exercises 6–8
E	**12** I am able to talk about the characteristics of Generation Z.	▸ p. 107, exercises 1–3
	13 I feel comfortable writing a mediation text from English to German.	▸ p. 109, exercise 4
	14 I can make my texts more interesting by using adjectives.	▸ p. 109, exercise 5
F	**15** I understand and can define Universal Basic Income.	▸ pp. 110–113, exercises 1–8
	16 I can use adjectives and adverbs correctly.	▸ p. 113, exercise 6
G	**17** I can give examples of cultural missteps business people make.	▸ pp. 114–116, exercises 1–4
	18 I can use idioms in my writing and speaking.	▸ pp. 116–117, exercises 5–9
Skills	**19** I know how to deal with listening tasks.	S ▸ pp. 123–125
	20 I am able to deal with creative writing tasks	S ▸ pp. 126–128

Consolidate

You want to go deeper into the the topic of work and consumers, and speed up your learning process? Scan this page with the PagePlayer app. There you'll find some suggestions for additional tasks.

Aufgabenteil I Hören

26

1 You will hear an interview with the mayor of Stockton, California, about an experiment with basic income payments.

While listening, choose the correct answers (a, b or c). There is only one correct answer.

1 Recipients of the $500 dollars have to …
  a have a bank account.
  b make at least $46,000.
  c earn less than the average citizen of Stockton.

2 The Stockton Economic Empowerment Demonstration programme has been running for …
  a 8 months. **b** 18 months. **c** 28 months.

3 The mayor of Stockton decided to experiment with basic income because he …
  a wanted to make more people in his city rich.
  b wanted to follow Dr. Martin Luther King's example.
  c was keen to find a way to help people living in poverty.

4 He says that people spent the money on …
  a extra treats for themselves.
  b cosmetics and expensive health care.
  c things they would otherwise not have been able to afford.

5 Critics of the idea said that the money would be spent on …
  a luxury items. **b** food only. **c** new cars.

6 Thomas, one recipient, said the money allowed him to spend more time on …
  a risky part-time work.
  b his free-time activities.
  c applications for full-time work.

7 The people received the money in the form of …
  a cheques. **b** debit cards. **c** cash.

8 Mayor Tubbs knows how the money was spent because …
  a the recipients had to complete questionnaires.
  b his team asked recipients how they spent it.
  c the transactions were monitored and people were interviewed.

27

2 You will hear an interview with Edna Green, an African businesswoman.

While listening, take notes on the following points. You need not write complete sentences.

1 Why did Edna need to sell mangoes as a child (2 aspects)?: …
2 Why were mangoes the perfect product (3 aspects)?: …
3 What is Edna's current occupation (2 aspects)?: …
4 Which character traits does she say you need to be a success in business (3 aspects)?: …
5 How does she think you should treat employees from different cultures?: …
6 What is her dream for the future?: …

3 You will hear five speakers talking about Generation Z and its characteristics. 28

While listening, match the headings A–G with the speakers 1–5. There are two more headings than you need.

Headings	
A	a new sense of togetherness
B	availability of things
C	belief in the tried and true
D	better safe than sorry
E	concerns about an entire industry
F	high demand for consumer goods
G	high standards of moral integrity

Speaker	Heading

Aufgabenteil II Lesen und Schreiben

Aufgabenstellung

1 Summarize the pros and cons of the gig economy as described in the text. (Material 1, pp. 131–132)

2 Analyse the way in which the author conveys his message. Refer to language and structure. (Material 1, pp. 131–132)

3 Choose <u>one</u> of the following:

A "The gig economy, in one form or another, is here to stay and we need to find a way of making it compatible with social equity and human dignity." (ll. 15–16)

Comment on the statement from the text.

B As an exchange student at an English school you are taking part in a project on working conditions in low-paid jobs.

Write an article for the school magazine, discussing how consumers' wants and needs influence adequate working conditions for workers in Germany.

Material 1

The gig economy is here to stay. Now let's humanise it

The US didn't have just one election on 3 November. All kinds of other public offices were up for election too. And in California, electors had an additional choice to make: whether to approve Proposition 22, a referendum on whether ride-hail and delivery companies (think outfits such as Uber, Lyft, Deliveroo) should get an exemption from California employment law that would allow them to continue treating workers as independent contractors rather than as employees with rights that come with conventional employment. The companies had spent $200m on a campaign to preserve their exemption and it worked: voters approved the proposition by 58% to 42%. [...]

Now, \$200m is peanuts to these money-burning enterprises, but it was peanuts well spent from their point of view. Having to shoulder the responsibilities of "real" employers would grievously undermine their business models and therefore the prospects of big eventual payouts for their investors. For the trade unions and the civil society groups who opposed the proposition, the outcome is somewhere between a disappointment and a disaster. For the rest of us, it's confirmation that a referendum is a lousy way of resolving a complex problem that's not going away. The gig economy, in one form or another, is here to stay and we need to find a way of making it compatible with social equity and human dignity.

Pandemics, as Yuval Noah Harari has observed, have a way of accelerating history. Only a year ago, I remember estimating that it would probably take a decade before remote working became accepted practice in many industries. And look what has happened; in a few months, entire industries and occupations have been Zoomed out. In those same months, we have discovered that Amazon has metamorphosed into the critical infrastructure of most western states. Less shopping and more working from home means more households are using Deliveroo and other gig economy platforms more frequently. A study by the consultancy firm McKinsey in August found that "approximately 35–55% of existing [European] consumers intend to continue using delivery more in the future".

What the pandemic has brought home to us is the extent to which our economies – and our industries – were being reshaped by technology and economic ideology. Evidence of this reshaping has been available for years to those who were disposed, or professionally obliged, to pay attention to it. But now it's inescapable. And the question is: will we use the lessons we've learned from the pandemic to reshape our world? In particular, how can we adapt our laws and institutions to exploit the benefits of new industries while reducing their downsides?

Here, the gig economy might provide a useful case study. At the moment, most of the challenges to platform-based enterprises such as Uber and Deliveroo have involved trying to shoehorn them into legal frameworks that were designed for a pre-platform age. This is a piecemeal approach that has so far produced erratic results. In February, for example, a French court ruled that a Deliveroo courier should be treated as an employee rather than a contractor. In September, Spain's supreme court made a similar ruling about another delivery startup, Glovo, after lower courts had made a series of contradictory rulings.

We can't go on like this. A better way of thinking about it would be to recognise that we're in a position analogous to that of Britain in the 1830s and 1840s when parliament passed the Factory Acts to regulate the conditions of novel kinds of employment as the Industrial Revolution roared ahead. The Factories Act of 1847, for example, colloquially known as the 10 Hours Act, met a long-standing demand by mill workers for a 10-hour day. Other legislation regulated the use of child labour and other practices.

We need that kind of comprehensive approach to the gig economy because, as other kinds of employment get automated away, it will be what provides employment for an increasing number of people (just as the factories of industrialising Britain provided jobs for people coming off the land). We should be thinking of what the French entrepreneur Nicolas Colin calls "a new social contract" that would cover workers against the new risks of the day – the impossibility of renting housing in cities when your income is derived from gig platforms; access to loans when and where you need them, not necessarily to buy a car but instead to learn new skills when it's time to move on. And, as he says, "to help workers organise so that they defend their interests themselves, but with a different approach from that which was embraced in the coalmines of the 19th century or the car factories of the 20th". Uber drivers of the world, unite: you have nothing to lose but your ratings.

(790 words) Source: *The Guardian*, 7 November 2020

Mündlicher Teil Kommunikationsprüfung

Partner A: look here. **Partner B**: look at File 13 on page 274.

Partner A: Sequence 1 (your five-minute talk)

Situation: You have entered an annual English debating competition and this year's theme is gender equality. At the beginning of the debate each candidate has to give a five-minute statement on the topic.

Use the cartoon and statistics below as a starting point to explain to your audience what gender inequality means and where it is most frequently experienced.

"Oh, you'll love working here. Nobody treats you any differently just because of your age, race, or gender."

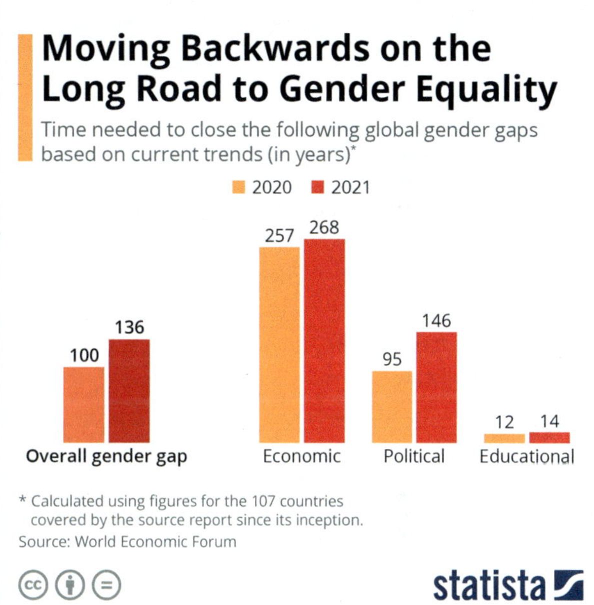

Partner A: Sequence 2 (you and the teacher / another student)

Continue the discussion on the need for gender equality with your teacher / your partner.

1 Outline some of the causes of gender inequality and suggest ways in which it can be overcome.

2 *"No country can ever truly flourish if it stifles the potential of its women and deprives itself of the contribution of half its citizens."* – Michelle Obama

Explain the economic, political and social consequences that gender inequality causes.

Topic 4 The USA – a divided nation?

Section B
Gun control

"A well regulated Militia, being necessary to the security of a free state, the right of the people to keep and bear arms, shall not be infringed." – Second Amendment to the US Constitution

school shooting

Section A
Past and present

colonization

Fact: By 1804, slavery had been abolished in the North but it wasn't until the end of the Civil War in 1865 that slaves were officially freed in all of the existing states.

A nation of contradictions

dreams

future

Section G
A vision of the future

Fact: "The Hill We Climb", a spoken word poem recited by Amanda Gorman at the inauguration of President Joe Biden, was completed in response to the storming of the US Capitol on 6 January 2021.

1 Read the facts and quotations about the United States above.

a Which of them are totally new to you?
b Which of them do you find surprising?

2 Rank Sections A–G on how interested you are in them.

3 The mind map shows you a preview of Topic 4. Copy it onto a piece of paper and add words and phrases from …

a the facts and quotations above.
b the Word bank opposite.
c your own ideas.
d Sections A–G you think are important.

Find information on each Section in the PagePlayer app!

reform

Section C
Polarization in US society

"When have we not been deeply divided?"
– Todd Gitlin, US sociologist

racism

Section D
Immigration to the USA

A better life

Fact: Currently the largest population of immigrants to the USA comes from Mexico, Central and South America.

"The road to success is not easy to navigate, but with hard work, drive and passion, it's possible to achieve the American Dream."
– Tommy Hilfiger, fashion designer

Section F
The American Dream

Fact: During the early 20th century, due to industrialization and immigration, the United States grew exponentially and became one of the world's leading industrial powers.

Section E
The role of the USA in the world

power

4 Note a few key words to say what you expect to learn in each Section.

5 Make a "KWL" (Know, Want to know, Learned) list for the Topic.

6 With a partner, compare …

a your mind maps and say why you added words where you did.
b your rankings from exercise 2.
c what you expect to learn in Sections A–G.

Then compare with another pair.

7 Save your work for reviewing when you've finished the Topic.

Word bank

adversity *Not*
to **colonize sth** *etw besiedeln*
equality *Gleichheit, Gleichberechtigung*
firearm *Schusswaffe*
liberty *Freiheit*
Native American *Ureinwohner/in Nordamerikas*
oppression *Unterdrückung*
permit *Genehmigung*
perseverance *Ausdauer*
pity *Mitleid*
settler *Siedler/in*
redemption *Wiedergutmachung*

Section A Past and present

Warm-up

1 Think: Make notes about the pictures below and how they relate to what you know about the USA and its history. Use the headings in the box.

2 Pair: Find a partner and compare your results.

3 Share: Compare your results with another pair.

A

B

Native Americans
Slavery
The Constitution
Immigration
The Civil War
The American Dream

C

D

E

F

29

The history of the USA: an overview

Native Americans

Long before the land that is now known as the United States was colonized by the Europeans, a large number of Native American cultures and tribes had already existed in North America for thousands of years. Following the discovery of the Americas by Christopher Columbus in 1492, an estimated 90% of these indigenous peoples died as a result of wars and ethnic cleansing as well as diseases brought by the Europeans to which the Native Americans had no immunity. After the founding of the United States, European settlers waged war on these tribes as they moved west. Many more Native American peoples were killed in massacres, their land was taken from them, and they were subjected to discriminatory, one-sided treaties and were forced to live on reservations.

The Constitution and the Bill of Rights

After their victory in the Revolutionary War (1775–1783), which won the colonies independence from England, the Founding Fathers of the United States drafted the American Constitution and the Bill of Rights. These two documents formed the basis of the new nation's government. The Constitution, which came into force in 1789, established the rights of the government, limiting its power over the people, and the Bill of Rights (1791) defined the rights of the people. Probably the most debated and discussed section of the Bill of Rights is the Second Amendment, which gives the people the right to own a gun.

5 **ethnic cleansing** *ethnische Säuberung(en)*
8 to **wage war on sb** *Krieg führen gegen jdn*
10 to **be subjected to sth** *etw unterworfen sein*
14 **Founding Fathers** *die Männer, die 1787 die Verfassung der USA entwarfen*

Good to know

The **Second Amendment** of the Bill of Rights states: "A well regulated Militia, being necessary to the security of a free State, the right of the people to keep and bear Arms, shall not be infringed (= *angetastet*)."

Slavery

Although a significant number of free, indentured and enslaved Africans were brought to North America as early as 1526, 1619 is widely viewed as the beginning of slavery in America. During the 17th century, enslaved Africans provided a cheap source of labor, which helped build what is now the United States. Although it is impossible to state exactly how many Africans were brought across the ocean, it is generally believed that during the 18th century alone, between six and seven million people were transported from Africa to America against their will.

[22] **indentured** *vertraglich verpflichtet*
[22] **enslaved** *versklavt*
[37] **the Confederacy** *die Konföderation* (Bund der Südstaaten)

The Civil War

Slavery had already been abolished in the northern states of the USA by 1804, but the southern states were very dependent on the institution because their main source of income, farming, necessitated cheap labor. In 1860, when Abraham Lincoln was elected the 16th president of the United States running on a platform to stop the expansion of slavery, seven southern states left the Union and founded the Confederacy, and in 1861 the American Civil War began. In 1865, the war ended with the defeat of the Confederacy, and as a result slavery was abolished. There was enormous animosity between the North and the South after the conclusion of the war, beginning the rift between people and ideals in the USA which continues today. As the southern states began to regain their power, they created a series of so-called "Jim Crow" laws. This oppression continued for more than 100 years, leading to the Civil Rights movement of the 1960s and later the Black Lives Matter movement in the early 21st century.

Good to know

Jim Crow refers to a collection of laws used to legalize racial segregation in the United States, particularly in the South. The laws were put in place after the American Civil War and remained in force until the mid-1960s. Among other restrictions, the laws controlled where and how African Americans could get an education, where they could live and work, and severly restricted their right to vote.

[40] **animosity** *Feindseligkeit*
[41] **rıft** *Bruch*
[42] to **regain** *wiedererlangen*
[43] **oppression** *Unterdrückung*

Immigration

By the 1500s, Spanish and French settlers began to colonize North America, followed by the English, who came in large numbers in the 17th century, seeking religious freedom and the possibility of a new life. Between 1815 and 1865 another major wave of immigration from Europe was led by the Irish, who came to escape famine in their own country. During this time, many German immigrants also came to buy cheap land and farm in the middle of the newly formed nation. In the first half of the 19th century, many Chinese were lured by the promise of riches from the California gold rush. At the turn of the 20th century, there was an influx of Italian immigrants and in the early part of that century, more than 2 million Eastern European Jews emigrated to the USA to escape persecution. Currently the largest population of immigrants coming to the USA is from Mexico and Central or South America. These people are fleeing persecution, poverty and violence in their home countries.

The role of the USA in the world

During the early 20th century, due to industrialization and immigration, the United States grew exponentially and became one of the world's leading industrial powers. Although initially reluctant to join the fight in World War I, the United States finally entered in 1917, one year before its end. In 1941, the Japanese attack on Pearl Harbor forced the United States to enter into World War II. After the end of the war, the United States and the Soviet Union emerged as the two major competing superpowers. When the Soviet bloc crumbled in 1991, the United States was left as the world's only superpower. At the beginning of the 21st century, the

[48] to **seek sth** *(nach) etw suchen, etw anstreben*
[53] to lure sb/sth *jdn/etw locken, ködern*
[54] **riches** *pl* *Reichtum*
[55] **influx** *Zustrom*
[56] **persecution** *Verfolgung*
[58] to **flee** *fliehen*
[67] to **crumble** *zerfallen, zerbröckeln*

United States' foreign policy was greatly influenced by the September 11th attacks in 2001, leading to wars in Afghanistan and Iraq. As we move into the mid-21st century, the United States is no longer the superpower it once was and the question is: who will take its place?

The American Dream

Although it was not known as The American Dream at the time, the roots of this idea date back to the earliest settlers. In 1620, the Pilgrim Fathers, a group of roughly 100 English Puritans, left England and sailed to present-day Massachusetts seeking religious freedom so they could live their lives free from persecution. The Revolutionary War was later fought so that the new nation could be founded on the ideal, as stated in the Declaration of Independence, that "all men are created equal". Westward expansion, which was driven by the search for inexpensive land for farmers and slave owners, was the ultimate American Dream, based on the competitive and individualistic belief that through hard work and perseverance people can create, for themselves and their families, the life they wish for. For new immigrants today, the United States still holds the promise of the American Dream through hard work and ingenuity.

(1013 words)

76 **Puritan** *strenge ProtestantInnen*
82 **perseverance** *Ausdauer*
85 **ingenuity** *Erfindungsreichtum*

Working with the text

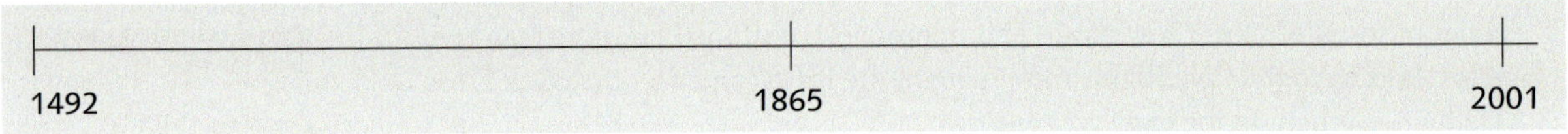

How to say or write it

- I also included …
- I don't think … is an important event.
- … is an interesting point.
- This point is very important because …
- Don't forget about …

4 Using information in the text, create a timeline of the history of the United States of America. Choose the events that you find most important to highlight on your timeline. Three dates are given to get you started.

5 Work with a partner and compare your timelines. Did you choose the same important events? Discuss your findings and discuss why you believe these aspects to be the most important. (Add any events that you think are missing after comparing timelines with your partner.)

Speaking

6 With a partner, look at the photos at the beginning of the Section (p. 136) again. Talk about these questions.

- Which events did the images make you think of originally?
- What new aspects of the history of the USA did you learn from the text?
- Do you see anything differently after reading the text? Explain your answers, giving examples if necessary.

Working with words

7 Copy and complete the table with the noun forms of the verbs.

Verb	Noun	Verb	Noun
persevere	…	immigrate	…
enslave	…	infringe	…
industrialize	…	discriminate	…
assimilate	…	abolish	…
oppress	…	found	…
colonize	…	persecute	…

8 Complete the sentences using the correct form of words from exercise 6.

1. Although many immigrants come the United States with almost nothing, through hard work and … they build a better life for themselves.
2. My grandfather and his brother left Italy and … to New York.
3. Slavery is an … of the rights of the people who are enslaved.
4. … describes the time during which machines began to replace workers.
5. The 13th Amendment to the United States Constitution … slavery.
6. Many Native Americans were killed during the … of North America.

Looking at language

Remember: Using conditionals

Conditional type 1 – *if* + simple present, *will*-future
If the laws ***are*** *fair, people* ***won't protest****.*

Conditional type 2 – *if* + simple past, *would* + infinitive
If the laws ***were*** *fair, people* ***wouldn't protest****.*

Conditional type 3 – *if* + past perfect, *would have* + past participle
If the laws ***had been*** *fair, the people* ***wouldn't have protested****.*

9 Complete the sentences using the words in brackets and say which conditional you used. Sometimes more than one answer is possible.

G ▸ Conditionals, p. 291

1. If Europeans … (not colonize) North America, the USA … (not be found).
   If Europeans hadn't colonized North America, the USA wouldn't have been founded. (conditional type 3)
2. … (slavery / end) in 1865 if the North … (not win) the Civil War?
3. Gun control … (not be) such a difficult issue if the Bill of Rights … (not include) the Second Amendment.
4. People … (continue) to protest in the USA if the government … (not deal) with its systemic issues.
5. If Americans … (try) to understand each other better, … (there still / be) so much political division?
6. The USA … (not enter) World War II if Japan … (not bomb) Pearl Harbor.
7. If the belief in the American Dream … (not be) so strong, many immigrants … (not come) to the USA.
8. The USA … (not remain) the world's only superpower in 2050 if China … (continue) to grow economically.

Crossover TV

The US-Dakota War

04

Good to know

There are 574 federally recognized Native American tribes (also called *bands*, *communities*, *nations*, *native villages* and *pueblos*) in the United States. Each community is culturally, ethnically, and linguistically diverse. Of these nations, 229 are located in Alaska; the rest are located in 35 other states.

Watching

You are going to watch a video about the 1862 war between the US government and the Dakota tribe in Minnesota.

10 Read the questions below then watch the video. Make notes to answer the questions.

1. What happened on 17 August 1862?
2. Which developments in the 1860s led to the US-Dakota War?
3. Why were the Dakota people suffering from starvation?
4. How did the US government treat the Dakota people at the time?
5. Which local factors made the Dakota feel they had to defend themselves?
6. What did some of the Dakota tribe want to do?
7. How does one descendant of the settlers criticize the Dakota?
8. How do the descendants of the Dakota tribe view the situation?
9. What was the result of the US-Dakota war?
10. What role does Fort Snelling play in the story of the war?

Speaking

11 **Poster:** Work in groups and decide which topic from the list below your group will deal with. Each group creates a poster about their topic and how it relates to the video.

Little Crow

- the Dakota tribe
- settlers in Minnesota
- the treaties of 1851
- reservations
- the Battle of Wood Lake
- the Dakota 38
- Fort Snelling

Abraham Lincoln

12 **Gallery walk:** Set up stations in the classroom, one station with an expert for each poster. In your group, walk around the different stations, taking notes on what you have learned. Ask the expert any questions you might have.

Exam preparation

S ▸ Dealing with a creative writing task, pp. 126–128

Writing checklist

Writing

13 You are an exchange student at a high school in Minnesota during the anniversary of the US-Dakota War. As part of a school project on the event, you are asked to give a speech giving an "outsider's" viewpoint.

Write a speech, referring to the information in the video and the posters, in which you comment on the historical events and their relevance for the USA today.

Section B Gun control

Warm-up

1 Do the quiz below about gun control in the USA. (Sometimes more than one answer is correct.)

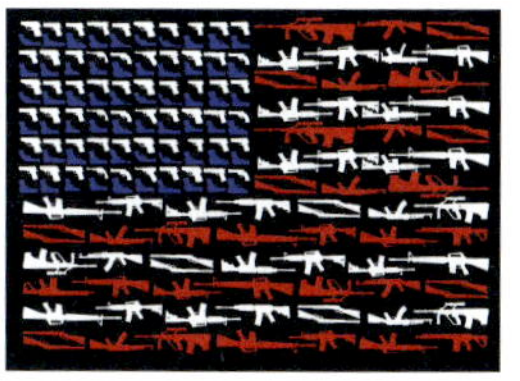

What do you know about firearms in the USA?

1 **What is the minimum age to buy a firearm in the USA?**
 a 16 c 21
 b 18 d 30

2 **Who is restricted from purchasing or possessing firearms?**
 a stalkers c felons
 b tourists d students

3 **Does the federal or state government regulate firearms?**
 a federal b state

4 **Who may sell firearms?**
 a anyone over 21 c children
 b supermarket employees d anyone who has a license and wants to make a profit

5 **Is a background check required to buy firearms?**
 a yes b no

6 **How many American states require a permit to purchase a handgun?**
 a 50 (all) c 3
 b 12 d 0

7 **How many states require a permit to purchase a shotgun?**
 a 50 c 3
 b 12 d 0

8 **Do you need a permit in most states to carry a firearm?**
 a yes, for all firearms c no, for shotguns
 b yes, for handguns d no, never

9 **What is the "gun show loophole"?**
 a Anyone can have a gun as long as it was given to them as a gift and they are not a criminal.
 b It is possible to buy a gun legally without a background check.
 c No one can buy a gun at a gun show
 d Anyone can sell a gun as long as it is not for profit.

firearm *Schusswaffe*
felon *Verbrecher/in*
permit *Genehmigung; Bewilligung*
gun show *Waffenschau, Waffenmesse*
loophole *Gesetzeslücke*

Working with the text

2 Scan the text on pages 142–143 and find the answers to the quiz.

S ▸ Reading difficult texts, pp. 39–40

Good to know

GCA: Gun Control Act of 1968

ATF: The Bureau of Alcohol, Tobacco, Firearms and Explosives

FFL: Federal Firearms License

NICS: National Instant Criminal Background Check System (part of the FBI)

Eight facts about gun control in the US

Proponents of stricter gun regulations fear for their safety in a country where there is an average of 88 guns per 100 people. The Brady Campaign to Prevent Gun Violence estimates that around 114,994 people are shot each year in the US. This includes murders, assaults, accidents, police intervention, suicide attempts and suicides.

Opponents of regulatory arguments, however, also fear a loss of safety. They argue that restricting the right to bear arms would leave citizens unable to protect themselves in their daily lives or, in a worst-case scenario, from a government turned against the people.

Though regulations vary from state to state, there are a few key conditions for obtaining guns in the US.

1 Is there a minimum age?

The Gun Control Act of 1968 (GCA), which regulates firearms at the federal level, requires that citizens and legal residents must be at least 18 years of age to purchase shotguns or rifles and ammunition. All other firearms — handguns, for example — can only be sold to people 21 and older.

2 Who's restricted from purchasing or possessing firearms?

Fugitives, people deemed a danger to society and patients involuntarily committed to mental institutions are among those who may not purchase firearms. People with prior felony convictions that include a prison sentence exceeding one year, or misdemeanors carrying sentences of more than two years, are also prohibited from purchasing firearms.

Federal law also blocks the sale of guns to people who have been found guilty of unlawfully possessing or using controlled substances within the past year.

Other restrictions apply to people who have been issued restraining orders by courts to prevent harassment, stalking or threatening behavior; people who have renounced their citizenship; dishonorably discharged military personnel; unauthorized migrants; and people temporarily visiting the US on nonimmigrant visas, for example as tourists.

3 Does the federal or state government regulate firearms?

Although state and local governments regulate whether residents may, for example, carry guns in public, laws regulating who may receive or possess guns are set out at the federal level [by The Bureau of Alcohol, Tobacco, Firearms and Explosives].

Shotguns, rifles, machine guns, firearm mufflers and silencers are regulated by the National Firearms Act of 1934. The purchase of semi-automatic weapons is legal in most states, as are automatic weapons made before 1986.

4 Who may sell firearms?

Like handgun owners, dealers interested in obtaining a Federal Firearms License (FFL) must be at least 21 years of age. They must have premises for conducting business and must alert a local law enforcement official at the time of submitting their applications to the federal bureau that regulates firearms. Just like gun owners, they must fulfill the same criteria regarding their history of prior convictions and mental state.

4 **murder** *Mord*
4 **assault** *Körperverletzung*
6 **regulatory** *regulatorisch, behördlich*
15 **rifle** *Gewehr*
15 **ammunition** *Munition*
18 **fugitive** *Flüchtige/r*
20 **prior** *vorherig*
20 **felony** *Verbrechen*
20 **conviction** *Verurteilung*
21 **misdemeanor** *AE Vergehen*
24 **controlled substance** *Rauschgift*
25 to **issue** *erteilen, erlassen*
25 restraining order *AE einstweilige Verfügung; Kontaktverbot*
26 **harassment** *Schikane, Mobbing, Belästigung*
27 dishonourably discharged *unehrenhaft entlassen*
35 muffler *AE Schalldämpfer*
35 silencer *BE Schalldämpfer*
40 premises *pl Geschäft(sräume)*
43 to fulfil sth *etw erfüllen, etw ausführen*

However, the law is unclear on what constitutes selling guns for profit. Any individual may sell firearms without a license if his or her motive isn't to make a profit for livelihood through repeated and regular sales.

5 Is a background check required to purchase a firearm?

Yes. The amendment to the 1968 Gun Control Act — known as the Brady Handgun Violence Prevention Act of 1993 — requires holders of FFLs to conduct a background check.

Estimated to take under 10 minutes by phone or online, the check gives the FFL holder an immediate answer: approve, delay or deny. A delay indicates the need for further research for three business days, after which point FFL holders can act at their own discretion if the research proves inconclusive.

6 Do states require permits to purchase firearms?

Only a dozen of the US's 50 states require purchase permits for handguns. Of those states, only three — California, Connecticut and Hawaii — require permits for the purchase of rifles and shotguns.

California, for example, requires applicants to pass a written test and enroll in a gun safety class to obtain purchase permits. States with this requirement do not recognize the "concealed carry reciprocity" policies of some states, which allow gun owners licensed in one state to bring their weapons to another.

7 Do states require permits to carry firearms?

Most states require permits to carry handguns. By contrast, virtually no state requires a permit to carry rifles and shotguns.

8 What is the "gun show loophole"?

According to the ATF, anyone can sell a gun without an FFL from their home, online, at a flea market or at a gun show as long as he or she is not conducting the sale as part of regular business activity. One example would be someone who sells a firearm from his or her personal collection. Others who are exempt include those giving guns as gifts. Only individuals whose "principal motive" is to make a profit via sale must obtain an FFL.

Commonly referred to as the "gun show loophole", this ambiguity also explains how a purchase can occur without a background check — and without breaking the law. A 2017 survey by Harvard and Northeastern universities estimates that roughly one in five transactions occur without a background check.

A gun may also be purchased on behalf of a third party as long as it is a gift and as long as the recipient does not violate federal restrictions on gun ownership to the best of the gift giver's knowledge. The same applies to the general transfer of guns. Children younger than 18 may possess guns that were given to them by parents or guardians as gifts provided that they have written permission.

(907 words) From: *Deutsche Welle*, 20 January 2021

45 to constitute sth *etw darstellen, etw ausmachen, etw bilden*
47 livelihood *Existenzgrundlage, Lebensunterhalt*
53 to **deny (sb) sth** *(jdm) etw verweigern*
55 **at sb's discretion** *in jds Ermessen*
55 **inconclusive** *ergebnislos, uneindeutig*
57 **dozen** *Dutzend*
60 **applicant** *Bewerber/in*
60 to **enroll** *(AE)* **in sth** *sich für etw anmelden*
62 **concealed carry** *AE verdecktes Tragen* (von Waffen)
62 **reciprocity** *Gegenseitigkeit*
65 **virtually** *praktisch, nahezu*
69 flea market *Flohmarkt*
71 **exempt** *ausgenommen, befreit* (von Pflichten)
74 **ambiguity** *Unklarheit, Uneindeutigkeit*
78 **on behalf of sb** *in jds Namen, für jdn*
79 to **violate sth** *gegen etw verstoßen, etw verletzen*
79 **ownership** *Besitzverhältnisse*
82 **guardian** *Vormund*

3 Read the text carefully and then complete the following tasks.

1. Outline the restrictions that exist on who may purchase firearms in the USA.
2. Point out the regulations that affect people who sell firearms in the USA.
3. Describe the requirements that states have for purchasing and carrying firearms.
4. Point out how people can sell guns without a Federal Firearms License.

Remember

When you are writing a summary, you should use the **simple present**: *The article describes ...*

S ▸ Writing a summary, p. 81

Research

4 Work in small groups. Half of the group researches arguments in favour of gun control; half of the group researches arguments supporting the individual freedom to carry arms. Present your arguments to the group.

Speaking

Skills training: Analysing a cartoon

Look at the cartoon and make sure that you understand all of the words and phrases included.

Step 1: Describe what you *see* on the page.
Step 2: Analyse the *message* of the cartoon.
Step 3: Comment on the cartoon, giving *your thoughts* on its message.

Exam preparation
Kommunikationsprüfung
Phrases for speaking

S ▸ Describing and analysing cartoons, pp. 82–83

5 **Partner A:** Look here. **Partner B:** Look at File 14 on page 275.

Partner A: Sequence 1 (your five-minute talk)

Use the given material as a starting point for an uninterrupted five-minute talk on gun control in the USA.

1 Describe the cartoon and explain its message in your own words.

2 Comment on the following quote and how it relates to the cartoon.

"If you take guns away from legal gun owners, then the only people who would have guns would be the bad guys."
– Bruce Willis, US actor

Partner A: Sequence 2 (you and the teacher / another student)

Now discuss the following questions with your partner.

1 What are the causes of gun violence in the USA?

2 Why is the issue of gun control so controversial in the USA?

Writing

Exam preparation
S ▸ Dealing with a creative writing task, pp. 126–128
Writing checklist

6 You are an exchange student at a high school in the USA. Write an article for the school magazine comparing the spread of firearms in Germany with the USA. Refer to the text and the cartoon above.

Section C Polarization in US society

Warm-up

1 Look at the photos and discuss with a partner how they represent division in the USA. Refer back to Section A to find more examples of polarization.

A

B

C

D

Working with the text

2 Skim the text and say which two issues caused the most division in the USA at the time the author wrote the text.

S ▸ Reading difficult texts, pp. 39–40

Here's why Americans have always been divided

Americans mark this Independence Day during a time of turmoil in the United States. While many debate whether to wear a mask in public, the COVID-19 pandemic is surging in most U.S. states. Outraged Black Lives Matter protesters have taken to the streets after the death of George Floyd while in police custody.

But the United States has faced great unrest, uncertainty and divisions before, and even in quiet times, discord is constantly rippling beneath the surface, according to sociologist Todd Gitlin of Columbia University.

Myth of unity

"America has always been divided. I think the myth of a unified country is a myth ... American beliefs have been contested ground from the start," Gitlin says. "I mean, pick a moment in history when we have always not been deeply divided."

In her 244-year history, the U.S. has endured deep divisions between its political parties, and over industrialization, the Civil War, immigration in the late 1800s, women's suffrage, whether to enter the first and second world wars, civil rights and anti-war protests in the 1960s, gay rights, abortion rights and numerous other battles. One reason for that disunity could be found at the very foundation of America, a melting pot of people who do not share a common origin story.

"We're not just a normal nation founded on agreement on a national story or a national consensus, which are usually embedded in a story of national origins," Gitlin says. "America is unified by an ideological doctrine. As a statement of belief, rather than a statement of identity."

Common beliefs

America's identity comes through the common beliefs laid out in the Declaration of Independence, which is celebrated on the Fourth of July. And using the holiday to air out one's grievances is not uncommon.

1 **turmoil** *Unruhen*
3 outraged *entrüstet, empört*
4 **police custody** *Polizeigewahrsam*
5 **unrest** *Unruhe(n)*
6 to ripple beneath the surface *unter der Oberfläche brodeln*
8 myth *Mythos, Märchen*
9 **unified** *vereint*
10 **belief** *Glaube, Überzeugung*
10 to contest sth *etw anzweifeln, etw bestreiten*
12 to endure *ertragen, erdulden*
15 **gay** *schwul, lesbisch*
16 **disunity** *Zerrissenheit*
19 **consensus** *Konsens*
25 to air out one's grievances *seinem Unmut Luft machen*

Good to know

Use a singular verb with the USA:

The United States **has** faced great unrest ...

26 **marginalized** *ausgegrenzt*
27 **occasion** *Anlass, Gelegenheit*
28 **liberty** *Freiheit*
31 **treatise** *Abhandlung*
34 **abolitionist** *Abolitionist/in (Anhänger/in der Sklavenbefreiung)*

Good to know

Frederick Douglass (1818–1895) was an African-American who was born into slavery in Maryland. He later escaped to New York where he became a famous leader of the abolitionist movement. He was also well known as a writer, speaker, intellectual and statesman.

38 hypocrisy *Heuchelei*
40 to embody sth *etw verkörpern*
41 **extended** *erweitert*
51 bigoted *engstirnig*
52 **resilience** *Widerstandsfähigkeit, Belastbarkeit*
52 **adversity** *Not, schlechte Zeit(en)*
53 **equity** *Gleichheit*
68 to **preserve sth** *etw bewahren, etw erhalten*

"People in the country who have felt marginalized or oppressed or cut out of the American Dream have always used the Fourth of July as an occasion to claim their membership in the nation, to claim their freedom and liberty and their equality with others," says Timothy Shannon, professor of history at Gettysburg College.

In July 1848, suffragettes launched the women's rights movement with the drafting of a "Declaration of Sentiments and Grievances," a treatise modeled on the Declaration of Independence. And, before there was a Labor Day holiday, the Fourth of July was central to the labor movement. On July 5, 1852, American abolitionist Frederick Douglass gave his now-famous speech that asked, "What to the Slave is the Fourth of July?"

Founding fathers' ideals

In praising the nation's founders' ideals of freedom, the former slave-turned-prominent-activist pointed out the hypocrisy of their ideals due to the existence of slavery.

"Are the great principles of political freedom and of natural justice, embodied in that Declaration of Independence, extended to us?" Douglass asked.

For some observers, today's Black Lives Matter protests against police brutality and injustice recall the turbulent 1960s, when people marched for civil rights, women's rights, and against the American war in Vietnam.

A history of protest

"In the 1960s, we saw protesters marching in the streets and people boycotting racist companies," says Jamie Goodall, a staff historian at the U.S. Army Center of Military History in Washington […].

"Today, we have protesters taking to the streets and individuals choosing to purchase from Black-owned companies, boycotting companies that contribute to racist and bigoted causes. We can look to these protesters as a sign of American resilience in the face of adversity. They're carrying the torch of their predecessors, continuing the fight for freedom and equity," Goodall added. […]

Fight over facemasks

The fight over whether to wear a facemask to protect others against the spread of COVID-19 could come down to how Americans view themselves in a country that increasingly makes people feel like they have to choose a side.

"Are we freestanding, isolated individuals who are self-made and do not owe collective responsibility to those less lucky?" Gitlin says. "Or are we connected in ways that require some sort of coordinated response to avoidable individual suffering?"

Towards a more perfect union

In some ways, this Fourth of July […] reminds America that although she hasn't quite fulfilled her promise, the work towards achieving those ideals continues.

"It's kind of our annual reminder that the nation was founded on a pretty radical political principle: all men are created equal," Shannon says. "That was not obviously the reality in 1776, in a country that had slavery, in a country where women were denied the right to vote ... But, as a nation, we have been called to live up to that ideal, and to do our best each generation to promote and preserve that notion of equality."

(785 words) From: *Voice of America*, 4 July 2020

3 Read the text closely and do the following tasks.

S ▸ Writing a summary, p. 81
S ▸ Words for tasks, pp. 79–80

1. Point out some of the issues that have divided in the USA during its history.
2. Describe how "Black Lives Matter" relates to other protest movements.
3. Illustrate how the debate over facemasks divides the country.
4. Explain the relevance of the Fourth of July to the idea of equality for everyone.

4 Examine how the author presents her opinion and analyse the means used to convince the reader of her position.

Exam preparation

S ▸ Dealing with a text analysis task, pp. 213–218

Looking at language

5 Work with a partner. Find at least five examples of the present perfect and the simple past in the text. Explain the difference in meaning to your partner.

G ▸ The simple past, p. 284; The present perfect, p. 284

Remember: Present perfect vs simple past

The **present perfect** is used to talk about something that happened in the past but is relevant for the present:
*The United States **has** always **been** a divided nation.*
This means that the United States was divided in the past and is still divided now.

The **simple past** describes something that happened in the past and is now finished:
*Slavery **was** legal in the southern states until 1865.*
This means that slavery was legal until 1865 but it is not legal now.

6 Use the verbs from the list to complete the paragraph, putting the verbs into either the present perfect or the simple past.

be | believe | divide | endure | face | feel | leave | point out | pride | protest

While the United States is a country which …[1] itself on unity, in reality it is a country that …[2] unrest and division since its founding. Beginning with the Civil War, which deeply …[3] the country into North and South, these divisions …[4] throughout the country's history. Marginalized people in the United States …[5] (always) left out of the American Dream and for many, the freedom declared by the country's Founding Fathers …[6] (not) part of their personal experience. Many people, including Frederick Douglass, the former slave and famous abolitionist, …[7] in the principles of the Founding Fathers but …[8] that these ideals were not carried through into practice. In the 1960s, people …[9] against the war in Vietnam, for women's rights, and for civil rights. The desire for equality …[10] (never) the consciousness of the nation and it is what many Americans are fighting for today.

Presentation

7 Work in small groups. Choose a controversial event or a movement in the USA that has recently been in the news. Do some research on the background and present your findings to the class.

S ▸ Presentation, pp. 260–261

Use the following ideas to structure your presentation:

- the event or movement itself
- problems or issues involved
- (famous) people involved
- some historic background
- national or global issue
- contribution to division in society

Section D Immigration to the USA

Warm-up

1 Read the stories below of some young immigrants to the USA, then talk about the following with a partner:

- how it feels moving to a new country with a different language as a child
- the difficulties children experience growing up in this situation
- the problems they might face after high school or university

Hi, I'm Fernanda. I came to the USA when I was two years old. My mom and I left our family behind in Mexico to join my father in Texas, who had already been living there for one year. He made the decision to come because there was so much violence in our hometown.

My name is Juan Carlo and I'm 23 years old. When I was four years old, I got on a plane with my parents and little brother and flew to the USA to escape the chaos in Venezuela. My parents gave up everything they had to give us a chance of a better life. They knew we wouldn't have that in our home country.

My name is Rosa. I was born in Peru and came to the USA when I was ten years old. I came with my brother to be with our mother. After six months, our tourist visas expired but we stayed. I've been to university but I don't know how I'll find a job without the proper paperwork.

Working with the text

S ▸ Reading difficult texts, pp. 39–40

2 Scan the first three paragraphs of the text on pages 149–150 to find the following information:

- the purpose of DACA and the DREAM Act
- who is eligible for the programme

Help for Dreamers?

DACA (Deferred Action for Childhood Arrivals) is a program that allows undocumented people who came to the United States as children to receive work permits. The DREAM Act (Development, Relief and Education for Alien Minors Act) is a bill in Congress that, if passed, would do the same thing. The DREAM Act is simply a more permanent version of DACA. The people who qualify are referred to as DREAMERS.

About 650,000 undocumented immigrants were enrolled in DACA as of September 30, 2019. While the majority of Dreamers are from Mexico or Central and South America, many were born in Asia, the Caribbean, Europe and Africa. The average Dreamer is 21 to 25 years old, female and not married.

In order to qualify for DACA, the undocumented immigrant must have come to the United States as a child (before their 16th birthday), have lived in the US continuously since that time, currently be in school, have graduated from high school or earned a GED, or have been in the Coast Guard or Military and been honorably discharged, and not have been convicted of a felony. Enrollment in the program must be renewed every two years.

Pros

DACA and the Dream Act benefit both the eligible immigrants and the United States. Firstly, and most importantly, most people who are eligible for the DACA program have grown up and been educated in the United States. Tax dollars have already been invested in these individuals and sending them back to their home country would be a waste of this money.

Furthermore, sending them back to their home country would be sending them to a place they do not actually know. They are well integrated into American society, having grown up in the US, and see themselves as American: they *are* essentially American, except that they do not have the documents to prove it.

Additionally, these immigrants are vital to American society. In 2020, some 900 DACA recipients served in the US military, 20,000 were school teachers and 27,000 were healthcare workers, including nurses, home health aides and technicians.

Moreover, the fact that they do not have official paperwork to live and work in the United States means that they can easily be taken advantage of by their employers, for example through lower wages or unsafe work conditions. DACA provides a safe alternative allowing people to work without fear of being sent back to their home country, to pay taxes, and to establish economic stability within their community.

Steps toward legalization that have been proposed through this legislation include the payment of a mandatory fine, payment of back taxes that may be owed, citizenship tests and additional background checks. If the 650,000 people currently under DACA each paid a $2,000 fine to resolve their illegal status and paid their unpaid taxes, several billion dollars in revenue would be generated for the United States as a result.

Good to know

The term **undocumented** refers to anyone living in a country without the appropriate legal paperwork to allow them to live, go to school and/or work there.

1 to defer sth *etw verschieben*
4 **act** *Gesetz*
5 alien *Ausländer/in*
5 **minor** *Minderjährige/r*
5 **bill** *Gesetzentwurf*
8 to refer to *bezeichnen*

Good to know

GED stands for General Education Development. It is a test that one can take to get the equivalent of a high school diploma in the United States.

20 **eligible** *berechtigt, geeignet*
34 aide *Hilfskraft*
37 **wages** *pl Lohn*
42 **mandatory** *verpflichtend, vorgeschrieben, obligatorisch*
42 back taxes *pl Steuerschulden*

48 **to encourage sth** *etw fördern*

56 to **reward** *belohnen*

60 to lessen sth *etw mindern, etw verringern*

61 **overpopulation** *Überbevölkerung*

63 fault *Schuld, Verschulden*

69 to **convict sb** *jdn verurteilen (für schuldig befinden)*

71 **ID card** *Ausweis*

72 to **commit (a crime)** *(ein Verbrechen) begehen*

Cons

Without a doubt, the DACA program encourages more illegal immigration. The first and most important point to remember is that when families make the decision to illegally immigrate to the United States, they do so in the hope that their young children will qualify for the DREAM Act and receive work permits. For example, in 1986 three million illegal immigrants were legalized and this encouraged more illegal immigrants to come to the country in the hope that they too would become legal residents. Between 1990 and 2007, the number of unauthorized immigrants in the US rose from 500,000 to 12.2 million per year.

Secondly, law breakers should not be rewarded with legal status. The people covered by DACA may have come to the US as children, but they are still in the US illegally. By providing a possibility for citizenship to people who have broken the law, whether knowingly or not, the value of citizenship for the people who have gone through the process legally is lessened. It is acceptable for a country to enforce its laws, which are meant to discourage overpopulation and the using up of resources within a nation. The parents of these children are guilty of knowingly putting their families at risk when entering a country illegally. It is not the fault of the United States that they entered illegally.

Furthermore, more people within a community means more competition for the jobs that exist. Employers can then hire people at lower wages because there are so many people competing for one job.

Lastly, these illegal immigrants are eligible for DACA only if they have not been convicted of a crime. The key word here, however, is convicted. There are many young illegal immigrants who do not pay income tax and often commit work-related crimes such as fraud, lying on tax forms, making fake ID cards, etc. Simply because they have not been convicted of these crimes does not mean that they have not been committed. Therefore, without doubt, there are people who should not be granted legal status because they are criminals and should actually not qualify for the DACA program, which in itself should not exist because allowing these illegal immigrants to stay in the country puts the country's existing citizens at risk.

(860 words)

Exam preparation

S ▸ Writing a summary, p. 81

3 Summarize the arguments in favour of and against DACA and the Dream Act.

Listening

30

4 You are going to listen to an interview with Pareen Mhatre, a Dreamer. While listening, take notes on the following points. You do not need to write complete sentences.

1 Pareen Mhatre's age when she came to the United States
2 the kind of visa Pareen's parents had
3 the kind of visa Pareen has now
4 reason why Pareen realized that her visa put her at a disadvantage
5 possible course of action for Pareen when her current visa expires
6 main cause of Pareen's clinical depression
7 her parents' motivation to move to the USA
8 Pareen's course of study
9 Pareen's career goal

Exam preparation

S ▸ Dealing with listening tasks, pp. 123–125

Good to know

An **H-1B visa** allows US employers to temporarily employ foreign workers in special occupations.

An **H-4 dependent visa** is given to family members of the visa holder.

Speaking

5 Discuss with a partner. Which of these quotes about Dreamers and the Dream Act do you agree or disagree with? Explain why.

"To target these young people is wrong … because they want to start new businesses, staff our labs, serve in our military, and otherwise contribute to the country we love. And it is cruel. What if our kid's science teacher … turns out to be a Dreamer? Where are we supposed to send her? To a country she doesn't know or remember, with a language she may not even speak?"
– Barack Obama, former US President

"The Dream Act will only encourage more illegal immigration. … The 1986 amnesty legislation legalized about three million illegal immigrants. But rather than put an end to illegal immigration, the amnesty only encouraged more."
– Lamar Smith, Republican politician

How to say or write it

- I completely agree that …
- To some extent, I agree that …
- I totally disagree that …
- I believe that …
- In my opinion, …
- I understand your point, but …
- That's partly true, but …
- I also think that …, but …

Looking at language

6 Use linking words and phrases to improve the style of the text below. Use the words and phrases in the list or any others that you know.

also | and | because | because of this | but | furthermore | in addition | since | so | then | when

My name is Juana. I am 20 years old. I was born in Bolivia. My birthday is 6 May. I immigrated to the US when I was two years old. My parents and brother also came. My brother was five then. My family quickly formed a new life in the US. Baltimore, Maryland is my home. It is all I've ever known. My parents wanted to move to the US. My mom requested a tourist visa for the four of us. My family was fortunate enough to receive it. I asked my parents why they wanted to move to the US. They said they realized they could give me and my brother a better future here than they could in Bolivia. Now I can see that political turmoil is still rampant in Bolivia. So is poverty. It would make anyone want to leave.

Our ten-year visa expired. I was twelve. At that moment, I realized I was labeled as an "illegal alien". We tried for ten years to gain legal residency. It didn't work. I was told at the age of 16 that I wasn't eligible for student aid for university. I needed a social security number. DACA saved me. I was able to get in-state tuition. This is much cheaper.

Undocumented immigrants come from different backgrounds. They have diverse cultures. They have so much to offer the US. I dream people will realize that.

Remember

We use **linking words** to connect two or more short sentences and to make our writing more interesting. Remember, if the linking word is at the beginning of a sentence, it should be followed by a comma.

Writing

7 The Statue of Liberty bears the famous inscription: "Give me your tired, your poor, your huddled masses, yearning to breathe free …"

Assess how relevant this statement is in the USA today. Use the information in the text and the factsheet in File 16 on page 276 to help you.

Exam preparation

S ▸ Writing an argumentative text, pp. 167–172
S ▸ Words for tasks, pp. 79–80
Writing checklist

Section E The role of the USA in the world

Warm-up

1 Form groups of three or four and look at the pictures below. What do these images mean to you and what is your reaction to them? Are they topics that you think of as specifically American or are they world wide issues?

A

B

C

D

E

F

Listening

2 Before listening, match the following words/phrases with the correct synonym from the list.

to break down | to criticize sb/sth | to feel sad about sb's troubles | to lose power | to make fun of sb | obvious | success | thinking about sb/sth all the time

1 to feel pity for sb
2 to ridicule sb
3 to fall apart
4 evident
5 to fade
6 obsessed with sb/sth
7 achievement
8 to call sb/sth out

31

Exam preparation

S ▸ Dealing with listening tasks, pp. 123–125

3 You will hear an interview with an expert on international relations. While listening, choose the correct answer (a, b or c). There is only one correct answer.

1 What happened in May 2020?
a Donald Trump was elected President of the USA.
b President George W. Bush was mocked and ridiculed.
c Protests took place against police violence in the USA.

2 What was the new feeling that people felt for the United States?
a pride **b** fear **c** pity

3 Which example is NOT given of a moment in time when the world disagreed with the direction of the United States?
a the Covid-19 pandemic
b the wars in Vietnam and Iraq
c American policies on climate change

4 What caused America's failings to become obvious to the rest of the world?
   a the Covid-19 pandemic
   b the election of Donald Trump
   c the election of George W. Bush

5 Between which two groups is there a huge political divide?
   a young and old
   b conservatives and liberals
   c employed and unemployed

6 According to Sarah Stevens, how much is Donald Trump responsible for the USA's current problems?
   a the problems all existed before his presidency
   b the problems were all caused by his presidency
   c the problems became very obvious during his presidency

7 Who do world leaders imagine will take the USA's place if it is no longer the world leader?
   a China   b Russia   c no clear alternative

8 Who brought thousands of people to the Brandenburg Gate when he spoke there?
   a Joe Biden   b George W. Bush   c Barack Obama

9 Why do people around the world watch the USA so closely?
   a because of its great successes
   b because it sets such high standards
   c because of its attitude towards racism, gun violence and poverty

10 What does Ms Reed say shows the unique nature of the United States?
   a the ability to protest   b multiculturalism   c health care

Good to know

George W. Bush, b. 1946, president 2001–2009

Barack Obama, b. 1961, president 2009–2017

Donald Trump, b. 1946, president 2017–2021

Joe Biden, b. 1942, president 2021–...

Looking at language

4 Choose the correct highlighted word(s) to complete the paragraph.

G ▸ Countable and uncountable nouns, p. 297

What will America be like in 2050? According to a new study by the Research Center for American Studies, the evidence shows / evidences show[1] that a large percentage of the population is pessimistic about the future of their country. Over 60% of American adults believe that the USA's influence is / influences are[2] decreasing rapidly in many parts of the world. More than half of Americans see the damage / damages[3] from 9/11 attacks as the most important event in their lifetime and predict that another attack at least as bad as that one will occur by 2050. Just over half of Americans also believe that the news is / are[4] not good as far as the American economy is concerned, and that by 2050 economic progress / progresses[5] will have stopped. Additionally, the data shows / datas show[6] that the gap between rich and poor will continue to grow and there will be a larger lower class by 2050. The USA is / USA are[7] equally divided in its view on how race relations will develop and the police is / police are[8] in the spotlight regarding brutality, especially where minorities are concerned. Politics plays / play[9] an important role in the future of the United States as well. Will the spread of false information / informations[10], or "fake news", affect the outcome of elections more in the future than it already has? The media has / have[11] a particularly important role to play in the future.

Working with charts

Exam preparation

S ▸ Describing and analysing diagrams, pp. 43–44

How to say or write it

The line graph compares military spending from … to …
The figures rose/increased slightly/steadily/constantly from … to …
… jumped/climbed significantly/sharply by …

The line fell/decreased gradually/slowly …
… plunged/dropped suddenly/dramatically

The figures for … are/were slightly/significantly higher/lower than …

The figures demonstrate/illustrate that …

It is (slightly) surprising that …
… but this can be explained by …

5 **Partner A:** Look here. **Partner B:** Look at File 17 on page 276.

Describe the figures in this chart to your partner.

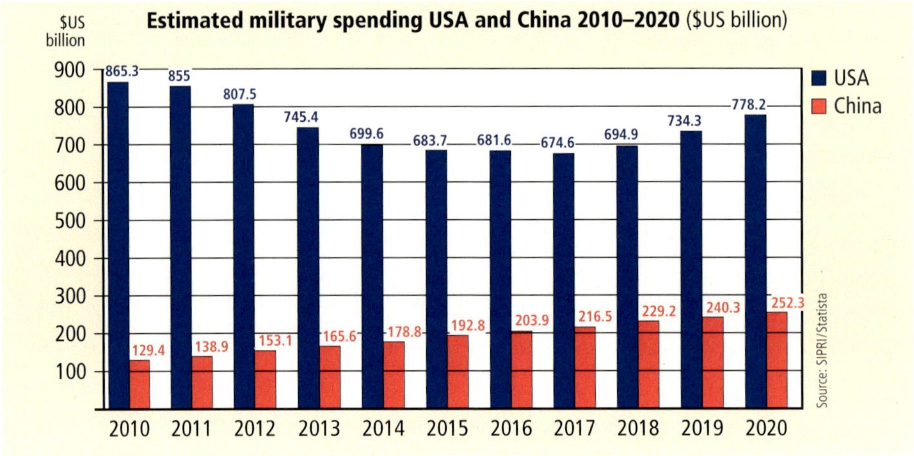

Listen to your partner's description of their chart.
Discuss the similarities and differences between the two sets of figures. What trends do they show?

6 Study the chart below, then do the following tasks with your partner.

1 Speculate on how the relationship between the USA and China will develop over the next 5–10 years. Use the information in the charts to explain your ideas.

2 Discuss whether it is fair to describe the USA as a "fading nation".

Writing

Exam preparation

S ▸ Writing an argumentative text, pp. 167–172

Writing checklist

7 Comment on the role of the United States in the world today making use of the charts and the interview with Sarah Stevens.

Section F The American Dream

Warm-up

1 Form a group of two or three students and write a definition of what you think the "American Dream" is.

2 Look at the quotes and discuss within your group how they do or do not represent your idea of the American Dream and what new ideas they present.

"The road to success is not easy to navigate, but with hard work, drive and passion, it's possible to achieve the American Dream."
—Tommy Hilfiger, US fashion designer

"For many, the American Dream has become a nightmare."
—Bernie Sanders, US senator

"I think the American Dream used to be achieving one's goals in your field of choice – and from that, all other things would follow. Now, I think the dream has morphed into the pursuit of money: Accumulate enough of it, and the rest will follow."
—Buzz Aldrin, US astronaut

"I have spent my life judging the distance between the American reality and the American dream."
—Bruce Springsteen, US singer-songwriter

Working with the text

3 Scan the text on the following pages to find the phrases in the list. Write definitions of them using your own words.

S ▸ Reading difficult texts, pp. 39–40

disposable cash | the gig economy | living from hand to mouth | peripatetic lifestyle | living it large

Nothing more than a dream

32

The American Dream is basically the idea that any American, regardless of their social status or the circumstances of their birth, can achieve anything, if they work hard enough and remain determined to succeed. For decades, success meant having a house, car, disposable cash and a family with whom you could enjoy the pleasures of life. There was nothing that couldn't be achieved if you were willing to put the hours in. However, times change, and dreams change along with them. The myth that anything is achievable hasn't changed, as far as what achievement means. The house/kids/car model is not enough anymore. Nowadays, the image of success is to live a life of constant adventure and passion, travelling the world, doing a job you love without a boss breathing down your neck, having total freedom about where you live and when you work – and how many people are admiring your amazing life, because of course everything you do will be posted on social media. Although the American Dream might have changed, the unattainability of it has most definitely not.

2 **birth** *Geburt*
7 **achievable** *erreichbar, realisierbar*
10 to **breathe down sb's neck** *jdm im Nacken sitzen*
13 **unattainability** *Unerreichbarkeit*

[21] to **attend sth** *etw besuchen*
[25] **prospect** *Aussicht, Perspektive*
[26] **vocational college** *Berufsschule*
[27] staple *Grundnahrungsmittel; hier etwa: Grundpfeiler*
[33] **vocation** *Berufung, Beruf*
[43] to eke out an existence *sich durchschlagen*
[45] **(social) safety net** *soziales Netz*
[49] to **starve** *(ver)hungern*
[52] **aspiration** *Ambition, Bestreben*
[52] quaint *idyllisch; bizarr*
[53] to **prize** *schätzen*
[58] **desperation** *Verzweiflung*
[58] **angle** *Winkel*

In the past, the American Dream was truly gettable, as long as you were white and well educated. For a large number of the population, there was no chance of finishing school, let alone getting a good job. Today, race is less of an issue (although followers of the Black Lives Matter movement may question whether sufficient progress has been made on that front), and education is theoretically available to everyone. Previous generations were perfectly aware that successful people went to college, and everyone else got a low-wage job. Nowadays, attending college is possible for most people ... if they can pay for it. Around 44 million Americans are struggling to pay off their student fees. They start out in the world of work up to their necks in 'good debt', from an education that has given them no real job prospects.

One option for education has always been vocational college. This type of education makes and always has made a lot of sense. Students don't learn about literature, history, and other staples of traditional education. Instead, they learn skills which can be used in the real world, and put on the path to earning a decent salary. In the past, it was believed that vocational colleges were only attended by those who were too poor or too stupid to attend an academic college. That stigma no longer applies, and vocational college education has increased in popularity. However, modern American society doesn't celebrate vocations. It celebrates play. Who wants a boring, stable job, when you could be having fun?

It seems a change in attitude was necessary to be able to accept the changes that have occurred in the job market. Former generations valued job security, worked for a single employer, enjoyed good benefits, and climbed their way up the corporate ladder. Even low-wage jobs, for example factory work, provided a level of stability and a regular pay check. Finding a job that provides a similar level of stability in this day and age is a near impossibility.

The gig economy has eroded job security. Workers are expected to eke out an existence from a series of short-term jobs, getting paid only for the hours they do, having no health insurance or other safety nets, and no guarantee of future employment. This is not only for people who are considered to be living in poverty. The vast majority of workers are forced to accept these conditions. It comes down to accepting this peripatetic lifestyle and being able to pay the rent and feed the family, or living in a cardboard box and starving in the street. Dressing this situation up as having freedom and being able to choose your own working hours is a myth that keeps this cycle running.

Looking back, the aspirations of the 1950s might seem quaint. Wanting a comfortable life with no real excitement, and prizing security above and beyond everything else, is somewhat cute, but truly boring. It's not the life most young Americans would choose for themselves, even if having it were a realistic option. But think about how future generations will judge what is happening now – the vast majority living from hand to mouth, with no security and no escape plan. Lives of quiet desperation photographed from the best possible angle to be shared and bragged about on social media. Young adults acquiring more financial debt than they can ever pay off before they've even started their first job. And all the while, telling ourselves that this is what we want, and that we're living our best lives and being our best selves.

Hopefully, we won't be judged too harshly. How can this generation aspire to savings, security and predictability when they are no longer part of the story? Scrimping and pinching to make ends meet was something our grandparents did. Living it large and buying things we can't afford is an ugly but inevitable part of modern life.

(836 words)

63 to **aspire** *aufstreben*
64 **predictability** *Berechenbarkeit*
65 to scrimp *knausern*
65 to pinch (pennies) *jeden Cent zweimal umdrehen*

4 Summarize the main ideas of the article about the new American Dream.

5 Analyse the means the author uses to convince the reader of their position.

Exam preparation

S ▸ Writing a summary, p. 81

S ▸ Dealing with a text analysis task, pp. 213–218

Working with words

6 Match words from box A and box B to make collocations. They are all in the text.

A	B
social | determined | sufficient | job (2x) | regular | health | safety | the vast | realistic	insurance | majority | nets | option | paycheck | progress | prospects | security | status | to succeed

Speaking

7 Work with a partner and discuss the following questions. Use collocations from exercise 6 where possible.

1 How does the old American Dream compare with the new American Dream?
2 How similar is the new American Dream to the hopes and aspirations of young people in Germany?
3 How are your ideas for the future different from those of your parents and grandparents?
4 Which aspects of the old and new American Dream appeal to you, and which do you find unattractive?

Writing

8 Comment on the statement "The American Dream is dead", referring to the text in this Section and the cartoon below.

Exam preparation

S ▸ Writing an argumentative text, pp. 167–172

Writing checklist

"I SOMETIMES FANTASIZE ABOUT A MODEST HOME AND A FAIRLY NEW USED CAR..."

Working with a song

9 Read the song *The American Dream* by the American rapper, songwriter and producer will.i.am. Then answer the questions.

The American Dream

They be talking equality
But they don't mean it for people like me
They say opportunity
But I don't see none in my streets
Statistically they say I'll be in a penitentiary
So I'ma get on that college track
And go to a Ivy League
I know that sounds impossible but I am possibilities
I'ma jump through all the obstacles and master geometry

I wrote that code, that C plus, plus
Robot autonomy
Yeah, they call me a dreamer
But now I'm at Georgetown University

The American Dream

Everyone agrees the future is technology
And I want to be up to speed
So give me that education I need
Just give me that STEM, that STEAM
Teach me the skills that I will need
To unlock all the roadblocks and get that master's degree
And fill the workforce vacancy
And introduce brand new industries
Because the jobs of the future
Are gonna come from someone just like me

I wrote that code, that C plus, plus
Robot autonomy
Yeah, they call me a dreamer
But now I'm at Brown University

The American Dream (Song by will.i.am)

5 penitentiary *Gefängnis*
7 **Ivy League** *die acht Eliteuniversitäten in den USA*
9 **obstacle** *Hindernis*
9 to master sth *etw meistern, etw bewältigen*
18 **STEM, STEAM** *Akronyme für "Science, Technology, Engineering, (Arts) and Mathematics"*
20 to unlock *aufschließen, entsperren*
20 roadblock *Straßensperre*
20 **degree** *Abschluss*

1 In line two, who are "people like me"?
2 Where do you think the person in the song lives?
3 What are the different meanings of the term "dreamer" in line 12?
4 What is the "workforce vacancy" that is referred to in line 21?
5 What part of the American Dream is the singer referring to?

Research

10 Do some research on the internet, then report back to the class.

- Who is will.i.am?
- What is will.i.am's background?
- Why did he write this song?
- What is the purpose of his foundation?

Section G A vision of the future

Warm-up

1 You are going to read Amanda Gorman's poem *The Hill We Climb.* Before you read, think about these questions:

- What does the title mean to you? What images does it bring to mind?
- Does it give a positive image or a negative one, or something in between? Explain your answer.

The Hill We Climb

Amanda Gorman

When day comes, we ask ourselves:
Where can we find light
In this never-ending shade?
The loss we carry, a sea we must wade.

We've braved the belly of the beast.
We've learned that quiet isn't always peace,
And the norms and notions of what "just is"
Isn't always justice.

And yet the dawn is ours before we knew it.
Somehow we do it.
Somehow, we've weathered and witnessed
A nation that isn't broken, but simply unfinished.

We, the successors of a country and a time
Where a skinny Black girl,
Descended from slaves and raised by a single mother,
Can dream of becoming president,
Only to find herself reciting for one.

And yes, we are far from polished, far from pristine.
But that doesn't mean we are striving to form a union that is perfect.
We are striving to forge our union with purpose,
To compose a country committed
To all cultures, colors, characters
And conditions of man.
And so we lift our gazes not
To what stands between us,
But what stands before us.
We close the divide,
Because we know to put
Our future first, we must first
Put our differences aside.

We lay down our arms
So we can reach our arms out to one another.
We seek harm to none, and harmony for all.

Good to know

Amanda Gorman (b. 1998) is an American activist and poet. She recited the poem *The Hill We Climb* on 20 January 2021 at the Inauguration of President Joe Biden in Washington D.C. The poem was specially written for the occasion and addressed the attack on the Capitol building that had happened two weeks earlier while Gorman was writing the poem.

4 to wade sth *etw durchwaten*
5 to brave sth *etw standhalten, etw trotzen*
9 **dawn** *Morgendämmerung*
11 to weather sth *etw überstehen*
13 **successor** *Nachfolger/in*
18 pristine *makellos*
20 to forge sth *etw formen, etw aufbauen*
21 to **compose** *zusammensetzen*
24 **gaze** *Blick*

Let the globe, if nothing else, say this is true:
That even as we grieved, we grew,
That even as we hurt, we hoped,
That even as we tired, we tried.
That we'll forever be tied together. Victorious.
Not because we will never again know defeat,
But because we will never again sow division.

Scripture tells us to envision that:
"Everyone shall sit under their own vine and fig tree,
And no one shall make them afraid."
If we're to live up to our own time, then victory
Won't lie in the blade, but in all the bridges we've made.
That is the promised glade,
The hill we climb, if only we dare it:
Because being American is more than a pride we inherit –
It's the past we step into and how we repair it.

We've seen a force that would shatter our nation, rather than share it,
Would destroy our country if it meant delaying democracy.
And this effort very nearly succeeded.
But while democracy can be periodically delayed,
It can never be permanently defeated.

In this truth, in this faith, we trust.
For while we have our eyes on the future,
History has its eyes on us.

This is the era of just redemption.
We feared it at its inception.
We did not feel prepared to be the heirs
Of such a terrifying hour.
But within it we've found the power
To author a new chapter,
To offer hope and laughter to ourselves.

So, while once we asked: How could we possibly prevail over catastrophe?
Now we assert: How could catastrophe possibly prevail over us?

We will not march back to what was,
But move to what shall be:
A country that is bruised but whole,
Benevolent but bold,
Fierce and free.

We will not be turned around,
Or interrupted by intimidation,
Because we know our inaction and inertia
Will be the inheritance of the next generation.
Our blunders become their burdens.
But one thing is certain:
If we merge mercy with might, and might with right,
Then love becomes our legacy,
And change our children's birthright.

35 to **grieve** *trauern*
38 **defeat** *Niederlage*
40 to sow *säen*
41 Scripture *die Heilige Schrift*
41 **to envision sth** *sich etw ausmalen*
42 vine *Weinrebe*
42 fig tree *Feigenbaum*
45 **blade** *Klinge*
46 glade *Lichtung*
55 **faith** *Glaube, Vertrauen*
58 **just** *gerecht*
58 redemption *Wiedergutmachung; Erlösung*
59 inception *Anfang*
69 **heir** *Erbe/Erbin*
65 to prevail *siegen, herrschen, die Oberhand gewinnen*
66 to assert *behaupten, versichern*
69 bruised *verletzt*
70 benevolent *gütig, wohlwollend*
73 **intimidation** *Einschüchterung*
74 inertia *Trägheit*
75 **inheritance** *Erbschaft*
78 to **merge sth with sth** *etw mit etw verschmelzen*
78 **mercy** *Gnade*
78 **might** *Macht*

So let us leave behind a country better than the one we were left.
With every breath from our bronze-pounded chests,
We will raise this wounded world into a wondrous one.

We will rise from the gold-limned hills of the West!
We will rise from the windswept Northeast, where our
forefathers first realized revolution!
We will rise from the lake-rimmed cities of the Midwestern states!
We will rise from the sun-baked South!

We will rebuild, reconcile, and recover,
In every known nook of our nation,
In every corner called our country,
Our people, diverse and dutiful.
We'll emerge, battered but beautiful.

When day comes, we step out of the shade,
Aflame and unafraid.
The new dawn blooms as we free it,
For there is always light,
If only we're brave enough to see it,
If only we're brave enough to be it.

(710 words) From: *The Hill We Climb*, by Amanda Gorman

82 to pound *hämmern, schlagen*
83 **wounded** *verwundet*
83 wondrous *wundersam*
84 gold-limned *hier: mit goldenem Rand*
85 windswept *windgepeitscht*
86 **forefather** *Vorfahr*
86 to **realize sth** *etw verwirklichen, etw ausführen*
87 to rim *mit einem Rand versehen*
88 sun-baked *ausgedörrt*
89 to **rebuild** *umbauen, erneuern*
90 nook *Ecke, Winkel*
92 **dutiful** *pflichtbewusst*
00 battered *(an)geschlagen*
95 aflame *in Flammen*
96 to **bloom** *(auf)blühen*

Working with the text

2 Discuss with a partner: What feelings and emotions does Amanda Gorman's poem bring up? Positive/Negative? Hopeful/Hopeless? How do these feelings compare to what you imagined when you thought about the title of the poem?

3 Refer to the poem to answer the following questions.

1. In line 6, what is the difference between "quiet" and "peace"?
2. In line 12, is her reference to the nation positive or negative? Explain why.
3. In lines 14–17, who is she referring to?
4. In lines 31 and 32, what are the "arms" she is describing?
5. In line 34, what is she referring to when she talks about the "globe". How does that relate to one of the Sections in this Topic?
6. In line 50, what is the "force" she is referring to?

4 Find examples of metaphors and allusions in the poem and explain them.

Good to know

An **allusion** is an indirect reference to an idea, event or person.

5 Refer to the list on pp. 211–212 and find other examples of stylistic devices in the poem, e.g. alliteration, contrast, enumeration, ...

S ▸ Stylistic devices, pp. 211–212

Writing

6 Write an "occasional poem" about a news event that moved you in some way – either to anger or sadness or joy. It will be easier for you if it is a topic that is very important to you.

Choose your own style – rhyming or non-rhyming – and length – and present it to the class. Remember to be specific about your ideas. It will be easier for you to write it and it will be more interesting for your readers.

Good to know

An **occasional poem** is a poem which is written for a specific occasion. It can be written to document an event or to comment on an event and it is often written to be read publicly.

Project Creating a video essay

You are going to create a short video essay about one aspect of the USA. Like many other kinds of presentations, a video essay is used to make a particular point or to tell an interesting or a moving story. You can use a mixture of videos, pictures, charts, texts, music and narration to create your video essay.

Step 1

As a class, brainstorm aspects of the four main areas that were discussed in this Topic. Divide the class into four groups and assign one of the four topics to each group.

American history

Gun control

The American Dream

Immigration

Tip

Make sure that you focus on something that really interests you. The more interested you are in the subject, the more engaged your audience will become.

Step 2

In your group, look at the brainstorming you did as a class on your topic and decide on a specific story you would like to tell. Try to formulate a question that you wish to answer with your video. This will help you to focus on the issues involved.

Step 3

Research your topic, focusing on your question. Find out as much information as you can and decide how to answer your question:

- Would you like to make an argument and present a specific point of view?
- Would you like to share information you think might be new to your viewers?
- Would you like to shock your viewers? Move them?

Choose an approach that appeals to the whole group and then come up with ideas to reach your goal.

Tip: fact checking

To give your video essay credibility, make sure that you double and triple-check the facts that you present. Viewers will quickly lose interest in your presentation if they realize that you haven't researched the topic properly.

Step 4

Next decide how to present your information. Would you like to use still pictures, for example photographs or drawings, filmed movement, videos of people speaking, music or written text? Or a combination of some or all of these?

Tip: content rights

For any content you wish to use that you have not created yourself, including photos, charts, drawings, music, etc., you must make sure that you have the rights, or permission, to use them.

- If you know the people involved, you can get written permission which states that they don't mind if you use their material.
- If you want to use copyrighted material, and you don't know personally the person or entity who owns the copyright, you must apply for permission to use the material, which can sometimes be quite expensive.

The easiest solution is to use something from the public domain which means that the copyright has expired (usually around 70 years after the death of the author/composer) or to create the content yourself. There are also websites that offer music and photos royalty-free for non-commercial purposes.

rights *pl Rechte*
permission *Erlaubnis*
copyright *Urheberrecht*

Step 5

Create an outline or a storyboard of your video. Some people like to do this as a written outline, others prefer to create a storyboard, which is like a comic strip of the order in which you would like to tell your story. In either case, make notes on how your video should run. Be as exact as you can about the timing as well as the images, words and music you want to present.

Step 6

Write a script for the written or spoken text that will be included in your video.

Step 7

Now it is time to put it all together using a video-making tool.

Step 8

When you are ready, present your video to the class!

Video essay checklist

- ✓ Have you discussed your topic thoroughly with your group, done your research and come up with an intriguing point of view?
- ✓ Have you planned out your evidence and examples to prove your point and/or tell your story?
- ✓ Have you made a plan for the structure of your video?
- ✓ Have you written and edited your script?
- ✓ Have you got permission for all of the audio/video clips and images that you would like to use?
- ✓ Have your practised reading your text and prepared everything that you would like to record?
- ✓ Have to recorded the video and audio?
- ✓ Have you edited the video together?

33

Words in context

Settlers and Native Americans

settler *Siedler/in*
Native American *amerikanische/r Ureinwohner/in*
colonization *Kolonisierung*
indigenous people *Ureinwohner*
territory *Gebiet*
tribe *Stamm*
reservation *Reservat*
oppression *Unterdrückung*

The European colonization of North America, which began on a large scale in the 17th century, meant the end of the traditional way of life of the Native Americans, the indigenous peoples who had been living on the continent for thousands of years. As the nation expanded westwards during the 19th century, the US government acquired new territories by fighting for them against the Mexicans, by buying them from other colonial nations, or by stealing them from the local Native American tribes. In long treks, such as the Trail of Tears (1838), they were forced to resettle on reservations that were often hundreds of miles from their tribal homeland. Native Americans are a small, heavily disadvantaged minority in the USA, and the history of their oppression by the white settlers and the government remains one of the unresolved conflicts in US society today.

Slavery and Civil War

slavery *Sklaverei*
Civil War *Bürgerkrieg*
Declaration of Independence *Unabhängigkeitserklärung*
colony *Kolonie*
slave trade *Sklavenhandel*
plantation *Plantage*
Confederacy *Konföderation, die Konföderierten Staaten von Amerika*
Union *Union, die Nordstaaten*
abolition *Abschaffung*
emancipation *Befreiung*
African-American *Afroamerikaner/in*
Jim Crow *Gesetze in den Südstaaten, die die Rassentrennung befestigten*
segregation *Rassentrennung*
Civil Rights Movement *Bürgerrechtsbewegung*
equal rights *Gleichberechtigung*

The Declaration of Independence (1776) of the thirteen original colonies against the British government stated that "all men are created equal". However, the wealth of the new nation was founded to a great degree on the slave trade. Over three centuries, an estimated 12 million Africans were kidnapped and shipped to the New World to work on the settlers' cotton or tobacco plantations. The Civil War (1861–1865) between the Confederacy (the southern states) and the Union (the northern states) was fought on the question of the abolition of slavery which had been outlawed in the North since 1804 but was still widespread in the South. Despite the emancipation of all slaves following the defeat of the Southern states, African-Americans still suffered racial discrimination. The Jim Crow laws that were introduced in many Southern states institutionalized segregation between Black and White Americans until the Civil Rights Movement of the 1960s. The Black Lives Matter protests of the 21st century are a continuation of the long fight for equal rights for all Americans.

Immigration

immigrant *Einwanderer/in*
ancestry *Abstammung, Herkunft*
to **escape poverty** *der Armut zu entfliehen*
religious persecution *Verfolgung aus religiösen Gründen*
melting pot *Schmelztiegel (der Kulturen)*
to **assimilate** *sich anpassen, sich integrieren*
national identity *Nationalbewusstsein, nationales Selbstverständnis*
American Dream *der amerikanische Traum*
sacrifice *Verzicht*

Huge waves of immigrants came to the USA from Europe following the Civil War, and many Americans are proud, for example, of their Irish or Italian ancestry. Many Irish people emigrated to escape poverty and others, such as Jewish families from Russia or Germany, fled from religious persecution. The USA was seen as a "melting pot", where all nationalities could assimilate to create one American national identity.

After the Second World War, new waves of immigrants from Asia and Latin America moved to the USA in search of the American Dream, the idea that anyone, regardless of their background, can create a better life for themselves and their family through hard work and sacrifice.

The so-called Hispanics are now the largest single ethnic minority in the USA, and many would nowadays describe the USA as a "salad bowl": it is a country of enormous ethnic diversity and many immigrant groups are very proud to be Americans yet at the same time maintain their ethnic identity.

Hispanic *Hispano-Amerikaner/in*
salad bowl *Salatschüssel*
ethnic diversity *ethnische Vielfalt*
ethnic identity *ethnische Identität*

Polarization in the USA

Immigration control is one of the issues that divides American society today. The attraction of the American way of life means that millions of undocumented immigrants now live in the country illegally, working mostly in low-paid jobs. Whether the government should build a border wall on the Mexican border and how to deal with Dreamers, the children of illegal immigrants are two questions that are hotly debated.

Gun control is another highly controversial issue.
The Second Amendment to the Constitution, which gives Americans the right to own and bear arms, is enshrined in the Bill of Rights. Its supporters believe that Americans should continue to have the right to own and carry firearms. Opponents would like gun ownership to be more strictly regulated. There are regulations prohibiting people who have violated certain laws from possessing firearms, and there are also local state laws which require people to submit to a background check if they want to buy a gun. There is, however, a loophole in the law that allows people to avoid background checks.

The conservative Republican Party and the slightly more liberal Democratic Party represent opposing views on almost all political debates: divisions on issues such as racism, immigration, health care, law enforcement and individual freedom usually run along party lines.

immigration control *Einwanderungskontrolle*
undocumented immigrant *Einwanderer/in ohne Papiere*
border wall *Grenzmauer*
Dreamer *minderjährige/r illegale/r Einwanderer/in*
illegal immigrant *illegale/r Einwanderer/in*
gun control *Reglementierung von Waffenbesitz*
Second Amendment *zweiter Zusatz zur amerikanischen Verfassung*
to **bear arms** *Waffen tragen*
Bill of Rights *die ersten 10 Ergänzungen zur amerikanischen Verfassung*
firearm *Schusswaffe*
gun ownership *Waffenbesitz*
regulation *Regelung*
background check *Prüfung des Strafregisters*
loophole in the law *Gesetzeslücke*
conservative *konservativ*
liberal *liberal*
racism *Rassismus*
health care *Gesundheitswesen, medizinische Versorgung*
law enforcement *Strafverfolgung, Gesetzesvollzug*
individual freedom *individuelle Freiheit*

The USA on the world stage

Following the end of the Second World War, the two superpowers – the USA and the Soviet Union – competed in the Cold War until the fall of communism in the 1990s. Despite the military defeat of the USA in the Vietnam War, the second half of the 20th century was a time of enormous economic development. The USA followed a foreign policy of promoting free-market capitalism around the world. A dynamic economy and diverse population made the USA the undisputed world leader in science, medicine, space exploration, entertainment and digital communication, leading to criticisms of cultural imperialism in some parts of the world. The USA is also by far the world's largest military power. The "9/11" terrorist attack on the World Trade Center in New York on September 11, 2001 led to the invasion, along with other nations, of Afghanistan and Iraq as part of the "War on Terror". These costly and bloody military interventions came to an end with the final withdrawal from Afghanistan in 2021. The increase in the economic power and influence of China around the world means that the USA may lose its superpower status in the 21st century.

Cold War *Kalter Krieg*
military defeat *militärische Niederlage*
Vietnam War *Vietnamkrieg*
foreign policy *Außenpolitik*
free-market capitalism *freier Marktkapitalismus*
diverse population *vielfältige/multikulturelle Bevölkerung*
cultural imperialism *Kulturimperialismus*
military power *militärische Macht*
terrorist attack *Terroranschlag*
invasion *Invasion, Eindringen*
War on Terror *Antiterrorkrieg, Bekämpfung des Terrorismus*
military intervention *Eingreifen, militärische Intervention*
withdrawal *Rückzug, Abzug*
influence *Einfluss*
superpower status *Status als Supermacht*

1 **Read the text and find highlighted words and phrases with the meanings below.**

1 the original inhabitants of North America
2 the document that started the war between the 13 colonies and England
3 the campaign during the 1960s for equal rights for African-Americans
4 the belief that you can achieve a better life through hard work and perseverance
5 people in the USA whose families come from Mexico, Central and South America
6 the law which gives Americans the right to buy and carry weapons

2 **Find highlighted words and phrases in the text that match these definitions.**

1 freeing sb from legal or political control
2 separating people from different groups and treating them differently
3 the family or group of people that you come from
4 to become part of a country or community rather than remaining in a separate group
5 a large range of groups of people from different countries and cultures
6 one country imposing their culture on a less powerful society

3 **Copy and complete the table with the correct form of the word.**

Verb	Noun (person)	Noun (abstract)
...	slave	...
...	...	... / colonization
...	settler	...
...	...	persecution
...	...	abolition
...	immigrant	...
...	...	oppression
to found	...	...

4 **Complete the sentences with the correct word from the list.**

reservations | plantations | melting pot | regulations | background check | loophole | superpower | diverse

1 China is now challenging the USA's status as a world ... .
2 Many Native American ... are located far away from their tribal homelands.
3 Slaves from Africa were forced to work on the cotton and tobacco ... in the southern states.
4 States require that people who want to purchase a weapon submit to a ... .
5 The gun show ... allows people to buy guns that are not sold for profit.
6 The mixture of nationalities and cultural backgrounds in the USA was thought of as a ... for many years.
7 The USA has the most ... population in the world due to its history of immigration.
8 There are a number of ... that stop people who have violated laws from buying firearms.

Writing an argumentative text

In the case of a **written discussion**, you will be expected to **objectively** weigh up the pros and cons of a situation and to come to a well-founded conclusion. Basically, the subject will either be controversial or be a question requiring you to give an answer.

Good to know

As part of your ***Abitur*** exam, you have the choice of whether to write a **written discussion** or **comment**, or to do a **creative writing task**.

Example task:
Discuss the pros and cons of introducing stricter gun control in the USA.

In the case of the **comment**, the task requires a well-argued **personal opinion piece** based on a situation or an hypothesis.

Planning

Step 1: Analysis

Analyse the question carefully by reading it several times to identify whether you are being asked to produce a **written discussion** or a **comment**.

The **verbs** used in the **task instructions** tell you exactly how the task should be done, i.e. which type of text you should write.

S ▸ Words for tasks, pp. 79–80

Instruction	Examples	Approach
Comment		
comment on / give your opinion	*Comment on whether stricter gun regulation could reduce gun-related violence in the USA.*	Formulate your position clearly (for/against/ undecided) and justify it comprehensively with arguments.
Written discussion		
discuss / weigh up the pros and cons	*There have repeatedly been calls for stricter gun control in the USA. Discuss the pros and cons of introducing stricter gun control in the USA.*	Analyse and balance opposing positions or aspects in detail and come to a justified conclusion.
evaluate / assess	*Evaluate arguments for and against stricter gun control in the USA.*	

You can find more help on writing **comments** in the PagePlayer app.

Good to know

If the question asks you to **discuss** an issue, you're not necessarily being asked for your own opinion.

NOTE: The following pages deal with **written discussions** and explain what is expected for the **example task** above.

Step 2: Brainstorming

A mind map is a very useful support tool when collecting and structuring your ideas. Identify the **pros** (= benefits/advantages) and **cons** (= downsides/disadvantages) to help you collect your arguments.

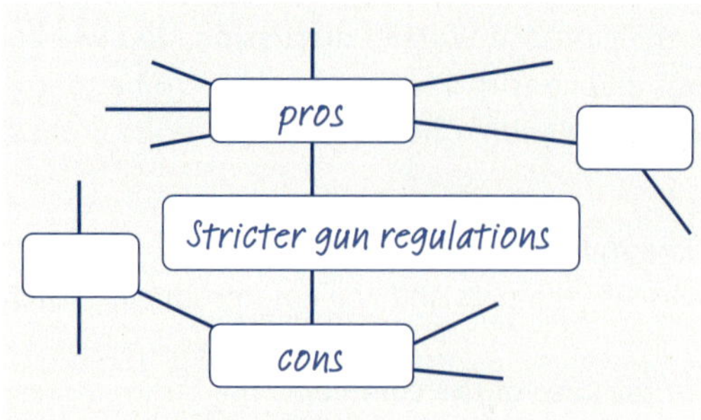

Exercise 1

▸ You can find further arguments in Topic 4, Section B.

Copy the mind map on the topic of *Stricter gun regulations* to your notes and complete it by writing down all your ideas for the main topics as keywords.

Step 3: Structure of the main body

Decide in **which order** you want your ideas from the mind map to appear by giving each point a number. This will help to structure the body of your text. There are several different methods you can use to help you.

Hourglass method
1 Introduction
2 Pro arguments
3 Con arguments
4 Conclusion

Note: Whichever method you decide to use, start with the position that you personally **do not agree with**. We recommend starting with the weakest argument and moving towards the strongest one, as readers tend to remember the final point better. Support each argument with facts and examples.

Zigzag method
1 Introduction
2 Argument 1 → Counterargument 1
3 Argument 2 → Counterargument 2
4 Argument 3 → Counterargument 3
5 Conclusion

Exercise 2

Create a structure using your arguments from exercise 2.

a Turn an A4 sheet of paper on its side and split it into three columns under the following headings:

Main argument	Examples	Facts

▸ You can find further examples and facts in Topic 4, Section B.

b Take three pro and three con arguments from your mind map and support them with appropriate examples and facts.
c Decide which of the arguments is the most important and number them 1, 2 and 3 in order of importance.
d Decide which structure you would like to use for your written discussion: the hourglass or zigzag method.

Writing

Step 4: Introduction

In short, the aim of the introduction is to **grab the reader's attention** and make them want to read the rest.

Its main functions are …

1 to present the topic using one of the following:
   a an anecdote
   b a quote
   c a provocative statement or
   d factual classification

2 to connect to the main body using, for example,
   a a direct question
   b an indirect question or
   c an invitation to the reader to continue reading

Exercise 3

Match each example (introductions 1–4 and connectors 1–3) with a function (1a–2c).

Example introductions:

1 *"Guns don't kill people – people kill people."*

2 *Six minutes and about twenty seconds – this is the length of Emma Gonzalez' speech that covered the same time it took the gunman to kill 17 people in her high school.*

3 *Throughout US history, the debate on gun control in connection with the Second Amendment has divided the nation.*

4 *Let's face it: gun control means control.*

Example connectors:

1 *Let's take a closer look at the issue.*

2 *So what exactly are the pros and cons of introducing stricter gun regulations?*

3 *At this point, you may be asking yourself what the pros and cons really are.*

Step 5a: Main body – topic sentences

Every argument should be given its own paragraph, and each paragraph should begin with a strong **topic sentence** which tells the reader what the paragraph will be about.

To develop the argument, follow the topic sentence with a plausible **explanation** and one or two **examples** to illustrate it. Wherever possible you should use **factual arguments** to make your point.

Important: In the main body, there is no place for your personal opinion – this should not be given until the conclusion.

Example introductions:

Proponents state that the more guns there are in society, the more likely it is they will be used.

Guns are also responsible for an increase in accidental deaths in the US.

Opponents, however, consider controlling guns will not solve the existing challenges created by guns such as crimes or mass shootings.

One of the biggest cons of stricter gun control is that it will not stop people who are determined to purchase a firearm.

Exercise 4a

1 Which topic sentence (a or b) is correct for the paragraph below?

... These laws will make it hard for people to acquire these weapons, limiting the ability of criminals to use them. Currently it is very easy to acquire a gun. This makes it possible for a person with a criminal record to get and use one. Many countries worldwide managed to reduce crime rates because they made it illegal for civilians to own guns.

a With strong gun control laws, the rates of murder and crime will decrease across the country.
b Regulation of gun ownership limits the right to self-defence.

2 Choose one of the example topic sentences above and write a complete paragraph to follow it including an explanation, examples and facts.

Step 5b: Main body – linking words

Good to know

These linking words are also useful when giving presentations.

Provide clarity to your overall arguments using **linking words**. These can help link paragraphs and will help you write your text in a logical, understandable manner without losing your **train of thought**.

Linking words will also help the reader to better understand the structure of your writing and follow your arguments.

Structuring arguments
First, ... / Second, ... / Next, ... / Further, ... / In addition, ...

Introducing examples
For example, ... / For instance, ... / To illustrate ...

Introducing comparisons
On the one hand, ... / On the other hand, ... / Despite ... / In spite of ... / Alternatively, ... / However, ...

Giving explanations
As ... / Since ... / The reason for ... is that ...

Giving results and consequences
As a result, ... / Consequently, ... / For this reason, ...

Summarizing
All in all, ... / To sum up, ... / To conclude, ...

Exercise 4b

1 Divide an A4 sheet of paper into columns for the different types of linking words. Then decide which category each of the following belong to.

a *In conclusion, it is clear that ...*
b *Finally, ...*
c *Moreover, ...*
d *This fact sounds convincing, but ...*
e *Besides, ...*
f *In brief, ...*
g *Therefore, ...*
h *On the whole, ...*
i *Additionally, ...*
j *By contrast ...*
k *Let me start with ...*
l *On the contrary, ...*
m *Lastly, ...*
n *To begin with, ...*
o *Another point ...*

2 Write the main body of your text. Make sure your paragraphs follow on from the topic sentence and that you make use of the correct linking words.

besides *außerdem*
in brief *kurz gesagt*
by contrast *dagegen, im Gegensatz zu*
on the contrary *(ganz) im Gegenteil*

Step 6: Conclusion

The final paragraph is where you draw **conclusions** on what you have written. This might be from a *for* or an *against* stance, or you might prefer to come to a compromise. The one thing you *must* do, though, is adopt a clear position.

It is also recommended that you round off the piece by referring back to the original question asked and making a prediction or suggestion for the future.

Important: The conclusion is not the place to introduce new arguments – it is where you state what your personal position is precisely and concisely.

Examples:

~~*Everybody has to decide what opinion he or she has.*~~

Weighing up the pros and cons, it becomes clear that ...

The pros clearly outweigh the cons.

To sum up, it is very hard to say whether the pros outweigh the cons or vice versa.

Looking to the future, ...

As stated at the beginning, ...

My personal opinion is that ...

to **weigh up sth** *etw (gegeneinander) abwägen*

to **outweigh sth** *(gegenüber etw) überwiegen, schwerer wiegen als etw*

vice versa *umgekehrt*

Exercise 5

Now write your conclusion. Check that you have clearly referred back to the original question. Decide whether it would be sensible to make a suggestion or prediction for the future.

Checking

Good to know

Pages 41–42 provide a good introduction to using a monolingual dictionary effectively.

S ▸ Using a dictionary, pp. 41–42

Step 7: Proofreading

Check your draft version for:
- spelling mistakes
- grammar mistakes
- vocabulary
- sentence structure and
- train of thought

Tip: Use a **monolingual dictionary** for this task. It offers a whole variety of support to help you improve your writing.

Frequent mistakes

Spelling:
there ◂▸ their
who's ◂▸ whose
it's ◂▸ its

Direct translations from German:
find a ~~work~~ job
~~it makes~~ it's fun
be interested ~~on/for~~ in sth
spend money ~~for~~ on sth
~~in the~~ be near / close by
~~At~~ First (of all), …
~~Also~~ Another reason is …
What~~'s~~ about …?
~~the~~ most (of the) people
~~a big part of~~ most (of the) people
I ~~mean~~ think/believe

Exercise 6

Once you have checked your own written discussion, swap it with a partner and check each other's work. Then provide feedback on each other's texts.

Use the following checklist and symbols/letters:

Giving feedback – important rules
Always be complimentary! Stay positive and remember that the idea behind giving feedback is to improve your partner's work. Be specific and give examples of how their writing can be improved.

Correction marks

S	Spelling
G	Grammar
E	Expression (e.g. wrong word choice)
O	Omission (something is missing here)
>	Start new paragraph
?	Not clear what is meant
!	Very important aspect in your text
☺	Excellent work (e.g. content or style)
[ ]	Section unnecessary (e.g. not appropriate or repetitive)
~	Section needs rewriting
( )	Section not convincing

Review

1 Rank the Sections A–G in this Topic based on how interesting they were to you. Then, look back at your work on the overview of this Topic (pages 134–135) and how you ranked them there (page 134, exercise 2). Have your rankings changed? Share your results with a group and tell them what you found most interesting.

2 Look at your KWL list (page 135, exercise 5). Fill out the "Learned" part of the list. Next, look at your "Want to know" list. What do you still want to know?

3 Make a list of ten words in the Topic that were new to you and you consider important to know. Then collect everyone's words and cluster them into groups. Finally, pick a word group and write a paragraph using all the words.

Evaluate

Do this task on your own. How much do you agree or disagree with the statements below? Rate each one on a scale of one to four. The references on the right show you which exercises you can review.

1 = totally disagree **2** = disagree **3** = agree **4** = totally agree

Section	Statement	
A	**1** I can talk about the history of the United States of America, especially related to the treatment of Native Americans.	▸ pp. 136–140, exercises 4–5, 9–13
	2 I understand the difference between the three different forms of conditional and know how to use them.	▸ p. 139, exercise 8
B	**3** I know what the basic regulations are for possession of a firearm in the United States and how loopholes exist.	▸ pp. 141–144, exercises 1–4
	4 I know how to write a summary.	▸ p. 143, exercise 3
	5 I am able to describe and analyse a cartoon.	▸ p. 144, exercise 5
C	**6** I can talk about division and polarization in the United States.	▸ pp. 145–147, exercises 1–4
	7 I understand the difference between simple past and present perfect.	▸ p. 147, exercises 5–6
D	**8** I know what DACA and Dreamers are.	▸ pp. 148–150, exercises 2–4
	9 I am able to discuss a controversial topic, agreeing or disagreeing with the person I am speaking to.	▸ p. 151, exercise 5
E	**10** I am able to comment on the role of the United States in the world today.	▸ p. 154, exercises 5–7
F	**11** I can define the American Dream.	▸ pp. 155–157, exercises 1–3
	12 I am able to talk about why the American Dream may no longer exist.	▸ pp. 155–157, exercises 4, 7
G	**13** I know how to analyse a poem.	▸ pp. 159–161, exercises 3–5
	14 I am able to write an occasional poem.	▸ p. 161, exercise 6
Skills	**15** I can write an argumentative text.	S ▸ pp. 167–172

Consolidation

You want to go deeper into the USA, its history and current situation, and speed up your learning process? Scan this page with the PagePlayer app. There you'll find some suggestions for additional tasks.

Aufgabenteil I Hören

34

1 You will hear an interview about the book *Poet Warrior* by Joy Harjo. While listening, choose the correct answers (a, b or c). There is only one correct answer.

1 Joy Harjo's book *Poet Warrior* is …
a a very personal story about the author's war memories.
b a biography of her spiritual life and her family.
c about all the indigenous people in North America.

2 Joy Harjo …
a survived a traumatic move to Indian territory.
b has a great-grandfather who was displaced from his homeland.
c was expelled from Oklahoma by the government.

3 Harjo thinks the expression "Native American" …
a should not be used to talk about indigenous people.
b is an adequate word to talk about indigenous people.
c should be completely replaced by the term "Native".

4 For Harjo, the 1960s was the time when …
a she was educated at a school with other Native artists.
b President John F. Kennedy and Martin Luther King were politically active.
c she enjoyed late-night parties at her school.

5 As an activist, she …
a expresses her beliefs through her art.
b never uses her art to make statements about justice.
c fights for the civil rights movement in particular.

6 Harjo's art …
a deals with the problems of global warming.
b encourages people to appreciate nature.
c focuses on the special needs of Natives.

35

2 You will hear a conversation between two students about a teacher in California who was suspended. While listening, take notes on the following points. You need not write complete sentences.

1 the reason a teacher in California was put on leave
2 the teacher's intention
3 the school district's comment on the incident
4 the Natives' condemnation of the teacher's behaviour
5 the type of training all teachers should attend

36

3 You will hear four people talking about immigration and the USA. While listening, match the opinions A to E with speakers 1 to 4. There is one more opinion than you need.

Opinions:	The idea of the American Dream …
A	has come true even though the view is very restricted.
B	is only true when it comes to business and making money.
C	is irrelevant for this person.
D	has been very costly.
E	is a very individual thing.

Speaker	Opinion

Aufgabenteil II Lesen und Schreiben

Aufgabenstellung

1 Summarize the aspects of America's racist history which are dealt with in the museum. (Material 1, pp. 175–176)

2 Analyse the means the author uses to convince the reader of the importance of fighting racism. (Material 1, pp. 175–176)

3 Choose <u>one</u> of the following:

A Racism is everywhere. Comment on how racism and discrimination can be overcome in our times.

B You are very impressed after reading about the museum and you decide to write an email to Bryan Stevenson, its creator. In your email, comment on the situation in Germany concerning racism against and the discrimination of various ethnic and religious groups.

Material 1

'Truth-telling has to happen': the museum of America's racist history

[...] A 30ft wave crashes over your head as you enter the museum, dragging you instantly down into the roiling waters. The waves keep coming at you in gun-metal grey surges, with nothing to cling to amid the loneliness of the sea.

Across the giant screen in front of you, words start emerging that ask you to reflect on "the terrifying, tragic and deadly ocean journey" which 12.7 million men, women and children were forced to make having been kidnapped from their homes in Africa and sold into slavery. For about 2 million of them, the voyage to the Americas would end "in a watery grave at the bottom of the Atlantic Ocean".

The cinematic representation [...] forms the start of an agonizing journey through the Legacy Museum: From Enslavement to Mass Incarceration.

As the name suggests, the visitor is taken on a white-knuckle ride through some of the most painful elements of America's long history of racial injustice – slavery, lynching, segregation, all the way to the present-day epidemic of police killings of African American teenagers and the societal addiction to putting Black people behind bars. [...] The new institution [...] lands at a time when racial violence is again on the rise and when "critical race theory" is being used as a ruse to prevent the history of America's racist past being taught in schools. [...]

From the trauma of slavery, the museum's journey takes you through the glimmer of hope that was emancipation and the Reconstruction period into the renewed subjugation of lynching. A wall of contemporary newspaper headlines records such unconscionable events as: "Lynched Because He Didn't Say 'Mr'" [...] and "Triple Lynching in Georgia – Lynchers Could Not Find the Negro They Wanted and So Took Three Others". [...]

Later rooms explore the battle to secure fundamental freedoms in the civil rights era, including Montgomery's own bus boycott. Then the Legacy Museum arrives at the present day.

It is here at the end of the museum's journey that Bryan Stevenson's (*the mastermind behind the Legacy Museum*) holistic vision becomes clear – history must be understood not only as an end in itself but as a cure to the sickness coursing through the veins of modern America.

"This is about changing the larger narrative," he said. "Most people in this country, to the extent they knew anything about slavery, they were taught it was benign and not that big a problem; they knew nothing about lynching; and when you get to segregation, well, Black people wanted it that way, they wanted their own schools. You end up in a place where you just don't think we've done anything so problematic that we need to talk about it."

The new Legacy Museum opens at an exceptional moment for America. On the positive side, last year's wave of Black Lives Matter protests inspired a rethinking of the past that led to scores of Confederate monuments being toppled, including the statue of Robert E Lee that was removed earlier this month in the slave-owning capital of Richmond, Virginia.

But such winds of change only go so far in Stevenson's reckoning. [...]

"We are in this phase where truth-telling has to happen. It's going to require more than taking down statures (...). The harder stuff is, what does it mean that most of us were born in this country at a time when there were legal restrictions on who you could love. What's the legacy of that?"

Then there is the negative side of the present moment. The museum makes plain that the sores of America's racial wounds remain very much open. It records the fact that Black children today are killed by police at six times the rate of white children. [...]

Many of the exhibits trigger chilling parallels with the modern day. A room that examines the myriad imaginative ways in which Black citizens were disenfranchised in the deep south – answer the question "How many bubbles are in a bar of soap?" or you don't get registered to vote – is resonant at a time when voter suppression is once again sweeping the country.

The disturbing images displayed at the museum of white men at public lynching spectacles, their faces contorted into wild grimaces, beg comparison to the expressions of the mob that stormed the US Capitol on 6 January. [...]

Visitors to the new museum are likely to emerge from the end of all this challenged and shaken. But the journey contains a note of healing. One of the final rooms is a large "reflection space" given over to the stories of 400 people who had the courage to stand up against racial injustice. Some are familiar – Rosa Parks, Billie Holiday, WEB Du Bois, John Lewis – others have all but been forgotten.

Stevenson hopes the room will inspire people to action [...]. After the truth-telling comes the remedy and repair. [...]

(798 words) From: *The Guardian*, 19 September 2021

Mündlicher Teil Kommmunikationsprüfung

Partner A: look here. **Partner B:** look at File 18 on page 277.

Partner A: Sequence 1 (your five-minute talk)

1 Describe the photo and the cartoon and interpret their message.

2 Use the given material as the starting point for an uninterrupted five-minute talk on gun control in the USA.

"I want to be a teacher when I grow up."

Partner A: Sequence 2 (you and the teacher / another student)

Discuss the following questions with your partner:

1 Do stricter gun laws hurt the freedom of US citizens?

2 *"If you're afraid to leave the house unless you're armed, you don't need a gun, you need a psychiatrist."*

– Oliver Markus Malloy, German-American novelist and comic artist

Why do people think they need to carry a gun?

Topic 5 The United Kingdom

Section A

The British Empire

Section B

The aftermath of colonialism

"Aotearoa is a name that will unify our country rather than divide it."
– Rawiri Waititi, Co-leader of New Zealand Māori Party

Common-wealth

colonial power

"For better and for worse, the Empire made us what we are, forming our national identity. A country that does not understand its own history is unlikely to respect that of others."
– Antony Beevor, British historian

A disunited kingdom?

diversity

Section F

British identity

Fact: Around 40 % of London residents identify as Asian, Black, Mixed or another ethnic group. Of the total population of England and Wales, 86 % identify as white British. (Source: www.gov.co.uk)

1 Read the facts and quotations about the United Kingdom above.

a Which of them are totally new to you?
b Which of them do you find surprising?

2 Rank Sections A–F on how interested you are in them.

3 The mind map shows you a preview of Topic 5. Copy it onto a piece of paper and add words and phrases from …

a the facts and quotations above.
b the Word bank opposite.
c your own ideas.
d Sections A–F you think are important.

Find information on each Section in the PagePlayer app!

Section C

The Windrush generation

Fact: Between 1947 and 1970, almost 500,000 people from Caribbean countries came to the UK to live and work at the invitation of the government. (Source: The National Archives)

immigration

Section D

Britain´s relationship to the EU

"Brexit was a fantastic example of a nation shooting itself full in the face."
– Hugh Grant, British actor

division

Section E

Independence for Scotland?

independence

Fact: In the late 19th century, Glasgow was one of the biggest cities in the world, known as the "Second City of the Empire".

4 Note a few key words to say what you expect to learn in each Section.

5 Make a "KWL" (Know, Want to know, Learned) list for the Topic.

6 With a partner, compare …

a your mind maps and say why you added words where you did.
b your rankings from exercise 2.
c what you expect to learn in Sections A–F.

Then compare with another pair.

7 Save your work for reviewing when you've finished the Topic.

Word bank

to betray sb *jdn verraten*
decolonization *Dekolonisierung*
to deport sb *jdn abschieben*
hostile *feindlich, feindselig*
independence *Unabhängigkeit*
multicultural *multikulturell*
referendum *Volksabstimmung*
reparation *Entschädigung, Wiedergutmachung*
sovereignty *Eigenstaatlichkeit, Souveränität*
trade *Handel*

Section A The British Empire

1

2

3

4

5

6

Warm-up

1 Describe the images and discuss their possible connection to the British Empire.

Watching

Crossover TV

The British Empire

05

2 Watch the first half of the video on the British Empire and answer the questions. You don't need to write full sentences.

1 What was the maximum amount of territory the British empire controlled?
2 What can be said about Spain and Portugal at the time?
3 What did Queen Elizabeth I really want Francis Drake to do on his voyage? (2 aspects)
4 Where was the first British colonial settlement?
5 What was the source of the riches obtained from the Caribbean colonies?
6 Why was India known as the "jewel in the crown"? (3 aspects)
7 When was Britain's "Imperial Century"?
8 What had future consequences for the Empire?

3 Now watch the second half of the video and complete the sentences.

1 In the decades following World War II, many British colonies became …
2 Many people think that the end of the British Empire was signalled by …
3 The Commonwealth aims to … (2 aspects)
4 The positive effects of the British Empire included … (2 aspects)
5 During the British Empire, people were forcibly brought to British colonies and …
6 The division of British India resulted in …
7 The government of Jamaica has asked Britain to compensate the country financially for … (two aspects)

Working with words

4 Complete the sentences with words from the video in the list below.

dismantled | displacements | legacy | monarch | sovereign | voyages | wealth

1 In the 15th century, explorers made long … (journeys) across the oceans.
2 The Empire generated great … (riches) for the British Crown.
3 By now, the vast majority of the British Empire has been … (taken apart).
4 Former colonies such as India and Australia are now … (autonomous, self-ruling) countries.
5 Historians are exploring the … (outcome, consequences) of the British Empire and how it changed the world.
6 There were a number of … (transfers, movements) of people across continents due to wars and famines.
7 Britain is no longer governed by a … (queen or king), but by a prime minister.

Working with the text

5 Skim the text below and on the following page and choose the correct statement (a, b or c).

In the author's opinion, …
a the UK should make a public apology for its role in the slave trade.
b both Britain and the US have apologized enough for the damage done through slavery.
c Britain needs to do more to educate people about the human rights abuses carried out during colonial times.

S ▸ Reading difficult texts, pp. 39–40

Good to know

The Observer was first published in 1791 and is the world's oldest Sunday newspaper. It generally has a centre-left political view.

The Observer view on Britain's role in the slave trade

37

Nearly two centuries after slavery was abolished, this country has still not fully acknowledged the shameful part it played. We must delay no longer.

"This is the story of this country ... generations of people who felt the lash of bondage, the shame of servitude, the sting of segregation, but who kept on striving and hoping and doing what needed to be done so that today, I wake up every morning in a house that was built by slaves." The most powerful speech of the Democratic convention in Philadelphia was made by Michelle Obama. Her words remind us of the extent to which the slave trade – and the terrible legacy it left the United States – is part of that country's national consciousness.

Not so in Britain. Our political leaders hardly make reference to the dominant role this country played in the global slave trade. British slave traders generated immense spoils by transporting 5.5 million African slaves to its Caribbean colonies, forcing them to work in terrible conditions on plantations in Jamaica, Barbados and beyond. A new database launched last week by academics at UCL, cataloguing the details of 20,000 British slave owners, illustrates the extent to which the historic wealth of the slave trade extends its reach into modern Britain: in the Georgian architecture of cities such as London, Liverpool and Bristol; in businesses such as Greene King and the Royal and Sun Alliance; in the several recent or serving MPs with slave owners in their family history.

4 the lash of bondage *die Knute der Sklaverei*
5 the shame of servitude *die Schande der Knechtschaft*
12 spoils *pl* *Beute, Ausbeute*
14 UCL = University College London

Good to know

Georgian architecture was popular during the reigns of kings George I–IV (1714–1830). The style was also used in former British colonies.

Georgian architecture in London

Good to know

Greene King is a brewery founded in 1799 by Benjamin Greene, who owned sugar plantations in the West Indies. After the abolishment of slavery, Greene received financial compensation. The company is now a partner of the International Slavery Museum in Liverpool.

The **Royal and Sun Alliance** is an insurance company. Many insurance companies insured slave owners during the era of slavery.

Tony Blair: Labour prime minister (1997–2007).

David Cameron: Conservative prime minister (2010–2016).

The extraction of this wealth came at terrible cost. Slaves were shackled and transported in appalling conditions aboard disease-ridden ships. Those who survived the journey were often treated with unspeakable physical and emotional cruelty. Countless lives were lost: by the time of abolition, the African slave population in the Caribbean stood at a small fraction of the total number of slaves who had arrived over the years.

The scars are still visible across Britain's former colonies. After abolition, former slaves were left in abject poverty, a legacy from which no country has recovered. In Jamaica, Britain's largest slave colony, 80% of its population lacked functional literacy at the time it was granted independence in 1962. In Britain, the wealth extracted from African slaves has continued to contribute to our society flourishing long after slavery was abolished.

But unlike in the United States, the horrors of British slavery unfolded on plantations on distant shores and its legacies affect populations Britain has long washed its hands of. So our role in this dark period has been all too easy to obscure. Tony Blair was the first British prime minister to address this grim period of Britain's past, but only after decades of political leaders ignoring it altogether. When David Cameron visited Jamaica last year, he called for Jamaica to "move on" from its past and spoke positively of Britain's role in abolition. He neither acknowledged Britain's role as a perpetrator, nor the fact that even the act of abolition was itself a terrible injustice. While British slave owners were paid huge amounts of compensation by the government – between £16bn and £17bn in today's prices; 40% of government expenditure in 1834 – their slaves were forced to work for a further four years without pay in order to further compensate their owners.

Britain's true role in the slave trade must feature more prominently in our collective history and our national consciousness: not so that our political leaders should constantly apologise for Britain's past wrongs, or that contemporary descendants of slave traders should bear an ongoing burden of shame, but so that we view Britain's role in the modern world in the context of our history.

Our international responsibilities cannot be understood devoid of that context. They are derived not just from the deep injustice of the structural inequalities that divide global north from global south but from the fact that in the past Britain has helped create those very inequalities.

Few would disagree with this principle in abstract. Yet it is rarely played out in concrete debates about international aid, migration and refugee policy. Too often, Britain is portrayed as a benevolent benefactor rather than a country with a burden of debt to some of the world's poorest nations. We cannot understand our role in the world using only a sanitised version of our history.

(719 words) Source: *The Guardian*, 25 September 2016

20 **extraction** *Gewinnung*
20 to shackle sb *jdn fesseln*
21 appalling *entsetzlich, schrecklich*
21 disease-ridden *krankheitsverseucht*
23 **cruelty** *Grausamkeit*
24 **fraction** *Bruchteil*
27 abject *erbärmlich, elend*
28 to **lack functional literacy** *nicht richtig lesen und schreiben können*
32 to unfold *sich entwickeln, sich abspielen*
35 to obscure sth *etw verbergen, verdunkeln*
35 grim *düster*
47 **contemporary** *zeitgenössisch*
48 ongoing *fortlaufend, andauernd*
50 devoid of sth *frei von etw, ohne etw*
54 in abstract *(rein) theoretisch*
56 benefactor *Wohltäter/in*

Exam preparation

S ▸ Writing a summary, p. 81

Exam preparation

S ▸ Dealing with a text analysis task, pp. 213–218

6 Outline the suffering and effects of slavery during colonial times, after abolition and in the present day.

7 Examine the ways in which the author presents her opinion and tries to convince the reader of her position.

Working with words

8 Complete the sentences with the correct form of the highlighted words in the text.

1 It's time to publicly ... the crimes committed by this country during its colonial past.
2 At that point in US history, education and other areas of public life were still .... .
3 Slavery is a crime which is still ... by some countries and individuals today.
4 The Australian government issued an ... for the way it has treated its indigenous population.
5 Former slaves should have been ... for the years in which they were forced to work for free.
6 Despite the formal ... of slavery, many people continued to work for little or no money.

9 Explain the meaning of the following words or phrases in the context of the text. Use your own words wherever possible. Compare your answers in class.

1 national consciousness (l. 9)
2 extends its reach into (l. 16)
3 abject poverty (l. 27)
4 flourishing (l. 30)
5 washed its hands of (l. 34)
6 move on from (l. 38)
7 burden of shame (l. 48)
8 sanitised version of our history (l. 58)

Writing

10 Comment on the quote and on how it relates to the cartoon and the article.

Exam preparation

S ▸ Writing an argumentative text, pp. 167–172

Writing checklist

"Slavery was an important part of the development of Britain ... You cannot understand the situation for black people in Britain without understanding these roots. The wealth generated from slavery is still with us, as is the poverty from centuries of exploitation."

– Kehinde Andrews, academic and author

Section B The aftermath of colonialism

Warm-up

1 Find the correct information about New Zealand in the word cloud below.

- the capital city
- the head of state
- the New Zealand rugby team
- a slang term for a person from New Zealand and a bird from there
- the name for the indigenous people of New Zealand
- the nation's founding document that was signed by the colonizers and the indigenous people
- the island group New Zealand belongs to
- the name of the indigenous ceremonial dance, performed before international rugby matches

queen or king of the United Kingdom
Oceania
haka
Christchurch
Polynesia
robin
president of New Zealand
Three Lions
All Blacks
céilí
Aboriginals
Māori
Wellington
kiwi
Declaration of Independence
Treaty of Waitangi

Working with words

2 Read the leaflet opposite and complete the text with the correct words relating to the British Empire and New Zealand.

Working with the leaflet

S ▸ Dealing with a text analysis task, pp. 213–218

3 Analyse how the author of the leaflet tries to convince the reader of her point of view.

Are you a Kiwi living in London?

Then come and join us on Waitangi Day, 6 February, at 11 a.m. outside New Zealand House.

Why should Kiwis come?
Well first of all because you'll meet lots of lovely Kiwis there! AND because you will be supporting the rights of the ...[1] **Aboriginal/Native/Māori** people!

Are you a Londoner who believes in human rights? Then you should join us too!
So the country you call New Zealand (and we call Aotearoa) was thought to have been discovered and ...[2] **developed/occupied/settled** by Polynesian people in the 1300s, who became the modern-day Māori people. The first European ...[3] **colonizer/explorer/settler** to travel to the islands was a Dutch man called Abel Tasman in 1642 (as you might have guessed from his surname, the Australian island of Tasmania is named after him!).

But he didn't step onto the ground of New Zealand because his boats were attacked and driven away by Māoris protecting their land. The next European to come to NZ was James Cook, who sailed around the islands and created the first map of the country. Subsequently, New Zealand was regularly visited by sailors, missionaries and ...[4] **buyers/sellers/traders**.

By 1840, the British crown was in the process of establishing ...[5] **a colony / a settlement / an exploration**. At first, the Māori welcomed the ...[6] **colonizing/settlement/trading** opportunities brought by the British and agreed to sign the Treaty of Waitangi with them. The Treaty allowed the indigenous islanders to keep possession of the land, forest and fisheries of New Zealand and become British subjects.

Good to know

The **Crown** is the government of a country, represented by a king or queen (in this case Queen Victoria).

A **subject** is someone who has the right to live in a country (usually one which has a monarchy) and is governed by that country.

Sounds OK so far, right? So what was the issue?
Well the first problem was that the Māori translation of the document contained a mistake: the word 'sovereignty' was wrongly translated as 'governance'. In practical terms, this meant that the Māori ended up losing much of their valuable land and ...[7] **autonomy/government/rule**. The imposition of the British economic and legal system, wars over land rights and the introduction of European diseases previously unknown in New Zealand, eventually lead to the impoverishment of the Māori.

And those effects are still felt today: Māori people still face racial ...[8] **discriminate/discriminated/discrimination**, suffer from worse health than white New Zealanders and are more likely to end up in prison.

If you care about the human rights of the indigenous people of New Zealand, then support our protest movement to fight against the ...[9] **injustice/justice/unjustice** committed by the European colonizers on our land. We are fighting for the return of our land rights, increased use of the Māori language and visibility of our culture and an end to racism.

Our protest movement has achieved some successes in the past: some of our land has been returned to us and the Māori language rightfully became an ...[10] **office/official/officious** language of New Zealand in 1987 (alongside English and sign language).

Come and join our protest on Waitangi Day this year and help us build on our successes and obtain all the rights that belong to us!

Working with the text

S ▸ Reading difficult texts, pp. 39–40

4 Read the text below and make notes on these aspects:

- what the Māori Party petition is asking for
- why this is important
- reaction of other politicians

Good to know

The Māori word for New Zealand, **Aotearoa**, is commonly translated as "land of the long white cloud".

Good to know

Use of **te reo**, the Māori language, is increasing in New Zealand, despite fears that it would eventually die out. Use of individual Māori words, proverbs and greetings are being increasingly used in everyday life and there have been recent debates about whether place names should be returned to their original Māori names.

New Zealand Māori Party launches petition to change country's name to Aotearoa

Party wants all original te reo Māori place names to be officially restored across the country in the next five years.

The Māori Party has launched a petition to change New Zealand's official name to Aotearoa, the te reo Māori, indigenous language name for the country.

"It's well past time that te reo Māori was restored to its rightful place as the first and official language of this country," Te Pāti Māori leaders, Rawiri Waititi and Debbie Ngarewa-Packer said in a statement launching the petition. "We are a Polynesian country – we are Aotearoa."

"Aotearoa is a name that will unify our country rather than divide it," Waititi said. "Others are trying to use it as a divisive tool, but this is an inclusive tool, where our ancestors consented to us all living on this whenua [land] together."

"New Zealand is a Dutch name. Even the Dutch have changed their name – from Holland to the Netherlands, for Christ's sakes!"

The petition also calls on the government to "identify and officially restore the original Te Reo Māori names for all towns, cities and places right across the country" over the next five years, completing the process by 2026.

"Tangata whenua are sick to death of our ancestral names being mangled, bastardised, and ignored. It's the 21st century, this must change," the petition reads.

Te Pāti Māori said successive governments and "the imposition of a colonial agenda in the education system" had resulted in widespread language loss among Māori, with fluency dropping from 90% to 20% over the past 90 years.

"It is the duty of the Crown to do all that it can to restore the status of our language. That means it needs to be accessible in the most obvious of places; on our televisions, on our radio stations, on road signs, maps and official advertising, and in our education system." they said.

Over time, New Zealanders, including state officials, political leaders and companies have increasingly come to use Aotearoa interchangeably with or alongside New Zealand – but the shift hasn't been made official.

Prime minister Jacinda Ardern said last year that an official name-change, was "not something we've explored," but that she supported more people using the name. "I hear more and more often the use of Aotearoa interchangeably with New Zealand and that is a positive thing," she said.

"Whether or not we change it in law I don't think changes the fact New Zealanders do increasingly refer to Aotearoa, and I think that's a transition that has been welcomed."

5 to **restore sth** *etw restaurieren, etw wieder herstellen*
10 **divisive** *entzweiend, spalterisch*
11 **ancestor** *Vorfahr/in*
11 to **consent** *zustimmen, einwilligen*
13 for Christ's sake(s) *um Himmels willen*
17 **ancestral** *angestammt, ererbt*
17 to mangle sth *etw zerfetzen, etw verstümmeln*
18 to bastardize sth *etw verfälschen*
22 **fluency** *Gewandtheit, Flüssigkeit (Sprache)*
32 **interchangeable** *austauschbar*

That transition also hasn't been without controversy. On the right, National party leader Judith Collins has called for a referendum on the use of Aotearoa for different reasons – saying the name was being implemented "by stealth," and National MP Stuart Smith has floated the idea of banning its use by public officials. Libertarian ACT party leader David Seymour said via Twitter: "People are already free to use Māori place names. What the Māori Party is saying is it would like to ban people from calling our country New Zealand."

The launch of the petition comes 49 years to the day after the Māori language petition was delivered to parliament – a drive which eventually led to Māori becoming an official language.

"I acknowledge the people who laid down that challenge," Waititi said. "In 2021, we continue to take up the challenge and continue to push further, to ensure that the mahi, the work that they have done, is not lost to the history books of time, but is continued to ensure that we are creating a better Aotearoa for our mokopuna, for the next generation to come."

He said in the first two and a half hours of the petition going online, it had garnered 3,000 signatures. "There is a mood for change," Waititi said.

(632 words) Source: *The Guardian*, 14 September 2021

38 stealth *Heimlichkeit, List*
39 to float sth *etw lancieren*
46 to **lay down** *niederlegen, aufzeichnen*
52 to garner signatures *Unterschriften sammeln*

5 Outline the main reasons behind the Maori Party's campaign.

Exam preparation
S ▸ Writing a summary, p. 81

Working with words

6 Guess the meaning of these expressions from the text from the context.

1 rightful place (l. 5)
2 divisive tool/inclusive tool (l. 10)
3 sick to death of sth (l. 17)
4 a drive (l. 44)
5 lay down/take up a challenge (ll. 46–47)
6 mood for change (l. 52)

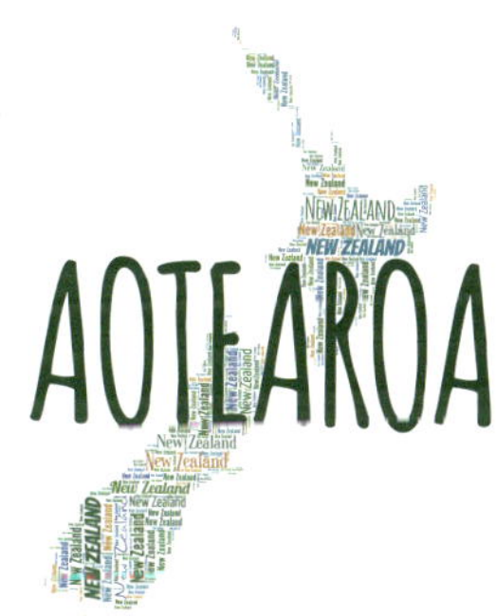

Writing

7 Choose <u>one</u> of the following tasks.

A Taking the text as a starting point, discuss the following quotation.

> *"[The name] New Zealand does erase who was there. I personally think when you use the term Aotearoa, it's more inclusive."*
> – Tina Ngata, Environmental, Indigenous and Human Rights Advocate

Exam preparation
S ▸ Writing an argumentative text, pp. 167–172

B You are an exchange student in New Zealand and have been asked to write an article for your school magazine about a current topic affecting its society. Write the article, using the quotation below as a starting point.

> *"People are already free to use Māori place names. What the Māori Party is saying is it would like to ban people from calling our country New Zealand."*
> – David Seymour (ll. 40–42)

Exam preparation
S ▸ Dealing with a creative writing task, pp. 126–128

Writing checklist

Listening

38

8 **You will hear a radio interview about New Zealand and the Commonwealth. While listening, complete the sentences.**

Exam preparation

S ▸ Dealing with listening tasks, pp. 123–125

1 Maia Parata would like New Zealand to …
2 Although the British monarch doesn't have any political power over a Commonwealth country, the role as head of state symbolizes the country's …
3 Another factor which the former British colonies have in common is that …
4 According to Jamie, the British Empire Games used to …
5 Maia doesn't think that the Commonwealth's charitable projects should be …

39

9 **Listen and choose the correct answer (a, b or c). Only one answer is correct.**

Good to know

The term **decolonization** describes the process by which a former colony becomes independent.

Barbados is an island country in the West Indies and was Britain's oldest colony. It was settled by English people in 1627 and remained under the rule of the Crown until 1966.

1 The island nation of Barbados has just …
  a declared its independence from Britain.
  b replaced the British monarch with a president.
  c elected a new president with extended political powers.

2 The majority of Barbados citizens …
  a have ancestors in Africa.
  b still work in the sugar production business.
  c are descendants of Europeans who came to the island during the Empire.

3 Maia thinks that Britain should pay reparations to Barbados to …
  a compensate people whose ancestors died as slaves.
  b return the material worth of what they took from the island in the past.
  c apologize for the damage they did during colonial times.

4 She believes that …
  a all Commonwealth countries will remove the monarch as their head of state.
  b Britain may remove their monarch as head of state in many former colonies.
  c Barbados' removal of the British crown may encourage other small countries to do the same.

5 Britain's dominance on the world stage has been further reduced by the …
  a effects of leaving the European Union.
  b increasing imbalance of power in the world.
  c the large number of nations leaving the Commonwealth.

40

10 **Listen and make notes on these points. You don't need to write full sentences.**

Jacinda Ardern
1 acknowledgment of Māori culture and traditions (2 aspects): …
2 appeal to other Commonwealth Heads of Government (2 aspects): …
3 symbolic effect of words and gesture: …

New Zealand
4 ways to create a more equal society (2 aspects): …
5 positive outcome of becoming a republic: …

S ▸ Presentation, pp. 260–261

11 **Research and present a Commonwealth country. Include the following aspects in your presentation:**

- location of the country
- period of colonization
- benefits for the British Empire
- independence and the Commonwealth
- current social and economic issues
- issues related to colonization

Section C The Windrush generation

1

2

3

4

5

Warm-up

1 Describe the images above. How do they relate to each other and the UK?

2 Look at the speech bubble and discuss how it relates to the images.

My name is Thomas. I came to the UK from Jamaica in 1948 on the Empire Windrush. I was only 17 and it was all a great adventure. When we arrived, it was freezing cold and pouring with rain, but I was hoping that the hearty welcome of the people would warm me up! And sure enough, when I arrived there was a crowd of people standing by the ship. They must be happy to see us! We had come to help rebuild our Mother Country and I was proud to be using the building skills I'd learnt in Jamaica to help.
But things were different. I felt like the white people didn't want us there at all. People in the shops were very rude to us, and on the building site our white boss called us stupid monkeys and other racist names. I was so disappointed and angry – and also confused. They asked us to come, so why are they treating us so badly?

Working with words

3 Complete the text with the words from the list. Use your dictionary to help you if necessary.

citizens | compensation | deported | detained | immigrants | inquiry | shortage | undocumented

The Windrush scandal

In the wake of the destruction of the Second World War, Britain faced a severe …[1] of workers and encouraged people from former colonies to settle and work in the UK. The 1948 British Nationality Act granted the right to live and work in the UK to any British 'subject', i.e. a person born in a British colony.

The Empire Windrush was a former cruise ship which brought the first large group of …[2] to London from Jamaica in 1948. It arrived with about 800 passengers from the Caribbean on board.

Between 1948 and 1970, almost half a million people moved from the Caribbean to Britain under the British Nationality Act, which meant that they did not need – and were not given – any official documents when they entered the UK. Throughout their lives, they received the same sort of documentation as other UK-born …[3], such as school and work records, but nothing documenting their right to remain in the UK, as it wasn't considered necessary.

In 2012, the British government implemented a "hostile environment" policy which put …[4] migrants under pressure to leave the UK voluntarily by making life unbearable for them, for example by cutting off access to public services such as healthcare and social housing. Members of the Windrush Generation received letters from the Home Office threatening to send them back to a country they might not have seen since their childhood. Some were …[5] in centres for illegal immigrants and then …[6]; others lost their jobs, homes or even died through being denied healthcare.

In June 2020, the UK Equality and Human Rights Commission launched a legal …[7] into the government's hostile environment policy. The Commission found that the government had broken the law and should pay …[8] to those affected. Many people are still suffering from the effects of the policy and have yet to receive any payment.

Working with the text

S ▸ Reading difficult texts, pp. 39–40

4 Skim the text on pp. 191–192 and choose the right option (a, b or c).

Anthony Brown …

a was deported to Jamaica, but later managed to return to the UK.

b studied law in Jamaica and came to the UK to help people affected by the Windrush scandal.

c was affected by the Windrush scandal, then decide to use his knowledge and experience to help others.

Anthony Brown: the man who resisted deportation – then fought tirelessly for Windrush survivors

41

When he applied to university in the 80s, Brown was told to leave the UK. Decades later, finally awarded a law degree, he set about helping people who had been targeted by the Home Office.

In 1982, Anthony Brown, then 21, was hoping for a place to study law. After his degree, he planned to join the police, to help counter the violent style of policing he had seen in television coverage of the recent Brixton riots. Instead, he received a letter telling him he was in the UK illegally and needed to report to Manchester airport for deportation. Brown, who was born in Jamaica but moved to England as a six-year-old in 1967, had been classified as an immigration offender.

His case was taken up by a group of campaigners who were determined to prevent his removal. Lawyers were brought in and petitions were circulated; marches followed and the campaign made the local television news. Brown's MP agreed to write to the home secretary and eventually Brown was granted discretionary leave to remain in Britain. For the activists, it was a triumph. Brown was grateful for the reprieve, but the experience had shaken him profoundly. "After the way the Home Office treated me, I became disillusioned. I was upset for a long time," he says. It was a small chapter in the history of immigration activism, which might have been forgotten had the harsh restrictions of the time not echoed explosively in the Windrush scandal that broke in 2018.

Brown quickly realised he was uniquely placed to offer support. "I knew what they were going through, because I'd faced it. I knew I was going to have to dedicate my time to taking this on," he says. Brown, who had finally managed to take an Open University law degree in his late 50s, stepped up within days to help hundreds of people in Manchester who had been misclassified as illegal immigrants. His experience of facing forced repatriation, and his knowledge of how to launch a campaign, made him an empathic and effective leader. The Windrush Defenders have helped approximately 500 people apply for documentation confirming their immigration status and providing advice to those hoping to secure compensation. [...]

Brown was born in Jamaica in 1960. His father, Derrick, had already left the country to return to the UK. He spent six years saving what he could to bring over his wife and children. [Anthony's] memories of the 14-day boat journey in 1967 are hazy. He has clearer recollections of the bone-deep coldness he felt on arriving in Britain – and he remembers a camera crew filming passengers as they disembarked. [...]

Good to know

The 1981 **Brixton riots** were a series of riots which took place in the London district of Brixton, mainly between young Black men and the police. The riots were sparked by racial tensions based around inequality and Black people being targeted by the police, especially under the "Stop and search" law.

to **resist sth** *sich gegen etw wehren*
2 to set about sth *sich auf etw stürzen*
9 **riot** *Aufstand, Aufruhr*
14 to classify *klassifizieren, einteilen*
15 **offender** *Straftäter/in*
17 to circulate *verbreiten, in Umlauf bringen*
19 discretionary leave *Ermessenserlaubnis*
21 **reprieve** *Aufschub, Gnadenfrist*
28 to **dedicate sth to sb/sth** *jdm/etw etw widmen*
29 Open University *britische Fernuniversität*
31 repatriation *Rückführung*
33 **documentation** *Unterlagen, Urkunde(n)*
39 **recollection** *Erinnerung*
41 to disembark *an Land gehen*

43 unwittingly *ohne es zu ahnen*
47 to **dislocate** *verrenken, auskugeln*
48 taunt *Hänselei*
50 to relent *einlenken, nachgeben*
53 to **tighten sth** *etw anziehen, etw verschärfen*
53 **unbeknown to sb** *ohne jds Wissen*
58 to rectify *berichtigen, richtigstellen*
60 **ultimately** *letztlich, letztendlich*
60 **indefinite** *unbefristet*
61 **heart attack** *Herzinfarkt*
61 to **prompt sb to do sth** *jdn veranlassen, etw zu tun*
74 to **sack sb** *jdn entlassen*
74 to **evict sb** *jdn zwangsräumen*
74 **pension** *Rente, Pension*

His childhood in the Stretford area of Manchester was happy. But when he was 13 his father was offered a university teaching post in Kingston and unwittingly made a decision that would cause life-changing immigration difficulties for Brown. He removed his two younger sons from school in Manchester and took them back to Jamaica to study. [Anthony] had spent more than half his life in England and found the return to Jamaica very dislocating. Having endured playground taunts about his skin colour for years, he was again targeted as an alien, by fellow pupils who called him "English boy". He was profoundly homesick. Eventually, his parents relented and allowed him to return to the family home in Stretford, aged 17, to finish school.

During the time Brown was preparing to leave the UK, the rules relating to Commonwealth migrants tightened, unbeknown to the family; legislation introduced in 1971 cancelled the right to British citizenship for anyone who left the country for more than two years. Brown had been out of England for about four years. Without realising it, he had become an immigration offender. It was only when he applied to university that he discovered that he was going to be treated as an overseas student [...]. When he wrote to the Home Office, attempting to rectify his situation, officials told him he needed to report for deportation. Although ultimately he was granted indefinite leave to remain, the shadow lingered. [...]

In 2012, Brown had a heart attack, which prompted him to re-evaluate his life. As soon as he had recovered, he enrolled at the Open University, aged 52, to start a law degree. "He graduated the month the Windrush scandal broke in 2018. In the immediate aftermath, Brown agreed to speak at a public meeting to discuss the problems unleashed by hostile environment policies. "I told people I'd been very scared and said that I knew people would be frightened. I think that gave people confidence to speak out," he says. They made a call for legally trained volunteers and the Windrush Defenders was set up. Brown and his colleagues occupied three interview rooms in the Windrush Millennium Centre, advising people on how to get documentation confirming their legal status in the UK.

His experiences with an earlier version of the hostile environment were minor compared with what had happened to some of those caught up in the scandal: people who had been mistakenly arrested, detained and removed from the country; sacked from their jobs and evicted from their homes; or denied healthcare or pensions despite decades spent paying UK taxes. Brown is sceptical about whether the Windrush compensation scheme is delivering justice. Since it launched, only 1,196 people have received payments. At least nine people have died before getting a payment; 500 have been waiting for more than a year for a decision. Sometimes, Brown finds it overwhelming to have the weight of dozens of people's difficult experiences in his head. What's upsetting is seeing people whose lives could have been so different," Brown says. "I want to get the Home Office into court."

(957 words) Source: *The Guardian*, 12 May 2021

Exam preparation

S ▸ Writing a summary, p. 81

5 Summarize the events in Anthony Brown's life relevant to his status as an immigrant to the UK.

Working with words

6 Complete the sentences with the correct form of the words from the list.

alien | endure | evict | homesick | linger | offend | simmer

1. My dad had a hard time at work, he … a lot of racist comments from his colleagues.
2. I felt really … when I first arrived in Britain, I couldn't stop thinking about the friends and family I'd left behind in Trinidad.
3. They … us from the flat because my parents couldn't pay the rent anymore.
4. I was the only Black kid at my school which made me feel like an … .
5. Racial tensions had been … for a long time until they finally exploded in the Brixton riots.
6. The police stopped and searched me but I hadn't committed any … .
7. The feeling of not being wanted still … today, I've never felt truly welcome here.

7 Explain what the author wants to express in the highlighted parts of the text. Re-write the sentence using your own words to express the same meaning. Compare your results with the class.

Listening

8 Listen to six people connected to the Windrush generation. Read the statements below. While listening, match the statements A to H with the speakers 1 to 6. There are two more statements than you need.

42

Headings	
A	Juggling different identities
B	The pain of homesickness
C	The battle to be taken seriously
D	You can't hate what you don't know
E	Experiencing discrimination whoever you are
F	Racism ties us to the past
G	Losing the race you couldn't compete in
H	A childhood trauma

Exam preparation

S ▸ Dealing with listening tasks, pp. 123–125

coolie *taboo* offensive word sometimes used by Europeans to describe workers in foreign countries

Person	Statement

Writing

9 Comment on the quote in the context of the history of the British Empire up to the present day.

"The Windrush era is a very important part of British history as it helps us understand how and why we became the multicultural society we are today, and also helps us understand the history of race relations in this country."

– Naomie Harris, British actor

Exam preparation

S ▸ Writing an argumentative text, pp. 167–172

Writing checklist

Section D Britain's relationship to the EU

Warm-up

1 Work in groups. Describe the images above. Share what you know about the topic with the class.

Working with words

2 Complete the text with the correct form of the word in brackets.

Good to know

Brexit stands for "**Br**itish **exit**" and refers to the process of the United Kingdom leaving the European Union.

The **European Economic Community (EEC)** was the predecessor organization of the European Union from 1958–1993.

distorted *verzerrt*
curved *gekrümmt*

In 1973, the UK joined the European Economic Community (EEC). Two years later, a referendum was held asking whether people thought the UK should remain in the EEC, and the result was ...[1] (approximate) 67% in favour of remaining. However, there remained a ...[2] (voice) minority of Eurosceptic politicians who spread anti-EU sentiment. Furthermore, conservative and Eurosceptic media outlets helped spread anti-EU sentiment with untrue or distorted stories about the EU and ridiculous laws it was allegedly going to force on Britain, such as ...[3] (ban) curved bananas.

In 2015, the British prime minister David Cameron, who believed that Britain should stay in the EU, announced that the country would hold a referendum on Britain's ...[4] (member) of the EU and people could vote to either leave the EU or remain in it. The campaign to remain in the European Union was largely supported by the government at the time, as well as the opposition Labour and Liberal Democrat parties.

The campaign to leave the EU was partly ...[5] (drive) by the right-wing Eurosceptic United Kingdom Independence Party (UKIP) and other figures in the Conservative party such as Boris Johnson. The Leave campaign was criticized for using ...[6] (exaggerate) or false facts in its campaign.

The vote on 23 June 2016 resulted in a narrow victory for leaving the EU (Leave: 51.9%; Remain: 48.1%). After the result, David Cameron resigned and Theresa May became prime minister. After a long period of ...[7] (negotiate) setting out Britain's future relationship with the EU, Britain finally left the EU on 31 January 2020, but the nation remains divided and its future ...[8] (certain).

Working with the text

3 Work in groups. Before you read the text, describe the cartoons and say what their message is.

'He's an ardent remainer.'

'And you voted Brexit didn't you Granddad?'

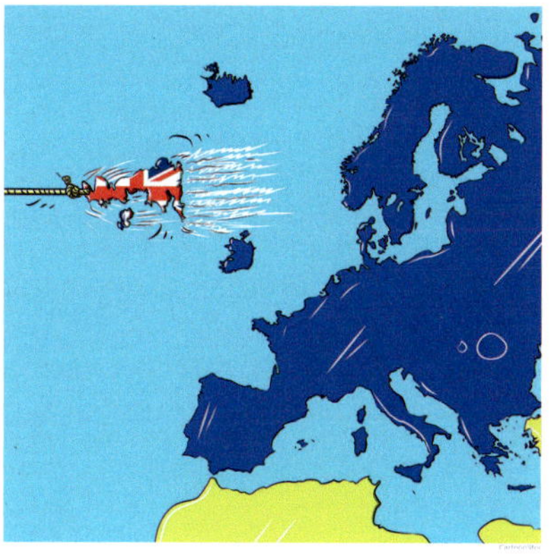

4 Now read the blog entry and comments and match the cartoons to the blog author and each of the comments. Share your answers with the class and say how you reached your decision.

ardent *glühend, begeistert*

Sami's blog **31 January 2020**

Why I'm furious about Brexit!

Dear fellow Gen-Zed people, how are you feeling today, on the great patriotic day that the UK has finally 'gone it alone' and left the EU? At last, we can replace those blue and gold flags with our own glorious red, white and blue one! And go back to the days when people needed visas to travel between neighbouring countries and we could be proud of ruling half the world!

Of course I'm exaggerating, but I'm furious about Brexit – and you should be too! Here's why:

When former Prime Minister David Cameron decided to call the referendum, it was a big risk. I know we had a referendum in 1973 and it went well (the majority of Britons wanted to join); and I know that Mr Cameron thought that the majority would vote "remain" because he thought that the best thing for Britain would be to stay in the EU. And I and many others agreed.

However, did he forget about the large percentage of people over 60, who are nostalgic for the "good old days" when Britain was still a superpower and a group of foreigners weren't imposing their ridiculous laws on us and coming to change our way of life? And did he fail to think about those who were happy to stay in the EU, but wanted to show that they weren't happy with the government and voted 'leave' as a sign that they were unhappy with (non-EU-related) things in our country (such as inequality)? Did he underestimate the extent and power of the lies put out by the 'Vote Leave Campaign', most famously, on the side of a bus? And did he lose sight of those of us whose futures Brexit really affects, who were under 18 at the time and too young to vote?; who were 'out-voted' by older people who may not even see the long-term consequences of their leave vote? Just look at the voting statistics! The answer is probably no ... but he took the risk anyway because he knew that, whatever the outcome, he and his Eton buddies will be just fine.

[3] glorious *ruhmreich, herrlich*
[5] to **rule** *herrschen*
[19] to **underestimate sb/sth** *jdn/etw unterschätzen*

Good to know

Eton College is an exclusive private boarding school for boys, which was attended by several British prime ministers (including David Cameron and Boris Johnson) and other senior politicians, especially in the centre-right Conservative party. It is often used by people who oppose those ministers to refer to their wealth, privilege and distance from "ordinary people".

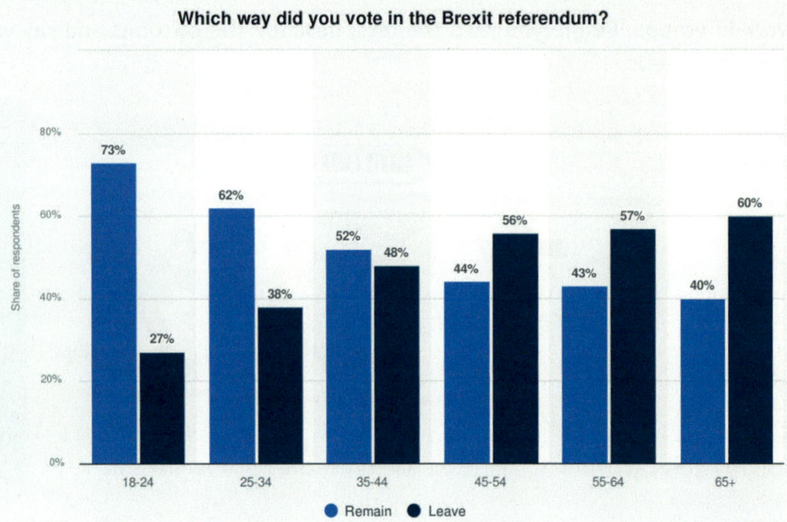

27 to **employ sb** *jdn beschäftigen, jdn einstellen (Personal)*

40 knock-on effect *Folgewirkung*

55 be bound to do sth *etw sicherlich tun werden*

So what have we lost? Well, let's start with my region, the North East of England. I'm from Sunderland, where a large international car manufacturer employs around 6,500 people in the city alone. If export tariffs on cars rise significantly, the manufacturer could move the factory overseas, resulting in significant job losses and economic damage. And for Gen Zed, this would mean less opportunities for apprenticeships, training and employment.

And what about small companies which import and export goods to mainland Europe? The founding principles of the EU are the freedom of movement for people, goods, services and capital, and losing those will have a whole variety of consequences for our generation. As with the car parts example, importing and exporting goods will now involve cross-border checks, which automatically means more paperwork – and costs – for everyone involved, making the UK a less attractive trading partner. And the loss of the free movement of people means that start-ups in the UK can't employ experts from neighbouring countries and young Brits will be less likely to join start-ups in the EU. The knock-on effect will be less innovation and fewer opportunities for us all.

Oh, and did you want to make valuable professional and personal contacts living in one of 27 different countries? Spend a year studying and improving your French in Paris or picking up some job skills during an internship in Stuttgart? Bad luck!

So, I think you've probably understood that I'm not very happy about Brexit by now. My question is: does anyone have anything positive to say about us leaving the EU? Please send me your inspiring ideas to cheer me up (or rant in solidarity!).

Comments:

Pat T.:

You're far too negative about Brexit! I was also too young to have voted in the referendum, but I would've voted Leave. I don't think things will be as bad as you say, although I'm sure we'll see some short-term negative effects. Some businesses might be reluctant to invest in the UK for a while because not all the agreements and final changes have been made yet. But that's bound to change and, while we might be making fewer trade deals with EU countries, think about all the opportunities we will have to become a truly international Britain again and explore trade deals with the rest of the world! Don't forget our historical ties with Commonwealth countries, either. There are many opportunities waiting for us there. Britain was always more of a global player than one that stayed in the small neighbourhood of Europe! Our special relationship with the US is also extremely important and our ties will be getting much stronger in years to come.

This is the start of a new and exciting era for the UK!

Aussieintown:

I think both Sammy and Pat have made some interesting points. I'm an Aussie living in the UK so I couldn't vote in the referendum anyway, but it's certainly been an interesting time ...

A lot of young Brits go to Australia and New Zealand and vice versa as part of working holiday schemes and that's thanks to the Commonwealth, so there are still ways to get out and do some work experience outside your own country (you're less likely to learn a new language, but you will come back with some Aussie or Kiwi slang!). So I do agree with Pat that Britain does have many other connections in the world, and there will be other opportunities for young people to work and study abroad.

However, for me the biggest loser from Brexit will be the environment. If Britain signs trade deals further afield, then won't the carbon flying the products (and extra people) all around the world increase carbon emissions? And secondly, we need more cooperation between countries to tackle international and regional climate issues and not being part of the EU means not having to stick to any joint rules. I REALLY hope the UK will stick to its climate targets through all these changes.

(999 words)

69 **vice versa** *umgekehrt*

77 further afield *weiter weg, weiter entfernt*

81 **joint** *gemeinsam, gemeinschaftlich*

Working with the text

5 Outline the arguments given in the blog text and comments for the UK remaining in the EU.

Exam preparation

S ▸ Writing a summary, p. 81

6 Examine how Sami conveys his attitude towards Brexit. Refer to language and structure.

Exam preparation

S ▸ Dealing with a text analysis task, pp. 215–220

Mediation

7 You are a member of a youth group "Young Futures in Europe" and have been asked to write a report on the issues surrounding Brexit for young people. During your online research, you find Sami's blog entry and the comments and decide to use them for your report.

Write your report in German using relevant information from the blog entry and comments.

S ▸ Mediation, pp. 257–259

Listening

8 **You are going to hear a radio interview on Britain's vote to leave the European Union. Before you listen to the interview, match the words to their definitions.**

1 detached	**a** reason for or purpose of sth
2 in the wake of	**b** so closely linked that they are difficult to separate
3 intertwined	**c** an example from the past on how to do or decide sth
4 precedent	**d** use sth in a positive way
5 reluctant	**e** coming after an event or person
6 shrink	**f** separate from
7 tap into	**g** doing sth slowly because you don't want to do it
8 the point of	**h** become smaller

43

9 **Listen to the interview, which was recorded just after the referendum result, and complete the sentences.**

Exam preparation

S ▸ Dealing with listening tasks, pp. 123–125

1. The presenter asks how Brexit …
2. The expert compares the impact of Brexit on Britain to …
3. In the early 20th century, Britain was … and …
4. After 1961, British governments believed that the country should … and …
5. Now Britain has left the EU, it will need to … and …
6. Britain influenced Europe by …
7. Britain joined the European Union because it …
8. Britain felt that it had a close relationship to … and …
9. According to the expert, in terms of government policy, Brexit was …

Working with words

10 **Complete the sentences with words and expressions from exercise 8.**

1. Many Remain voters asked what was … Britain leaving the EU.
2. Their successful colonial past was perhaps the … for their recent invasion of a neighbouring country.
3. A rise in nationalist sentiment occurred … their victory in the war.
4. The region has always felt … from rest of the country and wants to become independent.
5. After our long membership of the EU, our foreign policy has become … with that of the Union.
6. The EU has always been … to allow those countries to become members.
7. Now that the fighting has ended, the country needs to … its natural resources to generate income.
8. With the gradual loss of the Empire, British influence in the world began to … .

Speaking

11 **Use the quote below as the basis for a discussion on the future of the UK outside the European Union.**

> *"We champion freedom – but Brexit will mean that the next generation is less free to live, work and love across Europe."*
>
> – Jo Swinton, Scottish Liberal Democrat politician

Section E Independence for Scotland?

Warm-up

1 What do you know about Scotland? Do the following tasks with a partner.

1. Name the capital of Scotland and one other major Scottish city.
2. Describe the Scottish flag.
3. Name a typical item of clothing from Scotland.
4. Name a typical dish from Scotland.
5. Name a tourist attraction in Scotland.
6. Name a famous person from Scotland.

Good to know

Scotland and the UK

After centuries of wars, various annexations and unions and separations, the Treaty of Union between the Kingdom of England (which included Wales) and the Kingdom of Scotland was signed in 1707 and the United Kingdom of Great Britain was formed.

Let's spark a debate!

As I'm sure you've also seen, the old independence debate has been in the news again recently with the SNP calling for another referendum on the issue. So this week our readers' debate is between a lad from Lerwick and a lass from Glasgow! And once you've read what they think, we want to know what you think, so please visit our forum and have a debate!

Our debate question this week is: Should Scotland become independent from the rest of the UK?

Finn's view

It's time for us to go it alone, Scotland!

Until recently, I'd kind of sat on the fence about the independence issue and if I'd been able to vote in the first independence referendum, in 2014, I'm not sure which way I would've voted. Of course, it's always been a bit frustrating for Scotland that whoever wins elections in England will basically rule the whole of the UK because most UK citizens live there. However, while I've never been very fond of the government in Westminster, I was happy with our devolved parliament and being able to run many things for ourselves.

AND the UK was a member of the European Union after all, so I felt we could be proudly Scottish and British as part of a diverse group of nations.

But now that the UK has left the EU – and forced Scotland to leave with it – I think it's time for Scotland to take the bull by the horns and just leave the UK! The fact that a majority of Scottish voters wanted to stay in the EU but our

Good to know

The official languages in Scotland are English, British sign language and two native Scottish languages: Scots and Scottish Gaelic. In Scottish English a number of different words and expressions are used, many derived from the ancient Scots language. Examples include *aye* for yes, *naw* for no and *bonnie* for beautiful.

[17] **devolved** *dezentralisiert*

Good to know

All four nations of the UK were once run centrally from Westminster. In 1997, Scotland held a public vote on **devolution**: delegating some powers to local bodies. This led to the creation of the elected Scottish Parliament in Edinburgh. Scotland's **devolved parliament** is now responsible for running many of its own affairs such as education and housing. However, some policy areas remain in the hands of the Westminster government, such as defence and immigration.

39 **firm** *fest, sicher*
71 to untangle *entwirren*

wishes were ignored by the government in England, says to me that our nations want to go in different directions and the UK is holding Scotland back from a bright future joined together with other nations.

Of course, you can't just join (or re-join) the EU without going through all the economic and social checks and balances. But within the EU an independent Scotland would be classified as a medium-sized country, with similar interests to other medium-sized countries within the Union, such as financial services and green energy. And in terms of energy, Scotland has got plenty of resources. There's a fair amount of oil off the coast of Scotland, but more importantly for the future there are many sources of renewable energy being developed here such as wind or wave energy.

Another point in Scotland's favour is the level of education of our population; in fact, we're the most educated country in Europe with 45% of us having a university degree! And that means more expertise and creative ways of solving today's problems like climate change or poverty. We don't need to be held back by old England with its head still firmly stuck in the sand of its old imperial past.

Yes, I know that an independent Scotland could well be economically worse off at first and that there would be a lot of paperwork to deal with, but many Scots who run small businesses are already dealing with that in relation to new customs regulations brought in by Brexit! I think it's worth it to get our Scottish sovereignty at last and to take control of our destiny instead of just being dragged along by the rest of the UK.

Prisha's view

Scotland took part in two referendums within quite a short space of time: the independence referendum in 2014 and the Brexit referendum in 2016. I do wonder what would have happened if the Brexit referendum had been before the independence referendum as the majority of Scots voted to stay in the EU. Perhaps we would be an independent nation and new member of the EU by now. But hey, that boat has sailed and we need to look at where we are now and what's best for our future.

We should stay where we are!

However, that wasn't the case and I do think that we should just respect democracy and leave it at that. We wanted to stay in the UK and the UK as a whole voted to leave the EU, so, although I also voted Remain, I think it's only fair that we respect the Leave vote.

And there are other reasons to stay in the United Kingdom and I think by far the most important one is the economy. The rest of the UK is Scotland's main trading partner – around 60% of our exports go there! That's much more than we trade with the European Union and three times that of what we export to the rest of the world! If we left the UK, of course we should re-join the EU, but the benefits of being part of that market wouldn't make up for our trade with the UK.

Furthermore, if we were independent, we'd also need a land border with England and can you imagine how complicated and expensive that would make trade and the movement of people? Brexit has already been a bit of a bureaucratic headache as British laws have become so intertwined with European law and it's a mammoth task to untangle all that. So let's not add insult to injury by leaving the UK, OK?

The UK government also supports us financially with something called a "block grant" because we raise less tax and spend more per person than the rest of the UK! And I hate to say this BUT we're not exactly a healthy nation: our life expectancy is one whole year lower than the rest of the UK – and western Europe! In fact, some call Scotland "the sick man of Europe"! This difference is particularly marked in my city, Glasgow, where poverty and social problems are rife. How would we fund the health and social services that are needed to help people below the poverty line without support from the UK? And what currency would we use? Would we even be entitled to enter the Euro-zone with our poor economy? Your guess is as good as mine ...

I know things aren't perfect in the United Kingdom, but I think we need to stay in it and build our future as a proud nation.

(1037 words)

73 **life expectancy** *Lebenserwartung*
76 rife *weit verbreitet*
78 **currency** *Währung*
79 **entitled** *berechtigt*

Working with the text

2 Outline the arguments given in the text for and against Scottish independence.

Exam preparation
S ▸ Writing a summary, p. 81

3 Analyse how each person conveys their attitude to the issue of Scottish independence.

Exam preparation
S ▸ Dealing with a text analysis text, pp. 213–218

Working with language

4 Match the highlighted idioms from the text to their meanings.

1 to sit on the fence (l. 9)
2 to take the bull by the horns (l. 22)
3 head stuck in the sand (l. 39)
4 that boat has sailed (l. 55)
5 to add insult to injury (l. 71)
6 your guess is as good as mine (ll. 79–80)

a to have no idea
b to delay making a decision
c to deal with a potentially difficult situation
d to make a bad situation even worse
e to avoid dealing with a problem by ignoring it
f it's too late now

Listening

5 Listen to a radio show recorded just before the Scottish regional parliamentary elections and make notes on the following points. You don't need to write full sentences.

44

1 Scottish National Party (SNP)'s promise: ...
2 reason for previous Scottish rejection of independence: ...
3 SNP: why independence is necessary: ...
4 Alistair McDougal: view on UK government (2 aspects): ...
Example: *hard-line*
5 main argument against independence: ...
6 negative outcomes for independent Scotland (3 aspects): ...
7 what USA needs from UK: ...
8 consequence for West if Scotland leaves UK: ...

Exam preparation
S ▸ Dealing with listening tasks, pp. 123–125

Speaking

Exam preparation
Kommunikationsprüfung
Phrases for speaking

6 Partner A: look here. **Partner B:** look at File 19 on page 278.

Partner A: Sequence 1 (your five-minute talk)

1 Describe the cartoon and say how it relates to the quotation.

2 Use the given material as the starting point for an uninterrupted five-minute talk on the issues involved in the question of Scottish independence.

"We are Scotland's independence generation. And our time is now."

– Alex Salmond,
Scottish politician

Partner A: Sequence 2 (you and the teacher / another student)

Continue the discussion about independence for Scotland with your partner:

1 *"I've always been hopeful about Scotland's prospects. And I now believe more than ever that Scotland is within touching distance of achieving independence and equality."*

– Sir Sean Connery,
Scottish actor

Why do some Scottish people feel that their country should be independent?

2 Is independence the right path for Scotland?

Writing

Exam preparation
S ▸ Writing an argumentative text, pp. 167–172
Writing checklist

7 Weigh up the pros and cons of Scotland leaving the United Kingdom.

Section F British identity

Warm-up

1 Close your book and say what comes to mind when you hear the word 'British'. Which famous British people can you think of?

Sadiq Khan, politician

Emma Raducanu, tennis player

John Boyega, actor

2 Compare the people in the photos to the people you thought of in exercise 1. Say what you think is meant by the term 'British identity'.

Working with the text

3 Scan the text and say which issue is being debated. Create an alternative headline for the text in the form of a question.

Emma Raducanu victory sparks debate over multiculturalism in the UK

Some have hailed the tennis star as a model of British diversity, while others see pitfalls in holding her up as an example.

The Twitter bio of Emma Raducanu, whose victory in the US Open on Saturday has sent much of the UK into an extended state of joyful delirium, contains only four words: london|toronto|shenyang|bucharest.

It's a reflection of her pride and ease in her rich heritage which – thanks to 111 thrilling minutes in New York – has opened a debate about multiculturalism in her home nation, where she arrived as a two-year-old from Canada.

After the success of a fresh wave of sporting stars in 2021 – from the Olympics' BMX rider Kye Whyte and weightlifter Emily Campbell to Marcus Rashford, Bukayo Saka and other stars of the Euro finalists football team – Raducanu is being hailed as the face of a new proudly diverse era.

On Sunday Sadiq Khan, the mayor of London, tweeted that Raducanu – who was born in Canada to a Chinese mother and a Romanian father – reflected "London's story", writing: "Here in London, we embrace and celebrate our diversity. And if you work hard, and get a helping hand, you can achieve anything."

Raducanu, who soon after her victory over the Canadian teenager Leylah Fernandez tweeted a picture of herself holding the union flag in one hand and her newly acquired trophy in the other with the words "We are taking her HOMEEE", was congratulated by everyone from the Queen to Nigel Farage.

1 to hail sb *jdn feiern*
1 pitfall *(Stolper-)Falle, Schwierigkeit*
4 joyful *freudig*
7 thrilling *aufregend, spannend*
10 weightlifter *Gewichtheber/in*
20 to congratulate sb *jdn beglückwünschen*

Good to know

The **US Open** is a major tennis competition, which hosts top players from around the world.

Nigel Farage was one of the leading figures of the campaign for Britain to leave the European Union and is known as a right-wing populist figure.

Good to know

UKIP (United Kingdom Independence Party) is a right-wing populist and Eurosceptic political party, which campaigned for Britain leaving the EU. Nigel Farage was a key figure in the party, briefly leading it in 2016.

27 **swipe** *bissige Bemerkung*
28 to allude to sth *auf etw anspielen*
33 **refuge** *Zuflucht*
34 to **illuminate** *beleuchten*
34 **delusion** *Illusion, Täuschung*
35 pronouncement *Erklärung, Behauptung*
49 **exceptional** *außergewöhnlich*
52 to **overplay** *übertreiben*
53 to **hearten** *ermutigen*
56 **inexorable** *unaufhaltsam*
57 figurehead *Aushängeschild*

The latter came in for a barrage of criticism, as critics noted that in an interview the former Ukip leader described crime statistics relating to offences committed by Romanians as "eye-watering", adding: "I was asked a question if a group of Romanian men moved in next to you, would you be concerned. If you lived in London, I think you would be."

Match of the Day presenter and former captain of the England football team Gary Lineker couldn't resist a swipe. "He won't be able to afford to live next door to Emma Raducanu, so he needn't worry," he said, alluding to Raducanu's £1.8m US Open prize money.

But Sport England board member Chris Grant said he welcomed the comments from Farage, and the wall-to-wall positive coverage of the 18-year-old's achievements in parts of the media that are openly hostile to asylum seekers legally seeking refuge from danger.

"Her victory illuminates the reality of Britishness and the delusion at the heart of their other pronouncements," he said. "A girl who has one Chinese parent, one Romanian parent and was born in Canada but came to Bromley at the age of two is such a normal story in this country, and one that we should be proud of."

But Grant, speaking in an individual capacity, said the focus should be on Raducanu herself rather than on anything she does or doesn't represent.

"We have to be mindful about what we place on the shoulders of individuals," he said, adding that Raducanu's mental health had already been the subject of intense speculation following her withdrawal from Wimbledon. "As of today, there's going to be a massive spotlight on her from the point of view of immigration. That's another burden for her to carry, and it's probably not one she wants."

Sunder Katwala, of British Future, a thinktank that promotes debate about immigration and integration, said Raducanu's ease with her heritage was typical of her generation. But he warned people with liberal views on immigration using her as a "gotcha" argument.

"These are exceptional stories, which don't answer the broader public questions about if we are good at identity integration, equal opportunity and shared identities," he said. "They do give a popular image of the positive contribution of migration and integration, and that has that positive element, as long as it's not overplayed."

Grant said he was most heartened by the images of celebration beamed from Raducanu's tennis club, which included families of colour. "That a tennis club is a diverse place is socially significant in this country, and that's happening quietly and inexorably. That's why the Farage thing ultimately becomes irrelevant, because it's happening anyway. If that integration has figureheads like her, that's brilliant."

(794 words) Source: *The Guardian*, 12 September 2021

Exam preparation

S ▸ Writing a summary, p. 81

4 Outline the positive aspects of holding up Raducanu and other multicultural stars as examples of British diversity.

Exam preparation

S ▸ Dealing with a text analysis text, pp. 215–220

5 Analyse the means and strategies the author employs to present the issue in its complexity.

Working with words

6 Replace the underlined words with one of the highlighted words or phrases from the text.

1. The government has received a large number of disapproving comments for their new refugee policy.
2. The media placed too much emphasis on the fact that he's a gay man: he's an excellent player who just happens to have a boyfriend.
3. It's important to avoid potential problems in putting someone into the limelight so young.
4. I'd rather people focused on my skills as a sportsperson than my ancestry and family cultural tradition.
5. Commentators should be thoughtful and careful about the words they use to describe people.
6. We shouldn't discourage diversity in our club, but rather enthusiastically welcome and celebrate what makes us unique.

Writing

7 Do one the following tasks.

A Comment on the meaning of the following quote in the context of Emma Raducanu's image as a 'model of diversity'.

> *"We have to be mindful about what we place on the shoulders of individuals."*
> – Chris Grant (l. 40)

Exam preparation

S ▸ Writing an argumentative text, pp. 167–172

Writing checklist

B You are a member of a pro-diversity group which keeps a blog on diversity-related topics and have been asked to write the next blog entry. Write the entry commenting on Nigel Farage's statement about Romanian neighbours.

Exam preparation

S ▸ Dealing with a creative writing task, pp. 126–128

Writing checklist

Listening

8 Listen to an excerpt from an interview with Michael Andrew and choose the correct answer (a, b or c). There is only one correct answer.

45

Exam preparation

S ▸ Dealing with listening tasks, pp. 123–125

1. Michael Andrew has always felt …
   - **a** a conflict between his different identities.
   - **b** more at home in a Nigerian environment, like his childhood church.
   - **c** that he could easily switch between identities according to the situation.
2. When the national anthem of Great Britain was playing before a match, he …
   - **a** didn't sing along because he didn't feel a connection to the country.
   - **b** sang along because he didn't want to be the only team member not singing.
   - **c** quietly sang the Nigerian anthem instead because he felt more of a bond to Nigeria.
3. For him, the opportunity to play professional sport for his country …
   - **a** wasn't that special.
   - **b** was a great honour.
   - **c** made him feel more British.

Good to know

Michael Andrew is British-Nigerian and works as a teacher in Germany. In the past, he played American football for Great Britain.

Good to know

When Michael Andrew talks about racism in connection with the 2020 European football championships, he is referring to when three Black players were targeted with online racist abuse after failing to score penalty goals in the final match against Italy.

4 Before the European football championships began, he felt sure that the Black players would …
- **a** experience racism from football fans.
- **b** suffer racist bullying from their teammates.
- **c** receive racial abuse should something go wrong during the championship.

5 He identifies as …
- **a** Nigerian, because he feels too Black to be British.
- **b** British, because he has known the country all his life.
- **c** a Londoner, because he identifies more with the city than with Great Britain or Nigeria.

6 According to Andrew, if you want to call yourself a Londoner, you should …
- **a** have been born and brought up in the city.
- **b** think and act in the same way as other Londoners.
- **c** adopt the same mentality as other English people.

7 He believes that London is unique because …
- **a** it's ethnically very mixed.
- **b** Londoners are so relaxed.
- **c** the rule of law is different to other parts of England.

8 He says that he has a "cultural advantage" because he …
- **a** had a very diverse friendship group growing up.
- **b** grew up knowing the languages, food and attitudes of two very different countries.
- **c** can adapt to other countries more easily because he lived among many other cultures in London.

Working with words

9 Match the underlined words/phrases from the interview to their definitions.

to let sb down | a great privilege | deep connection | negative reaction | to know it in your heart of hearts | to say what you think

1. "When it came down to playing for Great Britain, something that is an honour for most people …"
2. "I didn't feel any kind of bond to Great Britain."
3. "… some of the Black boys on the England team missed the penalties and they got the whole racism backlash for it."
4. "I knew deep down that if anything happens they are going to revert to racism."
5. "London has never betrayed me in that kind of way."
6. "(Londoners) speak their mind."

Speaking

10 Research and present a diversity project either in the UK or in your region. Include the following in your presentation:

- information on the target group/s of the project
- what it does
- what it aims to achieve in the field of diversity
- whether you think it is successful and why (not)

Project A documentary film

You are going to research and create a documentary film about a former British colony. Your film should be around five minutes long and include the following aspects:

- **basic facts**: location; capital city; language(s) spoken; population; main religion(s)
- **pre-colonization**: inhabitants; culture; trade with other countries
- **colonization and colonial times**: how colonization came about; how inhabitants were treated by the colonizers; resources or goods the colonizers used/exported; ways in which the country was developed
- **independence**: how it came about; relationship to Britain and the Commonwealth; how the country has developed
- **migration:** movement of people to/from the UK; current situation
- **the country in the world:** famous people/events; exports; tourism

Step 1
Divide the class into groups. Each group should choose one former colony to focus on. Do not choose the USA (see Topic 4) or New Zealand (see Section B).

Step 2
Think about what kind of film you would like to make, for example a cut-out animation film, a documentary film, feature film, …

Step 3
Do research online about your country and brainstorm which information should be included and how your video will be structured.

Step 4
Assign roles to each member of your group; for example, narrator, speakers/actors, interviewer/interviewee.

Step 5
Write the first draft of your script and decide which sound effects and/or music and visuals you need and which location(s) you would like to use.

Step 6
Practise "performing" your film and decide what works well and what doesn't. Edit your script accordingly. When you are happy with everything, start filming!

Step 7
Review your film together and edit out any mistakes or unnecessary material.

Step 8
Show your film to the class and watch the other films. While watching, note down some brief constructive feedback on the other films.

Documentary film checklist
- ✓ Have you chosen the kind of documentary you want to make?
- ✓ Have you researched the subject and found interesting facts for your audience?
- ✓ Have you prepared your roles carefully, noting down what you want to say?
- ✓ Have you edited the material and cut out any unnecessary material?

Good to know

Some Commonwealth countries, such as Canada, Australia and New Zealand, are sovereign states but have the Queen as head of state. Other countries, such as South Africa, India and Pakistan, are republics and have their own heads of state. Some countries, such as Burma/Myanmar and Aden/Yemen, didn't join the Commonwealth after independence.

Tip

Less is often more! Think about which information your audience really needs to know and how you can keep their attention!

▸ Tip: content rights, p. 163

46

Words in context

The United Kingdom

union *Vereinigung, Union*
constitutional monarchy *konstitutionelle Monarchie*
head of state *Staatsoberhaupt*
to **govern** *regieren*
democratic *demokratisch*
to **elect** *wählen*
prime minister *Premierminister/in*
devolved *dezentralisiert*
parliament *Parlament*
foreign policy *Außenpolitik*
immigration *Einwanderung*

The United Kingdom of Great Britain and Northern Ireland is a union of four countries: England, Scotland, Wales and Northern Ireland. The main part of the island of Ireland is a separate country, the Republic of Ireland. The UK is a constitutional monarchy, which means that the head of state is a queen or king who only has limited power. The UK is governed by a democratically-elected central government led by a prime minster in London. Scotland, Wales and Northern Ireland have devolved parliaments which give them control over local issues but not over areas such as foreign policy and immigration.

A troubled union

independence *Unabhängigkeit*
to **partition sth** *etw teilen, trennen*
nationalist *Nationalist/in*
to **pursue sth** *etw verfolgen*
to **accuse sb** *jdn beschuldigen*
discrimination *Diskriminierung*
to **spark conflict** *einen Konflikt auslösen*
peace *Frieden*

In 1707, the kingdoms of England (including Wales) and Scotland signed the Acts of Union forming a single state. Ireland had long been colonized by Britain, but only became a part of the UK in 1801.

However, support for Irish independence grew, resulting in the Irish War of Independence (1919–21). After the war, Ireland was partitioned into the Republic of Ireland in the south and Northern Ireland, which remained in the UK and had a large protestant community who supported the union. Irish nationalists pursued a united independent Ireland and the Northern Irish government was accused of discrimination against the Catholic minority. This sparked conflict in the north during a period known as "the Troubles" (approx. 1969–98). In 1998, the Good Friday Agreement between the British and Irish governments brought relative peace.

The British Empire

empire *Weltreich*
territory *(Hoheits-)Gebiet*
acquisition *Erwerb*
trade *Handel*
natural resource *Rohstoff*
goods *pl Ware(n)*
to **generate wealth** *Reichtum aufbauen*
Crown *Krone*
to **expand** *ausbauen*
sphere of influence *Einflussbereich*
to **enslave** *versklaven*
to **displace sb** *jdn verschleppen*
benefit *Nutzen, Vorteil*

Although other European countries such as Spain and France also had empires, Britain's was the largest and it has had a lasting effect on the world. The main reason for colonizing and maintaining such a large amount of territory was the acquisition of and trade in natural resources and other goods with a view to generating wealth for the British Crown – and expanding Britain's sphere of influence. In order to achieve this, millions were enslaved or displaced and their way of life and culture were destroyed. However, some leaders within colonized countries cooperated – and profited – from the Empire and it brought some benefits to colonies such as infrastructure, schools and hospitals.

Postcolonial migration to the UK

decline *Niedergang, Talfahrt*
to **dismantle** *auflösen*
prosperity *Wohlstand*
democracy *Demokratie*

Following the two world wars, Britain went into economic decline and colonial independence movements grew, resulting in the dismantling of most of its Empire. At the same time, an association of former colonies, the Commonwealth, was formed, which aims to promote prosperity, democracy and peace.

To combat a severe labour shortage following the Second World War, Britain invited citizens of former colonies to the UK to fill job vacancies in public transport, manufacturing and the National Health Service. However, they often suffered racial abuse and discrimination.

In 2012, a "hostile" government policy towards illegal immigrants meant that many people who had come to the UK from former Caribbean colonies experienced unjust legal difficulties surrounding their right to remain in the UK, and some were even deported.

labour shortage *Arbeitskräftemängel*
citizen *Bürger/in*
racial abuse *rassistische Diskriminierung*
hostile *feindselig*
illegal immigrant *illegale/r Einwanderer/in*
unjust *ungerecht*
right to remain *Aufenthaltsrecht*
to **deport sb** *jdn abschieben*

Multiculturalism in the UK

Modern Britain is a multicultural society, although ethnic diversity is mostly seen in big cities such as London, Birmingham and Manchester, which have ethnically and racially diverse populations. A large percentage are descendants of immigrants from former British colonies, such as India, Pakistan, Jamaica and Nigeria. Second and third-generation immigrants continue to enrich British society in various ways such as cuisine (curry is often cited as the UK national dish), art, literature and music. The Notting Hill Carnival, created and led by the British Caribbean community, is an important part of Black British culture.

multicultural *multikulturell*
ethnic *ethnisch*
diversity *Vielfalt*
descendant *Nachkomme*
former *ehemalig*
second-generation *aus der zweiten Generation*
to **enrich** *bereichern*
cuisine *Küche, Kochkunst*
culture *Kultur*

The UK and the EU

The UK was a member of the European Union for 47 years. It left in 2020, as a result of a referendum on its membership in 2016, in which a narrow majority voted to leave. The process of leaving the EU – commonly known as "Brexit" – involved intense negotiation to achieve a withdrawal agreement. To some, the vote to leave the EU didn't come as a huge surprise, given the vocal criticism in the right-wing media and amongst eurosceptic Members of Parliament (MPs).

The majority of young Brits wanted to remain in the EU, but many were still too young to vote when the referendum was held. The long-term repercussions of Brexit on the UK economy and its relationship with the EU may take years to become completely clear.

referendum *Volksabstimmung*
membership *Mitgliedschaft*
narrow majority *knappe Mehrheit*
to **leave** *verlassen*
withdrawal agreement *Austrittsabkommen*
vocal criticism *laute/deutliche Kritik*
eurosceptic *Euroskeptiker/in*
Member of Parliament (MP) *Unterhausabgeordnete/r*
Brit *Brite/Britin*
to **remain** *verbleiben*
to **vote** *abstimmen*
long-term *langfristig*
repercussion *Auswirkung, Konsequenz*

Potential future challenges

The UK faces a number of different challenges in the coming years, from global issues such as climate change and pandemics, to geopolitical threats such as war and terrorism.

The UK is a member of several international organizations including NATO (North Atlantic Treaty Organization), a military alliance which was set up to ensure collective security. Membership implies collective action in the event of an attack on a member state.

Pro-independence voices in Scotland grew louder following Brexit. However, as the rest of the UK is its main trade partner, the risk of Scotland leaving the union may be too great. Long-standing conflicts within Ireland may flare up again, due to potential border issues brought about by the recent division of the island into an EU member and a non-member state.

to **face a challenge** *vor einer Herausforderung stehen*
geopolitical *geopolitisch*
threat *Gefahr*
war *Krieg*
terrorism *Terrorismus*
alliance *Bündnis*
security *Sicherheit*
member state *Mitgliedsstaat*
trade partner *Handelspartner*
long-standing *langjährig*
to **flare up** *aufflammen*
border *Grenze*

1 Copy and complete the table with the missing words. Use your dictionary if necessary.

Verb	Noun	Adjective
…	…	acquired
…	devolution	…
to enslave	… / …	…
…	…	expanded
…	involvement	
to migrate	… / …	migratory
to withdraw	…	withdrawn

2 Find highlighted words and phrases in the text to match the definitions.

1 to try to achieve sth over a long period of time; The region wants to … independence.
2 the act of buying, selling or exchanging goods or services; The UK has signed a new … deal with India.
3 to take apart or break apart; The aim of the treaty is for countries to … their nuclear weapons.
4 to forcibly remove a person from a country; The government wants to … illegal immigrants.
5 unfriendly; The press statement said they would create a … environment for criminals.
6 the effect of an action or decision, especially a negative effect; The … of the attack might include a wider war.

3 Match verbs from box A and box B to make collocations. Then complete the sentences with the correct words.

A	B
bring | face | generate | hold | spark | suffer	a challenge | a referendum | conflict | peace | racial abuse | wealth

1 The government hopes that the new treaty will … lasting … to the region.
2 The Scottish National Party would like to … new … on independence from the UK.
3 A number of immigrant workers … when they arrive in the UK.
4 The government will … serious … to their power in the next election.
5 The discovery of oil off the coast of Scotland continues to … for the whole UK.
6 Partitioning the country may … a serious … .

4 Match the words (1–7) to words of opposite meaning (a–g).

1 dictatorship	**a** benefit
2 disadvantage	**b** democracy
3 excess	**c** monarchy
4 leave	**d** peace
5 poverty	**e** prosperity
6 republic	**f** remain
7 war	**g** shortage

Stylistic devices

Rhetorical or literary devices are linguistic techniques which are used to add effect to a spoken presentation or written text.

Good to know

As a part of the **textual analysis** in your written ***Abitur*** examination, you are expected to be able to recognize stylistic devices and what effect they are intended to have on the reader.

Device	Definition	Example	Effect
alliteration	repeated identical consonant sounds at the beginning of successive words	*"What I recognize is that what we need in this country is strong and stable leadership."* Theresa May, former British Prime Minister	the repeated sounds accentuate what is being said, making it stick better in the reader's/listener's memory
contrast	placing opposing ideas or concepts together	*"If you want something said, ask a man. If you want something done, ask a woman."* Margaret Thatcher, former British Prime Minister	emphasizing arguments or ideas by directly contrasting them with their opposite
enumeration	listing of words, word groups or topics	*"... whose political personality is admired and even loved around the world for our inventiveness, for our humour, for our universities, our scientists, our armed forces, our diplomacy, ..."* Boris Johnson, British Prime Minister	gives an argument emphasis; can also be used to show there are multiple arguments for a theory
euphemism	paraphrasing using more pleasant-sounding words	*"painful engagements"* Tony Blair, former British Prime Minister, describing the wars in Afghanistan and Iraq	avoidance of terminology that could be considered negative
exaggeration	amplifying a message or statement so that it goes beyond what is actually true	*"The problem is that nobody believes him any more."* Edward Miliband, British politician, attacking David Cameron, former British Prime Minister	drawing attention to a statement using escalation; can be either serious or humorous
imagery	(mostly visually) descriptive or figurative language	*"I have as much chance of becoming Prime Minister as of ... finding Elvis."* Boris Johnson, British Prime Minister	anchoring of a clear image in the reader's/listener's mind
metaphor	describing a situation using an image as a comparison	*"This country has become a prisoner to the old arguments of 2016."* Boris Johnson, British Prime Minister	visualization and elucidation of abstract ideas; often used to make the assessment or position of the speaker clear
parallelism	use of similar words or expressions in the same phrase or subsequent phrases	*"Of course, Brexit means that something is wrong in Europe. But Brexit means also that something was wrong in Britain."* Jean-Claude Juncker, former President of the European Commission	emphasizes a single thought through repetition making it more memorable

Device	Definition	Example	Effect
repetition	using the same word or series of words over and over	*" … rebuilding family, rebuilding community, … rebuilding responsibility …"* David Cameron, former British Prime Minister	highlights a single statement and gives it emphasis
irony	making it clear to the reader/listener that the opposite is true	*"To keep insisting that the EU is about economics is like saying the Italian Mafia is interested in olive oil."* Boris Johnson, British Prime Minister	expresses open or indirect criticism or derision of a thing or person
pun	deliberate use of concepts with two meanings where both meanings are possible	*"Brexit stops Britain from being Great Britain."* Layla Moran, British politician	creation of a humorous effect using a deliberate but surprising change of meaning in one word
rhetorical question	a question where no answer is expected, because the answer is obvious	*"Is that what you want for your children? For other countries to race ahead of us, …? What folly that would be."* John Major, former British Prime Minister	the obviousness or absurdity of a statement is emphasized by seemingly questioning it

Exercise 1

Identify which stylistic device is used in each of the following quotations.

1 *"Education is not the privilege of the few but the right of the many."*
Tony Blair, former British Prime Minister

2 *"Real change is when everyone pulls together, comes together, works together."*
David Cameron, former British Prime Minister

3 *" … we shall defend our island, whatever the cost may be, we shall fight on the beaches, we shall fight on the landing grounds, we shall fight in the fields and in the streets, we shall fight in the hills; we shall never surrender."*
Winston Churchill, former British Prime Minister

4 *"If we left the European Union, it would be a one-way ticket, not a return."*
David Cameron, former British Prime Minister

5 *"What incentive do Labour's policies give to our young people planning for the future? What prospect for those seeking promotion? What hope for the parents and grandparents wanting to see their children and grandchildren making a career, building a better life? None. No incentives; no prospects; no hope; and no future."*
John Major, former British Prime Minister

Exercise 2

Write a series of statements on the themes covered in this Topic (e.g. Brexit or any other suitable theme) using as many different stylistic devices as possible. Then check if a partner is able to identify which rhetorical devices you chose.

Dealing with a text analysis task

This writing task will involve you analysing a set text according to a specific question. Most of the texts you'll be asked to analyse are written with a specific **intention** in mind. This text will then be used for you to write a structured, coherent textual analysis based on a question which may ask you to look at the content and linguistic aspects of a piece of writing.

Good to know

In your ***Abitur*** examination, you'll be asked to write a textual analysis based on a non-literary text.

The source texts in your exams will involve text types such as **reports** or **articles** in different forms which will generally be taken from reputable news sources in the English-speaking world. **Speeches** are also sometimes used as a basis for content/ linguistic textual analysis.

► António Guterres speech, p. 231

Writing your analysis – step-by-step guide

Step 1: Before analysing the text, you need to analyse the task

You may be asked to identify the **position** the author of the text has adopted using the **linguistic tools** they have used in their writing.

This might additionally involve the analysis of so-called **discontinuous texts** such as graphs, images and cartoons.

S ► Stylistic devices, pp. 211–212
S ► Describing and analysing diagrams, pp. 43–44
S ► Describing and analysing cartoons, pp. 82–83

Example task

Examine how the author tries to persuade the reader of her point of view. Refer to the article as well as to the illustration published with it.

Another possibility is you might be asked to explicitly identify the **linguistic tools** the author has used to try to convince their readers that their **understanding** or **opinion** is correct. This might involve additional **discontinuous texts** that you'll be expected to include in your answer.

Example task

Analyse the means used to convince the reader of the author's position. Refer to the article and the cartoon published with it.

Exercise 1

Read the following question on the text *Which is more dysfunctional – the US or the UK?* on pp. 217–218 and identify which parts of the question refer to the content of the article and which refer to linguistic aspects to be included in your analysis.

Analyse how the author conveys her attitude towards the UK and the USA. Refer to language and structure.

Step 2: Text attack! What kind of text is it and what is it about?

Find the parts of the text that support the arguments in your analysis and either assign them to the following aspects a–g or mark them directly in different colours.

a Text function

Different text functions can usually be identified according to the aim of the text:

Function	Text
informative	*presents or reproduces information, can take different forms:* *– descriptive (e.g. describing people, places, events, etc.)* *– expository (e.g. explaining facts, often including opinions)*
argumentative	*evaluates the pros and cons of an issue / a situation*
persuasive	*attempts to convince or influence the reader*

Good to know

Many texts make use of more than one of these functions. In a political speech, for example, the aim of the speaker is not only to persuade, but also to inform their listeners. However, the emphasis is usually on one function.

b Text type

Identify that text type you are dealing with. Common text types are **argumentative** and **persuasive texts** such as **editorials**, **columns** or **speeches**.

c Register

In non-literary texts, you need to identify the level of language (= register) that a writer uses in a particular text. It can be either **formal**, **neutral** or **informal**.

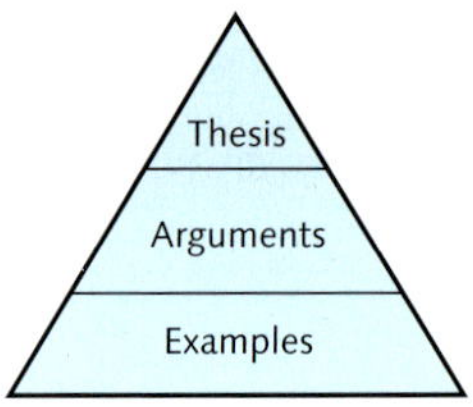

d Types of argument

When debating an issue, an opinion needs to be justified convincingly. To do this, a **thesis** or **proposition** is put forward, which is supported by **arguments** and **examples**. The strength of the proposition depends on the quality of the arguments used to support it. Examine the text for the following types of argument.

Thesis: *Schools should allow mobile phone use during the school day*.

Type of argument	Thesis supported by ...	Examples
practical argument	verifiable, indisputable statements of fact	*Most German teenagers have their own mobile phones nowadays.*
argument by authority	appeal to widely recognized experts or other authorities	*A recent study conducted by the Pew Research Center shows that nearly every U.S. teenager owns a smartphone.*
normative argument	link to widely recognized values or norms	*Parents want their children to be safe. During a crisis, mobile phones allow students to notify their parents that they are safe.*
argument by analogy	link to an example from a different area of life from which parallels can be drawn	*Mobile phones have now become standard equipment in much the same way that laptops or PCs can be found in most teenagers' bedrooms.*
indirect argument	rebuttal of the opposite opinion	*Mobile phones were once considered a distraction in the classroom. True, but educators have slowly found out that they can be turned into learning tools.*

verifiable *überprüfbar* • **indisputable** *unstrittig* • **rebuttal** *Entkräftung*

A **line of argumentation** is often created using the different types of argument in a logical sequence.

e Text structure

The structure of the text reflects the way in which the information is presented.

description	descriptions that provide the reader with a clear picture of the subject	
sequence and order	a chronological sequence of events	
comparisons and contrasts	similarities and differences between people, events, concepts, ideas, etc.	
cause and effect	the relation between causes and their effects on the situation/issue	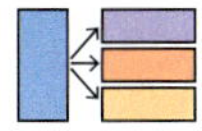
problem and solution	a presentation of the problem(s) and possible ways to solve it/them	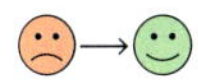

f Tone

Analyse the tone of the text – this will help you identify the author's attitude towards the topic of the text. There are a whole range of different possible options, including serious, humorous, ironic, witty, sentimental, warm-hearted, aggressive or sarcastic. Looking closely at the title can help, as it sometimes contains a clue as to the tone of the text.

g Stylistic devices

Identify which different stylistic devices are used in the text.

S ▸ Stylistic devices, pp. 211–212

Step 3: Structure the information you've collected

Keep the following key question in mind:
What effect is the author aiming to achieve by using this device?

Do not work through the text chronologically – you need to sort the examples you find in the text according to the different aspects you want to analyse. Make sure the examples you give are relevant and that you can show how they demonstrate the stylistic devices you have identified them as.

Dealing with quotations: Quotes are an important tool for connecting the content of the text and its meaning. There are two ways to quote from the text:

direct quotations	*"Privileged Immigrant Derangement Syndrome (PIDS)" (l. 4)*
indirect quotations	*The author refers to her English accent. (l. 8)*

Good to know

In your analysis, avoid quoting sections of the text which are too long. Any passages or phrases you refer to in your analysis must be identified as quotations.

Exercise 2

Use the step-by-step guide above to analyse the task (exercise 1, p. 213) on the text *Which is more dysfunctional – the US or the UK?*

Step 4: Writing your text analysis

Text analysis checklist

a Before you start to write, use the following checklist to make sure you've identified and provided examples for each aspect:

- ✓ **text function**
- ✓ **text type**
- ✓ **register**
- ✓ **types of argument**
- ✓ **text structure**
- ✓ **tone**
- ✓ **stylistic devices**

S ▸ Stylistic devices, pp. 211–212

b What effect(s) is/are achieved?

Introduction

Your introductory text should contain information on the source and author of the text, what text type it is, when it was published, what it is about and what its intention is.

Introductory sentence

In his/her/their [text type] "[title]" published in [name of newspaper/magazine] on [date] / in [year], [author's name] focuses on the topic of [general topic] and describes/stresses [positive/negative aspects/opportunities], using various means to convey his/her/their message.

to **stress sth** *etw betonen*
to **convey sth** *etw vermitteln*

Body

Now write your analysis with examples backing up what you said in your introductory sentence (about the intention of the text). Make sure you divide your points into meaningful paragraphs as this will help guide the reader through your text. Don't just give a list of devices and examples, but explain what the function and effect on the reader is meant to be. Add weight to your suggestions by providing line numbers or even suitable direct and indirect quotations where appropriate.

Examining register and choice of words

The author makes use of formal/neutral/informal language.
The author uses outdated/specialist terms / slang / colloquial elements.
This is indicated by l./ll. [line number(s)], where it is stated that …
This can be seen in l./ll. [line number(s)], where the author states …

Examining the tone

The tone of the text is serious/humorous/sarcastic/ironic/comic/critical. It also contains … elements.
The author creates a harmonious/gloomy/depressing/optimistic mood/atmosphere.
The ironic tone of the passage is in marked contrast to …

outdated *veraltet*
slang *Umgangssprache*
colloquial *umgangssprachlich*
This is indicated by … *Dies zeigt sich / wird deutlich in …*

to **contain** *beinhalten*
harmonious *harmonisch, stimmig*
gloomy *düster*
mood *Stimmung*
marked *deutlich*

Examining stylistic devices
The [stylistic device] has a(n) ... effect.
We also find [stylistic device].
The author employs/uses/applies [stylistic device] to show ...
This rhetorical device emphasizes/illustrates/suggests that ... / symbolizes / attracts the reader's attention ...
... is a symbol for ... / The symbol/image chosen by the author refers to ...

S ▸ Stylistic devices, pp. 211–212

to **employ sth** *etw anwenden*
to **apply sth** *etw anwenden*
rhetorical device *rhetorisches Mittel*
to **emphasize** *betonen*

Conclusion

Keep your concluding section short – refer back to your introduction and express the main point of your analysis in one sentence using different words. Do not add any new points, your personal opinion or evaluation.

Exercise 3

Write a complete textual analysis of the text *Which is more dysfunctional – the US or the UK?* according to the task in exercise 1, p. 213.

Which is more dysfunctional – the US or the UK? I've created a Global Embarrassment Index to figure it out

Living in the US, I have always seized every opportunity to insist things are better in Blighty. But now both countries look ludicrous.

For years now I have been living with a chronic condition that I've finally been able to diagnose as Privileged Immigrant Derangement Syndrome (PIDS). Let me explain: more than a decade ago I left my native Britain to go and work in New York. I wasn't fleeing persecution, poverty, or life in a failed state; I just wanted to live in the US. There were more opportunities, I didn't have to navigate the suffocating class system, and, most importantly, my English accent gave me a competitive edge. Women swooned at my vowel sounds (I'm not making that up: they swooned ... OK, I promise at least one woman swooned) and everyone assumed I was on tea-drinking terms with the Queen.

Anyway, that's the PI bit of PIDS. The D bit is this: when you spend extended time away from your home country, it's easy to build up a romanticised version of it in your head. I became a cheerleader for all things British; I even bought a pair of union jack wellies, and wore them with pride whenever it rained. As my long-suffering American wife can attest, I seized every opportunity to say how much better things were in Blighty than Stateside. We had a superior healthcare system; we weren't gun-nuts; our infrastructure was better; our political system wasn't as drenched with money, and was less corrupt. Even our rain was better. On and on I went about how the UK was infinitely superior to the US.

Then Brexit happened. Suddenly the US media (and the rest of the world) started looking at the UK with more sceptical eyes. Britain's global reputation started to plummet, as did the value of my accent. Still, it wasn't as if the US could feel superior for long: shortly after Brexit, it elected a reality TV star president. Since then both countries have been engaged in a race to the bottom. Even with an acute case of PIDS, it's hard to deny Britain is an out-of-control dumpster fire; every time I think things can't get more ludicrous, they do. The other day there were reports that Boris Johnson had concocted a strategy called Operation Save Big Dog to protect him from the fallout from "partygate". GB News just announced it will – dictatorship style – start broadcasting the national anthem daily at the beginning of its live programming. Today, I read a headline about Prince Andrew allegedly verbally abusing his maids for rearranging his teddy bears. How on earth are these real headlines from a real country? Then again, it's not as if things are better Stateside: it's been just more than a year, after all, since they had an attempted insurrection.

Back in 2017, reeling from Brexit and Donald Trump, I conducted a very scientific study in this column, looking at whether the UK or the US was more dysfunctional. The US narrowly won that round. Five years and infinite scandals on, it's worth revisiting that question. I'm afraid that, due to word limit constraints, I can't dwell on the ins and outs of my highly methodological Global Embarrassment Index™. If you want all the details, you'll have to wait until it passes peer review (AKA my wife takes a look). For now, we'll just skip to the conclusion. Which – drum roll, please – is that both sides of the Atlantic are equally dysfunctional. Johnson is undoubtedly more of a buffoon than Joe Biden but, at the end of the day, it's not gaffes, hypocrisy, and bad hair that matter: it's the fact that both countries are moving perilously quickly towards authoritarianism. In the UK, Johnson's government is pushing oppressive measures to criminalise protest, and arbitrarily deprive people of citizenship. In the US, certain states are busy banning books, and Biden's government is proving ineffectual in the fight to protect voting rights. What is happening on either side of the Atlantic may often be beyond parody but, believe me, the dissolution of democracy is no laughing matter.

(703 words) Source: *The Guardian*, 18 January 2022

Review

1 Rank the Sections A–F in this Topic based on how interesting they were to you. Then, look back at your work on the overview of this Topic (pages 178–179) and how you ranked them there (page 178, exercise 2). Have your rankings changed? Share your results with a group and tell them what you found most interesting.

2 Look at your KWL list (page 179, exercise 5). Fill out the "Learned" part of the list. Next, look at your "Want to know" list. What do you still want to know?

3 Make a list of ten words in the Topic that were new to you and you consider important to know. Then collect everyone's words and cluster them into groups. Finally, pick a word group and write a paragraph using all the words.

Evaluate

Do this task on your own. How much do you agree or disagree with the statements below? Rate each one on a scale of one to four. The references on the right show you which exercises you can review.

1 = totally disagree **2** = disagree **3** = agree **4** = totally agree

Section	**Statement**		
A	**1**	I can summarize a text about Britain's role in the slave trade.	► p. 181, exercise 5
	2	I can analyse the author's position in a difficult text.	► p. 182, exercise 6
	3	I can write an argumentative text on the topic of slavery.	► p. 183, exercise 9
B	**4**	I understand the issues related to colonialism in post-colonial societies.	► pp. 184–187, exercises 2–7
	5	I can understand a radio discussion about post-colonial New Zealand.	► p. 188, exercises 8–10
C	**6**	I can talk about the main aspects of the Windrush scandal.	► p. 189, exercises 1–2
	7	I can summarize relevant points from a text about a Windrush survivor.	► p. 192, exercise 5
	8	I can write an argumentative text about the Windrush scandal.	► p. 193, exercise 9
D	**9**	I can summarize arguments for and against Brexit from a blog.	► p. 197, exercise 4
	10	I can analyse the language and structure of a blog text.	► p. 197, exercise 5
	11	I can express the main points of an English blog in German.	► p. 197, exercise 6
	12	I can take part in a discussion on the future of the UK outside the EU.	► p. 198, exercise 10
E	**13**	I can understand a radio show discussing Scottish independence.	► p. 201, exercise 5
	14	I can discuss the issues surrounding Scottish independence.	► p. 202, exercise 6
	15	I can write an argumentative text about Scottish independence.	► p. 202, exercise 7
F	**16**	I can summarize the points in a text about multiculturalism in the UK.	► p. 204, exercise 4
	17	I can analyse the strategies employed by an author to present an issue.	► pp. 205–206, exercise 8
	18	I can understand an interview about growing up with a multicultural background in the UK.	► p. 204, exercise 5
Skills	**19**	I can recognize stylistic devices.	S ► pp. 211–212
	20	I know how to deal with a text analysis task.	S ► pp. 213–218

Consolidate

You want to go deeper into the topic of the UK, and speed up your learning process? Scan this page with the PagePlayer app. There you'll find some suggestions for additional tasks.

Aufgabenteil I Hören

47

1 **You will hear another part of the interview with Michael Andrew, a British-Nigerian teacher who lives and works in Lower Saxony.**

While listening, choose the correct answers (a, b or c). There is only one correct answer.

1 The neighbourhood Michael grew up in was ...
a not very diverse apart from the street in which he lived.
b already very multicultural with people from Nigeria, Vietnam and Britain.
c the opposite of diverse because British people lived there for the most part.

2 Within his surroundings Michael ...
a felt very much that he was black and that other people weren't.
b didn't feel any different than the others regarding his skin colour.
c had a lot to share with his friends who were of the same African heritage.

3 Being black ...
a was not discussed when he was young.
b prevented him from being allowed to play football.
c was a constant source of problems when he joined the football club as a child.

4 Things changed when he was a child of ten. He ...
a tried to cross a road even though he wasn't allowed to.
b pretended he wanted to cross the road to annoy the drivers.
c crossed the road and walked very slowly to annoy the drivers.

5 One driver ...
a called him names.
b tried to run him over.
c stopped the car and used the B-word.

6 This incident hurt him so much that he ...
a is still upset and dreams of the event.
b can still remember it 26 years after it happened.
c can still remember even though he is now 26 years old.

7 He started playing sports because ...
a all his friends joined the football team.
b he could be a child there like any other child.
c there was no racism in football at all in those times.

8 At a rugby match, ...
a the adults served as a role model to their children.
b the children insulted their opponents in a racist manner.
c the adults made racist comments while watching the match.

2 You will hear an opinion piece by Val McDermid, a famous crime writer, on Scottish independence. 48

While listening, complete the following sentences.

1 According to Val McDermid, the visible benefits for Scotland of EU membership were … and … and …
2 Scotland has changed to …
3 When voting about whether to stay or leave the EU, 62 per cent …
4 Westminster made a mistake because …
5 People in favour of Scotland's independence see the country as a place that …
6 The author knows that the road ahead is hard but she believes …

3 You will hear five young adults talking about Brexit and its consequences for them personally. 49

While listening, match the headings A–G with the speakers 1–5. There are two more headings than you need.

Headings	
A	job restrictions in the UK
B	like a phoenix from the ashes
C	relapse into past times
D	violent battles flaring up
E	together and yet apart
F	limited private and professional possibilities
G	watching from the margin

Speaker	Heading

Aufgabenteil II Lesen und Schreiben

Aufgabenstellung

1 Outline the negative effects that leaving the European single market has had on the UK in terms of the labour market and bureaucracy. (Material 1, pp. 222–223)

2 Examine the author's attitude towards Brexit. Refer to language and structure. (Material 1, pp. 222–223)

3 Choose one of the following:

A "Sooner or later, the free movement of goods, services, capital and labour will have to be restored, … ."

Comment on the author's statement, referring to the current situation.

B You are taking part in the Scottish Youth Forum in Glasgow where the consequences of Brexit for young people are being discussed. Many of the participants voted Remain in the 2016 referendum, including you.

Write a speech in support of a campaign to start a new referendum on rejoining the European Union.

Material 1

The evidence is all around us: life outside the single market is an utter disaster

A massacre is occurring. More than 35,000 healthy British pigs have been slaughtered and buried on farms since September, with an estimated 200,000 languishing in a backlog.

The reason is that abattoirs lack the staff to process them, largely due to Britain's exit from the pan-European labour market. In October, the environment department offered 800 six-month visas for foreign butchers. But it insisted they go through its laborious scheme for seasonal workers: barely 100 turned up. Whitehall also refuses to curb imports of European pork – which now makes up 60% of the UK market and rising. To the National Pig Association, Brexit means buy from Europe.

For pig farmers, we can read apple growers, flower producers, fishing fleets, road hauliers, house builders, medicine suppliers, care home managers – a whole range of workers on the frontline of Britain's economy. All have benefited in the past from the open market in European labour. All must now lobby Whitehall for permits, visas, waivers and, if not, compensation. Hundred-page documents must accompany every food convoy to and from Dover and Belfast, where hours of tailbacks quietly rot produce.

You might think all this comes from some statist socialist regime. Yet it is the brainchild of the right wing of the Conservative party, now in government. [...] Jobs must be categorised by specialism, shortage, pay and length of stay. Vast Whitehall charts must be mapping labour flows. The Home Office aversion to foreigners has bred a "hostile environment" culture. At the end of last year, private care homes were forced to sack 50,000 unvaccinated staff. To pretend to compensate, the government then offered care homes extra visas. It turned out they could be only for one year – despite the essence of care being continuity. As for getting a visa, it is said to take a minimum of 16 weeks.

I care about elderly people more than I do pigs, but the principle is the same. Both are victims not – repeat not – of the UK's decision to leave the European Union. They are victims of Boris Johnson's subsequent decision, to aid him in toppling Theresa May, to interpret Brexit as requiring Britain to depart the world's most efficient and benign economic entity, the single market. This had been in large part the creation in 1986 of the right's hero, Margaret Thatcher, to honour her free-market principles.

Leaving the EU had some arguments for it. Leaving the single market had none. "Soft" Brexit within that market would have been far been easier to negotiate. Leaving it has meant wrecked supply chains and terminated scientific collaboration. It has undermined recruitment patterns and destabilised Northern Ireland. It has crippled the fish industry and impeded billions of pounds of UK trade. Its consequences have wavered between nuisance and disaster.

Brexit has seen a consummation of the very thing Tories are supposed to hate – bureaucracy. Whitehall officials used to be accused of "gold plating" Brussels regulations. "Taking back control" has licensed their wildest dreams. Brexit is estimated to have required a civil service army of 50,000 new officials, more than the entire central bureaucracy of the EU in Brussels. The latest addition to this apparat is Jacob Rees-Mogg calling himself the "Brexit opportunities" minister. His first act has been desperate, to "implore" readers of the Sun to tell him what opportunities they could think of.

Rees-Mogg is now advocating an Institute of Economic Affairs suggestion to boost trade with other countries by abolishing non-tariff barriers and "recognising [their] regulations, without requiring reciprocity, starting with the EU". Why should they negotiate at all? Surely this negates the whole point of "taking back control". But then the government is also desperate to reopen trade talks with the US and China. The idea that Britain might "control" such talks is beyond naive.

The battered band of Brexiters is now seen as wandering in a hostile desert, mystified at why their promised land has failed to materialise. Former European partners were supposed to come *crawling to London begging* for business. We were told: “They need us more than we need them.” But Europe’s other nations have no interest in rewarding separatism of any sort. A Britain divided, weakened and ill-led is merely the subject of scorn and ridicule. Chaos at Dover is an excellent advertisement for European union.

Britain’s position as an island has to be one that trades openly with the mainland. Sooner or later, the free movement of goods, services, capital and labour will have to be restored, however painfully. It would greatly help if Labour’s Keir Starmer stopped vacillating and committed himself to that objective, as should candidates for Johnson’s succession. No, this is not revoking Brexit or rejoining the EU. It is just embracing sanity.

(783 words) Source: *The Guardian*, 17 February 2022

Mündlicher Teil Kommunikationsprüfung

Partner A: look here. **Partner B:** look at File 20 on page 279.

Partner A: Sequence 1 (your five-minute talk)

1 Describe the cartoon and statistics below and interpret their message.

2 Use the material below as a starting point for an uninterrupted five-minute talk on the British Empire and colonialism in regard to current developments.

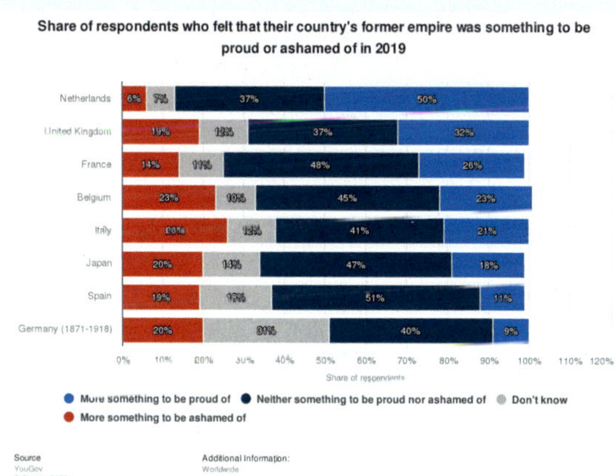

Partner A: Sequence 2 (you and the teacher / another student)

Continue the discussion on the British Empire and colonialism with your teacher / your partner:

1 *"Every empire, however, tells itself and the world that it is unlike all other empires, that its mission is not to plunder and control but to educate and liberate."*
– Edward W. Said, US-Palestinian literary critic and professor of post-colonial studies

Explain the connection between the Empire and the Commonwealth. Consider possible, upsides and downsides, as well.

2 Discuss the thesis that the Commonwealth is nothing more than nostalgia for the Empire on behalf of the former colonial power.

Topic 6 Equality

Section A

Civil rights in the USA

"I have a dream that my four little children will one day live in a nation where they will not be judged by the color of their skin, but by the content of their character."

– Dr Martin Luther King Jr, civil rights activist

Section B

Gender equality

Fact: Fact: In most countries, women only earn between 60& and 70% of men's wages – for the same work. (Source: Global Citizen)

"If you believe in equality, you're a feminist."

– Emma Watson, actor and activist

justice

feminism

access

Equal rights for everyone

Section F

Overcoming disabilities

Fact: Around 15% of the world's population lives with a disability, around 650 million people. (Source: WHO)

1 Read the facts and quotations about equality above.

a Which of them are totally new to you?
b Which of them do you find surprising?

2 Rank Sections A–F on how interested you are in them.

3 The mind map shows you a preview of Topic 6. Copy it onto a piece of paper and add words and phrases from …

a the facts and quotations above.
b the Word bank opposite.
c your own ideas.
d Sections A–F you think are important.

Find information on each Section in the PagePlayer app!

Section C

Multicultural society

Fact: 40% of US Fortune 500 companies in 2017 were founded by immigrants or children of immigrants. (Source: United Nations Foundation)

Migration is the expression of the human aspiration for dignity, safety and a better future. It is part of the social fabric, part of our very make-up as a human family.
– Ban Ki-Moon, former Secretary-General of the United Nations

integration

acceptance

Section D

Sexual and gender minorities

Fact: 70 countries criminalize same-sex relationships. (Source: Stonewall, LGBTQ+ charity)

I think the best day is when we no longer talk about being gay or straight … It's not a gay wedding, it's just a wedding.
– Pink, US singer

Section E

Social class

social mobility

Fact: Only 7% of people attend private schools in the UK, but people with private-school backgrounds account for 29% of the Members of Parliament.

4 Note a few key words to say what you expect to learn in each Section.

5 Make a "KWL" (Know, Want to know, Learned) list for the Topic.

6 With a partner, compare …

a your mind maps and say why you added words where you did.
b your rankings from exercise 2.
c what you expect to learn in Sections A–F.

Then compare with another pair.

7 Save your work for reviewing when you've finished the Topic.

Word bank

discrimination *Diskriminierung*
equal opportunities *pl Chancengleichheit*
gender *Geschlecht*
inequality *Ungleichheit*
inclusion *(soziale) Einbindung*
to judge sb *jdn beurteilen*
migration *Migration*
minority *Minderheit*
poverty *Armut*
prejudice *Vorurteil*
to segregate *trennen*
social mobility *(soziale) Mobilität*

Section A Civil rights in the USA

Warm-up

1 Look at the photos in the timeline. What do you know about the people/ situations they show? Share your ideas with a partner.

2 Complete the timeline with words from the list.

abolished | abolition | Black Lives Matter | boycott | Civil Rights | Civil War | I can't breathe | I have a dream | justice | Dr Martin Luther King Jr | resistance | Rosa Parks | segregation | slavery | supremacist | taking the knee | Yes we can!

Timeline of civil rights in the USA

1616 – Around 20 people from Angola were kidnapped and taken to Jamestown, Virginia, where they were sold as slaves. Their story is often used to symbolize the start of …[1] in the USA. During the following two centuries, millions of men, women and children were forcibly brought from Africa and 'imported' to the New World as slaves. By the end of the 1700s, slavery had been …[2] in the northern states, but the southern states resisted because slave labour was needed to produce crops such as cotton or tobacco.

1861 – The …[3] started when seven southern states separated from the Union and formed the Confederate States of America in which slavery was legal. They were later joined by a further four states. The northern states supported the Union and the …[4] of slavery.

1865 – The victory of the Union over the Confederacy officially ended slavery.

1870 – The 15th Amendment to the Constitution granted all citizens, including African Americans, the right to vote. Many white Southerners felt that they were losing power, leading to the foundation of violent white …[5] organizations, such as the Klu Klux Klan.

1870s–1960s – The southern states began to introduce laws enforcing racial …[6], known as "Jim Crow" (a derogatory term for black people) laws. This meant separate schools for black and white students, and separate public transport and leisure facilities.

1955 – Black bus passengers in Montgomery, Alabama had to sit at the back and give up their seat for white passengers if there were no seats left at the front. When the 'mother of the civil rights movement', …[7], was asked to give up her seat for a white man, she refused and was arrested. In response, African Americans started a bus …[8] which left the bus company almost bankrupt. In 1956, the Supreme Court ruled that the company's segregated seating was unconstitutional and the buses were desegregated.

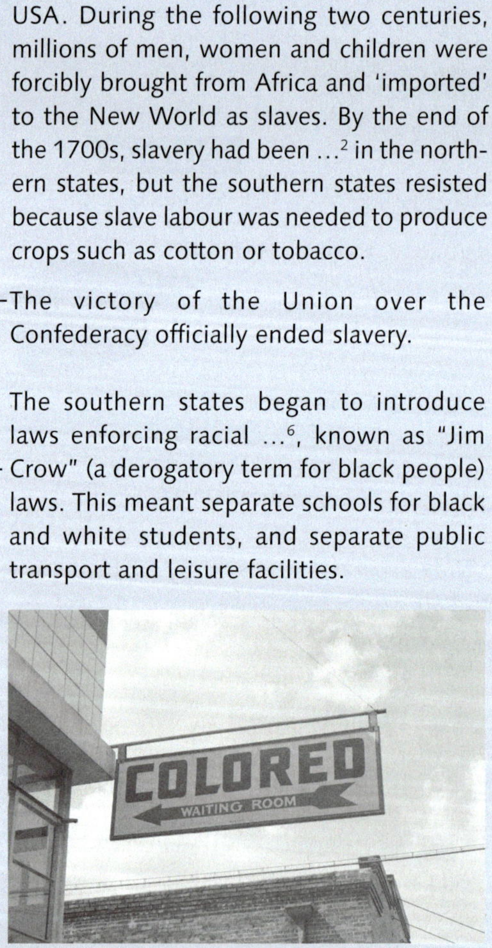

1963 – The March on Washington for Jobs and Freedom was perhaps the largest in the capital's history, with about 250,00 participants – both black and white people. The last speaker to address the crowd was the Baptist preacher …[9] who talked about the struggles of African Americans and the continuing need for nonviolent protest. In his famous speech, he said, "…[10] that my four little children will one day live in a nation where they will not be judged by the color of their skin, but by the content of their character."

1964 – Thanks to campaigners such as Martin Luther King, the Civil Rights Movement grew during the 1960s. In 1964, the …[11] Act became law, giving African American citizens more protection against discrimination. It also guaranteed equal employment and voting rights and ended the segregation of most public places.

1968 – The assassination of Martin Luther King by a white man led many African Americans to question non-violent …[12] to achieve equality.

Barack Obama

2008 – Barack Obama was the first African American to be elected president of the USA. His slogan "…"[13] inspired many people, especially African Americans.

2012 – An unarmed 17-year-old, Trayvon Martin, was shot and killed in Sanford, Florida. When the shooter was acquitted, there were nationwide protests. The hashtag …[14] began to be used as a protest against white supremacy and the killing of black civilians.

2016 – Three American football players from the San Francisco 49ers knelt during the national anthem at a match to protest against police brutality. This form of protest, "…"[15], has since been carried out at a number of other national and international sports events.

2020 – When George Floyd was accused of using a fake $20 note in a shop, he was handcuffed and pinned to the ground by a police officer who knelt on his neck for over eight minutes until he died. His death sparked a large number of protests using the slogans "…"[16] and "Black Lives Matter".

2021 – Kamala Harris became the first female and the first Vice President of colour in the history of the USA under President Joe Biden. In her victory speech, Harris acknowledged generations of American women or all races who had fought and sacrificed so much for equality, liberty and …[17] for all.

Speaking

3 Choose one of the following people or topics and present it to the class, showing where it belongs on the timeline of civil rights.

Black Power movement | Brown vs Board of Education | Charlotte Hawkins Brown | Freedom Summer Murders | Juneteenth | Los Angeles riots | Malcolm X | Selma to Montgomery March | student sit-in movement | Underground Railroad

Working with the text

S ▸ Reading difficult texts, pp. 39–40

4 Skim the text below about the "Little Rock Nine" and make notes on the following points:

- the identity of the Little Rock Nine
- what they wanted to do
- the historical background to the events described in the article

50

Minnijean Brown-Trickey: the teenager who needed an armed guard to go to school

The first black students leave Central High School, Little Rock, Ark., 2 October 1957

Brown-Trickey, now 79, was one of the Little Rock Nine, the first group of African American children to go to the city's Central High School in September 1957 – and in doing so, desegregate it. On the teenagers' first day at the Arkansas school, white residents were so furious they amassed in a 1,000-strong mob at the gates.

As they tried to walk into school, the children were subject to verbal abuse, spat on and denied admission. Three black journalists watching were also attacked.

It took a further three weeks for the students to actually step inside the building, thanks to fierce resistance from the Arkansas governor Orval Faubus, who used the mob as a pretext for barring the nine, putting the state's National Guard in their way. Brown-Trickey recalls how he warned of "blood in the streets" should the children be allowed to go to school.

Eventually the deadlock was broken by President Eisenhower, who sent in 1,200 troops from the army's elite 101st Airborne Division to take control. They dispersed the crowd and quelled the general unrest in Little Rock that had left black citizens afraid to go out after dark. The army unit then met the students every day to escort them into the building, and throughout the day each of the nine would have an armed guard between classes.

The Jim Crow laws in the south enforced strict racial apartheid, with segregated schools a key feature. Because white schools had resources poured into them, integration became a rallying cry in the struggle for civil rights. But many white parents were passionately keen not to "pollute" the education of their children with African Americans, whom they saw as inferior. […]

As a 16-year-old, she was well aware that African Americans lived "parallel lives to white people", and that the circumstances were devastatingly unequal. Segregation in the south was so total it was like living "in a complete bubble", she says. She recalls going into shoe stores and seeing the "plush seats at the front" for white customers, while she was consigned to the "wooden benches at the back".

Yet, despite growing up under this vicious system, Brown-Trickey says she not only always felt safe, but was constantly told by her family that she was also "beautiful, smart and talented". Originally, 80 students signed up for Central, but they dropped out after being told they would be barred from extracurricular activities and clubs. But, with her strong personality and confidence, Brown-Trickey was sure she would overcome this restriction.

armed *bewaffnet*
guard *Leibwächter/in*
7 to spit on sb *jdn bespucken*
7 **admission** *Zugang, Einlass*
10 **governor** *AE Gouverneur/in (USA: Regierungschef/in eines Bundesstaats)*
11 pretext *Vorwand*
11 to bar sb *jdn aussperren*
14 deadlock *Sackgasse, Pattsituation*
16 to quell *niederschlagen*
18 to **escort sb** *jdn begleiten, jdn eskortieren*
28 plush *Plüsch*
29 to be consigned to sth *auf etw verwiesen werden*
29 **bench** *Bank (zum Sitzen)*

In reality, even the army's protection could not keep her and her friends safe. Shockingly, all nine of the teenagers had to keep spare sets of clothes at school because they were routinely spat on or showered with cafeteria food. Their legs were always bruised and heels bloody as other students would kick out and step on them. When they were alone, the violence was worse.

How did she survive? Brown-Trickey said she chose to feel "sorry for the white kids at that school". She thought to herself they "can't even think", thus turning their efforts to make her feel inferior into a source of strength and pride that allowed her to persevere.

Home, however, was no longer a safe haven, either. The "punishment was total", she says; her father, a landscaper, found all his work had dried up. Their telephone constantly rung with threats that "they were 'coming to burn your house down, we're gonna kill you, grind your bones'". Her parents would even get phone calls from people who said they worked at the morgue, asking them to identify the body of a child.

Today, Brown-Trickey works extensively with young people. She finds inspiration in young activists, especially Malala Yousafzai, whose experiences she sees as a mirror to her own. While Brown-Trickey was not shot, she assures me that was not for lack of murderous intent.

The police killing of George Floyd meanwhile "felt like the 1960s, even worse because it was 50 years later [and] it's still not a better time". The current state of the nation provokes a deep sense of sadness, leading her to genuinely consider if she "wasted my life" in her struggles for justice.

Perhaps this is no surprise. The response to desegregation of education was white flight from the public school system, especially in the inner cities, which means that US public schools are more segregated today than they were in the late 60s. And African American girls remain far more likely to be suspended. Brown-Trickey laments that the "US has two values: violence and segregation, and they do them both really well".

Yet she is far from drowning in despair. She is very proud of the way young people are taking up the fight for racial justice through Black Lives Matter. And when speaking to young people she reminds them that it was only due to her and eight fellow students' refusal to back down that Eisenhower sent in the 101st Airborne and broke the barricade around Central High School. People may feel powerless, she says, but with organisation, strength and commitment, "you can make presidents act".

(852 words) Source: *The Guardian*, 26 November 2020

Good to know

The **National Guard** is part of the US army, composed of persons who are not full-time military personnel and may well have a civilian job at the same time. They take part in regular military training and may be deployed for certain security or military tasks when needed.

37 **spare** *Ersatz*
39 **heel** *Ferse*
46 landscaper *Landschaftsgärtner/in*
48 to grind *mahlen, zerreiben*
49 **morgue** *Leichenschauhaus*
53 to **assure sb** *jdm versichern*
54 **murderous** *mörderisch*
54 **intent** *Absicht*
57 to **provoke** *auslösen, hervorrufen*
59 **desegregation** *Aufhebung der Rassentrennung*
63 to **suspend sb** *jdn suspendieren*
63 to **lament** *beklagen*
68 **refusal** *Ablehnung, Verweigerung*

5 Read the text again and do the following tasks.

S ▸ Writing a summary, p. 81

1 Summarize the process of getting to and remaining safe at school for the Little Rock Nine and the difficulties they encountered there.
2 Outline the difficulties faced by Brown-Trickey's family and other people of colour in the area at the time.
3 Describe the positive and negative aspects of the situation today according to Brown-Trickey and illustrate your answer with examples.

Working with words

6 Complete the sentences with a suitable form of *(de)segregate*.

1 Many aspects of public life were … under the Jim Crow laws.
2 The process of … was an important factor for the Civil Rights movement in the USA.
3 The council decided to … housing to give everyone the same opportunities.
4 To a certain extent, … still exists in US schools today.
5 In my opinion, the US school system still … many non-white students and offers them inferior educational opportunities.

7 Match the highlighted collocations from the text with the descriptions.

1 "No justice, no peace!" became an important slogan which brought people together at Black Lives Matter demonstrations.
2 The continuing instances of police brutality meant that she was so depressed that she had no more energy and she gave up fighting racial injustice in her area.
3 The continuing violence on the streets meant that for many students, school was a place in which they were free from danger during the day.
4 Although they lived in the same city, black and white kids had very different daily realities.
5 The Little Rock Nine were not only made to suffer through verbal abuse, they also experienced physical violence.
6 We have sympathy with the teachers, because they have to bring together divided classes.

Listening

51

Exam preparation

S ▸ Dealing with listening tasks, pp. 123–125

Good to know

Jackie Robinson was the first African American to play in Major League Baseball in 1947.

8 You will hear an interview about events in the USA around the time of the Little Rock Nine. While listening, take notes on the following points. You need not write full sentences.

1 topic of Juan Williams' book and series: …
2 schools response to the Brown decision (2 aspects): …
3 civil rights protest also mentioned: …
4 Emmett Till's supposed "crime": …
5 what happened to Till as a result (2 aspects): …
Examples: *dragged from great-granduncle's house; cotton gin tied around neck*
6 the USA starting to examine race (2 aspects): …
Example: *question of race in the past*
7 question relating to foreign policy (2 aspects): …

Speaking

Exam preparation

Kommunikationsprüfung

Phrases for speaking

9 Work with a partner. Use the quotes as a basis for a discussion on racial inequality in the USA.

"When you say black lives matter, that's inherently racist … Black lives matter, white lives matter, Asian lives matter, Hispanic lives matter. That's anti-American and it's racist."
– Rudolph W. Giuliani, former mayor of New York

"If all lives did really matter, #blacklivesmatter wouldn't have been born in the first place."
– Abhijit Naskar, neuroscientist, author

Watching

10 You are going to watch the performance of a slam poem called *Sneezing is like racism*. Before you watch, brainstorm what the poem could be about and why the poet might have chosen this title.

11 Watch the video and choose the correct option (a, b or c).

1 The poet says that when you try to ignore a sneeze …
 a another part of your body will start itching instead.
 b it will come out even more violently than if you hadn't kept it in.
 c you will want to scratch your nose and your body will make strange movements until it comes out.

2 When he accidentally sneezed on a stranger, she …
 a gave him a disgusted look.
 b shouted racist abuse at him.
 c told him that he should have turned away from her.

3 He describes racism as when a person …
 a looks at you as if they really hate you.
 b judges you without knowing anything about you.
 c tells you that you are a bad person for no reason.

4 His ex-girlfriend's dad said that he didn't want him to date his daughter because he …
 a doesn't like black people.
 b is worried that he would hurt his daughter.
 c thinks it would be too dangerous for both of them.

5 White people tell black people that sneezing is …
 a only a joke.
 b black people's fault.
 c not a serious issue.

6 People respond to sneezing by …
 a completely ignoring it.
 b blaming it on an allergy.
 c posting an angry face on social media.

Crossover TV

Sneezing is like racism

06

Speaking

12 Watch the video again, then discuss the following points.

- the effect of the way S.C. delivers his poem
- why he uses sneezing as a simile for racism
- the dates he mentions and why he might have chosen them

S ▸ Stylistic devices, pp. 211–212

Writing

13 In recent years, there have been a number of protests in response to the police killings of African Americans, sometimes ending in violent clashes with the police. Protesters have often used the slogan "No justice, no peace" to express the injustice of those killings.

Discuss the meaning of the slogan referring to the history of civil rights in the USA.

Exam preparation

S ▸ Writing an argumentative text, pp. 167–172

Writing checklist

Section B Gender equality

Warm-up

"We need to reshape our own perception of how we view ourselves. We have to step up as women and take the lead."
– Beyoncé, singer and entrepreneur

"Whatever women do they must do twice as well as men to be thought half as good. Luckily, this is not difficult."
– Charlotte Whitton, former mayor of Ottowa

"Men and women have roles – th roles are different, but their rights are equal."
– Harri Holkeri, former pr minister of Finl

"A woman without a man is like a fish without a bicycle."
– Gloria Steinem, US journalist and activist

1 Look at the photos and quotes above and do the following tasks.
- Describe the photos and discuss your reaction to them.
- Read the quotes and talk about your first impressions of them.

2 Discuss ways in which the photos and quotes may support each other.

Working with the text

Good to know

António Guterres is a Portuguese politician and diplomat and was elected Secretary-General of the UN in 2017.

3 You are going to read an excerpt from a speech given by UN Secretary-General António Guterres on "Women and Power". In his speech, he outlines five areas in which achieving gender equality can transform our world.

Divide the class into five groups. Each group reads one section of the speech.

Groups A and B: look at page 233.
Group C: look at File 21 on page 280.
Group D: look at File 23 on page 281.
Group E: look at File 24 on page 281.

Read your text and summarize the main points.

First, conflict and violence. There is a straight line between violence against women, civil oppression and conflict.

Trillions of dollars are spent every year on peace and security. But we should be asking: whose peace? Whose security?

Interstate conflict makes headlines, but in some of the most violent parts of the world, levels of femicide – the killing of women – are comparable to a war zone. 137 women around the world are killed by a member of their own family every day. Impunity rates are above 95 percent in some countries.

In other words, we have men waging war on women – but no one is calling for a ceasefire or imposing sanctions. And how a society treats the female half of its population is a significant indicator of how it will treat others.

Rape and sexual slavery are routinely used as a tactic of war, and misogyny is part of the ideology of almost all violent extremist groups.

Conversely, involving women leaders and decision-makers in mediation and peace processes leads to more lasting and sustainable peace.

The United Nations is committed to putting women at the centre of our conflict prevention, peacemaking, peacebuilding and mediation efforts – and to increasing the numbers of our women peacekeepers.

Group A

[5] **interstate** *zwischenstaatlich*
[7] **impunity** *Straffreiheit*
[10] **ceasefire** *Waffenstillstand*
[12] **rape** *Vergewaltigung*
[12] **misogyny** *Frauenfeindlichkeit*
[14] conversely *umgekehrt, im Gegenzug*
[18] **peacekeeper** *Soldat/in einer Friedenstruppe*

Source: United Nations Organisation

Second, the climate crisis.

The existential emergency we are facing is the result of decisions that were taken mainly by men, but have a disproportionate impact on women and girls.

Drought and famine mean women work harder to find food and water, while heatwaves, storms and floods kill more women and girls than men and boys.

Women and girls have long been leaders and activists on the environment, from Wangari Maathai and Jane Goodall to the Fridays for Future movement. But the impact of gender inequality on climate action goes deeper.

Initiatives to reduce and recycle are overwhelmingly marketed at women, while men are more likely to put their faith in untested technological fixes.

There is plenty of evidence that women are more open than men to reducing their personal environmental impact.

And recent studies show that women economists and parliamentarians are more likely to support sustainable, inclusive policies.

There is a risk that safeguarding our planet is seen as "women's work" – just another domestic chore.

I am grateful to young people, Generation Z, including many of you here in this room, who are working for climate action and gender equality, while recognizing the reality of non-binary identities and solutions.

Macho posturing will not save our planet.

Gender equality, including men stepping up and taking responsibility, is essential if we are to beat the climate emergency.

Group B

[3] **disproportionate** *unverhältnismäßig*
[10] to **put one's faith in sth** *auf etw vertrauen*
[15] to **safeguard** *sichern, schützen, bewahren*
[16] **domestic chore** *Hausarbeit*
[19] **non-binary** *non-binär, divers*
[20] macho posturing *Macho-Gehabe*

Source: United Nations Organisation

Research and presentation

S ▸ Presentation, pp. 260–261

4 Work in your group. Using your summary from exercise 3 as a basis, research additional facts and/or statistics to illustrate the area that António Guterres describes. Try to use the highlighted collocations in your section in the presentation.

5 Give your presentation. The rest of the class listens and makes notes on the main points of each.

6 Discuss the five areas mentioned by Guterres. Say whether or not you agree with him. Brainstorm other areas in which you think promoting women's rights would benefit the world. Share your conclusions with the class.

Working with words

7 Complete the text with the words from the list.

benefits | breakthrough | childcare | disproportionate | divide | lack of | misogyny | overwhelmingly | sexual harassment

Box like a girl: a boxing club just for women and girls

FAQs

Why is the club for females only?

There's still a big gender …[1] in the boxing world and even today, it's very much a male-dominated sport. Boxing clubs and competitions are still …[2] aimed at men and boys and it can be hard for women and girls to find somewhere to train.

Despite a major …[3] in women's rights and opportunities over the last century, there's still a long way to go. And unfortunately, …[4] – the hatred of women – is still very much alive today. Even in the UK, a …[5] number of girls and women are subject to discrimination – or even violence – just because they are female.

Outside the home (and especially in male-dominated spaces like boxing clubs), many women and girls are subject to some form of …[6]. This doesn't necessarily involve physical violence, but men staring at their bodies or making sexualized comments can make them feel very uncomfortable – or even frightened.

What are the …[7] of boxing at your club?

Well, there are many – but we're just going to name a couple! First of all, boxing is a great way to build up bodily strength, fitness and agility, which help you to feel more self-confident and empowered.

Secondly, there is a …[8] opportunities for women and girls in the boxing world. We have trainers who can help you build up your boxing skills at whatever level – and help and advise those who want to take up professional boxing.

And we also offer …[9] facilities to entertain your little ones so that you can train in peace!

Listening

8 You will hear a podcast about women and sport. While listening, complete the sentences.

52

1 The German Olympic team decided to …
2 As a result of the action, the Norwegian team had to …
3 According to Dunja, during the Olympics, both female and male athletes should be able to …
4 The doctor of the US women's national gymnastics team was accused of …
5 Tarana Burke wanted to make it easier for victims of sexual abuse to …
6 According to Dunja, the #MeToo movement has made people around the world …
7 Dunja believes that one way to create change is to …
8 Ibtihaj Muhammed was the first woman to …

Good to know

The **Tokyo Summer Olympics** were originally scheduled to be held in the summer of 2020, but were moved to 2021 because of the COVID-19 pandemic.

#MeToo was first used on social media by Tarana Burke in 2006. The movement gained momentum in 2017 when sexual-abuse allegations in Hollywood became public.

Ibtihaj Muhammed is a Muslim-American fencer.

Speaking

9 Hold the following discussion in groups, then present your conclusions to the class.

You are members of the Olympic Committee and have been asked to decide on rules for sports outfits for athletes in the light of the actions by the German and Norwegian women's teams. You should include the following points in your discussion:

- the possible effect of changing women's sports outfits on society as a whole
- the role of male and female athletes in promoting gender equality

Writing

10 Choose one of the following writing tasks.

A Comment on the following statement.

If you believe in equality, you're a feminist.
– Emma Watson, actor and activist

B You are a youth delegate at the UN and have been asked to write an inspiring speech to be given on International Women's Day.

In your speech, describe one area which you think would create the most change and explain what must be done to achieve it.

Exam preparation

S ▸ Writing an argumentative text, pp. 167–172

Writing checklist

Exam preparation

S ▸ Dealing with a creative writing task, pp. 126–128

Writing checklist

Section C Multicultural society

Warm-up

1 Discuss the people in the speech bubbles using the terms in the list.

asylum seeker | belonging | to deport | discrimination | emigration | fear | first/second generation immigrant | to flee | identity | immigration | integration | migration | persecution | refugee | seasonal migrant worker | to seek asylum

Jazmin

I came to the UK with my family because I wanted my kids to be able to go to school without the risk of being injured by a bomb. It wasn't easy to leave family and friends behind and I really hope that we can go back home one day.

Murat

I travel to the USA from my home in Mexico regularly to find agricultural work. I usually stay for a season at a time, for example to harvest crops or pick fruit. It's really hard physical work, but it's worth it because the employment situation at home is really bad and I can take money home to my family.

My grandparents came to West Germany as guest workers. They only wanted to stay for a few years. Then my mother was born and they ended up staying. They still sometimes talk about going back to Turkey, but I wouldn't go. I have Turkish roots, but this is my home.

José

Anisa

Sam

I'm African-American, but I now live in Ghana. I was really tired of being stopped by the cops just because I'm black. And one day someone told me to "go back to Africa!" And I thought, why not? Of course there are cultural differences, but no one stares at me on the street anymore and I can just be myself.

I'm British-Indian but I don't fit into either culture 100%. When I was growing up, my parents spoke Bengali to me, but I always answered in English. Now I regret not learning the language properly: I'd love my kids to grow up bilingual and embrace both cultures.

Listening

53

2 You will hear a radio show about opposition to asylum seekers in Ireland. Listen once and choose the correct answer (a, b or c).

S ▸ Dealing with listening tasks, pp. 123–125

1 The background to the radio show is a …
- **a** street survey about attitudes to immigrants.
- **b** protest by asylum seekers about conditions in reception centres.
- **c** plan to use a hotel in a small town as a temporary home for asylum seekers.

2 The presenter talks to Rachel about …
- **a** modern-day and historical ways in which racial division is created.
- **b** racism and fear of foreigners in the USA compared to other countries.
- **c** the effects of racism on Irish society and how to improve the integration of immigrants.

3 Listen again and take notes on the following points. You need not write full sentences.

53

Exam preparation

S ▸ Dealing with listening tasks, pp. 123–125

1. protesters concerns about asylum seeker (3 aspects): …
   example: *extremist attacks*
2. results of 2001 study: …
3. right-wing media:
   - emotions used to stir up hatred of immigrants: …
   - common image used: …
4. historical behaviour of colonial powers: …
5. effects of increase in immigration in Canada (2 aspects): …
6. results of social media hate messages (2 aspects): …

Working with the text

4 Scan the text below quickly and say how it relates to the topic of the radio show.

S ▸ Reading difficult texts, pp. 39–40

Matchmaking Irish village finds harmony with asylum seekers

Lisdoonvarna's reluctant union has mostly paid off as fear of new arrivals gives way to friendship

It seemed a match made in hell. The village did not fancy the asylum seekers. The asylum seekers did not fancy the village.

Residents of Lisdoonvarna in County Clare, on Ireland's west coast, rejected a government plan to settle asylum seekers there in a lopsided vote: 197 against, 15 in favour.

Authorities ignored the vote and bussed in dozens of people from Africa, Asia, eastern Europe and the Middle East to a hastily converted hotel in April 2018. The newcomers feared hostility and isolation in a windswept village with few amenities and poor transport links.

It was a forced union laden with irony: Lisdoonvarna was famous for a venerable matchmaking festival that draws tens of thousands of visitors each September.

Now, 16 months later and with a new festival under way, it turns out that on one level the match has largely worked: villagers and asylum seekers have warmed to each other.

"They are very active in the community and are very well-liked," said Elsha Daly, the daughter of Willie Daly, Lisdoonvarna's official matchmaker. "People here have become very accepting of different cultures." Other residents – business owners, taxi drivers, older people – echoed the sentiment.

The new arrivals said initial anxiety had turned to relief as they encountered friendliness and generosity. Emboldened, several plan to attend the matchmaking festival, which started on Saturday and continues until the end of September.

"People are good to me. They make me feel welcome," said Mputu Wabalekelayi, 30, from the Democratic Republic of the Congo. The single mother of two is open to romance. "I want to see the music and dancing. Sharing is good. Maybe I'll meet somebody."

Lisdoonvarna Castle

Good to know

The **Lisdoonvarna matchmaking festival** is a popular festival with live music and dancing. Participants come from all over Ireland – and other parts of the world – so that a '**matchmaker**' can arrange dates for them with other participants.

matchmaking *Partnervermittlung*
[1] **reluctant** *widerwillig*
[1] **to give way to sth** *etw weichen*
[6] lopsided *schief, einseitig*
[9] hasty *schnell, voreilig*
[10] **hostility** *Feindseligkeit*
[12] laden *beladen*
[12] venerable *ehrwürdig*
[22] **generosity** *Großzügigkeit*
[22] to embolden sb to do sth *jdm Mut machen, etw zu tun*

29 to deter sb from sth *jdn von etw abhalten*
32 **shelter** *Unterkunft*
33 arsonist *Brandstifter/in*
36 to **channel sth** *etw lenken, etw ausrichten (auf)*
38 singleton *Single*
40 regency-style hotel *Hotel im Regentenstil*
43 to **knit** *stricken*
46 **sympathetic to** *wohlwollend gegenüber*
48 to avert sth *etw vermeiden, etw abwenden*
49 to afflict sb *jdn plagen*
49 dwindling *schwindend*
50 to scrub *schrubben*
52 **surly** *mürrisch*
54 to endorse sth *etw bestätigen*
55 to **credit sb with sth** *jdm etw zuschreiben*
56 to relish sth *etw genießen, etw auskosten*
60 bunting *Wimpel*
61 fairy-tale ending *märchenhaftes Ende*
62 on the verge of sth *an der Schwelle zu etw, kurz vor etw*
63 to **compound** *verschlimmern*
65 revels *pl* *Feier*
67 **bemused** *irritiert*
69 **intrigued** *fasziniert*

Sayed Ali, 20, who arrived from Bahrain, said rudimentary English would not deter him from socialising. "People say hello. I feel safe. It would be nice to meet girls."

Ireland's policy of accommodating asylum seekers in rural hotels – a response to overcrowding at shelters in Dublin – has prompted protests from residents who cite cultural differences and strain on public services. Arsonists in Roosky, County Roscommon, twice attacked an empty hotel earmarked for asylum seekers. Authorities cancelled the move.

Lisdoonvarna, in contrast, has channelled the spirit of its festival. Launched 160 years ago to find wives for farmers, it has broadened into a global, LGBTQ+ friendly event for singletons and music lovers. "Some matches are made in heaven but the best ones are made in Lisdoonvarna," says the slogan.

The 107 asylum seekers at the King Thomond, a three-star regency-style hotel just outside the village, have settled into the community without backlash. The children attend schools and many parents have found work. Volunteers from Lisdoonvarna and neighbouring villages visit the hotel to teach knitting, host coffee mornings and help with transport. [...]

Several factors smoothed the integration. A spa town, Lisdoonvarna is accustomed to foreigners. Residents sympathetic to hosting people fleeing persecution appear to have been underrepresented in the vote.

Increased school enrolment should help Lisdoonvarna avert the school closures that afflict other rural communities with dwindling populations. Hotels, B&Bs and restaurants are grateful to have workers willing to scrub pots and toilets – jobs difficult to fill.

Asylum centres can be grim, with bad food and surly staff, but the King Thomond is well-run, said Orla Ni Eili of the Clare Immigrant Support Centre. Asylum seekers there endorsed that.

Willie Daly, a fourth-generation matchmaker credited with 3,000 marriages, relished the prospect of matching asylum seekers with some of the estimated 40,000 visitors expected to pack the village in coming weeks. He meets clients in the Matchmaker bar and notes their details in a leather-bound folder tied with shoelace known as "the lucky book". [...]

Despite the festival bunting and "love is in the air" slogans, Lisdoonvarna is hardly a fairytale ending for asylum seekers. [...] Ending up in rural areas – a money-saving tactic for the state, which rents hotels on the verge of closure – can compound feelings of isolation and frustration.

"I'm stuck, not happy," said a woman who fled violence in eastern Europe. She had no intention of joining the revels. "The festival means nothing to me."

Another woman, aged 29, said she had fled an arranged marriage in the Middle East to a much older man. She was bemused at the prospect of being matched at a festival still associated with elderly bachelors.

Vikisha Sesay, 25, in contrast, was intrigued. Having escaped homophobia in Sierra Leone, Sesay hoped to meet other members of the LGBTQ+ community and to see Irish craic in action. "I want to experience it. Why not?"

(802 words) *Source: The Guardian*, 1 September 2019

Good to know

Craic (or 'crack') is Irish slang for having a fun with other people; e.g. *The party was good craic – we laughed a lot!*

5 Read the text in detail and do the following tasks.

1 Outline the series of events described in the text.
2 Point out the feelings of the locals and asylum seekers at different times.

S ▸ Writing a summary, p. 81

6 Analyse how the author arouses the reader's interest in the topic of the article.

Exam preparation

S ▸ Dealing with a text analysis task, pp. 215–220

Working with words

7 Match the words in the list to the definitions. The words are all from the text.

amenities | backlash | dwindling | enrolment | limbo | persecution | reluctant | underrepresented

1 not keen, or happy, to do something
2 becoming less or smaller
3 registration, for example to join a school or course
4 not enough of a certain type of person in a group or organization
5 a situation where you cannot take action because you are waiting for sb else to make a decision
6 facilities for people to use in a town or hotel
7 harassment and unfair treatment because of, for example, race, religion or sexuality
8 a strong feeling and/or action by a group of people in response to change

Looking at language: mixed tenses

8 Complete the text with the verbs in brackets in the most suitable tense.

I …[1] (be) in Dublin for several months now, waiting for my papers to be processed. For a long time, I …[2] (hope) that my application for asylum would be accepted quickly, but I have to be patient. I know others here …[3] (face) deportation and that scares me. When I was in my home country, the secret police …[4] (look for) me because I took part in pro-democracy protests. So I …[5] (run away) and kept moving from country to country until I reached Ireland. Yesterday I found out that the Irish authorities …[6] (transfer) me to a refugee centre in the countryside next month. I hope this means that they …[7] (accept) my application and let me start a new life here. I …[8] (be) ready for my future to begin!

Good to know

Pull factors are things which **attract** people to a particular country or region, such as a higher standard of living or better employment opportunities.

Push factors are things which push people away from their country or region, such as violence or a lack of opportunities.

Presentation

9 Work in groups of four. Two students should brainstorm and make a list of the "pull factors" for Ireland (reasons people move there). The other two research the historical "push factors" for Ireland (reasons Irish people emigrated).

Share your lists with the group and create a diagram or another kind of image to visualize the push and pull factors for migration, giving examples.

Writing

10 You are doing an exchange year in Castleton and recently witnessed the protests by local people against the plans to accommodate 200 asylum seekers in the town.

Write a contribution for the school blog (school magazine) giving your opinion of the plan and how it will affect the town.

Exam preparation

S ▸ Dealing with a creative writing task, pp. 126–128

Writing checklist

Section D Sexual and gender minorities

Warm-up

1 Read the texts, then look at the photos and say how they relate to the texts.

In the USA in the 1950s and 60s, gay bars were illegal and were often raided by the police. On 28 June 1969, in response to another police raid, a series of riots took place outside the **Stonewall Inn** on **Christopher Street** in New York which lasted several days. The riots are thought of as a key moment in the fight for gay rights in the USA.

Section 28 – or **Clause 28** – was a series of UK laws against the so-called promotion of homosexuality which were in force from 1988 to 2000 in Scotland and 2003 in England and Wales. The laws included a ban on teaching about homosexual relationships in schools. For decades, campaigners fought for the inclusion of non-heterosexual relationships when teaching about sex and relationships in England.

In September 2020, new regulations came into force in England which mean that all pupils now learn about different kinds of relationships as part of the curriculum. Although many have welcomed the move, there have also been widespread protests online, in the media and even in front of schools, especially from religious communities.

The **progress pride flag** is a well-known symbol of the lesbian, gay and bisexual community. New colours have recently been added to represent people of colour and trans people. It is commonly flown outside LGBTQ spaces and at Pride marches and festivals around the world. In many towns and cities in Germany, the annual gay pride event is known as Christopher Street Day, in memory of the events that occurred there in 1969.

Marriage equality is the application of legal marital status to both homosexual and heterosexual couples. The first country to officially certify **same-sex** or **gay marriage** was the Netherlands in 2001.

Laverne Cox is a transgender woman of colour who is an actor and advocate for LGBTQ rights. In 2014, she became the first transgender person to be nominated for a Primetime Emmy award.

Stefani Germanotta, better known as **Lady Gaga**, is a US singer-songwriter and actor who identifies as bisexual and supports international LGBTQ rights. She has spoken out about anti-gay bullying in schools in the US and the poor situation for gay people in several eastern European countries.

2 What other famous people do you know who identify with the LGBTQ community? Share what you know about them.

Working with the text

3 Scan the text and list the reasons why the author believes it is important to teach children about LGBT relationships in schools.

S ▸ Reading difficult texts, pp. 39–41

54

At last, a generation of schoolchildren will grow up knowing it's OK to be LGBT

A whole generation will attend schools that not only accept LGBT people and same-sex relationships, but also celebrate and offer support on the issues that young LGBT people face.

The guidance means that primary schools will teach about different families, which of course includes LGBT families. Contrary to what's been said by some online and in the media, this is just about showing kids that families can have two mums or two dads. Or to put another way: different families, same love.

If you, like me, were at school in the 1980s and 90s you endured an education system that erased LGBT people and history. In 1989, section 28 banned local authorities from "promoting homosexuality". Without any recognition or inclusion, and with teachers essentially banned from reprimanding those who used homophobic slurs, bullying flourished and scarred a generation of young people. Growing up as a gay boy in Kent was hard. Schools couldn't even acknowledge the existence of gay people, let alone talk about the challenges we faced – I felt totally isolated and afraid of being found out. All the while, the media wrote stories about lesbian, gay and bi people arguing that children would be "turned" gay if they were taught about same-sex relationships. I had few role models and was left feeling ashamed of who I was. During my entire school career I couldn't accept my sexuality, let alone be open about it.

The struggle to repeal section 28 took years. It only left the statute books in 2000 in Scotland and 2003 in England and Wales. Kent county council even voted to keep its own version of section 28, and that was only quashed when the 2010 Equality Act came into force. The damaging impact of this legislation is still felt in school hallways and classrooms across Britain. Stonewall's 2017 research showed that 40% of LGBT students were never taught anything about LGBT issues. Teaching about LGBT families not only means children from these families see themselves reflected in what they learn, but also helps all young people understand that there's nothing wrong or unusual about being LGBT.

However, if this is to be effective, the government (whoever that might be) has to invest in training to prepare teachers and schools. All schools need to have the resources and time to engage with parents and carers, and explain how they will teach these subjects in a way that benefits children from all backgrounds. To make this happen, we want people to write to their local authorities and be vocal in their support for inclusive education, so that every child can grow up and reach their full potential.

We know that 60% of the British public want primary school teachers to talk positively about different kinds of families, including those who are LGBT, to their students. We work in many schools where young people are already embedding LGBT inclusion in their schools – because it's so important for them. They're setting up LGBT networks among peers and teachers, as well as putting on

[4] **guidance** *Anleitung, Hilfestellung*
[4] **primary school** *Grundschule*
[5] **contrary to** *im Gegensatz zu*
[9] **local authority** *(Kommunal-)Behörde*
[11] to reprimand *maßregeln*
[12] slur *Beleidigung*
[12] **to scar** *entstellen (Narben hinterlassen)*
[20] to **repeal sth** *etw widerrufen, etw aufheben*
[20] **statute book** *Gesetzbuch*
[22] to quash sth *etw aufheben*
[24] hallway *Flur, Korridor, Gang*

Good to know

There are several abbreviations in use to refer to communities of different gender and/or sexual preference:

LGBT+ = lesbian, gay, bisexual, trans and related communities

LGBTQ = lesbian, gay, bisexual, trans, (gender) queer / gender questioning

[46] **affirmation** *Bestätigung*
[50] to foster sth *etw fördern*
[52] to **be under no illusion** *sich nichts vormachen*
[54] **rhetoric** *Redekunst, Phrasendrescherei*
[56] to perpetuate sth *etw aufrechterhalten, etw verewigen*
[56] to **coexist** *nebeneinander bestehen*
[59] to **inflame** *entfachen, entzünden*
[60] vigilant *wachsam, aufmerksam*
[63] **exception** *Ausnahme*
[64] to **heal** *heilen, verheilen*

assemblies to celebrate LGBT History Month or Pride. Life for most children has changed beyond recognition, but they are eager for more progress, particularly when 45% of LGBT young people still face bullying at school because of who they are. We must support them. I would have given anything to have had LGBT-inclusive education that taught me it was OK to just be me.

Inclusive teaching is an affirmation that you exist, and your identity is valid. It's also not just about lesbian, gay, bi and trans people. It's crucial that people realise that there's no hierarchy in this teaching. It's about acceptance for people from all backgrounds – be that race, gender, sexual orientation, faith, class and/or disability. This kind of teaching will help foster greater inclusion, acceptance and understanding in our classrooms, playgrounds and school corridors.

I'm under no illusion that it will be plain sailing or that there'll be no more disruptions outside schools. A vocal minority have gained a platform with anti-diversity rhetoric that seeks to target LGBT people and divide communities. Some protesters claim that a move towards inclusive education is against their religion. This perpetuates a harmful myth that faith and LGBT inclusion cannot coexist. Faith is a big part of many LGBT people's lives and many of them have spoken out in support of LGBT-inclusive education. Unfortunately, this situation is being used by some groups to further inflame Islamophobic and anti-faith attitudes. We must be vigilant to this and push against those who seek to sow division.

Inclusive education helps to create inclusive communities. Building a more welcoming society requires building bridges between diverse groups. If all schools teach acceptance – no exceptions – then that would be a good first step to healing some of the division that we've seen in society over the past decade.

(805 words) Source: *The Guardian*, 6 September 2019

Exam preparation

S ▸ Writing a summary, p. 81

4 Summarize the arguments in favour of teaching LGBT issues at schools.

Exam preparation

S ▸ Dealing with a text analysis task, pp. 215–220

5 Examine how the author presents his opinion and tries to convince the reader of his position.

Working with words

6 Complete the sentences with suitable words from the list.

acknowledge | affirmation | erase | inclusion | inflame | repeal | vocal

1. You can't … LGBTQ people from history books. We have existed for centuries and are still around today!
2. The school needs to … that homophobic language is being used by its pupils and educate them as to why it's not OK to use those words.
3. Legalizing gay marriage was a big step in the … of LGBTQ people in society.
4. If you try to argue with her in class, you'll just … the whole situation.
5. The head teacher has been very … in his support of LGBTQ representation at the school.
6. Her speech calling for an end to the discrimination of LGBTQ people in society was a real … of the struggles many of us face.
7. We are campaigning for the government to … the law banning the teaching of homosexuality in schools in our country.

7 Match the two halves of the collocations from the text.

A to come | to face | to engage | to change | to be | to speak | to sow |

B beyond recognition | division | plain sailing | issues or challenges | with people | out about/in support of | into force

8 Complete the sentences with suitable collocations from exercise 7.

1. We need to … from different communities to tackle the issue of homophobia.
2. I'm afraid there will be many challenges ahead. It won't be … .
3. We need to start preparing now because the new regulations … next month.
4. The atmosphere at school has … since the new head teacher took over.
5. Hate speech aims to … among different sections of the community.
6. The politician … the homophobia that LGBTQ people face.

Listening

9 You will hear a number of people giving their opinion about the changes to the new regulations. While listening, match the statements A–G with the speakers 1–5. There are two more statements than you need.

55

Statements	
A	Education is a weapon against prejudice.
B	Young people should learn about sexuality and relationships from their family, not at school.
C	People teaching about the topic should be given training and guidance.
D	Learning about gay relationships could encourage young people to become homosexual.
E	Students should learn about famous gay people because role models are important.
F	If we'd learned about diverse relationships at my school, I wouldn't have suffered so much.
G	Learning about LGBT relationship is really important for young people's health and well-being.

Exam preparation

S ▸ Dealing with listening tasks, pp. 123–125

Person	Statement

Speaking

10 Choose an English-speaking country. Research how LGBTQ issues are dealt with in schools. Compare what you have found out to the situation in Germany. Present your research to the class.

Writing

11 You have just read the article *At last, a generation of schoolchildren will grow up knowing it's OK to be LGBT.*

Write a letter to the editor in which you assess the difficulties and differences of opinion surrounding the issue.

Exam preparation

S ▸ Dealing with a creative writing tasks, pp. 126–128

Writing checklist

Section E Social class

Warm-up

1 Write down the first words that occur to you when you hear the term "social class".

2 Look at the images and decide which social class you associate them with (working class, middle class or elite).

3 Say which (if any) of the cultural symbols would be different in Germany.

S ▸ Reading difficult texts, pp. 39–40

Good to know

In the **UK**, most students go to government-funded **state** or **comprehensive schools,** which usually take students of any level of ability. There are also **academies,** which have more flexibility over their curriculum and may specialize in subjects such as science, modern languages or business.

'Working-class children get less of everything in education – including respect'

When Diane Reay, Cambridge University professor of education, started researching her book about working-class children's experiences of education, she had no idea just how much inequality she would uncover in state schools today. "The most important thing I found out was that we are still educating different social classes for different functions in society."

She expected to find the English state system was providing roughly the same education for all. "But it doesn't. Even within a comprehensive school, when they're all in the same building, the working classes are still getting less education than the middle classes, just as they had when my dad was at school at the beginning of the 20th century."

Reay's background informs her book and her opinions. The daughter of a coalminer, and the eldest of eight, she grew up on a council estate and received free school meals. [...]

"My parents had a strong sense that the educational system hadn't been fair to them and they had missed out. I learned as a small child I had to work at least twice as hard as the middle-class children to achieve the same result."

How much has changed? "This government is making inequality in education worse, not better," she says.

11 to **inform** sth *etw durchdringen*
12 **coal miner** *Bergarbeiter/in*
12 **eldest** *älteste/r/s*
15 to **miss out** *zu kurz kommen*

England does not have an education system that is serious about realising the potential of all children, she argues. Four-fifths of children from working-class minority ethnic families are taught in schools with high concentrations of other immigrant or disadvantaged students – the highest proportion in the developed world, according to a report by the Organisation for Economic Cooperation and Development.

"There are predominantly middle-class comprehensives and predominantly working-class and ethnically-mixed comprehensives – pupils in the more working-class comprehensives get less money per head. They get less qualified teachers. They get higher levels of teacher turnover and more supply teachers. Even if they are in the same schools as middle-class children, they are in lower sets and yet again they get less experienced teachers."

All the children she interviewed had a powerful sense of their position in the academic hierarchy. "Right from reception now some children are in sets aged four and they can tell they're only in 'the monkeys' and that's not a very good group to be in. That means they're not very clever." [...]

Research suggests it is the wealth and inclination of parents, rather than the ability and efforts of the child, that have the most bearing on a child's educational success today. "If you're a working-class child, you're starting the race halfway round the track behind the middle-class child. Middle-class parents do a lot via extra resources and activities."

Less affluent children also get a more restrictive educational offer, she discovered. "It wasn't until I talked to young people about their experiences that I realised how different and unequal their educations were. Because the schools that working-class children mostly go to are not doing well in the league tables, there's a lot of pressure on their teachers and heads to increase their league table position. That means they focus ruthlessly on reading, writing and arithmetic."

Some children in these schools talked wistfully about hardly ever doing art, drama or dance: "These children come from families where their parents can't afford to pay for them to do those activities out of school. It almost feels criminal. It feels very unfair."

The difference between amounts spent on educating children privately or in the state sector is stark. She cites research from University College London that found £12,200 a year is the average spending on a privately educated primary pupil, compared with £4,800 on a state pupil. For secondary, it's £15,000 compared with £6,200.

"Society has got more unfair, and the gap between the rich and poor is a lot greater than it was even 30 years ago. We've got to move back instead of going further in the direction of austerity, which seems to be punishing the poor."

[...] Another issue is widespread setting and streaming. "There's masses of research that shows it doesn't work – that, actually, if you put children in mixed-ability groups, the majority make greater progress.

"Plus, research on wellbeing shows that you need to decrease the social distance between people. There's mistrust, wariness and anxiety about people who are different from us. That obviously came out in the Brexit vote. If you put children together in their classroom, they start to learn that what they share is much greater than the differences between them."

(756 words) Source: *The Guardian*, 21 November 2017

27 turnover *Fluktuation, Personalwechsel*
27 supply teacher *Aushilfslehrer/in, Vertretungslehrer/in*
29 set *Satz, Zusammenstellung; hier Leistungsgruppe*
34 **inclination** *Neigung, Vorliebe*
37 **track** *Rennstrecke, Laufbahn*
39 **restrictive** *einschränkend*
45 wistful *wehmütig*
50 stark *krass*
52 **secondary (school)** *weiterführende Schule*
55 austerity *wirtschaftliche Einschränkung, Entbehrung*
60 **mistrust** *Misstrauen*
60 **wariness** *Vorsicht, Skepsis*

Good to know

School **league tables** are statistics which compare examination results at different schools. Parents can use them when choosing a school for their child. However, they do not show how well a school helps disadvantaged students, or the range of extra curricular activities, such as dance or art, that a school offers.

Exam preparation

S ▸ Writing a summary, p. 81

Working with the text

4 Outline the educational advantages enjoyed by middle-class children in England in comparison to working-class children.

Working with words

5 Match these words from the text to their synonyms. There are two options you don't need.

1	roughly (l. 6)	**a**	sadly
2	sense (l. 14)	**b**	feeling, understanding
3	predominantly (l. 24)	**c**	exactly, precisely
4	bearing (l. 35)	**d**	influence, effect
5	affluent (l. 39)	**e**	approximately, more or less
6	wistfully (l. 45)	**f**	rich, well-off
		g	mostly, mainly
		h	poor, disadvantaged

Speaking

6 In groups, brainstorm ways in which society could be made more equal. Choose the most effective and present it to the class.

S ▸ Describing and analysing diagrams, pp. 43–44

7 Describe the following statistics. Discuss what they show and their relevance for democracy. Compare your conclusions about the UK to the situation in Germany.

Good to know

Grammar schools in the UK are academically selective schools funded by the government. However, there are only 169 grammar schools in England and 69 in Northern Ireland.

So-called **public schools** are actually elite private schools that charge expensive fees. Many of them are boarding schools, which provide accommodation and all meals for pupils.

Schools in the UK – who attends which type of school?

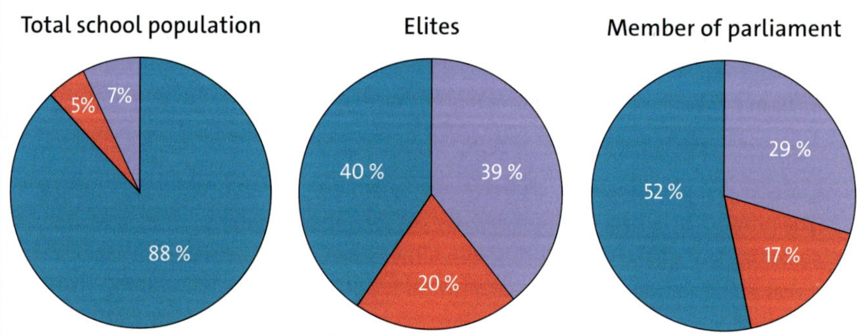

Writing

Exam preparation

S ▸ Writing an argumentative text, pp. 167–172

Writing checklist

8 Taking the text and the statistics in exercise 7 as a starting point, comment on this quote from the text.

> *"The most important thing I found out was that we are still educating different social classes for different functions in society."* (ll. 3–5)

Section F Overcoming disabilities

Warm-up

1 Look at the photos of four famous people who have all overcome disabilities. In groups, share what you know about them. If you need help, look at the box or find out about the person online.

Simone Biles, US gymnast and Olympic gold medallist

Prof. Stephen Hawking, British scientist and author

Greta Thunberg, Swedish climate activist

Jamie Oliver, British chef and author

Good to know

Attention Deficit Hyperactivity Disorder (ADHD) is a behavioural disorder which may make it difficult for a person to concentrate or control certain impulses.

People with **Asperger syndrome (Asperger's)** often struggle with social interaction and understanding non-verbal communication. They may also show repetitive behaviour or very specific and restricted interests.

Dyslexia is a learning disability which may mean that a person has difficulties with reading, writing and spelling words.

Motor neurone disease (*neuro* = related to the nerves) is a rare, degenerative disease which causes symptoms such as muscle weakness and usually shortens life expectancy.

2 Do you know any other famous people with disabilities? What are they famous for? Share what you know with the class.

Working with the text

3 Skim the text on the following pages and choose the correct option.

S ▸ Reading difficult texts, pp. 39–40

The author of the blog is …

a a young man with a disability who wanted to do an internship.
b an able-bodied blogger who campaigns for the rights of people with disabilities.
c the head of a company who would like to improve access to the workplace for people with disabilities.

Nazeem's blog

It's time to give people with disabilities equal opportunities in the workplace.

Hey! It's Naz here and I wanna tell you all about something that happened to me last week. I'm still really angry and I need to get this off my chest!

So I applied for an internship in the marketing department of a young fashion magazine. Perfect for me, right? You all know that I love fashion and have already written a couple of articles for magazines about cool clothes for people with disabilities. So, I sent in my CV and a week later they rang me to arrange an interview. The guy on the phone said that they were really impressed with my qualifications and enjoyed reading the articles I'd sent in. Sounds positive, right?

But then I had to ask about wheelchair access to the building as they are on the 2nd floor. And guess what? He said he was really sorry but the offices are in an old building with no lift. Now I was prepared for this coz I'd already looked up the building online and thought this might be the case. So I suggested doing the internship online (I have a laptop and everything I need at home). I even offered to do the interview in an accessible café around the corner from the company and to come there every week for meetings if necessary! But no. They said they were not 'equipped' to offer online internships.

Why do I and other people with disabilities have to put up with this kind of discrimination? I have the qualifications and necessary experience to do the internship and I'd be a great employee coz I'm really enthusiastic and would work twice as hard as someone without disabilities coz I want to show the world that we are just as good, if not better than able-bodied people!

All this anger and disappointment has inspired me to write about the issues people with disability face in the workplace – AND I'm going to send a link to this text to the guy at the marketing company!

First of all, a few facts:

- There are over 1,000,000,000 people with disabilities around the world – that's around 1 person in 6!
- There are many types of disability. Here are a few of them: people with mobility issues like me, people with cognitive issues, or whose speech, vision or hearing are impaired. Some people have visible disabilities, and some disabilities are invisible. The point is: we're all different!
- We are not only 'disabled' but we also belong to a large variety of ethnicities, cultures and traditions, we are LGBTQ+, we belong to different social classes, we speak different languages or we don't use words at all = we are really diverse!
- People with disabilities are the largest minority group in the world – so how come we are excluded from many conversations about diversity and inclusion? How about talking to us?

What's it like for us in the world of work?

For a start, people with disabilities are 50% less likely to get a job than non-disabled people and when they do work, it's often at a lower corporate level. So is it because we're less qualified? Well, studies actually show that those with an advanced university degree earn $21,000 less per year than people without disabilities,

17 to **equip** *ausrüsten, ausstatten*
30 **vision** *Sehkraft, Sehvermögen*
31 **impaired** *beeinträchtigt*

even though they have the same education levels. There's absolutely NO reason for this, coz studies have shown time and time again that employees with disabilities bring improved productivity and increased innovation.

Companies can even use us to boost their image: companies identified as disability-inclusion champions had 28% higher revenue, perhaps because consumer surveys say that people are more likely to buy from companies that show disabled people in their advertising. So we can even improve your company's reputation – great, right? And don't forget that disabled people are consumers too!

So how can employers make life easier for their awesome employees with disabilities?

Well, for many of us, our preferred working environment might be our home. And that's not because we're lazy and wanna take naps all day (although having a little sleep during the day is awesome!), but because we might need specialized equipment and that's set up at home. Or we have someone to help us with certain things and it's just easier to organize all that from home.

People who have autism and are sensitive to sound and light might just prefer to work in a quiet environment so they can concentrate better. So what about being flexible and allowing remote or hybrid working? It's not a big deal and it makes our lives a whole lot easier!

Of course, other people with disabilities would prefer to work in the company office with the rest of their team, but they face physical barriers (remember that fashion magazine office I talked about?). It would be great if companies bore people with disabilities in mind when choosing a company office. A lift that's big enough to accommodate a wheelchair and accessible toilets would be a great start. Sometimes making some smaller changes would also help, like putting in special ramps or widening doorways.

I'm sure there are many more helpful ideas that I haven't included here, so, if you'd like to add some of your own, please put them in the comment field below.

People with disabilities can make a positive contribution to the world of work – it's time to level the playing field for them.

(914 words)

[53] **awesome** *beeindruckend, fantastisch*

[70] to **widen sth** *etw erweitern, etw verbreitern*

[70] doorway *Eingang, Türdurchgang*

4 Read the text again and do the following tasks.

1 Describe what happened to Naz when he applied for an internship.
2 State the ways in which people with disabilities are discriminated against in the world of work.
3 Outline ways in which, according to Naz, employers can make workplaces more accessible to people with disabilities.

S ▸ Writing a summary, p. 81

5 Analyse how the author tries to persuade the reader of his point of view.

Exam preparation

S ▸ Dealing with a text analysis task, pp. 215–220

Working with words

6 Work with a partner. Look at the highlighted words or phrases in the text and work out the meaning from the context.

Listening

56

7 You are going to hear a radio interview with a group of young disabled people.

While listening, choose the correct options (a, b or c). There is only one correct answer.

Exam preparation

S ▸ Dealing with listening tasks, pp. 123–125

1 D.D.M.A. is …
- **a** a hip hop group.
- **b** the name of a radio show.
- **c** an organization campaigning for disabled rights.

2 D.D.M.A. also means …
- **a** artists with disabilities should be represented more in the music industry.
- **b** don't judge a person who is different because they might have a hidden disability.
- **c** audiences should focus on what people with disabilities can do, rather than what they can't do.

3 The 'Krip Hop' movement supports …
- **a** young artists from any minority group.
- **b** talented artists who happen to be disabled.
- **c** young disabled people who want to express themselves through hip hop.

4 People with disabilities are often left out of debates on diversity and equality because …
- **a** of communication or practical issues arising from their disability.
- **b** people who experience other kinds of discrimination are often prioritized.
- **c** there often aren't enough of them in one area to be able to form a protest group.

5 For people on the autism spectrum, some public places offer …
- **a** a time when everybody has to be as quiet as possible.
- **b** a special time of the day with quieter or no music and without flashing lights.
- **c** an area with special flashing lights where they can have a break and listen to relaxing music.

6 With respect to people with disabilities and relationships, able-bodied people often wrongly believe that …
- **a** a disabled person won't be able to care for them too.
- **b** they will have to live together with a disabled person's carer.
- **c** a person with disabilities won't need anyone to care for their emotional needs.

Mediation

S ▸ Mediation, pp. 259–261

8 Read the article on the following pages and make notes in German on these aspects.

- issues faced by people with disability
- solutions which have been implemented in other places and how they improve people's lives

What would a disabled-accessible city look like?

Most cities are utterly unfriendly to people with disabilities – but with almost one billion estimated to be urban-dwellers by 2050, a few cities are undergoing a remarkable shift

To David Meere, a visually impaired man from Melbourne, among the various obstacles to life in cities is another that is less frequently discussed: fear.

"The fear of not being able to navigate busy, cluttered and visually oriented environments is a major barrier to participation in normal life," says Meere, 52, "be that going to the shops, going for a walk in the park, going to work, looking for work, or simply socialising."

[...] Meere is just one of the hundreds of millions of people with disabilities who live in cities around the world. By 2050, they will number an estimated 940 million people, or 15% of what will be roughly 6.25 billion total urban dwellers, lending an urgency to the UN's declaration that poor accessibility "presents a major challenge".

For the physically disabled, barriers can range from blocked wheelchair ramps, to buildings without lifts, to inaccessible toilets, to shops without step-free access. Meanwhile, for learning disabled people or those on the autistic spectrum, the cluttered and hectic metropolitan environment can be a sensory minefield.

Although the Convention on the Rights of Persons with Disabilities and laws such as the Americans with Disabilities Act, Britain's Equality Act and Australia's Disability Discrimination Act aim to boost rights and access, the reality on the ground can be very different.

And yet, cities benefit from accessibility. One World Health Organisation study described how, like Meere, disabled people are less likely to socialise or work without accessible transport. Cities also miss out on economic gains: in the UK the "purple pound" is worth £212bn, and the accessible-tourism market an estimated £12bn.

Some cities, however, are leading the way.

Mapping apps make navigating cities a doddle for most people – but their lack of detail on ramps and dropped kerbs mean they don't always work well for people with a physical disability.

Take the hilly city of Seattle, where several neighbourhoods have no pavements at all, and many streets have a slope grade (or tilt) of 10% or even 20%.

The University of Washington's Taskar Center for Accessible Technology has a solution: a map-based app allowing pedestrians with limited mobility to plan accessible routes. AccessMap enables users to enter a destination, and receive suggested routes depending on customised settings, such as limiting uphill or downhill inclines. [...] Now the Taskar Centre's related OpenSidewalks project is taking it further by crowdsourcing extra information, such as pavement width and the location of handrails. [...]

As David Meere discovered, in Melbourne, Australia, an eight-month pilot scheme is currently transforming how visually impaired people navigate public space. The project at Southern Cross station rail terminal uses Bluetooth and free GPS smartphone app BlindSquare to create a beacon navigation system.

1 utter *völlig, vollkommen*
17 cluttered *überladen, voller Unordnung*
17 **sensory** *sensorisch*
17 **minefield** *Minenfeld, gefährliches Terrain*
28 doddle *Kinderspiel*
29 kerb *Bordstein*
31 **hilly** *hügelig*
31 **pavement** *Gehsteig, Bürgersteig*
32 **slope grade** *Gefälle*
32 tilt *Neigung*
37 incline *Steigung, Neigung*
38 **width** *Breite*
39 handrail *Geländer, Handlauf*
40 **pilot scheme** *Pilotprojekt*
42 rail terminal *Bahnhof*
44 **beacon** *hier: (akustisches) Warnsignal*

[44] **cue** *Zeichen, Hinweis*
[45] **escalator** *Rolltreppe*
[45] **outage** *Ausfall*
[46] **directional information** *Richtungsangaben*
[46] **unreliable** *unzuverlässig*
[53] **blindness** *Blindheit*
[54] **sighted** *sehend*
[55] **reversal** *Umkehr, Umkehrung*

Users receive audio cues via their smartphones, providing directions or real time information about issues such as escalator outages. Outside, the app provides real time directional information; inside, where GPS is unreliable, 20 wireless Bluetooth beacons means users still receive information. Audio cues include advice such as: "Approaching three escalators on left, followed by a set of doors – the doors on the left are automated."

The trial is led by the charity Guide Dogs Victoria, which plans to install similar systems at Melbourne Zoo, Albert Park (home to the Australian Grand Prix) and the Docklands area.

"In many situations, the person with low vision and blindness will have greater knowledge than the sighted person," says Alastair Stott of Guide Dogs Victoria. "It's a complete role reversal."

(619 words) Source: *The Guardian*, 14 February 2018

9 You are a member of a local campaign group for the rights of people with disabilities. The group leader has asked you to write a letter to the local council, outlining some of the difficulties people with disabilities face in everyday life and ways in which their lives can be made easier. You decide to use the article *What would a disabled-accessible city look like?* as a basis for your letter.

S ▸ Mediation, pp. 259–261

Write your letter in German, giving examples of what other cities have done.

Speaking

10 **Discuss the following points with a partner, then share your ideas with the class.**

1. Brainstorm barriers (physical and social) and prejudices people with physical or cognitive disabilities may face in everyday life in your local area.
2. Choose three and discuss ways in which these issues can be overcome.

Writing

Exam preparation

S ▸ Writing an argumentative text, p. 167–172

Writing checklist

11 **Taking the cartoon as a starting point, comment on the quote below.**

Being disabled should not mean being disqualified from having access to every aspect of life.
– Emma Thompson, British actor

Project A class debate

You are going to have a class debate on one of the issues related to equality that you have dealt with in this Topic.

Step 1

Decide on an issue that you want to debate. You can choose one of the statements below or come up with your own idea.

- African Americans should receive financial compensation for the suffering caused by slavery.
- Gender inequality in leading positions can only be solved by a 'quota' system.
- Refugees should have the right to remain and settle wherever they want.
- All buildings, including historical ones, must be adapted to make them accessible to people with physical disabilities.
- Schools should educate all children together, whatever their physical or mental abilities.

Step 2

Once you have chosen a topic for the debate, divide the class into four groups: two groups should agree with the statement and two groups disagree.

Step 3

Decide on the following additional roles:

- **A moderator**: this person is responsible for ensuring that both sides of the debate receive equal speaking time and that participants do not interrupt one another.
- Three **speakers** per group: these people will take it in turns to express the opinion of the group and deliver arguments against statements by the other groups.

Tip

Brainstorm possible counterarguments that opposing groups might come up with and decide how to deal with them.

Step 4

Research and formulate arguments and examples which support your point of view.

Step 5

The moderator introduces the debate and calls on each member of the individual groups to give their opening arguments. He/She signals when it is time for a change of speaker.

Tip

It's a good idea to agree on the maximum length of time for the debate, which the moderator will be responsible for keeping.

Step 6

The debate ends when all three speakers from each group have contributed to the debate and there are no more points of discussion. However, each group should have the opportunity to sum up their arguments briefly at the end of the debate.

Class debate checklist

✓ Have you clearly defined the issue to be debated?
✓ Have you prepared your roles carefully, noting down what you want to say?
✓ Has everyone had a chance to present their arguments?
✓ Has each group summed up their arguments briefly at the end?

57

Words in context

to **enslave sb** *jdn versklaven*
abolition *Abschaffung*
slavery *Sklaverei*
segregation *Rassentrennung*
Civil Rights movement *Bürgerrechtsbewegung*
non-violent *gewaltlos*
racism *Rassismus*
acquittal *Freispruch*
to **spark sth** *etw auslösen*
protest *Demonstration*
supremacy *Vorherrschaft*
to **migrate** *migrieren, auswandern*
to **flee conflict** *vor Konflikten fliehen*
to **seek asylum** *um Asyl bitten*
to **apply for asylum** *Asyl beantragen*
refugee camp *Flüchtlingslager*
to **reject a claim** *einen Antrag ablehnen*
to **deport** *ausweisen, abschieben*
to **overcome** *überwinden*
labour shortage *Arbeitskräftemangel*
suspicion *Misstrauen*
hostility *Feindseligkeit*
to **settle** *sich niederlassen*
descendant *Nachfahre, Nachkomme*
to **face discrimination** *mit Diskriminierung zu kämpfen haben*
to **struggle (with sth)** *(mit etw) kämpfen*
identity *Identität*
gender equality *Gleichstellung der Geschlechter*
feminism *Feminismus*
poverty *Armut*
violence *Gewalt*
femicide *Frauenmord*
to **empower sb to do sth** *jdn befähigen, etw zu tun*
misogyny *Frauenfeindlichkeit*
sexual harrassment *sexuelle Belästigung*
abuse *Missbrauch*
perpetrator *Täter/in*
to **bring sb to justice** *jdn vor Gericht bringen*
paternity leave *Vaterschaftsurlaub*
gender pay gap *geschlechtsspezifische Lohngefälle*
glass ceiling *gläserne Decke*

From racial segregation to #Blacklivesmatter

Centuries ago, Africans were brought over to what is now the USA and enslaved in terrible conditions. Even following the abolition of slavery, they endured the humiliation of racial segregation in education, public services and other facilities.

The Civil Rights movement pushed for change through non-violent protests such as the March on Washington, and, by 1964, most public places and institutions had, at least in theory, been desegregated. However, the fight against racism and unequal treatment is ongoing. Many black people have been killed by police officers, such as the unarmed teenager Trayvon Martin in 2012. His death and the subsequent acquittal of the shooter sparked protests against police brutality and white supremacy, and the hashtag Black Lives Matter gained wider usage.

Trying to belong

People migrate for a variety of reasons, for example to flee conflict or seek better opportunities.

Every year, thousands seek asylum in EU countries. The process of applying for asylum can be complex and many stay for extended periods in refugee camps, only to have their application rejected and be deported.

After the Second World War, people were invited to come and help overcome the labour shortages, for example the immigrants from former British colonies in the Caribbean, or the 'guest workers' who came to West Germany. Many expected a warm welcome, but were instead greeted with suspicion or even hostility. However, many settled permanently and their descendants are now second or third generation immigrants. Although migrants and their descendants bring a number of benefits to the societies they live in, many face discrimination and struggle with issues of identity and belonging.

The long road to gender equality

For decades, women have been fighting for more gender equality. Although feminism has brought about significant change, there is still a long way to go. Even today, women – and especially women of colour – are disproportionately affected by poverty, poorer health and are subject to gender-based violence and femicide.

In recent years, the #MeToo movement has empowered women (and men) to speak out about misogyny, sexual harassment and abuse. This has resulted in some perpetrators being brought to justice.

In some countries, women have attained greater job security through improved childcare options and paternity leave for fathers. However, inequality can still be seen in the gender pay gap and the 'glass ceiling', which means that women are often underrepresented in higher professional and political positions.

Sexual and gender minorities: the struggle for acceptance

Lesbian, gay, bisexual and transgender people and other gender or sexual minorities (LGBTQ+) suffer discrimination, persecution, and sometimes face imprisonment or death just for being who they are. Even in countries with progressive LGBTQ+ rights, they don't have the same rights as heterosexual and cisgender people. Furthermore, there are still worrying numbers of homophobic attacks and LGBTQ+ people still experience bullying and ostracization. Gay pride parades and other events take place across the world to push for equal rights, visibility and acceptance.

In recent decades, civil rights milestones have been reached in a number of countries, such as the decriminalization of homosexuality, same-sex marriage and the legal acknowledgement of transgender people's gender identity.

lesbian *lesbisch*
gay *homosexuell*
bisexual *bisexuell*
transgender *transgender*
minority *Minderheit*
imprisonment *Haft(strafe)*
heterosexual *hetero(sexuell)*
cisgender *(sich mit dem Geschlecht identifizierend, mit dem man geboren wurde)*
homophobic *homophob*
gay pride parade *Schwulenparade*
decriminalization *Entkriminalisierung*
homosexuality *Homosexualität*
same-sex marriage *gleichgeschlechtliche Ehe*
gender identity *Geschlechtsidentität*

Stuck in the class system

In most societies, some form of social class system exists, based on factors such as family background, wealth, profession and regional accent. The UK in particular is known for being a 'class-based' society with rigid class divisions. However, in recent years these have become more blurred, as people from working-class backgrounds climb the 'class ladder' by attaining higher educational qualifications which lead to better-paid jobs and perhaps a more middle-class lifestyle.

Social mobility can be extremely difficult to achieve. For example, a working-class child growing up in a poor area of the UK will most likely attend a state school which struggles to offer the same opportunities as a school in a more affluent area. Furthermore, the top jobs and political positions in the country are still predominantly in the hands of a wealthy elite, who are often educated at exclusive private schools.

social class *Bevölkerungsschicht*
wealth *Vermögen*
class-based society *klassenbasierte Gesellschaft*
class divisions *Trennlinien zwischen den Klassen*
working-class background *aus einer Arbeiterfamilie (stammend)*
class ladder *(sozialer) Aufstieg*
middle-class *der Mittelschicht zugehörig*
social mobility *gesellschaftliche Mobilität*
state school *öffentlich Schule*
affluent *wohlhabend*
elite *Elite*
private school *Privatschule*

Representing ability

People with disabilities are often left out of the fight for diversity. Possible reasons for this are that those with limited mobility may be unable to attend public demonstrations and protests, while others may have a cognitive or behavioural disability which hinders communication.

Fortunately, the stigma attached to people with disabilities taking part in public life is slowly disappearing. Laws have been put into place to make new buildings more accessible through wheelchair ramps and lifts. In education, barriers are being broken down allowing people with different disabilities to participate in mainstream education.

They have also become more visible in the media: RJ Mitte, an actor with cerebral palsy, starred in the popular series *Breaking Bad,* and George Webster, an actor who has Down's Syndrome, is a presenter on BBC children's TV. Webster also campaigns for better representation of disabled people in public life and to dispel myths about people with disabilities.

disability *Behinderung*
mobility *Beweglichkeit*
cognitive *kognitiv*
behavioural *Verhaltens-*
accessible *barrierefrei*
wheelchair *Rollstuhl*
ramp *Rampe*
lift *Aufzug*
barrier *Barriere, Hindernis*
cerebral palsy *Zerebralparese (Lähmung)*
to **campaign for sth** *sich für etw engagieren*
representation *Vertretung; Darstellung*
to **dispel a myth (about sth)** *mit einem Mythos aufräumen*

1 **Use the prefixes from the list to make words with the opposite meanings.**

de- | dis- (x2) | in- (x2) | un- (x2)

1 Many old buildings are …accessible to people with physical disabilities.
2 Our society is very …equal: there's a large gap between rich and poor.
3 Some of the protesters had guns, but the majority were …armed.
4 People of colour make up a …proportionate amount of the prison population in the US.
5 Many homosexuals tried to make themselves …visible in public to avoid arrest.
6 Civil rights activists fought for the …segregation of public transport.
7 She's physically fit but needs extra support at school because of her cognitive …ability.

2 **Match verbs from box A and box B to make collocations. Then complete the sentences with the correct words.**

A	B
bring | dispel | face | flee | overcome | seek | spark | treat	asylum | conflict | discrimination | labour shortages | myths | protests | to justice | with suspicion

1 Organizing events for refugees and local people helps to … … about refugees and promote friendship.
2 We are trying to … the … in our company by speeding up the visa application process for migrant workers.
3 The police have promised to … the perpetrators of the homophobic attacks … .
4 The racist comments made by the leader of the far-right political party are likely to … … across the country.
5 Why do people … us … when we have come here to help them?
6 She decided to … … in the UK because she was being persecuted in her own country for being a lesbian.
7 People with disabilities often … … on the job market.
8 Refugees are trying to cross the border to … the violent … in their country.

3 **Find highlighted words and phrases in the text to match the definitions.**

1 the process of making something legal
2 start to live somewhere permanently
3 the formal ending of something
4 putting people into jail for committing a crime
5 a device to help people who are unable to walk to move around
6 the opportunity to move to a higher level of society
7 social groups which do not belong to the majority
8 a period of time off work for a father to look after his baby

4 **Replace the underlined words with a word with a similar meaning from the list.**

affluent | benefits | endure | milestone | misogyny | non-violent | supremacy

1 His family was <u>wealthy</u>, so they could afford to send him to a private school.
2 The end of segregation was an important <u>achievement</u> in the history of the Civil Rights movement.
3 The black students at the school were forced to <u>suffer</u> bullying and humiliation.
4 Our feminist movement fights against <u>sexism</u> and gender inequality.
5 Increased diversity has brought a number of <u>advantages</u> to our company.
6 We are campaigning against police harassment with a series of <u>peaceful</u> protests.
7 Racist organizations such as the Klu Klux Klan believe in white <u>superiority</u>.

Mediation

Mediation means "getting a message across". You express ideas in one language through the medium of another. Mediation can be both written or oral, and sometimes takes the form of "interpreting" between people who speak different languages.

Example task

Situation: As a disability activist, you are participating in the International Day of Persons with Disabilities which takes place on 3 December each year.
You have volunteered to prepare a brochure for the participants reporting on the ways in which different cities help disabled persons overcome the obstacles they are often confronted with. You find a German newspaper article which deals with this issue – *Barrierefreiheit – Städte, die als Blaupause dienen können* (p. 259).

Task: Read the article and use the information in it for your brochure.

Step 1: Analysing the task

1 Form

The exact form of your mediation depends primarily on three factors you need to identify by reading the question carefully:

Audience	**Medium / Text type**	**Aim**
– fellow students	– brochure	to provide ...
– customers of a company	– announcement	– information
– family members	– email, letter	– advice
– readers of a newspaper	– podcast	– arguments
– etc.	– newspaper article	– etc.
	– etc.	

Register:
The factors outlined above determine the situational context and, as a result, which register you are expected to use (more informal or more formal).

2 Content

Start by narrowing down the relevant content: the way the question is worded usually helps you do this.

Exercise 1

1 Determine which form and content is correct for the following question:

Write an email with information on how refugees can become German citizens for a US American friend who is working on a paper on the topic "From refugee to citizen".

2 Determine which form and content is correct for the example task at the top of this page.

Step 2: Dealing with the original text

Skimming: Skim over the text quickly to get a rough impression of what it is about. Don't forget to include the title – and any illustrations or photos.

Scanning: Now go through the text paragraph by paragraph and write down the information you decided was important when you analysed the question (see Step 1).

Exercise 2

Use the two reading styles (skimming and scanning) for the text on p. 259.

Step 3: Writing the mediation

Before you start to write, read the question again to make sure that you are expressing the content you identified to the right audience using the correct text type.

Part of the writing process involves **paraphrasing**, i.e. writing things using different words. There are two main reasons why you need to paraphrase parts of the text:

1 Idioms in the source text

No matter what language the source text is written in, it can be very tricky to express idioms in another language – imagery varies greatly from one language to another. Use both bilingual and monolingual dictionaries to help you.

S ▸ Using a dictionary, pp. 41–42

Examples of idiomatic expressions

1. *The ball is in your court.* (Sie sind am Zug / dran.)
2. *to judge a book by its cover* (vorschnell nach dem äußeren Anschein urteilen)
3. Eselsbrücke *(method to make learning easier)*
4. sich aus dem Staub machen *(to leave)*

2 Simplification / shortening in the target text

Mediation is basically all about summarizing. Make sure you ignore any repetitions, examples, anecdotes and digression, and concentrate solely on the main topic. Quotes should be looked at individually, and only be used in your mediation text if they contain a core message and are not just there to look or sound good.

Example of simplification / shortening

Original text:

Bei der Umsetzung ließ sich das Architekturbüro von der Arizona State University hinsichtlich der Reizverringerung beraten, was zur Wahl einer besonders leisen Heizungs- und Belüftungsanlage und der Platzierung der Waschküche fern der Schlafzimmer führte.

Example of how this should be expressed in a mediation task:

This led to the installation of a quiet heating and ventilation system and to locating the laundry room away from the bedrooms.

Exercise 3

1. Find two German idioms in the source text of the example exercise and mediate their meaning in English.
2. Now write the text for your brochure (see example task on p. 257) for the participants at the conference.

Barrierefreiheit – Städte, die als Blaupause dienen können

Freuen Sie sich nicht auch, wenn Sie mit einem Rollkoffer unterwegs sind und anstatt einer Treppe eine Rampe vorfinden? Menschen mit Behinderung sind auf solche und andere Maßnahmen zur Barrierefreiheit im Alltag und allen Lebensbereichen angewiesen und werden diesbezüglich immer noch viel zu oft in ihre Schranken verwiesen. Einige Städte weltweit haben jedoch in den letzten Jahren gezeigt, wie es funktionieren kann.

Dänemark zählt dabei zu den federführenden Ländern. Das Freizeitzentrum Musholm in der Stadt Korsør, Eigentum der dänischen Stiftung für Menschen mit Muskeldystrophie, zählt in puncto Barrierefreiheit zu den weltweit modernsten Sport- und Ferienanlagen für Menschen mit Einschränkungen. Neben zahlreichen weiteren Preisen erhielt das Zentrum 2017 eine Auszeichnung des Internationalen Paralympischen Komitees für den Bau einer großen Mehrzweckhalle mit maximaler Barrierefreiheit. Dort entstanden u.a. eine 100 m lange Bahn für Rollstuhlrennen rund um die Halle und eine Kletterwand für Rollstuhlfahrer. Ein spezielles Flaschenzugsystem macht das Klettern auch für Menschen mit wenig Muskelkraft möglich. Das angrenzende Hotel ist selbstverständlich maximal barrierefrei und auch der private Badesteg der Anlage ist breit genug für Rollstühle und mit einer Rampe ausgestattet. So ermöglicht dieses Konzept Menschen mit Behinderung einen rundum aktiven, inklusiven Urlaub.

Aber auch im Bereich der Arbeitswelt zeigt Dänemark in der Hauptstadt Kopenhagen, wie Barrierefreiheit gelebt werden kann. Dort befindet sich das weltweit barrierefreieste Bürogebäude, das als Hauptsitz von ca. 30 Behindertenverbänden nach dem Prinzip des Universellen Designs gestaltet wurde. So sind alle Aufzüge mit zweiseitigen Zugängen ausgestattet, womit sich die sonst notwendige 180-Grad-Drehung mit dem Rollstuhl im Aufzug erübrigt. Außerdem verfügt das Gebäude über barrierefreie Handläufe mit taktilen Beschriftungen, damit blinde und sehbehinderte Menschen sich besser zurechtfinden.

In der Stadt Chester in England befindet sich im Zentrum der Altstadt eine einzigartige Sehenswürdigkeit: die Rows. Dabei handelt es sich um überdachte Gänge, die nebeneinanderliegende Häuser mit einer Art Galerie verbinden. Einige davon befinden sich im ersten Stock und sind mit Rampe und Aufzug behindertengerecht ausgestattet. 2016 gewann die Stadt den Access City Award, ein Preis, der jährlich von der EU ausgelobt wird.

Zudem entsteht mit dem Chester Northgate hier gerade ein Vorzeigeprojekt. Das gesamte Stadtzentrum wird rundum neugestaltet: Sämtliche Läden und Restaurants sind barrierefrei und ein Hotel hat Deckenlifte sowie sogenannte „Changing Places", die mehr bieten als reguläre Behindertentoiletten, da sie nicht nur größer sind, sondern zusätzlich mit einer höhenverstellbaren Pflegeliege, einem Liftsystem sowie einer Dusche ausgestattet sind. Auch im Storyhouse, einem gemischt genutzten Kulturzentrum in Chester, wird Barrierefreiheit großgeschrieben. Es wurde unter anderem auf der Grundlage von Feedback von Behinderten gestaltet und beherbergt eine Bibliothek, ein Theater und ein Kino, die allesamt rollstuhlgerecht gestaltet sind. Mit einem Angebot an barrierefreien Vorstellungen mit Audiodeskription und Zeichensprache werden hier auch hör- und sehgeschädigte Menschen berücksichtigt.

Doch nicht nur körperliche, sondern auch psychische Beeinträchtigungen fordern Barrierefreiheit. Menschen mit Autismus beispielsweise kämpfen mit Reizüberflutung und können überempfindlich auf Geräusche, Licht, Farben und Bewegung reagieren und Schwierigkeiten mit großen Menschenansammlungen haben. In Sonoma im US-amerikanischen Bundesstaat Kalifornien wird dem Rechnung getragen. Das Sweetwater Spectrum ist eine Anlage, die speziell auf die Bedürfnisse von Autisten angepasst ist. Die Unterkunft in ruhiger Umgebung für junge Erwachsene bietet Therapiepools und für Bewohner mit einem grünen Daumen einen Bereich zum Gärtnern. Bei der Umsetzung ließ sich das Architekturbüro von der Arizona State University hinsichtlich der Reizverringerung beraten, was zur Wahl einer besonders leisen Heizungs- und Belüftungsanlage und der Platzierung der Waschküche fern der Schlafzimmer führte. Die Wohnbereiche sind reizarm ausgestattet und verzichten auf überflüssige Dekoration und grelles Licht.

(599 words)

Presentation

Being able to present to an audience is a skill that we need at almost every stage of our lives beginning with school and lasting well into our working lives and careers. In a presentation, it is not just the content that is important but also how clearly and understandably this is presented.

Example task

Give a presentation on the topic of "Child labour – poverty and exploitation".

Step 1: Doing research

Good to know

When researching with search engines, using search operators such as *site:*, *related:*, *OR* and *AND* will help narrow down your search.

Prepare your topic well, making sure that any websites you use as information sources are reliable. It is sometimes helpful to look at a website's *About us* page which should clearly explain who has created the website and who is responsible for it. US websites with top level domains such as *.org*, *.edu* and *.gov* can generally be considered trustworthy and reliable.

Record your search results carefully in a structured way.

Step 2: Developing your ideas

Aim the content and format of your presentation clearly at your audience. Your **presentation cards** should ideally only contain a couple of keywords to help you formulate what you want to say in your own words. This will make your presentation flow more naturally.

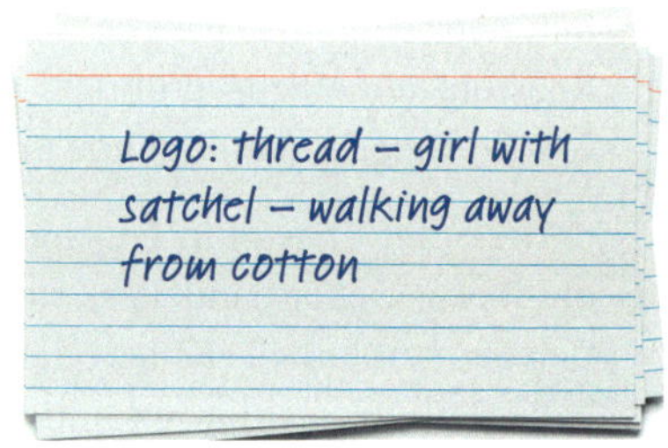

Stick to the most important key ideas, and structure your presentation so that it follows a **clear central theme**.

subsidiary

subsidiary site:youglish.com

Check your notes for accuracy regarding both the content and language. If you're not sure how to **pronounce** a word, check it in an online dictionary with pronunciation. You might need to look for videos if the word (e.g. a place name you don't recognize) doesn't appear in a normal dictionary.

Use suitable **visual materials** in your presentation to help make the content more memorable for your audience.

- Make sure you don't fill your slides with too much information when creating your presentation. Your audience's attention should be on *you*, not your slides.

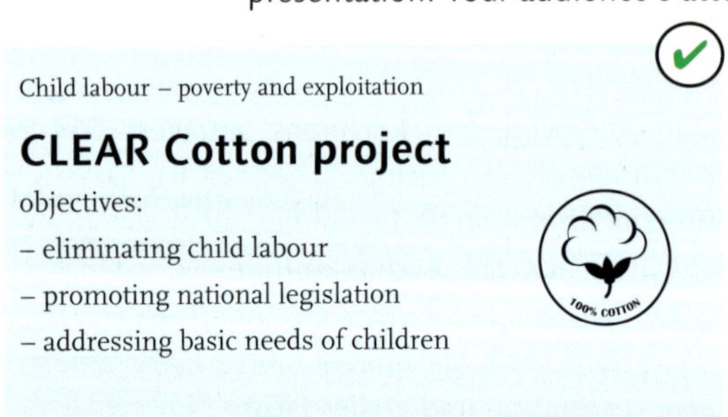

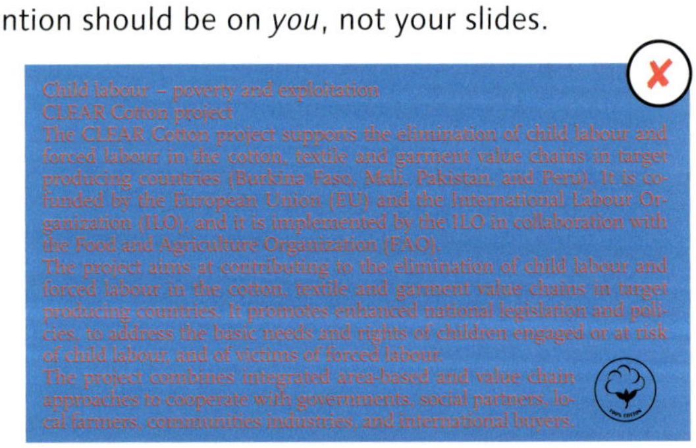

- If you're using a flipchart or whiteboard: decide what it should look like at the end of your presentation.

Step 3: Practising and rehearsing

There's no such thing as practising too much for a presentation! Rehearse your presentation in front of a mirror or record a video of yourself giving your presentation – you'll be surprised just how quickly you get used to it!

Practise standing still and pay attention to your **body language** (facial expressions and gestures); speak calmly and pronounce every word clearly.

Use verbal statements or cues (known as **signposting**) to structure your presentation and help your audience understand where you are in your presentation and what they can expect next.

Start the presentation by explaining what you'll be talking about and repeat the main message of your presentation at the end.

Introducing yourself and your topic
- Good morning/afternoon. My name is ...
- Today I am going to talk about ...
- The subject of my talk is ...
- My topic today is ...
- If you have any questions, please don't hesitate to interrupt me.
- I'd like to ask you to please save your questions for the end of the presentation.

to **hesitate** *zögern*
to **interrupt sb** *jdm ins Wort fallen*

Beginning your first point
- I'd like to begin by saying something about ...
- I want to start by explaining ...

Guiding your audience through your presentation
- There are a number of points I'd like to make.
- I'll start with ... . Then I'll talk about ...
- Firstly, / First of all, ... / Secondly, ... / And finally, ...
- And now, moving on to ...
- The next topic I'd like to focus on is ...
- Now I'd like to discuss ...
- Now we'll move on to ...
- Let's look at ...
- Why is this important? Because ...
- The significance of this is ...

significance *Bedeutung, Wichtigkeit*

Ending your presentation
- Let's summarize briefly what we've looked at.
- Let me remind you of some of the issues we've covered.
- In conclusion, ...
- I would like to finish by saying ...
- Thank you very much for your attention.
- If you have any questions, I'm happy to answer them now.

briefly *kurz*
issue *Problem, Thema*
to **cover sth** *etw (Thema usw.) behandeln*

Exercise

Research a topic appropriate to your syllabus according to the aspects mentioned above. You should look for an example of a TED Talk on the internet (max. length: 5 minutes) which you think was particularly successful.

Present to the rest of your class what you think the talk's strengths are with the help of short video clips, then discuss your findings in the group.

During the presentations, make a list of any new useful presentation skills your classmates find, and implement as many of them as possible when you give your next presentation.

Review

1 Rank the Sections A–F in this Topic based on how interesting they were to you. Then, look back at your work on the overview of this Topic (pages 224–225) and how you ranked them there (page 224, exercise 2). Have your rankings changed? Share your results with a group and tell them what you found most interesting.

2 Look at your KWL list (page 225, exercise 5). Fill out the "Learned" part of the list. Next, look at your "Want to know" list. What do you still want to know?

3 Make a list of ten words in the Topic that were new to you and you consider important to know. Then collect everyone's words and cluster them into groups. Finally, pick a word group and write a paragraph using all the words.

Evaluate

Do this task on your own. How much do you agree or disagree with the statements below? Rate each one on a scale of one to four. The references on the left show you which exercises you can review.

1 = totally disagree **2** = disagree **3** = agree **4** = totally agree

	Section		Statement
▸ p 230, exercise 8	**A**	**1**	I can understand an interview about the Civil Rights movement.
▸ p. 231, exercise 11		**2**	I can understand a slam poetry performance about racism.
▸ p. 231, exercise 13		**3**	I can write an argumentative text about racial injustice in the USA.
▸ pp. 232–233, exercise 3	**B**	**4**	I can summarize part of a speech on the need for gender equality.
▸ p. 235, exercise 8		**5**	I can understand a radio discussion about the #MeToo movement.
▸ p. 235, exercise 10		**6**	I can write an argumentative text about gender equality.
▸ pp. 236–237, exercises 2–3	**C**	**7**	I can understand a radio show about asylum seekers.
▸ p. 239, exercise 6		**8**	I can analyse a newspaper article.
▸ p. 239, exercise 10		**9**	I can write a creative text about integrating asylum seekers.
▸ p. 242, exercise 4	**D**	**10**	I can summarize a text teaching about LGBT issues in schools.
▸ p. 243, exercise 9		**11**	I understand various speakers giving their opinion on teaching LGBT relationships in schools.
▸ p. 243, exercise 11		**12**	I can write a letter to the editor expressing my opinion on the issue.
▸ p. 246, exercise 7	**E**	**13**	I can describe and analyse statistics on educational backgrounds.
▸ p. 246, exercise 8		**14**	I can write an argumentative text on education and social class.
▸ p. 250, exercise 7	**F**	**15**	I can understand a radio interview with disability activists.
▸ pp. 250–252, exercises 8–9		**16**	I can express the most important points of an English-language text in German (mediation).
▸ p. 252, exercise 11		**17**	I can write an argumentative text on disability and inclusion.
S ▸ pp. 257–259	**Skills**	**18**	I can deal with mediation tasks.
S ▸ pp. 260–261		**19**	I know how to give an informative presentation.

Review

You want to go deeper into the topic of equality, and speed up your learning process? Scan this page with the PagePlayer app. There you'll find some suggestions for additional tasks.

Aufgabenteil I Hören

1 **You will hear an interview with Sasha Issenberg about a book called "The Engagement".** 🔊 58

While listening, choose the correct answer (a, b or c). There is only one correct answer.

1 Sasha Issenberg is …
a a member of the LGBT community.
b the author of the book "The Engagement".
c a journalist who reviewed the book on Facebook.

2 In the USA, same-sex marriage …
a is illegal in a number of states.
b has been legal in the whole country since 2015.
c is legal only in the states of Hawaii and Massachussetts.

3 The aim of the book is …
a to tell the story of his lifetime.
b to inform readers about same-sex marriage.
c to depict an aspect of the cultural history of the USA.

4 The book also covers …
a the biography of the author's adult years.
b the biggest problem the LGBT community has.
c many political aspects such as social policy debates.

5 He admits that journalists …
a often focus on the political side of a protest movement.
b often write about problems within a protest movement.
c are often biased and therefore don't tell the whole story.

6 The LGBT movement …
a is a homogeneous movement of its own.
b is made up of several groups that collaborate.
c is made up of several groups that follow their own agenda.

7 Over the recent decades, …
a hate crime against LGBT has become much less of an issue.
b same-sex marriage has become a top priority for LGBT communities.
c discrimination against gay people in the military has remained the #1 topic.

2 **You will hear a radio interview with Kate, the mother of a trans child.** 🔊 59

While listening, complete the following sentences.

1 Kate noticed that Alex was different because …
2 She realized that Alex was trans when …
3 Kate's first reaction to Alex's behaviour was …
4 Alex showed persistence by …
5 One incorrect assumption about the number of transgender people is …
6 In the past, trans children kept their worries to themselves because …
7 The difference between transgender children and adults is that …

60

3 You will hear a podcast about Monica Whalton, a researcher on social mobility in the UK.

While listening, take notes on the following points. You need not write complete sentences.

1 consequences of insufficient social mobility (2 aspects): …
2 feelings of marginalized social classes (1 aspect): …
3 social background and career of the guest (2 aspects): …
4 her claim when it comes to who should make decisions in politics: …
5 current situation of young people in the UK (2 aspects): …

Aufgabenteil II Lesen und Schreiben

Aufgabenstellung

1 Summarize the author's view on (male and female) political leaders. (Material 1, pp. 264–265)

2 Analyse how the author tries to persuade the reader of his own view. (Material 1, pp. 264–265)

3 Choose one of the following:

A "All the 'feminine' traits that women have been told are weaknesses in the workforce (empathy, collaboration, altruism) are, in fact, strengths." (ll. 48–49).

Discuss the quotation.

B You are taking part in a web-based project on diversity and equality which is aimed at young adults. Your contribution to the project focuses on the topic: "Who are the better leaders – men or women?"

Write an article for the project website in which you discuss this question.

Material 1

It is crunch time for humanity. We need everyone to start leading like a woman

Is Boris Johnson really the best Britain can do? I don't care what your politics are. Do you honestly think that a guy who rambles on about Peppa Pig, U-turns on important decisions every five seconds and spent years refusing to disclose how many children he has is the most qualified person to lead the UK?

I am not saying Keir Starmer would be much better in the top job, mind you. I am saying there are 67 million people in the UK. Surely, among them, there is someone who would make a far better leader than Johnson?

If we lived in a meritocracy – if opportunity were equally distributed – then we would be doing a lot better than this. But we don't live in a meritocracy. We live in a world where success isn't so much about merit but money, a world in which there are established routes to power. In the case of Britain, these take in Eton and Oxford. Johnson is the fifth of the 15 prime ministers since 1945 to have been educated at Eton. Twenty-eight prime ministers went to

Oxford (13 of them to Christ Church). Fourteen went to Cambridge (six to Trinity College). Is this because the Eton-Oxbridge pipeline produces the people best suited to lead? Or is it that we just assume they will be good leaders?

We talk a lot about leadership, but we tend to talk around the subject. We don't often stop to interrogate our ideas about what qualities a leader should embody. We don't often examine the biases that make us assume someone has what it takes to be in charge. But it is crucial that we do this, because every crisis the world faces is ultimately a crisis of leadership.

Before we can solve anything – from the climate crisis to social inequality – we need to solve the mediocre-man crisis. We need to understand why so many incompetent men are in power. (...)

How do so many incompetent men bluster their way into high office? The short answer is confidence. Lots of studies show that confident people are more convincing – and humans have a lamentable tendency to confuse confidence with competence.

There is, of course, a class element to this. One of the most valuable aspects of an elite education may well be the entitlement it imbues. A series of recent studies by researchers from Stanford University and the University of Virginia found that "individuals with relatively high social class are more overconfident". Others buy into the hype. The result is that "advantages beget advantages".

But while class is a catalyst of confidence, so is gender. Research has found that girls as young as six believe brilliance is a male trait. Because the idea that geniuses are predominately male is so ingrained, society tends to reward men for overconfidence and narcissism, while punishing women for the same qualities. Women tend to be reviled if they self-promote "too much" – and so they are inclined to do it far less than men.

(...)

"Women are better leaders," Chamorro-Premuzic told the Financial Times. "I am not neutral on this. I am sexist in favour of women. Women have better people skills, [they are] more altruistic, better able to control their impulses. They outperform men in university at graduate and undergraduate levels." A 2019 study that analysed the performance assessments of more than 60,000 leaders found that women rate higher than men in 17 out of 19 leadership skills.

I agree with Chamorro-Premuzic on a lot, but I want to make something very clear: I don't think women are hardwired to be better leaders. I am not interested in having more women in power for the sake of it. Who cares about having more women in charge if those women simply lean into a toxic model of leadership that men have created?

I am interested in advancing a more "feminine" model of leadership, for men and women. Because while I don't believe that men *and* women are hardwired differently, we are certainly socialised differently. All the "feminine" traits that women have been told are weaknesses in the workforce (empathy, collaboration, altruism) are, in fact, strengths.

It is high time – and I think the pandemic has dramatically underscored this – that we stop telling women to "lean in" to a male style of leadership. Instead, we should tell everyone to start leading like women. (...)

As Christiana Figueres, the leader of the 2015 Paris accord (...), has noted, it is crunch time for humanity. Here is the thing, though: we aren't going to be able to change anything if we don't drastically change how we think about leadership.

(787 words) Source: *The Guardian*, 30 November 2021

Mündlicher Teil Kommunikationsprüfung

Partner A: look here. **Partner B:** look at File 25 on page 282.

Partner A: Sequence 1 (your five-minute talk)

Situation: You are taking part in a UNICEF Youth Conference on discrimination and equality. Each participant is expected to give a five-minute opening statement on the subject.

Use the cartoon and statistics below as a starting point to outline to your audience the different forms of discrimination.

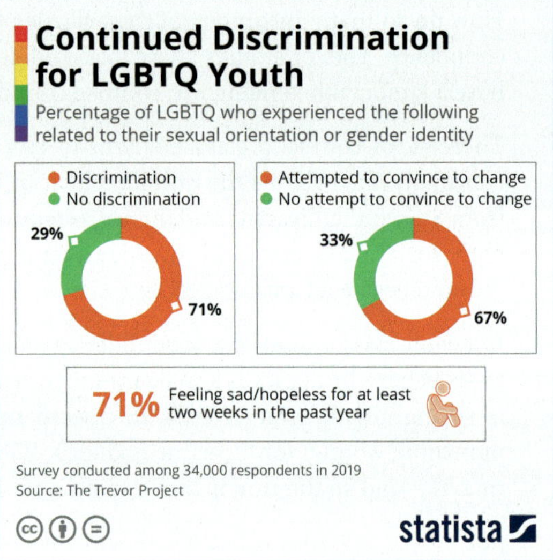

Partner A: Sequence 2 (you and the teacher / another student)

Continue the discussion on equality and discrimination with your teacher / your partner.

1 Discuss the following quote:

> *"Collective fear stimulates herd instinct, and tends to produce ferocity toward those who are not regarded as members of the herd."*
> Bertrand Russell, British philosopher

2 Develop ideas on how discrimination, bias and prejudice among people, groups and cultures can be overcome.

1 Topic 1, Section A, exercise 9

▸ Topic 1, p. 13

Group C: Forests

You are going to give a group presentation on the importance of forests and the dangers they face due to human impact.

Start by using the words in the list to help you create a mindmap or list of your ideas. Then add your own ideas and do some research online.

to absorb | to prevent | to provide | to slow sth | spread | store | carbon dioxide | forest fires | flooding | global warming | habitats | oxygen | rainforest | shade | soil erosion | exploitation | logging | mining | plantations | species

Questions

- Why are forests important for the planet and for humans?
- Which major forests are the most important for the survival of the planet and why?
- In what ways has humanity impacted forests?

Prepare and structure your presentation. If possible, find an image or images to illustrate it. Then give your presentation to the class.

to **prevent sth** *etw (ver)hindern, einer Sache vorbeugen*
soil erosion *Bodenerosion*
exploitation *Ausbeutung, Abbau* (von Rohstoffen)
logging *Abholzung*
plantation *Plantage*

Group D: Population growth

You are going to give a group presentation about population growth and the challenges it presents to the environment.

Start by using the words in the list to help you create a mindmap or list of your ideas. Then add your own ideas and do some research online.

carbon footprint | consumption | crowded | deforestation | depletion of natural resources | desertification | drought | famine | freshwater | intensive farming | light pollution | malnutrition | over-farming | overpopulation | pollution | reproductive health | strain on | war | water shortages

Questions

- How fast is the human population growing?
- What could this mean for the resources humanity needs to survive and thrive?
- In what ways does an increase in world population affect the environment?

Prepare and structure your presentation. If possible, find an image or images to illustrate it. Then give your presentation to the class.

depletion *Verringerung, Abbau*
desertification *Wüstenbildung, Versteppung*
famine *Hungersnot*
malnutrition *Unterernährung, falsche Ernährung*
reproductive health *Fortpflanzungsgesundheit*
shortage (of) *Mangel, Knappheit (an)*

▸ Topic 1, p. 16

2 Topic 1, Section B, exercise 5

Partner B

Study the graph and then do the tasks below.

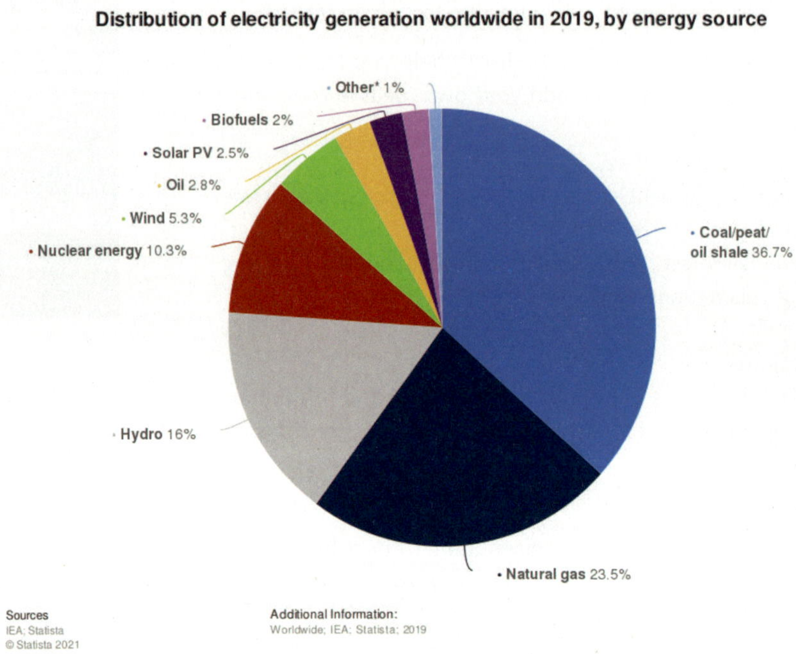

1 Listen to your partner's description of their graph. Ask relevant questions about the statistics and your partner's conclusions about them.

S ▸ Describing and analysing diagrams, pp. 43–44

2 Describe the graph above to your partner. Explain the conclusions that can be drawn from the statistics.

▸ Topic 1, p. 34

3 Topic 1, Project

Mediator

Your job: You should lead the conference and make sure each participant has equal opportunities to present their arguments.
Priorities: Make sure everyone has the chance to present their arguments and have equal talking time as far as possible. You will need to listen carefully and perhaps move the debate forward if participants get stuck on one point.
Before the conference: You will need to decide the following in advance:
- how long each person is allowed to speak
- when participants can respond to other speaker's point (avoiding interruptions!)
- when participants can ask and respond to other participants' questions and questions from the audience or press

Aim at conference: To reach a conclusion that is fair to everyone. The press should also be able to produce a report representing all sides of the debate.

4 Topic 1, Mock exam, Kommunikationsprüfung

▸ Topic 1, p. 49

Partner B: Sequence 1 (your five-minute talk)

1 Describe the picture and the cartoon and interpret their messages.

2 Use the material below as a starting point for an uninterrupted five-minute talk on climate change and the destruction of our planet.

Partner B: Sequence 2 (you and the teacher / another student)

Discuss the following questions:

1 What changes – political and individual – need to be made to slow down global warming?

2 *"We have enslaved the rest of the animal creation, and have treated our distant cousins in fur and feathers so badly that beyond doubt, if they were able to formulate a religion, they would depict the Devil in human form."*

– William Inge, American playwright

What other "crimes" have we committed and how can we undo the harm that we caused?

5 Topic 1, Project

▸ Topic 1, p. 34

Local scientific researcher(s)

Your job: You are a researcher at a science centre on the Galápagos Islands
Background: Your current research is about plastic washed up on the Islands and harm to the ocean sand local wildlife. You have found out that the largest percentage of the waste is from product packaging and empty toiletries bottles and tubes; much of which is produced by major Ecuadorian companies.
Priorities: Reduce plastic waste and find ways to preserve the local ecosystem
Aim at conference: Make sure conference participants understand the urgency of the issue and how it will affect them too; put pressure on companies to change their ways; convince politicians to prioritize this issue

▸ Topic 2, p. 55

6 Topic 2, Section A, exercise 8

Partner B: Sequence 1 (your five-minute talk)

1 Describe the photo and the cartoon and interpret their message.

2 Use the given material as a starting point for an uninterrupted five-minute talk on the advantages of genetically modified food.

"NO, I'M NOT THE WAITER. I'M THE GENETIC ENGINEER. HOW WOULD YOU LIKE YOUR LAMB?"

Partner B: Sequence 2 (you and the teacher / another student)

Discuss the following questions with Partner A:

1 *"Practically every food you buy in a store for consumption by humans is genetically modified food. There are no wild, seedless watermelons. There's no wild cows."*
– Neil deGrasse Tyson, US astrophysicist, author and broadcaster

Why is genetically modifying food different to cross-breeding?

2 Will be possible to feed the future population of the Earth without genetically modified food products?

▸ Topic 1, p. 34

7 Topic 1, Project

Members(s) of the press

Your job: To report news items to your readership
Background: You are members of various news outlets and your job is to report information article which will interest your readership and gain online readers or sell your newspaper.
Before you begin: Think about what is most important for your readership to know and which points will interest them most and why.
Aim at conference: Take notes and cover most the important parts of the conference. Come up with questions to ask the participants to gain information which will interest your readership.

8 Topic 2, Section C, exercise 9

▸ Topic 2, p.63

Partner B: Sequence 1 (your five-minute talk)

Situation: You are taking part in a youth forum on new developments in the field of artificial intelligence.

Use the given material as a starting point for an uninterrupted five-minute talk on our use of robots and artificial intelligence.

1 Describe and analyse the cartoon.

2 Comment on the quote and explain how it relates to the cartoon.

"Sir, the robots have gained sentience and are demanding better working conditions."

"Robots are not going to replace humans, they are going to make their jobs much more humane. Difficult, demeaning, demanding, dangerous, dull – these are the jobs robots will be taking."
– Sabine Hauert, co-founder of Robohub.org

Partner B: Sequence 2 (you and the teacher / another student)

Discuss the following questions with Partner A:

1 Why do some people see robots as a threat to humanity?

2 What do you imagine the future of robots to be? Compare the ideas from the video with the discussion of AI ethics in the article.

9 Topic 1, Project

▸ Topic 1, p.34

Representative(s) of a local environment group

Your job: You are one of the leaders of a local environment group, campaigning to save the unique natural environment of the Galápagos Islands.
Background: You and other members are passionate about environmental issues. You're furious about what you see as the lack of government action on waste and the irresponsible action of large companies only interested in making profits. In order to provoke a reaction from politicians and the companies and gain publicity, your organization has sometimes resorted to illegal tactics such as graffiti, vandalism of company machinery and disruptive protests.
Priorities: Achieve an end to plastic waste and other pollution from factories.
Aim at conference: Convince politicians to put pressure on companies to change their behaviour; force representatives of polluting companies to listen to your concerns.

▸ Topic 2, p. 89

10 Topic 2, Mock exam, Kommunikationsprüfung

Partner B: Sequence 1 (your five-minute talk)

Situation: You are taking part in an international conference on modern technology and nutrition. Each participant is expected to give a five-minute opening statement on the subject.

Use the statistics and cartoon below as a starting point to outline to your audience the controversy surrounding genetically modified food.

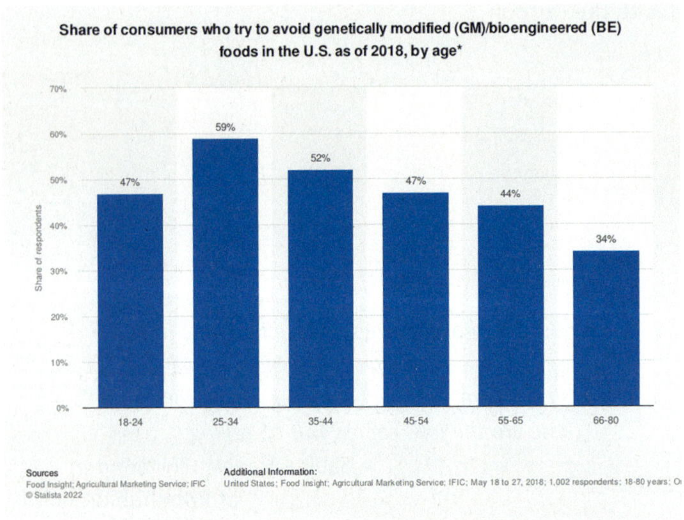

Describe and analyse the graph.

Describe and analyse the cartoon and refer it to the statistics.

Partner B: Sequence 2 (you and the teacher / another student)

Discuss the future of genetically modified food with your teacher / your partner.

1 Under what circumstances can you imagine a meaningful use of genetically modified foods?

> *"As we move forward, you cannot resolve the potential food crisis or shortages without science being part of the solution. Science has to be part of the solution but African governments …, most African companies do not accept genetically modified seeds.*
>
> – Kofi Annan, former UN Secretary-General

2 How can the fight against hunger be won?

11 Topic 3, Section C, exercise 10

▸ Topic 3, p. 102

Partner B: Sequence 1 (your five-minute talk)

1 Describe the cartoon and explain how it relates to the quote.

2 Use the given material as a starting point for an uninterrupted five-minute talk on the benefits and disadvantages of the global economy.

Outsourcing and globalization of manufacturing allows companies to reduce costs, benefits consumers with lower cost goods and services, causes economic expansion that reduces unemployment, and increases productivity and job creation.
– Larry Elder, US journalist

Partner B: Sequence 2 (you and the teacher / another student)

Discuss the following questions with Partner A:

1 Is globalization going to get rid of cultural differences and make everybody the same?

2 What can be done to keep the negative effects of globalization to a minimum?

12 Topic 1, Project

▸ Topic 1, p. 34

Representative(s) of a packaging manufacturer

Your job: Part of the management team for a packaging manufacturing company.
Background: Your company makes and sells plastic packaging to major brands; employs thousands of people and is important to the economy. Has been accused of contributing to the problem of plastic waste. An environmental group is taking aggressive action, causing expensive damage by breaking machinery, spraying graffiti and intimidating staff.
Priorities: Keep profits high and keep shareholders happy; convince the environmental group to stop carrying out actions against your company.
Aim at conference: To make as few changes as possible, while appeasing the environmentalists and protecting your profits.

▸ Topic 3, p. 133

13 Topic 3, Mock exam, Kommunikationsprüfung

Partner B: Sequence 1 (your five-minute talk)

Situation: You have entered an annual English debating competition and this year's theme is gender equality. At the beginning of the debate each candidate has to give a five-minute statement on the topic.

Use the cartoon and statistics below as a starting point to explain to your audience what gender inequality means and where it is most frequently experienced.

CartoonStock.com

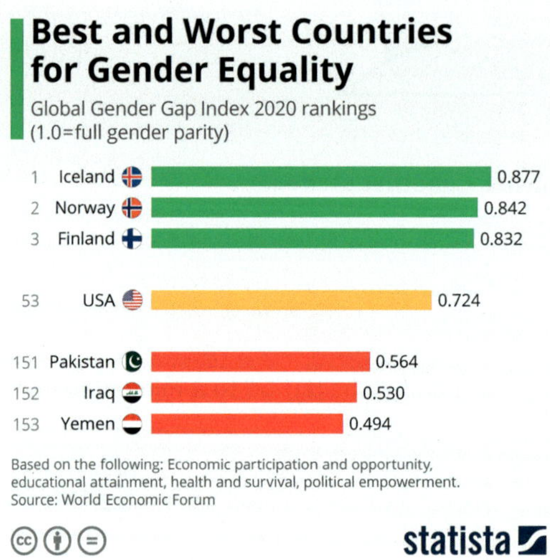

Partner B: Sequence 2 (you and the teacher / another student)

Continue the discussion on gender equality with your teacher / your partner.

1 Outline some of the reasons that cause gender inequality and suggest ways in which it can be overcome.

2 *"Gender equality is more than a goal in itself. It is a precondition for meeting the challenge of reducing poverty, promoting sustainable development and building good governance."*

– Kofi Annan, former UN Secretary-General

Elaborate on the connection between gender inequality and poverty.

14 Topic 4, Section B, exercise 5

▸ Topic 4, p. 144

Partner B: Sequence 1 (your five-minute talk)

1 Describe the cartoon and compare it with the quote.

2 Use the given material as a starting point for an uninterrupted five-minute talk on gun control in the USA.

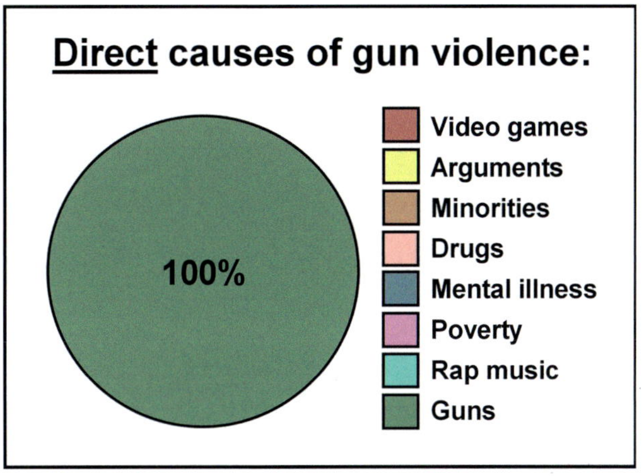

"There are hundreds of millions of gun owners in this country, and not one of them will have an accident today. The only misuse of guns comes in environments where there are drugs, alcohol, bad parents, and undisciplined children. Period."

– Ted Nugent, US singer

Partner B: Sequence 2 (you and the teacher / another student)

Discuss the following questions with your partner.

1 What are the causes of gun violence in the USA?

2 Why is the issue of gun control so controversial in the USA?

15 Topic 1, Project

▸ Topic 1, p. 34

Representative(s) of the tourist industry

Your job: Maintain high numbers of tourist visits to the Galápagos Islands, which involves preserving their natural beauty.
Background: Tourism is vital to the Galápagos Islands' economy, Islands are popular with more affluent tourists, who want to enjoy their natural beauty. Recent bad press reviews about plastic and other waste spoiling parts of the coastline; this may have a severe effect on future tourism and the economy, and result in local job losses. You're not very interested in environmental issues, but recognise the importance of preserving nature to preserve the economy!
Aim at conference: Find a solution to the problem of waste to keep the Islands looking beautiful.

▸ Topic 4, p. 151

16 Topic 4, Section D, exercise 7

USA: Immigration factsheet

3.93 million	Population of the USA 1790	
Ireland	IMMIGRANTS TO USA	**1.6 million**
Largest number	–> 1870	IMMIGRANTS TO USA
OF IMMIGRANTS TO USA	*from Germany*	*from Germany*
–> 1870	**2.37 million**	1880–1889
IMMIGRANTS TO USA	**1.9 million**	IMMIGRANTS TO USA
from Europe	IMMIGRANTS TO USA	*from Latin America*
1890–1899	1900–1909	1960–1969
96.8%	*from Italy*	**52%**
Largest nationality of successful applicants for Green Cards 2019		**Mexico**
192,000	*Illegal immigrants arrested on US-Mexico border September 2021*	
Estimated number of illegal immigrants in the USA		**10.5 million**

▸ Topic 4, p. 154

17 Topic 4, Section E, exercise 5

Listen to your partner's description of their chart.

Then describe the figures in this chart to your partner.

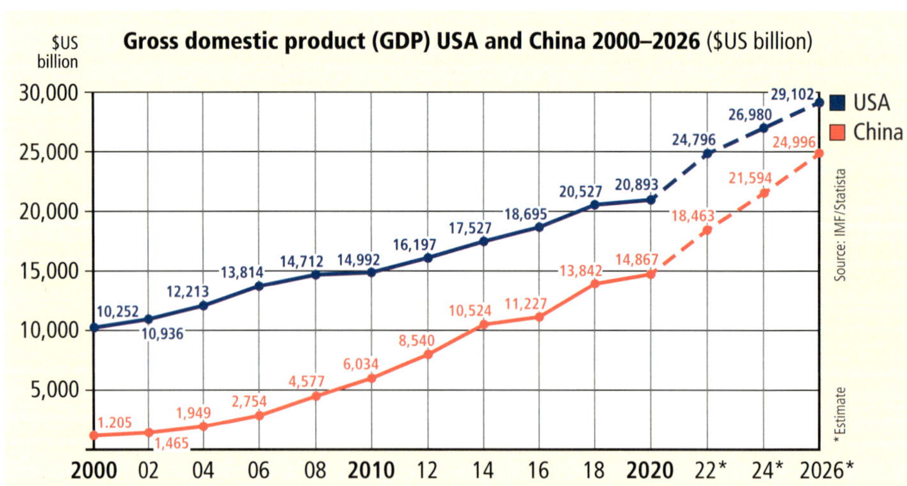

Discuss the similarities and differences between the two sets of figures. What trends do they show?

18 Topic 4, Mock exam, Kommunikationsprüfung

▸ Topic 4, p. 177

Partner B: Sequence 1 (your five-minute talk)

1 Describe the photo and the cartoon and interpret their message.

2 Use the given material as a starting point for an uninterrupted five-minute talk on gun ownership in the USA.

Partner B: Sequence 2 (you and the teacher / another student)

Discuss the following questions with your partner:

1 Do stricter gun laws hurt the freedom of US citizens?

2 *"If you're afraid to leave the house unless you're armed, you don't need a gun, you need a psychiatrist."*

– Oliver Markus Malloy, German-American novelist and comic artist

Why do people think they need to carry a gun?

▸ Topic 5, p. 202

19 Topic 5, Section E, exercise 6

Partner B: Sequence 1 (your five-minute talk)

1 Describe the cartoon below and say how it relates to the quotation.

2 Use the given material as the starting point for an uninterrupted five-minute talk on the issues surrounding the question of Scottish independence.

> *"I will say that anyone who supports Scottish independence should go to Athens. Because nothing works. It is a ruined, dirty place where people do not have money or future prospects. The day one after independence, Scotland would be worse."*
>
> – Philip Kerr, author

Partner B: Sequence 2 (you and the teacher / another student)

Discuss the following questions.

1 *"I've always been hopeful about Scotland's prospects. And I now believe more than ever that Scotland is within touching distance of achieving independence and equality."*

– Sir Sean Connery, Scottish actor

Why do some Scottish people feel that their country should be independent?

2 Is independence the right path for Scotland?

20 Topic 5, Mock exam, Kommunikationsprüfung

▸ Topic 5, p. 263

Partner B: Sequence 1 (your five-minute talk)

1 Describe the cartoon and statistics and say how they relate to the topic of the British Empire.

2 Use the given material as the starting point for an uninterrupted five-minute talk on the British Empire and colonialism in regards to current developments.

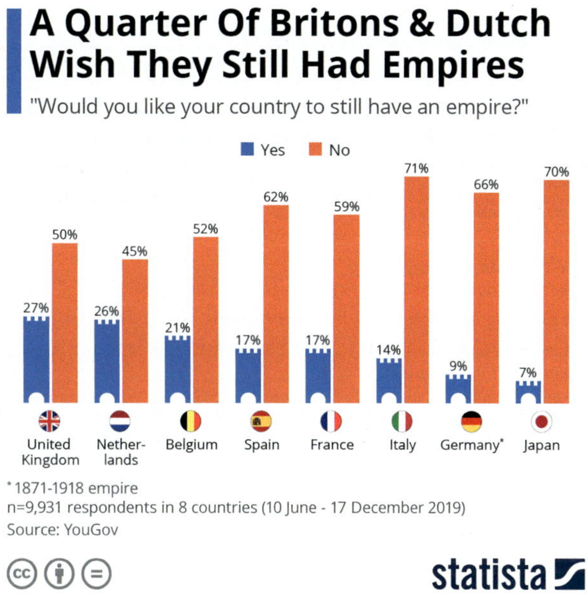

Partner B: Sequence 2 (you and the teacher / another student)

Discuss the following questions:

1 Examine the thesis that the Commonwealth is nostalgia on the behalf of the former Empire.

2 *"Until the lion learns how to write, every story will glorify the hunter."*
– J. Nozipo Maraire,
Zimbabwean doctor and writer

Explain the connection between the Empire and the Commonwealth.
Consider possible upsides and downsides, as well.

▸ Topic 6, p. 232

21 Topic 6, Section B, exercise 3

Group C

[1] **breakthrough** *Durchbruch*
[5] **pay gap** *Verdienstlücke*
[12] to fetch *holen, abholen*
[13] to **care for sb** *für jdn sorgen, sich um jdn kümmern, auf jdn aufpassen*
[15] **gross domestic product (GDP)** *Bruttosozialprodukt*
[16] flawed *fehlerhaft, mangelhaft*
[16] metric *Kennzahl, Metrik*
[16] **baseline** *Basis, Ausgangspunkt*
[18] to **strengthen** *kräftigen, stärken*
[20] to **tend to do sth** *dazu neigen, etw zu tun*
[20] **board** *Gremium, Ausschuss*
[22] to take a company public *ein Unternehmen an die Börse zu bringen*
[23] **on moral grounds** *aus moralischen Gründen*

Good to know

The **gender pay** gap is the average difference in pay for work (i.e., pay) for women and men.
A country's **gross domestic product (GDP)** is the total value of the goods and services it produces in one year.

The third area in which women's rights and equal opportunities can create a breakthrough is in building inclusive economies. Worldwide, women still earn just 77 cents for every dollar earned by men.

The latest research by the World Economic Forum says it will take until 2255 to close the gender pay gap.

How can I tell my granddaughters that their granddaughters' granddaughters will still be paid less than a man for the same work?

The gender pay gap is one reason why 70 percent of the world's poor are women and girls.

Another is that women and girls do some 12 billion hours of unpaid care work around the world every day – three times more than men.

In some communities, women can spend 14 hours a day cooking, cleaning, fetching wood and water and caring for children and the elderly. Economic models classify these hours as "leisure time".

Gross domestic product puts zero value on anything that happens in the home.

But this flawed metric is the baseline for economic decision-making, distorting policies and denying women opportunities. Women who do have an income are more likely than men to invest in their families and communities, strengthening economies and making them more resilient.

Women also tend to take a longer view. Corporate boards that include them are more stable and profitable.

The recent decision by one of the world's biggest investment banks not to take a company public unless it has a woman board member was not made on moral grounds. It was financial good sense.

Women's equal economic rights and opportunities are a global imperative if we are to build a fair globalization.

Source: United Nations Organisation

▸ Topic 1, p. 34

22 Topic 1, Project

Government representative(s)

Your job: You are (a) politician(s) and member(s) of the ruling political party in Ecuador. You represent the province of the Galápagos Islands in parliament.
Background: Local voters are calling for government action on environmental issues.
Priorities: Not to lose voters/power and to look after their interests.
Aim at conference: Come up with a solution which will appeal to conference participants and voters, and is realistic and acceptable to your political party.

23 Topic 6, Section B, exercise 3

▸ Topic 6, p. 232

Group D

Fourth, the digital divide.

When a couple complained last year that the man's credit limit was 20 times higher than his wife's, despite her higher credit score, the discrepancy was blamed on an algorithm. But with women occupying just 26 per cent of jobs in Artificial Intelligence, it is no surprise that many algorithms are biased towards men.

Digital technology can be an enormous force for good.

But I am deeply concerned by the male domination of technological professions in the universities, start-ups and Silicon Valleys of this world.

These tech hubs are already shaping the economies and societies of the future, with a huge impact on the evolution of power relations.

Unless women play an equal role in designing digital technologies, progress on women's rights could be reversed. Lack of diversity will not only expand gender inequality.

It will limit the innovation and scope of new technologies, making them less useful for everyone.

Source: United Nations Organisation

3 to **blame sth on sb/sth** *jdm/etw für etw die Schuld geben*
6 **force** *Triebkraft*
7 **domination** *Dominanz*
10 **evolution** *Entwicklung*
12 **lack (of)** *Mangel (an)*
14 scope *Rahmen, Umfang*

Good to know

A **credit score** is a record of a person's debt and their past record of paying off debts.

Silicon Valley is a region in northern California which is home to the headquarters of many of the largest tech companies and many tech start-ups.

24 Topic 6, Section B, exercise 3

▸ Topic 6, p. 232

Group E

Fifth and finally, political representation.

Women's participation in parliaments around the world has doubled in the last 25 years – to one quarter. Fewer than one-tenth of states are led by a woman.

But women's representation in government is not about stereotypical "women's issues" like opposing sexual harassment or promoting childcare.

Women in government drive social progress and meaningful changes to people's lives.

Women are more likely to advocate for investment in education and health; and to seek cross-party consensus and common ground.

When the numbers of women reach a critical mass, governments are more likely to innovate, and to challenge established orthodoxies. In other words, women in politics are redefining and redistributing power.

It is no coincidence that the governments that are redefining GDP to include well-being and sustainability are led by women. It is simple math.

Women's participation improves institutions.

Doubling the resources, capacity and expertise we put into decision-making benefits everyone.

Source: United Nations Organisation

2 to double *(sich) verdoppeln*
9 **cross-party** *parteiübergreifend*
9 **common ground** *Gemeinsamkeit(en)*
10 **critical mass** *kritische Masse*
11 to **innovate (sth)** *Neuerungen einführen, (etw neu) einführen*
11 orthodoxy *Lehrmeinung*
12 to **redefine sth** *etw neu definieren*
13 **coincidence** *Zufall*
16 to **benefit (sb)** *(jdm) nutzen, Nutzen bringen, profitieren*

▸ Topic 6, p. 266

25 Topic 6, Mock exam, Kommunikationsprüfung

Partner B: Sequence 1 (your five-minute talk)

Situation: You are taking part in a Unicef Youth Conference on Equality. At the beginning of the conference each delegate gives a five-minute statement on the topic.

Use the cartoon and statistics below as a starting point to outline to your audience the dangers of bias and prejudice.

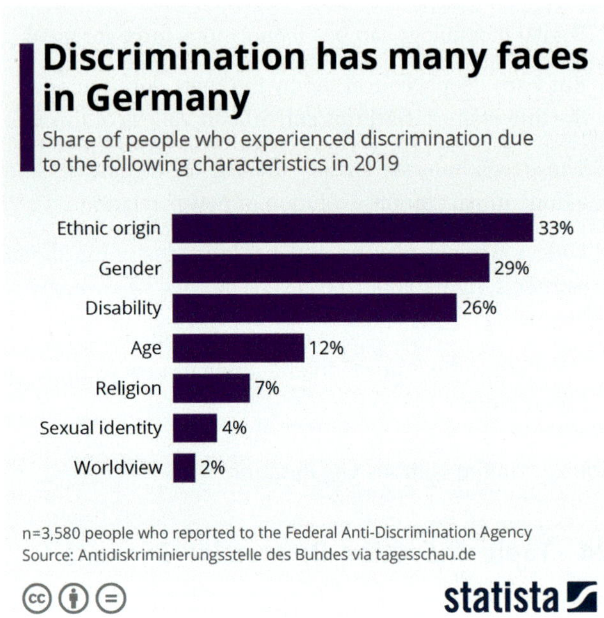

Partner B: Sequence 2 (you and the teacher / another student)

Discuss the following questions:

1 Develop ideas on how discrimination, bias and prejudice among people, groups and cultures can be overcome.

2 *"Equality is not the empirical claim that all groups of humans are interchangeable; it is the moral principle that individuals should not be judged or constrained by the average properties of their group."*

– Steven Pinker,
psychologist and author

Discuss the quote.

GRAMMAR SUMMARY

The simple present

1 I **go** to the disco most weeks, but **I don't go** every week.
2 Mr Brown **teaches** us English every day.
3 We **live** in Bavaria. Where **does** Mathew live?

Man verwendet das **simple present** für regelmäßige, sich wiederholende Ereignisse oder Handlungen (1, 2) und für Dauerzustände (3).

Das **simple present** wird häufig mit den folgenden Zeitangaben verwendet:
- *always, never, often, rarely, seldom, sometimes*
- *generally, mostly, normally, regularly, usually*
- *every day/week/month ..., every morning/afternoon ...*
- *on Mondays/Tuesdays ..., on weekdays*
- *in (the) summer/winter ...*
- *at Christmas/Easter, at weekends*

The present progressive

1 **I'm calling** to say that Ben's ill. He **isn't feeling** well.
2 He**'s staying** in bed today.

Man verwendet das **present progressive** (auch **present continuous** genannt) für Vorgänge oder Handlungen, die im Moment des Sprechens oder Schreibens vor sich gehen und noch nicht abgeschlossen sind (1).

Es wird auch für vorübergehende Situationen gebraucht (2).

Das **present progressive** wird oft mit den folgenden **Zeitangaben** verwendet: *at the moment, at present, now, this week/month*

⚠ Diese Verben bilden normalerweise keine **progressive**-Form: *be, believe, doubt, feel* (meinen), *hate, hear, imagine, know, like/dislike, love, mean, notice, prefer, realize, recognize, remember, see* (begreifen), *seem, suppose, think* (meinen), *understand, want, wish*

▸ exercises 5–6, p. 147

The simple past

1 We **wanted** to go to the USA last year, but in the end we **didn't go**.
2 Jasmin **went** on that school trip to London in March. **Did** you **go** too?

Man verwendet das **simple past**, um über Vergangenes zu berichten, insbesondere wenn im Vordergrund steht, **wann** etwas geschehen ist (1, 2).

Das **simple past** wird häufig mit den folgenden **Zeitangaben** verwendet:
- *yesterday, the day before yesterday, the week/month ... before last*
- *last night/week/month/summer/December/Easter ...*
- *two/three ... hours/days/years ... ago*
- *in 2015 / in the 20th century ...*
- *at that time, in those days*

The past progressive

1 The teacher **was talking** to Heather **during the break**.
2 I **wasn't doing** anything particular when Pete **came** round.

Wenn man ausdrücken möchte, dass eine Handlung zu einem bestimmten Zeitpunkt oder während eines bestimmten Zeitraums in der Vergangenheit **im Gange** war, verwendet man das **past progressive** (auch **past continuous** genannt) (1).

Das **past progressive** wird auch verwendet um auszudrücken, dass eine Handlung im Gange war, als ein neues Ereignis (plötzlich) eintrat (2).

⚠ Einige Verben haben **keine progressive-Form** (siehe die Liste unter **present progressive**).

▸ exercises 5–6, p. 147

The present perfect

1 I**'ve bought** a new car. I **haven't driven** many kilometres yet.
2 **How long has** it **been** warm with you? We**'ve had** sunshine **for** two weeks.
3 She**'s had** a cold **since** December.

Wenn man ausdrücken will, dass etwas geschehen ist, ohne dass der genaue Zeitpunkt des Ereignisses im Vordergrund steht, wird das **present perfect** verwendet (1).

Man verwendet das **present perfect** auch um mitzuteilen, seit wann oder wie lange ein Zustand oder eine Handlung bereits andauert (2, 3). Dafür wird in Fragen sehr oft *how long*, in Aussagen *for* bzw. *since* verwendet. (Im Deutschen steht dafür „seit" plus Gegenwart.)

Das **present perfect** wird oft mit den folgenden Zeitangaben verwendet:
- *already, still (not), (not) yet*
- *(not) ever, just, lately, never, recently*
- *so far this week/month ..., till/until now*

The present perfect progressive

1 **I've been learning** English since I was 10.
2 They**'ve not been speaking** to each other lately.

Das **present perfect progressive** (auch **present perfect continuous** genannt) verwendet man für Handlungen und Vorgänge, die in der Vergangenheit begonnen haben und zum Zeitpunkt des Sprechens bzw. Schreibens noch andauern (1).

Es wird auch für vorübergehende Situationen gebraucht, die noch nicht beendet sind (2).

⚠ Einige Verben haben normalerweise **keine progressive-Form** (siehe die Liste unter **present progressive**).

The past perfect

1 Nina **had** already **left** the coffee bar by the time I arrived.
2 When I visited John in hospital, he **had been** there for ten days.

Mit Hilfe des **past perfect** wird ausgedrückt, dass zwei Handlungen oder Vorgänge in der Vergangenheit aufeinanderfolgten (1).
Die Handlung, die zeitlich voranging, steht im **past perfect**.

Das **past perfect** wird auch verwendet um auszudrücken, dass ein Zustand vor einem Zeitpunkt in der Vergangenheit begonnen hatte und zu diesem Zeitpunkt noch andauerte (2).

Wenn zwei oder mehrere kurze Handlungen in der Vergangenheit direkt aufeinanderfolgten, wird für alle Handlungen das **simple past** verwendet: *The cat* ***ran*** *out when Joanne* ***opened*** *the door.*

The past perfect progressive

1 Rod **had been travelling** for three months when he ran out of money.
2 When I found Mary, I could see that she **had been crying**.

Das **past perfect progressive** wird verwendet, wenn man ausdrücken möchte, dass eine Handlung oder ein Vorgang vor einem Zeitpunkt in der Vergangenheit begonnen hatte und bis (oder fast bis) zu diesem Zeitpunkt andauerte.

The future (will)

1 In the future people **will use** public transport more. There **won't be** so many private cars.
2 We can only hope that everyone **will accept** this shift in attitudes.
3 You've forgotten your purse? Don't worry. I**'ll lend** you some money.

Das **will-future** wird verwendet, um Vorhersagen zu treffen (1) oder Hoffnungen bzw. Vermutungen über die Zukunft zu äußern (2).

Man verwendet es auch, wenn man sich spontan zu etwas entschließt, etwas anbietet oder etwas verspricht (3).

Das **will-future** kommt häufig mit den folgenden einleitenden Verben und Ausdrücken vor:
- *believe, expect, forecast, hope, imagine, suppose, think*
- *It's clear/obvious that ..., There's no doubt that ...*

The future (going to)

1 Look at these clouds. It**'s going to rain** soon.
2 This time I**'m going to get** good marks in the class test.

Das **going-to future** verwendet man für Ereignisse und Situationen, die nach Meinung der/des Sprechenden bald eintreten werden (weil es bereits Anzeichen dafür gibt) (1).

Es wird auch für Pläne und Absichten verwendet (2).

Modal auxiliary verbs

1 He **can speak** several languages.
2 You **must accept** your new situation.
3 We **needn't go** to work today.
4 **May** I **interrupt** you?

Um auszudrücken, was geschehen kann, muss, darf, soll usw., verwendet man ein modales Hilfsverb in Verbindung mit einem Vollverb (1–4).
Im Englischen steht ein Hilfsverb – anders als im Deutschen – **nie ohne** Vollverb:
Lena kann Spanisch. ⚠ *Lena can speak Spanish.* NICHT: ~~*can Spanish*~~

Abgesehen von *could* (wenn es für eine Fähigkeit gebraucht wird) kann man modale Hilfsverben nur im Präsens und – mit einer geeigneten Zeitangabe – mit zukünftiger Bedeutung verwenden, zum Beispiel:
- *You **can go** home now.* (Präsens)
- *You **can go** home an hour early tomorrow.* (Futur)
- *I **must write** these letters now.* (Präsens)
- *I **must write** a long report next week.* (Futur)

⚠ Um ein modales Hilfsverb in der Vergangenheit zu verwenden, muss ein geeignetes Ersatzverb verwendet werden:
must *The provider **had to** block access to the internet last December.*
can *I **couldn't** start the car yesterday.* (Fähigkeit)
*We **weren't allowed to** go home early last Friday.* (Erlaubnis)

Übersicht der modalen Hilfsverben nach Funktion

Funktion	Modale(s) Hilfsverb(en)	
Fähigkeit	*He **can** speak several languages.* *The first satellites **could** only transmit sound.*	
Möglichkeit	*With your qualifications you **could** work abroad.* *The boss **may** come in at any moment.* *He **might** ask you what you are doing.*	
Bitte	***Can** I have a word with Ms Sims, please?* ***Could** I speak to Ms Sims, please?* ***May** I interrupt you?* ***Might** I ask you a personal question?*	(neutral) (höflich) (betont höflich) (äußerst höflich)
Erlaubnis	*You **can** go in now.* *The boss is free. You **may** go in now.*	(neutral) (freundlich)
Verbot	*We **mustn't** be late for work tomorrow.*	
Vorschrift	*You **must** wear a hard hat in the factory.*	
freie Wahl	*Good food **needn't** be expensive.*	
Empfehlung	*You **should** get better qualifications.* *You **ought to** get better qualifications.* *You **must** get better qualifications.*	(neutral) (betont) (streng)

The definite article

1 **Sociologists** say that **violence** is increasing.
2 **Most** of us aren't interested, **half** of us have never heard of the place.
3 I came to **school** today **by car**. I parked in **George Street.**
4 I love **winter** weekends. Often I don't get up or have **breakfast** before 12.

Hat ein Substantiv eine allgemeine, uneingeschränkte Bedeutung – also „alle ohne Ausnahme" – dann steht es ohne Artikel (1).

Ferner wird der Artikel in den folgenden Fällen und Wendungen im Englischen – z.T. anders als im Deutschen – **nicht** verwendet:
- bei *most* in der Bedeutung „die meisten" und bei *half* (2),
- bei öffentlichen Gebäuden im allgemeinen Sinne, Straßennamen und Verkehrsmitteln (3)
- bei Tageszeiten, Mahlzeiten, Wochentagen, Monaten und Jahreszeiten im allgemeinen Sinne (4).

▸ exercise 5, p. 105

Reported speech (Aussagesätze)

1 "There are some jobs robots can't do."
The speaker **said** that there **were** some jobs robots **couldn't do**.

Wenn man einem Dritten berichten möchte, was jemand gesagt hat, verwendet man die **indirekte Rede**.

Bei Verwendung der indirekten Rede verwendet man ein einleitendes Verb wie *say, claim, remind, answer, think, mention* usw.

Steht das einleitende Verb in der Vergangenheit – also *said, answered, mentioned* usw. –, dann verschieben sich die Zeiten wie folgt:

direkte Rede		indirekte Rede
simple present *she works hard*	⟹	simple past *she worked hard*
present progressive *she is working hard*	⟹	past progressive *she was working hard*
simple past *she worked hard*	⟹	past perfect *she had worked hard*
past progressive *she was working hard*	⟹	past perfect progressive *she had been working hard*
present perfect *she has worked hard*	⟹	past perfect *she had worked hard*
present perfect progressive *she has been working hard*	⟹	past perfect progressive *she had been working hard*
past perfect *she had worked hard*	⟹	(keine Verschiebung)
past perfect progressive *she had been working hard*	⟹	(keine Verschiebung)
will *she will work hard*	⟹	*would* *she would work hard*
am/is/are going to *she is going to work hard*	⟹	*was/were going to* *she was going to work hard*
would/might, etc. *she would work hard*	⟹	(keine Verschiebung)
would have / might have, etc. *she would have worked hard*	⟹	(keine Verschiebung)

Die modalen Hilfsverben werden folgendermaßen verschoben:

Modalverb	Bedeutung	indirekte Rede
can	Fähigkeit	*could, was/were able to*
can	Erlaubnis	*was/were allowed to*
may	Möglichkeit	*might*
may	Erlaubnis	*was/were allowed to*
must	Pflicht	*had to*
mustn't	Verbot	*was/were not allowed to*
needn't	freie Wahl	*did not/didn't have to*

Außer wenn man über ein Gespräch berichtet, das am selben Tag stattgefunden hat, müssen fast alle **Zeit-** und einige **Ortsangaben** entsprechend der folgenden Tabelle verändert werden. (Angaben, die nicht aufgeführt sind, bleiben unverändert.)

direkte Rede	indirekte Rede
today	*(on) that day*
tomorrow	*the next day*
yesterday	*the day before*
the day after tomorrow	*two days later*
the day before yesterday	*two days before*
next day/Friday/week/Christmas …	*the following day/Friday/week/Christmas …*
last Friday/week/summer …	*the Friday/week/summer … before*
two years/months/weeks … ago	*two years/months/weeks … before*
now, at present	*then*
at the moment	*at that moment*
at this time	*at that time*
here	*there*
in this place	*at that place*
this	*that*
these	*those*

Reported speech (Fragesätze)

1 "What led to the widespread use of robots?"
A member of the audience **asked what had led** to the widespread use of robots.
2 "Is my job endangered?"
She **wanted to know if/whether** her job **was endangered**.

Bei Fragen **mit Fragewort** wird das Fragewort übernommen (1).

Bei Fragen **ohne Fragewort** verwendet man *if* bzw. *whether* (= ob) (2).

Alle anderen Änderungen erfolgen wie bei den Aussagesätzen (siehe **Aussagesätze** oben).

Reported speech (Bitten, Aufforderungen und Befehle)

1 "Show me the robot."
Lucy **asked the engineer to show her** the robot.
2 "Don't go too close to it."
He **told her not to go** too close to it.

Bei **Bitten** verwendet man meist *asked* (= bitten) + Person + Infinitiv (1).

Für **Aufforderungen** und **Befehle** verwendet man *told* (= sagen) + Person + Infinitiv (2).

Bei **negativen Sätzen** setzen wir *not* unmittelbar vor *to* (2).

Die Wörter *tell* und *ask* stehen immer mit einem Objekt:
"Don't enter the studio when the red light is on."
*Ben **told people / everybody / visitors** not to enter the studio when the red light was on.*

▸ exercises 5–6, p. 290

The passive

1 Measures **are being introduced** to reduce traffic pollution.
2 Pollution **is caused by** some thoughtless people.

Ist der Urheber einer Handlung unbekannt oder zweitrangig, verwendet man das Passiv. Man verwendet eine Zeitform von *be* + dritte Form des Verbs. Im Vordergrund steht also das Ergebnis des Vorgangs (1).

Möchte man den Urheber doch angeben, verwendet man *by* und den Namen auf keinen Fall *from* (2)!

Zeit	Zeitform von *be*	3. Form
simple present	*am/is/are*	*caused*
present progressive	*am/is/are being*	*introduced*
simple past	*was/were*	*buried*
past progressive	*was/were being*	*built*
present perfect	*has/have been*	*installed*
will-future	*will be*	*blocked*
going to-future	*am/is/are going to be*	*sacked*

Beim Verwendung von modalen Hilfsverben wird nach folgendem Muster verfahren:

bei Aussagen	Hilfsverb + *be* + 3. Form	*must be displayed*
bei Fragen	Hilfsverb + Subjekt + *be* + 3. Form	*Can ... be persuaded?*

The impersonal passive

1 **It is said that** petrol should cost more.
2 **The man is thought to** have gone to hospital. **He is believed to** be not very badly injured.

Das **impersonal passive** wird vor allem dann verwendet, wenn man sich objektiv bzw. unbeteiligt ausdrücken möchte. Daher kommt diese Struktur oft in Polizeiberichten, seriösen Zeitungsartikeln usw. vor.

Dabei wird häufig folgendes Satzmuster verwendet: *It is/was* ... + 3. Form des einleitenden Verbs + *that*-Satz (1).

Bei Verben des Berichtens, Vermutens usw. kann man eine Person (*the man, he* usw.) zum Subjekt des Satzes machen. Hinter dem Verb steht dann ein *to*-Infinitiv (2).

Conditionals

▸ exercise 8, p. 139

1 If we **invest** in new technology, a lot of people **will lose** their jobs.
2 If more people **retrained**, they **wouldn't have to worry** about finding a new job.
3 We **won't have** political censorship if we **don't start** to censor the internet.

Ein **Konditionalsatz** besteht aus zwei Teilen: dem ***if*-Teil** und dem **Hauptteil**. Der ***if*-Teil** drückt eine **Bedingung** aus, der Hauptteil deren **Folge**.

Je nach Sinn können *if*-Teil, Hauptteil oder Satzteile **verneint** werden (2, 3).

Bei **Konditionalsätzen** kommen folgende **Zeitmuster** am häufigsten vor:

Typ I *If + simple present*	+	*will*-future
Typ II *If + simple past*	+	*would* + Infinitiv
Typ III *If + past perfect*	+	*would have* + 3. Form des Verbs

if-Sätze werden gemäß der **Wahrscheinlichkeit** der zu erwartenden Folge eingesetzt:

– **Typ I:** Folge (fast) sicher:
If we ***invest in*** *new technology, a lot of people* ***will lose*** *their jobs.*
D. h. viele Leute werden (vermutlich) ihre Stellen verlieren, da wir (sehr wahrscheinlich) in die neue Technologie investieren werden.

– **Typ II:** Folge theoretisch möglich, aber kaum wahrscheinlich.
If we ***invested in*** *new technology, a lot of people* ***would lose*** *their jobs.*
D. h. es ist kaum zu erwarten, dass viele Leute ihre Stellen verlieren werden, da wir (wahrscheinlich) nicht in die neue Technologie investieren werden.

– **Typ III:** Folge unmöglich, da die Bedingung nicht erfüllt wurde und bereits in der Vergangenheit liegt.
If we ***had invested in*** *new technology, a lot of people* ***would have lost*** *their jobs.*
D. h. der Sprecher weiß bereits, dass niemand seinen Job verloren hat, da wir nicht in die neue Technologie investiert haben.

Gerund/Infinitive

1 Max **enjoys playing** football.
2 Can you **afford to buy** that DVD collection?
3 Cem and Julie **continued to meet / continued meeting** even though they had spilt up.
4 Alison **normally likes to go / likes going** to parties, but **today** she **would prefer to stay** at home.

Nach bestimmten Verben folgt stets die *-ing*-Form (**gerund**) (1). Am wichtigsten sind: *admit, avoid, consider, deny, enjoy, finish, imagine, mention, mind* (etwas dagegen haben), *miss, practise, risk, suggest*

Nach bestimmten Verben folgt stets der Infinitiv (**infinitive**) (2). Die wichtigsten Verben dieser Gruppe sind:
afford, choose, decide, expect, hope, mean, promise, refuse, want

Nach den Verben *begin, continue, intend, start, like, love, hate, prefer* können sowohl der **Infinitiv** als auch die ***-ing*-Form beliebig verwendet werden**. Nach *would like, would love, would hate, would prefer* steht jedoch stets der **Infinitiv** (3, 4).

forget/remember

***forget/remember* + *-ing*-Form** bezieht sich auf etwas, das in der Vergangenheit geschehen ist.
– *I still **remember getting** my first bicycle.*
– *I'll never **forget going** to the Rock Against Hunger concert last year.*

***forget/remember* + Infinitiv** dagegen bezieht sich auf etwas Zukünfiges.
– *Dad, please **remember / don't forget to pick me up** from the station.*
– *Oh dear. I **forgot / didn't remember to pick Sally up** from the station.*
In diesem letzten Satz drückt jemand aus, dass er vergessen hat, etwas zu tun, das damals in der Zukunft lag.

regret

***regret* + *-ing*-Form** drückt Bedauern über eine vergangene Situation bzw. einen vergangenen Vorfall aus. Häufig geht es dabei um verpasste Chancen.
– *I really **regret leaving** school without qualifications.*
– *I know they will **regret buying** such a big, expensive car.*

***regret* + Infinitiv** – fast immer mit einem Verb des Mitteilens wie *inform, say, tell* – wird zur Verkündung schlechter Nachrichten verwendet.
– *I **regret to say** that I can't attend the meeting tomorrow.*
– *We **regret to inform** you that the vacancy has now been filled.*

stop

Bedeutet *stop* „aufhören, etwas zu tun", steht das nachfolgende Verb in der ***-ing*-Form**. Bedeutet aber *stop* „kurz anhalten, um etwas anderes zu tun", folgt ein Verb im **Infinitiv**.

- *For heaven's sake **stop shouting** at me.*
- *I'm a little late because I **stopped to give** somebody a lift.*

try

Bedeutet *try* „etwas ausprobieren", steht das nachfolgende Verb in der ***-ing*-Form**. Bedeutet aber *try* „sich anstrengen, etwas zu tun", folgt ein Verb im **Infinitiv**.

- *I **tried phoning** Ellie, but she wasn't at home.*
- *We'**ll try to repair** your computer by the weekend.*

Used to

1 I **used to do** a lot of sport, but I haven't got time now.
2 I **didn't use to drink** coffee, but I do now because I enjoy it.
3 **Didn't** you **use to live** in London? – Yes, I did. But now I live in Stuttgart.

Used to + infinitive wird verwendet, um Handlungen, Zustände oder Gewohnheiten, die in der Vergangenheit bestanden haben, zu beschreiben. (1– 3) Im Deutschen werden dafür oft Sätze mit *früher* oder *damals* verwendet.

Adjectives and adverbs

▸ exercise 5, p. 109
▸ exercise 6, p. 113

1 John has a **new** DVD player. It wasn't **expensive**.
2 That CD sounds **terrible**.
3 We can make printouts **quickly** and **cheaply**.

Um **Personen** oder **Sachen** näher zu beschreiben, verwendet man **Adjektive** (1, 2).

Adjektive stehen **unmittelbar vor** Substantiven oder **unmittelbar nach** einer Form von *be* (bzw. *become* oder *seem*, die *be* ersetzen können) (1).

Adjektive können mit Verben wie *feel, look* (aussehen), *sound, smell* und *taste* eine **sinnliche Wahrnehmung** ausdrücken (2).

Um ein **Tätigkeitsverb** näher zu beschreiben, setzt man ein Adverb **unmittelbar hinter das Verb** bzw. Verb + Objekt (3).
⚠ Im Englischen können ein Verb und sein Objekt – anders als im Deutschen – nicht durch ein Adverb getrennt werden. Also NICHT: ~~*We can make quickly printouts*~~.

Die meisten Adverbien werden durch Anhängen von *-ly* an das entsprechende Adjektiv gebildet (3). Eine kleine Anzahl von Adverbien hat jedoch dieselbe Form wie die zugehörigen Adjektive; die häufigsten sind *fast, hard, early, late, long, daily*.

Adverbien werden auch verwendet, um **Adjektive**, **andere Adverbien** und **ganze Sätze** näher zu bestimmen:

- *MP3 players have become **surprisingly cheap**.* (Adverb + Adjektiv)
- *You can buy them **surprisingly cheaply**.* (Adverb + Adverb)
- ***Luckily** Gerd left a message on my mailbox.* (Satzadverb)

Comparison of adjectives and adverbs

1 A hundred years ago life was **slower** and people may have been **happier**.
2 Which technological innovation is the **most/least important**?
3 Today you can copy data **more easily than** ever before.

Einsilbige und **zweisilbige Adjektive**, die auf *-y* enden – zum Beispiel *easy, happy* und *lucky* –, werden mit *-(i)er* und *-(i)es* gesteigert (1).

Mehrsilbige Adjektive und **Adverbien**, die auf *-ly* enden, werden mit *more/most* gesteigert (2, 3).

Adverbien, die dieselbe Form wie das entsprechende Adjektiv haben (*fast, hard, early* usw.) werden mit *-er/-est* gesteigert.

Um Personen oder Sachen im Satz miteinander zu vergleichen, gibt es folgende Möglichkeiten:

– kein Unterschied	***as** good **as***	genau so gut wie
– Unterschied	***not as** good **as***	nicht so gut wie
– Unterschied	*better **than***	besser als

Word order – positions of adverbs of time, place and frequency

1 She goes shopping **every week**. She goes to the mall **in Wexham.**
2 **Last year** we went to India for our holidays.
3 Paul and Emily went to **the USA last year**.
4 Rob **is never** at home on Saturday afternoon. He **always goes** swimming.
5 I like to stay at home **now and then**.
6 Gina acted **strangely at the party last night**.

Zeitangaben (Wann?) und Ortsangaben (Wo?, Wohin?) stehen in der Regel am Satzende (1).

Um die Zeit eines bestimmten Ereignisses hervorzuheben, kann man die Zeitangabe an die erste Stelle setzen (2).

Stehen eine Zeitangabe und eine Ortsangabe zusammen am Satzende, dann gilt die Reihenfolge Ort vor Zeit (alphabetisch merken: O vor Z!) (3).

Besteht eine Häufigkeitsangabe aus einem Wort, z. B. *always, often, sometimes*, steht sie hinter dem Verb *be*, sonst vor dem Vollverb (4). ⚠ Sie darf nicht zwischen Vollverb und Objekt stehen, also NICHT: ~~*He goes always swimming*~~.

Besteht die Häufigkeitsangabe aus mehreren Wörtern, z. B. *every day, now and then*, steht sie wie eine Zeitangabe am Satzende (5).

Adverbien der Art und Weise stehen in der Regel am Satzende. Kommen noch Zeit- oder Ortsadverbien hinzu, lautet die Reihenfolge: Art und Weise – Ort – Zeit (AOZ) (6).

Relative clauses and contact clauses

▸ exercise 8, p. 94

1 Car manufacturers are designing cars **which/that** can use hydrogen fuel cells.
2 Wildernesses are being spoiled by tourists **who/that** want to go to "unspoiled" places.
3 Tony filled in a questionnaire **(which/that)** he found on the Internet.
4 Fred Foley is a photojournalist **whose** pictures sell for huge sums.
5 Call centre employees, most of **whom** come from India, work long hours.
6 Some non-GM crops are attacked by pests **against which** they have no resistance.

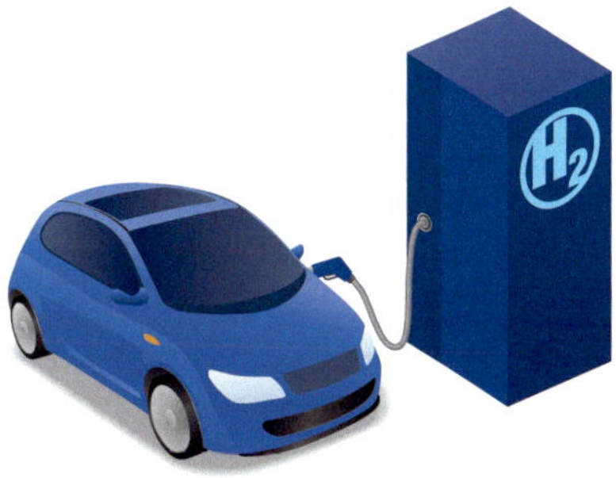

Relativsätze werden verwendet, um den Hauptsatz durch zusätzliche Informationen genauer zu bestimmen.

Für **Sachen** verwendet man das Relativpronomen *which* bzw. *that* (1) und für Personen *who* bzw. *that* (2).

Bezieht sich das Relativpronomen auf das **Objekt des Hauptsatzes**, dann kann man es weglassen (3). Solche Relativsätze heißen **contact clauses**.

Um **Besitz** bzw. **Zugehörigkeit** anzuzeigen, verwendet man *whose* unmittelbar vor dem **Substantiv** bei Personen und Sachen (4).

Steht eine **Präposition** vor dem **Relativpronomen**, wird *whom* für Personen und *which* für Sachen verwendet (5, 6). In solchen Fällen ist die Verwendung von *that* nicht möglich.

Defining and non-defining relative clauses

▸ exercise 7, p. 94

1 The first Europeans **who** settled in Australia came from Britain.
2 Sydney, **which** is famous for its unusually designed opera house, is situated on the south-eastern coast of Australia.

Im **ersten Beispielsatz** ist der Sinn des Hauptsatzes *The first Europeans came from Britain* ohne den Relativsatz *who settled in Australia* offensichtlich nicht zu verstehen. Solche Relativsätze sind also wesentlich notwendig für das Verständnis des gesamten Satzes – sie nennt man **defining relative clauses** (notwendige oder bestimmende Relativsätze).
⚠ Notwendige Relativsätze erhalten kein **trennendes Komma**.
Dies signalisiert, dass sie fester Bestandteil der Hauptaussage sind.

Im **zweiten Beispielsatz** ist die Aussage des Hauptsatzes *Sydney is situated on the south-eastern coast of Australia* auch ohne den Relativsatz völlig verständlich, weil der Relativsatz *which is famous for its unusually designed opera house* eine zusätzliche, also nebensächliche, Information enthält. Daher werden solche Relativsätze ***non-defining relative clauses*** (nicht notwendige oder nicht bestimmende Relativsätze) genannt.

▸ exercise 7, p. 54

Participle constructions

1 Malaria, preventable with treatment **costing** less than one pound per bed, is endemic.
2 Many men believe that any work **involved** with cooking is a woman's chore.
3 **Losing** more and more people to AIDS, Africa now needs effective help more urgently than ever before.
4 **Burdened** with declining life-expectancy, large parts of Africa are caught in a poverty trap.
5 **Having fetched** water from a river for many years, some women in developing countries are now happy to have modern systems.
6 Although **facing** extreme destitution, many residents haven't given up hope.
7 Donors should invest in projects that help local inhabitants become self-supporting, thereby **making** sure that the money isn't wasted.
8 Poor infrastructure is a key barrier to economic growth in Nepal, thus **causing** huge additional costs to the transport of commercial goods.
9 Life is becoming hard in the developing countries, **with** many small farmers **going** out of business.
10 AIDS represents a major challenge to sub-Saharan Africa, currently **killing** more than two million people every year.

Die englische Sprache ist geprägt durch die häufige Verwendung von Partizipialkonstruktionen. Diese ermöglichen einen eleganteren Sprachfluss. Partizipialkonstruktionen verkürzen:

- Relativsätze; dabei kann entweder das **present participle** (1) oder das **past participle** (2) verwendet werden.
- Adverbiale Nebensätze (3–9).

Wie bei der Verkürzung von Relativsätzen kommen auch bei der Verkürzung von adverbialen Nebensätzen das **present participle** (3, 6–9) und das **past participle** (4) zur Anwendung. Darüber hinaus wird hier auch noch das **perfect participle** verwendet (5), und zwar um die Vorzeitigkeit der Handlung im Nebensatz auszudrücken. *(Nachdem sie jahrelang Wasser aus dem Fluss geholt hatten, ...)*

Schließlich verknüpft man mit einer Partizipialkonstruktion zwei Hauptsätze zu einem einzigen Satz, und zwar ausnahmslos mittels **present participle** (10).

Countable and uncountable nouns, nouns that are only plural

▸ exercise 4, p. 153

1 Visit our website for more **information** on our firm. NICHT ~~informations~~
2 Have you read the paper today? The political **news** is interesting. NICHT ~~news are~~
3 Who can give me a piece of / some **advice**? NICHT ~~an advice~~

Einige wichtige **Substantive** sind **zählbar im Deutschen**, **nicht jedoch im Englischen**. Diese Substantive können also nicht direkt mit dem unbestimmten Artikel *a/an* oder mit einem Zahlwort verwendet werden. Hier ist eine Liste solcher Wörter, die Sie auswendig lernen sollten:
advice, baggage, damage, data, equipment, evidence, furniture, garbage *(Abfall)*, information, knowledge, luck, luggage, machinery, news, progress, research, rubbish, work (housework, homework)

Um diese Substantive zählbar zu machen, verwendet man Ausdrücke wie *a bit of, a piece of, some* (3).

⚠ Einige Substantive gibt es im Englischen nur im Singular oder nur im Plural.

4 Economics **is** a popular subject. Politics **doesn't interest** me.
5 The media **have** a lot of influence.
6 The police **are looking** for the murderer.
7 The scissors **need** sharpening.

Auf *economics, politics, physics* folgt ein Verb im Singular, trotz End-*s* (4).

Auf *media, police, scissors, trousers* etc. folgt immer ein Verb im Plural (5–7).

Unit word list

Dieses Wörterverzeichnis enthält alle Wörter in der Reihenfolge ihres Erscheinens (Seitenzahlen sind angegeben). Nicht aufgeführt sind Wörter, die nicht unbedingt zum aktiven Wortschatz gehören müssen. Daher eignet sich diese Liste hervorragend für die Vorbereitung auf Klausuren, sowie auf die Abiturprüfung.

Wörter aus Hörverständnisübungen sind gelb, aus Partner Files grün, aus Videos blau markiert.

Abkürzungen: AE = amerikanisches Englisch, BE = britisches Englisch, etw = etwas, jdm = jemandem, jdn = jemanden, jds = jemandes, pl = plural, sb = somebody, sth = something, < > Gegenteil

Topic 1 The environment

▸ page 8	**climate change** ['klaɪmət tʃeɪndʒ]	rising temperature and changing weather patterns caused by increased levels of carbon dioxide	*Klimawandel*
	greenhouse gas [ˌgriːnhaʊs 'gæs]	a gas that contributes to the greenhouse effect e.g. carbon dioxide and chlorofluorocarbons	*Treibhausgas*
	source [sɔːs]	origin, starting point	*Quelle*
	sustainability [səˌsteɪnə'bɪləti]	*adj* sustainable	*Nachhaltigkeit*
	climate crisis [ˌklaɪmət 'kraɪsɪs]	intense difficulty caused by climate change	*Klimakrise*
	geological epoch [ˌdʒiːəˌlɒdʒɪkl 'iːpɒk]	a period of time in which a layer of rock is formed	*erdgeschichtliches Zeitalter*
	renewables [rɪ'njuːəblz]	natural sources of energy that do not decrease from use	*erneuerbare Energien*
	upcycling ['ʌpsaɪklɪŋ]	reusing waste to make new products	*Abfallveredelung*
	quotation [kwəʊ'teɪʃn]	a group of words or a short piece of writing taken from a book, play, speech, etc.	*Zitat*
	preview ['priːvjuː]	a chance to see sth before it is generally available	*Vorschau*
▸ page 9	to **greenwash sth** ['griːnwɒʃ]	to create an environmentally friendly image of sth harmful	*etw ein grünes Image geben*
	on average [ɒn 'ævərɪdʒ]	middle point of all values	*im Durchschnitt*
	review [rɪ'vjuː]	looking back on sth	*Über-, Rückblick, Zusammenfassung*
	to **review sth** [rɪ'vjuː]	to check sth, to look at sth carefully	*etw wiederholen*
	campaign [kæm'peɪn]	to try to win an election	*Kampagne, Aktion*
	deforestation [diːˌfɒrɪ'steɪʃn]	clearing of large areas with trees	*Waldzerstörung*
	extinction [ɪk'stɪŋkʃn]	totally dying out, not being any more	*Ausrottung, Aussterben*
	fossil fuel ['fɒsl fjuːəl]	coal, fuel oil or natural gas, made from the remains of dead plants and animals	*fossiler Brennstoff*
	overconsumption [ˌəʊvəkən'sʌmpʃn]	using too much of sth	*Überkonsum*
	pollution [pə'luːʃn]	things in the environment that are harmful or poisonous	*(Umwelt-)Verschmutzung*
	resource [rɪ'sɔːs]	stock, supply of sth	*Ressource, Rohstoff*
	responsibility [rɪˌspɒnsə'bɪləti]	being in charge of sth	*Verantwortung*
	waste [weɪst]	to not use sth well	*Abfall*

Section A The human impact

▸ page 10	to **estimate** ['estɪmeɪt]	to guess or calculate costs, etc	*schätzen*
	to **melt** [melt]	e.g. The ice is melting in Antarctica.	*schmelzen, abschmelzen*

oxygen ['ɒksɪdʒən]	chemical found in the air that is necessary for life	*Sauerstoff*	
to scale [tə 'skeɪl]	everything the correct size	*maßstabsgetreu*	
estimate ['estɪmət]	to guess or calculate costs, etc	*Schätzung*	
drought [draʊt]	a long period of time with low rainfall	*Dürre*	
extinct [ɪk'stɪŋkt]	no longer existing e.g. the dodo bird	*ausgestorben*	
species, *pl* **species** ['spi:ʃi:z]	sort, type, kind	*Art* (Biologie)	
renewable [rɪ'nju:əbl]	replaceable, not depleted when used	*erneuerbar*	
such as ['sʌtʃ əz]	for example	*wie (zum Beispiel)*	
coal [kəʊl]	black or brown rocks used as fuel	*Kohle*	
characteristic [ˌkærəktə'rɪstɪk]	a feature or quality of sb	*Merkmal, charakteristische Eigenschaft*	
to **affect sth** [ə'fekt]	to have negative consequences for sth	*etw beeinflussen, sich auswirken auf etw*	▸ page 11
to **declare** [dɪ'kleə]	to make sth known	*verkünden*	
to **claim** [kleɪm]	to say that sth is true	*behaupten*	
current ['kʌrənt]	at the moment, present	*aktuell, derzeitig*	
to **indicate** ['ɪndɪkeɪt]	to show sth, to prove sth	*(an)zeigen, darauf hindeuten, hinweisen auf*	
entirely [ɪn'taɪəli]	completely, 100%	*völlig, ganz*	
to **emphasize sth** ['emfəsaɪz]	to make sth stronger in tone	*etw betonen, etw hervorheben*	
attempt [ə'tempt]	try	*Versuch*	
to **appreciate** [ə'pri:ʃieɪt]	to admire sth, to value sth	*anerkennen*	
scale [skeɪl]	size, amount	*Ausmaß, Umfang*	
to **back sth up** [ˌbæk 'ʌp]	to support sth, e.g. an argument	*etw untermauern, etw bekräftigen, etw belegen*	
advance [əd'vɑ:ns]	move forward	*Fortschritt*	
consumption [kən'sʌmpʃn]	*v* to consume	*Verbrauch, Konsum*	
major ['meɪdʒə]	important	*Haupt-, wesentlich, größer*	
carbon ['kɑ:bən]	a chemical element	*Kohle(nstoff)*	
sea level ['si: levl]	e.g. The melting ice caps are causing sea levels to rise dramatically.	*Meeresspiegel*	
entire [ɪn'taɪə]	whole	*ganz, vollständig*	
to **relate to sth** [rɪ'leɪt]	connected to sth	*mit etw in Zusammenhang stehen*	
to **relate to sth** [rɪ'leɪt]	to empathize	*sich mit etw identifizieren*	
researcher [rɪ'sɜ:tʃə]	*v* to research	*Forscher / in, Wissenschaftler / in*	▸ page 12
scientific [ˌsaɪən'tɪfɪk]	*n* science	*wissenschaftlich*	
carbon footprint [ˌkɑ:bn 'fʊtprɪnt]	e.g. Companies need to reduce their carbon footprint.	*CO_2-Bilanz*	
amount [ə'maʊnt]	how much you have or use	*Menge, Ausmaß, Umfang*	
to **breathe (in)** [bri:ð]	*n* breath	*(ein)atmen*	▸ page 13
exposure (to) [ɪk'spəʊʒə]	having contact with sth	*Belastung (durch)*	
exhaust fumes [ɪg'zɔ:st fju:mz]	gas created when fuel is burned	*Abgase*	
pollutant [pə'lu:tənt]	sth that makes the air or water unclean	*Schadstoff*	
radiation [ˌreɪdi'eɪʃn]	energy made up of electromagnetic waves	*Strahlung; Bestrahlung*	
to **prevent sth** [prɪ'vent]	to stop sth happening	*etw (ver)hindern, einer Sache vorbeugen*	
soil erosion ['sɔɪl ɪrəʊʒn]	earth taken away by wind and water	*Bodenerosion*	
exploitation [ˌeksplɔɪ'teɪʃn]	using sb or sth for one's own benefit	*Ausbeutung, Abbau (von Rohstoffen)*	
logging ['lɒgɪŋ]	cutting down trees	*Abholzung*	
plantation [plæn'teɪʃn]	a large area of land, esp. in a hot country where crops such as coffee, sugar, tobacco are grown	*Plantage*	
depletion [dɪ'pli:ʃn]	using up sth	*Verringerung, Abbau*	
desertification [dɪˌzɜ:tɪfɪ'keɪʃn]	when fertile land becomes a desert	*Wüstenbildung, Versteppung*	

	famine ['fæmɪn]	e.g. The famine caused 10,000 deaths.	*Hungersnot*
	malnutrition [ˌmælnjuː'trɪʃn]	health problems caused by not having enough food	*Unterernährung, falsche Ernährung*
	reproductive health [ˌriːprəˌdʌktɪv 'helθ]	sexual health and family planning	*Fortpflanzungsgesundheit*
	shortage (of) ['ʃɔːtɪdʒ]	not having enough of sth	*Mangel, Knappheit (an)*
	to **assess sth** [ə'ses]	to make a judgement on sth	*etw beurteilen*
	urgent ['ɜːdʒənt]	needing to be dealt with or done immediately	*dringend*

Section B The need for energy

▸ page 14	**wave** [weɪv]	up-and-down movement of the sea	*Welle*
	hydropower ['haɪdrəʊpaʊə]	energy created from water	*Wasserkraft*
	kinetic energy [kɪˌnetɪk '-], [kaɪˌnetik '-]	energy created from movement	*Bewegungsenergie*
	tidal ['taɪdl]	caused by the rise and fall of the sea	*Gezeiten-*
	to **promote sth** [prə'məʊt]	to support sth, to make sth grow	*etw fördern, etw unterstützen*
	soil [sɔɪl]	earth	*Erde, Boden*
▸ page 15	**power station** ['paʊə steɪʃn]	a place where energy is created	*Kraftwerk*
	wastewater ['weɪstwɔːtə]	e.g. sewage	*Abwasser*
	to **harvest** ['hɑːvɪst]	*n* harvest	*ernten*
	panel ['pænl]	e.g. solar panels	*Platte, Tafel, Kollektor*
	to **convert** [kən'vɜːt]	*n* conversion	*umwandeln, konvertieren*
	to **poison** ['pɔɪzn]	to contaminate sth	*vergiften*
	to **harm sb/sth** [hɑːm]	to hurt sb/sth	*jdm / etw schaden*
	dependent on sth [dɪ'pendənt ɒn]	needing sth to be able to live normally	*von etw abhängig*
	crop [krɒp]	plants grown for food	*Nutzpflanze, Feldfrucht*
▸ page 16	**oil rig** ['ɔɪl rɪg]	a structure with equipment for drilling oil	*Ölbohrinsel*
	to **take sth apart** [ˌteɪk ə'pɑːt]	to separate sth into different parts	*etw auseinandernehmen*
	to **dismantle sth** [dɪs'mæntl]	< > to build sth	*etw abbauen, etw zerlegen*
	tide [taɪd]	the regular rise and fall in the level of the sea	*Gezeit(en), Tide*
	hydrogen ['haɪdrədʒən]	the lightest gas with no smell or colour	*Wasserstoff*
	legacy ['legəsi]	sth left behind or handed down	*Erbe, Altlast*
	predictable [prɪ'dɪktəbl]	foreseeable	*voraussagbar, vorhersehbar*
	excess [ɪk'ses]	extreme behaviour that is unacceptable or illegal	*Überschuss*
	to **be opposed to sth** [bi ə'pəʊzd tə]	to be against sth	*gegen etw sein*
	to **campaign for/against sth** [kæm'peɪn]	to fight for/against sth	*sich für / gegen etw einsetzen*
	former ['fɔːmə]	that used to have a particular position or status in the past	*ehemalig*
	islander ['aɪləndə]	sb who lives on an island	*Inselbewohner / in*
	spring tide [ˌsprɪŋ 'taɪd]	the greatest difference between high and low tides	*Springflut*
	to **fail** [feɪl]	to be unsuccessful in a test or exam	*versagen, scheitern*
	coastal ['kəʊstl]	on the coast	*Küsten-*
	scalable ['skeɪləbl]	able to change size	*skalierbar, größenvariabel*
	laboratory [lə'bɒrətri]	place for scientific research	*Labor*
	various ['veəriəs]	different types of	*verschieden, mehrere, allerlei*
	based ['beɪst]	located, situated	*ansässig*
	proof of concept [ˌpruːf əv 'kɒnsept]	process showing that sth is feasible	*Machbarkeitsnachweis*

settled ['setld]	agreed, decided	*beschlossen, abgemacht*
foundation [faʊn'deɪʃn]	the act of starting a new institution, organization or country	*Grundlage, Fundament; Stiftung*
transition [træn'zɪʃn]	the process of changing in some way	*Übergang, Umstellung*
to **remain** [rɪ'meɪn]	to stay	*bleiben*
valuable ['væljuəbl]	worth a lot, very important	*wertvoll*
net [net]	that is the final number	*netto, Netto-*
reliance (on sth) [rɪ'laɪəns]	needing or depending on sth	*Abhängigkeit (von etw)*
to **rely on sb/sth** [rɪ'laɪ ɒn]	to be able to count on sb/sth	*sich auf jdn / etw verlassen*
remains *pl* [rɪ'meɪnz]	sth that is left behind	*(Über-)Reste, Relikte*
settlement ['setlmənt]	colony	*Siedlung, Kolonie*
to **occur** [ə'kɜː]	to happen	*stattfinden, passieren, geschehen*
to **extract sth** [ɪk'strækt]	to take sth out e.g. from the earth	*etw gewinnen* (Bodenschätze)
to **achieve sth** [ə'tʃiːv]	to do sth successfully	*etw erreichen, etw leisten*
goal [gəʊl]	sth you want to do or get	*Ziel, Absicht*
liquid ['lɪkwɪd]	fluid	*Flüssigkeit*
to **fracture** ['fræktʃə]	to break	*brechen, aufbrechen*
to **access sth** ['ækses]	to be able to get (to) sth	*auf etw zugreifen, Zugang haben zu etw*
domestic [də'mestɪk]	relating to the home	*inländisch, Inlands-*
concern [kən'sɜːn]	worry	*Sorge, Befürchtung*
release [rɪ'liːs]	letting sb go free	*Freisetzung*
to **contaminate sth** [kən'tæmɪneɪt]	to make sth dirty, poisoned	*etw verunreinigen, etw kontaminieren*
incident ['ɪnsɪdənt]	something that happens, often unusual or unpleasant	*Vorfall*
safety measure ['seɪfti meʒə]	doing sth to protect sb/sth	*Sicherheitsmaßnahme*
threat [θret]	sth bad that might happen to sb/sth	*Bedrohung*
dependence [dɪ'pendəns]	relying on or being controlled by sb/sth	*Abhängigkeit*
participant [pɑː'tɪsɪpənt]	*v* to participate	*Teilnehmer / in*
to **host (a debate)** [həʊst]	to be a presenter (for a debate)	*(eine Debatte) moderieren*
representative [ˌreprɪ'zentətɪv]	sb who officially speaks on behalf of a group of people, e.g. in parliament	*Vertreter / in, Beauftragte / r*

▸ page 17

Section C Greenwashing

brand [brænd]	a type of product manufactured by a company under a particular name	*Marke*
cardboard ['kɑːdbɔːd]	e.g. cardboard box	*Pappe, Karton*
packaging ['pækɪdʒɪŋ]	*n* package	*Verpackung*
classic ['klæsɪk]	typical	*klassisch*
to **suppose** [sə'pəʊz]	to think, to believe	*vermuten, annehmen*
to **be willing to do sth** [bi 'wɪlɪŋ tə]	to be happy to do sth	*bereit sein, etw zu tun*
to **cover sth up** [ˌkʌvər 'ʌp]	to make it look like sth bad didn't happen	*etw vertuschen*
to **emit sth** [ɪ'mɪt]	to produce sth then give it out	*etw emittieren, etw ausstoßen, etw abstrahlen*
manufacturing [ˌmænju'fæktʃərɪŋ]	processing raw materials into a finished product	*Fertigung, Herstellung*
harmless ['hɑːmləs]	< > harmful	*harmlos, ungefährlich*
to **certify** ['sɜːtɪfaɪ]	to show to be true	*bescheinigen, zertifizieren*
certification [ˌsɜːtɪfɪ'keɪʃn]	providing an official document	*Bescheinigung*
file [faɪl]	*v* to file	*Datei, Ordner, Akte*
operation [ˌɒpə'reɪʃn]	being in activity, functioning	*Arbeitsablauf, Arbeitsgang, Betrieb, Geschäft*
to **mislead (-led, -led)** [ˌmɪs'liːd]	to give the wrong idea, impression	*täuschen*

▸ page 18

▸ page 19

	annual ['ænjuəl]	every year	*jährlich*
	to **withdraw (-drew, -drawn)** [wɪð'drɔː]	to take out	*zurückziehen*
	to **distract sb** [dɪ'strækt]	to move sb's attention away from sth	*jdn ablenken*
	vast [vɑːst]	very large, enormous	*riesig, sehr groß*
	to **conduct sth** [kən'dʌkt]	to carry out sth, to do sth	*etw (durch)führen, etw leiten*
	corporate ['kɔːpərət]	related to a business or company	*Unternehmens-; Geschäfts-*
	emitter [ɪ'mɪtə]	source of pollution	*Emissionsquelle, Emittent*
▸ page 20	**agreement** [ə'griːmənt]	contract, understanding	*Vereinbarung*
	carbon capture and storage [ˌkɑːbn ˌkæptʃə n 'stɔːrɪdʒ]	catching and storing CO_2	*CO_2-Abscheidung und -Speicherung*
	capacity [kə'pæsəti]	e.g. The capacity of this water bottle is 1 litre.	*Kapazität, Leistung*
	numerous ['njuːmərəs]	many	*zahlreich*
	to **propose sth** [prə'pəʊz]	to suggest sth formally	*etw vorschlagen, etw unterbreiten, etw darlegen*
	spokesman/-woman/-person ['spəʊksmən, -wʊmən, -pɜːsn]	a man/woman/person who speaks for a group	*Sprecher/in*
	intensity [ɪn'tensəti]	strength, power	*Intensität*
	consistent [kən'sɪstənt]	< > changing, contradictory	*konsistent, widerspruchsfrei*
	to **reject** [rɪ'dʒekt]	< > to accept sb	*ablehnen, zurückweisen*
	(carbon) offset [ˌkɑːbən 'ɒfset]	compensation (for carbon emissions)	*Klimakompensation*
	treatment ['triːtmənt]	*v* to treat	*Behandlung*
	treaty ['triːti]	official agreement between countries	*(Staats-)Vertrag*
	to **involve** [ɪn'vɒlv]	*n* involvement	*einbeziehen*
	accusation [ˌækju'zeɪʃn]	e.g. You did this! It is your fault!	*Vorwurf, Anschuldigung*
	regarding [rɪ'gɑːdɪŋ]	with regards to	*bezüglich, betreffend*
▸ page 21	to **insist** [ɪn'sɪst]	e.g. I insist you do exactly as I say!	*darauf bestehen, beteuern*
	clothing ['kləʊðɪŋ]	clothes	*Bekleidung, Kleidung*
	manufacturer [ˌmænju'fæktʃərə]	producer	*Hersteller/in, Produzent/in*
	contribution [ˌkɒntrɪ'bjuːʃn]	thing given to help sth	*Beitrag*
	in relation to [rɪ'leɪʃn]	in connection with	*in Bezug auf*

Section D The importance of forests

▸ page 22	**referred to as** [rɪ'fɜːd]	called/named sth by sb	*bezeichnet als*
	percentage [pə'sentɪdʒ]	the number of sth as if it is part of a total which is 100	*Prozentsatz, Anteil*
	transmission [træns'mɪʃn]	circulation	*Übertragung*
	destruction [dɪ'strʌkʃn]	*v* to destroy	*Zerstörung, Vernichtung*
	loss [lɒs]	the state of no longer having sth	*Verlust*
	to **enable** [ɪ'neɪbl]	to make it possible for sth to happen	*ermöglichen, befähigen*
	expansion [ɪk'spænʃn]	growth	*Ausweitung, Expansion*
	mine [maɪn]	*n* miner	*Bergwerk, Mine*
▸ page 23	to **associate sth with sth** [ə'səʊʃiət]	to connect sb/sth with sth in one's mind	*etw mit etw verbinden, etw mit etw assoziieren*
	trade [treɪd]	*v* to trade	*Handel*
	to **cultivate sth** ['kʌltɪveɪt]	to grow sth	*etw anbauen; etw züchten*
	deposit [dɪ'pɒzɪt]	layer, accumulation	*Vorkommen*
	widespread ['waɪdspred]	over a large area	*(weit) verbreitet, allgemein, groß*
	to **slaughter** ['slɔːtə]	to kill	*schlachten*
	to **chop down** [ˌtʃɒp 'daʊn]	to cut (a tree) so it falls down	*fällen*
	to **expose** [ɪk'spəʊz]	< > to cover	*aussetzen* (einer Sache)
	to **stress** [stres]	to underline sth	*betonen, hervorheben*
	parcel ['pɑːsl]	package	*Paket; Parzelle*
	interface [ɪntəfeɪs]	interaction, connection	*Schnittstelle*
	fever ['fiːvə]	rise in body temperature	*Fieber*

inevitable [ɪn'evɪtəbl]	unable to be avoided or stopped	*unausweichlich, unvermeidbar*	
veterinary (medicine) ['vetnri, 'vetrənəri]	medical care for animals	*Tiermedizin*	
price tag ['praɪs tæg]	a paper saying how much sth costs	*Preisschild*	▸ page 24
to **wipe** [waɪp]	to clean, erase	*wischen, wegwischen*	
to **facilitate sth** [fə'sɪlɪteɪt]	to make sth possible	*etw ermöglichen, etw vermitteln, etw vereinfachen*	
previous ['priːviəs]	before, earlier	*vorherig, früher*	
addition [ə'dɪʃn]	adding sth to sth else	*Ergänzung*	
to **investigate sth** [ɪn'vestɪgeɪt]	to look carefully at sth	*etw ermitteln, etw untersuchen*	
thought [θɔːt]	*v* to think	*Gedanke*	▸ page 25
to **outline sth** ['aʊtlaɪn]	to summarize the main points	*etw skizzieren, etw grob beschreiben*	

Section E The fashion industry

to **donate** [dəʊ'neɪt]	to give money	*spenden*	▸ page 26
fact sheet ['fækt ʃiːt]	a paper with useful information	*Datenblatt, Merkblatt*	
respondent [rɪ'spɒndənt]	people answering a survey/ questionnaire	*Befragte/r*	
toxic ['tɒksɪk]	poisonous	*giftig, Gift-*	
eventually [ɪ'ventʃuəli]	in the end	*letztendlich, schließlich*	
to **commit (oneself) to sth** [kə'mɪt]	to promise to do sth	*sich auf etw einlassen, sich auf etw festlegen*	
production line [prə'dʌkʃn laɪn]	a line of machines and workers in a factory, which assembles a product piece by piece	*Fließband, Produktion(sstraße)*	
emphasis, *pl* **emphases** ['emfəsɪs]	importance given to sth	*Betonung, Schwerpunkt, Akzent*	
landfill site ['lændfɪl saɪt]	an area of land where waste/rubbish is buried	*Mülldeponie*	▸ page 27
developing country [dɪˌveləpɪŋ 'kʌntri]	a country with poor industry and economy	*Entwicklungsland*	
fabric ['fæbrɪk]	e.g. This scarf is made of very soft fabric.	*Gewebe, Stoff, Tuch*	
to **address sth** [ə'dres]	to think about and deal with a problem	*etw angehen, sich mit etw befassen*	
resale ['riːseɪl]	selling sth again	*Weiterverkauf, Wiederverkauf*	
to **record sth** [rɪ'kɔːd]	*n* record	*etw dokumentieren, etw verzeichnen, etw aufzeichnen*	
hub [hʌb]	the centre of sth	*Knotenpunkt, Hauptumschlagplatz*	
to **launch** [lɔːntʃ]	to bring a new product on the market	(Produkt) *auf den Markt bringen, einführen*	▸ page 28
delivery service [dɪ'lɪvəri sɜːvɪs]	a company/person that transports goods to a final destination	*Lieferdienst*	
token ['təʊkən]	a voucher that can be exchanged for sth	*Gutschein*	
retailer ['riːteɪlə]	seller to individual customers	*Einzelhändler/in*	
goods *pl* [gʊdz]	things to buy	*Waren, Güter*	
guilt [gɪlt]	<> innocence	*Schuld(gefühle)*	
devastating ['devəsteɪtɪŋ]	causing a lot of damage and destruction	*verheerend*	
to **host** [həʊst]	to moderate an event	*veranstalten*	
greatly ['greɪtli]	very much	*erheblich*	
to **loan** [ləʊn]	< > to borrow	*ausleihen*	
to **fund sth** [fʌnd]	to finance sth	*etw finanzieren*	
significance [sɪg'nɪfɪkəns]	importance, meaning	*Bedeutung, Stellenwert*	

	fee [fiː]	money requested for a specific job	*Gebühr*
	to **treasure** ['treʒə]	to appreciate, care for sth	*schätzen, pflegen*
	circular ['sɜːkjələ]	round	*kreisförmig, rund*
	chief executive [ˌtʃiːf ɪg'zekjətɪv]	managing director	*Geschäftsführer / in*
▸ page 29	to **urge sb** [ɜːdʒ]	to try and convince sb	*jdn drängen*
	EC (= European Commission) [ˌiː 'siː]	the executive branch of the EU	*Europäische Kommission*
	shortcoming ['ʃɔːtkʌmɪŋ]	deficit	*Mangel, Defizit*
	carpooling ['kɑːpuːlɪŋ]	several people driving together in one car	*Fahrgemeinschaft(en)*

Section F Climate activism

▸ page 30	**collocation** [ˌkɒlə'keɪʃn]	a group of words which usually go together	*Kollokation* (inhaltliche Kombinierbarkeit sprachlicher Einheiten)
	to **confront sb with sb/sth** [kən'frʌnt]	to face up to and deal with a problem	*jdn mit jdm / etw konfrontieren*
	to **glue** [gluː]	to stick sth to another thing	*kleben*
	lawsuit ['lɔːsuːt]	legal process	*Gerichtsverfahren, Prozess*
▸ page 31	**justice** ['dʒʌstɪs]	fairness in the way people are treated	*Gerechtigkeit*
	income ['ɪnkʌm]	money from work, business, investments	*Einkommen*
	vulnerable ['vʌlnərəbl]	weak and easily hurt	*verletzlich, verwundbar*
	to **evaluate sth** [ɪ'væljueɪt]	*n* evaluation	*etw bewerten, etw beurteilen*
	leaves *pl* [liːvz]	foliage on trees and plants	*Blätter, Laub*
	wrapping ['ræpɪŋ]	packaging	*Verpackung*
	twig [twɪg]	small tree branch	*Zweig*
	effort ['efət]	attempt	*Anstrengung, Bemühung(en)*
	to **snap** [snæp]	to break	*(zer)brechen*
	branch [brɑːntʃ]	limb of a tree	*Ast, Zweig* (auch: *Zweigstelle*)
	root [ruːt]	where sb/sth comes from	*Wurzel*
	commitment (to) [kə'mɪtmənt]	a promise to do sth	*Engagement (für), Bekenntnis (zu)*
	unethical [ʌn'eθɪkl]	not morally correct	*unethisch, nicht vertretbar*
▸ page 32	**desperate** ['despərət]	e.g. The man was starving, he desperately needed some food.	*verzweifelt*
	to **inspire** [ɪn'spaɪə]	My teacher inspired me to study abroad.	*inspirieren, anregen*
	elderly ['eldəli]	older	*älter*
	rider ['raɪdə]	sb who travels by bike or horse	*Fahrer / in (Passagier / in)*
	passionate ['pæʃənət]	*n* passion	*leidenschaftlich*
	workmate ['wɜːkmeɪt]	colleague	*Kollege / in*
	to **receive sth** [rɪ'siːv]	to get sth, to be given sth	*etw erhalten, etw empfangen*
	to **be done** [dʌn]	to be finished with sth	*fertig sein*
	astonishing [ə'stɒnɪʃɪŋ]	amazing	*überraschend*
	to **waste sth** [weɪst]	They wasted their time playing computer games all day.	*etw verschwenden, etw vergeuden*
	part ..., part ... [pɑːt]	the things that make up sth bigger	*teils ..., teils ...*
	encouragement [ɪn'kʌrɪdʒmənt]	*v* to encourage	*Ermutigung*
	craft [krɑːft]	making things by hand	*Handwerk*
	reflection [rɪ'flekʃn]	I decided, on reflection, not to apply for the job.	*Betrachtung*
	to **preach** [priːtʃ]	to speak like a priest	*predigen*
	mentor ['mentɔ]	sb who helps you if you have a problem	*Mentor / in*
	to **yell** [jel]	to speak very loudly	*schreien, brüllen*
	crop failure ['krɒp feɪljə]	food plants which are damaged or cannot grow properly	*Missernte, Ernteausfall*
	throughout ... [θruː'aʊt]	the whole way	*der / die / das ganze ... (hindurch)*
	globe [gləʊb]	I'd love to travel around the globe one day.	*Globus, Welt*

to **be aimed at sb** [bi 'eɪmd ət]	e.g. Who is the course aimed at?	*sich an jdn richten*	▸ page 33
inventor [ɪn'ventə]	e.g. Thomas Edison was the inventor of the light bulb	*Erfinder/in*	
particular [pə'tɪkjələ]	used to emphasize one individual person, thing or type of thing and not others	*bestimmt, speziell*	
vermicomposting [ˌvɜːmɪ'kɒmpɒstɪŋ]	compost made using worms	*Wurmkompostierung*	
carbon sequestration [ˌsiːkwə'streɪʃn]	to break apart	*CO_2-Abscheidung und -Speicherung*	
to **separate** ['sepəreɪt]	to move sb/sth apart	*trennen, abspalten*	
to **leak** [liːk]	to lose contents	*auslaufen, lecken*	
flavouring ['fleɪvərɪŋ]	sth that makes food or drink taste stronger	*Aroma(stoff)*	
to **exceed** [ɪk'siːd]	to be greater than a particular amount of sth	*überschreiten*	

Words in context

irreversible [ˌɪrɪ'vɜːsəbl]	< > reversible	*unumkehrbar*	▸ page 36
to **raise awareness about sth (rose, risen)** [ˌreɪz ə'weənəs]	to make people interested in/care about sth	*auf etw aufmerksam machen*	
carbon neutrality [ˌkɑːbən njuː'træləti]	when the amount of carbon dioxide released into the environment is the same as the amount removed	*Klimaneutralität*	
to **renew** [rɪ'njuː]	to restore, make new again	*erneuern*	
sufficient [sə'fɪʃnt]	enough, having the right amount	*ausreichend, hinreichend*	
to **overheat** [ˌəʊvə'hiːt]	to let sth get too hot	*(sich) überhitzen*	
catastrophic [ˌkætə'strɒfɪk]	*n* catastrophe	*katastrophal, verhängnisvoll*	
heatwave ['hiːtweɪv]	abnormally hot weather	*Hitzewelle*	
vital ['vaɪtl]	absolutely necessary	*lebensnotwendig, unerlässlich*	
endangered [ɪn'deɪndʒəd]	< > protected	*bedroht*	
pollination [ˌpɒlə'neɪʃn]	e.g. Bees are one of the most important insects for pollination.	*Bestäubung*	
to **release sth** [rɪ'liːs]	to let sth free	*etw freisetzen*	
ecosystem ['iːkəʊsɪstəm]	a complex biological network	*Ökosystem*	
overpopulated [ˌəʊvə'pɒpjuleɪtɪd]	having too many people for the available space	*überbevölkert*	
to **pollute sth** [pə'luːt]	to make sth, e.g. air, water, soil unclean	*etw verschmutzen*	
double edged sword [ˌdʌbl edʒd 'sɔːd]	sth with good and bad outcomes	*zweischneidiges Schwert*	▸ page 37
nuclear power station [ˌnjuːkliə 'paʊə steɪʃn]	a place where nuclear energy is produced	*Kernkraftwerk*	
shutdown ['ʃʌtdaʊn]	to stop, close down	*Herunterfahren, Abschaltung*	
to **phase out** [ˌfeɪz 'aʊt]	to wind sth down	*auslaufen lassen*	
to **consume** [kən'sjuːm]	*n* consumption	*verbrauchen, konsumieren*	
to **regenerate** [rɪ'dʒenəreɪt]	to renew, restore	*sich regenerieren*	
biodegradable [ˌbaɪəʊdɪ'greɪdəbl]	able to break down or rot naturally	*biologisch abbaubar*	
garbage patch ['gɑːbɪdʒ pætʃ]	a place to leave waste and trash	*Müllstrudel*	
to **measure** ['meʒə]	to find out how big, long, heavy sth is	*messen*	
to **injure sb** ['ɪndʒə]	*n* injury	*jdn verletzen*	
microbead ['maɪkrəʊbiːd]	very small particle	*Mikrokügelchen*	
hygiene ['haɪdʒiːn]	*adj* hygienic	*Hygiene*	
household ['haʊshəʊld]	e.g. We are five in our household: mum, dad, granny, my sister, and me.	*Haushalt, Haushalts-*	
drain [dreɪn]	to take sb's energy	*Abfluss*	
to **tackle sth** ['tækl]	to deal with sth, to fight sth	*etw (z.B. ein Problem) angehen, etw bewältigen*	

	factory farming ['fæktri fɑːmɪŋ]	industrial method of raising farm animals	*Massentierhaltung*
▸ page 38	to **radiate** ['reɪdieɪt]	to give out, give off	*strahlen*
	sustained [sə'steɪnd]	ongoing, continued	*anhaltend, ununterbrochen*
	birth control ['bɜːθ kəntrəʊl]	e.g. condoms, the pill, etc	*Geburtenkontrolle*
	severe [sɪ'vɪə]	extremely bad or serious	*ernst*
	to **decompose** [ˌdiːkəm'pəʊz]	to decay, to break down	*sich zersetzen, zerfallen*

Topic 2 Technology

▸ page 50	**genetically modified (GM)** [dʒəˌnetɪkli 'mɒdɪfaɪd]	containing DNA that has been modified	*genetisch verändert*
	CEO (Chief Executive Officer) [ˌsiː iː 'əʊ]	the head of a business, company	*Vorstandsvorsitzende/r*
	to **alter sth** ['ɔːltə]	to change sth	*etw (ver)ändern*
	artificial [ˌɑːtɪ'fɪʃl]	not real, made up	*künstlich*
▸ page 51	**broad** [brɔːd]	strong	*breit, weit*
	protection [prə'tekʃn]	*v* to protect	*Schutz*
	purchase ['pɜːtʃəs]	sth you buy	*Kauf, Ankauf*
	absent ['æbsənt]	< > present	*abwesend*
	along with [ə'lɒŋ wɪð]	plus, together with	*(zusammen) mit, neben*
	synthetic [sɪn'θetɪk]	< > natural	*künstlich, synthetisch*
	to **not bother to do sth** ['bɒðə]	to not do sth because you think it isn't important	*es nicht für nötig halten, etw zu tun*
	to **distinguish (between)** [dɪ'stɪŋgwɪʃ]	to see the difference (between sth and sth else)	*unterscheiden (zwischen)*

Section A Genetically modified food

▸ page 52	to **modify sth** ['mɒdɪfaɪ]	to change sth slightly	*etw (ver)ändern, etw modifizieren*
	genetic engineering [dʒəˌnetɪk endʒɪ'nɪərɪŋ]	changing of genes in plants or animals for a desired effect	*Gentechnik, Gentechnologie*
	to **cross-breed** ['krɒs briːd]	to produce sth from two different species	*kreuzen, durch Kreuzung züchten*
	variety [və'raɪəti]	different things to choose from	*Sorte, Art, Variante*
	resilient [rɪ'zɪliənt]	able to withstand difficult conditions	*widerstandsfähig*
▸ page 53	**obvious** ['ɒbviəs]	clear	*offensichtlich, klar*
	to **ensure** [ɪn'ʃʊə]	to make sure, be certain	*sicherstellen*
	as well as [əz 'wel əz]	in addition to, also	*sowohl … als auch …, ebenso wie, sowie*
	resistance (to) [rɪ'zɪstəns]	opposition (to)	*Widerstand (gegen)*
	to **begin with** [tə bɪ'gɪn wɪð]	to start	*anfänglich*
	long-term [ˌlɒŋ 'tɜːm]	< > short-term	*langfristig, Langzeit-*
	toxin ['tɒksɪn]	poison	*Gift*
	nutrient ['njuːtriənt]	a substance that a plant needs to grow	*Nährstoff*
	to **decrease** [dɪ'kriːs]	< > to increase	*abnehmen, zurückgehen*
	to **witness** ['wɪtnəs]	to see sth, to experience sth	*(mit)erleben*
	to **dominate sth** ['dɒmɪneɪt]	to be the most important	*etw beherrschen, etw dominieren*
	investment [ɪn'vestmənt]	money put into a product or service for which you expect a profit	*Investition*
	return [rɪ'tɜːn]	profit from an investment	*Ertrag, Rendite*
	to **pose a question** [pəʊz]	to bring attention to a problem	*eine Frage aufwerfen*
	advocate ['ædvəkət]	sb who speaks in favour of sb/sth	*Befürworter/in*
▸ page 54	**nutritious** [nju'trɪʃəs]	full of vitamins and minerals	*nahrhaft*
	herbicide ['hɜːbɪsaɪd]	a poison used to kill plants	*Unkrautvernichtungsmittel*

error in judgement [ˌerər ɪn 'dʒʌdʒmənt]	bad decision	*Fehleinschätzung*	
thoroughly ['θʌrəli]	totally, completely	*gründlich, aufmerksam*	
properly ['prɒpəli]	correctly	*richtig, ordentlich, korrekt*	
fortunate ['fɔːtʃənət]	lucky	*glücklich*	
condition [kən'dɪʃn]	*phr* in good/poor condition	*Bedingung, Zustand*	
seedless ['siːdləs]	having no seeds	*kernlos*	▸ page 55
humane [hjuː'meɪn]	compassionate, considerate	*human, menschenwürdig*	
directed at [də'rektɪd]	said in an aggressive way	*gerichtet an*	

Section B Food production

appealing [ə'piːlɪŋ]	e.g. a very appealing idea	*ansprechend*	▸ page 56
to **intend sth** [ɪn'tend]	to plan, mean sth	*etw beabsichtigen*	
to **eradicate** [ɪ'rædɪkeɪt]	to destroy	*ausrotten*	
roast [rəʊst]	cooked in an oven	*gebraten*	
substitute ['sʌbstɪtjuːt]	replacement	*Ersatz*	▸ page 57
fundraising ['fʌndreɪzɪŋ]	to collect money for a special reason	*Spendensammeln, Geldbeschaffung*	
to **branch out** [ˌbrɑːntʃ 'aʊt]	to go in a different direction	*sich verzweigen*	
to **rate sth** [reɪt]	to measure, value sth	*etw einstufen, etw bewerten*	
taste [teɪst]	*n* taste	*Geschmack*	
to **project sth** [prə'dʒekt]	to plan sth for the future	*etw prognostizieren, vorhersagen*	
poultry ['pəʊltri]	e.g. chicken, turkey, goose, etc	*Geflügel*	
to **outweigh sth** [ˌaʊt'weɪ]	to be greater, more significant	*etw übertreffen*	
to **recover** [rɪ'kʌvə]	to become healthy, get better	*sich erholen*	
to **substitute** ['sʌbstɪtjuːt]	to replace sb/sth	*jdn / etw ersetzen*	
reasonable ['riːznəbl]	appropriate, OK	*vernünftig*	
to **crack a code** [ˌkræk ə 'kəʊd]	to figure out a message, information	*einen Code knacken*	▸ page 58
to **replicate** ['replɪkeɪt]	to copy, reproduce	*nachbilden*	
texture ['tekstʃə]	how sth feels	*Konsistenz, Beschaffenheit*	
sensation [sen'seɪʃn]	feeling	*Gefühl, Empfinden*	
soy [sɔɪ]	a type of bean	*Soja*	
processed ['prəʊsest]	treated, modified, made different	*verarbeitet*	
loaf, *pl* **loaves** [ləʊf, ləʊvz]	e.g. a loaf of bread	*Laib*	
oven ['ʌvn]	a device used for cooking, roasting or baking	*Backofen*	
thoughtful ['θɔːtfl]	understanding, considerate	*wohlüberlegt, gut durchdacht*	
regulations *pl* [ˌregju'leɪʃnz]	rules, laws	*Vorschriften, Bestimmungen*	
oat [əʊt]	type of grain	*Hafer*	
actual ['æktʃuəl]	real, true	*tatsächlich, konkret*	
to **market** ['mɑːkɪt]	to make sth available for people to buy	*vermarkten*	▸ page 59
developer [dɪ'veləpə]	a company that builds and sells houses on land	*Entwickler / in*	
outstanding [aʊt'stændɪŋ]	excellent, brilliant, extraordinary	*hervorragend, überragend, außergewöhnlich*	
appetizing ['æpɪtaɪzɪŋ]	looking tasty, delicious	*appetitanregend*	
instance ['ɪnstəns]	example, case	*Beispiel, Fall*	
to **label** ['leɪbl]	to name sth	*beschriften, etikettieren, benennen*	
spice [spaɪs]	powder or seeds with a strong taste used in cooking	*Gewürz*	
heat [hiːt]	warmth, spiciness	*Schärfe*	
to **team up with sb** [ˌtiːm 'ʌp wɪð]	to work together with sb	*mit jdm zusammenarbeiten, sich mit jdm zusammentun*	
mashed potatoes [ˌmæʃt pə'teɪtəʊz]	potatoes mixed with milk and butter	*Kartoffelpüree*	
to **spice** [spaɪs]	to add powder or seeds to change the taste of food	*würzen*	
to **suspect sth** [sə'spekt]	to think that sth is not really OK	*etw vermuten*	

	to **appeal to sb** [ə'pi:l tə]	to seem like a good idea	*für jdn attraktiv sein, jdn ansprechen*
	peace [pi:s]	*adj* peaceful	*Frieden*

Section C Robots and artificial intelligence

▸ page 60	**assistance** [ə'sɪstəns]	help, support	*Hilfe, Unterstützung*
▸ page 61	**ethicist** [ˌeθɪ'sɪst]	sb with a moral code	*Ethiker / in*
	ethics *pl* ['eθɪks]	good rules of how to behave morally correct	*Ethik*
	breed [bri:d]	e.g. a poodle is a breed of dog	*Züchtung, Rasse*
	to **limit sth** ['lɪmɪt]	to allow only a particular amount of sth	*etw begrenzen, etw einschränken*
	imagination [ɪˌmædʒɪ'neɪʃn]	ability to think of things that aren't real or not yet in existence	*Phantasie, Vorstellungskraft*
	to **recreate** [ˌri:kri'eɪt]	to do/make sth again	*wiederherstellen, nachbauen*
	to **flourish** ['flʌrɪʃ]	to grow well	*florieren, blühen, gedeihen*
	to **shape sth** [ʃeɪp]	to form sth	*etw formen*
	equation [ɪ'kweɪʒn]	balance of one thing with another	*Gleichung*
	supplement ['sʌplɪmənt]	sth extra	*Ergänzung*
	to **put sb on trial** ['traɪəl]	to bring sb before a judge	*jdn vor Gericht stellen*
	to **punish sb** ['pʌnɪʃ]	to make sb pay for their mistakes	*jdn bestrafen*
	to **hold sb accountable (for sth)** [ˌhəʊld ə'kaʊntəbl]	to make sb take responsibility for sth	*jdn (für etw) zur Rechenschaft ziehen*
	to **foresee sth (foresaw, foreseen)** [fɔ:'si:]	to guess what will happen in the future	*etw voraussehen, etw vorhersehen*
	to **assign sb sth** [ə'saɪn]	to give sb sth, e.g. a job, role	*jdm etw zuweisen*
	unanticipated [ˌʌnæn'tɪsɪpeɪtɪd]	not expected	*unerwartet*
▸ page 62	**intimate** ['ɪntɪmət]	very personal	*intim, eng, persönlich*
	functionality [ˌfʌŋkʃə'næləti]	usefulness	*Funktionalität*
	data set ['deɪtə set]	collection of information	*Datensatz*
	to **model sth on sth** ['mɒdl]	to make sth so it is similar to sth else	*etw einer Sache zum Vorbild nehmen, etw einer Sache nachbilden*
	racial bias [ˌreɪʃl 'baɪəs]	discrimination against sb based on their ethnicity	*rassistische Voreingenommenheit*
	loneliness ['ləʊnlinəs]	feeling of sadness when sb has no contact with other people	*Einsamkeit*
	care worker ['keə wɜ:kə]	sb whose job is to look after other people	*Pfleger / in*
	conscious ['kɒnʃəs]	knowing(ly)	*bewusst*
	predictor [prɪ'dɪktə]	sb/sth that says what will happen in the future	*Indikator*
▸ page 63	to **confront sth** [kən'frʌnt]	to face up to and deal with sb/sth	*sich einer Sache stellen*
	capable of ['keɪpəbl əv]	having the ability to do sth	*fähig zu, imstande zu*

Section D The internet of things

▸ page 64	**utility records** *pl* [ju:'tɪləti rekədz]	e.g. phone, gas, water, electricity bills	*Versorgungsdaten*
	collection [kə'lekʃn]	group of clothes released by a designer at the same time	*Sammlung*
▸ page 65	to **stem from** [stem]	to start/begin from	*herrühren von*
	to **unearth sth** [ʌn'ɜ:θ]	to uncover, reveal sth	*etw ausgraben, etw aufstöbern*
	to cite sth [saɪt]	to make reference to sth	*etw zitieren, etw angeben*
	to **pursue sth** [pə'sju:]	to follow or chase sth	*einer Sache nachgehen, etw verfolgen*
	violation [ˌvaɪə'leɪʃn]	action that breaks a law or a contract	*Verstoß, Verletzung* (von Gesetzen, Rechten)
	surveillance [sɜ:'veɪləns]	act of watching others	*Überwachung*

indeed [ɪn'diːd]	in fact	*tatsächlich, in der Tat*	
concerning [kən'sɜːnɪŋ]	serious, worrying	*besorgniserregend*	
continuous [kən'tɪnjuəs]	without a break	*kontinuierlich, anhaltend*	
involvement (in) [ɪn'vɒlvmənt]	participation (in)	*Beteiligung (an), Einbindung (in)*	
reminder [rɪ'maɪndə]	sth that makes you remember sth	*Erinnerung, Mahnung*	
brokerage ['brəʊkərɪdʒ]	buying and selling for clients	*Börsenhandel*	
agency ['eɪdʒənsi]	business or organization	*Behörde; Agentur*	
law enforcement ['lɔː ɪnfɔːsmənt]	the police, FBI, etc.	*Gesetzesvollzug, Polizeigewalt*	
sensitive ['sensətɪv]	able to understand other people's feelings	*sensibel,* (Daten:) *vertraulich*	
oddity ['ɒdəti]	sth strange	*Eigentümlichkeit*	
to **capture** ['kæptʃə]	to catch	*einfangen, erfassen*	
nosy ['nəʊzi]	curious in a negative way	*neugierig*	
court [kɔːt]	a place where legal decisions are made	*Gericht(shof)*	
warrant ['wɒrənt]	legal document signed by a judge that gives the police authority to do sth	*richterliche Anordnung*	
affordable [ə'fɔːdəbl]	almost everyone can pay for it	*erschwinglich*	
insecure [ˌɪnsɪ'kjʊə]	with no security	*unsicher*	
absence ['æbsəns]	lack of sth	*Abwesenheit*	▸ page 66
deportation [dɪpɔː'teɪʃn]	sending sb/many people out of a country	*Abschiebung*	
restriction [rɪ'strɪkʃn]	*v* to restrict	*Beschränkung, Einschränkung*	
lock [lɒk]	*v* to lock	*Schloss*	▸ page 67
doorbell ['dɔːbel]	a button near a door that makes a noise to announce visitors	*Klingel, Türglocke*	
to **adjust sth** [ə'dʒʌst]	to change sth	*etw einstellen*	
priority [praɪ'ɒrəti]	the most important thing	*Priorität, Vorrang*	
cautious ['kɔːʃəs]	careful	*vorsichtig*	
appliance [ə'plaɪəns]	e.g. washing machine, dishwasher, microwave, etc.	*Gerät, Haushaltsgerät*	
regulation [ˌregju'leɪʃn]	rule, law, control	*Regulierung, Vorschrift*	

Section E Digital manipulation

to **undermine** [ˌʌndə'maɪn]	to make sth less important	*untergraben*	▸ page 68
artificial intelligence (AI) [ɑːtɪˌfɪʃl ɪn'telɪdʒəns]	highly intelligent computers	*künstliche Intelligenz*	
apology [ə'pɒlədʒi]	*v* to apologize	*Entschuldigung*	
from scratch [skrætʃ]	from the very beginning	*ganz von vorne, von Grund auf*	▸ page 69
to **spy** [spaɪ]	to collect information about sb/sth without their permission	*ausspionieren*	
subsidiary [səb'sɪdiəri]	a company that is owned or controlled by another company	*Tochtergesellschaft, Filiale*	
fraudster ['frɔːdstə]	sb who tricks another person	*Betrüger/in*	
to **mimic sb (mimicked, mimicked)** ['mɪmɪk]	to copy what sb says or does	*jdn nachahmen*	
insurer [ɪn'ʃʊərə]	sb who makes a contract to save a person or company from losing money	*Versicherer*	
scam [skæm]	making money by tricking people	*Schwindel, Betrug*	
reportedly [rɪ'pɔːtɪdli]	apparently, on the surface	*Berichten zufolge*	
detection [dɪ'tekʃn]	finding out sth that was hidden	*Entdeckung, Aufdeckung*	
to **transpose** [træn'spəʊz]	to make sth change places	*austauschen*	
to **render** ['rendə]	to calculate and change sth	*rendern (berechnen und ausgeben)*	
strand [strænd]	e.g. a strand of hair	*Strähne*	

	fringe [frɪndʒ]	the edge of sth	*Rand*
	jewelry ***AE*** ['dʒuːəlri]	e.g. a gold necklace, a silver ring	*Schmuck*
	inconsistent [ˌɪnkən'sɪstənt]	not staying the same	*uneinheitlich, unstimmig*
	illumination [ɪˌluːmɪ'neɪʃn]	lighting sth	*Beleuchtung*
	reflection [rɪ'flekʃn]	showing an image	*Reflexion, Spiegelbild*
	to **harass sb** ['hærəs]	to annoy, stress sb	*jdn schikanieren, jdn belästigen*
	to **intimidate** [ɪn'tɪmɪdeɪt]	to frighten sb so they do what you want	*einschüchtern, bedrohen*
	imaging ['ɪmɪdʒɪŋ]	making pictures	*Bildverarbeitung*
	stock [stɒk]	a share in a public company	*Aktie, Anleihe*
	footage ['fʊtɪdʒ]	video recording(s)	*Film-/Bildmaterial*
	to **mock sb** [mɒk]	to tease, make fun of sb	*sich über jdn lustig machen*
	to **erode** [ɪ'rəʊd]	to damage, wear away	*zerfressen, beschädigen*
	doubt [daʊt]	feeling of uncertainty	*Zweifel*
▸ page 70	to **admit to sth** [əd'mɪt]	to confess to e.g. a crime	*etw zugeben, (ein)gestehen*
	attorney [ə'tɜːni]	lawyer	*(Rechts-)Anwalt / Anwältin*
	to **be unlikely to do sth** [ʌn'laɪkli]	e.g. winter is unlikely to be warm and sunny	*etw wahrscheinlich nicht tun*
▸ page 71	**fraud** [frɔːd]	crime of deceiving people in order to get their money	*Betrug*
	frame [freɪm]	e.g. a picture frame	*Rahmen*
	to **polish sth** ['pɒlɪʃ]	to make a surface smooth and shiny	*etw (auf)polieren*
	to **establish sth** [ɪ'stæblɪʃ]	to set sth up	*etw beweisen*
	likeness ['laɪknəs]	similarity in appearance	*Abbild*
	obligated ['ɒblɪgeɪtɪd]	be forced to do sth	*verpflichtet*
	content ['kɒntent]	e.g. There is a lot of content in this book.	*Inhalt*
	to **deliver** [dɪ'lɪvə]	to bring and hand over sth	*liefern, übermitteln*
	meltdown ['meltdaʊn]	collapse, breakdown	*Schmelze*
	eager ['iːgə]	wanting to do or have sth	*bestrebt, darauf aus*
	to **distribute sth** [dɪ'strɪbjuːt]	to give out, share sth	*etw verteilen, etw vertreiben*
	legislator ['ledʒɪsleɪtə]	sb who makes laws	*Abgeordnete / r*

Section F Artificial humans

▸ page 72	**viable** ['vaɪəbl]	that will be successful	*realisierbar, durchführbar*
	motion ['məʊʃn]	movement	*Bewegung*
	shift of expression [ˌʃɪft əv ɪk'spreʃn]	a change in the emotions shown on sb's face	*Ausdrucksänderung*
	notion ['nəʊʃn]	opinion, concept	*Vorstellung, Auffassung*
	ethnicity [eθ'nɪsəti]	ethnic background	*Ethnizität, Volkszugehörigkeit*
	rumour ['ruːmə]	unconfirmed information	*Gerücht*
	to **tell apart** [ˌtel ə'pɑːt]	to see the difference (between sth and sth else)	*auseinander halten*
	random ['rændəm]	with no clear line or idea	*zufällig, beliebig*
	to **grant** [grɑːnt]	to agree or allow	*gewähren, einräumen*
▸ page 73	**ankle** ['æŋkl]	part of the body between the leg and foot	*Knöchel, Sprunggelenk*
	naked ['neɪkɪd]	not wearing anything	*nackt*
	socket ['sɒkɪt]	e.g. The sockets in the UK are different to those in Europe.	*Steckdose*
	smooth [smuːð]	< > rough	*glatt; reibungslos*
	eyelash ['aɪlæʃ]	hair that grows around the eye	*Wimper*
	to **retrieve** [rɪ'triːv]	to get sth back	*abrufen, wiederfinden*
	to **converse** [kən'vɜːs]	to talk with sb	*sich unterhalten*
	working life [ˌwɜːkɪŋ 'laɪf]	the time sb spends at work	*Betriebsdauer*
	tight [taɪt]	small, narrow	*eng*
	to **drain of sth** [dreɪn]	to deplete sth	*etw verlieren*
	to **acquire sth** [ə'kwaɪə]	to get sth	*etw erwerben; etw annehmen*

beyond [bɪ'jɒnd]	further than sth	*jenseits, außerhalb*	
to **observe sth** [əb'zɜːv]	to watch sth carefully	*etw beobachten*	
handsome ['hænsəm]	good looking	*attraktiv, gut aussehend*	
animating ['ænɪmeɪtɪŋ]	giving life to sth	*belebend, beseelend*	
competitor [kəm'petɪtə]	sb who takes part in a competition	*Konkurrent / in, Konkurrenz*	▸ page 74
to **disgrace sb** [dɪs'greɪs]	to bring shame on sb	*jdn in Verruf bringen*	
capability [ˌkeɪpə'bɪləti]	the ability to do sth	*Fähigkeit, Potenzial*	

Words in context

fertilizer ['fɜːtəlaɪzə]	a substance spread on land, plants, etc. to make them grow well	*Dünger, Düngemittel*	▸ page 76
to **comprise sth** [kəm'praɪz]	to be made of sth	*etw umfassen, aus etw bestehen*	
distribution [ˌdɪstrɪ'bjuːʃn]	*v* to distribute	*Verteilung*	
processing ['prəʊsesɪŋ]	working on, changing sth	*Verarbeitung*	
preservation [ˌprezə'veɪʃn]	protecting sth	*Konservierung*	
to **disconnect** [ˌdɪskə'nekt]	to cut a connection	*abtrennen, die Verbindung unterbrechen*	
to **interact** [ˌɪntər'ækt]	to work with and influence	*interagieren, aufeinander eingehen*	
face to face [ˌfeɪs tə 'feɪs]	< > via email, telephone, etc.	*persönlich*	
remotely [rɪ'məʊtli]	from far away	*aus der Ferne*	▸ page 77
to **reproduce** [ˌriːprə'djuːs]	to copy sth	*nachbilden*	
cognition [kɒg'nɪʃn]	thinking	*Wahrnehmung, Erkenntnis*	
accordingly [ək'ɔːdɪŋli]	in an appropriate way	*(dem)entsprechend*	
to **perceive sth** [pə'siːv]	to begin to understand sth	*etw wahrnehmen, etw erkennen*	
rudimentary [ˌruːdɪ'mentri]	basic	*unterentwickelt, rudimentär*	
perceptive [pə'septɪv]	insightful	*scharfsinnig; einfühlsam*	
course of action [ˌkɔːs əv 'ækʃn]	the next steps	*Vorgehen, Maßnahmen*	▸ page 78

Topic 3 Work and consumers

relation [rɪ'leɪʃn]	e.g. the earth is small in relation to the sun	*Beziehung, Verhältnis*	▸ page 90
entrepreneur [ˌɒntrəprə'nɜː]	sb who owns their own business	*Unternehmer / in*	
management consultant [ˌmænɪdʒmənt kən'sʌltənt]	sb who helps a company solve issues and improve performance	*Unternehmensberater / in*	
to **evolve** [ɪ'vɒlv]	to develop	*sich weiter entwickeln*	▸ page 91
unemployment [ˌʌnɪm'plɔɪmənt]	< > employment	*Arbeitslosigkeit*	
universal [juːnɪ'vɜːsl]	general	*universell, allgemein, weltweit*	
employer [ɪm'plɔɪə]	person who gives sb a job	*Arbeitgeber / in*	

Section A Advertising

signature ['sɪgnətʃə]	*v* to sign	*charakteristisch, unverkennbar*	▸ page 92
delighted [dɪ'laɪtɪd]	very happy	*froh, erfreut*	
manner ['mænə]	way	*Art, Wesen*	
to **encourage** [ɪn'kʌrɪdʒ]	to give support to sb/sth	*ermuntern, ermutigen*	
dependable [dɪ'pendəbl]	can be trusted, relied on	*zuverlässig, verlässlich*	
to **gift** [gɪft]	to give sth to sb	*schenken*	
to **sustain sth** [sə'steɪn]	to continue sth	*etw (aufrecht)erhalten*	
insatiable [ɪn'seɪʃəbl]	always wanting more	*unersättlich*	
to **satisfy sb** ['sætɪsfaɪ]	to give sb what they want	*jdn zufriedenstellen, jdn befriedigen*	
to **degrade sb** [dɪ'greɪd]	to treat sb without respect	*jdn erniedrigen*	▸ page 93
fame [feɪm]	*adj* famous	*Ruhm*	
to **broaden sth** ['brɔːdn]	to make sth bigger, wider	*etw erweitern*	
to **prolong sth** [prə'lɒŋ]	to make sth go on for a longer time	*etw verlängern, etw herauszögern*	

	transient ['trænziənt]	temporary, short term	*vorübergehend*
	relentless [rɪ'lentləs]	without stopping, without mercy	*unerbittlich, unbarmherzig*
	essentially [ɪ'senʃəli]	basically	*im Wesentlichen*
	to **deceive** [dɪ'siːv]	to make sb believe sth that is not true	*täuschen, (be)trügen*
▸ page 94	to **accompany sb** [ə'kʌmpəni]	to go with sb/sth	*jdn begleiten*
	blend [blend]	a mix of different things	*Mischung*
	to approach sb [ə'prəʊtʃ]	to speak to sb for the first time	*an jdn herantreten*
	invoice ['ɪnvɔɪs]	a bill (which lists goods or services provided)	*Rechnung*
	to aim for sth [eɪm]	to work towards sth	*etw anstreben*
	to be likely to do sth ['laɪkli]	to have a high probability of doing sth	*etw wahrscheinlich tun (werden)*
	extent [ɪk'stent]	how large, important, etc. sth is	*Umfang, Ausmaß*
	guideline ['gaɪdlaɪn]	e.g. Read the guidelines before you start.	*Richtlinie*
	disclosure *fml* [dɪs'kləʊʒə]	releasing (sensitive) information	*Offenlegung*

Section B Ethical consumption

▸ page 96	to **reflect sth** [rɪ'flekt]	to be a sign of the nature of sth or of sb.'s attitude or feeling	*etw reflektieren, etw widerspiegeln*
	to **treat sb** [triːt]	to handle sb/sth	*jdn behandeln*
	contradictory [ˌkɒntrə'dɪktəri]	opposite, incompatible	*widersprüchlich*
	guilty ['gɪlti]	< > innocent	*schuldig*
▸ page 97	**morality** [mə'ræləti]	principles concerning right and wrong or good and bad behaviour	*Moral* (Wertesystem)
	corporation [ˌkɔːpə'reɪʃn]	big business	*Konzern*
	to **exploit sb** [ɪk'splɔɪt]	to use sth in a way that helps you	*jdn ausnutzen, jdn ausbeuten*
	overwhelming [ˌəʊvə'welmɪŋ]	very strong, extreme	*überwältigend*
	necessity [nə'sesəti]	*adj* necessary	*Notwendigkeit*
	sacrifice ['sækrɪfaɪs]	the fact of giving up sth important in order to get or do something that seems more important	*Opfer*
	judgement ['dʒʌdʒmənt]	*v* to judge	*Wertung*
	wallet ['wɒlɪt]	e.g. Women have purses, men have wallets to keep their cash in.	*Geldbeutel, Brieftasche*
	compassionate [kəm'pæʃənə]	understanding, caring	*mitfühlend, barmherzig*

Section C Globalization

▸ page 99	**tax** [tæks]	money paid to the government	*Steuer*
	to **rethink** ['riːθɪŋk]	to think again about an issue	*überdenken*
	to **source sth** [sɔːs]	to get sth from a particular place or supplier	*etw beziehen, beschaffen*
	to **speed sth up** [ˌspiːd 'ʌp]	to accelerate sth	*etw beschleunigen*
	executive [ɪg'zekjətɪv]	manager	*Führungskraft*
	durable ['djʊərəbl]	lasting a long time	*haltbar, langlebig*
	bicycle ['baɪsɪkl]	vehicle with two wheels and no motor	*Fahrrad*
	to **derail** [diː'reɪl]	to block or interrupt	*entgleisen (lassen)*
	supply chain [sə'plaɪ tʃeɪn]	the stages of getting a product from producer to consumer	*Lieferkette*
▸ page 100	to **shift** [ʃɪft]	to move	*(sich) verlagern*
	trillion ['trɪljən]	1,000,000,000,000	*Billion*
	nearshoring [ˌnɪə'ʃɔːrɪŋ]	relocating a business to a nearby country	*Produktions(zurück)verlagerung in die Nähe*
	offshoring [ˌɒf'ʃɔːrɪŋ]	relocating a business to a foreign country far away	*Produktionsverlagerung ins Ausland*
	coffin ['kɒfɪn]	a box for a dead body	*Sarg*
▸ page 101	to **disrupt sth** [dɪs'rʌpt]	to cause an extreme change to sth	*etw stören, etw behindern*

to **exchange sth** [ɪks'tʃeɪndʒ]	to give sth and get another thing in return	*etw (ein-, aus-) tauschen*	
silk [sɪlk]	e.g. a silk scarf	*Seide*	
to **trade** [treɪd]	*n* trade	*handeln, Handel (be)treiben*	
raw material [ˌrɔː mə'tɪəriəl]	material before it is made into sth else	*Rohstoff*	
to **take advantage of sth** [ˌteɪk əd'vɑːntɪdʒ əv]	to exploit or abuse sth	*sich etw zunutze machen, etw ausnutzen*	
expertise [ˌekspɜː'tiːz]	e.g. He has a lot of expertise in cooking.	*Fachkenntnisse, Sachverstand*	
to **gain sth** [geɪn]	to get sth, to acquire sth	*etw erwerben, etw erlangen*	
to **deny sth** [dɪ'naɪ]	to say that sth is not true	*etw leugnen, etw bestreiten*	
cost of living [ˌkɒst əv 'lɪvɪŋ]	the price of normal life e.g. rent, food, bills, etc.	*Lebenshaltungskosten*	
union ['juːniən]	a group of workers who want to improve working conditions	*Gewerkschaft*	
to **defend sb/sth** [dɪ'fend]	to protect sb/sth against attack	*jdn / etw verteidigen*	
working conditions *pl* [ˌwɜːkɪŋ kən'dɪʃnz]	the environment in which sb works	*Arbeitsbedingungen*	
unskilled [ˌʌn'skɪld]	unqualified	*ungelernt*	
transnational [ˌtrænz'næʃnəl]	involving several countries	*länderübergreifend, grenzüberschreitend*	▸ page 102

Section D Gender inequality

to **request sth** *fml* [rɪ'kwest]	to ask for sth	*etw (an)fordern, etw erbitten, um etw bitten*	▸ page 103
to **legislate** ['ledʒɪsleɪt]	to set laws	*Gesetze erlassen*	
default [dɪ'fɔːlt]	normal, typical, standard	*Standard*	
adoption [ə'dɒpʃn]	taking on or appropriating sth/sb	*Übernahme, Aneignung*	
maternity [mə'tɜːnəti]	motherhood	*Mutterschaft*	
substantially [səb'stænʃəli]	essentially, for the most part	*erheblich, im Wesentlichen*	▸ page 104
adverse ['ædvɜːs]	hostile, unfavourable	*nachteilig, ungünstig*	
accountancy [ə'kaʊntənsi]	bookkeeping	*Buchhaltung, Rechnungswesen*	
pregnant ['pregnənt]	going to have a baby	*schwanger*	
pregnancy ['pregnənsi]	the time when a baby develops inside a woman's body	*Schwangerschaft*	
hospitality [ˌhɒspɪ'tæləti]	the food, drink, and entertainment industry	*Hotel- und Gaststättengewerbe*	
promotion [prə'məʊʃn]	getting a better job at the same company	*Beförderung*	
seniority [ˌsiːni'ɒrəti]	having a higher rank or status	*Führungsebene*	
expectation [ˌekspek'teɪʃn]	*v* to expect	*Erwartung*	▸ page 105

Section E Generation Z

sophisticated [sə'fɪstɪkeɪtɪd]	having a lot of experience and knowledge	*gebildet, erfahren, kultiviert*	▸ page 107
competitive [kəm'petətɪv]	able and keen to successfully compete with others	*wettbewerbsorientiert, leistungsorientiert*	
determined [dɪ'tɜːmɪnd]	ready to work hard to achieve a result and not allow sb/sth to stop you	*(fest) entschlossen*	
to **adapt** [ə'dæpt]	to become used to sth	*(sich) anpassen*	▸ page 108
to **challenge sb** ['tʃælɪndʒ]	to do sth difficult	*jdn herausfordern*	
sophistication [səˌfɪstɪ'keɪʃn]	worldliness, experience	*Ausgereiftheit, Erfahrung*	
to **customize sth** ['kʌstəmaɪz]	to change, modify sth	*etw anpassen, etw individuell gestalten*	
tough [tʌf]	difficult	*hart, schwer*	
generic [dʒə'nerɪk]	typical, everyday	*generisch, allgemein, typisch*	
in the aftermath of sth ['ɑːftəmæθ]	the days/events immediately following a disaster	*in der Folge von etw*	

	mindset ['maɪndset]	sb's way of thinking, sb's attitude	*Mentalität, Denkweise*
	to **miss out on sth** [ˌmɪs 'aʊt]	to not have the chance to experience sth	*etw verpassen*
	to **suffer from sth** ['sʌfə frəm]	to have a health problem or an illness	*unter etw leiden*
	intense [ɪn'tens]	extreme, very strong	*intensiv*
	DIY (do-it-yourself) [ˌdiː aɪ 'waɪ]	e.g. a DIY store	*Heimwerker-, Heimwerken*
	collaborative [kə'læbərətɪv]	working together	*gemeinschaftlich, partnerschaftlich*
▸ page 109	**award** [ə'wɔːd]	*n* award	*Auszeichnung, Preis*
	predecessor ['priːdɪsesə]	thing that came before sth else	*Vorgänger / in, Vorläufer / in*
	driven ['drɪvn]	hard-working, ambitious	*besessen, ehrgeizig*
	to **recruit sb** [rɪ'kruːt]	to hire sb	*jdn anwerben, jdn neu einstellen*
	excerpt ['eksɜːpt]	piece, fragment	*Auszug, Ausschnitt*
	entrepreneurial [ˌɒntrəprə'nɜːriəl]	making money by starting one's own business	*unternehmerisch*

Section F Unemployment and universal basic income

▸ page 110	**laid off** [ˌleɪd 'ɒf]	losing your job	*arbeitslos*
	freelance ['friːlɑːns]	self-employed	*selbstständig, freiberuflich*
	paycheck *AE* ['peɪtʃek]	money your company pays you at the end of each month	*Gehalt(sscheck)*
	to **make ends meet** [meɪk ˌendz 'miːt]	to earn just enough money to live on	*über die Runden kommen*
	lease [liːs]	contract that sb has rented a flat/ house	*Miete, Pacht*
	obituary [ə'bɪtʃuəri]	news article that reports sb's death	*Nachruf*
	pleasant ['pleznt]	nice, good	*angenehm*
	retirement [rɪ'taɪəmənt]	stopping work e.g. at age 67	*Ruhestand, Rente*
	uncertainty [ʌn'sɜːtnti]	< > predictability	*Ungewissheit, Unsicherheit*
	breadwinner ['bredwɪnə]	sb who earns money for his/her family	*Brotverdiener / in*
	essentials *pl* [ɪ'senʃlz]	the most important things	*lebensnotwendige Güter*
▸ page 111	**with no strings attached** [nəʊ ˌstrɪŋz ə'tætʃt]	having no restrictions or conditions	*ohne Auflagen*
	guinea pig ['gɪni pɪg]	small furry animal kept as a pet	*Meerschweinchen; Versuchsperson*
	odd [ɒd]	strange, weird	*gelegentlich*
	relief [rɪ'liːf]	pleasant feeling after completing/ finishing sth	*Erleichterung, Entlastung*
	to **recall** [rɪ'kɔːl]	to remember sth	*sich erinnern*
	to **brand sth** [brænd]	to make a product easy to recognize, identify	*etw kennzeichnen, mit seinem Zeichen versehen*
	to **implement sth** ['ɪmplɪmənt]	to put sth in place, e.g. a new law	*etw einführen, etw umsetzen, etw einsetzen*
	insecurity [ˌɪnsɪ'kjʊərəti]	unprotected, open to danger	*Unsicherheit*
▸ page 112	**secure** [sɪ'kjʊə]	safe, sure	*sicher*
	trial ['traɪəl]	test, try	*Versuch, Studie*
▸ page 113	**profound** [prə'faʊnd]	intense, great	*tief greifend, tief gehend, fundiert*
	duly ['djuːli]	correctly, properly	*ordnungsgemäß*
	revenue ['revənjuː]	income	*Einkünfte, Einnahmen*

Section G Intercultural competence

▸ page 114	**celebration** [ˌselɪ'breɪʃn]	*v* to celebrate	*Feier*
	manners *pl* ['mænəz]	*phr* to learn good/bad manners	*Manieren, Umgangsformen*
	ripe [raɪp]	The apples are ripe. We can pick them now.	*reif*
	to **broker** ['brəʊkə]	to arrange, negotiate	*makeln, vermitteln*

not a clue [klu:]	no idea	*keine Ahnung*	▸ page 115
clash [klæʃ]	conflict	*Konflikt, Zusammenstoß*	
fairly ['feəli]	quite a lot	*ziemlich, recht*	
accustomed [ə'kʌstəmd]	usual, normal	*gewöhnt, gewohnt*	
bow [baʊ]	*v* to bow	*Verbeugung*	
shade [ʃeɪd]	shadows, out of the light	*Schattierung, (Farb-)Ton*	
to **frown upon sth** [fraʊn]	to think sth is a bad idea	*etw missbilligen*	
awkward ['ɔ:kwəd]	uncomfortable, embarrassing	*unangenehm, peinlich*	
to **translate** [træns'leɪt]	*n* translation	*übersetzen*	
recipient [rɪ'sɪpiənt]	sb who receives/gets sth	*Empfänger/in*	
to **make the effort** [ˌmeɪk thi 'efət]	to use extra energy to achieve sth	*sich die Mühe geben*	
to **apologize** [ə'pɒlədʒaɪz]	*n* apology	*sich entschuldigen*	
hurdle ['hɜ:dl]	obstacle, problem	*Hürde, Hindernis*	
tender ['tendə]	soft, sensitive	*zart*	
initially [ɪ'nɪʃəli]	at the beginning	*anfangs, anfänglich*	
to **stick to sth** ['stɪk tə]	to stay with sth	*bei etw bleiben, sich an etw halten*	
offence [ə'fens]	insult	*Beleidigung*	
to **neglect sb/sth** [nɪ'glekt]	< > to take care of sb/sth	*jdn/etw vernachlässigen*	
to **stock** [stɒk]	to keep a supply of sth	*einlagern, vorrätig halten, am/auf Lager haben*	▸ page 116
to **dip** [dɪp]	to put sth in liquid, then take it out	*(ein)tauchen*	
toe [təʊ]	e.g. You have five toes at the end of your foot.	*Zeh*	
thorough ['θʌrə]	100%	*gründlich, sorgfältig*	
venture ['ventʃə]	taking a risk	*Vorhaben, Unternehmen, Wagnis*	
latter ['lætə]	the last one	*letztere/r/s*	
negotiation [nɪˌgəʊʃi'eɪʃn]	discussing terms and conditions	*Verhandlung, Vermittlung*	
to **resolve sth** [rɪ'zɒlv]	e.g. to resolve an issue	*etw (auf)lösen*	
collaboration [kəˌlæbə'reɪʃn]	working together	*Zusammenarbeit, Gemeinschaftsprodukt(ion)*	
to **offend sb/sth** [ə'fend]	*adj* offensive	*jdn/etw verletzen, kränken*	
sensibility [ˌsensə'bɪləti]	feelings, emotions	*Befindlichkeit, Feinfühligkeit*	
temper ['tempə]	mood	*Laune*	▸ page 117

Words in context

to **take sth for granted** [ˌteɪk fə 'grɑ:ntɪd]	to accept sth without question	*etw als selbstverständlich betrachten*	▸ page 120
to **engage sb** [ɪn'geɪdʒ]	to get sb involved (in sth)	*jdn fesseln*	
package holiday ['pækɪdʒ hɒlədeɪ]	a holiday arranged by a travel agent, which includes all travel, meals, accommodation	*Pauschalreise*	
to **broadcast (broadcast, broadcast)** ['brɔ:dkɑ:st]	to transmit a programme by radio or television	*senden* (im Rundfunk)	
continual [kən'tɪnjuəl]	non-stop	*ständig, ununterbrochen, kontinuierlich*	
recreational [ˌrekri'eɪʃənl]	for free time	*Freizeit-, Erholungs-*	
debt [det]	money owed	*Schulden*	
to **purchase sth** *fml* ['pɜ:tʃəs]	< > to sell sth	*etw kaufen, erwerben*	
primarily [praɪ'merəli]	e.g. Who is the account primarily for?	*vorrangig, hauptsächlich*	
groundbreaking ['graʊndbreɪkɪŋ]	innovative	*bahnbrechend*	
trade barriers *pl* ['treɪd bæriəz]	e.g. Some countries have trade barriers to protect their economy.	*Handelsschranke, Handelshemmnis*	
suffrage ['sʌfrɪdʒ]	the right to vote	*Wahlrecht*	▸ page 121
to **discourage** [dɪs'kʌrɪdʒ]	< > to encourage	*entmutigen*	

	glass ceiling [ˌglɑːs ˈsiːlɪŋ]	invisible barrier which stops women from being promoted as high as men	*gläserne Decke* (unsichtbare Barriere, die Frauen am beruflichen Aufstieg hindert)
	to **occupy sth** [ˈɒkjupaɪ]	to take control of a space	*etw einnehmen, etw besetzen, etw innehaben*
	gender imbalance [ˈdʒendə ɪmbæləns]	e.g. men being promoted instead of women shows a gender imbalance in the business world	*Ungleichgewicht zwischen den Geschlechtern*
	casual staff [ˈkæʒuəl stɑːf]	Employees who work for a company for a short time	*Aushilfskräfte, Gelegenheitsarbeiter / in(nen)*
	retail [ˈriːteɪl]	selling goods to the general public	*Einzelhandel*
	gig economy [ˈgɪg ɪkɒnəmi]	< > permanent work	*Gig Economy* (auf Freiberuflern basierendes Wirtschaftsmodell)
	to **suit** [suːt]	e.g. I think I would suit the job very well.	*passen*
	to **be inclined to do sth** [ɪnˈklaɪnd]	to be likely to do sth	*geneigt sein, etw zu tun*
	apart from [əˈpɑːt frəm]	except for, other than	*abgesehen von, außer*
	to **be made redundant** [rɪˈdʌndənt]	to lose one's job	*entlassen werden, den Arbeitsplatz verlieren*
► page 122	**carer** [ˈkeərə]	*v* to care	*Betreuer / in, Pfleger / in*
	in terms of … [ɪn ˈtɜːmz əv]	with regard to	*was … betrifft / angeht*
	local [ˈləʊkl]	near to where you are	*Einheimische / r*
	commerce [ˈkɒmɜːs]	*adj* commercial	*Handel*
	redistribution [ˌriːdɪstrɪˈbjuːʃn]	sharing sth differently than before	*Umverteilung*
	to **enforce sth** [ɪnˈfɔːs]	to make sure a rule etc. is respected	*etw durchsetzen, etw vollstrecken*

Topic 4 The USA – a divided nation?

► page 134	**contradiction** [ˌkɒntrəˈdɪkʃn]	e.g. I love sth and I also hate it	*Widerspruch*
	to **infringe** [ɪnˈfrɪndʒ]	to limit sth (e.g. sb's rights)	*verletzen*
	amendment [əˈmendmənt]	an important addition to the US constitution	*Ergänzung, Zusatz*
	to **recite sth** [rɪˈsaɪt]	to say sth aloud, in front of an audience	*etw vortragen*
	arm [ɑːm]	e.g. gun, tank, bomb, etc	*Waffe*
► page 135	**polarization** [ˌpəʊləraɪˈzeɪʃn]	splitting into two separate groups	*Polarisierung*
	passion [ˈpæʃn]	powerful emotion, enthusiasm	*Leidenschaft*

Section A Past and present

► page 136	**ethnic cleansing** [ˌeθnɪk ˈklenzɪŋ]	mass murder of a group of people	*ethnische Säuberung(en)*
	to **wage war on sb** [ˌweɪdʒ ˈwɔː]	to attack e.g. a group of people	*Krieg führen gegen jdn*
	to **be subjected to sth** [səbˈdʒektɪd]	to be forced (to do sth)	*etw unterworfen sein*
	discriminatory [dɪˈskrɪmɪnətəri]	treating a group of people differently from, and worse than, other groups	*benachteiligend, diskriminierend*
	Bill of Rights [ˌbɪl əv ˈraɪts]	the first ten amendments to the US constitution	Grundrechte-Zusatzartikel der amerikanischen Verfassung
	victory [ˈvɪktəri]	defeating an enemy or opponent	*Sieg*
	to **draft** [drɑːft]	to prepare a first version of a document	*entwerfen, aufsetzen* (Schriftstück)
► page 137	**enslaved** [ɪnˈsleɪvd]	being kept in a state of slavery	*versklavt*
	the Confederacy [kənˈfedərəsi]	the 11 southern states which seceded from the US in 1860	*die Konföderation* (Bund der Südstaaten)
	to **regain** [rɪˈgeɪn]	to get sth back	*wiedererlangen*
	oppression [əˈpreʃn]	the systematic unfair or cruel treatment of people	*Unterdrückung*
	to **seek sth** [siːk]	to look for sth, to try to achieve sth	*(nach) etw suchen, etw anstreben*

riches *pl* ['rɪtʃɪz]	money, wealth	*Reichtum*	
influx ['ɪnflʌks]	arrival in great numbers	*Zustrom*	
persecution [,pɜːsɪ'kjuːʃn]	treating sb badly because of their race or beliefs	*Verfolgung*	
to **flee** [fliː]	to run away from sth	*fliehen*	
superpower ['suːpəpaʊə]	one of the most powerful countries in the world, e.g. the USA, China, Russia	*Supermacht*	
ultimate ['ʌltɪmət]	final, most important	*ultimativ*	▸ page 138
perseverance [,pɜːsə'vɪərəns]	to continue doing sth, although it is difficult	*Ausdauer*	
ingenuity [,ɪndʒə'njuːəti]	creativity, imagination, inventiveness	*Erfindungsreichtum*	
to **persevere** [,pɜːsə'vɪə]	to keep going despite difficulties	*durchhalten*	
to **enslave** [ɪn'sleɪv]	to make sb a slave	*versklaven*	
to **industrialize** [ɪn'dʌstriəlaɪz]	to develop industries	*industrialisieren*	
abolition [,æbə'lɪʃn]	the end of slavery	*Abschaffung*	
to **oppress** [ə'pres]	to treat sb in a cruel, unfair way	*unterdrücken*	
to **discriminate (against)** [dɪ'skrɪmɪneɪt]	to treat sb differently from, and worse than, sb else	*diskriminieren*	
to **persecute sb** ['pɜːsɪkjuːt]	to treat sb in a cruel and unfair way, esp. because of their race, religion or political beliefs	*jdn verfolgen* (z.B. aus politischen Gründen)	
enslavement [ɪn'sleɪvmənt]	< > liberation, emancipation	*Versklavung*	
industrialization [ɪn,dʌstriəlaɪ'zeɪʃn]	an economy based on making material goods	*Industrialisierung*	
assimilation [ə,sɪmə'leɪʃn]	integration of people, ideas, culture	*Anpassung, Angleichung*	
to **assimilate** [ə'sɪmɪleɪt]	to integrate into sth, possibly by giving up what make you different	*sich anpassen*	
colonization [,kɒlənaɪ'zeɪʃn]	travelling to a new area and taking control of it	*Besiedlung, Kolonisierung*	
immigration [,ɪmɪ'greɪʃn]	the movement of foreign people into a country to live permanently	*Einwanderung*	
establishment [ɪ'stæblɪʃmənt]	starting, setting up	*Einrichtung*	
discrimination (against sb) [dɪ,skrɪmɪ'neɪʃn]	treating a group of people in a worse way than others	*Diskriminierung (eines Menschen)*	
division [dɪ'vɪʒn]	splitting, keeping separate	*Trennung, Spaltung*	▸ page 139

Section B Gun control

federal ['fedərəl]	e.g. a federal law	*auf Bundesebene geltend*	▸ page 140
to **be located in** [bi ləʊ'keɪtɪd ɪn]	e.g. Vienna is located in Austria	*sich in ... befinden, in ... liegen*	
starvation [stɑː'veɪʃn]	death caused by not having enough to eat	*Hunger*	
to **owe sb sth** [əʊ]	e.g. I borrowed £10 from Fred, so now I owe Fred £10.	*jdm etw schulden*	
to **last** [lɑːst]	to continue to function	*dauern, andauern*	
firearm ['faɪərɑːm]	weapon, gun	*Schusswaffe*	▸ page 141
to **possess sth** [pə'zes]	to have, own sth	*etw besitzen*	
permit ['pɜːmɪt]	document permitting sth	*Genehmigung; Bewilligung*	
shotgun ['ʃɒtgʌn]	a long gun that is held at the shoulder	*Schrotflinte*	
handgun ['hændgʌn]	small gun that can be held in one hand	*Handfeuerwaffe, Kurzwaffe*	
loophole ['luːphəʊl]	a defect in a set of rules	*Gesetzeslücke*	
murder ['mɜːdə]	*v* to murder	*Mord*	▸ page 142
assault [ə'sɔːlt]	attack with intention to harm or injure sb	*Körperverletzung*	
suicide ['suːɪsaɪd]	the act of killing yourself	*Selbstmord*	
opponent [ə'pəʊnənt]	person or thing you are fighting against	*Gegner / in*	
regulatory ['regjələtəri]	organisational, controlling	*regulatorisch, behördlich*	

	to **restrict (to)** [rɪ'strɪkt]	to limit the amount of sth	*einschränken, beschränken (auf)*
	rifle ['raɪfl]	a gun with a long barrel which you hold to your shoulder to fire	*Gewehr*
	ammunition [ˌæmjə'nɪʃn]	e.g. bullets	*Munition*
	fugitive ['fjuːdʒətɪv]	sb who escapes captivity	*Flüchtling*
	involuntarily [ɪn'vɒləntrəli]	in a way that is not by choice	*unfreiwillig*
	prior ['praɪə]	before	*vorherig*
	felony ['feləni]	a serious crime	*Verbrechen*
	conviction [kən'vɪkʃn]	a prison sentence	*Verurteilung*
	prohibited [prə'hɪbɪtɪd]	forbidden	*verboten*
	controlled substance [kənˌtrəʊld 'sʌbstəns]	a drug or other chemical whose use is regulated by the government	*Rauschgift*
	to **issue** ['ɪʃuː]	to give out	*erteilen, erlassen*
	harassment ['hærəsmənt]	aggressive pressure or irritation	*Schikane, Mobbing, Belästigung*
	semi-automatic [ˌsemi ɔːtə'mætɪk]	self-loading (firearm)	*halbautomatisch*
	dealer ['diːlə]	sb who buys and sells sth	*Händler/in*
	to **submit** [səb'mɪt]	to put forward, present	*einreichen, vorlegen, zusenden*
	state [steɪt]	present condition	*Zustand, Status*
▸ page 143	to **deny (sb) sth** [dɪ'naɪ]	to refuse sb sth	*(jdm) etw verweigern*
	at sb's discretion [dɪ'skreʃn]	doing sth the way sb thinks is best	*in jds Ermessen*
	inconclusive [ˌɪnkən'kluːsɪv]	proving nothing	*ergebnislos, uneindeutig*
	dozen ['dʌzn]	twelve	*Dutzend*
	applicant ['æplɪkənt]	the person who applies for a job	*Bewerber/in*
	to **enrol in sth** [ɪn'rəʊl]	to officially register (as a student, soldier, etc)	*sich für etw anmelden*
	concealed carry *AE* [kənˌsiːld 'kæri]	hidden weapon	*verdecktes Tragen* (von Waffen)
	reciprocity *fml* [ˌresɪ'prɒsəti]	exchanging things for mutual benefit	*Gegenseitigkeit*
	virtually ['vɜːtʃuəli]	almost or very nearly	*praktisch, nahezu*
	exempt [ɪg'zempt]	free from sth	*ausgenommen, befreit* (von Pflichten)
	ambiguity [ˌæmbɪ'gjuːəti]	uncertainty, doubt	*Unklarheit, Uneindeutigkeit*
	on behalf of sb [ɒn bɪ'hɑːf]	as a representative of sb	*in jds Namen, für jdn*
	to **violate sth** ['vaɪəleɪt]	< > to respect sth	*gegen etw verstoßen, etw verletzen*
	ownership ['əʊnəʃɪp]	possession	*Besitzverhältnisse*
	guardian ['gɑːdiən]	sb who takes care of another person	*Vormund*
▸ page 144	to **represent sth** [ˌreprɪ'zent]	e.g. any opinions expressed in this interview do not represent the values held by our company	*etw darstellen*

Section C Polarization in US society

▸ page 145	**turmoil** ['tɜːmɔɪl]	< > peace	*Unruhen*
	police custody ['pəliːs kʌstədi]	being arrested and held by the police	*Polizeigewahrsam*
	unrest [ʌn'rest]	< > calm	*Unruhe(n)*
	unified ['juːnɪfaɪd]	< > separated	*vereint*
	belief [bɪ'liːf]	accepting that sth is true	*Glaube, Überzeugung*
	gay [geɪ]	a person, normally a man, who is sexually attracted to other men	*schwul, lesbisch*
	disunity *fml* [dɪs'juːnəti]	disagreement, conflict	*Zerrissenheit*
	consensus [kən'sensəs]	everyone sharing the same opinion	*Konsens*
	grievance ['griːvəns]	a reason to complain about sth	*Beschwerde*
▸ page 146	**marginalized** ['mɑːdʒɪnəlaɪzd]	treated as insignificant	*ausgegrenzt*
	occasion [ə'keɪʒn]	moment, chance	*Anlass, Gelegenheit*
	liberty ['lɪbəti]	freedom	*Freiheit*
	abolitionist [ˌæbə'lɪʃənɪst]	sb who wants to end slavery	*Abolitionist/in* (Anhänger/in der Sklavenbefreiung)
	extended [ɪk'stendɪd]	*v* to extend	*erweitert*

resilience [rɪ'zɪliəns]	able to recover quickly	*Widerstandsfähigkeit, Belastbarkeit*	
adversity *fml* [əd'vɜːsəti]	difficult situation on a larger scale	*Not, schlechte Zeit(en)*	
equity *fml* ['ekwəti]	equal right(s), justice, etc.	*Gleichheit*	
to **preserve sth** [prɪ'zɜːv]	to protect sth, to keep sth safe	*etw bewahren, etw erhalten*	
desire [dɪ'zaɪə]	want, need	*Wunsch, Verlangen*	▸ page 147
consciousness ['kɒnʃəsnəs]	awareness	*Bewusstsein*	

Section D Immigration to the USA

to **expire** [ɪk'spaɪə]	to run out, to come to an end	*ablaufen, verfallen*	▸ page 148
paperwork ['peɪpəwɜːk]	written documents	*Formalitäten*	
childhood ['tʃaɪldhʊd]	< > adulthood	*Kindheit*	▸ page 149
act [ækt]	law, bill	*Gesetz*	
minor ['maɪnə]	sb under the age of 18	*Minderjährige/r*	
bill [bɪl]	sth which tells you how much you have to pay	*Gesetzentwurf*	
eligible ['elɪdʒəbl]	having the legal right to do sth	*berechtigt, geeignet*	
healthcare worker ['helθkeə wɜːkə]	e.g. nurse, doctor, physiotherapist	*Bedienstete/r im Gesundheitswesen*	
wages *pl* [weɪdʒ]	money for work paid by the hour, day or week	*Lohn*	
mandatory ['mændətəri]	obligatory, sth one must do	*verpflichtend, vorgeschrieben, obligatorisch*	
to **encourage sth** [ɪn'kʌrɪdʒ]	to give support to sb/sth	*etw fördern*	▸ page 150
to **reward** [rɪ'wɔːd]	to give sb sth good after they do sth	*belohnen*	
cruel [kruːəl]	horrible, brutal	*grausam, gemein*	
overpopulation [ˌəʊvəˌpɒpju'leɪʃn]	too many people living in one place	*Überbevölkerung*	
fault [fɔːlt]	defect, problem	*Schuld, Verschulden*	
to **convict sb** [kən'vɪkt]	to find sb guilty of a crime in court	*jdn verurteilen* (für schuldig befinden)	
ID card [ˌaɪ 'diː kɑːd]	form of identification	*Ausweis*	
to **commit (a crime)** [kə'mɪt]	do sth bad (esp. a crime)	*(ein Verbrechen) begehen*	
to **put sth at risk** [ˌpʊt ət 'rɪsk]	to put sth in danger	*etw gefährden*	
scholarship ['skɒləʃɪp]	financial help for sb who wants to continue education	*Stipendium*	
aid [eɪd]	help and assistance	*Hilfe, Unterstützung*	
to **encounter sth** [ɪn'kaʊntə]	to be faced with sb/sth	*etw begegnen, auf etw treffen*	
toll [təʊl]	money that must be paid	*Gebühr, Tribut*	
sb is diagnosed with sth ['daɪəgnəʊzd]	sb is told by a doctor they have an illness, etc	*bei jdm wird etw festgestellt/diagnostiziert*	
anxiety disorder [æŋ'zaɪəti dɪsɔːdə]	uncontrollable feelings of fear and worry	*Angststörung*	
upsetting [ʌp'setɪŋ]	causing unhappiness, disappointment, worry	*ärgerlich*	
budget reconciliation bill [ˌbʌdʒɪt ˌrekənsɪli'eɪʃn bɪl]	parliamentry procedure regarding money in the US	*Haushaltsgesetzgebungs-verfahren in den USA*	
to **exclude sb/sth** [ɪk'skluːd]	< > to include sb/sth	*jdn/etw ausschließen*	
to **major in sth** ['meɪdʒə]	to study with a special focus on one topic	*etw (als Hauptfach) studieren*	
equitable *fml* ['ekwɪtəbl]	fair	*gerecht*	
occupation [ˌɒkju'peɪʃn]	job	*Beruf, Tätigkeit, Beschäftigung*	
to **succeed** [sək'siːd]	adj successful	*erfolgreich sein, Erfolg haben*	▸ page 151
to **contradict** [ˌkɒntrə'dɪkt]	to disagree with sb/sth, to go against sb/sth	*widersprechen*	
residency *fml* ['rezɪdənsi]	living in a country	*Wohnsitz*	
inscription [ɪn'skrɪpʃn]	e.g. sth written on a monument	*Inschrift*	

Section E The role of the USA in the world

▸ page 152	to **feel pity for sb** ['pɪti]	to have sympathy for sb	*mit jdm Mitleid haben*
	ally ['ælaɪ]	sb who supports a different group of people	*Alliierte/r, Verbündete/r*
	to **ridicule sb** ['rɪdɪkju:l]	to make fun of sb	*jdn lächerlich machen*
	presidency ['prezɪdensi]	e.g. Obama's presidency was from 2009 to 2017	*Präsidentschaft*
	to **fall apart** [ˌfɔ:l ə'pɑ:t]	e.g. The skirt was so old it fell apart.	*auseinanderfallen, platzen*
	turn of events [ˌtɜ:n əv ɪ'vents]	a sudden change in a situation	*Wende der Ereignisse/des Schicksals*
	replacement [rɪ'pleɪsmənt]	*v* to replace	*Ersatz, Ersetzung, Austausch*
	obsessed with [əb'sest wɪð]	cannot stop thinking about	*besessen von*
	achievement [ə'tʃi:vmənt]	a good result from hard work	*Errungenschaft, Leistung*
	ambivalence [æm'bɪvələns]	having mixed feelings	*Zwiespältigkeit*
	eloquence ['eləkwəns]	fluency, expressiveness	*Wortgewandtheit, Eloquenz*
▸ page 153	**articulate** [ɑ:'tɪkjələt]	good at speaking	*wortgewandt*
	bountiful *fml* ['baʊntɪfl]	< > mean, not enough	*reichlich; großzügig*
	abundant *fml* [ə'bʌndənt]	more than enough	*reich, reichlich (vorhanden)*
	coincidental [kəʊˌɪnsɪ'dentl]	happening by chance	*zufällig*
▸ page 154	**steady** ['stedi]	continuous, unchanging	*kontinuierlich, stabil*

Section F The American Dream

▸ page 155	to **accumulate** [ə'kju:mjəleɪt]	to collect, gather together	*(sich) ansammeln, (sich) anhäufen*
	to **judge** [dʒʌdʒ]	to form an opinion about sb	*(be)urteilen, ermessen*
	birth [bɜ:θ]	< > death	*Geburt*
	achievable [ə'tʃi:vəbl]	able to be reached	*erreichbar, realisierbar*
	to **breathe down sb's neck** [ˌbri:ð daʊn ... 'nek]	to watch sb very closely	*jdm im Nacken sitzen*
	unattainability [ʌnəˌteɪnə'bɪləti]	impossible to get	*Unerreichbarkeit*
▸ page 156	to **attend sth** [ə'tend]	to go to sth	*etw besuchen*
	prospect ['prɒspekt]	future possibility	*Aussicht, Perspektive*
	vocational college [vəʊˌkeɪʃənl 'kɒlɪdʒ]	a school to learn skills for work	*Berufsschule*
	vocation [və'keɪʃn]	profession, job	*Berufung, Beruf*
	(social) safety net ['seɪfti net]	a program to support poor or vulnerable people	*soziales Netz*
	to **starve** [stɑ:v]	to die from not having enough food	*(ver)hungern*
	aspiration [ˌæspə'reɪʃn]	hope and ambition	*Ambition, Bestreben*
	to **prize** [praɪz]	to appreciate	*schätzen*
	desperation [ˌdespə'reɪʃn]	< > hopefulness	*Verzweiflung*
	angle ['æŋgl]	e.g. a square has four 90° angles	*Winkel*
▸ page 157	to **aspire** [ə'spaɪə]	to want to be sth	*aufstreben*
	predictability [prɪˌdɪktə'bɪləti]	being able to guess what will happen	*Berechenbarkeit*
▸ page 158	**penitentiary** [ˌpenɪ'tenʃəri]	prison	*Gefängnis*
	Ivy League [ˌaɪvi 'li:g]	e.g. Harvard, Yale, Princeton	die acht Eliteuniversitäten in den USA
	obstacle ['ɒbstəkl]	sth that stops progress	*Hindernis*
	STEM, STEAM [stem], [sti:m]	e.g. Science, Technology, Engineering, (Arts), Maths	Akronyme für "Science, Technology, Engineering, (Arts) and Mathematics"
	degree [dɪ'gri:]	qualification when you leave university	*Abschluss*
	vacancy ['veɪkənsi]	e.g. a job vacancy	*offene Stelle*

Section G A vision of the future

dawn [dɔ:n]	beginning of the day when the sun rises	*Morgendämmerung*	▸ page 159
successor [sək'sesə]	< > predecessor	*Nachfolger / in*	
to **compose** [kəm'pəʊz]	to write music, poetry	*zusammensetzen*	
gaze [geɪz]	long look	*Blick*	
one another [ˌwʌn ə'nʌðə]	e.g. At Christmas, people give presents to one another.	*einander, sich (gegenseitig)*	
to **grieve** [gri:v]	to feel sad after sb has died	*trauern*	▸ page 160
to **tie together** [ˌtaɪ tə'geðə]	to join, link, connect	*miteinander verbinden, zusammenbinden*	
victorious [vɪk'tɔ:riəs]	being the winner	*siegreich*	
defeat [dɪ'fi:t]	losing a competition or battle	*Niederlage*	
to **envision sth** [ɪn'vɪʒn]	to imagine sth	*sich etw ausmalen*	
blade [bleɪd]	the sharp edge of a knife, sword	*Klinge*	
faith [feɪθ]	strong religious belief	*Glaube, Vertrauen*	
era ['ɪərə]	a period of history	*Ära, Epoche*	
just [dʒʌst]	fair	*gerecht*	
heir [eə]	sb who will inherit sth	*Erbe / Erbin*	
terrifying ['terɪfaɪɪŋ]	very scary	*furchterregend*	
chapter ['tʃæptə]	part of a book	*Kapitel*	
intimidation [ɪnˌtɪmɪ'deɪʃn]	scaring, terrorizing	*Einschüchterung*	
inaction [ɪn'ækʃn]	doing nothing	*Tatenlosigkeit*	
inheritance [ɪn'herɪtəns]	wealth and property received by sb from sb who has died	*Erbschaft*	
to **merge sth with sth** [mɜ:dʒ]	to combine two or more things to make one thing	*etw mit etw verschmelzen*	
mercy ['mɜ:si]	compassion, forgiveness	*Gnade*	
might [maɪt]	power	*Macht*	
wounded ['wu:ndɪd]	injured, hurt	*verwundet*	▸ page 161
forefather ['fɔ:fɑ:ðə]	ancestor	*Vorfahr*	
to **realize sth** ['ri:əlaɪz]	to achieve sth	*etw verwirklichen, etw ausführen*	
lake [leɪk]	body of freshwater e.g. Loch Ness in Scotland	*(Binnen-)See*	
to **rebuild** [ˌri:'bɪld]	to reconstruct sth after it has been damaged	*umbauen, erneuern*	
dutiful ['dju:tɪfl]	doing what sb is supposed to do	*pflichtbewusst*	
to **bloom** [blu:m]	e.g. flowers bloom in the spring	*(auf)blühen*	
occasional poem [əˌkeɪʒənl 'pəʊɪm]	poetry written for a special occasion	*Festgedicht*	
narration *fml* [nə'reɪʃn], [næ'reɪʃn]	story telling	*Erzählung, Geschichte*	▸ page 162
credibility [ˌkredə'bɪləti]	the quality of being believable	*Glaubwürdigkeit*	
entity ['entəti]	sth which exists	*Organisation, Firma, Rechtspersönlichkeit*	▸ page 163
royalty-free ['rɔɪəlti fri:]	free from ongoing payments	*gebührenfrei, lizenzfrei*	
purpose ['pɜ:pəs]	intention	*Absicht, Zweck*	
intriguing [ɪn'tri:gɪŋ]	fascinating	*faszinierend, verblüffend*	
to **edit sth** ['edɪt]	to cut out or rewrite text	*etw editieren, etw überarbeiten*	

Words in context

to **resettle** [ˌri:'setl]	to go to live in a different place	*umsiedeln*	▸ page 164
wealth [welθ]	*adj* wealthy	*Wohlstand, Reichtum*	
outlawed ['aʊtlɔ:d]	< > legal	*geächtet*	
emancipation [ɪˌmænsɪ'peɪʃn]	liberation, setting free	*Befreiung*	
ancestry ['ænsestri]	background, origins	*Abstammung, Herkunft*	

▸ page 165	**salad bowl** ['sæləd bəʊl]	a large bowl for serving vegetables such as lettuce, tomatoes, etc	*Salatschüssel*
	enshrined [ɪn'ʃraɪnd]	fixed permanently, protected	*festgeschrieben, verankert*
	to **prohibit sb from sth** [prə'hɪbɪt]	to stop/forbid sb from sth	*jdm etw untersagen*
	to **oppose sth** [ə'pəʊz]	< > to support sth	*gegen etw opponieren, sich gegen etw widersetzen*
	exploration [ˌeksplə'reɪʃn]	travelling around a place in order to learn about it	*Erforschung, Erkundung*
	invasion [ɪn'veɪʒn]	entering a foreign country/region	*Invasion, Eindringen*
	costly ['kɒstli]	expensive	*kostspielig, teuer*
	withdrawal [wɪð'drɔːəl]	taking sth out, away	*Rückzug, Abzug*
▸ page 166	**inhabitant** [ɪn'hæbɪtənt]	sb who lives in a place	*Einwohner / in, Bewohner / in*
	to **impose sth on sb** [ɪm'pəʊz]	to force sth on sb	*jdm etw aufzwingen*
	tribal homeland [ˌtraɪbl 'həʊmlænd]	the place where a group's culture and identity was formed	*Stammesgebiet*

Topic 5 The United Kingdom

▸ page 178	**empire** ['empaɪə]	e.g. the British Empire	*Imperium, Reich*
	the Commonwealth ['kɒmənwelθ]	a group of countries including the UK and countries that were formerly part of the British Empire	Staatenbund aus Großbritannien und ehemaligen britischen Kolonien
	to **unify** ['juːnɪfaɪ]	to bring together	*vereinigen*
▸ page 179	**Caribbean** [ˌkærə'biːən]	e.g. Barbados, Jamaica, etc, and the surrounding area	*Karibik, karibisch*
	archive ['ɑːkaɪv]	a collection of records and documents	*Archiv*

Section A The British Empire

▸ page 181	**displacement** [dɪs'pleɪsmənt]	moving or forcing sb/sth from its place or position	*Vertreibung*
	sovereign ['sɒvrɪn]	self-governing	*unabhängig*
	explorer [ɪk'splɔːrə]	a traveller who goes to a new, unfamiliar area	*Forschungsreisende(r), Entdecker / in*
	to **govern sth** ['gʌvn]	*n* government	*etw regieren*
	human rights *pl* [ˌhjuːmən 'raɪts]	the basic rights that everyone has to be treated fairly and not in a cruel way, especially by their government	*Menschenrechte*
	abuse [ə'bjuːs]	e.g. alcohol abuse, drug abuse	*Missbrauch*
	convention [kən'venʃn]	large meeting or conference	*Versammlung, Tagung*
	hardly ['hɑːdli]	e.g. A waitress hardly has time to sit down.	*kaum*
	trader ['treɪdə]	sb whose business is buying and selling	*Händler / in*
	database ['deɪtəbeɪs]	collection of information saved on a computer	*Datenbank*
	to **extend sth** [ɪk'stend]	to make sth longer	*etw erweitern, etw ausdehnen*
	MP (= Member of Parliament) [ˌem 'piː, ˌmembər əv 'pɑːləmənt]	sb who is elected to Parliament	*Parlamentsabgeordnete / r*
	reign [reɪn]	the period of time a particular king or queen rules	*Regierungszeit*
▸ page 182	**extraction** [ɪk'strækʃn]	getting sth out of sth else	*Gewinnung*
	cruelty ['kruːəlti]	*adj* cruel	*Grausamkeit*
	fraction ['frækʃn]	a small group within a larger one, who hold different opinions	*Bruchteil*
	to **lack functional literacy** [ˌlæk ˌfʌŋkʃənl 'lɪtərəsi]	to be unable to read, write, do basic maths	*nicht richtig lesen und schreiben können*
	distant ['dɪstənt]	far away	*(weit) entfernt, fern, entlegen*
	neither … nor … [ˌnaɪðə 'nɔː]	not one thing and not another thing	*weder … noch …*

perpetrator ['pɜːpətreɪtə]	person who does sth (criminal)	*Verursacher / in, (Straf-)Täter / in*	
injustice [ɪn'dʒʌstɪs]	< > justice	*Ungerechtigkeit*	
compensation [ˌkɒmpən'seɪʃn]	sth (usually money) given to sb to make up for loss or injury	*(finanzieller) Ausgleich*	
expenditure [ɪk'spendɪtʃə]	payments	*Ausgaben*	
to **compensate sb** ['kɒmpənseɪt]	to give sb money to compensate for sth bad	*jdn entschädigen*	
contemporary [kən'temprəri]	happening now, modern	*zeitgenössisch*	
descendant [dɪ'sendənt]	offspring, younger relative	*Nachfahre, Nachkomme*	
to **portray** [pɔː'treɪ]	to show/describe sb in a particular way	*darstellen, schildern*	
to **insure sb** [ɪn'ʃʊə]	to protect sb against sth	*jdn versichern*	

Section B The aftermath of colonialism

surname ['sɜːneɪm]	family name e.g. Schmidt, Yildiz	*Nachname*	▸ page 185
fishery ['fɪʃəri]	an area of water where fish are caught and can be sold	*Fischerei, Fischzucht*	
sovereignty *fml* ['sɒvrənti]	a country's independence and authority to make its own decisions	*Eigenstaatlichkeit, Souveränität*	
governance ['gʌvnəns]	rule, control	*Regierungshandeln, Herrschaft*	
imposition [ˌɪmpə'zɪʃn]	sth you are forced to do or look at	*Auferlegung, Verhängung*	
impoverishment [ɪm'pɒvərɪʃmənt]	becoming poor	*Verarmung, Verelendung*	
to **restore sth** [rɪ'stɔː]	to return or re-establish sth	*etw restaurieren, etw wieder herstellen*	▸ page 186
rightful ['raɪtfəl]	< > wrong, undeserved	*rechtmäßig*	
divisive [dɪ'vaɪsɪv]	causing/provoking people to disagree with each other	*entzweiend, spalterisch*	
ancestor ['ænsestə]	forefather, older relative	*Vorfahr / in*	
to **consent** *fml* [kən'sent]	to agree to sth	*zustimmen, einwilligen*	
ancestral [æn'sestrəl]	from, or related to, a member of a family	*angestammt, ererbt*	
to **result in sth** [rɪ'zʌlt]	to cause sth to happen	*zu etw führen, etw ergeben*	
fluency ['fluːənsi]	able to speak and write easily and accurately	*Gewandtheit, Flüssigkeit* (Sprache)	
official [ə'fɪʃl]	person working for the government	*Beamte / r, Funktionär / in*	
increasingly [ɪn'kriːsɪŋli]	more and more	*zunehmend, in zunehmendem Maße*	
interchangeable [ˌɪntə'tʃeɪndʒəbl]	similar, replaceable	*austauschbar*	
to **lay down** [ˌleɪ 'daʊn]	to insist on a rule or principle	*niederlegen, aufzeichnen*	▸ page 187
to **erase** [ɪ'reɪz]	to rub sth out	*(aus)löschen, ausradieren*	
dedicated ['dedɪkeɪtɪd]	passionate, committed	*engagiert, passioniert*	
campaigner [kæm'peɪnə]	activist	*Aktivist / in*	
decolonization [diːˌkɒlənaɪ'zeɪʃn]	making a state independent	*Dekolonisierung*	
to **signify sth** ['sɪgnɪfaɪ]	to mean sth, to stand for sth	*etw bedeuten, etw bezeichnen*	
to **presume sth** [prɪ'zjuːm]	to guess that sth is true	*etw annehmen, etw vermuten, etw voraussetzen*	
to **eliminate sth** [ɪ'lɪmɪneɪt]	to kill sth, to delete sth	*etw eliminieren, etw unterbinden*	
worthy (of sth) ['wɜːði]	deserving attention or respect	*(einer Sache) würdig, wert*	
unpaid [ˌʌn'peɪd]	not given any money for work	*unbezahlt*	
reparation [ˌrepə'reɪʃn]	making sth right after sth bad has happened	*Entschädigung, Wiedergutmachung*	
to **repay** [rɪ'peɪ]	to do sth in return for sth	*zurückzahlen*	
to **diminish** [dɪ'mɪnɪʃ]	to become smaller, less	*(sich) verringern, abnehmen*	
removal [rɪ'muːvl]	taking away	*Entfernung, Abschaffung*	
proverb ['prɒvɜːb]	a short sentence stating truth or a piece of advice	*Sprichwort*	

	respective [rɪ'spektɪv]	e.g. After the school trip we all went back to our respective houses.	*jeweilig*
	gesture ['dʒestʃə]	sth you do with your hands	*Geste*
	cloak [kləʊk]	a coat with no sleeves, worn by Batman, etc	*Umhang*
	acknowledgment [ək'nɒlɪdʒmənt]	sb showing that they have noticed sth/sb else	*Anerkennung*

Section C The Windrush generation

▸ page 189	to **pour** [pɔː]	to make sth flow quickly and strongly	*gießen, schütten*
	hearty ['hɑːti]	cheerful, friendly	*herzlich*
	not … at all [ət 'ɔːl]	e.g. I don't like football at all.	*überhaupt nicht*
▸ page 190	to **deport** [dɪ'pɔːt]	to force sb to leave a country	*abschieben*
	to **be detained** [dɪ'teɪnd]	to be imprisoned, kept in police custody	*in Gewahrsam genommen werden*
	inquiry [ɪn'kwaɪəri]	investigation, examination	*Untersuchung*
	shortage (of) ['ʃɔːtɪdʒ]	not having enough of sth	*Mangel, Knappheit (an)*
	subject ['sʌbdʒɪkt]	citizen (of a monarchy)	*Staatsbürger/in*
	hostile ['hɒstaɪl]	very unfriendly	*feindlich, feindselig*
	unbearable [ʌn'beərəbl]	too much to handle, deal with	*unerträglich*
	payment ['peɪmənt]	*v* to pay	*Bezahlung, Zahlung*
▸ page 191	to **resist sth** [rɪ'zɪst]	to have a negative attitude towards	*sich gegen etw wehren*
	tirelessly ['taɪələsli]	with great effort and energy	*unermüdlich*
	to **be awarded sth** [ə'wɔːd]	to be given a prize	*etw zuerkannt bekommen, etw verliehen bekommen*
	policing [pə'liːsɪŋ]	police work	*Polizeiarbeit*
	riot ['raɪət]	violence and disturbance by a crowd	*Aufstand, Aufruhr*
	offender [ə'fendə]	sb who committed a crime	*Straftäter/in*
	grateful ['greɪtfl]	thankful	*dankbar*
	to **dedicate sth to sb/sth** ['dedɪkeɪt]	e.g. the ancient Greeks deciated shrines to Aphrodite	*jdm/etw etw widmen*
	documentation [ˌdɒkjumen'teɪʃn]	paperwork	*Unterlagen, Urkunde(n)*
	recollection *fml* [ˌrekə'lekʃn]	memory	*Erinnerung*
▸ page 192	to **dislocate** ['dɪsləkeɪt]	to move sth from its proper place or position	*verrenken, auskugeln*
	to **tighten sth** ['taɪtn]	< > to loosen sth	*etw anziehen, etw verschärfen*
	unbeknown to sb *fml* [ˌʌnbɪ'nəʊn]	e.g. Unbeknown to me, everyone at school knew my secret.	*ohne jds Wissen*
	ultimately ['ʌltɪmətli]	e.g. Ultimately, we want to win.	*letztlich, letztendlich*
	indefinite [ɪn'defɪnət]	unlimited, unrestricted	*unbefristet*
	heart attack ['hɑːt ətæk]	*phr* to suffer from a heart attack	*Herzinfarkt*
	to **prompt sb to do sth** [prɒmpt]	to do sth which makes sb take action	*jdn veranlassen, etw zu tun*
	defender [dɪ'fendə]	protector	*Verteidiger/in*
	colleague ['kɒliːg]	sb you work with	*Kollege/-in*
	to **advise sb on sth** [əd'vaɪz]	to recommend what to do	*jdn über etw beraten*
	to **sack sb** [sæk]	to end sb's job, employment	*jdn entlassen*
	to **evict sb** [ɪ'vɪkt]	to force sb to leave the place in which they live	*jdn zwangsräumen*
	pension ['penʃn]	monthly payment you get when you are retired	*Rente, Pension*
▸ page 193	to **linger** ['lɪŋgə]	to stay longer than necessary	*verweilen, fortbestehen*
	to **simmer** ['sɪmə]	to cook slowly	*köcheln*
	to **explode** [ɪk'spləʊd]	to blow up violently	*explodieren*
	descent [dɪ'sent]	moving downwards	*Herkunft, Abstammung*
	to **march** [mɑːtʃ]	to walk like a soldier	*marschieren*
	spicy ['spaɪsi]	with lots of spices	*würzig, pikant*

jerk chicken [ˌdʒɜːk 'tʃɪkɪn]	marinated chicken dish from the Caribbean	*mariniertes gegrilltes Hühnchen*
calculation [ˌkælkju'leɪʃn]	adding up the amount of sth	*Rechnung, Berechnung*
manual labourer [mænjuəl 'leɪbərə]	sb who works with their hands e.g. a carpenter	*Handarbeiter/in*
inferior [ɪn'fɪəriə]	worse, of less worth	*minderwertig, unterlegen*
to **sort sth out** [ˌsɔːt 'aʊt]	to make sth clear, to organize sth	*etw klären, etw lösen*
relieved [rɪ'liːvd]	glad, no longer worried	*erleichtert*
to **bring up** [ˌbrɪŋ 'ʌp]	e.g. They are bringing up three children.	*erziehen, aufziehen*
to **retrace** [rɪ'treɪs]	to go back over a place sb has been before	*zurückverfolgen, wieder auffinden*
which is why [ˌwɪtʃ ɪz 'waɪ]	e.g. I watch TV all night, which is why I am tired today	*weshalb, weswegen*
to **persist** [pə'sɪst]	to remain, to continue	*fortbestehen*
homesickness ['həʊmsɪknəs]	bad feelings caused by being away from home	*Heimweh*
whoever [huː'evə]	person or people, it doesn't matter exactly who they are	*wer/wen/wem auch immer*

Section D Britain's relationship to the EU

sentiment ['sentɪmənt]	feeling	*Stimmung*	▸ page 194
right-wing [ˌraɪt 'wɪŋ]	< > left-wing	*rechtsgerichtet*	
to **resign** [rɪ'zaɪn]	to give up your job	*zurücktreten*	
to **rule** [ruːl]	to govern an area or people	*herrschen*	▸ page 195
to **underestimate sb/sth** [ˌʌndər'estɪmeɪt]	e.g. I underestimated the weight of these boxes. I can't lift them.	*jdn/etw unterschätzen*	
to **employ sb** [ɪm'plɔɪ]	to hire sb	*jdn beschäftigen, jdn einstellen* (Personal)	▸ page 196
vice versa [ˌvaɪs 'vɜːsə]	the other way around	*umgekehrt*	▸ page 197
joint [dʒɔɪnt]	together with	*gemeinsam, gemeinschaftlich*	
in the wake of [weɪk]	following sth	*infolge*	▸ page 198
detached [dɪ'tætʃt]	separate from	*getrennt*	
intertwined [ˌɪntə'twaɪnd]	connected, twisted together	*verflochten*	
precedent ['presɪdənt]	a similar action or event that happened earlier	*Präzedenzfall, Beispiel, Tradition*	
to **shrink** [ʃrɪŋk]	to get smaller, to become less	*schrumpfen*	
to **scramble** ['skræmbl]	to climb or crawl	*klettern, krabbeln*	
collapse [kə'læps]	*n* collapse	*Einsturz*	
to **overturn** [ˌəʊvə'tɜːn]	to tip sth over	*umstürzen, kippen*	
to **defeat sb** [dɪ'fiːt]	to win against sb	*jdn besiegen, jdn schlagen*	
destiny ['destəni]	fate	*Schicksal, Bestimmung*	
provincial [prə'vɪnʃl]	rural, small-town	*provinziell*	
ambition [æm'bɪʃn]	sth you want to do or achieve very much	*Ehrgeiz, Ziel, Ambition*	
titan ['taɪtn]	giant, very large	*Titan, Riese*	
reputation [ˌrepju'teɪʃn]	the general opinion people have about sb	*Ansehen, Ruf*	

Section E Independence for Scotland?

annexation [ˌænek'seɪʃn]	taking over (part of) a country illegally	*Anschluss, Annektierung*	▸ page 199
separation [sepə'reɪʃn]	situation where a couple starts living separately	*Trennung*	
lad *infml* [læd]	boy	*Junge*	
lass *ScottE* [læs]	girl	*Mädchen*	
to **sit on the fence** [fens]	to be unable to decide	*zwischen den Stühlen sitzen*	
to **be fond of sb/sth** ['fɒnd əv]	to like sb/sth	*jdn gernhaben, etw mögen*	

	devolved [dɪ'vɒlvd]	decentralised	*dezentralisiert*
	after all [ˌɑːftər 'ɔːl]	in the end	*schließlich (doch), immerhin*
▸ page 200	**injury** ['ɪndʒəri]	*v* to injure	*Verletzung*
	creation [kri'eɪʃn]	sth that has been made or invented	*Schaffung*
	affairs *pl* [ə'feəz]	business	*Angelegenheiten*
	defence [dɪ'fens]	the act of protecting sb/sth from attack	*Verteidigung*
▸ page 201	**life expectancy** ['laɪf ɪkspektənsi]	the length of time sb is expected to live	*Lebenserwartung*
	currency ['kʌrənsi]	the type of money that is used in a country	*Währung*
	entitled [ɪn'taɪtld]	justified	*berechtigt*
	considerably [kən'sɪdərəbli]	noticeably, significantly	*erheblich, beträchtlich*
	U-turn ['juː tɜːn]	a complete change to a different direction	*Kehrtwende*
	to **betray sb** [bɪ'treɪ]	to be disloyal or unfaithful to sb	*jdn verraten*
	to **flip** [flɪp]	to overturn	*(sich) umdrehen*
	to **assume** [ə'sjuːm]	to think or accept that sth is true but without proof of it	*annehmen, davon ausgehen*
	to **weaken** ['wiːkən]	to make sth weaker	*schwächen*
▸ page 202	to **weigh sth up** [ˌweɪ 'ʌp]	to think about sth carefully	*etw abwägen, etw einschätzen, etw beurteilen*

Section F British identity

▸ page 203	to **come to mind** [ˌkʌm tə 'maɪnd]	to suddenly think of sth	*einfallen*
	bio ['baɪəʊ]	story about sb's life	*Biographie*
	thrilling ['θrɪlɪŋ]	very exciting	*aufregend, spannend*
	to **embrace** [ɪm'breɪs]	to positively accept sth	*annehmen, akzeptieren, mit offenen Armen begrüßen*
	to **congratulate sb** [kən'grætʃuleɪt]	to tell sb they have done a good job	*jdn beglückwünschen*
▸ page 204	**refuge** ['refjuːdʒ]	a place to hide	*Zuflucht*
	to **illuminate** [ɪ'luːmɪneɪt]	to light up	*beleuchten*
	delusion [dɪ'luːʒn]	mistaken belief, misunderstanding	*Illusion, Täuschung*
	exceptional [ɪk'sepʃənl]	unusual or uncommon, special	*außergewöhnlich*
	to **overplay** [ˌəʊvə'pleɪ]	to make sth bigger than it needs to be	*übertreiben*
	to **hearten** ['hɑːtn]	to cheer up, encourage	*ermutigen*
	inexorable [ɪn'eksərəbl]	impossible to stop	*unaufhaltsam*
▸ page 205	**enthusiastically** [ɪnˌθjuːzi'æstɪkli]	doing sth with intense interest, enjoyment	*begeistert*
	anthem ['ænθəm]	a song which identifies a particular group	*Hymne*
	bond [bɒnd]	strong connection between people	*Bindung, Verbindung*
	honour ['ɒnə]	glory	*Ehre*

Words in context

▸ page 208	**troubled** ['trʌbld]	having many problems	*mit Problemen belastet, geplagt*
	to **accuse sb of sth** [ə'kjuːz]	to say, 'You did this!'	*jdn einer Sache beschuldigen, jdm etw vorwerfen*
	acquisition [ˌækwɪ'zɪʃn]	buying or taking possession of sth	*Erwerb*
	to **displace sb** [dɪs'pleɪs]	to move sth out of its usual place	*jdn vertreiben*
	prosperity [prɒ'sperəti]	wealth	*Wohlstand*
▸ page 209	**unjust** [ˌʌn'dʒʌst]	unfair	*ungerecht*
	to **enrich** [ɪn'rɪtʃ]	to make sb/sth richer	*bereichern*
	vocal ['vəʊkl]	expressing opinions freely and loudly	*lautstark, entschieden*
	repercussion [ˌriːpə'kʌʃn]	consequence	*Auswirkung, Konsequenz*
	alliance [ə'laɪəns]	strategic partnership	*Bündnis, Allianz*
	to **imply sth** [ɪm'plaɪ]	to say indirectly, hint	*etw beinhalten*

to **flare up** [ˌfleər ˈʌp]	to suddenly become worse	*aufflammen*	
migratory [ˈmaɪɡrətri]	moving, travelling	*migratorisch, Wander-, Zug-*	▸ page 210
forcibly [ˈfɔːsəbli]	aggressively	*gewaltsam; nachdrücklich*	
to **partition** [pɑːˈtɪʃn]	to divide, split up	*abtrennen, aufteilen*	
dictatorship [ˌdɪkˈteɪtəʃɪp]	< > democracy	*Diktatur*	

Topic 6 Equality

acceptance [əkˈseptəns]	*v* to accept	*Akzeptanz, Annahme*	▸ page 225
to **criminalize** [ˈkrɪmɪnəlaɪz]	to make sth illegal	*illegalisieren*	
straight *infml* [streɪt]	directly	*hetero(sexuell)*	

Section A Civil Rights in the USA

supremacist [suːˈpreməsɪst]	racist	*Rassist/in, Verfechter/in der Rassentrennung*	▸ page 226
to **separate** [ˈsepəreɪt]	to move sb/sth apart	*(sich) trennen, (sich) loslösen*	
confederate [kənˈfedərət]	allied, united	*alliiert, verbündet*	
leisure facility [ˈleʒə fəsɪləti]	place to spend free time e.g. swimming pool	*Freizeiteinrichtung*	
to **desegregate** [ˌdiːˈseɡrɪɡeɪt]	to end separation by race	*die Rassentrennung aufheben*	
preacher [ˈpriːtʃə]	minister of religion	*Prediger/in*	▸ page 227
struggle [ˈstrʌɡl]	fight	*Kampf*	
assassination [əˌsæsɪˈneɪʃn]	murdering an important person for politcal reasons	*Attentat, Mordanschlag*	
unarmed [ˌʌnˈɑːmd]	not carrying a weapon	*unbewaffnet*	
supremacy [suˈpreməsi]	the belief that sb is better than sb else	*Vorherrschaft*	
handcuffed [ˈhændkʌft]	e.g. The police handcuffed the perpetrator.	*in Handschellen*	
to **pin to the ground** [pɪn]	to use body weight to hold sb down	*auf den Boden drücken*	
to **sacrifice sth** [ˈsækrɪfaɪs]	to give up sth important in order to get or do something that seems more important	*etw opfern*	
vs (versus) [ˈvɜːsəs]	against	*gegen*	
armed [ɑːmd]	with a weapon	*bewaffnet*	▸ page 228
verbal abuse [ˌvɜːbl əˈbjuːs]	using demeaning language to make sb feel bad	*Beschimpfung(en)*	
admission [ədˈmɪʃn]	being allowed to enter a place	*Zugang, Einlass*	
Governor *AE* [ˈɡʌvənə]	a person who is chosen to be in charge of the government of a state in the USA	*Gouverneur/in* (USA: Regierungschef/in eines Bundesstaats)	
troop [truːp]	group of soldiers	*Truppe*	
airborne division [ˈeəbɔːn dɪvɪʒn]	e.g. the airforce	*Luftlandedivision*	
to **escort sb** [ɪˈskɔːt]	to guide, accompany sb	*jdn begleiten, jdn eskortieren*	
rallying cry [ˈræliɪŋ kraɪ]	words or phrases which unite people against an enemy	*Parole, Schlachtruf*	
to **be keen on sth** [bi ˈkiːn ɒn]	to like sth	*auf etw versessen sein*	
bench [bentʃ]	a place outside to sit down	*Bank* (zum Sitzen)	
to **sign up for sth** [ˌsaɪn ˈʌp]	to join, to register	*sich für/bei etw anmelden*	
to **drop out of sth** [ˌdrɒp ˈaʊt]	to stop doing sth e.g. to drop out of school	*aus etw aussteigen, etw abbrechen*	
spare [speə]	replacement	*Ersatz*	▸ page 229
heel [hiːl]	part of the foot e.g. high-heeled shoes	*Ferse*	
safe haven [ˌseɪf ˈheɪvn]	a safe, secure place	*Rückzugsort*	
morgue [mɔːɡ]	a place where dead bodies are stored	*Leichenschauhaus*	
to **assure sb** [əˈʃʊə]	to tell sb sth positively to convince them	*jdm versichern*	

	murderous ['mɜːdərəs]	wanting to kill	*mörderisch*
	intent [ɪn'tent]	reason, purpose	*Absicht*
	to **provoke** [prə'vəʊk]	to make sb have a feeling or do sth	*auslösen, hervorrufen*
	desegregation [ˌdiːˌsegrɪ'geɪʃn]	ending separation by race	*Aufhebung der Rassentrennung*
	to **suspend sb** [sə'spend]	to stop sth for a short time	*jdn suspendieren*
	refusal [rɪ'fjuːzl]	*v* to refuse	*Ablehnung, Verweigerung*
	personnel [ˌpɜːsə'nel]	human resources	*Personal*
	powerless ['paʊələs]	without the ability or possibility to do anything	*machtlos, unfähig*
▸ page 230	**depressed** [dɪ'prest]	e.g. My grandma was depressed after my grandpa died.	*deprimiert*
	reality [ri'æləti]	the real world	*Realität, Wirklichkeit*
	to **comply with sth** [kəm'plaɪ wɪð]	to act according to sth, e.g. a law	*etw erfüllen, etw befolgen, sich an etw halten*
	framework ['freɪmwɜːk]	basic structure	*Rahmen, Grundlage*
	supposedly [sə'pəʊzɪdli]	usually believed or understood	*vermeintlich, angeblich*
	to **whistle at sb** ['wɪsl]	e.g. When I want my dog to come to me, I whistle.	*jdm hinterherpfeifen*
	(cotton) gin [ˌkɒtn 'dʒɪn]	a machine for separating cotton from its seeds	*Baumwollentkörnungsmaschine*
	to **tie** [taɪ]	to fasten with string or rope	*binden*
	in the midst of sth [mɪdst]	at the centre of sth	*inmitten von etw*
	neuroscientist ['njʊərəʊsaɪəntɪst]	sb who studies the human brain	*Neurowissenschaftler / in*
▸ page 231	to **sneeze** [sniːz]	e.g. In spring, I get hayfever and sneeze a lot.	*niesen*
	to **itch** [ɪtʃ]	e.g. a mosquito bite itches	*jucken*
	to **scratch sth** [skrætʃ]	e.g. I tried to pet the cat but it scratched me.	*(sich an) etw kratzen*
	disgusted [dɪs'gʌstɪd]	offended, sickened	*angeekelt*

Section B Gender equality

▸ page 232	to **reshape** [ˌriː'ʃeɪp]	to form sth differently	*umgestalten, neu formen*
	perception [pə'sepʃn]	opinion, belief	*Wahrnehmung*
▸ page 233	**interstate** ['ɪntəsteɪt]	motorway *BE*	*zwischenstaatlich*
	impunity [ɪm'pjuːnəti]	freedom from punishment	*Straffreiheit*
	ceasefire ['siːsfaɪə]	a signal to stop fighting	*Waffenstillstand*
	rape [reɪp]	*v* to rape sb	*Vergewaltigung*
	misogyny *fml* [mɪ'sɒdʒɪni]	men hating women	*Frauenfeindlichkeit*
	peacemaking ['piːsmeɪkɪŋ]	< > warmongering	*Friedensschaffung*
	peacebuilding ['piːsbɪldɪŋ]	creating or sustaining peace	*Friedenskonsolidierung*
	peacekeeper ['piːskiːpə]	sb, esp. a soldier, who tries to prevent conflict	*Soldat / in einer Friedenstruppe*
	disproportionate [ˌdɪsprə'pɔːʃənət]	too large or too small	*unverhältnismäßig*
	to **put one's faith in sth** [feɪθ]	to make a decision to trust sb/sth	*auf etw vertrauen*
	to **safeguard** ['seɪfgɑːd]	to protect sb/sth from harm or danger	*sichern, schützen, bewahren*
	domestic chore [dəˌmestɪk 'tʃɔː]	e.g. vacuum cleaning, washing the dishes, etc	*Hausarbeit*
	non-binary [nɒn 'baɪnəri]	not female, not male	*non-binär, divers*
	equal opportunities ***pl*** [ˌiːkwəl ɒpə'tjuːnətiz]	giving the same chances in life, work and society to all people	*Chancengleichheit*
	breakthrough ['breɪkθruː]	an important new development	*Durchbruch*
	pay gap ['peɪ gæp]	unfair difference in the money people earn	*Lohngefälle*
	care work ['keə wɜːk]	e.g. nursing, social work, parenting	*Betreuungsarbeit, Pflegearbeit*
	to **fetch** [fetʃ]	to get, bring	*holen, abholen*
	to **care for sb** ['keə fə]	to make sure sb is safe and has everything they need	*für jdn sorgen, sich um jdn kümmern, auf jdn aufpassen*

gross domestic product (GDP) [ˌgrəʊs dəˌmestɪk ˈprɒdʌkt]	the total value of goods and services produced in a country	*Bruttosozialprodukt*	
flawed [flɔːd]	containing a lot of mistakes	*fehlerhaft, mangelhaft*	
metric [ˈmetrɪk]	system	*Kennzahl, Metrik*	
baseline [ˈbeɪslaɪn]	a starting point	*Basis, Ausgangspunkt*	
policy [ˈpɒləsi]	the way a state or institution does sth	*Politik, Vorgehensweise*	
to **strengthen** [ˈstreŋθn]	to make sth stronger	*kräftigen, stärken*	
to **tend to do sth** [ˈtend tə]	to usually behave in a particular way	*dazu neigen, etw zu tun*	
board [bɔːd]	group of people who make decisions for a company	*Gremium, Ausschuss*	
to **take a company public** [ˌteɪk ə ˌkʌmpəni ˈpʌblɪk]	to issue shares in a company	*ein Unternehmen an die Börse zu bringen*	
on moral grounds [ɒn ˌmɒrəl ˈgraʊndz]	doing/not doing sth based on ethics or principles	*aus moralischen Gründen*	
credit score [ˈkredɪt skɔː]	a number which represents sb's financial situation	*Kreditwürdigkeit*	
to **blame sth on sb/sth** [bleɪm]	to say that sb/sth is responsible for sth bad that has happened	*jdm / etw für etw die Schuld geben*	
force [fɔːs]	strength, energy	*Triebkraft*	
domination [dɒmɪˈneɪʃn]	having power or control over sb/sth	*Dominanz*	
profession [prəˈfeʃn]	job	*Beruf*	
evolution [ˌiːvəˈluːʃn]	development	*Entwicklung*	
lack (of) [læk]	when sth is missing	*Mangel (an)*	
scope [skəʊp]	range	*Rahmen, Umfang*	
to **double** [ˈdʌbl]	to increase by the same amount	*(sich) verdoppeln*	
cross-party [ˌkrɒs ˈpɑːti]	a combination of two or more political parties	*parteiübergreifend*	
common ground [ˌkɒmən ˈgraʊnd]	shared interests or opinions	*Gemeinsamkeit(en)*	
critical mass [ˌkrɪtɪkl ˈmæs]	the minimum amount to start a chain reaction	*kritische Masse*	
to **innovate (sth)** [ˈɪnəveɪt]	to create, design, formulate sth	*Neuerungen einführen, (etw neu) einführen*	
orthodoxy [ˈɔːθədɒksi]	traditional belief(s)	*Lehrmeinung*	
to **redefine sth** [ˌriːdɪˈfaɪn]	to look at sth in a new way, give it new meaning	*etw neu definieren*	
coincidence [kəʊˈɪnsɪdəns]	luck, chance	*Zufall*	
to **benefit (sb)** [ˈbenɪfɪt]	to get sth good out of a situation	*(jdm) nutzen, Nutzen bringen, profitieren*	
female [ˈfiːmeɪl]	< > male	*Frau, weibliche Person*	▸ page 234
hatred [ˈheɪtrɪd]	< > love	*Hass, Abscheu*	
not necessarily [nɒt ˌnesəˈserəli]	maybe, but maybe not	*nicht unbedingt*	
agility [əˈdʒɪləti]	ability to move quickly and easily	*Beweglichkeit, Gewandtheit*	
self-confident [ˌself ˈkɒnfɪdənt]	secure about yourself	*selbstbewusst, selbstsicher*	
to **empower sb to do sth** [ɪmˈpaʊə]	to give power to sb to do sth	*jdn befähigen, etw zu tun*	
to **entertain sb** [ˌentəˈteɪn]	to allow yourself to think about doing sth	*jdn unterhalten*	
gymnast [ˈdʒɪmnæst]	sb who does gymnastics	*Turner / in*	▸ page 235
leotard [ˈliːətɑːd]	short skin-tight, one-piece garment	*Gymnastikanzug, Trikot*	
unitard [ˈjuːnətɑːd]	long skin-tight, one piece garment	*Ganzkörpertrikot*	
loose [luːs]	< > tight	*locker, lose*	
federation [ˌfedəˈreɪʃn]	group of states	*Verband, Föderation*	
to **prescribe** [prɪˈskraɪb]	e.g. The doctor prescribed some pills	*vorschreiben, verordnen*	
inappropriate [ˌɪnəˈprəʊpriət]	not suitable for the situation	*unangemessen, ungeeignet, unpassend*	
revealing [rɪˈviːlɪŋ]	(clothing) allowing much of the body to be seen	*offenherzig (Kleidung), freizügig*	
to **devalue sb** [ˌdiːˈvæljuː]	to reduce importance or worth	*jdn abwerten*	

	to **molest sb** [mə'lest]	to sexually misuse sb	*jdn (sexuell) belästigen, jdn missbrauchen*
	allegation [ˌælə'geɪʃn]	to say sb has done sth wrong or illegal	*Beschuldigung, Anschuldigung, Vorwurf*
	dress code ['dres kəʊd]	clothes sb is expected to wear at work or at an event	*Kleiderordnung*
	fencer ['fensə]	sb who does a sport using swords	*Fechter/in*

Section C Multicultural society

▸ page 236	**asylum seeker** [ə'saɪləm siːkə]	sb who wants to stay in a new country for safety reasons due to a threat in the home country	*Asylsuchende/r*
	seasonal ['siːzənl]	relating to a particular time of the year	*jahreszeitlich, saisonal*
	to **regret** [rɪ'gret]	to feel sad about sth that happened or that you did	*bedauern, bereuen*
	bilingual [ˌbaɪ'lɪŋgwəl]	being able to speak two languages	*zweisprachig*
	opposition (to) [ˌɒpə'zɪʃn]	defiance, disapproval	*Widerstand (gegen)*
	to **accommodate** [ə'kɒmədeɪt]	to fit in with	*unterbringen*
	anger ['æŋgə]	*adj* angry	*Zorn, Wut*
	in the first place [ɪn ðə 'fɜːst pleɪs]	to begin with	*an erster Stelle, eigentlich, ursprünglich*
	principally ['prɪnsəpli]	mainly, mostly	*grundsätzlich, hauptsächlich*
	to **make up sth** [ˌmeɪk 'ʌp]	to invent a story	*etw bilden, etw ausmachen*
	Gosh! [gɒʃ]	expression of surprise	*Meine Güte!*
	superior [suː'pɪəriə]	manager, boss	*überlegen, höherwertig*
	to **intermarry** [ˌɪntə'mæri]	to marry sb from a different ethnic, racial, or social group	*Mischehen schließen*
	grip [grɪp]	holding sth with strength	*Griff*
	equal ['iːkwəl]	e.g. All men are created as equals.	*Gleiche/r, Gleichgestellte/r*
	to **retain sb/sth** [rɪ'teɪn]	to keep sth	*jdn/etw behalten, etw beibehalten, etw bewahren*
▸ page 237	**matchmaking** ['mætʃmeɪkɪŋ]	arranging romance or marriages	*Partnervermittlung*
	reluctant [rɪ'lʌktənt]	unwilling, not wanting to do sth	*widerwillig*
	union ['juːniən]	joining together	*Verbindung, Vereinigung*
	to **give way to sth** [gɪv 'weɪ]	to be replaced by sth	*etw weichen*
	to **settle sb** [setl]	to move to a new place and stay there	*jdn ansiedeln*
	hostility [hɒ'stɪləti]	aggression, negativity	*Feindseligkeit*
	matchmaker ['mætʃmeɪkə]	sb who arranges romances, marriages	*Heiratsvermittler/in*
	generosity [ˌdʒenə'rɒsəti]	being kind, big-hearted	*Großzügigkeit*
▸ page 238	to **socialize (with)** ['səʊʃəlaɪz]	to meet other people	*sich treffen (mit), unter Leute gehen*
	shelter ['ʃeltə]	a safe place to stay	*Unterkunft*
	to **channel sth** ['tʃænl]	to direct sth	*etw lenken, etw ausrichten (auf)*
	heaven [hevn]	in the Christian belief, place where good people go after they die	*Himmel*
	to **knit** [nɪt]	to create sth e.g. a sweater, out of wool, using two sticks	*stricken*
	to **smooth sth** [smuːð]	to make a problem seem less serious	*etw glätten, etw ebnen*
	sympathetic to [ˌsɪmpə'θetɪk]	being understanding of sth	*wohlwollend gegenüber*
	closure ['kləʊʒə]	a feeling that sth has ended	*Schließung*
	surly ['sɜːli]	unfriendly, bad-tempered	*mürrisch*
	to **credit sb with sth** ['kredɪt]	to say that sb has done sth well	*jdm etw zuschreiben*
	to **pack sth** [pæk]	to fill (a bag) with things needed for travel	*etw füllen*
	client ['klaɪənt]	sb who pays sb else for a service	*Kunde/Kundin*

folder ['fəʊldə]	file, binder	*Mappe, Ordner*	
shoelace ['ʃu:leɪs]	a cord that holds a shoe in place	*Schnürsenkel*	
to **compound** [kəm'paʊnd]	to make sth worse	*verschlimmern*	
bemused [bɪ'mju:zd]	confused, muddled	*irritiert*	
intrigued [ɪn'tri:gd]	fascinated	*fasziniert*	
to **arouse** [ə'raʊz]	to cause, trigger	*wecken, erregen*	▸ page 239
registration [ˌredʒɪ'streɪʃn]	e.g. Registration closes at 5 p.m.	*Anmeldung*	
to **scare sb** [skeə]	to shock sb, to make sb scared	*jdn ängstigen*	
to **visualize sth** ['vɪʒuəlaɪz]	to imagine sth, to see sth in your mind	*etw bildlich darstellen, etw visualisieren*	

Section D Sexual and gender minorities

raid [reɪd]	surprise attack	*Razzia*	▸ page 240
to **nominate** ['nɒmɪneɪt]	to suggest sb for election	*nominieren*	
lesbian ['lezbiən]	a woman who is sexually attracted to other women	*lesbisch*	
commemoration (of) [kəˌmemə'reɪʃn]	celebration to remember sb/sth	*Gedenken (an)*	
clause [klɔ:z]	group of words	*Klausel, Bestimmung*	
curriculum [kə'rɪkjələm]	educational programme	*Lehrplan*	
to **speak out** [ˌspi:k 'aʊt]	to express your opinion about sth	*seine Meinung sagen*	
marital status [ˌmærɪtl 'steɪtəs]	whether you're single, married, divorced, etc.	*Familienstand*	
guidance ['gaɪdəns]	help, advice	*Anleitung, Hilfestellung*	▸ page 241
primary school ['praɪməri sku:l]	children go to this school when they are between 6 and 9 years old	*Grundschule*	
local authority [ˌləʊkl ɔ:'θɒrəti]	local government	*(Kommunal-)Behörde*	
to **repeal sth** [rɪ'pi:l]	to make a law invalid	*etw widerrufen, etw aufheben*	
statute book ['stætʃu:t bʊk]	law book	*Gesetzbuch*	
to **change sth beyond recognition** [bɪˌjɒnd rekəg'nɪʃn]	to make sth unrecognizable	*etw so verändern, dass es nicht wiederzuerkennen ist*	▸ page 242
affirmation [ˌæfə'meɪʃn]	< > denial	*Bestätigung*	
to **be under no illusion** [ɪ'lu:ʒn]	to be fully aware of what is happening	*sich nichts vormachen*	
to **be plain sailing** [ˌpleɪn 'seɪlɪŋ]	to be uncomplicated, straightforward	*eine glatte Sache sein*	
rhetoric ['retərɪk]	speech or writing that is intended to influence people	*Redekunst, Phrasendrescherei*	
to **coexist** *fml* [ˌkəʊɪg'zɪst]	to live alongside	*nebeneinander bestehen*	
to **inflame** [ɪn'fleɪm]	to make a situation worse	*entfachen, entzünden*	
exception [ɪk'sepʃn]	a special case	*Ausnahme*	
to **heal** [hi:l]	to make/get well again	*heilen, verheilen*	
to **legalize** ['li:gəlaɪz]	< > to prohibit	*legalisieren*	
open-minded [ˌəʊpən 'maɪndɪd]	willing to learn about new ideas without prejudice	*aufgeschlossen, offen*	▸ page 243
supportive [sə'pɔ:tɪv]	ready to help and be supportive	*hilfreich, verständnisvoll*	
to **come out** [ˌkʌm 'aʊt]	to tell people that you are non-heteronormative	*sich outen*	
letter to the editor [ˌletə tə ði 'edɪtə]	a letter or email written to the editor of a newspaper, addressing an issue	*Leserbrief*	

Section E Social class

comprehensive (school) [kɒmprɪ'hensɪv sku:l]	secondary school (UK) that takes all students, regardless of academic achievement or wealth	*Gesamtschule*	▸ page 244
to **inform sth** [ɪn'fɔ:m]	to give facts or information	*etw durchdringen*	
coal miner ['kəʊl maɪnə]	sb who extracts coal from the ground	*Bergarbeiter/in*	
eldest ['eldɪst]	the oldest person in a group	*älteste/r/s*	
to **miss out** [ˌmɪs 'aʊt]	e.g. My mobile's broken! I'm gonna miss out big time!	*zu kurz kommen*	

	to **specialize in sth** ['speʃəlaɪz]	to focus on sth (and be good at it)	*sich auf etw spezialisieren*
▸ page 245	**inclination** [ˌɪnklɪ'neɪʃn]	an interest in or liking for sth	*Neigung, Vorliebe*
	restrictive [rɪ'strɪktɪv]	limiting	*einschränkend*
	secondary (school) ['sekəndri]	the school after primary school	*weiterführende Schule*
	mistrust [ˌmɪs'trʌst]	< > trust	*Misstrauen*
	wariness ['weərinəs]	carefulness, awareness	*Vorsicht, Skepsis*
▸ page 246	**grammar school** ['græmə skuːl]	academic secondary school	*Gymnasium*
	selective school [sɪ'lektɪv skuːl]	a school which chooses students based on their abilities	Schule mit Aufnahmebedingungen
	boarding school ['bɔːdɪŋ skuːl]	school where students live full time	*Internat*

Section F Overcoming disabilities

▸ page 247	**behavioural** [bɪ'heɪvjərəl]	relating to behaviour	*Verhaltens-*
	repetitive [rɪ'petətɪv]	doing or saying the same things the same way again and again	*sich wiederholend*
	learning disability ['lɜːnɪŋ dɪsəbɪləti]	condition in the brain which interferes with the ability to learn	*Lernbehinderung, Lernschwäche*
	to **shorten** ['ʃɔːtn]	e.g. Thomas prefers to shorten his name to Tom.	*(ver)kürzen*
▸ page 248	to **equip** [ɪ'kwɪp]	to prepare sb for a particular task	*ausrüsten, ausstatten*
	disappointment [ˌdɪsə'pɔɪntmənt]	sadness because wishes weren't fulfilled	*Enttäuschung*
	vision ['vɪʒn]	ability to see	*Sehkraft, Sehvermögen*
	impaired [ɪm'peəd]	weak or damaged	*beeinträchtigt*
	how about …? [ˌhaʊ ə'baʊt]	e.g. How about we go out and get ice cream?	*wie wäre es mit …?*
▸ page 249	**awesome** *AE* ['ɔːsəm]	really good	*beeindruckend, fantastisch*
	to **widen sth** ['waɪdn]	to extend sth	*etw erweitern, etw verbreitern*
▸ page 250	**thrilled** ['θrɪld]	very excited	*begeistert*
	initials *pl* [ɪ'nɪʃlz]	e.g. Joe Biden's initials are J.B.	*Initialen*
	to **dis sb** *infml* [dɪs]	to speak to sb without respect	*jdn dissen*
	cripple ['krɪpl]	bad word for a disabled person	*Krüppel*
	offensive [ə'fensɪv]	rude in a way that causes sb to feel upset or insulted	*beleidigend, anstößig*
	to **reclaim** [rɪ'kleɪm]	to get sth back	*zurückgewinnen*
	amongst [ə'mʌŋst]	in the middle of	*zwischen, unter*
	cerebral palsy [ˌserəbrəl 'pɔːlzi]	disability caused by brain damage at birth	*Zerebralparese (Lähmung)*
	to **patronize sb** ['pætrənaɪz]	to act nice but feel superior to sb	*jdn von oben herab behandeln, bevormunden; jdn beschützen*
	accessibility [əkˌsesə'bɪləti]	being easy to reach	*Barrierefreiheit*
	to **arise** [ə'raɪz]	come about	*sich ergeben, entstehen, auftreten*
	to **prioritize sth** [praɪ'ɒrətaɪz]	to decide that sth is most important	*etw der Wichtigkeit nach ordnen, etw priorisieren*
▸ page 251	**urgency** ['ɜːdʒənsi]	importance, having top priority	*Dringlichkeit*
	metropolitan [ˌmetrə'pɒlɪtən]	describing a large city	*großstädtisch*
	sensory ['sensəri]	describing hearing, sigh, touch, etc	*sensorisch*
	minefield ['maɪnfiːld]	situation with unseen dangers	*Minenfeld, gefährliches Terrain*
	to **lead the way** [liːd ðə 'weɪ]	to be the best	*vorangehen*
	hilly ['hɪli]	< > flat	*hügelig*
	pavement ['peɪvmənt]	sidewalk *AE*	*Gehsteig, Bürgersteig*
	slope grade ['sləʊp greɪd]	how slanted, steep or flat a surface is	*Gefälle*
	width [wɪdθ]	the measurement of sth from side to side	*Breite*
	pilot scheme ['paɪlət skiːm]	experimental trial	*Pilotprojekt*
	beacon ['biːkən]	signal light	hier: *(akustisches) Warnsignal*

cue [kjuː]	a signal for sb to do or say sth	*Zeichen, Hinweis*	▸ page 252
escalator [ˈeskəleɪtə]	moving staircase	*Rolltreppe*	
outage [ˈaʊtɪdʒ]	power supply become unavailable	*Ausfall*	
directional information [dəˌrekʃənl ɪnfəˈmeɪʃn]	e.g. traffic lights ahead!	*Richtungsangaben*	
unreliable [ˌʌnrɪˈlaɪəbl]	not to be trusted	*unzuverlässig*	
blindness [ˈblaɪndnəs]	not being able to see	*Blindheit*	
sighted [ˈsaɪtɪd]	being able to see	*sehend*	
reversal [rɪˈvɜːsl]	change to the oppsite direction	*Umkehr, Umkehrung*	
disqualified [dɪsˈkwɒlɪfaɪd]	< > allowed	*ausgeschlossen*	

Words in context

humiliation [hjuːˌmɪliˈeɪʃn]	embarrassment, shame	*Demütigung, Erniedrigung*	▸ page 254
usage [ˈjuːsɪdʒ]	*v* to use	*Nutzung*	
to **migrate** [maɪˈgreɪt]	to move from one country to another to live and work there	*auswandern, migrieren*	
suspicion [səˈspɪʃn]	*adj* suspicious	*Misstrauen; Verdacht*	
to **attain** [əˈteɪn]	to achieve, accomplish sth	*erreichen, erlangen*	
paternity leave [pəˈtɜːnəti liːv]	time a father takes off work to look after a baby	*Vaterschaftsurlaub*	
imprisonment [ɪmˈprɪznmənt]	< > freedom	*Haft(strafe)*	▸ page 255
milestone [ˈmaɪlstəʊn]	a significant stage in development	*Meilenstein*	
to **star in sth** [stɑː]	to have the main role (in a film, theatre production, TV series)	*in etw die Hauptrolle haben*	
to **dispel a myth** [dɪˌspel ə ˈmɪθ]	to establish the truth	*mit einem Mythos aufräumen*	

A–Z word list

Dieses Wörterverzeichnis enthält das gesamte Lernvokabular aus **Crossover 2 – 6th edition** in alphabetischer Reihenfolge. Nicht aufgeführt sind Wörter, die nicht unbedingt zum aktiven Wortschatz gehören müssen.

Abkürzungen:	AE = amerikanisches Englisch	jdm = jemandem	pl = plural	P = Partner files
	BE = britisches Englisch	jdn = jemanden	sb = somebody	T = Audio transcript
	etw = etwas	jds = jemandes	sth = something	V = Video transcript

A

abolition 138 *Abschaffung*
abolitionist 146 *Abolitionist / in* (Anhänger/in der Sklavenbefreiung)
absence 66 *Abwesenheit*
absent 51 *abwesend*
abundant *fml* 153 *reich, reichlich (vorhanden)*
abuse 181 *Missbrauch*
abuse, verbal ~ 228 *Beschimpfung(en)*
acceptance 225 *Akzeptanz, Annahme*
to **access sth** 17 *auf etw zugreifen, Zugang haben zu etw*
accessibility 250T *Barrierefreiheit*
to **accommodate** 236T *unterbringen*
to **accompany sb** 94 *jdn begleiten*
accordingly 77 *(dem)entsprechend*
accountable, to **hold sb ~ (for sth)** 61 *jdn (für etw) zur Rechenschaft ziehen*
accountancy 104 *Buchhaltung, Rechnungswesen*
to **accumulate** 155 *(sich) ansammeln, (sich) anhäufen*
accusation 20 *Vorwurf, Anschuldigung*
to **accuse sb of sth** 208 *jdn einer Sache beschuldigen, jdm etw vorwerfen*
accustomed 115 *gewöhnt, gewohnt*
achievable 155 *erreichbar, realisierbar*
to **achieve sth** 16 *etw erreichen, etw leisten*
achievement 152T *Errungenschaft, Leistung*
acknowledgment 188 *Anerkennung*
to **acquire sth** 73 *etw erwerben; etw annehmen*
acquisition 208 *Erwerb*
act 149 *Gesetz*
action, course of ~ 78 *Vorgehen, Maßnahmen*
actual 58 *tatsächlich, konkret*
to **adapt** 108 *(sich) anpassen*
addition 24 *Ergänzung*
to **address sth** 27 *etw angehen, sich mit etw befassen*
to **adjust sth** 67T *etw einstellen*
admission 228 *Zugang, Einlass*
to **admit to sth** 70 *etw zugeben, (ein)gestehen*
adoption 103 *Übernahme, Aneignung*
advance 11 *Fortschritt*
advantage, to **take ~ of sth** 101T *sich etw zunutze machen, etw ausnutzen*
adverse 104 *nachteilig, ungünstig*
adversity *fml* 146 *Not, schlechte Zeit(en)*
to **advise sb on sth** 192 *jdn über etw beraten*
advocate 53 *Befürworter / in*
affairs *pl* 200 *Angelegenheiten*
to **affect sth** 11 *etw beeinflussen, sich auswirken auf etw*
affirmation 242 *Bestätigung*
affordable 65 *erschwinglich*
after all 199 *schließlich (doch), immerhin*
aftermath, in the ~ of sth 108 *in der Folge von etw*
agency 65 *Behörde; Agentur*
agility 234 *Beweglichkeit, Gewandtheit*
agreement 20 *Vereinbarung*
artificial intelligence (AI) 68 *künstliche Intelligenz*
aid 150T *Hilfe, Unterstützung*
to **aim for sth** 95T *etw anstreben*
to **be aimed at sb** 33 *sich an jdn richten*
airborne division 228 *Luftlandedivision*
allegation 235T *Beschuldigung, Anschuldigung, Vorwurf*
alliance 209 *Bündnis, Allianz*
ally 152T *Alliierte / r, Verbündete / r*
along with 51 *(zusammen) mit, neben*
to **alter sth** 50 *etw (ver)ändern*
ambiguity 143 *Unklarheit, Uneindeutigkeit*
ambition 198T *Ehrgeiz, Ziel, Ambition*
ambivalence 152T *Zwiespältigkeit*
amendment 134 *Ergänzung, Zusatz*
ammunition 142 *Munition*
amongst 250T *zwischen, unter*
amount 12 *Menge, Ausmaß, Umfang*
ancestor 186 *Vorfahr / in*
ancestral 186 *angestammt, ererbt*
ancestry 164 *Abstammung, Herkunft*
angel 50 *Engel*
anger 236T *Zorn, Wut*
animating 73 *belebend, beseelend*
ankle 73 *Knöchel, Sprunggelenk*
annexation 199 *Anschluss, Annektierung*
annual 19 *jährlich*
one another 159 *einander, sich (gegenseitig)*
anthem 205 *Hymne*
anxiety disorder 150T *Angststörung*
apart, to **tell ~** 72 *auseinander halten*
apart, to **take sth ~** 16T *etw auseinandernehmen*
apart from 121 *abgesehen von, außer*
to **apologize** 115 *sich entschuldigen*
apology 68 *Entschuldigung*

to **appeal to sb** 59T *für jdn attraktiv sein, jdn ansprechen*
appealing 56 *ansprechend*
appetizing 59T *appetitanregend*
appliance 67 *Gerät, Haushaltsgerät*
applicant 143 *Bewerber/in*
to **appreciate** 11 *anerkennen*
to **approach sb** 95T *an jdn herantreten*
archive 179 *Archiv*
to **arise** 250 *sich ergeben, entstehen, auftreten*
arm 134 *Waffe*
armed 228 *bewaffnet*
to **arouse** 239 *wecken, erregen*
articulate 153 *wortgewandt*
artificial 50 *künstlich*
artificial intelligence (AI) 68 *künstliche Intelligenz*
as well as 53 *sowohl … als auch …, ebenso wie, sowie*
as, such ~ 10 *wie (zum Beispiel)*
aspiration 156 *Ambition, Bestreben*
to **aspire** 157 *aufstreben*
assassination 227 *Attentat, Mordanschlag*
assault 142 *Körperverletzung*
to **assess sth** 13 *etw beurteilen*
to **assign sb sth** 61 *jdm etw zuweisen*
to **assimilate** 138 *sich anpassen*
assimilation 138 *Anpassung, Angleichung*
assistance 60 *Hilfe, Unterstützung*
to **associate sth with sth** 23 *etw mit etw verbinden, etw mit etw assoziieren*
to **assume** 201T *annehmen, davon ausgehen*
to **assure sb** 229 *jdm versichern*
astonishing 32T *überraschend*
asylum seeker 236 *Asylsuchende/r*
at all, not … ~ 189 *überhaupt nicht*
attack, heart ~ 192 *Herzinfarkt*
to **attain** 254 *erreichen, erlangen*
attempt 11 *Versuch*
to **attend sth** 156 *etw besuchen*
attorney 70 *(Rechts-) Anwalt/Anwältin*
authority, local ~ 241 *(Kommunal-)Behörde*
on average 9 *im Durchschnitt*
award 109 *Auszeichnung, Preis*
to **be awarded sth** 191 *etw zuerkannt bekommen, etw verliehen bekommen*
awareness, to **raise ~ about sth (rose, risen)** 36 *auf etw aufmerksam machen*
awesome *AE* 249 *beeindruckend, fantastisch*
awkward 115 *unangenehm, peinlich*

B

to **back sth up** 11 *etw untermauern, etw bekräftigen, etw belegen*
barriers, trade ~ *pl* 120 *Handelsschranke, Handelshemmnis*
based 16T *ansässig*
baseline 233P *Basis, Ausgangspunkt*
beacon 251 hier: *(akustisches) Warnsignal*
to **begin with** 53 *anfänglich*
on behalf of sb 143 *in jds Namen, für jdn*
behavioural 247 *Verhaltens-*
belief 145 *Glaube, Überzeugung*
bemused 238 *irritiert*
bench 228 *Bank* (zum Sitzen)
to **benefit (sb)** 233P *(jdm) nutzen, Nutzen bringen, profitieren*
to **betray sb** 201T *jdn verraten*
beyond 73 *jenseits, außerhalb*
beyond, to **change sth ~ recognition** 242 *etw so verändern, dass es nicht wiederzuerkennen ist*
bias, racial ~ 62 *rassistische Voreingenommenheit*
bicycle 99 *Fahrrad*
bilingual 236 *zweisprachig*
bill 149 *Gesetzentwurf*
Bill of Rights 136 Grundrechte-Zusatzartikel der amerikanischen Verfassung
bio 203 *Biographie*
biodegradable 37 *biologisch abbaubar*
birth 155 *Geburt*
birth control 38 *Geburtenkontrolle*
blade 160 *Klinge*
blend 95T *Mischung*
blindness 252 *Blindheit*
to **bloom** 161 *(auf)blühen*
board 233P *Gremium, Ausschuss*
boarding school 246 *Internat*
bond 205 *Bindung, Verbindung*
bother, to **not ~ to do sth** 51 *es nicht für nötig halten, etw zu tun*
bountiful *fml* 153 *reichlich; großzügig*
bow 115 *Verbeugung*
bowl, salad ~ 165 *Salatschüssel*
branch 31 *Ast, Zweig* (auch: *Zweigstelle*)
to **branch out** 57 *sich verzweigen*
brand 18 *Marke*
to **brand sth** 111 *etw kennzeichnen, mit seinem Zeichen versehen*
breadwinner 110T *Brotverdiener/in*
breakthrough 233P *Durchbruch*
to **breathe down sb's neck** 155 *jdm im Nacken sitzen*
to **breathe (in)** 13 *(ein)atmen*
breed 61 *Züchtung, Rasse*
to **bring up** 193T *erziehen, aufziehen*
broad 51 *breit, weit*
to **broadcast (broadcast, broadcast)** 120 *senden* (im Rundfunk)
to **broaden sth** 93 *etw erweitern*
to **broker** 114 *makeln, vermitteln*
brokerage 65 *Börsenhandel*

C

calculation 193T *Rechnung, Berechnung*
campaign 9 *Kampagne, Aktion*
to **campaign for/against sth** 16 *sich für/gegen etw einsetzen*
campaigner 188T *Aktivist/in*
capability 74 *Fähigkeit, Potenzial*
capable of 63 *fähig zu, imstande zu*
capacity 20 *Kapazität, Leistung*
to **capture** 65 *einfangen, erfassen*
capture, carbon ~ and storage 20 *CO_2-Abscheidung und -Speicherung*
carbon 11 *Kohle(nstoff)*
carbon capture and storage 20 *CO_2-Abscheidung und -Speicherung*
carbon footprint 12 *CO_2-Bilanz*
carbon neutrality 36 *Klimaneutralität*
ID card 150 *Ausweis*
cardboard 18T *Pappe, Karton*
care worker 62 *Pfleger/in*
to **care for sb** 233P *für jdn sorgen, sich um jdn kümmern, auf jdn aufpassen*
care work 233P *Betreuungsarbeit, Pflegearbeit*
carer 122 *Betreuer/in, Pfleger/in*
Caribbean 179 *Karibik, karibisch*

carpooling 29 *Fahrgemeinschaft(en)*
carry, concealed ~ *AE* 143 *verdecktes Tragen* (von Waffen)
casual staff 121 *Aushilfskräfte, Gelegenheitsarbeiter/in(nen)*
catastrophic 36 *katastrophal, verhängnisvoll*
cautious 67T *vorsichtig*
ceasefire 233 *Waffenstillstand*
ceiling, glass ~ 121 *gläserne Decke* (unsichtbare Barriere, die Frauen am beruflichen Aufstieg hindert)
celebration 114 *Feier*
CEO (Chief Executive Officer) 50 *Vorstandsvorsitzende/r*
cerebral palsy 250T *Zerebralparese* (Lähmung)
certification 18T *Bescheinigung*
to **certify** 18T *bescheinigen, zertifizieren*
chain, supply ~ 99 *Lieferkette*
to **challenge sb** 108 *jdn herausfordern*
to **channel sth** 238 *etw lenken, etw ausrichten (auf)*
chapter 160 *Kapitel*
characteristic 10 *Merkmal, charakteristische Eigenschaft*
chief executive 28 *Geschäftsführer/in*
childhood 149 *Kindheit*
to **chop down** 23 *fällen*
chore, domestic ~ 233 *Hausarbeit*
circular 28 *kreisförmig, rund*
to **cite sth** 65 *etw zitieren, etw angeben*
to **claim** 11 *behaupten*
clash 115 *Konflikt, Zusammenstoß*
classic 18T *klassisch*
clause 240 *Klausel, Bestimmung*
client 238 *Kunde/Kundin*
climate change 8 *Klimawandel*
climate crisis 8 *Klimakrise*
cloak 188T *Umhang*
closure 238 *Schließung*
clothing 21 *Bekleidung, Kleidung*
clue, not a ~ 115 *keine Ahnung*
coal 10 *Kohle*
coal miner 244 *Bergarbeiter/in*
coastal 16T *Küsten-*
code, dress ~ 235T *Kleiderordnung*
code, to **crack a ~** 58 *einen Code knacken*
to **coexist** *fml* 242 *nebeneinander bestehen*
coffin 100 *Sarg*
cognition 77 *Wahrnehmung, Erkenntnis*
coincidence 233P *Zufall*
coincidental 153 *zufällig*
collaboration 116 *Zusammenarbeit, Gemeinschaftsprodukt(ion)*
collaborative 108 *gemeinschaftlich, partnerschaftlich*
collapse 198T *Einsturz*
colleague 192 *Kollege/-in*
collection 64 *Sammlung*
college, vocational ~ 156 *Berufsschule*
collocation 30 *Kollokation* (inhaltliche Kombinierbarkeit sprachlicher Einheiten)
colonization 138 *Besiedlung, Kolonisierung*
to **come to mind** 203 *einfallen*
to **come out** 243T *sich outen*
commemoration (of) 240 *Gedenken (an)*
commerce 122 *Handel*
to **commit (oneself) to sth** 26 *sich auf etw einlassen, sich auf etw festlegen*
to **commit (a crime)** 150 *(ein Verbrechen) begehen*
commitment (to) 31 *Engagement (für), Bekenntnis (zu)*
common ground 233P *Gemeinsamkeit(en)*
the Commonwealth 178 Staatenbund aus Großbritannien und ehemaligen britischen Kolonien
compassionate 97 *mitfühlend, barmherzig*
to **compensate sb** 182 *jdn entschädigen*
compensation 182 *(finanzieller) Ausgleich*
competitive 107 *wettbewerbsorientiert, leistungsorientiert*
competitor 74 *Konkurrent/in, Konkurrenz*
to **comply with sth** 230T *etw erfüllen, etw befolgen, sich an etw halten*
to **compose** 159 *zusammensetzen*
to **compound** 238 *verschlimmern*
comprehensive (school) 244 *Gesamtschule*
to **comprise sth** 76 *etw umfassen, aus etw bestehen*
concealed carry *AE* 143 *verdecktes Tragen* (von Waffen)
concept, proof of ~ 16T *Machbarkeitsnachweis*
concern 17 *Sorge, Befürchtung*
concerning 65 *besorgniserregend*
condition 54 *Bedingung, Zustand*
conditions, working ~ *pl* 101T *Arbeitsbedingungen*
to **conduct sth** 19 *etw (durch)führen, etw leiten*
the **Confederacy** 137 *die Konföderation* (Bund der Südstaaten)
confederate 226 *alliiert, verbündet*
to **confront sb with sb/sth** 30 *jdn mit jdm/etw konfrontieren*
to **confront sth** 63 *sich einer Sache stellen*
to **congratulate sb** 203 *jdn beglückwünschen*
conscious 62 *bewusst*
consciousness 147 *Bewusstsein*
consensus 145 *Konsens*
to **consent** *fml* 186 *zustimmen, einwilligen*
considerably 201T *erheblich, beträchtlich*
consistent 20 *konsistent, widerspruchsfrei*
consultant, management ~ 90 *Unternehmensberater/in*
to **consume** 37 *verbrauchen, konsumieren*
consumption 11 *Verbrauch, Konsum*
to **contaminate sth** 17 *etw verunreinigen, etw kontaminieren*
contemporary 182 *zeitgenössisch*
content 71T *Inhalt*
continual 120 *ständig, ununterbrochen, kontinuierlich*
continuous 65 *kontinuierlich, anhaltend*
to **contradict** 151 *widersprechen*
contradiction 134 *Widerspruch*
contradictory 96 *widersprüchlich*
contribution 21 *Beitrag*
controlled substance 142 *Rauschgift*
convention 181 *Versammlung, Tagung*
to **converse** 73 *sich unterhalten*
to **convert** 15 *umwandeln, konvertieren*
to **convict sb** 150 *jdn verurteilen* (für schuldig befinden)
conviction 142 *Verurteilung*
corporate 19 *Unternehmens-; Geschäfts-*
corporation 97 *Konzern*

cost of living 101T *Lebenshaltungskosten*
costly 165 *kostspielig, teuer*
course of action 78 *Vorgehen, Maßnahmen*
court 65 *Gericht(shof)*
cover up, to **cover sth up** 18T *etw vertuschen*
to **crack a code** 58 *einen Code knacken*
craft 32T *Handwerk*
creation 200 *Schaffung*
credibility 162 *Glaubwürdigkeit*
credit score 233P *Kreditwürdigkeit*
to **credit sb with sth** 238 *jdm etw zuschreiben*
to **criminalize** 225 *illegalisieren*
cripple 250T *Krüppel*
crisis, climate ~ 8 *Klimakrise*
critical mass 233P *kritische Masse*
crop 15 *Nutzpflanze, Feldfrucht*
crop failure 32T *Missernte, Ernteausfall*
to **cross-breed** 52 *kreuzen, durch Kreuzung züchten*
cross-party 233P *parteiübergreifend*
cruel 150 *grausam, gemein*
cruelty 182 *Grausamkeit*
cry, rallying ~ 228 *Parole, Schlachtruf*
cue 252 *Zeichen, Hinweis*
to **cultivate sth** 23 *etw anbauen; etw züchten*
currency 201 *Währung*
current 11 *aktuell, derzeitig*
curriculum 240 *Lehrplan*
custody 70 *Sorgerecht*
custody, police ~ 145 *Polizeigewahrsam*
to **customize sth** 108 *etw anpassen, etw individuell gestalten*

D

data set 62 *Datensatz*
database 181 *Datenbank*
dawn 159 *Morgendämmerung*
dealer 142 *Händler/in*
debt 120 *Schulden*
to **deceive** 93 *täuschen, (be)trügen*
to **declare** 11 *verkünden*
decolonization 188T *Dekolonisierung*
to **decompose** 38 *sich zersetzen, zerfallen*
to **decrease** 53 *abnehmen, zurückgehen*
to **dedicate sth to sb/sth** 191 *jdm/etw etw widmen*
dedicated 188T *engagiert, passioniert*
default 103 *Standard*
defeat 160 *Niederlage*
to **defeat sb** 198T *jdn besiegen, jdn schlagen*
defence 200 *Verteidigung*
to **defend sb/sth** 101T *jdn/etw verteidigen*
defender 192 *Verteidiger/in*
deforestation 9 *Waldzerstörung*
to **degrade sb** 93 *jdn erniedrigen*
degree 158 *Abschluss*
delighted 92 *froh, erfreut*
to **deliver** 71T *liefern, übermitteln*
delivery service 28 *Lieferdienst*
delusion 204 *Illusion, Täuschung*
to **deny (sb) sth** 143 *(jdm) etw verweigern*
to **deny sth** 101T *etw leugnen, etw bestreiten*
dependable 92 *zuverlässig, verlässlich*
dependence 17 *Abhängigkeit*
dependent on sth 15 *von etw abhängig*
depletion 13P *Verringerung, Abbau*
to **deport** 190 *abschieben*
deportation 66 *Abschiebung*
deposit 23 *Vorkommen*
depressed 230 *deprimiert*
to **derail** 99 *entgleisen (lassen)*
descendant 182 *Nachfahre, Nachkomme*
descent 193T *Herkunft, Abstammung*
to **desegregate** 226 *die Rassentrennung aufheben*
desegregation 229 *Aufhebung der Rassentrennung*
desertification 13P *Wüstenbildung, Versteppung*
desire 147 *Wunsch, Verlangen*
desperate 32T *verzweifelt*
desperation 156 *Verzweiflung*
destiny 198T *Schicksal, Bestimmung*
destruction 22 *Zerstörung, Vernichtung*
detached 198 *getrennt*
to **be detained** 190 *in Gewahrsam genommen werden*
detection 69 *Entdeckung, Aufdeckung*
determined 107 *(fest) entschlossen*
to **devalue sb** 235T *jdn abwerten*
devastating 28 *verheerend*
developer 59T *Entwickler/in*
developing country 27 *Entwicklungsland*
devolved 199 *dezentralisiert*
diagnosed, sb is ~ with sth 150T *bei jdm wird etw festgestellt/diagnostiziert*
dictatorship 210P *Diktatur*
to **diminish** 188T *(sich) verringern, abnehmen*
to **dip** 116 *(ein)tauchen*
directed at 55 *gerichtet an*
directional information 252 *Richtungsangaben*
to **dis sb** *infml* 250T *jdn dissen*
disappointment 248 *Enttäuschung*
disclosure *fml* 95T *Offenlegung*
to **disconnect** 76 *abtrennen, die Verbindung unterbrechen*
to **discourage** 121 *entmutigen*
discretion, at sb's ~ 143 *in jds Ermessen*
to **discriminate (against)** 138 *diskriminieren*
discrimination (against sb) 138 *Diskriminierung (eines Menschen)*
discriminatory 136 *benachteiligend, diskriminierend*
to **disgrace sb** 74 *jdn in Verruf bringen*
disgusted 231 *angeekelt*
to **dislocate** 192 *verrenken, auskugeln*
to **dismantle sth** 16T *etw abbauen, etw zerlegen*
disorder, anxiety ~ 150T *Angststörung*
to **dispel a myth** 255 *mit einem Mythos aufräumen*
to **displace sb** 208 *jdn vertreiben*
displacement 181 *Vertreibung*
disproportionate 233 *unverhältnismäßig*
disqualified 252 *ausgeschlossen*
to **disrupt sth** 101 *etw stören, etw behindern*
distant 182 *(weit) entfernt, fern, entlegen*
to **distinguish (between)** 51 *unterscheiden (zwischen)*
to **distract sb** 19 *jdn ablenken*
to **distribute sth** 71 *etw verteilen, etw vertreiben*
distribution 76 *Verteilung*
disunity *fml* 145 *Zerrissenheit*
division 139 *Trennung, Spaltung*
divisive 186 *entzweiend, spalterisch*

executive 99 *Führungskraft*
executive, chief ~ 28 *Geschäftsführer / in*
exempt 143 *ausgenommen, befreit* (von Pflichten)
expansion 22 *Ausweitung, Expansion*
expectation 105 *Erwartung*
expenditure 182 *Ausgaben*
expertise 101T *Fachkenntnisse, Sachverstand*
to **expire** 148 *ablaufen, verfallen*
to **explode** 193 *explodieren*
to **exploit sb** 97 *jdn ausnutzen, jdn ausbeuten*
exploration 165 *Erforschung, Erkundung*
explorer 181 *Forschungsreisende(r), Entdecker / in*
to **expose** 23 *aussetzen* (einer Sache)
exposure (to) 13 *Belastung (durch)*
expression, shift of ~ 72 *Ausdrucksänderung*
to **extend sth** 181 *etw erweitern, etw ausdehnen*
extended 146 *erweitert*
extent 95T *Umfang, Ausmaß*
extinct 10 *ausgestorben*
extinction 9 *Ausrottung, Aussterben*
to **extract sth** 16 *etw gewinnen* (Bodenschätze)
extraction 182 *Gewinnung*
eyelash 73 *Wimper*

F

fabric 27 *Gewebe, Stoff, Tuch*
face to face 76 *persönlich*
to **facilitate sth** 24 *etw ermöglichen, etw vermitteln, etw vereinfachen*
fact sheet 26 *Datenblatt, Merkblatt*
factory farming 37 *Massentierhaltung*
to **fail** 16T *versagen, scheitern*
failure, crop ~ 32T *Missernte, Ernteausfall*
fairly 115 *ziemlich, recht*
faith 160 *Glaube, Vertrauen*
faith, to **put one's ~ in sth** 233 *auf etw vertrauen*
to **fall apart** 152T *auseinanderfallen, platzen*
fame 93 *Ruhm*
famine 13P *Hungersnot*
fault 150 *Schuld, Verschulden*
federal 140 *auf Bundesebene geltend*
federation 235T *Verband, Föderation*
fee 28 *Gebühr*
felony 142 *Verbrechen*
female 234 *Frau, weibliche Person*
fence, to **sit on the ~** 199 *zwischen den Stühlen sitzen*
fencer 235T *Fechter / in*
fertilizer 76 *Dünger, Düngemittel*
to **fetch** 233P *holen, abholen*
fever 23 *Fieber*
file 19 *Datei, Ordner, Akte*
firearm 141 *Schusswaffe*
first, in the ~ place 236T *an erster Stelle, eigentlich, ursprünglich*
fishery 185 *Fischerei, Fischzucht*
to **flare up** 209 *aufflammen*
flavouring 33 *Aroma(stoff)*
flawed 233P *fehlerhaft, mangelhaft*
to **flee** 137 *fliehen*
to **flip** 201T *(sich) umdrehen*
to **flourish** 61 *florieren, blühen, gedeihen*
fluency 186 *Gewandtheit, Flüssigkeit* (Sprache)
folder 238 *Mappe, Ordner*
to **be fond of sb/sth** 199 *jdn gernhaben, etw mögen*
footage 69 *Film- / Bildmaterial*
footprint, carbon ~ 12 *CO2-Bilanz*
force 233P *Triebkraft*
forcibly 210P *gewaltsam; nachdrücklich*
forefather 161 *Vorfahr*
to **foresee sth (foresaw, foreseen)** 61 *etw voraussehen, etw vorhersehen*
former 16T *ehemalig*
fortunate 54 *glücklich*
fossil fuel 9 *fossiler Brennstoff*
foundation 16T *Grundlage, Fundament; Stiftung*
fraction 182 *Bruchteil*
to **fracture** 17 *brechen, aufbrechen*
frame 71T *Rahmen*
framework 230T *Rahmen, Grundlage*
fraud 71 *Betrug*
fraudster 69 *Betrüger / in*
freelance 110T *selbstständig, freiberuflich*
fringe 69 *Rand*
to **frown upon sth** 115 *etw missbilligen*
fugitive 142 *Flüchtling*
fumes, exhaust ~ 13 *Abgase*
functional, to **lack ~ literacy** 182 *nicht richtig lesen und schreiben können*
functionality 62 *Funktionalität*
to **fund sth** 28 *etw finanzieren*
fundraising 57 *Spendensammeln, Geldbeschaffung*

G

to **gain sth** 101T *etw erwerben, etw erlangen*
garbage patch 37 *Müllstrudel*
gas, greenhouse ~ 8 *Treibhausgas*
gay 145 *schwul, lesbisch*
gaze 159 *Blick*
gender imbalance 121 *Ungleichgewicht zwischen den Geschlechtern*
generic 108 *generisch, allgemein, typisch*
generosity 237 *Großzügigkeit*
genetic engineering 52 *Gentechnik, Gentechnologie*
GM (genetically modified) 50 *genetisch verändert*
geological epoch 8 *erdgeschichtliches Zeitalter*
gesture 188T *Geste*
to **gift** 92 *schenken*
gig economy 121 *Gig Economy* (auf Freiberuflern basierendes Wirtschaftsmodell)
gin, (cotton) ~ 230T *Baumwollentkörnungsmaschine*
to **give way to sth** 237 *etw weichen*
glass ceiling 121 *gläserne Decke* (unsichtbare Barriere, die Frauen am beruflichen Aufstieg hindert)
globe 32T *Globus, Welt*
to **glue** 30 *kleben*
GM (genetically modified) 50 *genetisch verändert*
goal 16 *Ziel, Absicht*
goods *pl* 28 *Waren, Güter*
Gosh! 236T *Meine Güte!*
to **govern sth** 181 *etw regieren*
governance 185 *Regierungshandeln, Herrschaft*
Governor *AE* 228 *Gouverneur / in* (USA: Regierungschef/in eines Bundesstaats)
grammar school 246 *Gymnasium*
to **grant** 72 *gewähren, einräumen*
granted, to **take sth for ~** 120 *etw als selbstverständlich betrachten*

grateful 191 *dankbar*
greatly 28 *erheblich*
greenhouse gas 8 *Treibhausgas*
to **greenwash sth** 9 *etw ein grünes Image geben*
grievance 145 *Beschwerde*
to **grieve** 160 *trauern*
grip 236T *Griff*
gross domestic product (GDP) 233P *Bruttosozialprodukt*
on moral grounds 233P *aus moralischen Gründen*
groundbreaking 120 *bahnbrechend*
guardian 143 *Vormund*
guidance 241 *Anleitung, Hilfestellung*
guideline 95T *Richtlinie*
guilt 28 *Schuld(gefühle)*
guilty 96 *schuldig*
guinea pig 111 *Meerschweinchen; Versuchsperson*
gymnast 235T *Turner/in*

H

handcuffed 227 *in Handschellen*
handgun 141 *Handfeuerwaffe, Kurzwaffe*
handsome 73 *attraktiv, gut aussehend*
to **harass sb** 69 *jdn schikanieren, jdn belästigen*
harassment 142 *Schikane, Mobbing, Belästigung*
hardly 181 *kaum*
to **harm sb/sth** 15 *jdm/etw schaden*
harmless 18T *harmlos, ungefährlich*
to **harvest** 15 *ernten*
hatred 234 *Hass, Abscheu*
to **heal** 242 *heilen, verheilen*
healthcare worker 149 *Bedienstete/r im Gesundheitswesen*
heart attack 192 *Herzinfarkt*
to **hearten** 204 *ermutigen*
hearty 189 *herzlich*
heat 59T *Schärfe*
heatwave 36 *Hitzewelle*
heaven 238 *Himmel*
heel 229 *Ferse*
heir 160 *Erbe/Erbin*
herbicide 54 *Unkrautvernichtungsmittel*
hilly 251 *hügelig*
to **hold sb accountable (for sth)** 61 *jdn (für etw) zur Rechenschaft ziehen*
holiday, package ~ 120 *Pauschalreise*
homeland, tribal ~ 166 *Stammesgebiet*
homesickness 193 *Heimweh*
honour 205 *Ehre*
hospitality 104 *Hotel- und Gaststättengewerbe*
to **host** 28 *veranstalten*
to **host (a debate)** 17 *(eine Debatte) moderieren*
hostile 190 *feindlich, feindselig*
hostility 237 *Feindseligkeit*
household 37 *Haushalt, Haushalts-*
how about ...? 248 *wie wäre es mit ...?*
hub 27 *Knotenpunkt, Hauptumschlagplatz*
human rights *pl* 181 *Menschenrechte*
humane 55 *human, menschenwürdig*
humiliation 254 *Demütigung, Erniedrigung*
hurdle 115 *Hürde, Hindernis*
hydrogen 16T *Wasserstoff*
hydropower 14 *Wasserkraft*
hygiene 37 *Hygiene*

I

ID card 150 *Ausweis*
identifiable 11 *erkennbar, identifizierbar*
to **illuminate** 204 *beleuchten*
illumination 69 *Beleuchtung*
illusion, to **be under no ~** 242 *sich nichts vormachen*
imagination 61 *Phantasie, Vorstellungskraft*
imaging 69 *Bildverarbeitung*
imbalance, gender ~ 121 *Ungleichgewicht zwischen den Geschlechtern*
immigration 138 *Einwanderung*
impaired 248 *beeinträchtigt*
to **implement sth** 111 *etw einführen, etw umsetzen, etw einsetzen*
to **imply sth** 209 *etw beinhalten*
to **impose sth on sb** 166 *jdm etw aufzwingen*
imposition 185 *Auferlegung, Verhängung*
impoverishment 185 *Verarmung, Verelendung*
imprisonment 255 *Haft(strafe)*
impunity 233 *Straffreiheit*
inaction 160 *Tatenlosigkeit*
inappropriate 235T *unangemessen, ungeeignet, unpassend*
incident 17 *Vorfall*
inclination 245 *Neigung, Vorliebe*
to **be inclined to do sth** 121 *geneigt sein, etw zu tun*
income 31 *Einkommen*
inconclusive 143 *ergebnislos, uneindeutig*
inconsistent 69 *uneinheitlich, unstimmig*
increasingly 186 *zunehmend, in zunehmendem Maße*
indeed 65 *tatsächlich, in der Tat*
indefinite 192 *unbefristet*
to **indicate** 11 *(an)zeigen, darauf hindeuten, hinweisen auf*
industrialization 138 *Industrialisierung*
to **industrialize** 138 *industrialisieren*
inevitable 23 *unausweichlich, unvermeidbar*
inexorable 204 *unaufhaltsam*
inferior 193T *minderwertig, unterlegen*
to **inflame** 242 *entfachen, entzünden*
influx 137 *Zustrom*
to **inform sth** 244 *etw durchdringen*
to **infringe** 134 *verletzen*
ingenuity 138 *Erfindungsreichtum*
inhabitant 166 *Einwohner/in, Bewohner/in*
inheritance 160 *Erbschaft*
initially 115 *anfangs, anfänglich*
initials *pl* 250T *Initialen*
to **injure sb** 37 *jdn verletzen*
injury 200 *Verletzung*
injustice 182 *Ungerechtigkeit*
to **innovate (sth)** 233P *Neuerungen einführen, (etw neu) einführen*
inquiry 190 *Untersuchung*
insatiable 92 *unersättlich*
inscription 151 *Inschrift*
insecure 65 *unsicher*
insecurity 111 *Unsicherheit*
to **insist** 21 *darauf bestehen, beteuern*
to **inspire** 32T *inspirieren, anregen*
instance 59T *Beispiel, Fall*
to **insure sb** 182 *jdn versichern*
insurer 69 *Versicherer*
intelligence, artificial ~ (AI) 68 *künstliche Intelligenz*

to **intend sth** 56 *etw beabsichtigen*
intense 108 *intensiv*
intensity 20 *Intensität*
intent 229 *Absicht*
to **interact** 76 *interagieren, aufeinander eingehen*
interchangeable 186 *austauschbar*
interface 23 *Schnittstelle*
to **intermarry** 236T *Mischehen schließen*
interstate 233 *zwischenstaatlich*
intertwined 198 *verflochten*
intimate 62 *intim, eng, persönlich*
to **intimidate** 69 *einschüchtern, bedrohen*
intimidation 160 *Einschüchterung*
intrigued 238 *fasziniert*
intriguing 163 *faszinierend, verblüffend*
invasion 165 *Invasion, Eindringen*
inventor 33 *Erfinder / in*
to **investigate sth** 24 *etw ermitteln, etw untersuchen*
investment 53 *Investition*
invoice 95T *Rechnung*
involuntarily 142 *unfreiwillig*
to **involve** 20 *einbeziehen*
involvement (in) 65 *Beteiligung (an), Einbindung (in)*
irreversible 36 *unumkehrbar*
islander 16T *Inselbewohner / in*
to **issue** 142 *erteilen, erlassen*
to **itch** 231 *jucken*
Ivy League 158 die acht Eliteuniversitäten in den USA

J

jerk chicken 193T mariniertes gegrilltes Hühnchen
jewelry *AE* 69 *Schmuck*
joint 197 *gemeinsam, gemeinschaftlich*
to **judge** 155 *(be)urteilen, ermessen*
judgement 97 *Wertung*
judgement, error in ~ 54 *Fehleinschätzung*
just 160 *gerecht*
justice 31 *Gerechtigkeit*

K

to **be keen on sth** 228 *auf etw versessen sein*
kinetic energy 14 *Bewegungsenergie*
to **knit** 238 *stricken*

L

to **label** 59T *beschriften, etikettieren, benennen*
laboratory 16T *Labor*
to **lack functional literacy** 182 *nicht richtig lesen und schreiben können*
lack (of) 233P *Mangel (an)*
lad *infml* 199 *Junge*
laid off 110T *arbeitslos*
lake 161 *(Binnen-)See*
landfill site 27 *Mülldeponie*
lass *ScotE* 199 *Mädchen*
to **last** 140 *dauern, andauern*
latter 116 *letztere / r / s*
to **launch** 28 (Produkt) *auf den Markt bringen, einführen*
law enforcement 65 *Gesetzesvollzug, Polizeigewalt*
lawsuit 30 *Gerichtsverfahren, Prozess*
to **lay down** 187 *niederlegen, aufzeichnen*
to **lead the way** 251 *vorangehen*
to **leak** 33 *auslaufen, lecken*
learning disability 247 *Lernbehinderung, Lernschwäche*
lease 110T *Miete, Pacht*
leave, paternity ~ 254 *Vaterschaftsurlaub*
leaves *pl* 31 *Blätter, Laub*
legacy 16T *Erbe, Altlast*
to **legalize** 242 *legalisieren*
to **legislate** 103 *Gesetze erlassen*
legislator 71 *Abgeordnete / r*
leisure facility 226 *Freizeiteinrichtung*
leotard 235T *Gymnastikanzug, Trikot*
lesbian 240 *lesbisch*
letter to the editor 243 *Leserbrief*
level, sea ~ 11 *Meeresspiegel*
liberty 146 *Freiheit*
life expectancy 201 *Lebenserwartung*
to **be likely to do sth** 95T *etw wahrscheinlich tun (werden)*
likeness 71T *Abbild*
to **limit sth** 61 *etw begrenzen, etw einschränken*
to **linger** 193 *verweilen, fortbestehen*
liquid 17 *Flüssigkeit*
literacy, to **lack functional ~** 182 *nicht richtig lesen und schreiben können*
living, cost of ~ 101T *Lebenshaltungskosten*
loaf, *pl* **loaves** 58 *Laib*
to **loan** 28 *ausleihen*
local 122 *Einheimische / r*
local authority 241 *(Kommunal-) Behörde*
to **be located in** 140 *sich in … befinden, in … liegen*
lock 67T *Schloss*
logging 13P *Abholzung*
loneliness 62 *Einsamkeit*
long-term 53 *langfristig, Langzeit-*
loophole 141 *Gesetzeslücke*
loose 235T *locker, lose*
loss 22 *Verlust*

M

major 11 *Haupt-, wesentlich, größer*
to **major in sth** 150T *etw* (als Hauptfach) *studieren*
to **make the effort** 115 *sich die Mühe geben*
to **make up sth** 236T *etw bilden, etw ausmachen*
malnutrition 13P *Unterernährung, falsche Ernährung*
management consultant 90 *Unternehmensberater / in*
mandatory 149 *verpflichtend, vorgeschrieben, obligatorisch*
manner 92 *Art, Wesen*
manners *pl* 114 *Manieren, Umgangsformen*
manual labourer 193T *Handarbeiter / in*
manufacturer 21 *Hersteller / in, Produzent / in*
manufacturing 18T *Fertigung, Herstellung*
to **march** 193T *marschieren*
marginalized 146 *ausgegrenzt*
marital status 240 *Familienstand*
to **market** 59 *vermarkten*
mashed potatoes 59T *Kartoffelpüree*
matchmaker 237 *Heiratsvermittler / in*
matchmaking 237 *Partnervermittlung*
raw material 101T *Rohstoff*
maternity 103 *Mutterschaft*
to **measure** 37 *messen*
meet, to **make ends ~** 110T *über die Runden kommen*
to **melt** 10 *schmelzen, abschmelzen*
meltdown 71T *Schmelze*

member, MP (= Member of Parliament) 181 *Parlamentsabgeordnete/r*
mentor 32T *Mentor/in*
mercy 160 *Gnade*
to **merge sth with sth** 160 *etw mit etw verschmelzen*
metric 233P *Kennzahl, Metrik*
metropolitan 251 *großstädtisch*
microbead 37 *Mikrokügelchen*
midst, in the ~ of sth 230T *inmitten von etw*
might 160 *Macht*
to **migrate** 254 *auswandern, migrieren*
migratory 210P *migratorisch, Wander-, Zug-*
milestone 255 *Meilenstein*
to **mimic sb (mimicked, mimicked)** 69 *jdn nachahmen*
mind, to **come to ~** 203 *einfallen*
mindset 108 *Mentalität, Denkweise*
mine 22 *Bergwerk, Mine*
minefield 251 *Minenfeld, gefährliches Terrain*
miner, coal ~ 244 *Bergarbeiter/in*
minor 149 *Minderjährige/r*
to **mislead (-led, -led)** 19 *täuschen*
misogyny *fml* 233 *Frauenfeindlichkeit*
to **miss out** 244 *zu kurz kommen*
to **miss out on sth** 108 *etw verpassen*
mistrust 245 *Misstrauen*
to **mock sb** 69 *sich über jdn lustig machen*
to **model sth on sth** 62 *etw einer Sache zum Vorbild nehmen, etw einer Sache nachbilden*
modify, genetically modified (GM) 50 *genetisch verändert*
to **modify sth** 52 *etw (ver)ändern, etw modifizieren*
to **molest sb** 235T *jdn (sexuell) belästigen, jdn missbrauchen*
on moral grounds 233P *aus moralischen Gründen*
morality 97 *Moral* (Wertesystem)
morgue 229 *Leichenschauhaus*
motion 72 *Bewegung*
MP (= Member of Parliament) 181 *Parlamentsabgeordnete/r*
murder 142 *Mord*
murderous 229 *mörderisch*

N

naked 73 *nackt*
narration *fml* 162 *Erzählung, Geschichte*
nearshoring 100 *Produktions(zurück)verlagerung in die Nähe*
not necessarily 234 *nicht unbedingt*
necessity 97 *Notwendigkeit*
neck, to **breathe down sb's ~** 155 *jdm im Nacken sitzen*
to **neglect sb/sth** 115 *jdn/etw vernachlässigen*
negotiation 116 *Verhandlung, Vermittlung*
neither … nor … 182 *weder … noch …*
net 16T *netto, Netto-*
net, (social) safety ~ 156 *soziales Netz*
neuroscientist 230T *Neurowissenschaftler/in*
to **nominate** 240 *nominieren*
non-binary 233 *non-binär, divers*
nor, neither … ~ … 182 *weder … noch …*
nosy 65 *neugierig*
notion 72 *Vorstellung, Auffassung*
nuclear power station 37 *Kernkraftwerk*
numerous 20 *zahlreich*
nutrient 53 *Nährstoff*
nutritious 54 *nahrhaft*

O

oat 58 *Hafer*
obituary 110T *Nachruf*
obligated 71T *verpflichtet*
to **observe sth** 73 *etw beobachten*
obsessed with 152T *besessen von*
obstacle 158 *Hindernis*
obvious 53 *offensichtlich, klar*
occasion 146 *Anlass, Gelegenheit*
occasional poem 161 *Festgedicht*
occupation 150 *Beruf, Tätigkeit, Beschäftigung*
to **occupy sth** 121 *etw einnehmen, etw besetzen, etw innehaben*
to **occur** 16 *stattfinden, passieren, geschehen*
odd 111 *gelegentlich*
oddity 65 *Eigentümlichkeit*
offence 115 *Beleidigung*
offender 191 *Straftäter/in*
offensive 250T *beleidigend, anstößig*
official 186 *Beamte/r, Funktionär/in*
offset, (carbon) ~ 20 *Klimakompensation*
offshoring 100 *Produktionsverlagerung ins Ausland*
oil rig 16T *Ölbohrinsel*
one another 159 *einander, sich (gegenseitig)*
open-minded 243T *aufgeschlossen, offen*
operation 19 *Arbeitsablauf, Arbeitsgang, Betrieb, Geschäft*
opponent 142 *Gegner/in*
opportunities, equal ~ *pl* 233P *Chancengleichheit*
to **oppose sth** 165 *gegen etw opponieren, sich gegen etw widersetzen*
to **be opposed to sth** 16 *gegen etw sein*
opposition (to) 236 *Widerstand (gegen)*
to **oppress** 138 *unterdrücken*
oppression 137 *Unterdrückung*
orthodoxy 233P *Lehrmeinung*
outage 252 *Ausfall*
outlawed 164 *geächtet*
to **outline sth** 25 *etw skizzieren, etw grob beschreiben*
outstanding 59T *hervorragend, überragend, außergewöhnlich*
to **outweigh sth** 57 *etw übertreffen*
oven 58 *Backofen*
overconsumption 9 *Überkonsum*
to **overheat** 36 *(sich) überhitzen*
to **overplay** 204 *übertreiben*
overpopulated 36 *überbevölkert*
overpopulation 150 *Überbevölkerung*
to **overturn** 198T *umstürzen, kippen*
overwhelming 97 *überwältigend*
to **owe sb sth** 140 *jdm etw schulden*
ownership 143 *Besitzverhältnisse*
oxygen 10 *Sauerstoff*

P

to **pack sth** 238 *etw füllen*
package holiday 120 *Pauschalreise*
packaging 18T *Verpackung*
palsy, cerebral ~ 250T *Zerebralparese* (Lähmung)
panel 15 *Platte, Tafel, Kollektor*
paperwork 148 *Formalitäten*
parcel 23 *Paket; Parzelle*
MP (= Member of Parliament) 181 *Parlamentsabgeordnete/r*
part …, part … 32T *teils …, teils …*
participant 17 *Teilnehmer/in*
particular 33 *bestimmt, speziell*
to **partition** 210P *abtrennen, aufteilen*
passion 135 *Leidenschaft*
passionate 32T *leidenschaftlich*
paternity leave 254 *Vaterschaftsurlaub*

to **patronize sb** 250T *jdn von oben herab behandeln, bevormunden; jdn beschützen*
pavement 251 *Gehsteig, Bürgersteig*
pay gap 233P *Lohngefälle*
paycheck *AE* 110T *Gehalt(sscheck)*
payment 190 *Bezahlung, Zahlung*
peace 59 *Frieden*
peacebuilding 233 *Friedenskonsolidierung*
peacekeeper 233 *Soldat / in einer Friedenstruppe*
peacemaking 233 *Friedensschaffung*
penitentiary 158 *Gefängnis*
pension 192 *Rente, Pension*
to **perceive sth** 77 *etw wahrnehmen, etw erkennen*
percentage 22 *Prozentsatz, Anteil*
perception 232 *Wahrnehmung*
perceptive 77 *scharfsinnig; einfühlsam*
permit 141 *Genehmigung; Bewilligung*
perpetrator 182 *Verursacher / in, (Straf-)Täter / in*
to **persecute sb** 138 *jdn verfolgen* (z.B. aus politischen Gründen)
persecution 137 *Verfolgung*
perseverance 138 *Ausdauer*
to **persevere** 138 *durchhalten*
to **persist** 193T *fortbestehen*
personnel 229 *Personal*
to **phase out** 37 *auslaufen lassen*
pilot scheme 251 *Pilotprojekt*
to **pin to the ground** 227 *auf den Boden drücken*
pity, to **feel ~ for sb** 152T *mit jdm Mitleid haben*
place, in the first ~ 236T *an erster Stelle, eigentlich, ursprünglich*
to **be plain sailing** 242 *eine glatte Sache sein*
plantation 13P *Plantage*
pleasant 110T *angenehm*
to **poison** 15 *vergiften*
polarization 135 *Polarisierung*
policing 191 *Polizeiarbeit*
policy 233P *Politik, Vorgehensweise*
to **polish sth** 71T *etw (auf)polieren*
pollination 36 *Bestäubung*
pollutant 13 *Schadstoff*
to **pollute sth** 36 *etw verschmutzen*
pollution 9 *(Umwelt-) Verschmutzung*
to **portray** 182 *darstellen, schildern*
to **pose a question** 53 *eine Frage aufwerfen*
to **possess sth** 141 *etw besitzen*
mashed potatoes 59T *Kartoffelpüree*
poultry 57 *Geflügel*
to **pour** 189 *gießen, schütten*
power station 15 *Kraftwerk*
power, nuclear ~ station 37 *Kernkraftwerk*
powerless 229 *machtlos, unfähig*
to **preach** 32T *predigen*
preacher 227 *Prediger / in*
precedent 198 *Präzedenzfall, Beispiel, Tradition*
predecessor 109 *Vorgänger / in, Vorläufer / in*
predictability 157 *Berechenbarkeit*
predictable 16 *voraussagbar, vorhersehbar*
predictor 62 *Indikator*
pregnancy 104 *Schwangerschaft*
pregnant 104 *schwanger*
to **prescribe** 235T *vorschreiben, verordnen*
preservation 76 *Konservierung*
to **preserve sth** 146 *etw bewahren, etw erhalten*
presidency 152T *Präsidentschaft*
to **presume sth** 188T *etw annehmen, etw vermuten, etw voraussetzen*
to **prevent sth** 13P *etw (ver) hindern, einer Sache vorbeugen*
preview 8 *Vorschau*
previous 24 *vorherig, früher*
price tag 24 *Preisschild*
primarily 120 *vorrangig, hauptsächlich*
primary school 241 *Grundschule*
principally 236T *grundsätzlich, hauptsächlich*
prior 142 *vorherig*
to **prioritize sth** 250 *etw der Wichtigkeit nach ordnen, etw priorisieren*
priority 67T *Priorität, Vorrang*
to **prize** 156 *schätzen*
processed 58 *verarbeitet*
processing 76 *Verarbeitung*
production line 26 *Fließband, Produktion(sstraße)*
profession 233P *Beruf*
profound 113 *tief greifend, tief gehend, fundiert*
to **prohibit sb from sth** 165 *jdm etw untersagen*
prohibited 142 *verboten*
to **project sth** 57 *etw prognostizieren, vorhersagen*
to **prolong sth** 93 *etw verlängern, etw herauszögern*
to **promote sth** 14 *etw fördern, etw unterstützen*
promotion 104 *Beförderung*
to **prompt sb to do sth** 192 *jdn veranlassen, etw zu tun*
proof of concept 16T *Machbarkeitsnachweis*
properly 54 *richtig, ordentlich, korrekt*
to **propose sth** 20 *etw vorschlagen, etw unterbreiten, etw darlegen*
prospect 156 *Aussicht, Perspektive*
prosperity 208 *Wohlstand*
protection 51 *Schutz*
proverb 188T *Sprichwort*
provincial 198T *provinziell*
to **provoke** 229 *auslösen, hervorrufen*
public, to **take a company ~** 233P *ein Unternehmen an die Börse zu bringen*
to **punish sb** 61 *jdn bestrafen*
purchase 51 *Kauf, Ankauf*
to **purchase sth** *fml* 120 *etw kaufen, erwerben*
purpose 163 *Absicht, Zweck*
to **pursue sth** 65 *einer Sache nachgehen, etw verfolgen*

Q

quotation 8 *Zitat*

R

racial bias 62 *rassistische Voreingenommenheit*
to **radiate** 38 *strahlen*
radiation 13 *Strahlung; Bestrahlung*
raid 240 *Razzia*
to **raise awareness about sth (rose, risen)** 36 *auf etw aufmerksam machen*
rallying cry 228 *Parole, Schlachtruf*
random 72 *zufällig, beliebig*
rape 233 *Vergewaltigung*
to **rate sth** 57 *etw einstufen, etw bewerten*
raw material 101T *Rohstoff*
reality 230 *Realität, Wirklichkeit*
to **realize sth** 161 *etw verwirklichen, etw ausführen*
reasonable 57 *vernünftig*

to **rebuild** 161 *umbauen, erneuern*
to **recall** 111 *sich erinnern*
to **receive sth** 32T *etw erhalten, etw empfangen*
recipient 115 *Empfänger / in*
reciprocity *fml* 143 *Gegenseitigkeit*
to **recite sth** 134 *etw vortragen*
to **reclaim** 250T *zurückgewinnen*
recognition, to **change sth beyond ~** 242 *etw so verändern, dass es nicht wiederzuerkennen ist*
recollection *fml* 191 *Erinnerung*
reconciliation, budget ~ bill 150T Haushaltsgesetzgebungsverfahren in den USA
to **record sth** 27 *etw dokumentieren, etw verzeichnen, etw aufzeichnen*
to **recover** 57 *sich erholen*
to **recreate** 61 *wiederherstellen, nachbauen*
recreational 120 *Freizeit-, Erholungs-*
to **recruit sb** 109 *jdn anwerben, jdn neu einstellen*
to **redefine sth** 233P *etw neu definieren*
redistribution 122 *Umverteilung*
redundant, to **be made ~** 121 *entlassen werden, den Arbeitsplatz verlieren*
referred to as 22 *bezeichnet als*
to **reflect sth** 96 *etw reflektieren, etw widerspiegeln*
reflection 32T; 69 *Betrachtung; Reflexion, Spiegelbild*
refuge 204 *Zuflucht*
refusal 229 *Ablehnung, Verweigerung*
to **regain** 137 *wiedererlangen*
regarding 20 *bezüglich, betreffend*
to **regenerate** 37 *sich regenerieren*
registration 239 *Anmeldung*
to **regret** 236 *bedauern, bereuen*
regulation 67 *Regulierung, Vorschrift*
regulations *pl* 58 *Vorschriften, Bestimmungen*
regulatory 142 *regulatorisch, behördlich*
reign 181 *Regierungszeit*
to **reject** 20 *ablehnen, zurückweisen*
to **relate to sth** 11; 11 *sich mit etw identifizieren; mit etw in Zusammenhang stehen*
relation 90 *Beziehung, Verhältnis*
in relation to 21 *in Bezug auf*
release 17 *Freisetzung*
to **release sth** 36 *etw freisetzen*
relentless 93 *unerbittlich, unbarmherzig*
reliance (on sth) 16T *Abhängigkeit (von etw)*
relief 111 *Erleichterung, Entlastung*
relieved 193T *erleichtert*
reluctant 237 *widerwillig*
to **rely on sb/sth** 16T *sich auf jdn / etw verlassen*
to **remain** 16T *bleiben*
remains *pl* 16T *(Über-)Reste, Relikte*
reminder 65 *Erinnerung, Mahnung*
remotely 77 *aus der Ferne*
removal 188 *Entfernung, Abschaffung*
to **render** 69 *rendern (berechnen und ausgeben)*
to **renew** 36 *erneuern*
renewable 10 *erneuerbar*
renewables 8 *erneuerbare Energien*
reparation 188T *Entschädigung, Wiedergutmachung*
to **repay** 188T *zurückzahlen*
to **repeal sth** 241 *etw widerrufen, etw aufheben*
repercussion 209 *Auswirkung, Konsequenz*
repetitive 247 *sich wiederholend*
replacement 152T *Ersatz, Ersetzung, Austausch*
to **replicate** 58 *nachbilden*
reportedly 69 *Berichten zufolge*
to **represent sth** 144 *etw darstellen*
representative 17 *Vertreter / in, Beauftragte / r*
to **reproduce** 77 *nachbilden*
reproductive health 13P *Fortpflanzungsgesundheit*
reputation 198T *Ansehen, Ruf*
to **request sth** *fml* 103 *etw (an)fordern, etw erbitten, um etw bitten*
resale 27 *Weiterverkauf, Wiederverkauf*
researcher 12 *Forscher / in, Wissenschaftler / in*
to **resettle** 164 *umsiedeln*
to **reshape** 232 *umgestalten, neu formen*
residency *fml* 151 *Wohnsitz*
to **resign** 194 *zurücktreten*
resilience 146 *Widerstandsfähigkeit, Belastbarkeit*
resilient 52 *widerstandsfähig*
to **resist sth** 191 *sich gegen etw wehren*
resistance (to) 53 *Widerstand (gegen)*
to **resolve sth** 116 *etw (auf)lösen*
resource 9 *Ressource, Rohstoff*
respective 188T *jeweilig*
respondent 26 *Befragte / r*
responsibility 9 *Verantwortung*
to **restore sth** 186 *etw restaurieren, etw wieder herstellen*
to **restrict (to)** 142 *einschränken, beschränken (auf)*
restriction 66 *Beschränkung, Einschränkung*
restrictive 245 *einschränkend*
to **result in sth** 186 *zu etw führen, etw ergeben*
retail 121 *Einzelhandel*
retailer 28 *Einzelhändler / in*
to **retain sb/sth** 236T *jdn / etw behalten, etw beibehalten, etw bewahren*
to **rethink** 99 *überdenken*
retirement 110T *Ruhestand, Rente*
to **retrace** 193T *zurückverfolgen, wieder auffinden*
to **retrieve** 73 *abrufen, wiederfinden*
return 53 *Ertrag, Rendite*
revealing 235T *offenherzig* (Kleidung), *freizügig*
revenue 113 *Einkünfte, Einnahmen*
reversal 252 *Umkehr, Umkehrung*
review 9 *Über-, Rückblick, Zusammenfassung*
to **review sth** 9 *etw wiederholen*
to **reward** 150 *belohnen*
rhetoric 242 *Redekunst, Phrasendrescherei*
riches *pl* 137 *Reichtum*
rider 32T *Fahrer / in* (Passagier/in)
to **ridicule sb** 152T *jdn lächerlich machen*
rife 201 *weit verbreitet*
oil rig 16T *Ölbohrinsel*
right-wing 194 *rechtsgerichtet*
rights, Bill of R~ 136 Grundrechte-Zusatzartikel der amerikanischen Verfassung
rightful 186 *rechtmäßig*
riot 191 *Aufstand, Aufruhr*
ripe 114 *reif*
risk, to **put sth at ~** 150T *etw gefährden*
roast 56 *gebraten*
root 31 *Wurzel*
royalty-free 163 *gebührenfrei, lizenzfrei*

storage, carbon capture and ~ 20 *CO_2-Abscheidung und -Speicherung*
straight *infml* 225 *hetero(sexuell)*
strand 69 *Strähne*
to **strengthen** 233P *kräftigen, stärken*
to **stress** 23 *betonen, hervorheben*
with no strings attached 111 *ohne Auflagen*
struggle 227 *Kampf*
subject 190 *Staatsbürger/in*
to **be subjected to sth** 136 *etw unterworfen sein*
to **submit** 142 *einreichen, vorlegen, zusenden*
subsidiary 69 *Tochtergesellschaft, Filiale*
substance, controlled ~ 142 *Rauschgift*
substantially 104 *erheblich, im Wesentlichen*
substitute 57 *Ersatz*
to **substitute** 57 *jdn/etw ersetzen*
to **succeed** 151 *erfolgreich sein, Erfolg haben*
successor 159 *Nachfolger/in*
such as 10 *wie (zum Beispiel)*
to **suffer from sth** 108 *unter etw leiden*
sufficient 36 *ausreichend, hinreichend*
suffrage 121 *Wahlrecht*
suicide 142 *Selbstmord*
to **suit** 121 *passen*
superior 236T *überlegen, höherwertig*
superpower 137 *Supermacht*
supplement 61 *Ergänzung*
supply chain 99 *Lieferkette*
supportive 243T *hilfreich, verständnisvoll*
to **suppose** 18T *vermuten, annehmen*
supposedly 230T *vermeintlich, angeblich*
supremacist 226 *Rassist/in, Verfechter/in der Rassentrennung*
supremacy 227 *Vorherrschaft*
surly 238 *mürrisch*
surname 185 *Nachname*
surveillance 65 *Überwachung*
to **suspect sth** 59T *etw vermuten*
to **suspend sb** 229 *jdn suspendieren*
suspicion 254 *Misstrauen; Verdacht*
to **sustain sth** 92 *etw (aufrecht) erhalten*
sustainability 8 *Nachhaltigkeit*
sustained 38 *anhaltend, ununterbrochen*
sword, double-edged ~ 37 *zweischneidiges Schwert*
sympathetic to 238 *wohlwollend gegenüber*
synthetic 51 *künstlich, synthetisch*

T

to **tackle sth** 37 *etw* (z.B. ein Problem) *angehen, etw bewältigen*
tag, price ~ 24 *Preisschild*
to **take advantage of sth** 101T *sich etw zunutze machen, etw ausnutzen*
to **take sth apart** 16T *etw auseinandernehmen*
taste 57 *Geschmack*
tax 99 *Steuer*
to **team up with sb** 59T *mit jdm zusammenarbeiten, sich mit jdm zusammentun*
to **tell apart** 72 *auseinander halten*
temper 117 *Laune*
to **tend to do sth** 233P *dazu neigen, etw zu tun*
tender 115 *zart*
in terms of ... 122 *was ... betrifft/angeht*
terrifying 160 *furchterregend*
texture 58 *Konsistenz, Beschaffenheit*
thorough 116 *gründlich, sorgfältig*
thoroughly 54 *gründlich, aufmerksam*
thought 25 *Gedanke*
thoughtful 58 *wohlüberlegt, gut durchdacht*
threat 17 *Bedrohung*
thrilled 250T *begeistert*
thrilling 203 *aufregend, spannend*
throughout ... 32T *der/die/das ganze ... (hindurch)*
tidal 14 *Gezeiten-*
tide 16T *Gezeit(en), Tide*
tide, spring ~ 16T *Springflut*
to **tie** 230T *binden*
to **tie together** 160 *miteinander verbinden, zusammenbinden*
tight 73 *eng*
to **tighten sth** 192 *etw anziehen, etw verschärfen*
tirelessly 191 *unermüdlich*
titan 198T *Titan, Riese*
toe 116 *Zeh*
token 28 *Gutschein*
toll 150T *Gebühr, Tribut*
tough 108 *hart, schwer*
toxic 26 *giftig, Gift-*
toxin 53 *Gift*
trade 23 *Handel*
trade barriers *pl* 120 *Handelsschranke, Handelshemmnis*
to **trade** 101T *handeln, Handel (be) treiben*
trader 181 *Händler/in*
transient 93 *vorübergehend*
transition 16T *Übergang, Umstellung*
to **translate** 115 *übersetzen*
transmission 22 *Übertragung*
transnational 102 *länderübergreifend, grenzüberschreitend*
to **transpose** 69 *austauschen*
to **treasure** 28 *schätzen, pflegen*
to **treat sb** 96 *jdn behandeln*
treatment 20 *Behandlung*
treaty 20 *(Staats-)Vertrag*
trial 112 *Versuch, Studie*
trial, to **put sb on ~** 61 *jdn vor Gericht stellen*
tribal homeland 166 *Stammesgebiet*
trillion 100 *Billion*
troop 228 *Truppe*
troubled 208 *mit Problemen belastet, geplagt*
turmoil 145 *Unruhen*
turn of events 152T *Wende der Ereignisse/des Schicksals*
twig 31 *Zweig*

U

ultimate 138 *ultimativ*
ultimately 192 *letztlich, letztendlich*
unanticipated 61 *unerwartet*
unarmed 227 *unbewaffnet*
unattainability 155 *Unerreichbarkeit*
unbearable 190 *unerträglich*
unbeknown to sb *fml* 192 *ohne jds Wissen*
uncertainty 110T *Ungewissheit, Unsicherheit*
to **underestimate sb/sth** 195 *jdn/etw unterschätzen*
to **undermine** 68 *untergraben*
to **unearth sth** 65 *etw ausgraben, etw aufstöbern*
unemployment 91 *Arbeitslosigkeit*
unethical 31 *unethisch, nicht vertretbar*
unified 145 *vereint*
to **unify** 178 *vereinigen*

Bildquellen

Cover: (Foto) Shutterstock.com / Oliver Foerstner; (Gestaltung & Produktmarke) Rosendahl Berlin - Agentur für Markendesign **S. 8/Section A:** Shutterstock.com / TR STOK; **S. 8/Section B:** Shutterstock.com / Gyuszko-Photo; **S. 8/Section F:** Shutterstock.com / I. Noyan Yilmaz; **S. 8/Illu:** Shutterstock.com / Qualit Design; **S. 9/Section C:** Shutterstock.com / Ivan Marc; **S. 9/Section D:** Shutterstock.com / Al'fred; **S. 9/Section E:** Shutterstock.com / Photographee.eu; **S. 10:** Cornelsen / Uwe Rogal; **S. 11:** Shutterstock.com / Nattakorn_Maneerat; **S. 13/1:** Shutterstock.com / TR STOK; **S. 13/2:** Shutterstock.com / Vlad61, **S. 14/1:** Shutterstock.com / Gyuszko-Photo; **S. 14/2:** Cornelsen / Uwe Rogal; **S. 16/1:** WILLIAM EDWARDS / AFPTV / SSE RENEWABLES / NOVA INNOVATION / GREENPEACE / AFP; **S. 16/2:** Statista.com; **S. 17:** Shutterstock com / VectorMine; **S. 18:** Shutterstock.com / Ivan Marc; **S. 19:** Cartoonstock / Ron Morgan; **S. 21:** Shutterstock.com / PhotoSGH; **S. 22:** Shutterstock.com / Al'fred; **S. 26/1:** Shutterstock.com / Photographee.eu; **S. 26/2:** Cornelsen / Uwe Rogal; **S. 28:** Shutterstock.com / Blan-k; **S. 30/1:** mauritius images / Chromorange; **S. 30/2:** mauritius images / alamy stock photo / SOPA Images Limited; **S. 30/3:** mauritius images / alamy stock photo / MARK LAING; **S. 30/4:** mauritius images / alamy stock photo / Angela Swann; **S. 31:** Shutterstock.com / rolandtopor; **S. 32:** Shutterstock.com / Luna Vandoorne; **S. 33/1:** Shutterstock.com / mynewturtle; **S. 33/2:** Shutterstock.com / I. Noyan Yilmaz; **S. 33/3:** Shutterstock.com / alterfalter; **S. 34/1:** Shutterstock.com / iluistrator; **S. 34/2:** Shutterstock.com / Jess Kraft; **S. 34/3:** Shutterstock.com / Rich Carey; **S. 36:** Shutterstock.com / Marc Bruxelle; **S. 37:** Shutterstock.com / Larina Marina; **S. 39:** Shutterstock.com / In-Finity; **S. 40:** Shutterstock.com / BenzSuthep; **S. 43/1:** Shutterstock.com / Blan-k; **S. 43/2:** Shutterstock.com / AVIcon; **S. 43/3:** Shutterstock.com / Chippo Medved; **S. 43/4:** Shutterstock.com / Drk_Smith; **S. 44/1:** Cornelsen / Uwe Rogal; **S. 44/2:** Statista.com; **S. 44/3:** Cornelsen / Uwe Rogal; **S. 45:** Shutterstock.com / Qualit Design; **S. 49/1:** Shutterstock.com / Marti Bug Catcher; **S. 49/2:** Cartoonstock / Jesse Springer; **S. 50/Section A:** Shutterstock.com / machimorales; **S. 50/Section B:** Shutterstock.com / Pixsooz; **S. 50/Section F:** Shutterstock.com / Olga Nikonova; **S. 50/Illu:** Shutterstock.com / Flash Vector; **S. 51/Section C:** Shutterstock.com / Miriam Doerr Martin Frommherz; **S. 51/Section D:** Shutterstock.com / robuart; **S. 51/Section E:** Shutterstock.com / MDV Edwards; **S. 52/1:** Shutterstock.com / LiuSol; **S. 52/2:** Shutterstock.com / fizkes; **S. 52/3:** Shutterstock.com / Rocketclips, Inc.; **S. 52/4:** Shutterstock.com / stockphoto mania; **S. 52/5:** Shutterstock.com / carmen2011; **S. 55/1:** Shutterstock.com / machimorales; **S. 55/2:** Cartoonstock / Mike Baldwin; **S. 56/1:** Shutterstock.com / Foodio; **S. 56/2:** Shutterstock.com / shakim888; **S. 56/3:** Shutterstock.com / Vladislav Noseek; **S. 56/4:** Shutterstock.com / hlphoto; **S. 56/5:** Shutterstock.com / Dzha33; **S. 56/6:** Shutterstock.com / Q77photo; **S. 56/7:** Shutterstock.com / NTL Photography; **S. 59:** Shutterstock.com / Pixsooz; **S. 60/1:** Shutterstock.com / Miriam Doerr Martin Frommherz; **S. 60/2:** Shutterstock.com / Terelyuk; **S. 60/3:** Shutterstock.com / metamorworks; **S. 60/4:** EMMANUELLE BAILLON / AFP VIDEOGRAPHICS / AFP; **S. 63:** Cartoonstock / Jeremy Nguyen; **S. 64/1:** Shutterstock.com / SkyPics Studio; **S. 64/2:** Shutterstock.com / korisbo; **S. 65:** Shutterstock.com / whiteMocca; **S. 66:** Shutterstock.com / robuart; **S. 68/1:** Shutterstock.com / MDV Edwards; **S. 68/2:** Shutterstock.com / THP Creative; **S. 68/3:** Shutterstock.com / MDV Edwards; **S. 68/4:** Shutterstock.com / THP Creative; **S. 72/1:** Shutterstock.com / Phonlamai Photo; **S. 72/2:** Shutterstock.com / Olga Nikonova; **S. 74:** Shutterstock.com / homeworlds; **S. 75:** Shutterstock.com / Aleksandr Merg; **S. 76/1:** Shutterstock.com / Africa Studio; **S. 76/2:** Shutterstock.com / Aleksandar Malivuk; **S. 77:** Shutterstock.com / thinkhubstudio; **S. 82:** Cartoonstock / Jody Zellman; **S. 83:** Cartoonstock / Pat Byrnes; **S. 84:** Shutterstock.com / Flash Vector; **S. 88:** Statista.com; **S. 89:** Cartoonstock / Fran; **S. 90/Section A:** Shutterstock.com / Daxiao Productions; **S. 90/Section B:** Shutterstock.com / Stokkete; **S. 90/Section G:** Shutterstock.com / ArtisticPhoto; **S. 90/Illu:** Shutterstock.com / Mascha Tace; **S. 91/Section C:** Shutterstock.com / Nomad_Soul; **S. 91/Section D:** Shutterstock.com / Prazis Images; **S. 91/Section E:** Shutterstock.com / Rawpixel.com; **S. 91/Section F:** Shutterstock.com / Rawpixel.com; **S. 92/1:** Shutterstock.com / Seahorse Vector; **S. 92/2:** dpa Picture-Alliance / empics / PA Wire / Isabel Infantes; **S. 95:** Shutterstock.com / Daxiao Productions; **S. 96/1:** Shutterstock.com / Stokkete; **S. 96/2:** Shutterstock.com / megaflopp; **S. 96/3:** Shutterstock.com / William Potter; **S. 98:** Deutsche Welle; **S. 99/1:** Shutterstock.com / Toria; **S. 99/2:** Shutterstock.com / Nomad_Soul; **S. 100:** Shutterstock.com / titov dmitriy; **S. 102:** Cartoonstock / Karsten Schley; **S. 103/1:** Shutterstock.com / Prazis Images; **S. 103/2:** Cartoonstock / Jonathan Brown; **S. 104:** Shutterstock.com / Big Joe; **S. 106:** Statista.com; **S. 107/1:** Shutterstock.com / DisobeyArt; **S. 107/2:** Shutterstock.com / browndogstudios; **S. 108:** Shutterstock.com / Rawpixel.com; **S. 110/1:** Cartoonstock / Harley Schwadron; **S. 110/2:** Shutterstock.com / Rawpixel.com; **S. 111:** Shutterstock.com / Bakhtiar Zein; **S. 114/1:** Cornelsen / Uwe Rogal; **S. 114/MGL-Flagge:** Shutterstock.com / aarrows; **S. 114/J-Flagge:** Shutterstock.com / Alex Vector; **S. 114/MEX-Flagge:** Shutterstock.com / Globe Turner; **S. 114/ROK-Flagge:** Shutterstock.com / Globe Turner; **S. 115:** Shutterstock.com / aijiro; **S. 116:** Shutterstock.com / Pressmaster; **S. 117/1:** Shutterstock.com / ArtisticPhoto; **S. 117/2:** Cartoonstock / Mark Godfrey; **S. 118/1:** Shutterstock.com / hoangpts; **S. 118/2:** Cornelsen / Uwe Rogal; **S. 119/1:** Shutterstock.com / tynyuk; **S. 119/2:** Shutterstock.com / ClassicVector; **S. 119/3:** Shutterstock.com / mei yanotai; **S. 119/4:** Shutterstock.com / Iconic Bestiary; **S. 119/5:** Shutterstock.com / Katia_Om; **S. 119/6:** Shutterstock.com / Nsit; **S. 120:** Shutterstock.com / Golden Sikorka; **S. 121:** Shutterstock.com / Daisy Daisy; **S. 126:** Shutterstock.com / artKULO; **S. 127:** Cornelsen / Uwe Rogal; **S. 128:** Cornelsen / Uwe Rogal; **S. 129:** Shutterstock.com / Mascha Tace; **S. 133/1:** Cartoonstock / Loren Fishman; **S. 133/2:** Statista.com **;** **S. 134/Section A:** Shutterstock.com / Shu-Hung Liu; **S. 134/Section B:** Shutterstock.com / patrimonio designs ltd; **S. 134/Section G:** Shutterstock.com / Kathy Hutchins; **S. 134/Illu:** Shutterstock.com / Tatsiana Tsyhanova; **S. 135/Section C:** Shutterstock.com / AlessandroBiascioli; **S. 135/ Section D:** Shutterstock.com / Nadino; **S. 135/ Section E:** Shutterstock.com / Harun Ozmen; **S. 135/ Section F:** Shutterstock.com / rSnapshotPhotos; **S. 136/A:** Shutterstock.com / Everett Collection; **S. 136/B:** Shutterstock.com / Everett Collection; **S. 136/C:** Shutterstock.com / Mike Flippo; **S. 136/D:** Shutterstock.com / Chess Ocampo; **S. 136/E:** Shutterstock.com / cybrain; **S. 136/F:** Shutterstock.com / Sanchai Kumar; **S. 137/1:** Shutterstock.com / Shu-Hung Liu; **S. 137/2:** Shutterstock.com / Everett Collection; **S. 138:** Shutterstock.com / rozbyshaka; **S. 140/1:** mauritius images/Science Source; **S. 140/Little Crow:** mauritius images / Science Source; **S. 140/Lincoln:** Shutterstock.com / Everett Collection; **S. 141/1:** Shutterstock.com / sl vector grapy; **S. 141/2:** Shutterstock.com / Lutsenko_Oleksandr; **S. 144:** Cartoonstock / Lindsay Foyle; **S. 145/A:** Shutterstock.com / AlessandroBiascioli; **S. 145/B:** Shutterstock.com / 5D Media; **S. 145/C:** Shutterstock.com / ELG Photography; **S. 145/D:** Shutterstock.com / Rena Schild; **S. 146:** Shutterstock.com / Everett Collection; **S. 148/1:** Shutterstock.com / AJR_photo; **S. 148/2:** Shutterstock.com / blvdone; **S. 148/3:** Shutterstock.com / Nadino; **S. 148/4:** Shutterstock.com / america365; **S. 149/1:** Shutterstock.com / khaleddesigner; **S. 149/2:** Shutterstock.com / Bee-Bright; **S. 151/1:** Shutterstock.com / Rido; **S. 151/2:** Shutterstock.com / spyarm; **S. 152/A:** Shutterstock.com / Fiora Watts; **S. 152/B:** Shutterstock.com / Sepp photography; **S. 152/C:** Shutterstock.com / Sergey Novikov; **S. 152/D:** Shutterstock.com / Harun Ozmen; **S. 152/E:** Shutterstock.com / Lucian3D; **S. 152/F:** Shutterstock.com / esfera; **S. 154:** Cornelsen / Uwe Rogal; **S. 155:** Shutterstock.com / rSnapshotPhotos; **S. 156/1:** Shutterstock.com / wavebreakmedia; **S. 156/2:** Shutterstock.com / mihai's place; **S. 157:** Cartoonstock / Jack Corbett; **S. 158:** mauritius images / Cinema Legacy Collection; **S. 159:** dpa Picture-Alliance / newscom / PAT BENIC; **S. 162/1:** Shutterstock.com / VikiVector; **S. 162/2:** Shutterstock.com / Everett Collection; **S. 162/3:** Shutterstock.com / Jacob Lund; **S. 162/4:** Shutterstock.com / MarclSchauer; **S. 162/5:** Shutterstock.com / Lightspring; **S. 163:** Shutterstock.com / Quarta; **S. 164:** Shutterstock.com / Artiom Photo; **S. 165:** Shutterstock.com / Simone Hogan; **S. 168:** Shutterstock.com / Artem Novosad; **S. 171:** Shutterstock.com / Ivelin Radkov; **S. 173:** Shutterstock.com / Tatsiana Tsyhanova; **S. 177/1:** Shutterstock.com / wk-1003mike; **S. 177/2:** Cartoonstock / Kim Wark; **S. 178/Section A:** Shutterstock.com / William Barton; **S. 178/Section B:** Shutterstock.com / stockphoto mania; **S. 178/Section F:** Shutterstock.com/View Apart; **S. 178/Illu:** Shutterstock.com / Sentavio; **S. 179/Section C:** Shutterstock.com / Diego Cervo; **S. 179/Section D:** Shutterstock.com / Ivan Marc; **S. 179/Section E:** Shutterstock.com / Stefano Bobini; **S. 180/1:** Shutterstock.com / Joe Gough; **S. 180/2:** Shutterstock.com / Matis75; **S. 180/3:** Shutterstock.com / Prachaya Roekdeethaweesab; **S. 180/4:** Shutterstock.com / corlaffra; **S. 180/5:** Shutterstock.com / Feng Yu; **S. 180/6:** Shutterstock.com / Africa Studio; **S. 180/7:** stock.adobe.com / copyright Mary Evans Picture Library 2017 / Archivist; **S. 181:** Shutterstock.com / William Barton; **S. 183:** Cartoonstock / Tom Toro; **S. 184/1:** Shutterstock.com / Jiri Foltyn; **S. 184/2:** Shutterstock.com / Shay Yacobinski; **S. 184/3:** Shutterstock.com / Kitraveler; **S. 186:** Shutterstock.com / stockphoto mania; **S. 187:** Shutterstock.com / Colored Lights; **S. 189/1:** Shutterstock.com / Tuangtong Soraprasert; **S. 189/2:** mauritius images / alamy stock photo / Contraband Collection; **S. 189/2:** mauritius images / Loop Images; **S. 189/3:** mauritius images / alamy stock photo / Tim Ring; **S. 189/5:** Shutterstock.com / kipgodi; **S. 189/6:** Shutterstock.com / Diego Cervo; **S. 191:** mauritius images / alamy stock photo / Mark Kerrison; **S. 194/1:** Shutterstock.com / Ink Drop;

S. 194/2: Shutterstock.com / Lightspring; **S. 194/3:** Shutterstock.com / lazyllama; **S. 195/1:** Cartoonstock / Matt Percival; **S. 195/2:** Cartoonstock / John Lightbourne; **S. 195/3:** Cartoonstock / Ghamir Ali; **S. 196:** Statista.com; **S. 199/1:** Shutterstock.com / Stefano Bobini; **S. 199/2:** Shutterstock.com / Helen Hotson; **S. 199/3:** Shutterstock.com / Cookie Studio; **S. 200:** Shutterstock.com / WAYHOME studio; **S. 202:** Cartoonstock / Mark Winter; **S. 203/1:** mauritius images / alamy stock photo / Mark Thomas; **S. 203/2:** mauritius images / alamy stock photo / Juergen Hasenkopf; **S. 203/3:** dpa Picture-Alliance / empics / PA Wire / Ian West; **S. 205:** Michael Andrew; **S. 207:** Shutterstock.com/Nicoleta Ionescu; **S. 208:** Shutterstock.com/Sakchai.K; **S. 209:** Shutterstock.com / Ivan Marc; **S. 216:** Shutterstock.com / Frenggo; **S. 219:** Shutterstock.com / Sentavio; **S. 223/1:** Cartoonstock / Jorodo; **S. 223/2:** Statista.com; **S. 224/Section A:** mauritius images / TopFoto; **S. 224/Section B:** Shutterstock.com / Monika Wisniewska; **S. 224/Section F:** Shutterstock.com / StudioByTheSea; **S. 224/Illu:** Shutterstock.com / Marta Sher; **S. 225/Section C:** Shutterstock.com / Red Stock; **S. 225/Section D:** Shutterstock.com / Jeff Whyte; **S. 225/Section E:** Shutterstock.com / PremiumVector; **S. 226/1:** mauritius images / alamy stock photo / Nick Bakhur; **S. 226/2:** mauritius images / Glasshouse; **S. 227/1:** mauritius images / TopFoto; **S. 227/2:** mauritius images / alamy stock photo / Ian Dagnall; **S. 227/3:** mauritius images / alamy stock photo / Todd Strand; **S. 228:** dpa Picture-Alliance / AP Photo / AP / Ferd Kaufman; **S. 231:** WAN Media; **S. 232/1:** stock.adobe.com / pressmaster; **S. 232/2:** Shutterstock.com / Monika Wisniewska; **S. 232/3:** Shutterstock.com / Monkey Business Images; **S. 232/4:** Shutterstock.com / Gorodenkoff; **S. 232/5:** Shutterstock.com / Monkey Business Images; **S. 232/6:** dpa Picture-Alliance / Luiz Rampelotto / EuropaNewswire; **S. 234:** Shutterstock.com / Dean Drobot; **S. 235:** Shutterstock.com / Gyorgy Barna; **S. 236/1:** Shutterstock.com / Red Stock; **S. 236/2:** Shutterstock.com / Ebtikar; **S. 236/3:** Shutterstock.com / BearFotos; **S. 236/4:** Shutterstock.com / yurakrasil; **S. 236/5:** Shutterstock.com / italianstock; **S. 237:** Shutterstock.com / EML; **S. 240/1:** Shutterstock.com / Jeff Whyte; **S. 240/2:** mauritius images / alamy stock photo / Ovidiu Hrubaru; **S. 240/3:** Shutterstock.com / Lisa F. Young; **S. 240/4:** mauritius images / Cinema Legacy Collection; **S. 244/1:** Shutterstock.com / Viktorija Reuta; **S. 244/2:** Shutterstock.com / ElkhatiebVector; **S. 244/3:** Shutterstock.com / Tatiana Gulyaeva; **S. 244/4:** Shutterstock.com / Alexey V Smirnov; **S. 244/5:** Shutterstock.com / VectorPot; **S. 244/6:** Shutterstock.com / ALEXEY GRIGOREV; **S. 244/7:** Shutterstock.com / Viktorija Reuta; **S. 244/8:** Shutterstock.com / PremiumVector; **S. 247/1:** mauritius images / alamy stock photo / UPI; **S. 247/2:** mauritius images / Norbert Michalke; **S. 247/3:** mauritius images / Siegfried Kuttig; **S. 247/4:** mauritius images / alamy stock photo / Shakeyjon; **S. 248:** Shutterstock.com / StudioByTheSea; **S. 252:** Cartoonstock / Juan Carlos Partidas; **S. 253:** Shutterstock.com / Visual Generation; **S. 254:** Shutterstock.com / Krakenimages.com; **S. 255:** Shutterstock.com / Sabrina Bracher; **S. 260:** Shutterstock.com/W4V3; **S. 261:** Shutterstock.com/Zlatko Guzmic; **S. 262:** Shutterstock.com / Marta Sher; **S. 266/1:** Cartoonstock / Carré; **S. 266/2:** Statista.com; **S. 267/1:** Shutterstock.com / Skylines; **S. 267/2:** Shutterstock.com / Virrage Images; **S. 268:** Statista.com; **S. 269/1:** Shutterstock.com / VladisloveM; **S. 269/2:** Cartoonstock / Kendra Allenby; **S. 270/1:** Shutterstock.com / Reinhold Leitner; **S. 270/2:** Cartoonstock / Benita Epstein; **S. 271:** Cartoonstock / Drew Panckeri; **S. 272/1:** Statista.com; **S. 272/2:** Cartoonstock / Steve Greenberg; **S. 273:** Cartoonstock / Fran; **S. 274/1:** Cartoonstock / Fran; **S. 274/2:** Statista.com; **S. 275:** Cartoonstock / Paul Kinsella; **S. 276:** Cornelsen / Uwe Rogal; **S. 277/1:** Shutterstock.com / Marie Kanger Born; **S. 277/2:** Cartoonstock / Paul Fell; **S. 278:** Cartoonstock / Chris Madden; **S. 279/1:** Cartoonstock / Karsten Schley; **S. 279/2:** Statista.com; **S. 282/1:** Cartoonstock / Karsten Schley; **S. 282/2:** Statista.com; **S. 283/1:** Shutterstock.com / Yindee; **S. 283/2:** Shutterstock.com / GoodStudio; **S. 284:** Shutterstock.com / Irina Strelnikova; **S. 285/1:** Shutterstock.com / N.Savranska; **S. 285/2:** Shutterstock.com / GoodStudio; **S. 285/3:** Shutterstock.com / Keji; **S. 287:** Shutterstock.com / tati._.9; **S. 288:** Shutterstock.com / EgudinKa; **S. 292:** Shutterstock.com / Vectorium; **S. 294:** Shutterstock.com / Artisticco; **S. 295:** Shutterstock.com / metamorworks; **S. 297:** Shutterstock.com / Artram

Illustrationen:
Cornelsen / Carlos Borrell: S. 250, S. 251, S. 252

Textquellen

S. 19, 22, 27, 92, 103, 114: Copyright Guardian News & Media Ltd 2021; **S. 48, 56, 61, 64, 68, 87, 131, 175, 181, 186, 191, 203, 217, 222, 228, 237, 241, 244, 251, 264:** Copyright Guardian News & Media Ltd 2022; **S. 72:** Machines Like Me, by Ian McEwan. ISBN: 978-1-787-33167-9 (Jonathan Cape / Vintage 2019); **S. 99:** ©2020 National Public Radio, Inc. News report titled "What Bikes Tell Us About A Changing Global Economy" by Greg Rosalsky was originally published on NPR.org on August 25, 2020, and is used with the permission of NPR. Any unauthorized duplication is strictly prohibited.; **S. 108:** Gen Z@Work by David Stillman and Jonah Stillman; **S. 111, 142:** Deutsche Welle; **S. 145:** Voice of America (VOA)/Dora Mekouar, 04.07.2020; **S. 158:** Copyright Adams Jr, William James/Text, (OT) Will.I.am; **S. 159:** The Hill We Climb. An inaugural poem for the country by Amanda Gorman. Penguin Young Readers / Imprint Chatto & Windus 2021; **S. 233:** UN speech by Antonio Guterres: "Women and power", https://www.un.org/sg/en/content/sg/statement/2020-02-27/secretary-generals-remarks-the-new-school-women-and-power-scroll-down-for-french-version.

The British Isles

Canada & United States of America

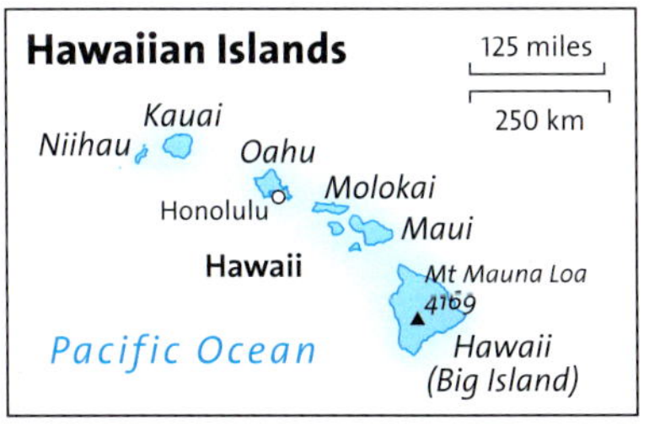

Abbreviations CANADA:
NB = New Brunswick
P.E.I. = Prince Edward Island

Abbreviations UNITED STATES:
CT = Connecticut
DE = Delaware
NH = New Hampshire
NJ = New Jersey
MA = Massachusetts
MD = Maryland
PA = Pennsylvania
RI = Rhode Island
VT = Vermont

European Union